PSYCHOLOGICAL RESEARCH:
THE IDEAS BEHIND THE METHODS

PSYCHOLOGICAL RESEARCH

THE IDEAS
BEHIND THE METHODS

DOUGLAS G. MOOK

PROFESSOR EMERITUS OF PSYCHOLOGY

UNIVERSITY OF VIRGINIA

W. W. NORTON & COMPANY

NEW YORK   LONDON

The text of this book is composed in Meridien
with the display set in Frutiger
Page makeup by Roberta Flechner
Composition by Matrix Publishing Company, Inc.
Manufacturing by Maple-Vail
Book Design by Martin Lubin Graphic Design

Library of Congress Cataloging-in-Publication Data
Mook, Douglas G., 1934–
    Psychological research : the ideas behind the methods / Douglas G. Mook.
      p. cm.
    Includes bibliographical references and index.
    ISBN 0-393-97620-3
    1. Psychology—Research—Methodology.   I. Title.

  BF76.5 .M67 2001
  150′.7′2—dc21   00-048079

W. W. Norton & Company, Inc., 500 Fifth Avenue, New York, N.Y. 10110
www.wwnorton.com

W. W. Norton & Company Ltd., Castle House, 75/76 Wells Street, London W1T 3QT

1 2 3 4 5 6 7 8 9 0

This one is for Melody—of course

CONTENTS

CHAPTER 8 **EXPERIMENTAL CONTROL II: CONFOUNDED VARIABLES** 256

CHAPTER 9 **EXPERIMENTS WITH MORE THAN ONE INDEPENDENT VARIABLE** 292

CHAPTER 10 **SINGLE-SUBJECT AND "SMALL-N" EXPERIMENTS** 330

CONTENTS

CHAPTER 11 **QUASI-EXPERIMENTS** 372

CHAPTER 12 **THE RELIABILITY AND GENERALITY OF FINDINGS** 408

CHAPTER 13 **ETHICAL CONSIDERATIONS IN RESEARCH** 444

CHAPTER 14 **RESEARCH PSYCHOLOGY, POP PSYCHOLOGY, AND INTUITIVE PSYCHOLOGY** 472

Before I learned better, I used to reply "experimental psychologist" to questions about what I did for a living. Far more often than not, or so it seems now, I would at once confront a stereotype: "Oh boy, do I have an uncle you'd want to meet!" or perhaps "Oh, rats? Mazes?" Or even "Uh oh! Are you taking notes?"

The fact is that many of the educated, intelligent people I encounter have never left these stereotypes behind. More disturbing still, that includes many former psych majors, some of whom have told me quite seriously that all they remember from the "experimental course" was Pavlov's drooling dogs!

Most texts on method, in my experience, do not address these misconceptions. They tend to assume a certain mind-set toward research that, in fact, beginners don't have. It has to be built. If it is not, students all too often retain the impression of a research methods course as just a hurdle to be cleared, so that they can get on to the "real stuff."

This book confronts the misconceptions directly, and it takes the view that research *is* the real stuff. From the outset, it emphasizes that research has changed our thinking about important issues; it has shown us when we were wrong, and thus allowed us to correct our mistakes. This, it is emphasized, is fundamental to science: If we know when we're wrong, we can correct our mistakes, and, while still not in possession of Absolute Truth, at least be *less* wrong than we were before. That sets up later discussions about theory testing, falsifiability, and the like.

In this spirit, the book was written with certain guiding ideas in mind:

1. It builds on real examples with real implications. It shows the reader why the researcher was interested in the question in the first place, and what the results tell us—about the specific question, but also about the broader context.

2. It taps into students' existing knowledge. Many standard procedures of good research are not mysterious or esoteric, but just *sensible precautions* against certain kinds of mistakes. Many instances of these are already familiar even to beginning students. For instance, the "double-blind" control in medical research makes good sense to most students. But we need to show them that problems of observer effects, observer bias, and the like are more general than that—and so are the solutions. True, some other important concepts, like the powerful notion of *randomization*, are not as intuitive as all that. But when these are explained, students find that they too make good sense.

3. This extension of familiar ideas is possible because—and this is another recurring theme—*whatever the content area may be, the principles of research are the same*. Notions of comparison, control, randomization, and other basics are as applicable to a clinical evaluation study as to an experiment in perceptual development or conditioned taste aversion.

Many of the traps and pitfalls are the same, too. As just one example: The problem of unintended *observer effects* is dramatically illustrated by the case of Clever Hans, the arithmetical horse. But if the story of Clever Hans had been more widely known, we might have spared ourselves the "facilitated communication" fiasco of a few years ago, which resulted from the same problem, detected—eventually—in the same way (Chapter 5).

To emphasize this common core of ideas, the examples in this book are deliberately made diverse; a study in neuropsychology may be deliberately juxtaposed with a study in social cognition or outcome research. The point of this is to show that procedures that look drastically different on the surface may nonetheless have the same underlying logic.

In all of this, the attempt is to induce , or at least introduce, a researcher's outlook. Apart from specific tricks of the trade, like "blind" observing or random assignment, a trained researcher will have developed *habits of thought* that can be applied to any empirical question whatever. We can learn to ask such questions as: "But what if the causal relation were the other way around?" or "But was observer bias controlled for?" or even simple old "How do you/they know that?" A few simple questions like that, *if* they come to mind as "habits of the head," can nail much of the nonsense we hear—or the nonsense we are about to speak.

4. The intuitive approach extends to the treatment of statistics. The usual presentation is heavily algebraic. That approach, I think, encourages many students (not all, of course) to treat statistical analyses as computations to be done, and interpreted, by rote. If this happens, a good student may do well in a statistics class, and even be able to tell us whether a difference is statistically significant or not, but still not quite grasp what it is all *for*.

This book takes a geometric rather than an algebraic approach; the attempt is to let students *see* what they are doing, the better to see why. Because of this rather unorthodox emphasis, the book should be useful as look-at-it-this-way" review for students who have had a course in statistics, as well as an accessible introduction for those who have not.

These sections on statistics come at the ends of chapters, separated from the main bodies. I tried interspersing them as boxes within the text (it breaks up the text too much), and also moving them all to an appendix after the main text (it moves statistical matters too far away from the research examples they draw upon.) The present way seems to me best. I have made some attempt to coordinate each section with the chapter's coverage, but there is necessarily some poorness of fit here and the coordination is less than we would like. Of course an instructor is at liberty to rearrange, or ignore, any or all of these sections; and setting them off as separate sections should make this easy to do if desired.

Two matters of style should be addressed. In showing the extension of familiar ideas into new domains, we are holding a conversation with the reader. We are explaining something to him or her, as we would do over a cup of coffee. Believing that conversations over coffee are more pleasant and more enlightening than lectures, I have deliberately written the book in an informal, conversational style.

Second, there's the ubiquitous pronoun problem: How to be gender neutral? The generic masculine is quite rightly obsolete, but too many instances of "he or she" and "his or her" make the text awkward and obese. My solution is to use both masculine and feminine as generics (unless of course the context dictates otherwise), and to use one or the other arbitrarily in any given case. There still retains some awkwardness, to be sure, and I ask the reader's patience. I think it is, as someone has said of democracy, the worst possible solution except for all the others.

While preparing this book, I worked with a series of editors at Norton: Don Fusting, Cathy Wick, Jon Durbin, and Rich Rivellese. Each in his or her own way brought wisdom and encouragement to the project, and I'm very grateful to them. Aaron Javsicas guided the book through the production process with patience and good humor. Gale Miller put the final touches on the text, and made it better, as copyeditor.

The book also profited immeasurably from the comments of reviewers who read sections of it in draft: Josh Blustein, Patrick Carroll, George Fago, Carolyn Ristau, Toni Wegner, and Debra Zellner. Paul Rozin and Scott Parker read the entire manuscript, some of it more than once as revision followed revision. Debra Zellner even test taught the penultimate draft over a semester at Shippensburg University, and my debt of gratitude to her extends also to her students, many of whom returned constructive and useful criticisms.

Then there were friends who, as friends, read and commented on draft sections: Melody Browning-Mook, Marcie Ewasko, Steffani Martin, Deborah Mook, Janet Perlman, and Sue Wagner.

The insightful comments of all these friends and colleagues steered me away from many chasms of awkwardness, opacity, or downright blunder, and I thank them all. Even so, the final decisions as to what to say and how to say it were my own—which makes me solely responsible for whatever may still be awkward, opaque, or wrong.

But my greatest debts are to successive groups of people, and to one very special person. The students in my classes in research methods have taught me how to think about research, as I was learning to teach them how to do the same. My wife, Melody, has given me confidence, caring, constructive criticism, and coffee besides. The dedication of this book is feeble acknowledgment of the joy she has brought me.

PSYCHOLOGICAL RESEARCH:

THE IDEAS BEHIND THE METHODS

CHAPTER 1

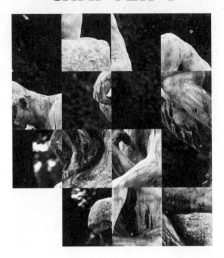

TESTING OUR IDEAS

Some may consider this an overbroad characterization, but to me every time we exercise self-criticism, every time we test our ideas against the outside world, we are doing science.

—CARL SAGAN (1995, p. 27)

IN THIS CHAPTER, WE'LL DISCUSS:

- How research findings show us when our ideas are wrong, thus allowing us to improve them
- How science tests its conclusions against the facts
- How this process differs from appeals to authority, common sense, personal experience, or intuition in supporting our conclusions
- How we can go wrong by basing conclusions on fraudulent research, bad research, or no research at all
- Why "research consumers" as well as practicing scientists can benefit from understanding the research process
- The difference between applied and basic research

Our ideas change.

Not so long ago, it was believed that yellow fever was caused by an excess of blood. The treatment was to bleed the patient so as to relieve the excess—a "treatment" that surely killed more patients than it cured.

Why? Because, for one thing, systematic research, which would have allowed us to *look and see* that the treatment was worse than the disease, was not conducted until much later.

Now that was long ago; true. So let's look at a more recent example. *Autism*, a disorder that appears early in life, is characterized by a failure to form social relationships. The sufferer is often totally indifferent to other persons, treating them more like pieces of furniture than like people. We don't know what causes this condition. But in the 1950s and into the 1970s, many of us thought that we knew. Some influential mental-health professionals concluded that autism was the result of bad parenting—the child sensed parents' rejection and was "tuning out" in an attempt to escape from it. One writer blamed the disorder on "icebox parents." The effect of all this was to place a decades-long guilt trip on already stressed and desperate real-life parents (Dolnick, 1998).

Why? For the same reason that blood-letting survived so long: *assumptions went unchecked*. Children's behavioral problems were simply *assumed* to result from disturbances in their relationships with parents. It was not until the 1970s that researchers took the obvious step: *Look and see* whether the parents of autistic children differ, as a group, from other parents. They did not (e.g., DeMyer, 1979). And today, we no longer "blame the victims" in this way—not for this disorder at least. But families were devastated in the meantime.

One more example? Consider this one, which may be closer to home for about half of my readers:

Not long ago at all, it was widely believed by educators, physicians, and scientists that women simply did not belong in college. Their intellects were too weak, and their nervous systems too fragile, to stand up to the stress of a college curriculum. We can laugh at that idea now, of course, because we have checked it. We have done the experiment—and it was just that—of admitting women into college, and then *looking and seeing* whether they could handle it. The results are clear: They can handle it just fine, as well as men or perhaps a shade better. In the same courses, too.

All these are example of *how* our ideas change, but also of *why* they change. They change because someone makes them change. People take observations, they try things, they do experiments. What they see shows us when our ideas are wrong, and need to be revised and improved.

This book is about that process. It will show you how scientists go about taking observations, trying things, doing experiments— *looking and seeing*. It will show some of the pitfalls in the road, and how they may be avoided, filled in, or bypassed. It is—in a word— about how the research that changes our ideas gets done.

WHAT DO WE THINK AND WHY DO WE THINK IT?

Thus Aristotle laid it down that a heavy object falls faster than a light one does. The important thing about this idea is not that it was wrong, but that it never occurred to Aristotle to check it.

—NOBEL LAUREATE ALBERT SZENT-GIIORGI

It ain't the things we don't know that get us into trouble. It's the things we know that ain't so.

—ARTEMUS WARD

We are all of us drowning in a sea of information and advice. From every point of the compass, we are told how to be slimmer, how to be better lovers, what we should do about crime, what we should do when the baby cries, how to increase said baby's IQ, and on and on. We are offered advice by the media, the Internet, our friends and relations, and even from books (Figure 1.1).

The articles, of course, will be written by Experts. Often they will boast that "Science tells us . . . ," or flash the badge "Studies show. . . ." They may point to what "everybody knows," or what is "just common sense." Or they may say, "Check your own experience and see if you don't find this to be so."

The problem is that some of what we are told is true, and some of it just isn't so. How do we know which is which? How do we tell whether an item of "information" is so or not so? When we are told, "Here is how to [treat yellow fever or treat our children or have an educated citizenry or be slimmer or sexier or richer]," how do we separate good advice from bad?

The solution is to ask: What is this "information" based on? If we are told that this or that is so, it is only sensible to ask: *"How do you know?"* or, more gently, *"Why do you think so?"* If we get an answer,

"I utilize the best from Freud, the best from Jung, and the best from my Uncle Marty, a very smart fellow."

FIGURE 1.1
We are offered information from many sources, good and bad.

we can ask the next obvious question: *"Are your reasons good ones?"* Science, we might say, *is* the art of finding good answers to the "Why do you think so?" question.

Now it is true that science is only one of several ways of backing up what we say—that is, of answering the "Why do you think so?" question. However, it has a unique advantage over other ways: It tests its conclusions and corrects its mistakes. To see this and why it is important, let's compare it with some other possible "ways of knowing."

AUTHORITY

The appeal to authority goes like this: "How do we know that this is so? Because So-and-so says it, and he ought to know."

A tremendous amount of our knowledge comes to us this way— we believe it because we were told it, by someone who ought to know. Very often we are right to believe it. We cannot verify for ourselves that $e = mc^2$, or that Columbus crossed the Atlantic in 1492. Nor can we verify from our own observations that London is the capital of England, or even that London is *in* England, if we have never been there. Even if we could test these ideas, obviously an attempt to test *all* the things we are told would leave us no time to do anything else.

However, we do know something more in these cases. We know that the conclusions *have been tested*, and that they have stood up under the tests. Physicists have *tested* the principles on which Einstein's famous equation rests, and confirmed them many times. Historians know about Columbus because they have gone, or could go, to earlier documents. If we have never been to London ourselves, we can talk to those who have, and their observations will assure us that it is where we think it is.

But in other cases, what we are told by So-and-so, who ought to know, may not have been tested at all. When it has not, it is unsupported opinion—no matter who says it.

Take the belief that women do not belong in college. At one time, many authorities, who all ought to know, assured us of that. This for two reasons at least. First, women were assumed to be intellectually inferior to men. One commentator, a *highly respected anthropologist* who surely ought to know, laid it down that women's intellectual inferiority to men was "so obvious that only its degree [was] worth discussion." (Hang on, Reader: His words, not mine.) Second, it was "well known" that women's nervous systems were delicate and fragile. Physicians (who ought to know) worried that women's attempts to use their brains in an "unnatural" way, by taking on college study, could disrupt their reproductive systems and threaten the very future of the species (Harrington, 1987)!

We can laugh at all this today, but that's because something has happened. Can women handle a college curriculum? Test it! *Look and see*! Today, we don't have to argue about the matter; we simply say that women have in fact been admitted to college, and they have done just fine. We have *tested* the idea that women cannot handle college. And the idea has flunked the test.

Note, however: If the authorities of a century ago had had their way, the experiment would never have been tried—and we still would not know whether women can handle college or not. For the admission of women to colleges in large numbers was just that—an experiment. And women's success at college is an experimental finding. As such, it's a beautiful example of how experimental findings, by testing preconceptions, can turn our thinking around.

In this example we see the difference between the appeal to authority and the scientist's attitude toward her conclusions. The scientist does not say, "Believe this because I say so, and I'm an authority." Nor does she say, "Believe this because So-and-so says so, and he's an authority." She says, "Here are the facts. Look and see for yourself." Offered information, she will say: "What are the facts that back up that information? Show me!" Facts have unhorsed Authority many, many times.

Yet the authorities get right back on their horses. In our own time, a media "expert," who it seems ought to know, tells us that 50% of American families are dysfunctional. It puts a new perspective on this remark when we ask our questions: Why does she think so? How could she know that? What *facts* could support it? Are there survey data that back it up? If so, how is "dysfunctional" defined by the surveyors? Surely different definitions would give us different percentages. . . . As we think about it, we begin to wonder whether the 50% figure is any more solid than thin air. Thin hot air.

COMMON SENSE

If appeal to authority takes the form "So-and-so says so, and he ought to know," what we call "common sense" says: "*Everybody* knows . . . ," or, "Why, it's *obvious*. . . ."

Well, what is obvious or known to all has a way of changing. Today, it is just common sense that if we're sick, we have some germs in our systems. Not long ago, and still today in some parts of the world, it would be just common sense to fear that a spell has been cast upon us. Today, it is just common sense that women can handle higher education just fine. Not long ago, it was just common sense that they could not.

How much else of what we call "common sense" fails when put to the test? Here is a sample of statements that the conventional wisdom would likely accept:

1. The more confident a person is of what he remembers, the more confident *we* can be that his memory is accurate.

2. Experienced therapists, applying their clinical insight, are better than laypersons at predicting whether a person will be violent in the future.

3. We can best understand what a person does by knowing her or his underlying personality characteristics.

4. Subliminal stimuli, on tape or flashed on a movie screen, can march past our conscious minds to affect us unconsciously.

5. Trust your feelings; they never lie. We may have our facts wrong, but we cannot be wrong about what we are feeling.

6. A young person who is outstanding academically is likely to be shy, nonathletic, socially inept, and generally nerdy.

Some of these ideas, like Numbers 2, 4, and 6, we may believe just because we've heard them asserted so often—by Authorities who ought to know. For others, like Numbers 1, 3, and 5, we may feel that we need no reasons; they're just *obvious* truths. Common sense.

There is, however, a problem. All of the above are false. They are things that "everybody knows," but that simply are not so. Why do I call them false? Because the data—whole bodies of data in each case—contradict them. We will use some of these assertions, and others like them, as case studies in what follows.

PERSONAL EXPERIENCE

The following has happened to me any number of times. I tell my conversation partner about some well-established research finding, only to be met with "I don't agree with that." Why not? Because "It doesn't fit my experience." Thus, there is an implicit criterion for belief: "It is true if it fits my experience."

What to do? My partner may be bright and well educated, but she doesn't stop to consider that, first, she may be an exception to what is generally true, as may be her friends who are important parts of her experience. This is the problem of *sampling bias*. Second, any one person's "experience" is subject to our tendency to notice, remember, and call to mind things that confirm our beliefs better than ones that don't—the problem of *observer bias*. Third, in the normal course of human events, so many things are going on at once that it may be literally impossible to tell just why this or that happened—the problem of *confounded variables*. My companion's "personal experience" just doesn't stand up against systematically collected data, controlling for biases and based on many cases, and incorporating the needed comparisons. But how do I say that politely?

THE PROBLEM OF OBSERVER BIAS

Perhaps—since the reader will have patience with me, if my dinner companion will not—I can do it by again appealing to some facts. In this connection, let me tell you about what should be one of the most famous experiments in psychology.

Ray Hyman is a professor of psychology at the University of Oregon. He is also, as it happens, an accomplished stage magician, and one who follows the various claims of the paranormal that abound. At one point he became interested in palmistry, read up on it, and tried it out on a sample of friends and students. He looked at their palms and, based on his readings, told his "subjects" what their palms told him about their personalities.

The result? "Wow!" his subjects said. "Yes! That's right on target! How can you possibly know so much about me?" So enthusiastic were their endorsements that Hyman began to think that there might be something to this palm-reading business after all. But as an experimenter, Hyman also ran the "control," or *comparison*, condition. For the next series of subjects who came his way, Hyman told them the *opposite* of what their palms told him was true of them.

What do you think happened? That's right. "Wow! Yes! How did you know? You're exactly right about me!" In a word, what Hyman had shown was not that palm-reading yields insights, but rather what has been shown in many other experiments as well: If we look inside ourselves for evidence that X is the case, we will find it. It is a case of *observer bias*: our well-documented tendency to see what we expect to see, in ourselves and in others as well.

The interesting thing is that when I tell my classes this story, they anticipate me. Their knowing grins are in place well before I get to the punchline. But we seem not to draw the more general conclusion: Knowledge drawn from personal experience is *often* subject to just such biases as these. To separate good from bogus conclusions, we must test our conclusions, controlling for such biases.

The worst of it is that to all too many people, this kind of nonsense is what psychology is all about! It's enough to make one want to write a book.

THE PROBLEM OF CONFOUNDED VARIABLES

There is another limitation of personal experience as a source of knowledge. In some cases (not all, but which are which?), it is simply impossible to separate one possible cause from another in the complex "real world" from which our experience comes.

Let's think about Aristotle's idea that heavy objects fall faster than light ones. Actually, it would seem that all of us have verified that idea countless times. Watch feathers fall, or leaves. They meander slowly, slowly to the ground. Let a brick fall, and straight down it goes—and fast! Who could doubt that heavy objects fall faster than light ones?

In fact, no one did seriously doubt it for over a thousand years—until it was realized that a feather and a brick differ in two ways, not one. They differ (1) in weight, but also (2) in their susceptibility to air resistance and air currents. Since (1) and (2) vary together, we don't know which of them produces the difference in rate of fall. They are, as we say, *confounded*.

When we separate (1) and (2), we find that (2) is the important one. Compare objects that differ in weight, but are all heavy enough to make the air a negligible factor, and we find that they fall at exactly the same rate. Or, even better: Take the air away and work in a vacuum. Then we will see that even feathers and leaves fall just as fast as any brick.

Now, to create a vacuum is to create a highly artificial situation. Vacuums do not occur in the nature most of us inhabit (unless we are astronauts); indeed, it used to be said that nature abhors them! Thus, to separate air resistance from weight, we must create a condition that nature-as-you-find-it does not provide us. No amount of "personal experience" in natural situations will permit that separation.

That example comes from physics. Let's look at such a case within psychology. We'll look at this experiment in more detail later, but we can preview it here.

Tapes are widely advertised that we are to play while we're asleep. When we do so (it is claimed), the taped messages bypass our conscious minds and go directly to the unconscious. There they can teach us French, or enhance our self-esteem . . . almost anything, it seems. An easy, painless way to become educated, confident, slim, tall . . .

Now, the tape manufacturers do offer us facts, in the form of testimonials. "Boy oh boy," says Robert F., "these tapes really helped me with my self-esteem" (or French, or whatever). The data, in other words, come from the personal experiences of those who have used them.

But when these tapes are evaluated by sound methods, they have turned out, consistently, to be utterly worthless. What we find is this: Robert F. will report—sincerely—a big improvement in his self-esteem if he *thinks* he has been listening to a self-esteem tape, even if it was really a French tape. Conversely, Alice Q. will report a marked improvement in her French if she *thinks* she has been listening to a French tape, even if it was really a self-esteem tape. All self-reported improvement occurs where the subjects *expect* it to occur—not in the domain in which the tapes, if they had any effect, should produce it.

Here again, notice that it takes special conditions to produce this separation—to separate the effects of the tape itself from the effects of subjects' expectations. In the everyday world of commerce, if one thinks one is buying (say) a French tape, it'll *be* a French tape. To separate the effects of the tape's *real* content from the effects of its *believed* content, we need a special, "unnatural" situation, analogous to the physicist's vacuum, in which the separation can be made.

One final remark on this topic. We have seen that personal experience or everyday observation has limitations as a road to understanding: Biases and confounded variables can lead us astray. Am I suggesting then that the research scientist is somehow immune to these ways of making mistakes?

Not at all. In fact, quite the contrary—the scientist is fully as susceptible to these traps as anyone else. The difference is that scientists *know it*. They will make a conscious effort to control for their own biases as observers, and to incorporate the needed comparisons—if necessary, deliberately creating an artificial situation in which these things can be done.

That is to say, scientists will do these things when thinking as scientists! When wearing another hat, scientists, you may be sure, can fall into these traps with just as much enthusiasm as laypersons.

INTUITION

Yet another source of our beliefs is intuition, which says: "I just *know* that this or that is true, that's all."

Intuition and scientific thinking are not incompatible—not at all. The scientist may see, intuitively, an explanation for something—a theory may occur in an out-of-the-blue flash of insight. In one famous instance (of many), the chemist Kekule saw the structure of the benzene ring in a dream! In psychology, an important insight into the nature of our emotions was suggested to a researcher by a passage in Thomas Mann's novel, *The Magic Mountain*.

Thus, the scientist may have flashes of intuitive insight like anyone else. However, the scientist *checks his intuitions*, to see if they are correct. That is the only difference, but it's a big one.

For there is a problem with "just knowing." Suppose I "just know" that such-and-such is the case, whereas you "just know" that it isn't. Whose intuitions do we rely on? Yours or mine? It would seem that in such a case, either we let facts decide (thus doing science), or we agree to disagree—or we fight about it.

That latter possibility shows us the down side of "intuition" and "gut feeling" as a way of knowing. Consider another true story: In the 1930s and 1940s, there was a political leader who "just knew" that a particular ethnic group—Jewish people—was the source of much of the world's troubles. This politician rose to become dictator of a great modern nation. Thus empowered, validated, and feeling good about himself, he trusted his intuitions, went with his gut, and set in motion a systematic plan for the extermination of the group that he "just knew" was responsible for humankind's ills.

Fortunately, there were many who did not share Adolf Hitler's intuition—and who did not just agree to disagree. Fortunately, we won.

A LOOK BACK

When we are offered information, it is only sensible for us to ask the speaker: "How do you know?" or "Why do you think so?" In the previous paragraphs, we've looked at some possible replies to that question. One reply is: "So-and-so says so, and he ought to know. Period." Another is: "Everyone knows that. Period." A third is: "My experience shows it to be so. Period." It is the "period" that all these answers have in common, that distinguishes them from scientific conclusions and is their greatest weakness. *They do not check their conclusions.* Or if they do, then they are doing science, whether they realize it or not. (Whether they are doing *good* science is another matter, as we'll see.) Carl Sagan's remark is worth quoting again. "[E]very time we exercise self-criticism, every time we test our ideas against the outside world, we are doing science."

How then does a scientist justify her conclusions? If asked "Why do you think so?" she will say something like this: "I think this conclusion is well-established because it has been tested, not once but many times, against facts. It has been tested under conditions that *could* have shown it to be false, if false it were [the *falsifiability criterion*, discussed later]. And it has survived those tests—so far."

"So far"—not "period"! Here we see what is characteristic of the scientist's attitude toward her conclusions: They are held tentatively, subject to correction. There is always tomorrow; and tomorrow, some new facts may come in that will lead her to modify her conclusions or even to change them fundamentally. And she knows this, and welcomes it, for this is the great strength of the scientific method: *It corrects its mistakes.* It permits us to know when we are wrong. That idea is so simple, yet so important, that we should state it as a

Principle: If we test our ideas, we can know when we are wrong. And if we know when we are wrong, we can correct our mistakes. If we don't, we can't.

We will have much more to say about that principle in the next chapter.

It is this built-in error-correction device that distinguishes science from other claims to knowledge, and makes it unique. It is ironic that we so often hear, "Scientists think they know it all!" That's exactly what they don't think. And those who tell us that "science itself is . . . just another faith or belief system or myth, with no more justification than any other" (see Schick & Vaughn, 1995, p. 218) do not, I think, understand this feature of science.

But of course I could be wrong.

RESEARCH: GOOD, BAD, AND BOGUS

We have looked at the scientist's answer to the question, "Why do you think so?" His reply will be: "Because the idea has been tested against facts, and has stood up under the tests." But remember that there is a follow-up question: We can go on to ask, "Are your reasons good ones?" Here that question becomes: "Were the tests good tests? Indeed, were they really tests of your conclusion at all?"

Life would be simpler if one could assume that all research is good research, and that when someone says "Studies show . . . ," the studies exist and they do in fact "show." Unfortunately, the world is not so simple.

FRAUDULENT "RESEARCH"

First, we must realize that claims can be based on outright fraud. An example? You may remember, some years back, a great flap about "subliminal advertising." In a movie theater, very brief messages— "Eat X" or "Drink Y"—were flashed on the screen. The flashes were so brief that people in the theater were quite unaware that the messages were there at all. Yet the sales of X and Y suddenly soared.

Remember those experiments, and the stir they caused? Then listen, for here comes a public-service announcement:

They never happened.

They never happened. The "researcher" who conducted these studies later admitted publicly that he had made the findings up, in order to get research funding. The whole flap was phony from beginning to end.

INCOMPETENT RESEARCH

Then there are the cases in which the problem is not fraud, but simple incompetence. One may offer actual research data in support of a conclusion, where the research is simply so poorly done as to be useless.

The "research" on autism is an example. Therapists seized on an explanation of the disorder, and bent the facts to fit the theory. Other researchers seized on "therapeutic success" as evidence for the theory, overlooking the biases in judgment and the confounded variables that, if uncontrolled, can make a treatment look successful whether it is or not. Bruno Bettelheim, the best-known autism "researcher," claimed a stunning 80% cure rate. But a colleague, a biologist, commented, "*He* decided on the diagnosis, and *he* decided when they were cured. . . . You let me decide who's got what and when they're cured, and I can have an eighty percent cure rate, too" (quoted by Dolnick, 1998, p. 213).

Have we learned better? We have not. The self-help shelves in any bookstore are good sources of just this kind of "research." Often, claims are backed up by "personal experience" or "clinical experience" that is labeled "research." However, as we've seen, personal experience (clinical or otherwise) is loaded with opportunities for bias of many kinds, and its assumptions are seldom put to any real test. It is a treacherous guide.

It is this kind of literature that has given rise to the popular impression of psychology as soft, squishy, all a matter of opinion where one person's opinion is as good as another's. That kind of psychology is!

WHY STUDY RESEARCH METHODS?

We have looked at some ways in which scientists have changed our ideas, and improved them; and we have previewed a few of the problems and pitfalls that good research must surmount. But now, as the saying goes, let's talk about you.

RESEARCH PRODUCERS AND
RESEARCH CONSUMERS

The professional scientist is a *"research producer."* He or she makes a career of discovery, of testing our ideas and helping to advance our knowledge. Now, only a few of my readers will become professional scientists. Only some will be psychology majors, and of those, chances are, only a few again will become research psychologists. However, it's important to realize this: Even those who don't do research themselves will want to be able to *use the research produced by others.* They may not be research producers, but they will be "research consumers."

But intelligent research consumers also need some familiarity with research methods. Indeed, *an understanding of research methods is as necessary for the research consumer as it is for the practicing scientist.* Why? Because the thinking that one does, in evaluating research, is the *same kind of thinking* as the thinking that a scientist does in planning and conducting research.

Since this point is an important one, let's elaborate it a bit. The research producer says, "What must I do to gain knowledge about this or that, or to answer this or that specific question about it?" She then goes on to ask, in effect: "What do I have to do to get a *good* answer to my question? How can I do it? What are the ways in which I might go wrong and get a misleading answer? How can I prevent such mistakes from throwing me off the track?"

The research consumer says, "Here is some knowledge about this or that offered to me. Should I believe it?" He then goes on to ask *exactly the same kinds of questions*: "What did this researcher (or research team, or leading authority, or whoever) have to do to get a *good* answer to the question? Did she do it? What are the ways she might have gone wrong, and did she take the needed steps to prevent such mistakes?"

We need to know how to do this, because we are flooded with information. We are offered advice on how to deal with every conceivable social and personal problem. But some of that information is "so" and some just simply is not so, and we must learn how to distinguish these. We need to develop what Carl Sagan (1995) called "baloney detectors." The best way to do this, I think, is to form the habit of asking: How do you know? Have you tested it? What evidence is there for the information you offer me? Is it *good* evidence? Is it based on good research or bad? To ask that last question, we must learn what the problems and the pitfalls of research are.

There we have it. We must know what the problems of research are, to do research intelligently as producers—but also to evaluate research intelligently as consumers. This book is about the problems, as well as the process, of research. It is therefore addressed to you, Reader—whatever your career plans may be.

BASIC AND APPLIED RESEARCH

One final point, and we can move on.

We have seen how the research consumer—you and I—can benefit from the study of research methods. These are the reasons for studying these methods, and the reason—or one reason—for this book. But what about the research producers—scientists plying their trade? Why do they do what they do? What are their motives and their rewards? Well, there are two *kinds* of reasons for the scientist's quest for knowledge, and we should distinguish them.

APPLIED RESEARCH

The *applied* researcher does his work with a practical problem in mind. He may be seeking a new and better way of treating depression, for example, or autism, or eating disorders. He wishes his findings to be directly *applied* to the solution of a human problem—hence the term.

Applied research goes beyond treating disorders. It may be an attempt to do something better, as when an applied scientist experiments with a new method for teaching math, in hopes that it will work better than what we're doing now. Or the research may be an attempt to *predict* where a problem is likely to arise. If we can identify the people most at risk for depression, or AIDS, or school failure, we can better concentrate our preventive measures where they are most needed.

Then again, rather than predicting where things will go wrong, we might be trying to predict where they will go right! An industrial psychologist may design a test, or a battery of tests, to predict who is likely to do well at a particular job. The SATs, which do take us some way in predicting success at college, are products of applied research of this kind.

In practice, it is true, the work an applied scientist does may seem far removed from the problem itself. A cancer researcher may grapple with a problem in enzyme kinetics, not thinking about cancer at all while doing so. But the researcher could, if asked, explain to us how the immediate problem bears on the bigger one—the search for a cure.

BASIC RESEARCH

Contrasted with this is the *basic researcher*, who is not trying—not now, at least—to contribute to a specific practical problem. Her goal is simply to enhance our understanding. Her question is: How does it work?—where "it" may be memory, or the visual system, or the behavior of subatomic particles.

The basic researcher's motives can easily be misunderstood. Because she is not attacking a practical problem directly, one may get the impression that she is indifferent to human betterment. She is not. Nor is she gathering facts at random and putting them on a shelf, in the vague hope that someone, someday, may find a use for them.

Rather, basic researchers realize that *understanding* is always of value. If we understand better how the brain works—the normal, undamaged, undiseased brain—then that understanding cannot help but make us better able to deal with any number of neurological disorders. If we understood how memory works, in the normal case, then again that understanding would make disorders of memory easier to understand, and to treat. Of these practical uses of our increased knowledge, some can perhaps be foreseen, but many cannot.

An analogy from the physical sciences may help make this clear. Think of what we need to know in order to build a television set. Just for starters, we obviously need to know a lot about electricity. But the early explorers of electricity—Benjamin Franklin and Sir William Gilbert and the rest—were not *trying* to build a television set. There was no way to know that such a remarkable device was even possible, *until* we had the basic knowledge in hand.

So we might say it this way: The basic researcher's work is intended to move us toward an understanding of the *principles* underlying some class of events—electricity or memory or nervous-system functioning—rather than trying directly to improve the system or correct some specific breakdown in it. That is because she realizes that we are in a better position to repair, improve, or troubleshoot any system if we know how it's supposed to work in the first place.

CROSS TALK

We have distinguished between *basic* and *applied research* here, because we will encounter these terms often and should be familiar with them. We should not, however, make the distinction too hard and fast. First, basic and applied researchers have much to say to each other and make fruitful use of each other's ideas and findings.

Second, nothing says that the same research producer may not do research of both kinds—even both kinds at once, in the same investigation! Suppose a researcher develops, on the basis of basic research and theory, an idea for a new method of treating depression. Now the researcher does an "applied" experiment, to test the effectiveness of the method in depressed patients.

If the treatment can be shown to be effective, this obviously will be of *practical* benefit (applied). But also, those same results will support the *theory* about how depression occurs and how it works that suggested the new method in the first place (basic). The applied research is also basic research, and it could lead to both practical and theoretical advances. The discovery of "learned helplessness" and its implications for depression (Chapter 9) is a clear example of this double-barreled process.

A LOOK BACK

Here, then, are two possible starting points in the search for knowledge. We may seek it for its use in solving a practical problem—*applied research*. Or we may seek it on the grounds that all knowledge is useful in the long run—*basic research*. However, these different starting points do not mean that researchers divide into two separate and isolated camps—or, at least, it need not and should not mean that. Basic and applied researchers have much to learn from each other. And a particular research program—even a particular experiment—can advance both theoretical and practical knowledge at the same time.

THE RESEARCH ADVENTURE

Developing a critical eye for evidence—Sagan's "baloney detector"— is, we might say, the *practical* reason for studying research methods, whether one intends to *be* a researcher or not. There are two additional reasons, though, and we ought not lose sight of them.

First, one may study research methods for the same reasons one studies Shakespeare—one becomes more interested, and interesting, as a *person*. The scientific method is a major achievement of civilization. It has affected every facet of the society in which we live. To understand it is to understand our civilization and our society that much more clearly.

Second, there is the plain fact that research is an adventure. It's a detective story, a whodunit, in which the scientist/detective asks, "What is going on and how do we find out?" That can be a lot of fun.

Watch any child. Listen to the stream of questions: Why is the sky blue? Why do cats meow? Where did I come from? The list goes on endlessly and happily. Well, the scientist may ask questions in much the same spirit: How does learning take place? Why do birds sit on their nests? How do we see other people? How do we see anything at all?

Then comes the real challenge: How do we find out? What do we do and how do we do it? We'll do some hard thinking, which, as in chess or Go, can be great fun in its own right. Perhaps we'll do some gadgeteering, as when we build an electronic device to collect our data for us. There will come the nuts and bolts of actual data collection, and the playing with graphs and printouts in deciding how to analyze the data and present the data effectively. At the end, in the best cases, will come the thrill of discovery: "Oh! So *that's* what is going on! So *that* is how it works!" Your author has experienced that thrill. He will convey it, if he can, in the pages that follow.

It need not be sophisticated. There is that same childlike pleasure in discovering very simple things—things like, say, how a fly lands on a ceiling. How does he do it, anyway? Does he do a half outside loop or a half barrel roll? And how do we find out (here we match our wits with the fly's, a greater challenge than we might suppose)? Well, we can find out by close observation, but first (nuts and bolts!) we must learn how to use a movie camera.

The question has in fact been answered—with a surprise for us! Outside loop or barrel roll? Neither (see Dethier, 1962).*

A book about research, then, is a book of adventure stories. It is about how men and women have matched wits with nature, as a climber pits herself against a mountain. In reading about mountain-

---

*If you're curious (good!): The fly flies along just under the ceiling, reaches up to grasp the ceiling with its forefeet, and flips itself over to land upside down on the ceiling. That is why (as we can verify for ourselves) the fly ends up facing backward in the direction from which it came.

climbing adventures (for pleasure), we learn about the techniques of mountain climbing. In this book, by watching investigators investigate, we will learn about the techniques of investigation. So this book, too, can be read for pleasure, if I have at all succeeded in what I have tried to do.

SUMMARY

Our ideas change as research findings lead us to change them. Research—looking and seeing—shows us when our ideas need correction. It also can tell us which items of "information," among the flood of such items we're subjected to, we should take seriously.

When offered information, we can learn to ask: "How do you know?" or "Why do you think so?" If we get an answer, we can learn to ask the next obvious question: "Are your reasons good ones?"

Scientific research tests its conclusions against observable facts, and thus corrects its mistakes. Asked to back up a conclusion ("Why do you think so?"), a scientist will point to the data—the facts—on which the conclusion is based, and by which it has been tested. In this, science contrasts with other ways of justifying our beliefs: authority ("So-and-so says so"), common sense ("It's obvious . . ."), personal experience ("I find it to be true"), or intuition ("I just know"). These ways of "knowing" do not test their conclusions. Or if they do, and are prepared to change their conclusions if they are wrong, then they are doing science. The principle is: *If we know when we are wrong, we can correct our mistakes. If we don't, we can't.*

Of course, not all tests are good tests, and not all "facts" are solid facts. Outright fraud can occur. Short of that, research may simply be so poorly done that the results are useless. In short, it is not true that one opinion is as good as another, if one opinion is supported by sound data and the other is not. And obtaining sound data may not be easy.

So we must learn to distinguish good research from bad research. The "research producer," the professional scientist, must of course know the logic (and the pitfalls) of research in order to do it well. But "research consumers"—all of us—must also understand the problems of research in order to *evaluate* it well—to develop "baloney detectors" that will help us avoid being misled by conclusions based on bad data, fraudulent data, or no data at all.

Scientists themselves may have more than one reason for doing research. In *applied research*, the scientist expects the research findings to be directly *applied* to a practical problem. In *basic research*, the scientist may not have a particular practical problem in mind, but seeks to better understand how a system works, realizing that we are in a better position to repair, improve, or troubleshoot any system if we know how it's supposed to work in the first place. The distinction is not hard and fast, however. A given investigator may engage in both kinds of research. Even a single research finding may be of practical use (applied), and also advance our understanding of how things work (basic). Finally, research is exciting and fun—which means that a book about research should be, too. Well, your author has tried!

MAKING FRIENDS WITH STATISTICS: A LOOK AHEAD

Many students approach the study of research methods with a certain feeling of tension deep down inside. You see, we have heard that research methods involve statistics; we believe that statistics is mathematics; and mathematics is not, shall we say, a domain in which all of us feel comfortable.

If you are comfortable with mathematics, you will not need these words of reassurance; but many of my readers will be people like me. As it happens, your author was a math phobic from the first grade on, and was still one when he was a college student in the late Middle Ages. Nor was he reassured when his statistics textbook said, early on, that even a person who knows little mathematics can understand statistics, provided that the weakness in math "is not accompanied by an emotional reaction to symbols."

I remember reading that remark and thinking: "Great. In other words, you'll get along just fine as long as you don't have the problem (math anxiety) that is, in fact, the very problem so many people do have! It's like saying, 'You can be perfectly comfortable at the South Pole as long as it doesn't get cold.'"

But it does turn out that a person who knows little math—like me—can understand statistics. (If I can do it, you can do it!) The anxiety is unnecessary. We can overcome it if we keep three principles in mind:

1. *Statistics isn't mathematics; it's logic.*

It is true that professional statisticians do some very high-powered mathematical wizardry. That is their profession, and we will leave them to it. We don't have to do it ourselves.

It is also true that we have to do some arithmetic. But it will be mindless arithmetic; a computer can do it better than we can. The statistical thinking comes in both before and after the arithmetic is done, and the thinking is straightforward logic. If A, then B. But we find that not-B; therefore, not-A. That kind of thinking.

2. *You already know a lot about statistics.*

Do you doubt it? Consider: The basketball game has a few seconds to go; and the home team, with the ball, is two points behind. If we can score a basket, we will tie the game and send it into overtime. To whom, then, do we try to get the ball? To our best shooter, of course. If Player 9 is our best scorer, having thus far in the season made (say) 72% of her shots, whereas Player 21, the next best scorer, has 58%, and so on down, then we want to let Player 9 have the shot if we can.

Does that make sense? Then look at how much we understand already:

a) The notion of a *summary statistic*: 72% is a single number that *summarizes* Player 9's shooting performance in the season thus far.

b) The notion of *probability*: Player 9 is not guaranteed to make the next shot, any more than Player 14, with only (say) 42%, is guaranteed to miss it. But it makes sense that Player 9 is *more likely* than Player 14 to hit the basket next time. Why? See *d* below.

c) The concept of a *correlation*: On average and with exceptions, the higher a player's hit rate over the season to date, the higher it will turn out to be for the rest of the season. That kind of "the more of *this,* the more of *that*" statement is what we mean by a *correlation*.

d) The notion of *prediction* based on correlation: If hit rate to date will be correlated with hit rate for the rest of the season, then we *predict*—not perfectly, but better than with unaided guesswork—that the player with the higher average is the more likely to make *any* given shot over the rest of the season—including the shot that is coming up now. That is why we want Player 9, not Player 14, to get the ball and attempt the shot now.

Can it really be that simple? Yes.
And finally:

3. *Mathematical symbols are labor-saving devices, nothing more.*

It is the strange-looking symbols that call forth that tense, cautious feeling that many of us experience. But those symbols are only a new form of shorthand—anything we say by using them, we could say in plain English.

Let's take an example. Here is one of the first symbols a beginner in statistics is likely to encounter:

$$\Sigma$$

This can be menacing to a math phobic. It looks like Greek (which it is); it's new and strange; it looks mean and angular and, well, mathematical. But all it is is a *summation* sign. It means "the sum of."

Of what? Actually, Σ never walks alone. It always comes before something else, as in "ΣX," which means "the sum of X." That expression says: "You have a set of numbers that are scores on some variable, which we'll call X. Add up all the numbers there are and write down their sum, and let ΣX stand for that sum thereafter."

All that takes a long time to say or to write. So we use the shorter expression, ΣX, to represent it.

That's all.

HOW TO READ A GRAPH

If you are already familiar with graphs, you can skim this section, but don't skip it because we will be looking further at these data later on.

Look first at the left graph (Figure 1.2A), with its dots connected by lines. What the graph shows is the proportion of 25-year-old Americans who were married (the lines with the dark circles), and who were cohabiting but unmarried (light circles), in 5-year blocks from 1940 to 1965. We see right away that the proportion of married people decreased over that time period (the line gets lower as we follow it from left to right), whereas the proportion cohabiting increased (the line gets higher left to right). That is one advantage of a graph: It allows us to see trends at a glance.

The graph also gives us more specific information if we want it. What proportion were cohabiting in 1950? On the horizontal axis, we read over to "1950." From there our eye moves up (as shown by the vertical arrow) to the line that represents cohabitors. Then we read over to the ver-

tical axis (following the horizontal arrow). This tells us that about 17% of 25-year-olds were cohabiting in that year. Similarly, if we want to know the percentage who were married in 1960, then (following the arrows) we move from "1960" up to the line for "marrieds," then over to the vertical axis to find the percentage. It's about 61%.

Another way of presenting data is shown in Figure 1.2B, which shows the same data as a *bar graph*. Again, we see at once that something is increasing (one set of bars gets taller as we go left to right), and something else is decreasing (the other set of bars gets shorter). If we want to know the proportion of marrieds in 1950, we find the bar for "married" for 1950 (the shaded bar for that year). Then we read from the top of the bar leftward to the vertical axis (I'm letting you do that in your mind's eye this time, as we normally would). Then we read from that axis the corresponding figure. It's about 73%.

Incidentally, the term *graph* refers to the whole figure. The individual circles in A, or the individual bars in B, are often referred to as *data points*.

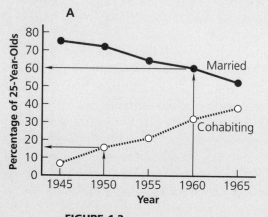

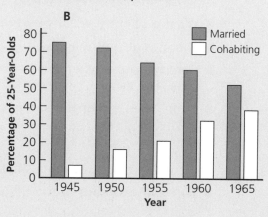

FIGURE 1.2
Panel A: A line graph showing the downward trend in marriages and the upward trend in cohabitation among 25-year-olds, from 1945 to 1965. Panel B: The same data presented as a bar graph (data from Bumpass & Sweet, 1989).

CHAPTER 2

THEORY AND DATA
IN PSYCHOLOGY

Science is built up with facts, as a house is with stones. But a collection of facts is no more a science than a heap of stones is a house.

—JULES HENRI POINCARE

IN THIS CHAPTER, WE'LL DISCUSS:

- What a scientist means by the term *theory*
- Theories at multiple levels
- How we know when we're wrong: testing our theories against the facts (the data)
- Hypotheses, predictions, and confirmations or disconfirmations
- Why we don't "prove" theories, but instead add to the "weight of evidence" pro or con
- Why theories must be falsifiable
- Three case studies of the theory-testing process in real research

Consider what happens when you click the switch on your reading lamp, and the lamp doesn't light. Something is obviously wrong, but what? Well, check the possibilities. Is the cord plugged into the wall? Look and see, and plug it in if it isn't. Does the light work now? No? Perhaps it's the bulb. Replace the bulb with a new one, and see if it works then.

If it doesn't, well, perhaps a fuse is blown or circuit breaker is open. Try replacing the fuse, or check the circuit breaker position to see if it is open. If that doesn't help, maybe it's the switch that's defective; we can replace the switch with a new one. . . . You get the picture.

If we have done these things, then we have engaged in a perfectly valid *scientific investigation*. We have checked out the possibilities, one by one, by setting things up so that we could *look and see* whether that was where the problem was. Thus, as so often, we find that we already understand many of the principles of research that this book is going to talk about in this and later chapters. We only need to put what we know in new contexts.

When we replaced the light bulb, for example, we were doing a simple *experiment*. We caused something to vary—old bulb versus new one. This is what an experiment is: We make a manipulation and note its effects. On the other hand, looking to see whether the lamp was plugged in, or whether a circuit breaker had opened, shows that we can learn by simple *looking*, without making anything vary. And often, "just looking" leads to experiment. Look and see if the cord is unplugged (an observation). If it is, plug it in and see if that corrects the problem (an experiment).

Notice a few other things. First, we checked out the possibilities, and in each case we *respected what the data told us*. Obviously, we want the problem to be something simple, like an unplugged plug or a blown-out bulb, for these are the easiest things to correct. But if our observations tell us that these are not the problem, we don't argue with the observations. This may seem an obvious point, but when we're debating more important or emotionally laden questions, we may find it very difficult to look at the data objectively, irrespective of what we *want* the answer to be.

Second, we checked the possibilities *one at a time*. We didn't change the bulb, change the switch, replace the plug, and tear out the wiring in the walls all at once. The research process is like that: We study a little bit of the complex system at a time, and do not try to study everything at once.

And a final point. Our investigation at each step was guided by a *hypothesis*, or *prediction*, about what we should expect to see if the explanation were such-and-such. If the problem is the bulb, then the light should work with a new bulb. We test that idea: Change the bulb and see. And these ideas in turn fit into a *theoretical* structure, believe it or not—a structure that goes way beyond why this particular lamp wasn't doing its job right then. To see this, we must look more closely at what a *theory* is.

THEORY

The word *theory* has some unfortunate connotations. We tend to think of a theory as a hunch, or a guess, or an idea in somebody's head—one, perhaps, that he dreamed up while sitting in an armchair. This is what we mean when we say, "Oh, well, that's just a theory." We hear that said even about the theory of evolution: "It is, after all, just a theory." Often we will hear the field of psychology dismissed as "just a lot of theories."

It doesn't help that a lot of what passes for psychology is, in fact, unsupported opinion. The section called "psychology" in any bookstore will be chockablock with "theories" in this sense. There will be whole bookfuls of ideas that live in authors' heads and, as far as we can tell, only there.

But there is a different use of the word *theory,* one that we're going to explore now. In this sense, a theory is simply a statement of *general principles* through which we can understand nature a little better. Let us see what this means.

THEORIES AS PRINCIPLES

Imagine this scenario. We flip a switch, and the light bulb does light up. So our simple-minded "theory" of light bulbs—flip the switch, and the bulb will light unless something is wrong—is supported. But *why* do light bulbs light up when we flip a switch? Our roommate, who is a physics major, happens to be there. We ask her, "Why did the bulb light up?"

She might say: "Well, when the switch was flipped, two pieces of metal came into contact with each other. Electric current flowed through that connection, through the wires attached to the bulb, and also through the little wire (the filament) inside the bulb itself. Now when electricity flows, heat is produced. The filament heated up; and when it got hot enough, it began to glow, just as white-hot steel gives off a glow. That glow is the light that we see."

Notice that at every step of this explanation, there is an appeal to a general principle. It is true *in general* that metals conduct electricity—*all* metals, not just this bit of metal. It is true *in general* that the flow of electric current generates heat, and that metals glow if they are made hot enough. Our roommate's explanation showed how the specific event—*that* light bulb lighting up just *then*—was a specific case of general principles that apply to all such cases. (This is why we speak of our simple-minded statement—switch a light on, and it will light unless something's wrong—as a theory. It applies to all incandescent lights, not just this or that one.)

In short, a scientific theory is a statement, or set of statements, that describe *general principles* or, at least, what we think *might* be general principles. It is statements of general principles that the scientist seeks.

Why? For two reasons. First, general principles allow us to relate one event to another. They *organize our knowledge*. If we know the principles of electricity, we can better understand lightning and light bulbs and electric toasters and much besides. Second, it is principles that permit us to *use our knowledge*. If we understand electricity, then we can put together an electric circuit for some special purpose. It may be different from any circuit that has ever been built before, but if we know the principles, we can be confident that our widget will work. That is the process that has given us electric lights, telephones, television, computers, and space travel—the use of general principles to *predict* whether this or that new device will work, and implement it if we predict that it will.

THE LADDER OF PRINCIPLES

Let's push our example further. Our roommate has given us an explanation of why light bulbs light up—not just *this* light bulb, but all incandescent bulbs. Now suppose we sit down with her and kick these ideas around. "You know," she might say, "these same principles allow us to understand how electric toasters work. And electric ovens. The underlying principles are the same: Metals conduct current, and heat up when you pass current through them." So already we have hold of some principles that go far beyond the specific event we began with.

Now we push her: "Yes, yes. But why do metals heat up when current passes through them? Why does current flow through metals at all?" We are now asking for explanations of the principles themselves.

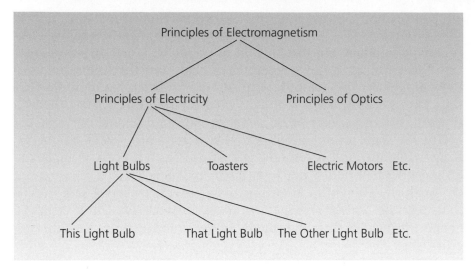

FIGURE 2.1
The hierarchy of principles.

What will the reply consist of? It will appeal to other principles that are *more general still*. The principles of electricity are special cases of the principles of electromagnetic theory—a more general theory that also allows us to explain the behavior of compass needles and other magnetic phenomena, *and* the laws of optics—for light, it turns out, is itself electromagnetic. Push still further, and eventually we will get to the most general physical theories we have: quantum mechanics and Einstein's theory of general relativity.

Thus, theories in science form a hierarchy (Figure 2.1). There are what we might call "local" or low-level theories, by which we can explain limited classes of phenomena—light bulbs, say. Higher up the ladder, more general theories explain the low-level ones, and relate them to each other. The higher we go, the more general we get, and the wider is the range of specific events we are able to explain.

PRINCIPLES IN PSYCHOLOGY

The above examples were drawn from physics, because there the ladder of explanatory principles is clearly laid out for our inspection. In psychology, we also seek general principles by which to explain, for example, how memory works or how learning takes place, but we are some way away from that ambitious goal. We understand electric circuits far, far better than we understand memory. But the goal remains the same—the search for principles—so let us look at an example of this from psychological research, just to show the parallel.

To remember someone's name, we know that it's often helpful to repeat the name over and over to ourselves, in the person's presence. Now that is already a generalization—we speak of "a person," not Sandy Smith or Pat Jones—but it's a special case of a broader generalization. Often we find that if two events occur together enough times, we will form a kind of mental connection between them. (We used to call the connection an *association*, but nowadays we call it a *retrieval cue*, for seeing the one event is a "cue" for "retrieving" the other.) This "principle of association" may tie together many specific events—learning a foreign-language vocabulary, learning people's names, the formation of conditioned reflexes, and much besides.

A LOOK BACKWARD—AND FORWARD

We see that the term *theory*, as used by scientists, is a very far cry from the popular notion of a hunch, a guess, or something somebody dreams up in an armchair. A theory is a statement of general principles, by which particular events can be explained and understood. This can occur at multiple levels. Low-level, "local" theories can explain limited classes of events. They can themselves be explained in terms of other, higher-level theories that are more general still.

The principles rest not on speculation only, but on a database of systematic observation. The observations may come first, and the theory arise out of them. Or one may begin with a theory; but even so, it must be checked—again with observations. Thus, by checking our theories against the facts of observation, and correcting the theories as the facts demand, we improve our theories and hence our understanding. This leads us into our next major topic.

ON KNOWING WHEN WE'RE WRONG: TESTING OUR THEORIES

Early in this chapter, we noted the misconception that a theory is "just an idea in somebody's head." Now, it is true that a scientific theory may *begin* as an idea in somebody's head. The difference is that it doesn't stay there. It is brought from the head into the real world, and *tested*.

In other words, having arrived at a (tentative) explanation, scientists check that explanation with further observations. That way, if an explanation is mistaken, sooner or later we will discover the fact. We will know when we are wrong. And remember our principle: *If we know when we are wrong, we can correct our mistakes; if we don't, we can't.*

TESTING THEORIES

How do we test a theory? By deriving from it a prediction, or *hypothesis*, about what the results of an experiment or other study should be. We say, "*If* the theory is right, *then* X should happen." That is our hypothesis. Then we do the experiment or run the study, look at the data, and ask: "Okay. Did X happen, or not? Do the data come out as the theory says they should?" There is a kind of loop, in other words, from theory, to the predicted data (the hypothesis), to the actual data, and then to the implications of those data for the theory (Figure 2.2).

What do we say then? We speak carefully.

First, suppose the data *do not* come out as the theory says they should. The prediction, we say, is *disconfirmed*. Then we know that something is wrong. Maybe we did the study wrong; we must check our procedures. (Did we replace a bad bulb with another bad one?)

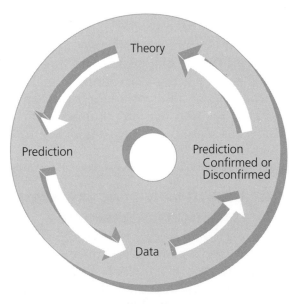

FIGURE 2.2
The theory-data cycle.

Maybe the theory does not really have to make that false prediction; we must check our logic. But if we can rule out these problems, then we will say that the theory itself cannot be right.

That doesn't mean that we scrap the theory root and branch. Maybe it just needs to be modified, so that it doesn't make that wrong prediction anymore. Or maybe it holds only under certain conditions and not others, and our finding may help to specify these *boundary conditions* (e.g., no electric light will work during a power blackout!). With luck, the data may even show us *where* and *how* our ideas need correction. Then the corrected theory can be tested in turn. So even a failed prediction can bring our ideas closer to the truth.

Or in the extreme, perhaps we must indeed scrap the theory altogether, go back to the drawing board, and try for one that will be closer to the truth. Whichever way it goes, we will have found out that our present theory cannot be right, and so we can correct our misunderstanding.

Second, suppose the data *do* come out as the theory says they should. The prediction is *confirmed*. Now we speak even more carefully.

Have we *proved* the theory to be correct? No. The theory predicts that X should happen, and X did happen—but X may have happened for some other reason altogether, and our theory could still be wrong.

This doesn't mean that a confirming instance is useless. If a prediction is confirmed, we are likely to have a little more confidence in the theory that gave rise to it. At the very least, we can say that we gave the theory a chance to be disconfirmed, and it wasn't. It passed the test—this time.

Moreover, if we predict that X should occur and it does, that finding will be a *disconfirming* instance for any alternative theory which says that X should *not* occur. This is especially true if the theory has made a prediction that is, as we say, *counterintuitive*—that is, it runs *counter* to our *intuitions*. It predicts a surprising result. If a prediction of that sort is made and confirmed, this can add substantially to the weight of evidence in favor of the theory. The theorist can then say, "My theory can explain this result, and I can't see how any other theory could." We have, we might say, ruled out *all* alternatives that we can now see.

In summary: When a prediction is *disconfirmed*, we take this as clear evidence that something is wrong—either with the theory, or with the investigation itself. If a prediction is *confirmed*, we may speak of this as supporting the theory, if only by making trouble for other, competing theories. But we never speak of *proving* a theory, once and for all. There are always further tests to be made—and that takes us to our next topic.

THE THEORY-DATA CYCLE

A single instance of theory-testing, of the kind we've just discussed, is actually only a single "turn" of an ongoing, cyclic process shown in Figure 2.2. There is a continuous back-and-forth movement between our theories and the facts of observation—the data—by which we test our theories. I call it the *theory-data cycle*.

One can enter the cycle at either level. A scientist may indeed begin with a preliminary theory in the form of a hunch or a guess—an idea in the head. "Perhaps," he says, "such-and-such is going on; perhaps these are the principles that apply." But the very next thing he will do is to ask, "Now how can I check that idea? How can I test it?" He will design a study to test his idea; then he will do the study and collect the relevant data (from theory to data). Then, back to the theory: What do the data tell us about it? (From data back to theory!) If the data *disconfirm* the theoretical prediction, he may modify the theory and then test the modified form—or, possibly, he may scrap the theory and start over. If the data *support* the theory, he will hold onto the theory for the time being, and test it again in some other way.

Alternatively, a researcher may begin by gathering data, doing exploratory experiments and so collecting some basic facts about her subject matter. At some point, she will move from data to theory: Looking over the facts, she will say, "Aha! I think I see what is going on. I'll bet these are the principles that apply" (data to theory). But then, just as in the previous case, she will ask: "Okay. How can I test that idea?" Once again, she will check her idea by testing it against further observations (theory to data).

Thus, wherever we begin, we find ourselves cycling through this process of testing and correcting. We check our theories against the data; if the theory is wrong, the data will tell us so; we will modify the theory and test again; and if we are still wrong, the data will tell us that too. The process is continuous and is never complete. There are always more tests to be made.

BAD VIBES AND LITTLE GREEN MEN: THE FALSIFIABILITY CRITERION

Let's recall our principle once again: If we know when we are wrong, we can correct our mistakes; if we don't, we can't.

Therefore, before we take a theory seriously, scientists will insist

FIGURE 2.3
But if our theory is unfalsifiable, we won't know when we're wrong.

that it be testable or, as we often say, *falsifiable*. This simply means that we must have some way of knowing that it is wrong, if it is. There must be some *possible* set of data, some *possible* experimental outcome, that could reveal the theory's falsity by disconfirming the prediction(s) it makes. Hence this very commonsensical requirement is sometimes called the *falsifiability criterion*.

What about a theory, then, that cannot be falsified? What if there are no *possible* data that could show it to be mistaken? At first glance, it sounds as if that would be a very powerful theory indeed. Not so: It is very easy to create a theory like that, but such a theory has no power at all (Figure 2.3).

Keith Stanovich, in his wonderful book *How to Think Straight about Psychology* (1998), shows how easy it is. He says:

> I have discovered the underlying brain mechanism that controls behavior. You will soon be reading about this discovery (in the *National Enquirer,* available at your local grocery). In the left hemisphere of the brain, near the language area, reside two tiny green men. . . . And, well, to make a long story short, they basically control everything. There is one difficulty, however. The green men have the ability to detect any intrusion into the brain (surgery, X rays, etc.), and when they do sense such an intrusion, they tend to disappear. (I forgot to mention that they have the power to become invisible.) (p. 25)

Well, there's a theory for us. Can we falsify it? Can we show Professor Stanovich that he is wrong? I don't see how. We won't see the little green men if we look, but then we wouldn't. They hide. The theory says so. So, if we look and see little green men, that would support the theory. If we look and we don't see little green men, that would support the theory too. The theory would win either way!

Now all this, Stanovich admits, is so utterly ridiculous as to be almost insulting. But that's because we don't believe in the little green men in the first place. What if we did? Well, Stanovich goes on to discuss what has been called the Catch-22 of ESP research:

> It works as follows: A "believer" . . . claims to have demonstrated ESP in the laboratory. A "skeptic" . . . is brought in to confirm the phenomenon. Often, after observing the experimental situation, the skeptic calls for more controls. . . . When the controls are instituted, the phenomena cannot be demonstrated. . . . [But then] the believer invokes the Catch-22 of ESP: Psychic powers, the believer maintains, are subtle, delicate, and easily disturbed. The "negative vibes" of the skeptic were probably responsible for the disruption of the "psi powers." The powers will undoubtedly return when the negative aura of the skeptic is removed. (p. 26)

(Incidentally, I have talked with researchers in parapsychology and have even run some experiments with them; and I can assure you that Stanovich is not making this up. Exactly that kind of argument has been made to me, when proper controls have made a "paranormal phenomenon" go away.)

Now, all this makes sense on the surface. But if we think about it, we see that the argument is the exact logical equivalent of the little-green-men theory. If we control our experiment properly, the ESP finding disappears. Is this because it was really an illusion caused by poor control in the first place? Oh, no—it's because ESP powers don't like well-controlled experiments! So they hide—like the little green men—until the controls go away.

But we see what that means: If there really are no ESP powers, we have no way of showing that fact. The theory—that ESP powers exist—is unfalsifiable. There are no possible observations that could show the ESP researcher that he is wasting his time, because any possible negative observations could be explained away by appeal to the skittishness of the powers. The theory is data-proof.

Well—if we don't know when we're wrong, we can't correct our mistakes. If in fact ESP does not exist, but if no possible experimental outcome could convince the researcher of this, he will go on wasting his time. A pity.

But it is not only in parapsychology that untestable theories are found. As Stanovich goes on to discuss, many scientists have concluded that psychoanalytic theory is unfalsifiable in much the same way. It is a rich, flexible theory, and that looks at first like a great strength; but in fact it is a great weakness, because the theory is so rich and flexible that it could account for anything that might conceivably happen. If X occurs, a psychoanalyst could explain it; if not-X occurs, a psychoanalyst could explain that too—for any X! Again, the theory would win either way; and if it is wrong, we have no way of knowing that it is.

As a result, we cannot speak of psychoanalysis as a well-established theory that has survived repeated tests. It hasn't survived *any* tests, because no tests are possible (Crews, 1996). So, is the theory mistaken? Does it give us, not understanding, but only the illusion of understanding? There is no way to know.

THEORY-TESTING AND THE "WEIGHT OF THE EVIDENCE"

I am often asked, "Do you believe in UFOs?" I'm always struck by how the question is phrased, the suggestion that this is a matter of belief and not of evidence. I'm almost never asked, "How good is the evidence that UFOs are alien spaceships?"

—SAGAN, 1995, p. 82

You can find a study that will prove anything.

—FREQUENTLY HEARD

A moment ago, we said that we "speak carefully" about the implications of evidence confirming, or disconfirming, a theoretical prediction. Let us elaborate that a bit, for it allows us to correct what may be a misleading impression of theory-testing in our discussion thus far, and to put a frequently heard remark in perspective.

We said that no single confirming finding can prove a theory correct. At most, we say that a finding supports a theory and, perhaps, makes trouble for competing theories. But *prove* a theory correct? No. New information might require us, tomorrow or the next day, to change our ideas and to improve them.

Similarly, a single disconfirming finding seldom leads us to scrap a theory root and branch. It is not as if a theory is destroyed by the very first failure of its predictions. As we noted earlier, the disconfirming study may itself have been done wrong, or it might be that the original theory needs only to be modified, not discarded.

Rather than think of a theory as confirmed or disconfirmed in one fell swoop, then, we might think of any single test of theory as adding to the *weight of the evidence*, for or against (Figure 2.4). Con-

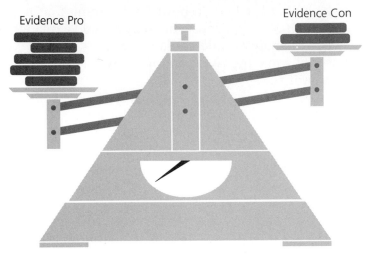

FIGURE 2.4
A single study doesn't "prove" or "disprove" a theory, but instead adds to the weight of evidence for or against.

firming instances add weight to the "for" side of the balance. Disconfirming instances add weight on the "against" side. And where we have no data, as in the alien spaceships question—why, we do what Carl Sagan does. We recognize that the pans are in balance with no weights on them. There is no evidence either way. We draw no conclusions, and keep an open mind.

Now, it is true that as evidence mounts, the balance may tip way over in one direction or the other. Eventually, the evidence against a theory may so far outweigh the evidence in its favor that the theory simply is discarded—not in some ceremony by a scientific court, but just because we gradually cease to take it seriously. In psychology, this happened to the once-popular "drive-reduction" theory of motivation (p. 37), and the "refrigerator parents" account of autism Chapter 1).

At the other end, suppose a theory has masses of data that support it, and few or no data that seriously challenge it. Then, at some point, we begin to speak of that theory, still not as *proven* (unless we're speaking carelessly), but as *well supported*, or even as *well established*. In physics, Einstein's theory of relativity has such a status. In biology—make no mistake—so does Darwin's theory of evolution. In psychology, I think the so-called "duplicity theory" of vision would qualify. This is the theory that in humans and some other animals, the visual system has two kinds of light-sensitive elements, the rods and the cones, each with its own set of properties and responsibilities. The evidence for this theory—psychophysical, anatomical, histochemical—is overwhelming. The evidence against it, so far as I know, is nil.

All this is what is overlooked by the remark, "You can find a study that will prove anything." Yes, we can, if we look at studies one by one. But where there is a mass of evidence—many studies, all or most supporting the same conclusion—then the conclusion must be taken seriously, as "well supported" by the evidence.

A LOOK BACK

What we have been talking about in this section is often referred to as the *self-corrective* nature of science. By testing our theories, we discover when they're wrong, and so we can improve them.

For the research producer, then, testing of theories is a powerful error-correction device. It's useful for the research consumer, too. When we read a bit of advice from a self-styled expert, it's instructive to ask: "But have these ideas been tested against real data? Have they survived repeated tests? Have they, come to think of it, survived any tests at all? *Can* they be tested?"

We can spot a lot of nonsense that way.

THREE CASE STUDIES

Thus far, we have discussed theory and theory-testing in the abstract (except for our light bulb example). It would be helpful at this point to look more closely at some specific instances of these ideas in action, in psychological research. Let us consider three such instances.

EXAMPLE 1: A TALE OF TWO MOTHERS

Babies form strong "attachments" to their adult caregivers. They may be calmed by the presence of the attachment figure, and distressed when she or he goes away; and when they are able to move around, they may follow the caregiver, keeping in close touch. We see this in human babies, and also in baby monkeys, who are able to get around almost immediately after birth. They spend many hours clinging tightly to the fur of the mother. Why?

Well, one theory goes like this. The monkey (or human) mother is a source of food. The baby gets hungry, nurses from the mother, and experiences a pleasant reduction in hunger. Now, that hunger reduction occurs repeatedly in the presence of the mother, and so the sight and feel of her become associated with the pleasure of hunger reduction. Here we have what has been called the "cupboard theory" of mother–infant attachment. The mother acquires positive value for the baby, because she is the cupboard from which food comes.

The underlying idea goes beyond attachment alone. The cupboard theory was a special case of a much more general theory, held both by early behaviorists and by Freud. That is the notion that all motives, however complex, are ultimately based on a handful of basic needs or drives—like hunger, for instance—and the attempt to reduce them. Thus, a test of the cupboard theory is also a test of this more general drive-reduction theory. The ladder of principles (pp. 27–29)!

HARLOW'S EXPERIMENT

An experimental psychologist, Harry Harlow, was studying primate behavior at the University of Wisconsin. For a number of reasons, he had long had doubts about drive-reduction theory in general and the cupboard theory in particular. So he set out to test the cupboard theory directly (Harlow, 1958).

First, what are the alternatives? A baby monkey spends a lot of time clinging to its mother. The cupboard theory says: This is because the mother is associated with the food that the baby *needs*. Another possibility is that the mother provides a warm, fuzzy, clingable surface that the baby *likes*; Harlow refers to this as *contact comfort*. Survival needs like hunger may have little to do with it.

When a baby clings to its mother, is it because she offers food or because she offers contact comfort? The problem is that, in nature, a mother offers both of these at once, and so we cannot tell which of the two is the important one. To determine that, we have to separate them, and the only way to do that is to build mothers of our own.

So Harlow built two foster monkey mothers—the only mothers his lab-reared baby monkeys had (Figure 2.5). One of the mothers was made of bare, bony wire mesh, but had a bottle of milk built in, with a nipple that the baby could drink through. She offered *food but not comfort*. The other mother was covered with fuzzy terry cloth and warmed by a light bulb suspended inside her—but she had no milk. She offered *comfort but not food*.

Which mother should the babies prefer? Well, what would our two theories predict? The cupboard theory predicts that the babies

FIGURE 2.5
Harlow's monkey mothers, cold wire with food and warm terrycloth without food (courtesy Harlow Primate Laboratory, University of Wisconsin).

should form an "attachment" to the source of food and prefer the wire mother. The contact-comfort theory predicts that the babies should prefer the source of comfort—the cloth mother.

And that is what happened. Harlow's data showed that the little monkeys would cling to the terry-cloth mother for 12 to 18 hours a day. When they got hungry, they would climb down, go over and nurse from the wire mother, and then at once go back to the warmth and clingability of the cloth mother. In short, they cared much more for contact-comfortable mothers than for food-associated ones.

Given these findings, Harlow went on to test the contact-comfort theory in other ways (the *theory-data cycle*, pp. 30–32). If the babies were actually forming an "attachment" to the cloth mother, we might expect her to provide a certain comfort in frightening situations. Observations supported this idea. If an unfamiliar object (like a toy teddy bear) were placed in the cage, the baby monkey would rush to the cloth mother and cling to her—if she was there. If only the wire mother were there, then the baby would avoid the frightening object *and* the mother. Rather than cling to her, he would huddle in a corner until the frightening object went away.

A LOOK BACK

In this case study, we see a clear example of how we test our ideas. The cupboard theory of attachment is falsifiable; it makes a prediction about the outcome of this experiment, and the prediction could be disconfirmed. And it was. Hence the experiment counts as evidence against the cupboard theory, and as evidence supporting the contact-comfort theory.

We also see how an experiment can test our ideas at more than one level (Figure 2.6). Harlow's data make trouble not only for the cupboard theory, but also for the more general drive-reduction theory of motivation. Indeed, by the time of this research, the evidence against that theory was already quite strong (see later discussion), but Harlow's data added a heavy block to the pan of the balance marked "against."

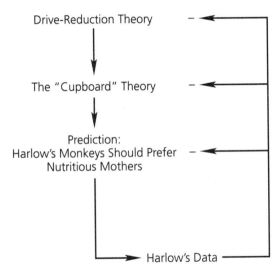

FIGURE 2.6
Disconfirmation at multiple levels. Harlow's data weigh against both the "cupboard" theory of infant attachment and the more general drive-reduction theory of motivation.

EXAMPLE 2: THE "APATHETIC BYSTANDER"

This really happened:

> Kitty Genovese is set upon by a maniac as she returns from work at 3 A.M. Thirty-eight of her neighbors in Kew Gardens [in New York City] come to their windows when she cries out in terror; none come to her assistance even though her stalker takes over half an hour to murder her. No one even so much as calls the police. She dies (Latané & Darley, 1970, p. 1).

Stories like these could be multiplied manyfold, and many explanations for these "terrifying failures of human compassion" (Latané & Darley, 1970, p. 2) have been put forward: Large cities, and the anonymity that goes with them, lead to alienation of the individual from the group. We are so fearful that we react to disaster by withdrawing from it. We are apathetic or indifferent or unconsciously sadistic. And so on. Notice that all these explanations appeal to some *internal* state, something that we carry around within ourselves: alienation, fear, apathy, and the like.

A team of social psychologists, Bibb Latané (rhymes with *matinee*) and John Darley, found these explanations unconvincing. After all, there is the other side. "People often help others, even at great risk to themselves. For every 'apathy' story, one of outright heroism could be cited" (Latané & Darley, 1970, p. 4). Apparently even city-dwellers are not always apathetic or indifferent; they act that way under some conditions, but not under others. So the question is: What are these "conditions"?

In particular: Could it be that the crucial determinant is not within ourselves, but in the *situation*? And might it have to do not with our feelings or motives, but with our cognitions—with our interpretation of the situation? Consider:

> When only one bystander is present in an emergency situation, if help is to be given it must be he who gives it. The situation is not so clear when a crowd of bystanders are present. Then the responsibility for intervention is diffused among the bystanders and focuses on no single one. In these circumstances, each person may feel less responsibility to help the victim. "Why me?" he can say (Latané & Darley, 1970, p. 1557).

In other words, if there is a crowd of onlookers and no one helps, maybe it's *because* there's a crowd of onlookers!

THE "SMOKE-FILLED ROOM" EXPERIMENT

This idea can be tested, and Latané and Darley did so with a classic series of experiments. In one of these, subjects were sitting in a waiting room, filling out a questionnaire. They believed that they were waiting to participate in an experiment; they didn't know that they were already in one. Then an emergency was staged: Smoke began to pour into the room from a vent in the wall. Question: Would the subject leave the waiting room to report the "emergency" or otherwise offer help?

There were two experimental conditions, and each subject was assigned *at random* to one or the other (see later). In one, the subject was waiting by himself; it was up to him to take action. In the other, the subjects were waiting in groups of three, so that "diffusion of responsibility" could occur: Each subject could ask himself, "Is it my responsibility to take action, or will one of these other people do it?" Sure enough: Fewer subjects took action, and took longer to act if they did, in the grouped condition (Figure 2.7).

Several other experiments, variations on this theme, were conducted, and the findings were consistent: In many settings, and for many kinds of emergencies, the mere presence of multiple bystanders makes it less likely that any of them will offer help. Moreover, it

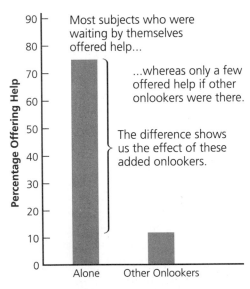

FIGURE 2.7
Data for the "smoke-filled room" experiment. Subjects waiting with others were less likely to respond to an emergency than those waiting by themselves (data from Latané & Darley, 1970).

does depend on how the bystander interprets the situation, and what messages he receives from others. If the bystander *believes* that other people are around, even if they are not, that is enough: He is less likely to offer help!

Latané and Darley (1970) sum up the implications of their studies thus:

> "There's safety in numbers" according to an old adage, and modern city dwellers seem to believe it. . . . It may be that people are less likely to find themselves in trouble if there are others present. But if a person does find himself in trouble, safety in numbers may be illusory. . . . In fact, the opposite seems to be true. A victim may be more likely to get help or an emergency to be reported, the fewer people who are available to take action. (p. 156)

A LOOK BACK

Here we have a case in which a prediction was *confirmed* by the data, and the confirmation was all the more forceful because the prediction was *counterintuitive* (p. 31). We say that there is "safety in numbers," and intuitively it seems obvious that if many onlookers are present, the likelihood that *someone* will intervene should increase. Our intuition is wrong.

There is more. The standard explanations of failures to help are in terms of alienation, apathy, indifference, "dehumanization," and similar personality characteristics thought to be produced by modern urban environments. But the subjects in the smoke experiment were assigned *at random* to wait alone, or to wait with others. Thus, each group of subjects should have contained about as many alienated, apathetic, and indifferent people as the other group did. But the two groups behaved differently. Therefore, it was the presence of other onlookers, *and nothing else*, that made subjects behave so differently in the two situations. The external social situation was a much more powerful influence than internal personal or personality factors. Finally, in some of their studies, Latané and his co-workers measured a whole series of personality variables, to see whether those who helped and those who did not would differ on any of them. They didn't.

Thus, like Harlow's experiment, this one addressed a specific question that bears on a more general issue. Besides disconfirming the "safety in numbers" prediction and confirming the counterintuitive "danger in numbers" one, these data take their place along with many others to suggest a more general, higher-level conclusion: External, situational factors can be much more powerful influences on our actions than internal personality factors are. We will return to this idea.

EXAMPLE 3. THERAPEUTIC TOUCH

Our third example is different again. It is an experiment conducted with humans; and, unlike the first two, which were examples of *basic research* guided by theory, this is an example of *applied research* (Chapter 1).

You may have heard of the technique known as *Therapeutic Touch* (TT), which enjoyed quite a vogue for awhile. At this writing, TT is still taught in more than 100 colleges and universities in 75 countries. Considered primarily a nursing technique, it is used by nurses in at least 80 hospitals in North America. Nursing journals have published many articles testifying to its usefulness.

Many thousands of people have been trained to treat patients through the use of TT. Dr. Dolores Krieger, its originator, has said that since she published her first paper on TT 28 years ago she has trained more than 47,000 practitioners. Her students have gone on to train thousands more.

Practitioners of TT say that the human body emits (or, indeed, *is*) an energy field. Trained therapists can be taught to detect these fields, which extend beyond the body. Moreover, patients who are ill have disturbances in their fields: hot spots or cold spots or areas that feel tingly to the therapist. The therapist can then "rebalance" a person's field by touching the field (not the body). It has been claimed that such manipulations can calm colicky babies, relieve symptoms of Alzheimer's disease, even treat cancer—and more. The practitioners insist that the energy field is real, and that anyone can be trained to feel it. (One practitioner said the field feels like "warm Jell-O or warm foam.")

EMILY ROSA'S EXPERIMENT

Okay: Trained therapists believe they can detect these energy fields. But can they? A researcher, Emily Rosa, decided to find out (Rosa, Rosa, Sarner, & Barrett, 1998).

The subjects were 21 trained Therapeutic Touch practitioners. The procedure was elegantly simple: The subject and the experimenter were separated by a screen, so that the subjects could not see their own hands or the experimenter's. The subject extended both hands palm up, and the experimenter simply placed one hand close to, but not touching, one or the other of the subject's hands. By flipping a coin for each trial, the experimenter decided whether to approach the subject's left hand or right hand on that trial. The subject was asked to decide which hand was being almost-touched in this way (Figure 2.8). If the subjects could detect the energy field surrounding the experimenter's hand, they should be able to tell where the experimenter's hand was: left or right.

They didn't. Twenty-one trained practitioners, on average, identified the correct location of the experimenter's hand just 47% of the time. They would have been right about half the time by chance alone. A second, follow-up study was just as discouraging—41% correct on average, again slightly below chance level.

Further analysis of the data ruled out some of the excuses the subjects offered—after the data were shown to them!—for their failures: (1) Perhaps, the subjects said, the experimenter left a "memory" of her hand behind, making it difficult on later trials to tell the real hand from the memory. But the data said: First attempts were no more accurate than later ones. (2) Some subjects said that the left hand is the "receiver" of energy and the right hand is the "transmitter," so it is harder to detect the field when it is above the right hand. But the data said: Accuracy was no greater for the left hand

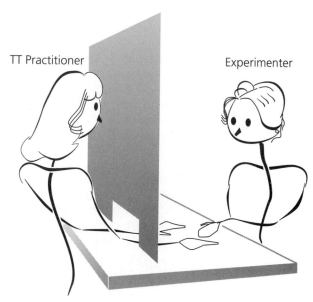

FIGURE 2.8
Emily Rosa's experiment (from Sarner, 1998).

than for the right. Finally, it's always possible that further training might improve accuracy. But these data said: Accuracy was not related to length of time the therapist had been practicing.

◀ A LOOK BACK

The conclusion is clear. Trained TT practitioners sincerely believe that they can detect a person's "energy field." They are mistaken. If they could, they could tell with better-than-chance accuracy whether such a "field" is impinging on their left hand or their right (prediction). They couldn't (disconfirmation). And the process was repeated in replying to objections. Was one trial leaving a "memory" that interfered with later ones? If so, performance should be better on first trials than on later ones (prediction). It wasn't (disconfirmation). Was only one hand a "receiver" for the fields? If so, performance should be more accurate with one hand than with the other (prediction). It wasn't (disconfirmation).

In addition, once again the narrow experimental question—Can the judges tell which hand is being almost touched?—bears on a much broader one that can be investigated in other ways. Trained TT practitioners were sure that they could perform well at this simple task. They were mistaken. Thus, this study can be added to the many others that tell us this: *We are quite good—much better than we think—at deluding ourselves.* In later chapters, we'll see further instances of this important and humbling fact.

AND FOR DESSERT . . .

I should tell you one thing more. The experimenter published the report of this study, with co-authors, in the prestigious *Journal of the American Medical Association*, when she was eleven years old. She had done the study as a fourth-grade science fair project, at the age of nine.

Her paper went through the same process of peer review (Chapter 12) as any other submission to that journal—and, like most such submissions, had to undergo revisions before it was accepted! The reviewers found it a procedurally and statistically valid study. The journal's editor commented that "practitioners should disclose these results to patients, third-party payers [that is, health insurers] should question whether they should pay for this procedure, and patients should save their money unless or until additional honest experimentation demonstrates an actual effect" (Lundberg, 1998, p. 1004).

This is one of many, many cases where a few well-performed experiments, if done *at the outset*, could have saved a great deal of time, effort, money, and pain.

A LOOK BACK

We have seen three examples of research in action. They differ in just about every way possible from each other, yet the underlying logic is the same for all. This is what the theory says should happen—the hypothesis or prediction. We do the study and ask: Does it happen?—the test. And the data say yes or no—confirmation or disconfirmation.

The studies have some other points in common, too. Let's look at a few.

THE "WEIGHT OF THE EVIDENCE" REVISITED

We mentioned earlier that no single experiment is likely to demolish a theory, and that still goes. However, in all the cases we've considered, the specific findings make contact with the results of other investigations. Harlow's conclusion—nutrition is not enough—is supported by other studies using quite different procedures—studies of human parent–child interactions (pp. 119–123), and even studies of blood chemistry (p. 49). Similarly, for the bystander-intervention studies, a variety of findings supports their conclusion (see Chapter 12).

Even the Therapeutic Touch experiment does not stand alone. At least one informal replication with one subject supports it. James Randi, director of the James Randi Educational Foundation in Fort Lauderdale, FL, tells us he had been trying to test therapeutic touch for years, and has even offered a prize to any practitioner who could detect a human energy field under controlled conditions. He has advertised in nursing journals and elsewhere. But only one person has answered; and she, in a similar test, succeeded in only 11 out of 20 attempts—almost exactly at chance. "She got up in a huff and muttered something about negative vibrations," Randi says—Catch-22 (quoted by Kolata, 1998, pp. 46–47)—and left. Second, as noted earlier, the study bears on a broader issue—how easily we can delude ourselves—that is supported by many other findings as well as this one.

There's another reason why it usually takes many findings to change our ideas—one is seldom enough. Different investigations act as cross-checks on each other. We've mentioned that when a prediction is disconfirmed, it's always possible that the study itself was done wrong. Maybe the methodology was not right, or perhaps some error crept in to bias the results. Yes—for any single study. But if a number of studies all point to the same conclusion, then we would have to argue that all of them allowed the same error, or equivalent errors that made them all come out the same wrong way. After awhile, that begins to look pretty implausible. It becomes much more likely that our ideas need to change.

FROM BIG QUESTIONS TO SMALL

STUDIES—AND BACK AGAIN

Any single investigation is going to be limited in scope. It will ask small, specific, answerable questions.

For example, we may ask: Will babies prefer nutritious or comfortable mothers? But we must be even more specific. There are endless ways of building model monkey mothers; Harlow chose only one. There are endless ways of measuring baby monkeys' preferences; Harlow chose one. Similarly, there is an endless variety of emergencies that might be staged; for each experiment, Latané and Darley chose only one. There is an endless number of ways we could set up an energy-field-detection experiment; Emily Rosa chose only one. And so on.

Since the conditions are so specific, and have to be, one's first reaction may be that the findings themselves are so limited as to be trivial. Politicians and the media can make fun of them: So baby monkeys prefer just *this* cloth mother to just *that* wire one—a choice they will never face under natural conditions anyway. Who cares? Why is it even worth finding out?

The way to put that reaction in perspective is to remember three things. First, we can think of these procedures as giving us *examples* of more general and important processes. If the cupboard theory were correct, baby monkeys should, in *this* setting, have preferred the wire mothers. If trained therapists can detect human energy fields, they certainly should have been able to do so in *this* simplified situation. If they can't, that's a problem for the theory.

Second, remember that experiments do not stand alone. In each case, we can point to other specific findings supporting the same conclusion. In our own time, for example, we find that social isolation in monkeys—even if they are not hungry, thirsty, or in pain—can actually affect the chemistry of the body (Suomi, 1991). It can produce an increase in levels of cortisol, a hormone made by the adrenal gland that, among other things, interferes with the immune system. These experiments didn't use wire mothers, but they do underscore the theoretical point: Nutrition is not enough.

Third, and perhaps most important: An experiment may be a test of theory at several levels at once. In this way, it may bear on fundamental questions about human and animal nature. Harlow's data make trouble for the cupboard theory, but also for the more general drive-reduction theory on which it is based. The "emergency" experiments bear on the issue of situational influences on what we do. And the TT experiments remind us once more of how easily we can delude ourselves.

In short: Small-scale, modest studies can combine to shed light on very broad issues. We can build large, beautiful, and very useful houses out of small stones.

SUMMARY

As scientists use the term, a *theory* is not just a hunch or a conjecture or an idea in somebody's head. It may begin "in the head," but it doesn't stay there.

A theory in our sense is a statement about the general principles that apply to classes of objects or events (e.g., to light bulbs in general), not just specific ones (this or that light bulb), or it may be a tentative statement about what general principles we think *might* apply. We seek general principles because they help us organize our knowledge and because it is the principles that we put to use, as when we invent a new device or procedure.

Theories can be stated at many levels. A "theory of light bulbs" would be a special case of a broader theory dealing with electrical phenomena in general. This in turn would be a special case of even broader physical theories, such as relativity.

But theories at any level must submit to checks; they must be tested against the data, the observed facts. That is how we know when we are wrong, and so are able to correct our mistakes and improve our theories. We determine what data we should obtain if our theory is correct—that is, what our theory *predicts* will happen. We then go to the data to see whether it does happen. If it does (if our prediction is confirmed), we have evidence in support of the theory—but we have not "proved" it to be right. If it does not (if our prediction is disconfirmed), we have evidence against the theory—but we have not "proved" it to be wrong. Perhaps it only needs modifying. Thus, any single study will seldom either demolish or enthrone a theory. Rather, it adds to the *weight of evidence* for or against. If that weight is strongly against a theory, eventually it will cease to be taken seriously, as has happened with drive-reduction theory and ESP research. If the weight of evidence is strongly in a theory's favor, as with relativity or the theory of evolution, we may come to speak of it as "well supported"—but still not as *proved*. There are always further tests to be made.

Thus, there is a continuous cyclic relation between data and theory (the theory-data cycle). Starting with a theory, we may make a prediction about what the data should show (from theory to data). Then, based on the data, we hold onto our theory for now, or we modify or discard it (from data to theory). Or we may begin by gathering data, and let a theory emerge from these (from data to theory). But the resulting theory will be tested against further observations (from theory to data).

The way we know when we're wrong is to test our ideas. However, this can only occur if our ideas *can* be tested—if, as we say, they are *falsifiable*. If no possible data would count as evidence against a theory, then that theory cannot be tested and, if it is wrong, we can never discover the fact.

Three case studies were presented. In each, a specific hypothesis (i.e., prediction) was tested; but also, in each case, the results have implications for much broader theoretical issues. Harlow's "wire and cloth mother" experiments told against the "cupboard" theory of mother–infant attachment, but also against the more general drive-reduction theory of motivation. Latané and Darley's "smoke-filled room" experiment supported the hypothesis that multiple onlookers may actually discourage helping behavior, but it also supported a much more general idea: Situational factors can be powerful determinants of how we behave. Rosa's experiment showed that even trained Therapeutic Touch practitioners cannot detect whatever "energy fields" pervade the human body. It also can be added to the many studies, of many kinds, that show us (if we will listen) how easily we can delude ourselves. Thus small-scale, modest studies can shed light on very broad issues.

MAKING FRIENDS WITH STATISTICS: STATISTICAL SIGNIFICANCE

Now let's shift focus, and look at one of the ways statistical reasoning is used in the research process. The case studies we looked over earlier in this chapter will provide some useful examples to work with.

The expression *statistical significance* sounds like a very esoteric and threatening idea. Indeed, discussion of it often comes at the end of a beginning statistics course, just to emphasize how difficult it is. Instead, we are going to confront it and tame it at the beginning of our journey.

Whenever we obtain a set of data, we need to ask: Do these data really tell us something, or did they come about by accident—did they just "happen to happen" this time? We have to realize that, strictly speaking, any data *could* have come about by chance. It's always possible. But we can ask: Is it *plausible* that these data came about by accident? If the answer is "No," we go ahead and draw our conclusion. And one way of answering that question is to test the *statistical significance* of our finding.

When we say that a finding is statistically significant, we are making the following three-step argument:

1. Data such as these *could* have come about by chance; true. But

2. We can show that that would happen very rarely. Therefore

3. We're pretty sure it didn't happen this time.

That's all! Step 2 can involve statisticians in some high-powered calculations, and it may require you and me to do some arithmetic, but the logic is just that simple.

To see how it works, consider a concrete instance. We'll gather some imaginary data and test its significance by what is called the *sign test*.

AN EXAMPLE: MORE MONKEY BUSINESS AND THE SIGN TEST

Suppose we decide to repeat Harlow's experiment and see whether we can replicate his findings. We build a cold, wiry, but nutritious mother monkey, and a warm terrycloth one but with no milk to offer. We have available, say, six lab-reared baby monkeys to use as subjects. We let each monkey have some time in a room that contains both model mothers, and we see which one it spends more time with. For short, we will then say that the baby monkey has "chosen" that model mother over the other.

We simplify our data as follows: For each monkey, if it spends more time with the cloth than with the wire mother, we record a plus sign next to its name or number. If it spends more time with the wire mother, we record a minus sign. (We could do it the other way around; it doesn't matter as long as we are consistent.) Hence the name, *sign test*.

Suppose that *all six* of our baby monkeys choose the cloth mother over the wire one. That sounds like strong evidence that the monkeys *prefer* the cloth mother. But, the carping critic carps, couldn't they have done that just by chance, even if they really had no preference one way or the other?

Strictly speaking, the answer is, as always, yes. It *could* have happened. But we can add: It's *implausible* that it did. What that means and how we know that, we will now see—so hang on.

THE NULL HYPOTHESIS

We begin by assuming that, in fact, our data did come about just by accident. They "just happened." Statisticians call this the *null hypothesis*. "Null" means "nothing," so we are assuming that "nothing is really going on here." The monkeys had no preference; rather, each one was as likely to choose one model mother as the other. We make that assumption, not because we believe it, but because it allows us to do some calculations. We ask: *If* the null hypothesis is true, then how often would we get data that are as consistent as this?

Consider: If there were no preference, then each monkey could as easily have chosen wire as cloth. It is as if each monkey flipped a coin—heads choose cloth, tails choose wire. The *probability* that all six would choose the cloth mother, then, is the same as the probability that if we tossed six honest coins, all six would come up heads!

And that's easy to calculate. The probability that one coin would come up heads is just 1/2, or 0.5. The probability that

both of two coins would come up heads is 1/2 × 1/2, or 0.25. The probability that three out of three coins would come up heads is 1/2 × 1/2 × 1/2, or 0.125. Continuing, we see that the probability that all of six coins would come up heads is $1/2^6$—0.5 multiplied by itself 6 times. That is 1/64, or 0.0156. We double that (we'll see why in a minute) to get 0.031. That is the *probability* that all six of six coins would come up the same way—all heads or all tails.

Why do we multiply by two? Because we would have said the same thing if the data had been equally consistent in the opposite direction: six out of six monkeys choosing wire. Thus, our final figure is the probability that we would get data that consistent, *in either direction*, if there is really no preference one way or the other. (We are doing what is called a *two-tailed test* of the null hypothesis. Later, we will see why it is called that, and what a one-tailed test would be.)

STATISTICAL SIGNIFICANCE

Having done this simple calculation, we end up with a number that gives us the *probability* of obtaining a set of data as consistent as these data are, *if* the null hypothesis is true. That phrase takes a long time to say or write, so we abbreviate it and speak of the *p-value* for our data (*p* for probability). Here, our *p*-value is 0.031, or 1/32.

That probability is pretty low. Such consistency would happen very rarely by chance if the coins are honest—and the equivalent event would happen very rarely if the monkeys had no preference! It is much more plausible to suppose that baby monkeys really do prefer cloth mothers to wire ones.

Therefore, here's what we can say: *If these data are matters of chance only, then something has "just happened," this time, that would happen less than 5% of the time by chance—that is, its p-value is less than 0.05.* We would be likely to say: We will discount that possibility, and accept that low risk of making a mistake if we do. If we speak Statistics, we say, "We will *reject the null hypothesis*" as implausible. We will go on to assume that our data are not just accident, but indicate a real preference for cloth over wire. When we reach that conclusion—that mere accident is too implausible to worry about—then we say that our data are *statistically significant.*

Notice how this follows exactly the three-step argument above: (1) These data could have come about by chance. This could be one of those 1-in-32 coincidences. But (2) we have shown that that would happen *only* about 1 time in 32—that is, pretty rarely. Therefore (3) we're pretty sure it didn't happen *this* time, and therefore that a real preference exists.

How rarely is "very rarely"? That is something we have to decide; but, for now, we will just adopt a convention: We will reject the null hypothesis, and draw a conclusion from our data, *if the p-value is 0.05 (5%) or less.* In this case, we would reject the null hypothesis under that convention, since 0.031 is less that 0.05.

Remember that that criterion is entirely arbitrary, and we're using it now only to get on with. Later, we'll discuss how we would go about setting it in actual practice.

This business of statistical significance seems like a rather backward kind of logic. Actually, it isn't. We use that logic whenever we are told something that *could* be true, but implies something implausible. Ms. R. Data is found standing over a dead body with a smoking gun in her hand; we later find that the fatal bullet was fired from that gun. But, Ms. Data insists, she's innocent of the crime. Now that is logically possible, but I'm afraid we will doubt her word anyway. Why? Because *if* she were innocent, it's very unlikely that we would find her in such circumstances!

So in our monkey experiment. Data so one-sided *could* have arisen even if there were no real preference. But *if* there were none, it's very unlikely that we would obtain the data we did obtain. That's what we are saying when we say that our six monkeys showed a *statistically significant preference* for the cloth model mother.

GENERALIZING THE SIGN TEST: SOME PRACTICE EXAMPLES

Now let's play with what we have learned. This will test our understanding of these ideas—and also generalize them.

CALCULATING p-VALUES

Here are some examples in which we can easily calculate p-values directly, as we did above.

1. Suppose we had twelve baby monkeys rather than six. All twelve of them preferred the cloth mother. What is the probability that we would get such consistency by chance, if there really is no preference?

Answer: Just 0.5 to the twelfth power (0.5 times itself twelve times), times 2. That turns out to be 0.00049. It is wildly implausible that such results have occurred by chance.

2. We give six college students a sample of each of two ice creams, Brand A and Brand B. All six subjects tell us they prefer Brand A. Is that a significant preference?

Answer: Yes, it is. The situation is exactly analogous to the six monkeys' preference for the cloth mother. As there, the probability that such consistent data would occur just by chance, in the absence of preference, is $0.5^6 \times 2$, or 0.031.

1. An election is coming up between two candidates for office, Ann Algorithm and P.C. Laptop. In a pre-election survey we select ten voters at random and ask whom they intend to vote for. All ten prefer Algorithm. Do we predict a victory for Algorithm, or is it too close to call?

Answer: Here, our null hypothesis is that the voters in the population are evenly divided between the two candidates. If so, for each voter we select, it should again be a toss-up: Each voter is as likely to be pro-Algorithm as pro-Laptop. And if *that* is so, our happening to select ten pro-Algorithm voters is as unlikely as ten heads with ten honest coins: $1/2^{10}$, or 0.0009. Double that (for we'd have said the same thing if all ten had favored Laptop), and we have 0.0019 as our *p*-value. Since 0.0019 is less than 0.05, we have a statistically significant preference for Algo-

rithm, and we would feel quite confident in predicting that she will win.

USING THE TABLE OF *p*-VALUES

We've been making things easy on ourselves to this point. We have dealt with data that were perfectly consistent—that is, all subjects did the same thing. What if they are not so consistent? Consider Problem 1 above: What if only ten of the twelve monkeys had chosen cloth, and the other two had chosen wire? Would we still have a significant preference for cloth, in the data as a whole?

We could calculate the probability of obtaining that degree of consistency if choices were random (any good introductory book in statistics would show us how). It would, however, require quite a lot of arithmetic. How nice it is, therefore, that someone has done all that arithmetic for us, once and for all!

Flip back to Appendix B1 (page 512), and have it handy for what follows. What it does is give us calculated *p*-values for various outcomes, for up to 25 cases.

We have 12 monkeys. So we read down the left-hand column, labeled *N* (for number of cases) until we get to 12. Now the numbers running across the top row, labeled *Number of Exceptions*, represent the number of exceptions to the overall trend of the data. Here, the overall trend is a preference for the cloth mother; 10 of the 12 monkeys chose her. But there are two exceptions to that trend, so we read across the rows for the number corresponding to an *N* of 12, and a number-of-exceptions of 2. There we find a *p*-value of .019. We must multiply that by two, for reasons given earlier, and we get .038 as our p-value. That is the probability of obtaining data as consistent as these, *if* there really were no preference (the null hypothesis).

Is the preference for the cloth mother still significant? It is. The p-value is still less than 5% (0.038 is less than 0.05).*

PRACTICE WITH THE TABLE

Once again, let's play with what we have learned to see how easy it really is.

1. Suppose there were 10 monkeys, and 9 of them preferred cloth over wire. Is that a significant preference?

Answer: Yes. For N (number of cases) = 10, and number of exceptions = 1, the p-value is .011, times 2 = .022, less than .05. Chance would rarely produce data as consistent as these, if there really were no preference.

2. Of 20 college students, 16 prefer Brand A to Brand B; only 4 exceptional cases prefer B to A. A significant preference for Brand A?

---

*We notice that the table is incomplete; some values are missing. That's to save ink and make the table easier to read. Thus, for 10 cases, we see that if there are 3 exceptions, the trend is nonsignificant (p is .172, greater than 0.05 even before we double it). So if there were even more exceptions, the trend couldn't possibly be significant and the p-values needn't be presented. Conversely, with 20 cases, data with only 3 exceptions are already very unlikely to be the result of chance; so if there were even fewer exceptions, chance would be even more wildly unlikely and the p-value need not be specified. So again, those p-values are omitted from the table.

Answer: Again, yes. For N = 20 and number of exceptions = 4, the p-value is .006, times 2 = .012. Random choices would seldom produce even this degree of consistency.

3. Suppose again that we have 6 baby monkeys; but this time, let there be an exception to the trend. Suppose 5 monkeys choose the cloth mother, but the 6th chooses the wire one. Is there still a significant preference for the cloth mother in the sample as a whole?

Answer: With N = 6, one exception gives us a p-value of .109. (Uh-oh.) And we must double that, for a final value of 0.218. So this time, if there really is no preference one way or the other, the likelihood of our seeing that degree of consistency is greater than .05. This time, the preference is *not significant*.

What do we say then? That rates a bit of discussion.

WHAT ABOUT NONSIGNIFICANT FINDINGS?

We have decided on this criterion: If our data are so consistent that the p-value is 5% or less, we will call the difference significant. Here, the p-value is roughly 20%. Not low enough.

What do we say, then? Have we shown that there is *no* preference? Not at all! After all, 5 of 6 monkeys made the same choice, and that's pretty consistent. It just is *not consistent enough* to satisfy us. We would not be comfortable drawing a conclusion if there is even that much inconsistency in the data, so we simply say:

The data are inconclusive. They are not consistent enough for us to draw a conclusion; hence we will draw none.

That leaves the issue open. If we wish, we (or someone else) can try the experiment again, perhaps making it more sensitive with better control or more subjects (see Chapter 7). But as to the present data, if they are nonsignificant, that just means they are not clear enough to draw conclusions from. So we draw none.

Now there are exceptions to this. We saw one earlier in the Therapeutic Touch experiments (pp. 44–46). Here, the therapists were given a task that should have been ridiculously easy, *if* trained therapists can detect energy fields that humans emit. If they can't (the null hypothesis), we would expect about 50% correct responses. What we saw was almost exactly that. In cases like that, we can say "There is *no* indication of better-than-chance accuracy *and there should have been*." Then we may go on to draw a positive conclusion: The therapists were mistaken in thinking they could do the task. All this looks forward to the discussion of the errors we can make in drawing conclusions from statistical tests. But again, that discussion must be postponed for now.

◀ A LOOK BACK

Let's now look back over what we have learned, because the underlying logic is the same for any test of significance. We look at our data, and we ask: What is the probability—the likelihood—that data such as these would arise, *if* the null hypothesis is true? Sometimes we can calculate that. In other cases, someone has done the calculations for us and we can look up the answer in a table. Now, if the probability is low enough that data like ours would come about by accident, then we assume that something other than accident has produced them. Something "real" is going on. So—if certain assumptions hold—we can be reasonably confident—not dead sure, but reasonably confident—that the data really do tell us something, and did not "just happen" by accident.

Finally, if we have data that are *not* clear enough to support a conclusion—our results are not significant—then, except in unusual cases, we draw no conclusion. With rare exceptions, we don't conclude that *no* real effect or difference exists; we simply acknowledge that the data are inconsistent, and therefore inconclusive.

A LOOK FORWARD: SOME QUESTIONS AND ASSUMPTIONS

Although the underlying logic is very simple, the use of significance tests makes certain assumptions. We can be misled if the assumptions don't hold. Here are two examples.

THE INDEPENDENCE ASSUMPTION

Many statistical techniques depend on the assumption that the various observations we take are *independent* of each other—that is, one is not affected by another. The sign test makes this assumption. Let's see why, and what it means.

Imagine this: Suppose all our baby monkeys were being held together, in a pen, waiting to be tested. One by one we send them out, and we see whether each monkey chooses the wire mother or the cloth mother. Suppose further that the little monkeys can see each other all the while.

Now, let's make some more suppositions: (1) Suppose that baby monkeys in fact don't care whether it's a wire or a cloth mother they go to (the null hypothesis). But (2) suppose the first monkey just happens to go to the cloth mother. And (3) suppose that baby monkeys tend to imitate each other.

Then do you see what would happen? The second monkey would also go to the cloth mother, and the third, and the fourth, and so on—not because baby monkeys prefer cloth to wire mothers, but because they imitate each other. If Harlow had allowed that to happen (he didn't), he might have drawn a conclusion that was all wrong. He might have thought he was seeing a preference for one model over the other, when all he really was seeing was a random selection by the first monkey, and then imitation by the others.

Harlow was far too capable an experimenter to allow such a thing. He made sure that each monkey baby made its choice independently of what any other monkey did. But the problem of independence can arise in more subtle ways, and in many kinds of research. It could play havoc with survey data too, as we'll see in a later chapter.

We now have the concept of *statistical significance* in our tool kit. How simple it is!

CHAPTER 3

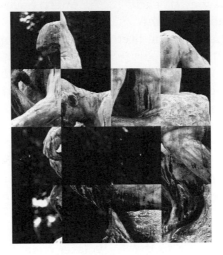

DATA

The great tragedy of Science is the slaying of a beautiful hypothesis by an ugly fact.

—THOMAS HUXLEY

IN THIS CHAPTER, WE'LL DISCUSS:

- What is meant by "systematic data"
  The importance of comparison
  The "present/present" bias
- Variables and their values
  Relations among variables
  Operationalizing the variables
- Objective data
- The problem of subjective data
  How to make data objective
  Some myths about objectivity
- Reliability and validity of measures

Huxley's quip is a restatement of the idea we touched on earlier. Offered information, we may ask the questions: How do you know? Why do you think so? Is your reason a good one? For the scientist, the reason for accepting a theory—provisionally, and subject to correction—is that it has been tested against the *facts* that we observe—the *data*. Facts tell us when we are wrong, and thus permit our understanding to advance—if we let them, and are willing to let our ideas change as the facts require.

SYSTEMATIC DATA

We want our conclusions to rest on data—on facts. But there are data and data, facts and facts. Not all data are created equal.

THE IMPORTANCE OF COMPARISON

Let's refer back to Chapter 1 for a minute. There we saw (pp. 3–4) that, for many years, the treatment for yellow fever was bloodletting. Eminent and intelligent doctors (like Dr. Benjamin Rush, a prominent physician and one of the signers of the Declaration of Independence) used it in treating patient after patient. This "treatment" surely killed more patients than it cured.

Why did it remain popular? If patients on average were worse off with it than without it, wouldn't capable doctors, like the good Dr. Rush, quickly discover the fact?

Not necessarily. Not unless (1) they kept systematic records of the patients who received bloodletting and those who did not, and (2) included in those records the outcomes, tallying the patients in each group who recovered and those who did not. Then, putting all those records together, they would have seen that the prognosis was actually better for the untreated "control" subjects. But they didn't do that. Such systematic record keeping is very much a modern invention.

There is another problem, too, with the data as they stood. The physicians considered only patients who were treated, and either recovered or did not. The trouble is that such data *could not have disconfirmed the underlying theory*. A patient is treated and recovers. Fine: That supports the theory. Another patient is treated and dies. Too bad, but no problem for the theory: He was too sick to recover and would have died anyway. The theory, in a word, was *not falsifiable* with data like these (Chapter 2). A therapeutic success supports it; a therapeutic failure does not challenge it. The theory is data-proof. Either way, it wins!

Now, if systematic data had been kept, physicians could have seen that over a large number of cases, the *proportion* who recovered was actually lower when bloodletting was used than when it was not. But to calculate these proportions we need careful tallies of successes and failures, with and without the treatment.*

Looking backward over all this, here is what we see. The physicians of the 1700s did have facts to go on: Some patients treated with their methods did recover. The problem is that those facts were not useful facts. The element of *comparison* was missing. It could have shown the physicians that their treatment was not only not better, but worse, than no treatment at all.

Of course, we know better now—don't we? Let us see.

THE "PRESENT/PRESENT BIAS"

Here is a demonstration you can try out on your friends. Suppose that we have a sample of persons with some disorder, who are treated or are not, and who improve or do not. (The disorder could be yellow fever and the treatment bloodletting. The disorder could be anxiety and the treatment psychotherapy. It doesn't matter; the idea is the same.)

Now, show your friends the table below, and ask: "Is improvement associated with treatment?" Whatever the answer is, then ask: "Why do you think so?"

	Treated	*Untreated*
Improved	20	10
Unimproved	80	40

You will get some interesting answers. Many will say that improvement is associated with treatment, because more people improve with treatment than without it. Others will say the relationship is negative, because the majority of people who are treated do not improve.

---

*At about this point we can expect to hear the wildly irrelevant remark: "A patient is not a statistic!" No, a patient is not. But if a higher proportion of untreated patients survive than treated ones, *that* is a statistic, and it is trying to tell us something.

Surprisingly few will get the correct answer: There is no relationship at all between the treatment and improvement. Improvement is present in 20% of the people who are treated, and in 20% of the people who are not. The proportions are identical.

Notice this, however: In order to calculate and compare those proportions, *we need to know all four cells of the table*. This includes the "absent/absent" cell—the apparently irrelevant cases that are *not* treated and do *not* improve. But those cases are not irrelevant at all. Do you doubt it? Compare the above table with this one:

	Treated	Untreated
Improved	20	10
Unimproved	80	1

In this case, treatment has a *negative* effect. Only 20% of the treated patients improve, but 90% of the untreated patients do.

But now suppose the data looked like this:

	Treated	Untreated
Improved	20	10
Unimproved	80	490

Now the treatment is *positively* associated with improvement. Improvement occurs in 20% of the people who are treated, and in only 2% of the people who are not.

But—and this is the point—in moving from table to table here, from no relation to a negative one to a positive one, *all I have changed* is the tally in the absent/absent cell! The other three cells are identical in all three sets of (imaginary) data. Changing that one cell changes the relationship drastically, from zero to negative to positive.

Moral: To know whether a relationship is positive, negative, or absent altogether, we need all four cells, including that fourth cell—no treatment, no improvement.

That's just one demonstration of an important underlying idea. If we want to know whether some condition, X, is associated with another condition, Y, we find it natural to focus on the "present/present" cell—X present, Y present. That tendency is what we'll call the *present/present bias*. It can lead us to neglect some facts that we really need to have.

Suppose we want to know whether redheads have fiery tempers. At first, the question suggests that we should observe hot-tempered redheads. However, the question really means: Do redheads tend *more than the rest of us* to have hot tempers? To answer that, we need data on "the rest of us." A tally of placid non-redheads is required, if we are to get an answer.

All this may seem obvious now that we point it out, but—obviously—it is not. Take a real example that looks quite different, but illustrates the same point (see Dawes, 1994). An article in *Discover* magazine urges readers who fly in airplanes to "know where the exits are and . . . exactly how to get to them." Why? Because interviews with 200 survivors of fatal airline accidents found that "more than 90% of them had their escape routes mentally mapped out beforehand." Sound impressive? It shouldn't. What about the *nonsurvivors*? For all we know, maybe 90% of them—or 100%!—had their escape routes mentally mapped, too. Of course we can't ask them, for they did not survive. So if we want to know whether such "mental rehearsal" saves lives, we must ask the question in some other way.

Underlying all of this is a simple but fundamental idea. It is so important that we can state it like this:

Principle: We cannot relate anything to anything unless they both vary.

Saying it another way: Most research projects require a *comparison*. Between what and what? Between one and another value of *each* of the *variables* involved. We'll see in a minute what that means.

A LOOK BACK

What do we mean by *systematic observation*? First, we mean observation under conditions where both data that support a conclusion, and data that argue against it, are tallied with equal care. And some of the latter must be possible—that is, there must be *possible* data that *could* argue against the idea we have in mind. That's our *falsifiability* idea again: If we're wrong, we want to know it. The good Dr. Rush was wrong, but had no way of knowing it, and many tragedies resulted.

Second, our variables must *vary*. To know whether any X is related to any Y, it's no good just looking at high or low values of X or of Y, or even of both. In particular, we cannot afford to focus just on positive or "present" instances: treatment present, survival present, and so on. We need to *compare* these with "negative" or "absent" instances—untreated and unimproved, or even-tempered nonredheads. So we must observe those instances, too.

In other words, we need to deal with relations among *variables*. Let us see what that means.

THE ANATOMY OF DATA: VARIABLES AND VALUES

Any single study is a modest thing. Research may begin with a big question, like "How does the brain work?" We cannot design a study to answer a question like that. We must narrow it down until we have a question that data can answer. We have such a question when we ask about the relations among a manageably small number of *variables*.

VARIABLES AND THEIR VALUES

A *variable* is just what its name implies. It is something that *varies*. It is anything that might be this, or might be that. . . . When we specify what it is, we are assigning a specific *value* to that variable.

Algebra deals with variables. Consider the statement $x = y + z$. That statement has three variables, *x*, *y*, and *z*. If we assign values to two of them—let $y = 3$ and $z = 2$—we can calculate what *x* has to be, and get a shining truth of arithmetic: $5 = 3 + 2$. Or, we *could* assign a value to *x* rather than calculating it: $8.886 = 3 + 2$. That, too, is a statement in arithmetic, though it is a false one.

Not all variables take numbers for their values. For example, *species* is a variable. We don't know its value until we know whom or what we are talking about. For the variable *species*, my value is *human being*. So is yours; thus, you and I have the same value for that variable. My cat has a different value. For *species*, her value is *cat*.

Gender is a variable: Its possible values are *male* and *female*. *Type of treatment for yellow fever* is a variable: One may prescribe this, that, or the other treatment, or no treatment at all, and all these options are possible values of that variable.

These examples are what we call *categorical variables*. The values are categories: male or female, human or cat or Rhesus monkey, treated for yellow fever with bloodletting or with something else or not treated at all, alive or dead following the onset of that disease.

Then there are *quantitative variables*, which take quantities or numbers for their values. Height and weight are quantitative variables. If you are 6 feet tall, then 6 is your value for the variable *height in feet.* (If it were *height in inches*, you'd have a different value: 72.)*

How fast can we run the 100-meter dash, in seconds? That is a quantitative variable, and its value for each of us might be our fastest time over a series of trials. Your value might be 12 seconds. Mine today might be around 18. Others will be slower than you but faster than I, so their values would fall between these.

Let's see how these ideas apply to examples we have seen.

RELATIONS AMONG VARIABLES

Very often, an investigation asks how two or more variables are related to each other. Harlow's work is an example. He built two model mothers, one comfortable, the other nutritious. These were two values of a categorical variable, *type of model mother.* Then he asked how this variable was related to another variable, a quantitative one: *time.* How much time would a baby monkey spend with each mother? Would the time spent in contact be greater for the nutritious mother, as the "cupboard" theory would predict? Or greater for the cloth mother, as the contact-comfort theory would predict? As we saw, the type-of-model variable was indeed related to the time-in-contact variable, and in the direction predicted by contact-comfort theory.

The Latané and Darley study shows the same process. A categorical variable—subject alone, or in a group—was related to each of two variables: another categorical one (whether the subject offered help or not) and a quantitative one (how promptly the subject took action if he did so at all). And in the Therapeutic Touch study,

---

*Many writers distinguish among different *levels* of quantification. Some, following the influential analysis by S. S. Stevens (1951), distinguish between *ordinal* and *interval* scales of measurement.

An *ordinal scale* gives us rank-order information only. Within a class of students, we might form an ordinal scale of height if we had the students line up by height and then call out numbers, shortest to tallest. Then, if Gene is 2 and Joan is 3, we know that Joan is taller than Gene, but not how much taller. *Percentiles* are another example: If Anna scored at the 90th percentile on an exam, and Andrew at the 60th percentile, we know that Anna scored higher than Andrew—but again, we don't know how much higher.

An *interval scale* has a fixed unit of measurement, so it does give us information about "how much." If we measure height in inches (the unit), then if Joan is 5'8" and Gene is 5'6", we know that Joan is taller than Gene and we know how much taller—just 2 inches.

Whether we are dealing with ordinal or interval data can affect our choice of statistical procedures for data description and analysis. The issues here, however, are beyond the scope of this book. In our "Making Friends with Statistics" sections, I will assume throughout that we have interval data to work with, unless indicated otherwise.

the question was whether one categorical variable (where the experimenter's hand was) was related to another one (where the subject thought it was). The two variables turned out not to be related—though they should have been, if the TT idea were true.

The general rule is simply this: *We have a researchable question when we have narrowed it down to a question about specific variables and the relation(s) among them.* All investigations we examine will deal with variables, and a manageably small number of them—seldom less than two, and seldom more than a handful.

OPERATIONALIZING THE VARIABLES

Still we are not through. Having decided what variables we will zero in on, we now must *operationalize* the variables. In plain English, this means that we must say: "Look, we have to do something specific. What shall it be?"

The term *operation,* used this way, does not imply a surgical procedure. It implies *doing something.* Think of a military operation, in which units take action—do something specific—to attain some objective. Just so, a researcher performs an operation—does something specific—in order to gather data relevant to a question. But again: Exactly what shall that "something" be?

Harlow narrowed his question to: How is the *type of mother* (one variable) related to the *preference* an infant expresses (another variable)? But how, *specifically,* shall we make our two mothers? What about the nutritious mother—what food shall she offer? In a bottle or a cup? Can a baby monkey sip from a cup? And so on. We want the terrycloth mother to be warm—how warm? Specific decisions had to be made about each of these questions and many more. Some were based on what was known about monkeys, some on what was convenient or inexpensive, some on what other researchers had done and some—of necessity—by guesswork.

Similar specific decisions had to be made for the bystander-intervention study. What emergency shall be staged? In what setting? What, specifically, shall be measured? And so on.

In doing this, it is true that we have to turn our backs on a great deal—indeed, on *all* of the things we could do but do not do, at least not yet. This doesn't bother us, for the "other things" will be studied in good time. What we cannot study today, we will study tomorrow; or, if we don't, we can be sure that someone else will.

OBJECTIVE DATA

The popular image of psychological research takes one of two forms (Figure 3.1). One pictures a clinician meeting with his client/patient. The other pictures rats confronted with complex mazes of the kind no researcher has used for almost a century.

The images are misleading. In fact, it is interesting to note that of all the examples we have used so far, *not one* fits either of these images. Let us run back over these examples, as instances of the use of *objective data* in psychology.

COUNTING EVENTS

First of all, our data may consist of simple *counts* of different kinds of events. How many bystanders offer help under each condition, and how many do not? How often does the Therapeutic Touch practitioner call out the correct hand, and how many times the incorrect one? Or consider a rat in a box, pressing a lever to earn food. How many times does it press, per unit time? Our data may consist of these counts.

"I'm going to be late, dear. It's total craziness here."

"Bathroom? Sure, it's just down the hall to the left, jog right, left, another left, straight past two more lefts, then right, and it's at the end of the third corridor on your right."

P. BYRNES.

FIGURE 3.1
Two popular images of psychological research.

PHYSICAL MEASURES

Besides counting events, we may also *measure* variables, asking not "Did an event of type X occur or not," but rather "How much of variable Y does this event embody?" The idea of measurement is familiar for *physical variables*, like distance, weight, and time; and, indeed, physical measurements are very often used as data in psychology. How much did a subject eat? Weigh his plate before and after the meal. And the use of *time* is very widespread in psychology. Harlow measured *how much time* a baby monkey spent with each of the model mothers. Latané and Darley, besides *counting* the number of subjects who took action under each condition, measured *how promptly* they did so. We can also learn a lot about events by noting *how long they take*—another use of time as a measure. We'll see some instances of this later.

But let us look at a different example of the use of objective measures.

A CASE STUDY: PAVLOV'S EXPERIMENTS

Ivan P. Pavlov was not a psychologist. He was a physiologist, concerned with the question: How does the nervous system work? That's much too broad to be a researchable question, so he narrowed his thinking down: How does the nervous system control the secretions of the digestive tract? Still too broad. There's a lot of nervous system in there, and a lot of digestive tract.

So Pavlov narrowed down again (in the studies that concern us here) to the study of salivary secretions. When an assistant placed food in a dog's mouth, Pavlov would collect saliva (through a tube into the mouth), and measure the amount of salivation that occurred in response to the food, under various conditions. Thus his data consisted of *amount of saliva*, a quantitative variable that could be operationalized by counting drops, or by measuring fluid volume. (Pavlov used both.) Then that variable—amount of saliva—could be related to a number of other variables, each made to vary in some specific way.

But there was a problem. After awhile, as the assistant approached the dog, the dog would begin to salivate *before* any food was placed in its mouth! Clearly that would not do. If we want to study salivation as a response to food in the mouth, how can we do that if salivation begins when there *is* no food in the mouth?

Then again, maybe what is happening here is even more interesting than the original question.* Pavlov thought so. He realized that he was watching the brain form a new connection or pathway—an *association*, as we like to say—between the sight of the assistant, who brought food, and the dogs' salivation in anticipation of that food.

THE CONDITIONING EXPERIMENTS

Pavlov set out to study the formation of such associations. Now, however, the assistant was an unnecessary complication, and the dog had had experience with him before. To study the formation of a brand-new association, Pavlov needed to start with a "signal" that had *no association at all* with food before the experiment began. Hence, the famous bell (or it could be any of a number of things). The experimental procedure was this: Sound a bell, and a very brief time after that, pop some food in the dog's mouth. (The latter was done by way of a pneumatic system that would blow a measured amount of food directly into the dog's mouth. That way, there was no approach of an assistant to complicate matters.)

If we do that a few times, we will see the *conditioning* phenomenon. A salivary response, which initially required food, now begins to occur to the bell alone. (We can show this by occasional test trials in which the food is omitted. Or, if the bell precedes the food by a brief period, we may see salivation in response to the bell before the food comes.) The salivary response, we say, has become a *conditioned response* or a *conditioned reflex*.

FOLLOW-UPS

This example lets us look back on some familiar ideas. First, we saw in the last chapter that one may begin research by exploring, gathering a systematic body of data, and letting the principles—the theory—develop out of the data. Pavlov's work is a good example. He and his co-workers explored the effects of varying the kind of signal used (a bell, the sound of a metronome, a light going on, a light going off, etc.), the effects of varying the interval between the signal for food and the food itself, the effects of presenting the signal without the food ("experimental extinction"), and much more.

---

*This sort of thing happens so often that it has been given a name. It is called *serendipity*—the art (or luck) of finding something interesting while looking for something else.

A CS (such as a tone)...

is paired repeatedly with a UCS (such as food), which
elicits a UCR (such as salivation).

After many such pairings, a new connection or association is formed,
so that the CS can now elicit the response by itself.

The response is then a conditioned response (CR).

FIGURE 3.2
A low-level theory of classical conditioning. A "connection" is formed between the
conditioned stimulus (CS) and the response.

Meanwhile other researchers, following Pavlov's lead, were extending the findings to other reflexes and other species, humans included.

All these findings fit together into a *theory* of the conditioning process. It is low level enough to be rather simple; we can even draw a picture of it (Figure 3.2). Yet it is general enough to summarize a wide variety of specific experiments.

We begin with some signal or stimulus—the *unconditioned stimulus*, or UCS—which already triggers some reflex reaction. The response is the *unconditioned response*, or UCR. It can be any of a number of specific things—food in the mouth which evokes salivation, a puff of air on the eye which evokes a blink, or a mild shock on the foot which elicits foot withdrawal. Any of these will do. We pair that signal with another signal that initially does *not* trigger the response in question. This is the (to be) *conditioned stimulus*, or CS. It too can be different in different experiments: It can be a tone, the sound of a metronome ticking, a light going on, a light going off, a touch on the skin; again, any of these will do. Now, after a few such pairings, we will begin to see the original response, the UCR, occurring in response to the CS alone. When that happens, we call it a *conditioned response* or a *conditioned reflex*.

Conditioning is typically a gradual process. Figure 3.3 shows some results in human subjects, with a brief tone as CS and a puff of air in the eye as UCS, eliciting a blink of the eyelid. The strength of the CR, measured by how often the blink occurred before the puff did, gradually rises over successive pairings of tone and puff ("trials").

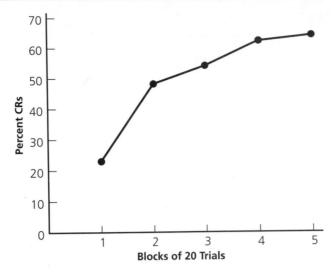

FIGURE 3.3
The development of a conditioned response over repeated pairings (data from Grice & Hunter, 1964).

Figure 3.2 shows a generalized, summary picture of many, many such experiments in many species. Present any CS along with any UCS, trial after trial, and we will see a connection or association forming, so that the CS comes to trigger the response (now a CR) on a greater and greater proportion of the trials.

Now, this simple picture is in fact too simple, and has had to be modified since Pavlov's day. (We'll see some reasons for this later.) But that's all right. How can we learn if we don't change our minds about some things? Again, the key is knowing when we're wrong, and modifying our ideas so they're less wrong.

Two things more should be noted. First—and Pavlov made much of this—every variable in a conditioning experiment is an *objective* one. The tone, the food, the salivary flow—all these are "out there" for anyone to see and measure. Different observers can look at them and check each other. That is what *objective* means.

This was a great advance in itself. For many centuries, philosophers had been talking about *associations* between one idea and another "in the mind." However, ideas in the mind *are* in the mind, locked up inside each person or animal where no one else can see them. Disagreements about these mental events were not easy to resolve (Humphrey, 1951). But in Pavlov's work, the association was between a stimulus and a response. What properties did these associations have? Since the data were "out there" for anyone to ob-

FIGURE 3.4

How *does* conditioning work? Snoopy is in good company if he wonders about that.

serve, we could *look and see*! True, the "connection in the brain" (or somewhere; see Figure 3.4) is hypothetical, but direct study of the brain can look for where it is and how it works. Such research, using Pavlov's procedures, is still in progress today (Thompson, 1986).

Second, Pavlov's experiments, like Harlow's, were far removed from real life and were intended to be. But the underlying *principles* of conditioning could shed some light on a number of real-life concerns. It's not just about dogs, or just about salivation. Conditioning may well play a role in some of our *attitudes*, positive or negative; it may play a role in the *fears* we acquire; it may even be used as a *therapeutic* procedure, as we will see. It has very wide ramifications indeed (Rozin & Zellner, 1987).

It also raises *theoretical issues* about the nature of learning and of consciousness. Let's see an example.

CAN CONDITIONING OCCUR WITHOUT AWARENESS?

An obvious interpretation of the conditioning phenomenon goes like this: After food-in-the-mouth has been paired with a bell for a number of times, the dog learns to *expect* food when it hears the bell. Similarly, a human subject comes to expect the puff of air to the eyeball when he hears the tone. In short, conditioning occurs because the subject learns to say, "Ah, here is the CS again, and that means that the UCS is coming."

But is that necessarily true? Can conditioning occur without conscious awareness? After long debate, it is becoming clear that the answer is yes.

In one experiment, Clark and Squire (1998) paired a tone with a puff of air in human subjects, with a seemingly minor difference

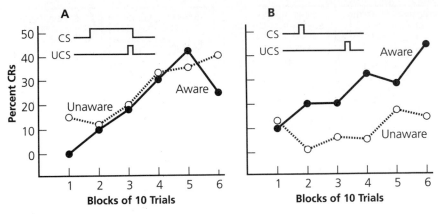

FIGURE 3.5
Conditioning in humans who did, or did not, realize what was going on; and in which there was, or was not, a brief gap between CS and UCS. Lack of this realization slowed or abolished conditioning, but only if the gap was there (from Clark & Squire, 1998).

between two conditions. In one, the tone came on, the air puff followed after 1 second, and the two ended together (Figure 3.5A). In the other, the tone came on briefly, then went off, and the puff followed after an interval of 500 milliseconds (Figure 3.5B).* This is known as *trace conditioning*. It seems that the puff must become associated with a "trace" of the tone somewhere in the brain, for the tone itself is no longer there when the puff comes.

Finally, all subjects were asked whether they were aware of the relation between the CS and the UCS.

It seems very strange that that very short blank interval should make any difference, but it did! Under the no-blank-interval condition (Panel A), some subjects reported that they were aware of the CS-UCS relationship; others said that they had not noticed it. But both groups formed conditioned eyeblink responses! And conditioning occurred at about the same rate for both. Awareness versus unawareness made no difference.

If there was a gap between tone and puff (Panel B), the picture changed. Now, subjects formed conditioned reflexes if they were aware of the CS-UCS relation. In those who were unaware of it, no conditioning occurred.

What do we conclude? Under one condition (the time gap, B), conditioning *was* dependent on the subject's conscious awareness of

---

*A millisecond (abbreviated ms or msec) is a thousandth of a second.

what was going on—specifically, that the CS predicted the UCS. But under a slightly different condition (no time gap, A), there was no such dependency. Subjects who were not aware of what was going on conditioned just as fast as those who were aware. Clearly, then, conditioning without awareness *can* occur. Clearly, too, a very subtle change in experimental conditions can have a great impact on the results.

This experiment looks forward to an issue we'll consider in more detail later. One of the measures Clark and Squire took was an *objective measure*: Does the eye blink or does it not? As in Pavlov's experiments, the data are "out there" for anyone to see. But when subjects were asked, "Were you aware of how the tone and the puff were related?" the answers were *subjective*. Only the subjects could know whether their answers were honest and accurate; there is no way anyone else could check what they said. Here, we're not too worried about this, because the question was simple and the subjects had no reason to lie. But in other cases, the lack of cross-check can raise real problems, as we'll now see.

THE PROBLEM OF SUBJECTIVE DATA

Not all data are objective. In some cases, we must ask our subjects to tell us about their private, subjective experiences. These are not "out there" for anyone to see, but "in here" where only the subject herself can see them.

JUDGMENTS ABOUT OTHERS: RATINGS

Sometimes the data consist of judgments, or ratings, by human observers. For example:

- How aggressively do you think this child is behaving on the playground? (Or, perhaps, Rate his aggressiveness on a scale of 1 to 10.)

- How well do you think this patient or client is functioning?

- How likely do you think it is that this offender will offend again?

Someone may have to make that judgment *now*, before an important decision—grant parole, or not?—is made.

Such ratings give us very crude information. We may be quite sure that Child A is behaving more aggressively than Child B, without being sure just why we think so. But for that very reason, there may be no alternative to a global "rating" by a human judge or judges. At minimum, there should be more than one judge. If two or more judges agree that Child A is being more aggressive than Child B, we may be more confident that the difference really is "out there," and not just in the eye of any one beholder.

One characteristic of subjective ratings that we worry about particularly is their susceptibility to *bias*. In one experimental study,* panels of mental-health professionals were shown a videotape of a younger man talking to an older man about his feelings and experiences. But some of the clinicians were told that the young man was a patient, whereas the others were told he was a job applicant. After seeing the videotape, the professionals were asked for their observations about the young man: What kind of person was he?

Remember, the videotape was the same for all. But the judges' reactions were not. Those who saw the "job applicant" described him in such terms as "attractive, candid, and innovative." He "seems fairly realistic . . . recognizes injustices of large systems." But those who saw the same conversation, thinking the young man was a patient, saw him as a "tight, defensive person," "frightened of his own aggressive impulses . . . tends to use denial . . . to center his problems in situations and other people" (Langer & Abelson, 1974). Since the tape was the same, these striking differences can only reflect the judges' biases in interpreting what they saw.

In this case, even agreement among judges would not reassure us—maybe all the judges share the biases! On the other hand, if the judges were prevented from knowing whether the young man was patient or job applicant, that would give the bias no room to operate. But this is not always possible either, as in the case of a prisoner to be, or not be, paroled.

We'll only touch on the topic of observer bias here. We'll discuss it further later on, along with some tactics that can *sometimes* be used to combat it (Chapter 5).

---

*This sort of thing happens often in psychology. A potential source of error in our studies is demonstrated—with a study! This is not surprising. What we are saying is this: Our data show that human beings are susceptible to such biases. Well, scientists are human beings too! If other humans are subject to these biases, then, chances are, so are we as scientists—and we had better take steps to prevent our own biases from introducing just such distortions.

THE PROBLEM OF SELF-REPORT

Things get even trickier when subjects make judgments about themselves. Here, we have no cross-check at all on what the subject tells us. We just have to take his word. But, by doing so, we may ask questions that cannot be answered in any other way. We may ask a subject, perhaps, "Were you dreaming when we woke you, and if so, of what?" Or we might ask, "Can you see this faint light right now, or not?" Or, "What do you remember about this-or-that event?" We are asking the subjects about their own private experiences of dreaming, seeing, or remembering.

Data based on such self-observations are called *self-report* data. That is a good term for them, for the word *report* reminds us that our data consist of what a subject *says*. We do not have a direct "readout" of dreams, perceptions, and the like. We must take the subject's word. Yet by doing so, we have learned much.

AN EXAMPLE FROM PERCEPTION: THRESHOLDS

Suppose we ask: What is the faintest light that a subject can just barely see? We would answer this by presenting a faint light (through a microscope eyepiece perhaps) and asking the subject whether he can see it. If we present a light that is too faint, the subject will say, "No, I can't see it." Then if we gradually increase its intensity, at some point (called the *threshold*) it will become intense enough to be seen, and the subject will say, "Okay; now I see it."

In Figure 3.6, we see the results of an experiment like this. A faint light, too faint to be seen, was gradually increased until the subject could see it. This was done repeatedly, as the subject sat in the dark. We see that the value of the threshold—the point at which the light became visible—got lower and lower.

Now the threshold is an *inverse measure of sensitivity*: The lower the threshold, the more sensitive the visual system is. It gets more and more sensitive as the subject sits longer and longer in the dark. There is also a "kink" in the curve—threshold drops, levels off, and then drops some more. It looks as if there are two processes going on, a rapid one and then a slower one that kicks in only after about 20 minutes. That turns out to be exactly right, as we'll see in a later chapter.

Now on the one hand, these data are entirely subjective. If a subject says, "Yes, I can see the light now," only he can know whether he is telling the truth; you and I cannot. On the other hand, data

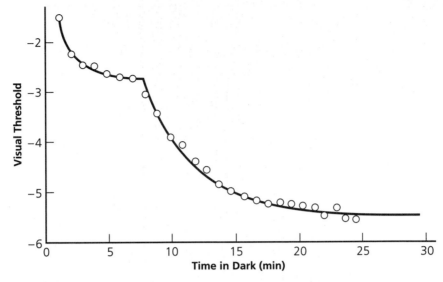

FIGURE 3.6
The time course of "dark adaptation"—the increase in visual sensitivity with time in the dark. A lower threshold means greater sensitivity (from Hecht, 1934).

such as these have given us some of the most precise and reliable data in all of psychology!

How can that be? Because these data (kink and all) can be replicated from one subject to another, and the findings can be related to other data—physiological, anatomical, chemical, behavioral—and they all fit together. These correspondences add what we call *construct validity* (p. 90) to the use of these self-reports as data. The different measures, objective and subjective, support each other.

AN EXAMPLE FROM PSYCHOBIOLOGY:
DREAMS AND REM SLEEP

Let us turn to an even clearer example of purely subjective data. Beginning back in the late 1950s, a new method was invented for the study of sleeping and dreaming. An experimental subject would be put to bed in a "sleep laboratory," with electrodes pasted to his scalp so that brain waves (the EEG) could be measured; and also to his eyelids, so that movements of the eyes could be detected by electronic sensing devices (Figure 3.7).

What we find is that after the subject has been asleep for a while, his eyes will begin to move around rapidly under his closed lids. This phase of sleep is therefore called "rapid-eye-movement" or *REM sleep*, though there are changes in the EEG that characterize it too. This

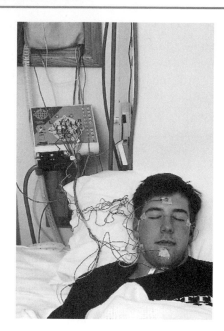

FIGURE 3.7
A subject in a sleep lab, strange as it seems, is able to sleep with electronic sensing devices, at the ends of light flexible wires, taped to his face.

research led to a discovery that opened up whole new lines of research: If we wake the subject from REM sleep, he will nearly always tell us that he was dreaming. He is much less likely to do so if awakened during other phases of sleep.

Exploration with this method changed our thinking about dreams in a number of ways. First, nearly everyone dreams. Many people say that they do not, but this probably means that they forget their dreams rapidly after waking. If they are awakened during REM sleep and asked *right away* about their dreams, most people will report having them. Second, it seems that the dream is not just a brief, compressed "flash"; it takes about as long as the dreamed events would take. And there is much more (see Dement, 1990).

Does the eye-movements measure give us an *objective* indication that the subject is dreaming? Not really. The eye movements themselves are recorded objectively, yes. But the subject has to *tell us* what, if anything, he was dreaming—and that is self-report. There are no objective means by which we can check those self-reports for accuracy.

And inaccuracies just might be there. Might a subject in a sleep laboratory be inventing dreams in order to please us, the experimenters? Or could he be filling the gaps in what he remembers with invented material, and then confusing the inventions with the actual dreams? This process, called *confabulation*, is something we all do on occasion. Is the subject doing something like that?

We are not too worried about this, however, because again the self-reports line up with other data. For example, the results of modern brain-imaging techniques, applied during REM sleep, have been compared with subjects' reports of their dreams. We find that if the subject reports a visual dream, parts of the brain involved in processing visual information become active (Hong, Gillin, Dow, Wu, & Buchsbaum, 1995). When a subject tells us he dreams about a conversation, it is cells in the language areas of the brain that become active (Hong et al., 1996). Together, these findings lend support to the idea that REM sleep is indeed accompanied by internal "imagined" perceptions—dreams.

AN EXAMPLE FROM MEMORY: "FLASHBULBS"

Then again, the data may make the opposite verdict: There are some kinds of self-report that we *know* may not be trustworthy. Reports of what we *remember* can be of this kind.

Some very dramatic or disturbing events leave us with what have been called *flashbulb memories*—we "see" the event as a clear and vivid image in our minds, as if the scene were lit up by a flashbulb. We remember where we were, who we were with, what happened— all with startling clarity. Hearing the news of the assassination of John F. Kennedy produced such an experience in many of us. So did the explosion of the space shuttle *Challenger*.*

When *Challenger* exploded, Neisser and Harsch (1992) saw an opportunity to check the accuracy of such "flashbulb memories." The day following the disaster, they gave a short questionnaire to students in their classes, asking them to recall where they were, whom they were with, and the like, when they heard of it. The class members were mostly freshmen, and the experimenters were able to contact them again when they were seniors. They then asked the students to answer the same questions as before, plus one additional one: The students rated the confidence they had in the accuracy of their memories.

The results were worrisome on two counts. First, overall accuracy was amazingly low: About a quarter of the sample scored flat zero on accuracy—literally *nothing* they said matched their earlier re-

---

*On January 28, 1986, the space shuttle *Challenger* exploded 73 seconds after liftoff, killing its crew of seven. Television screens worldwide showed the tragedy as it unfolded, and few who saw it happen will forget it.

port! One such student described the event the day after it happened, as follows: "I was in my religion class and some people walked in and started talking about [it]. . . ." But three years later she recalled: "When I first heard about the explosion I was sitting in my freshman dorm room with my roommate and we were watching TV. It came on as a news flash and we were both totally shocked. . . ." Another student remembered three years later than she had heard the news while at home with her parents. In fact, she had been away at college.

The second worrisome finding was that the students' *confidence* in the accuracy of their memories was virtually unrelated to how accurate they actually were. Memories that were recorded with great confidence, three years later, were about as likely to be wrong as ones reported with little or no confidence. Both right and wrong memories had the same flashbulb, "I can see it now" quality.

Moreover, students did not correct their memories. When finally confronted with these great discrepancies, one might have expected them to say, "Oh, yes, now I remember how it really was." None did! The "new" false memories *were* their memories for that event. As one subject said, "I still remember everything happening the way I told you. I can't help it"—when what she "remembered" was all wrong.

In this study the drifts in memories were spontaneous: No one tried to influence the students' memories. Yet they drifted substantially anyway, and the subjects were unaware that any drifts had occurred! Actually, this is not surprising if we think about it. In order to be aware that our memory had drifted, we would have to have a "copy" of the original, uncorrupted memory to compare the present memory with. It seems that none remains. (Wouldn't hypnosis bring it back? In a word, no—see Chapter 8.)

Certainly all this should make us wonder about the usefulness of even the most vivid "memories" of the past as indicators of what really happened back then. For this is one study among very many— the *weight of the evidence* again!—that show (1) that memory is highly susceptible to distortion, and (2) that confidence in our memories has surprisingly little to do with their accuracy. This has immediate implications for the legal system, for example. We know that juries tend to place a great deal of trust in *eyewitness testimony* (e.g., Loftus, 1979)—and now we know that they shouldn't!

And yet, obviously, not all memories are so distorted. Comparing memories of events with diary records taken at the time, some investigators (e.g., Linton, 1982) find (objectively!) that they may be surprisingly accurate even after many years. When should we take subjective memories at face value and when should we not? We are not sure.

A LOOK BACK

What about all this, then? When are self-report data to be trusted and when not? Often, self-reports give us information that we could not obtain in any other way; no one can tell us about a person's inner experience but the person herself. When we want to investigate such matters, we are very glad that our subjects can talk to us! That is the good news.

The bad news, and the reason researchers distrust self-reports, is simply this: We must *take the subject's word* for what his experiences are. There is no way we can check what he says for inaccuracies.

What to do? Tread warily. Obviously, if our subject has reason to lie (as in a criminal trial), we take her testimony with a grain of salt and look for more objective evidence. At the other extreme, where self-reports support and are supported by other kinds of data, we are likely to consider them reliable—as in threshold experiments or reports of dreams. But we are left with the large gray area in the middle, where we are not sure what to make of self-reports. We use them when there is no alternative—when we must, we must— but we keep a skeptical eye on them, and we keep looking for alternatives.

MAKING DATA OBJECTIVE

Because of these uncertainties, we look for objective measures when we can find them. Often, with a bit of thought, we can.

Consider Harlow's experiments again. He might have had observers *rate* how attached each baby monkey appeared to be, to the wire mother on the one hand or the cloth one on the other. Instead, he measured *time spent* with each—an objective measure. Latané and Darley could have asked their subjects, "How sympathetic did you feel toward those who seemed in danger?" Instead, they too took objective measures that anyone could verify: whether or not the subject went to offer help, and, if so, how promptly.

Or consider the flashbulb-memory experiment again. Strictly speaking, all of the data are subjective. Only the subject knows what he or she remembers. No observers were in the rooms to record, for each person, what actually happened when the news came. If there had been, then we could say: This, *objectively*, is what happened; and we could say, as an *objective* fact, that memories get much less accurate over time. All this would be possible because anyone could (in principle) have stepped into the role of observer here, and so the record of what happened is *independent of any particular observer*. That is what *objective* means.

More generally, we can say that any memory is subjective in itself. Only its "owner" knows what his memory of an event is like. But if we can ask how *accurately does a person answer questions* about what happened, that is objective, and we can learn much about memory that way.

Even mental imagery can be studied objectively. Images in your mind are private, subjective events. We could ask you to *describe* your images; but attempts to study imagery that way quickly bogged down in confusion (Humphrey, 1951). Instead, we can set you a problem that requires you to *use* imagery. Then we can measure—*objectively*—how quickly or accurately you can solve such a problem. The modern study of imagery was ushered in when researchers realized this (Chapter 6).

In clinical research too, the trend is away from global "ratings" of patients' or clients' well-being or adequacy of functioning, and toward the identification of particular "target behaviors" that can be tallied by anyone. Rather than rating a public speaker's anxiety, we can ask: Does she speak in a whisper? Hide behind the lectern? Hold her elbows against her sides? Clench her teeth? These may seem less rich in the information they provide, but at least they permit crosschecks among observers (Paul, 1966).

SOME MYTHS ABOUT OBJECTIVITY

The idea of studying human behavior and the human mind *objectively* seems to ruffle many feathers. We often hear one or both of two objections to it. One is that such an attempt demeans those who are studied; it "treats humans (and other animals) as if they were objects." The other is that objective investigation turns its back on the *subjective* side of human nature, our hopes and thoughts and fears. These inner states and events are a person's private possessions, known only to him or her—but they are also the most important of our possessions, the very stuff of our personhood.

Neither criticism is well-founded.

The first one reflects a simple misunderstanding of how scientists use the word *objective* and its relatives. If I say that I want to study your behavior *objectively*, I am not calling you an object. I am not calling you anything. What I am saying is this: "I want what I say about you to be as free as possible from any one person's biases, wishes, and preconceptions—including your own, and mine. I want it to be something that anyone could check for himself, and so correct the errors that you or I might make." In all this, far from denying your humanity, I am recognizing it: Humans are fallible.

The second idea—that objective study means we must ignore or deny the subjective, internal aspects of the human mind—is easier to deal with. It is simply false. How well do you remember an event? In a sense, that's subjective. Only you can "see" that memory. But if we check your memory against what actually happened, we can get an *objective* estimate of the memory's accuracy—and thus learn something about it.

Our emotions are subjective. Our mental images are subjective. Yet there are vast literatures out there, filled with *objective* findings about the properties of these inner events, what sorts of things affect them and what one can do with them. We have seen examples and will see more as we go.

In short, the search for objectivity is neither insult nor illusion. We can get objective handles even on the subjective side of humanness. And far from dehumanizing our subjects, we are acknowledging their very human fallibility—and our own.

THE RELIABILITY AND
VALIDITY OF MEASURES

We use a procedure, or operation, for assigning values to a variable—that is, for *measuring* that variable. How, then, do we evaluate the procedures themselves? Are they good ones, which will give us good answers to our questions? There are actually two questions we ask at this point.

RELIABILITY

The question of reliability is just what the word implies: Can we *rely* on this measurement we just made? If we checked it, or if someone else did, would the result be the same? To the extent that the answer is yes, the measurement procedure is reliable.

Consider this: You are taking some tricky measurement in a laboratory, deciding, for example, just where a pointer is pointing on a scale. "Looks like 10.6," you say, and you write the reading down. But then you look again, just to be sure, and indeed it still looks like 10.6. That's *test-retest reliability*.

Or, you may turn to your lab partner, and say: "I make it 10.6. Check me." The partner does, and says, "Right, I agree." That's *interobserver reliability*.

In short, we can determine reliability in either or both of two ways: (1) Having measured a variable, we can measure it again at another time and see if we get about the same value both times. If we do, then *test-retest reliability* is high. Or (2) we can let two or more observers measure the same variable at the same time, and see how closely they agree. If agreement is close, then *interobserver reliability* is high.

As to which to use, often the decision is obvious. We might be observing events that do change rapidly over time; perhaps the behavior of kids in a playground or chimps in the jungle. Here, test-retest reliability would make no sense. Of course our subjects will be seen to do different things at different times, because they *are* doing different things. But interobserver reliability, in which we see whether two or more observers agree on what it is that a person or chimp is doing at a given time, would be a useful check. Conversely, if we want to know whether a person is chronically depressed, one score on a scale of depression could mislead us—it might just reflect a sad mood right then. And the fact that two or more scorers agree with each other (interobserver reliability) would not reassure us. But if the person continues to score high when retested (test-retest reliability), we would feel safer in considering him chronically depressed.*

MEASURING RELIABILITY

The reliability of a measure is itself a variable; reliability can be high or low or in between. And it can be measured.

---

*Perhaps this is the place to mention that with pencil-and-paper tests, where there are many questions to be answered but all are designed to tap the same underlying process, specialized measures of reliability can be used. One may, for instance, see whether the odd-numbered items and the even-numbered ones give about the same result, or the first versus the second half of the items. In each case, if these "parts" of the test agree with each other, that is evidence that the whole thing is reliable.

To make these ideas clear, we will have to introduce some statistical devices: the notion of a *scatterplot* and of a *correlation coefficient*. We won't really stop to make friends with these ideas yet—later chapters will do that—but we will say hello to them here, and get a feel for what they can do.

THE SCATTERPLOT

Suppose I measure the variable *length of big toe in millimeters* for everyone in a classroom. I use an ordinary millimeter ruler to do so. Now, are my measurements reliable? I could do the measures again (test-retest), or have someone else do so (interobserver), to see how reliable they are.

In Figure 3.8, I imagine that we have done this. The measurements are in Panel A. In Panel B, I have plotted the big-toe lengths, as I first measured them, for each of four subjects, on the vertical Y-axis. On the horizontal X-axis, I plot the lengths as measured a second time (test-retest) or by a second observer (interobserver)—it doesn't matter which. Thus, each of the dots in the figure represents a single person's big-toe length, as measured twice.

For big-toe length, we would expect the two measures to be about the same for each person. They are, and we see that the little circles,

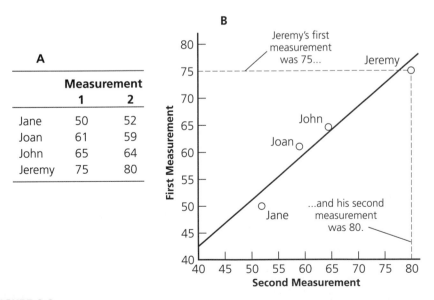

FIGURE 3.8
Two measurements of big-toe length in each of four imaginary subjects. Panel A shows the data; Panel B presents them graphically as a "scatterplot."

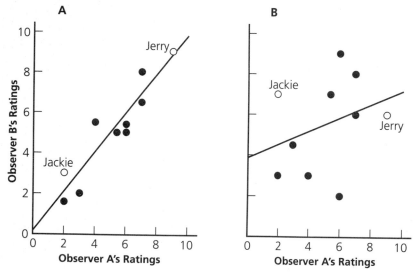

FIGURE 3.9
Interobserver reliability, high (Panel A) or low (Panel B).

each representing a person (or rather a toe), all fall *almost* exactly on the sloping line that would indicate perfect agreement: one measure identical to the other. The two measures will not be *exactly* the same, because there is going to be some measurement error (e.g., variations in placement of the ruler) that will lead to slightly different scores even for the same person. So the data points are *"scattered"* slightly around the graph, or *plot*—hence the expression, *scatterplot*.

Now, change the scenario and consider some new data. Suppose we are observing a group of 10 first-graders on a playground. Our task is to rate, on a scale of 1 to 10, how aggressively each child is behaving. Suppose two independent raters do this. Then, later, they compare notes to see how well they agree. They could plot Observer A's ratings on the X (horizontal) axis against Observer B's ratings for the same children on the Y (vertical) axis.

Now if the data looked like those in Figure 3.9, Panel A, we would know that our ratings have quite high interobserver reliability. Observer A thinks Jerry's aggressiveness rates a score of 9; Observer B thinks so too. Observer A rates Jackie at 2; Observer B rates her 3. And so on. Not perfect agreement, but no big disagreements either. Again, the points are scattered around the plot a bit, but they hover close to the sloping line that would indicate perfect agreement.

But suppose the data look like Panel B. Here, there is much less agreement. The two observers are watching the same children at the same time, but whereas Observer A gives Jerry a rating of 9, Observer B thinks he rates only a 6. Observer A sees Jackie behaving very calmly and rates her at 2, but Observer B thinks she's being passive-aggressive and rates her a full 7. And so on. Not good agreement at all. The scatterplot shows this at a glance; the data points in B are, on average, much farther away from that "perfect agreement" line than the points in A are.

In fact, for most purposes the reliability of the ratings in Panel B would be considered unacceptably low. If we were these researchers, we would look for more reliable measures or, perhaps, better-trained observers. And that is one reason for our using two observers in the first place—to test the reliability of the ratings.

HOW TO MAKE AND READ SCATTERPLOTS

The scatterplots in Figure 3.8 are based on imaginary data from four subjects only, just to simplify matters. The data on which the plot is based are shown to the left; the plot itself, on the right. We assume that each subject's big-toe length was measured twice, so we have a "first measurement" and a "second measurement" for each person.

First, let's consider how the figure was made. We see that Jeremy's big-toe length, measured the first time, was 75, so we draw a dashed line straight over from the vertical axis at 75. The second measurement was 80, so we draw a dashed vertical line up from 80. The place where they intersect is where we place the data point (the small circle) for Jeremy. We do the same thing for all the other subjects, though their dashed lines are not shown. Thus Jane's point is directly to the right of 50 (her first measurement), and directly above 52 (her second).

In reading a scatterplot, we just reverse the process. Suppose we did not have the numerical data, but only the scatterplot itself. We could still see that Jane's point is directly to the right of 50 and directly above 52, so we would know that those are her first and second measurements, respectively. In a similar way, we could read the first and the second measurement for each of the other subjects directly from the graph.

But why make the graph at all? Why not just present the numerical data? The advantage of scatterplots is that once we're accustomed to seeing them, we can tell at a glance both the direction and the strength of a relationship between two variables—even if the plot is based on hundreds of cases rather than just four. Thus in Figure 3.9 we see at a glance that interobserver reliability is quite high in Panel A, and lower in Panel B—even without looking at the numbers.

Reading scatterplots "at a glance" like that takes a bit of practice, but soon—trust me!—it becomes second nature. This chapter, and later ones, provide such practice.

VALIDITY

A measuring device is *reliable* to the extent that it gives us consistent results, considered all by itself. It is *valid* to the extent that it *measures what it is supposed to measure.**

The two ideas are quite different. Suppose I were to say to a class, "I'm going to estimate everyone's intelligence. I'll do it by measuring the length of each person's left big toe, in centimeters." Students would quite rightly object. Now, my left-big-toe measurements might be very reliable indeed. But, obviously, big-toe length is not going to be very strongly related to intelligence. My test is *reliable*, but it is not *valid* as an intelligence test.

The notion of validity comes in when there is some underlying variable that interests us, but that we cannot measure directly for one reason or another. Therefore, we use something else that we *can* measure directly, to *estimate* the value of that underlying variable. Intelligence is a good example. We have no means of directly measuring how intelligent a person is. But there are a number of ways we could estimate it: We might see how well he does on a standardized test. His test score—which we can measure directly in terms of, say, number of items right—could allow us to make an estimate of how intelligent he is. Similarly we might measure directly, in seconds, how fast he is able to solve a set of problems, and use that as our estimate. Or, if we were foolish, we could use big-toe length as our estimate. No law prevents it. It would have pretty low validity, that's all.

As with reliability, validity is a matter of degree. We do not (or should not) say that this or that measure is, or is not, valid. Instead, we ask: *How* valid is it? Validity is a variable, and in measuring it we assign it a value. And, again, as with reliability, there are a number of ways of doing that.

---

*Some writers express it a bit differently: A measuring device is valid to the extent that *we know what it measures.* This acknowledges that a device may be more valid for one purpose than for another—an important point.

FACE VALIDITY

A measure has *face validity* to the extent that it is a *plausible* measure of the variable we want to estimate. In other words, if it looks as if it should be a good measure, then it has face validity. Operationally, we might check it by asking a panel of judges "How reasonable do you think this is as a way of estimating intelligence?"—or whatever the underlying variable may be.

Obviously, big-toe length has very low face validity as a measure of intelligence. Rapidity of problem solving would be scored higher by our judges. So, chances are, would grade-point average—we could measure that directly, and it would seem reasonable to estimate intelligence on the basis of it.

PREDICTIVE VALIDITY

This kind of validity can sometimes be measured directly. It is a matter of how closely the measure we're considering is related to, or *correlated with*, the variable we want to estimate. We can see how closely the two are related, *if* we can measure each one. If the relationship is close, we can then use the one measure to estimate, or *predict*, the other. Hence *predictive validity*.

Suppose we are working for a company that wants to predict how well people will do as salespersons. We develop, let us say, a paper-and-pencil test of sales aptitude. Now, is our test valid? From the test score, can we estimate how well a person will do in sales?

Here's how we find out. We administer the test to a large sample of job applicants; some will score high, some low, some in between. Then we hire *all* those applicants, and track their performance over a period of time, measuring, say, number of dollars in sales brought in.

Now take a look at Figure 3.10. Here are scatterplots again! On the vertical axis Y, we plot sales performance. On the horizontal X axis, we plot score on the test. Thus, each person becomes a dot in the figure; for example, Alex scored 39 on the test, and brought in $38,000 in sales. Barbara scored 98 and brought in $100,000. This follows similarly for all other applicants.

Now we can take one look at these two plots and see that the relationship is much tighter for Panel A than for Panel B. In A, if we know only a person's X score and what the scatterplot looks like, then we can *predict* pretty well what his or her Y score will be when we look it up. If the data for our validity study looked like that, we'd know that our test has high validity. If instead the scatterplot looked like Panel B, our test would have rather low validity.

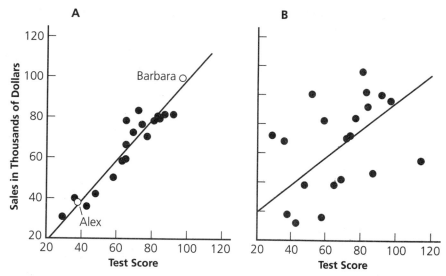

FIGURE 3.10
Predictive validity. In Panel A, validity is high; in B, lower.

Alternatively, the two scatterplots could represent two different tests, one for each panel. Then the scatterplots tell us at a glance that one test (for Panel A) has much higher validity than the other (for Panel B). We would likely keep the one test for future use, and discard the other.

Why? Because if our data look like Panel A, then we know that we can use the test to *predict* the sales performance of other applicants whom we haven't yet hired. So we might advise our employers to hire, in the future, only those who score high on that test. The company will then have a better sales force than if they hire everybody who comes along, and they might save *lots* of money in training costs and the like. On the other hand, if the data look like Panel B, we would likely throw the test away and try to construct a more valid one—assuming we still have our jobs.

Finally, notice that face validity and predictive validity can be quite different. A measure might turn out to have high predictive validity even if its face validity is low. Suppose we do find that big-toe length is, in fact, tightly correlated with intelligence as measured in some other way. (I don't think we would, but suppose we did.) Then our big-toe measure would have high predictive validity, whether that made any sense to us or not. And that might be useful knowledge that we could apply to other persons not yet measured. We want to estimate a person's intelligence? Measure his big toe! That's much easier and quicker than sitting him down with an intelligence test would be.

Conversely, a measure might be very plausible (high face validity) but, as an empirical matter—that is, as a matter of fact—have very low predictive validity. Thus, one's *confidence in his memory* for this or that event has high face validity as a measure of the *accuracy* of that memory. It *looks as if* it should be a good measure. But, surprising as it is, confidence turns out to have very low predictive validity. We do poorly if we try to predict, from a subject's self-reports of confidence, how accurate her memory will be when we check it. Again, this is shown not by any one study but by a whole literature. It is found, time and again, that a person may express great confidence in her memories ("Yes, I remember very clearly what happened then"), and yet be no more accurate than a person whose confidence is low. This has ramifications in, for example, courtroom testimony. Jurors are likely to pay more attention to a confident eyewitness than to a less-confident one. They shouldn't!

CONSTRUCT VALIDITY

When we ask about the *construct validity* of a measure, we are asking, in effect: Does this measure relate to other measures in a way that makes sense? We've seen examples earlier: Self-reports in threshold experiments, and in dream research, are justified by their relation to other data that do not depend on self-report. As another example, if we have a new test of intelligence and find that it is correlated with grades in school, job performance, and the results of other intelligence tests, these findings would establish the construct validity of our new intelligence test.

RELATIONS BETWEEN RELIABILITY AND VALIDITY

Validity, we have seen, is not the same thing as reliability. A test can be reliable (like big-toe length) but not very valid for its intended purpose (measuring intelligence). So a measure may have high reliability but low validity.

However, the converse is not true. *A measure cannot be more valid than it is reliable.* It may be *less* valid than it is reliable (like big-toe length as a measure of intelligence), but it cannot be more so.

In the case of predictive validity, where validity and reliability can both be measured numerically, we could work through a formal mathematical proof of this. We won't do it here; but, intuitively, the idea makes sense. Validity has to do with how closely related our measure is to some other variable that we want to estimate, like hunger or intelligence. If a test is not even closely related *to itself*, how can it be closely related to anything else? But that is the issue of reliability: How closely are scores on the measure related to scores on the *same* measure, when it is applied again (test-retest) or by someone else (interobserver)? For this reason, we will sometimes see researchers deliberately accepting a reduction in face validity, if it pays off in increased reliability.

SUMMARY

Our ideas are tested against the facts. And these facts are known as *data*.

We may have to think through just what facts we need. If we ask whether a treatment is effective or whether redheads have hot tempers, we need *comparisons*—we need to know how many redheads are hot tempered, how many are not, *and* how many nonredheads have hot tempers and how many not. Instead, our tendency is to focus on the "present-present" cases: hot-tempered redheads, or patients who improved with treatment. These data don't answer our questions.

A question becomes researchable when it is narrowed down to relations among variables. A *variable* can vary—that is, it can take on different *values*. A variable may be *categorical*—male/female, offers help/does not, alone/not alone, cloth/wire; or it may be quantitative—how much time a baby spends with each model mother, how promptly a person offers help, how many drops of saliva a dog produces, how many training trials a subject has had. Having selected our measures, we must *operationalize* them—we must make a series of decisions about what, *specifically*, we are going to do to make those measurements.

Our data may be objective or subjective. *Objective* data are "out there" for anyone to see. We may tally events, or take physical measures (e.g., of time, or of volume of saliva).

Subjective data are more problematic. The data are "in here" where only one person can see them. *Ratings* by observers are subjective judgments, but we may have no alternative to their use, and at least different observers can check each other's ratings. But such data are highly susceptible to biases, which different observers may share.

Self-report data are even trickier. If a subject tells us what his private experience is like, this can't be checked by anyone else; we must take the subject's word. But we can still ask whether self-reports are consistent among subjects and are reliably related to other data. Sensory thresholds and reports of dreaming during REM sleep are examples. At the other extreme, other data can tell us to be suspicious of certain kinds of self-reports. "Flashbulb memories" can be very vivid and subjects can be very confident of them, but they may be very inaccurate nonetheless.

Because of these uncertainties, much effort may go into *making* the data objective. Pavlov turned "associations in the mind" into objective stimulus-response relations. Latané and Darley turned "willingness to help" into frequency and promptness of offering help. Accuracy of memory can be measured objectively by how well the subject answers questions about an event—if, that is, we know what the right answers are! A person's degree of "anxiety" can be estimated from a tally of overt actions, where these are "out there" to be seen by anyone.

There are some common myths about objectivity. One is that it treats the subject as an "object," but that is not what we mean by the term. Another is that it denies the private, subjective events that are an important part of our mental lives. It doesn't; on the contrary, it tells us how to study them.

When we use a measurement instrument or procedure, we will want to know how reliable it is, and how valid. A measure is *reliable* to the extent that we would get the same result if we were to repeat it (test-retest reliability), or to the extent that two different observers would get the same result (interobserver reliability). It is *valid* to the extent that it measures what we want it to measure. There are different things this might mean. A measure has *face validity* to the extent that it seems reasonable as a measure of what we are interested in. It has *predictive validity* to the extent that it predicts (is correlated with) the variable we are interested in estimating. It has *construct validity* to the extent that it gives us measurements that are related to other data in ways that make sense. The three are not the same. Our confidence in our memories for some event has high face validity as a measure of their accuracy, but it turns out to have low predictive validity. When accuracy can be measured directly, we often see that confidence does not predict accuracy very well at all.

A method of measurement may be less valid than it is reliable, but it cannot be more so. Reliability sets the upper limit of validity. As a result, scientists may opt for a method of measurement that seems less valid than another, if it has higher reliability.

MAKING FRIENDS WITH STATISTICS: FREQUENCY DISTRIBUTIONS

When we have actually completed a research project, we will have accumulated a mass of *data.* A mass of numbers, perhaps, as in Figure 3.11—and that's just part of one day's session for one rat! Or we will have protocols detailing monkeys' movements or children's playground activities. Or *something.* And there will be a lot of it. Too much, chances are, to allow us just to look at it and see what all those data tell us.

Even a simple examination in a college class can give us (the exam givers) more information than we can easily absorb. Figure 3.12A shows part of a record of grades for an exam I recently gave in a class of 32 students. There are simply too many numbers to absorb all at once—and what's shown is only part of the record!

What we need to do is simplify this mass of data, to the point where we can see what the data show. A very handy first step is to convert the data to what we call *frequency distributions.* Actually, we are all familiar with the idea here; so let's start with a familiar example.

FIGURE 3.11
From a computer printout of the intervals between one lick and the next, in a single rat. The first column shows the time (in seconds) from the beginning of the session, until a lick occurred. The second column shows the time at which the next lap after that occurred. So the difference between them is the interval (in seconds) between each lap and the following one (third column). Read those numbers without the decimal points and we have the interlap interval in milliseconds, or thousandths of a second. Only part of one session is shown; there were a total of 3,829 laps, and that's just one session for one rat!

Look again at Figure 3.10A—the exam scores (the possible number of points was 30). As you see, it's a mass of numbers,

Lap	Time of Lap Onset	Time of Next Lap Onset	Interlap Interval (sec)
1	3.189	3.350	0.161
2	3.350	3.460	0.110
3	3.460	3.569	0.109
4	3.569	3.840	0.271
5	3.840	3.949	0.109
6	3.949	4.119	0.170
7	4.119	4.229	0.110
8	4.229	4.390	0.161
9	4.390	4.500	0.110
10	4.500	4.670	0.170
11	4.670	4.779	0.109
12	4.779	4.890	0.111
13	4.890	5.050	0.160
14	5.050	5.220	0.170
15	5.220	5.329	0.109
16	5.329	5.489	0.160
17	5.489	5.600	0.111
18	5.600	5.770	0.170
19	5.770	5.930	0.160
20	5.930	6.100	0.170
21	6.100	6.210	0.110
22	6.210	6.369	0.159
23	6.369	6.479	0.110
24	6.479	6.649	0.170
25	6.649	6.760	0.111
3612	1122.350	1122.510	0.160
3613	1122.510	1145.859	23.349
3614	1145.859	1145.960	0.101
3615	1145.960	1146.130	0.170
3516	1146.130	1146.290	0.160

A		B	
The raw exam scores are too many and too disorganized to make sense of. But...		**...a frequency distribution of scores gives a picture of the performance of the entire class at a glance.**	
Cheryl	29	33	/
Svertlana	29	32	////
Laura	30	31	/
Lonnie	18	30	////
James	24	29	////
Karen	32	28	
Jennifer	22	27	///
Paul	32	26	/
Joseph	33	25	///
Ben	31	24	//
Marianna	27	23	
Natalie	25	22	//
Christina	30	21	//
		20	/
		19	//
		18	/
		17	/
(and so on for all 32 students)			

FIGURE 3.12
Raw scores and a frequency distribution for examination scores.

and it's hard to see what the overall performance looked like even for these few students.

So, in Figure 3.12B I have tallied the *number of students* who received each possible raw score. Such a tally sheet is called a *frequency distribution*. It gives me, for each score, the number of students who obtained that score—or, as we say, the *frequency* of that score in the class. So, speaking technically, we say that in the figure the *frequencies* of the various scores are *distributed* over those scores—hence *frequency distribution.*

Now the data are much easier to make sense of. By simply counting tallies, I can

see that three students received a score of 25, four received 32, and similarly for other possible scores. Notice that I have made the data easier to inspect, but at the cost of some information. The tallies do not tell me *which* students received a score of 25—only that *some* three students did.

That's fine for a class of 32 students, but if I had a class of 400 or 4,000 students, even counting tallies would be a chore. In such a case, I could make things even easier for myself by changing the way I record frequencies. For example, using my class of 32, I could let each score be represented, not by a tally mark, but by a block; stack the blocks; and look at the heights of the stacks. We then get the picture shown in Figure 3.13A. Now I can just draw a scale on the vertical axis, and read off the frequency of each score from that axis. Looking at a score of 25, I note the height of the corresponding column and then, moving over to the vertical axis, read off the frequency with which that score appeared.

When frequency distributions are presented that way, with frequency represented by height of a bar for each score, they are often referred to as *histograms*. The data in the present histogram, of course, are identical to those in the original crude tally sheet. It's easier to read them now, that's all.

"SITTING" AND "HANGING" FREQUENCY DISTRIBUTIONS

When we encounter frequency distributions in the psychological literature, we will usually see them represented as in Figure 3.13A. The bars will be "sitting" side by side on the horizontal axis, and the frequencies are read from the height of the bars as shown on the vertical axis.

For some purposes, however (especially when we get into correlation and re-gression later on), it will be easier to visualize what is going on if we give the bar graph a quarter turn and show it as a "hanging" frequency distribution. Here, the scores have been put on the vertical axis, and the number of cases that have each score is shown by the length of the

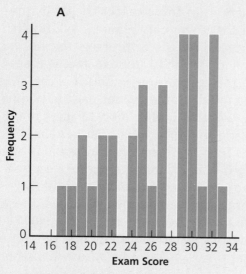

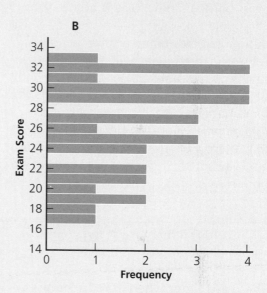

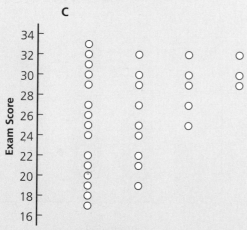

FIGURE 3.13
Histograms for the tallies in Figure 3.11, showing three ways to plot the same data. Panel A, a sitting histogram; Panel B, a hanging histogram; and C, a hanging "bubble" histogram.

bar along the horizontal axis. Figure 3.13B presents the same data as Figure 3.13A, but as a "hanging" frequency distribution of this kind. Look at the two figures and satisfy yourself that they present exactly the same data. It's only a matter of whether frequency is shown by the *height* of its bar (A), or by the *length* left to right of its bar (B). The choice is arbitrary.

Indeed, presenting a frequency distribution involves many arbitrary choices. Later on, some ideas will be easiest to visualize if we represent each score by a little circle. Figure 3.13C again presents the same data, but each score is a circle. Again, satisfy yourself before going on that these various figures are just different ways of showing the very same distribution of scores.

GROUPED FREQUENCY DISTRIBUTIONS

There are times when "raw" measures, even presented as frequency distributions, are awfully cumbersome to work with. This is especially likely if there are many possible scores, and the frequencies for particular scores are low. In such cases, we often simplify the data even further into *grouped* frequency distributions.

Again, let's start with a familiar example. Our frequency distribution of exam scores is not all that complicated, but students want to know how these scores translate into letter grades. There are 36 possible exam scores (0 to 35), but only five letter grades: A, B, C, D, and F. (Unless I also use A−, B+, and the like—for simplicity, let's suppose I don't do that.)

I group the scores from 30 through 33, and call them all A. I group the scores 25 through 29, and call them all B. 20 through 24 is C, and 15 through 19 is D, I'm afraid. Any score below 15 (there weren't any, as it happens) would be an F. Now, taking the results of that grouping, I can make a new histogram with letter grades on the horizontal axis, and frequencies of those grades shown by the height of the bars (Figure 3.14). Again, I can read off the vertical axis to find (for example) that 10 students received an A on this exam. (And, of course, I can always change the letter grades back to numbers, should it be useful to do so: let A = 4, B = 3, and so on.)

Then there are cases in which grouping is not just convenient, but necessary. Look back at the interlap-interval (ILI) data shown in Figure 3.11 earlier. Those are just a few of the more than 3,800 such intervals recorded for just that one rat on that one day. The intervals were measured

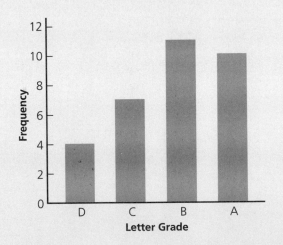

FIGURE 3.14
"Grouped" frequency distribution for the exam scores in Figure 3.11.

to the nearest millisecond (thousandth of a second, abbreviated msec), so one number could differ from another by as little as one msec. But there were also long pauses in drinking, lasting (on this session) up to more than 23 seconds—23,000 milliseconds!

That means that if we made a frequency distribution of the raw scores, there would have to be over 23,000 little tic marks along the horizontal axis. Then either the bars in the graph would have to be microscopically narrow, or the graph would have to stretch clear across the room. Clearly it would be very difficult to read, either way.

So I told the computer to *group* the ILIs in 50-msec "bins." Thus the first such "bin" was a tally of ILIs from 1 to 50 msec (there weren't any), the next, 51 to 100 msec, and so on. And then we get a picture of their distribution that is clear and easy to read (Figure 3.15). While drinking was in progress, the greatest number of ILIs was in the fourth bin (i.e., between 150 and 200 msec), and scores got fewer as the ILIs rose above that value or fell below it. Finally, intervals of 450 msec or more, representing pauses in drinking, were tallied in a separate "wastebasket" tenth bin; there were fewer than 100 of those. All this we see at a glance. That's the power of grouping!

SAMPLING FROM
FREQUENCY DISTRIBUTIONS

Now we know how to assemble sets of scores into a *frequency distribution*. Suppose we have done that, and suppose we take a *sample* of *one case*, at random, from that frequency distribution. For ex-

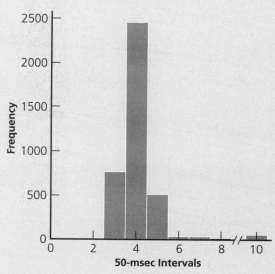

FIGURE 3.15
Grouped data for interlick intervals.

ample, look again at the frequency distribution of letter grades (Figure 3.14). Suppose we select one person's score, at random, from that distribution. What is the *probability* that it will be an A?

The histogram tells us at once that there were 10 grades of A in the distribution, and we know that there were 32 scores all told. Now *random sampling* means that any member of the distribution is as likely to be selected as any other member (Chapter 5). What then is the probability that we will select an A? Just 10/32, or 0.31. What is the probability that the score we select will be either an A *or* a B—that is, B or higher? Well, there are 21 scores that are A *or* B, so our probability is 21/32, or 0.66. Simple. (It was a good class!)

Here's another way of stating the same idea. Look at the *area* enclosed by the histogram, that represents a grade of

A. We can verify that it is 31% of the area enclosed by the whole thing. So that relative area, or proportional area, corresponds to the *probability* that we would select an A score if we sampled at random from that distribution. Similarly, we see at a glance that the area corresponding to an A *or* a B (the two right-hand bars together) is about 2/3 of the area under the whole thing. This is close to the 0.66 we calculated by counting.

Why look at it this way? Take a look at Figure 3.16A. In these data, we see that the area corresponding to A is a third of the total area. So if we sample at random, the probability that we will select an A is 1/3, or 0.33. But notice: We can say this even though, in this figure, *there are no numbers on the vertical axis at all*. We have not specified whether we are dealing with 30 cases or 300 or 300,000. In the latter two cases, of course, actual counting

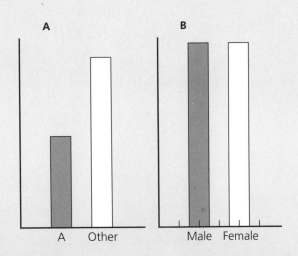

FIGURE 3.16
The areas within a histogram can represent the probabilities of various outcomes. For explanation see text.

would be very tedious, and we don't have to do it. We can just look at the areas enclosed by the bars, and calculate the probabilities of various outcomes with random sampling.

Another example? In Figure 3.16B, we show the relative numbers of males and females in some population or other. We see at once that there are about as many females as males. So, if we sample at random, we are about as likely to select a female as a male. How many females? How many males? It doesn't matter! As long as we know the *proportions* involved, we can represent them as a histogram in this way, whatever the numbers may be, and we can specify the *probability* of drawing a female by looking at the *proportion of the total area of the figure* that corresponds to female cases.

Understand this idea thoroughly before going on. Remember that a *probability* corresponds to a *proportion* that can be represented by an *area*—and be sure you see why this is so. It is an idea that is going to do a lot of work for us later.

CHAPTER 4

OBSERVATION AND DESCRIPTION

You can observe a lot by watching.

—YOGI BERRA

IN THIS CHAPTER, WE'LL DISCUSS:

■ How observational research differs from experimental research

■ Some methods used in observational research:

Case studies

Surveys and interviews

Participant observation

Direct observation of behavior

■ How observational studies can:

Test hypotheses

Provide an overview of a problem area

Answer further questions raised by the original findings

Show us how we can replace opinion with data

In the previous chapter, we saw some examples of what data look like and what can be done with them. Now we begin to address the nuts-and-bolts questions, such as: How shall we proceed to gather good data—solid facts on which to base our beliefs?

We can divide research methods into two broad classes. In one—experimental research—the investigator intervenes to make something happen. He deliberately causes something to vary. In a word, he *manipulates some variable*. Then he observes the effect of that manipulation. That is what an experiment is.

In the second kind—nonexperimental research—the investigator does not deliberately *make* something happen, but instead sets out to describe some aspect of nature as he finds it. He observes and describes it carefully, without attempting to influence events. We will call this very broad class of methods *observational research*. This chapter and the next one will be devoted to it.

In observational research, it's true that the researcher may intervene in the situation in order to gather data—as, for example, when a pollster asks someone to answer questions. However, this doesn't make the procedure experimental. The difference is that the pollster is not investigating the *effect* of his intervention per se. Indeed, he typically assumes that the intervention will have no effect at all, but only allow him to find out something about the subject— her opinion on some issue, or whom she intends to vote for—that would be true whether the pollster found it out or not. Of course this assumption may not always be justified (see "observer effects" later).

But now let us zero in on some examples of observational research. We will see what sorts of things can be learned by careful observation.

CASE STUDIES

In the simplest case, it may be important that some event occurs at all, even if only rarely. The mere fact that it *can* occur may tell us something interesting. In such instances, we may devote a great deal of study to just a few cases or even only one. Hence the term *case study*.

AN EXAMPLE FROM NEUROPSYCHOLOGY:
BROCA'S SPEECH AREA

In 1861, the French physician Paul Broca (1824–1880), a distinguished pathologist and neuroanatomist, encountered a patient called "Tan." The patient was given that name because that was the only word he could say! Except for that one word, he could not speak. He suffered from what we now call *expressive aphasia*—the inability to produce speech.

"Tan" was placed in Broca's care, but he died only six days later. An autopsy revealed damage to the brain at a certain area (now called Broca's Area) on the surface of the left frontal lobe (Figure 4.1). In the little time he had, Broca studied "Tan" very intensively, trying to pinpoint just what the difficulty was. This patient had trouble *producing* speech, though he could understand it perfectly well. Why?

It was not paralysis; the speech muscles were working just fine. "Tan"'s comprehension of language was intact, and his general intelligence seemed normal. Later case studies have supported this conclusion, showing that patients with *Broca's aphasia* can understand speech, many can write, and intelligence may be unimpaired.

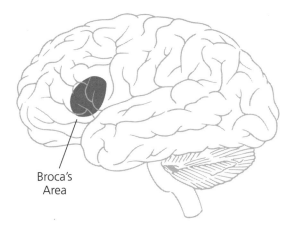

Broca's
Area

FIGURE 4.1
Broca's area, on the frontal lobe of the left hemisphere of the brain.

Rather, Broca concluded, such patients suffer from the failure of a specialized memory mechanism. It is as if they cannot *remember* how to use their speech apparatus to form words.

Six months after the death of "Tan," Broca had the opportunity to study a second patient. The symptoms were very similar to "Tan"'s and, it developed, so was the damage to the brain. Broca concluded that he had located an area of the brain that was specialized for speech production.

That conclusion fed into a longstanding controversy. Could one assign specific functions to different areas of the brain at all? Many students of brain function doubted it, and there were logical—and theological—reasons to doubt it. Grant that the brain is the organ of mind. Then, if a mind is single and indivisible—you speak of your mind, not of your minds!—it would seem that the brain also must work as a unit, or so the argument went.

Now, here were Broca's two cases and the others that followed: damage *just here* in the brain, associated with *just this* defect—difficulty in producing speech. Encouraged by Broca's convincing demonstrations, other scientists, in the decades following, sought—and found—other instances of such "localization of function" in the brain.

These findings and the surrounding controversy remind us again that small findings can bear on big issues. Does a person have one mind, or many? Does the mind have parts? If it does, does the *soul* have parts? (See Churchland, 1986, for discussion.) Questions about the very nature of humanity lie behind these limited, "localized" clinical case studies.

Broca himself was well aware of this:

[T]he days were over when one could say without hesitation . . . that the soul being single, the brain, in spite of neuroanatomy, must be single also. Everything concerning the connection of mind with matter had been called into question, and in the midst of the uncertainties that surrounded the solution to this great problem, anatomy and physiology, until then reduced to silence, finally had to raise its voice.

STRENGTHS AND LIMITATIONS OF CASE STUDIES

Case studies can be useful in telling us what *can* happen; for example, that a specific failure can be linked to a specific area of brain damage. The very fact that such things *can* happen may be important, for they bear on more general ideas, such as whether there is localization of function in the brain. They also may suggest new ideas or new lines of study, and they may add to the "weight of evidence" favoring or challenging a theoretical principle (Chapter 2), as Broca's studies did.

But case studies have two important limitations. First, they tell us that this or that sort of event *can* happen, but they do not tell us anything about what typically *does* happen. Sigmund Freud's work, for example, depended on case studies (though we present none here, for they are extremely long and involved). And his theory has been criticized on just those grounds—among others. From his conclusion that neurotic symptoms *can* express certain unconscious urges, he went on to claim that *all* behavior has such sources. Many writers feel that Freud's theory of the human mind simply went too far beyond his data, which consisted of a few case studies of very atypical people: affluent Viennese persons with symptoms.

Second, case studies are especially susceptible to two sources of error. These can damage any research project, but are especially dangerous here because of the close, repeated contact between the observer-scientist and his subject matter. First, there is the problem of *observer bias*. The observer (e.g., a therapist) may see what she expects to see; or she may select, from all that she sees, those events that she expects or that fit her theory. Thus a psychoanalyst may, consciously or not, attach importance to those events that fit the theory and less importance to those that do not.

Then there is the problem of *observer effects*. Even if an observer sees what is going on in an unbiased way, she may have unintended effects on what goes on. An observer or a therapist, by listening attentively to some remarks but not to others, or asking for elaboration of some remarks but not others, may steer the conversation in the direction in which she, the observer or therapist, thinks it should go. For all these reasons, scientists tend to treat case studies with caution.

SURVEYS: INTERVIEWS AND QUESTIONNAIRES

Whereas case studies are likely to focus on one or a few instructive "cases," survey research is more likely to ask: What is true of large groups of cases—many people, or many groups, on which we obtain data? A survey may be small-scale or large; but either way, individual cases will not be the focus of attention. Rather they will be treated as parts of a whole *sample* of cases. And the sample in turn may be considered a part of a larger *population*, to which we want our conclusion to apply.

Survey research as used in political or opinion polling, or in market research, is familiar to the reader, and we will say relatively little about it here. It does face technical problems. The *sampling* of cases can be tricky, and the phrasing of survey questions is an art in

"Next question: I believe that life is a constant striving for balance, requiring frequent tradeoffs between morality and necessity, within a cyclic pattern of joy and sadness, forging a trail of bittersweet memories until one slips, inevitably, into the jaws of death. Agree or disagree?"

FIGURE 4.2
The construction of survey questions is an art in itself. *This* survey was not constructed by an artist.

itself (Figure 4.2)—a highly specialized one, and we cannot get into it here (see Babbie, 1989).

Let us look at just one example of how such surveys can bear on questions of psychological interest.

A DEMOGRAPHIC SURVEY:
COHABITATION AND DIVORCE

Remember the decrease in the proportion of young American adults who were married, and the increase in those who were living together unmarried, from the 1940s to the 1960s (Chapter 1)? Here is one objective indicator of the marked change in American society's attitudes toward sexuality—a psychological phenomenon in its own right—over that period.

It suggests some further questions. We might ask, for instance: Is it a good idea for couples to live together before marrying? Maybe such a "trial marriage," in which the partners learned all about each other first, would serve to prevent many unsuitable marriages, thus reducing the risk of divorce later. (In a survey of nearly 300,000 American college students, 51% agreed that "a couple should live together before marriage"; Astin, Korn, & Riggs, 1993). Or we could just as well argue the opposite: Maybe those who cohabit first are more likely to regard marriage itself as an experiment rather than a commitment, and so be *more* likely to divorce if they become dissatisfied.

We could argue it either way—or we could look and see. *The data tell us* that couples who cohabited before marriage were more likely to divorce than those who did not, by as much as two to one. This has been found in the United States (Greeley, 1991), in Canada (Balakrishan, Rao, Lapierre-Adamcyk, & Krotki, 1987), and in Sweden (Bennett, Blanc, & Bloom, 1988). The evidence is pretty weighty!

Now, a note of caution about these studies. They do not necessarily mean that the prior cohabitation *causes* a greater risk of divorce later on. *Correlation does not imply causality* (something we all know, and routinely forget). Maybe cohabitation in itself makes no difference either way, but perhaps people with certain attitudes and values are more likely than others (1) to cohabit before marriage *and* (2) to dissolve the marriage if it becomes unsatisfying. What we *can* say is that cohabitation does not make divorce *less* likely, though it might have. Remember? We don't prove theories; we rule out alternatives (Chapter 2)!

AN EXAMPLE FROM SOCIAL PSYCHOLOGY: THE BENNINGTON STUDIES

Surveys need not be big, nationwide projects. They are often conducted on a much smaller scale in psychological research. Let us turn to some examples of what can be learned that way.

In the late 1930s, Bennington College in Vermont was almost brand new (Figure 4.3). It had been established in 1932 as an experimental college for women. It was a close-knit community, in which most faculty lived on campus, usually as masters of student dorms. The college was small—in 1936 it consisted of 300 people, students and faculty. Finally, it was imbued with enough of the experimental spirit that a large majority of its members was willing to participate in a research project, headed by Theodore Newcomb, concerned with the attitudes, and attitude changes, that seemed to occur in students as they studied there (Newcomb, 1943).

Bennington had a reputation for social awareness and political liberalism among its faculty, and among the students who had been there a while. Incoming students, on the other hand, tended to be from affluent families that had, on average, quite conservative attitudes. Newcomb and his co-workers wondered: What happens when people with one set of attitudes are placed in close, long-term contact with a "society" whose attitudes are different?

FIGURE 4.3
Bennington College in 1933.

The researchers conducted intensive interviews with students who had been at Bennington for varying periods of time; and, for a number of students, they were able to repeat the interviews as the students advanced from freshman to senior. The researchers found a consistent drift toward more liberal attitudes on political and social issues. These attitudes were *operationalized* in many ways—pencil-and-paper "attitude scales," which candidates for political office the students favored, and their opinions on various social issues of the day. As just one example, when questioned before the 1936 election, about two-thirds of the incoming class preferred the Republican (and more conservative) Alfred Landon to the Democrat, Franklin D. Roosevelt. Juniors and seniors preferred Roosevelt 3 to 1.

Consistently on all such measures, students tended to move away from their initial conservative attitudes and values, toward more liberal ones. Not all did, but, on average, the trend was clear.

There was substantial social pressure toward such a change. The faculty, Newcomb tells us, made a conscious effort not to push their views on students, but older students were less restrained. Indeed, those students whose attitudes did not change tended to be, or to become, rather isolated; they were named less often by other students as friends or as "admired," or as suitable to be leaders, than were those students whose attitudes did change.

That raises questions: Did the students' attitudes really change as a result of the Bennington experience? Or were they only paying lip service to the attitudes that prevailed at Bennington, while keeping their private and more conservative attitudes to themselves?

Well, one way of addressing that question is to ask: Were there *lasting* changes in attitudes? Once away from the social pressures they encountered at Bennington, did these women maintain their more liberal views, or did they move back to the more conservative attitudes they had entered college with?

Twenty-five years later, Newcomb and his co-workers were able to locate 94% of the women they had interviewed originally—a remarkable feat in its own right—and study them again (Newcomb, Koenig, Flacks, & Warwick, 1967). Many were reinterviewed; where this was not possible, they responded to mailed questionnaires. New questions had to be devised, of course, because the issues that separated liberals from conservatives in the 1960s were different from those that had distinguished them in the 1930s. The women were questioned (among many other things) about their attitudes toward a variety of social issues, and toward certain public figures identified as conservative (e.g., Dwight Eisenhower, Joseph McCarthy) or as liberal (e.g., Adlai Stevenson) in the early 1960s.

Would these Bennington alumnae remain more liberal years later? But wait—more liberal than whom? We need a *comparison group* here (Chapter 3). From the Survey Research Center at the University of Michigan, the investigators were able to obtain survey data from women roughly comparable to the Bennington group in age, income, and geographical location; and, on average, the Bennington alumnae expressed more liberal views than these "controls" did. But Newcomb saw a tighter comparison: What if we interview the *sisters* of women who had gone to Bennington, where the sisters had gone to college elsewhere or not at all? That gives us a comparison group closely matched to the Bennington graduates for family ethnicity, affluence, and parental attitudes. In addition, the *sisters-in-law* of Bennington graduates were questioned. This increased the size of the sample while still providing a partial control for ethnicity and social class, for people tend to marry people who are similar to themselves in these respects. As it turned out, Bennington alumnae in the 1960s did, on average, express more liberal attitudes and values than their non-Bennington sisters and sisters-in-law did.

Apparently, then, the change in attitude was genuine—and lasting. Further questioning suggested that if it was *social pressure* that produced the attitude change, it was *social support* that maintained it. Bennington women tended to select, or be selected by, husbands with more liberal attitudes than non-Bennington women did. They also tended to describe their close friends as having such attitudes and values.

There is much more, but this is enough to show us what interview and questionnaire data can do. Finally, the conclusions fit in with many other data, observational and experimental, on what happens to those who deviate from a group's majority attitude. The deviant is likely to be pressured to change his attitude toward the majority view; and, if the pressure doesn't work, he is likely to be rejected and isolated by the group (Schachter, 1951). This literature has some practical implications, too: If you want to change someone's attitude, the best way may be to immerse him in a group that already holds the attitude you wish to bring about in him.

AN EXAMPLE FROM CULTURAL PSYCHOLOGY: EXPLANATIONS OF ACTION

Here is another example of what we can learn from small-scale surveys. In the United States, when we are asked to explain someone else's actions—"Why did she do that?"—we tend to do it in a particular way, by referring the action to underlying personality traits: "She did it because she's that kind of person." We take it for granted that what determines a person's actions is the "kind of person" he or she is. It may come as a surprise to learn that this "habit of thought" is by no means universal.

Miller (1984) interviewed people of two cultures—Hindus living in India, and Americans living in the United States. She asked them to think of various examples of actions performed by their friends, and to explain why these actions were performed. Sure enough, the Americans explained their friends' behavior in terms of personality traits: "He or she is that kind of person." But the Indian respondents favored a different kind of explanation. They more often referred to outside situational factors: "He did it because the situation was such and such."

Perhaps the two cultures differ, then, as to the kinds of explanations for someone's actions that come most readily to mind. Perhaps Americans think first of personality variables, whereas Indians look to the situation. However, there is a loophole here. All these "situations" were ones that the interviewees thought up. It might be that Americans are more likely to think of situations where the causes really *are* personal, whereas in India, actions may come to mind that really *are* determined by the situation. So, to check this possibility, Miller took some of the scenarios generated by Indians, and gave them to Americans to comment on. Sure enough: Where the Indians had given situational explanations for the actions, Americans explained the *same* actions, in the *same* situations, by reference to the personality of the actor.*

Thus Americans prefer the one kind of explanation, Indians the other, even for the same events. If we are Americans, that tells us that the way we tend to explain things in this society is not universal. Not everyone jumps to the same conclusions as we!

PARTICIPANT OBSERVATION

Let us now turn to another way of observing events. Rather than asking questions, as in an interview or questionnaire, scientists may study the behavior of a group of individuals "from the inside." They may actually become part of the group, and observe it from the perspective of a member. Because the scientists participate in the group's activities while also studying them, this method is known as *participant observation*.

AN EXAMPLE FROM SOCIAL PSYCHOLOGY: THE "SEEKERS"

The following episode took place in the 1950s. Mrs. Marian Keech was a middle-aged woman who believed she was receiving messages from outer space. One evening in September, such a message informed her that, in December, most of the world would be destroyed by a great flood. She, and those close to her, would be rescued by flying saucers coming in from outer space. Mrs. Keech attracted a

---

*For example, one scenario concerned a lawyer on his way to work on his motorcycle, with a friend as passenger. There was an accident and the friend was injured. After taking his friend to the hospital, the lawyer went on to work rather than staying at the hospital with his friend. Why? Most Americans assumed that it was something about *him*: "The lawyer is obviously irresponsible." But most Indians assumed that it was something about the *situation* rather than the person: "It was his responsibility to be in court to represent his client."

small but loyal group of followers who believed her messages and prepared with her to meet the catastrophe. The commitment of some members of the group was quite striking: They quit their jobs and gave away their possessions; some even sold their homes. Why not? They would not need them on another planet!

A team of social psychologists (Festinger, Riecken, & Schachter, 1956) heard about the group, and decided to watch from close at hand what would happen when the flood failed to arrive. They and their student observers penetrated the group, claiming to be believers themselves. They were able to sit in on the group's discussions and keep careful records of what was said and done.

It is important to realize that the believers—the Seekers, they called themselves—were perfectly normal people. There was a physician among them, and several college students. They were quiet and reclusive, making no attempt to publicize their beliefs and refusing to grant interviews to reporters.

In the end, there was no flood and no spacepeople came. What did the group do?

We might have expected a reaction such as, "Well, we were wrong" (Figure 4.4). But *we'd* be wrong. After a predicted "rescue" had failed to occur not once but twice, the group showed every indication that their beliefs had not weakened, but instead had strengthened. The change was quite dramatic. Group members began making speeches and handing out leaflets, and Mrs. Keech made

FIGURE 4.4
After prophesy fails, we might expect a reaction like this. What really happened was quite different.

tapes for the media. These were things that they had never done before.

Was this because only the most devout and activist members remained with the group after the predicted Doomsday had come and gone? Fortunately, because Festinger et al. had kept detailed notes, they were able to go back through these, check that possibility, and rule it out. Those members who were now proselytizing and publicizing had, before the crisis of Doomsday, expressed no more commitment and activism than other group members had.

It would appear that even in perfectly sane people, a strong belief can survive even the clearest evidence that it is wrong. Indeed, a belief can not only survive such disconfirmation, but also show every sign of intensifying following it.

How could that be? In explaining it, Festinger et al. appeal to the theory of *cognitive dissonance*. The idea is this: We are uncomfortable if our actions conflict with our beliefs and values. We don't like to be inconsistent. Suppose then that we are confronted with such an inconsistency: We believe one thing, but our actions suggest the opposite belief. Then, if the actions have already occurred and cannot be changed, we may modify our beliefs instead, to bring them into line with our actions.

The Seekers (or many of them) had devoted a great deal of time and energy to promoting their liason with the extraterrestrial beings and, once an actual date was set for the rescue, some had quit their jobs and sold their homes. Clearly such actions would be inconsistent with a change in their beliefs: "Oh well, it was all a mistake." One member (the physician) said: "I've had to go a long way. I've given up just about everything. I've cut every tie; I've burned every bridge. I've turned my back on the world. I can't afford to doubt. I have to believe" (Festinger et al., 1956, p. 168).

So the group members who stayed on felt strong pressures toward sticking to their guns, and convincing themselves that they had done the right things; they had just got the details wrong, that was all. How could they support their belief that they had done the right thing? By convincing others! Hence, perhaps, the new willingness to publicize their beliefs and argue for them publicly.

One other observation sheds light on this episode. Those who did begin to publicize the group's belief were those who *remained with the group* after the disconfirmations. Those who drifted away, though they may have been just as committed earlier, did not do these things. It appears that just as *social pressure* can promote attitude change (as at Bennington), so too can *social support* promote the constancy of an opinion, even in the face of the clearest possible evidence that it is wrong.

The method of participant observation has given us some real adventure stories. One graduate student in sociology joined a Satanic cult, and described its (rather innocent) activities "from inside" (see Babbie, 1989). Eventually, he grew uncomfortable at the deception, which does raise ethical concerns. He went to the cult's leader and confessed that he had penetrated the group for research purposes. The leader was quite untroubled by this; indeed, he told the student that it was a properly Satanic thing to do!

DIRECT OBSERVATION OF BEHAVIOR

Rather than asking subjects questions, or participating in their activities, a researcher may observe their behavior directly, from outside the situation. "Just watching," in a careful and systematic way, can tell us much.

AN EXAMPLE FROM ETHOLOGY: SEX AND THE STICKLEBACK

A research tradition that has affected many areas of psychology is known as *ethology*: the study of animal and human behavior in its natural setting (see Tinbergen, 1951).

A classic in ethology is the observations on the reproductive behavior of the *three-spined stickleback*, a freshwater fish. This seemingly simple, instinctive sequence of events turned out to be marvelously complex.

In the spring, a male stickleback fish comes into reproductive condition, as shown by certain changes in his color caused by reproductive hormones. He will build an underwater nest (an ingenious tubular structure made of bubbles), and he will then patrol back and forth around the entrance to the nest.

He is now prepared to react in either of two ways to the approach of another stickleback. If the approacher is another male, our male fish is likely to make a characteristic "threat display," standing on his head with fins outspread (Figure 4.5). If the approacher is female, he will do a characteristic "zigzag" dance; this is the way he courts a female. (How does the fish distinguish a male from a female? Hang

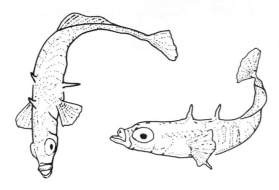

FIGURE 4.5
A male stickleback fish threatens an intruder with his head-down posture (from ter Pelkwijk & Tinbergen, 1937).

on.) To an experienced fish watcher, these "displays" are clearly recognizable—but it does take some practice.

If courtship is successful, there follows a meticulously choreographed mating sequence, with each member of the pair responding to the actions of the other. The male leads the female to his nest, pointing to its entrance with his nose. She swims through the nest and deposits the eggs; he swims through after her and deposits sperm to fertilize them. He then chases her callously away, but he does take over the job of caring for the eggs until they hatch, "fanning" them by moving his fins so as to direct a stream of oxygen-rich water over them.

Once we identify these action patterns, they can serve as jumping-off points for further investigation—and that is a great strength of "just watching" as a first step in research. Having seen what courtship and mating look like in this species, we can ask such questions as: What is it about an approaching fish that triggers threat on the one hand or courtship on the other? Or, whatever the cues are, does a stickleback have to learn to use them? Answering these questions requires us to manipulate certain aspects of the situation while holding others constant—in a word, to do *experiments*.

By moving from observing to experiments, ethologists have shown that each reaction is triggered by a characteristic *releasing stimulus*. An intruder male is identified by its red underbelly, and even crude models (introduced into the aquarium tank by an experimenter) will be threatened if they have that underside, whereas even very detailed model fish will not be threatened if they lack it. Similarly, a swollen underbelly identifies a female; crude models with it will be courted, whereas detailed models without it will not. Experiments have also shown that these reactions do not require training:

Even if a male has been brought up in isolation, never seeing another fish, he will react in the characteristic way the first time he does see one, or an appropriate model of one.

What's interesting about that? It revolutionized the way we look at behavior, that's all. By the 1930s or 1940s, most psychologists had thrown the concept of "instinct" out the window. They argued forcefully that all behavior, above the level of simple reflexes, was learned. But these ethological observations showed them, and us, that very complex sequences of actions could occur in the absence of any experiences that could have "taught" them. The concept of *instinctive behavior* made a strong comeback in light of such findings.

HUMAN ETHOLOGY I:

FACIAL EXPRESSIONS

"Just watching" can tell us much about human behavior, too. The next time you see two friends greet each other, look carefully at their eyebrows. You will see the characteristic "eyebrow flash"—a quick lifting and lowering of the eyebrows. Observations show that this gesture also occurs in cultures very different from our own, ones that have been separated from each other for many thousands of years (Figure 4.6).

Again, observation leads the way to further exploration with other methods. As just one example: Can the members of one culture recognize the facial expressions of members of a very different

FIGURE 4.6
The "eyebrow flash," used in greeting by (Panel A) a Papuan and (Panel B) a Waika Indian of the Orinoco in South America (from Eibl-Eibesfeldt, 1970).

FIGURE 4.7
Two people from very different cultures, a man of the Fore of New Guinea and an American woman, smile happily. Members of each society have no trouble seeing what this expression means in members of the other (from Ekman, 1973, 1975).

one? They can (Figure 4.7). Case study data are also relevant here. In Figure 4.8, we see a little girl laughing in the normal way: open mouth, with head thrown back and narrowed eyes. This unfortunate girl was born both blind and deaf. It is not obvious how she could have *learned* to make that expression. Perhaps, then, certain facial expressions in humans *begin* as instinctive action patterns, analogous to courtship or attack in the stickleback.

FIGURE 4.8
A child born both blind and deaf shows the characteristic facial expression that goes with laughter (from Eibl-Eibesfeldt, 1970).

Of course humans are more complicated than stickleback fish, and even if certain facial expressions arise without having to be learned, learning can certainly modify them later. We are taught certain "display rules" by the society we grow up in, and these rules tell us what expressions are appropriate, when. Some cross-cultural observations are relevant here. In Japan, one is taught to mask any negative emotion with a polite smile, and the "eyebrow flash" is considered rude and is deliberately suppressed.

Notice that in this case an entire culture becomes a kind of "case study," rather than an individual. And the fact of cultural variations in "display rules" tells us something important: Even if facial expressions *can* develop without the need for learning, they still may be greatly modified by the learning experiences we encounter as we grow up within a society.

HUMAN ETHOLOGY II: BOOK CARRYING

As a final example, here is an observation you can easily check for yourself. As you wander around the campus or the streets of your town, notice how men and women carry their books. Women are likely to carry their books with arm bent, cradling them against their chests. Men are likely to carry them with arms straight, books supported by the fingers (Figure 4.9). This difference has been observed

FIGURE 4.9
Males and females carry loads of books in different ways. The man is from Chile, the woman from Togo.

in a number of colleges in the United States and Canada and, in addition, in two Central American colleges (Jenni & Jenni, 1976); and I have confirmed them in my own workplace (see later discussion of this topic). Observations at public libraries show that it extends to the elderly as well as to college-age people.

For a thought problem (or perhaps a class project!), see if you can think of some reasons why this might be so. And then—the real test—think of some observations you might take to check your ideas. The consistency of the difference is quite remarkable; something interesting must be going on. Perhaps you will help us understand what it is.

TESTING HYPOTHESES WITH OBSERVATIONS

Thus far, most of our examples have dealt with exploratory research, asking questions in an open-ended way. What happens when people greet each other? When one stickleback meets another? When a strongly held opinion is disconfirmed? How do males and females carry books? And so on.

But observational research can also be used to test specific hypotheses, just as our experiments in Chapter 2 did. Rather than asking "What happens when . . . ?" we can say, "This theory predicts that such and such should happen. Does it?" Then the data will confirm or disconfirm the prediction, and add to the weight of evidence for the theory or against it.

Here are some examples.

AN EXAMPLE FROM CLINICAL PSYCHOLOGY: SMOKING, OBESITY, AND SELF-HELP

Certain behavioral disorders are notoriously difficult to correct. It is fairly easy to lose weight, but it is very difficult to keep it off. It is easy to stop smoking—but to stay stopped is another matter. Indeed, follow-up studies of clients in treatment programs report that a discouragingly high percentage of smokers or overeaters relapse within the first year—around 80% or more.

But then, all the people who were studied in those investigations were ones who had come to clinics for help. Perhaps the picture will be brighter if we look at those who have not done that, but have fought their problems on their own.

To test this idea, Schachter (1982) took a sample of people in the psychology department where he taught, and also in a small New England town where he spent his summers and knew many residents. He asked his subjects whether they had, or had ever had, a weight problem or a smoking problem or both; what they had done about it; and what had happened. So this was another small-scale survey and a questionnaire/interview study, like the Bennington one.

The resulting data looked much more optimistic than the clinical literature. About 40% of the people who had once smoked, had quit; and many had remained smoke-free for years. A roughly comparable percentage of those who had once had weight problems said, when interviewed, that they had lost their excess weight and kept it off—again, often for many years.

Why, then, are the data from clinics so much less encouraging? Maybe the people who go to clinics are those with the most severe problems, who have not been able to deal with their problems themselves. Well, that too can be tested. Schachter asked his subjects whether they had sought professional help for their problems. Sure enough: Those in his sample who had sought help tended to be the most overweight, or the heaviest smokers or ex-smokers.

Thus, the very discouraging statistical outlook for people with these problems may be misleading. It may be a matter of *sampling bias* (Chapter 5): Perhaps the cases who seek professional help, and so appear in our statistics, are the ones whose problems are especially difficult to overcome. For the rest of us, the difficulty may be less—perhaps much less. A comforting conclusion!

AN EXAMPLE FROM SOCIAL DEVELOPMENT:

MATERNAL RESPONSIVENESS AND INFANT CRYING

In this second example, we see *direct observation of behavior* used to test a theory—or rather a pair of them. Before describing it, let us set the stage a bit.

WHAT'S A PARENT TO DO?

Suppose that a baby has been fed, changed, and put in his crib—and he cries. All his needs have been met. Presumably he would just like some company and some "contact comfort." What is the parent to do—respond to the crying, or ignore it?

We could argue the case either way! And either way we would find substantial support from both common sense and psychological theory. Suppose that:

1. The attention a caretaker can bring—the warmth, the jiggling, the contact comfort—acts as a reward or, as we say, a *reinforcer*. Then, if the baby's crying brings about that comfort, crying will be reinforced—and a persistently crying baby should result.

2. There is the similar view of Dr. Benjamin Spock, the world-famous pediatrician. Dr. Spock is often called an advocate of permissiveness, but he took a hard line on this one: If you come running to the baby every time she cries, she will soon learn that she can manipulate you! You don't want to raise a manipulative baby, do you?

3. There is the view of one grandparent, who warns you: "You are going to spoil that baby rotten if you go running to answer her cries!"

All very convincing, and offered with great authority. The problem is that we can muster just as much common sense, and just as much authority, on the other side. Thus:

1. If the baby learns that he cannot manipulate you, then he is also learning that he cannot depend on your responding to the signals he gives. This disrupts an important component of the attachment process (John Bowlby).

2. The baby may fail to form "basic trust" in you and in people generally (Erik Erickson).

3. True, the baby will not be reinforced for crying, but if reinforcement is not dependent on what the baby does, he may form "conditioned helplessness" (Martin Seligman).

4. Then there is the other grandparent, who will say in effect: Go with your impulses! You know you want to go and comfort the baby, so do it!

So, from the first point of view—call it "reinforcement theory" for short—the advice to the parent is clear: Let the baby cry. Crying should drop out if it is unrewarded, and after awhile you'll have a baby who does not cry unless he is in real distress. But by the second account—call it "attachment theory" for short—a baby who is only tended when she needs feeding or changing is like a baby monkey with a wire mother: She will become insecure and fretful—a fussy, crying baby. So the attachment theorist's advice to the parent is: Go ahead. Comfort the baby.

SOME PREDICTIONS

What should the parent do? The two theories make exactly opposite predictions about the outcomes of the parents' actions.

If reinforcement theory is right, parents who respond promptly to babies' cries should reinforce crying, and have babies who cry a lot. Parents who don't respond as often or as promptly are not rewarding their babies' crying, and should have babies who don't cry much.* If we look over a sample of families, the amount of crying that occurs in different homes should be *positively correlated* with parents' responsiveness (Figure 4.10A). Responsive parents should tend to have babies who cry a lot (closed circles). Unresponsive parents should tend to have babies who cry less (open circles).

If attachment theory is right, the prediction is reversed (Figure 4.10B). Responsive parents should tend to have secure, nonfussy babies (closed circles). Unresponsive parents should tend to have insecure, fussy babies (open circles). So, amount of crying should be

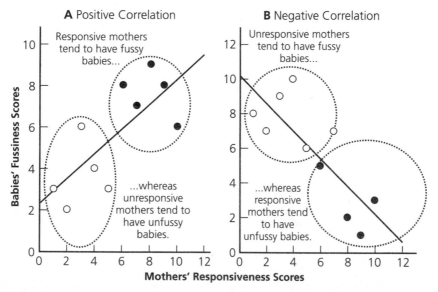

FIGURE 4.10
Pitting two theories against each other. The "reinforcement" view would predict a positive correlation between mothers' responsiveness and their babies' fussiness (Panel A). The "attachment" view predicts a negative correlation (Panel B).

---

*Reinforcement theorists quarrel with this rather naive analysis. They point out that unresponsive parents, who wait until they can't stand it any more before responding, may be reinforcing loud, persistent crying. This objection has been raised (Gewirtz & Boyd, 1977) and replied to (Ainsworth & Bell, 1977).

negatively correlated with parents' responsiveness. The more responsive the parent, the *less* the baby should cry (Figure 4.10B).

Thus we make predictions—that is, specify in general what the data *should* look like if a certain theory holds—and we can do this before we gather any data at all. In this case, we can pit two theories against each other, just as Harlow did (Chapter 2), by finding a situation in which they make opposite predictions. Then we gather some actual data, and look and see what actually happens.

THE BELL AND AINSWORTH STUDY

A team of investigators (Bell & Ainsworth, 1972) repeatedly spent whole afternoons with a sample of mother–infant families during the child's first year. Bell and Ainsworth noted (among other things) how often the babies cried, and how often and how promptly the mothers went to attend to them when they did. This was an observational study, not an experiment, because the researchers did not introduce any changes to see what effect they would have. They simply observed carefully what went on in each of the homes that they visited (direct observation of behavior).

What happened? The correlation was negative. *More* responsive mothers tended to have *less* fussy babies than did mothers who often ignored their babies' cries or were slow to respond to them. The data looked like Panel B, not Panel A, in Figure 4.10.

As Bell and Ainsworth (1972, p. 1187) sum it up, parents should not be afraid of spoiling their babies by responding to them. The data "suggest the contrary—that those infants who are conspicuous for fussing and crying . . . and who fit the stereotype of the 'spoiled child,' are those whose mothers have ignored their cries or have delayed long in responding to them." The concerns of Dr. Spock, of reinforcement theorists, and of hard-line grandparents simply are not borne out by the data.

A LOOK BACK

This study is a good example of how correlational data can be used to test predictions. Of course, this one study does not demolish what we have called the "reinforcement" theory of mother–infant attachment, but it takes its place in what is now a substantial literature, emphasizing the role of communication, and of responsiveness to that communication, in attachment formation.

Notice too that we speak of these data as posing problems for a theory, not as "proving" that another theory is true. The "attachment theory" could have been disconfirmed by the data; it wasn't, and so we could say that it has survived one test. Still, there are other ways of interpreting the data. Maybe it is true that an unresponsive mother is likely to make the baby fussy. Or it could be the other way around: Maybe a baby who is already fussy, for whatever reason, exhausts the mother and makes her unresponsive! Or maybe neither of these is true—there could be some third variable that affects both the mother *and* the baby. For instance, in homes with a lot of noise going on, both mother and baby might be stressed, tense, and therefore fussy (the baby) and unresponsive (the mother). Homes with less noise could leave the baby placid *and* the mother rested and responsive. The data are compatible with that idea, too.

This principle—*correlational data do not establish what causes what*—is so important, and so often forgotten, that it rates a discussion all to itself. We will come back to it.

Returning to the Bell and Ainsworth study, let's see how it incorporates some familiar concepts. The mother's responsiveness was *operationalized* in several ways: For example, the *number* of cries, and the *number* of times the mother responded to them, were counted. Another measure was *time*—a physical variable (Chapter 3). When a cry was heard, the observer would quietly start a stopwatch, and stop it when the mother left what she was doing and went to deal with the baby. The reliability of these measures was spot-checked by sessions in which more than one observer kept records, without communicating with each other. The *interobserver reliability* of the measures (Chapter 3) was acceptably high.

Perhaps most important of all, these data show that the original question—Will we make the baby more fussy if we respond to its cries, or if we don't?—need not be argued in a vacuum. It is possible to direct research to questions of this sort, and so let our conclusions be grounded in solid facts.

THE VALUE OF OBSERVATIONAL RESEARCH

Back in Chapter 2, we talked about the *theory/data cycle*—the back-and-forth interplay between our ideas and the facts (pp. 29–32). We also pointed out that a researcher can enter the cycle from either "place." He may begin with a theory and seek to test it; the examples in Chapter 2 were of that kind.

But he may also enter the cycle by collecting data first—by exploring something that he observes happening. The guiding idea here is not so much "Here is what this theory predicts should happen," but rather, "Something interesting is happening here; let's find out more about it." Pavlov's work is an example, and most of the research summarized in this chapter (with exceptions) is also in that spirit.

Thus many questions are "open-ended" ones: What happens when students from a conservative background find themselves in a liberal social environment? What do stickleback fish do when they encounter one another? What regularities can we see in how the facial muscles move when people greet each other? This patient cannot speak; why? And so on. Simple as they are, these questions (What happens? What is it like? Under what conditions does it happen, and what are its consequences?) give us an overview that can move us a long way toward understanding. A bird's wing would be a most puzzling structure if we didn't know that birds can fly.

As we explore, more specific questions come to mind that we can zero in on. How does a male stickleback tell male from female? Must he learn to do so? Do Bennington students only conform to the immediate situation, or are there lasting changes in attitude? Do people in different cultures use similar facial expressions in similar circumstances? Thus exploratory observation sets up questions to be addressed, perhaps by more systematic methods. The "transition to experiment," which we have seen in the stickleback case, is an instance of this.

Then too, observation without interference can test specific hypotheses. Schachter's study is one example. Are our clinical outcome statistics for smoking and obesity misleadingly pessimistic, because of a *sampling bias* in favor of those with more severe problems? Schachter's data (together with others) suggest that the answer is yes. Does being responsive to a baby's cries make for a spoiled, fussy baby? Bell and Ainsworth's observations (along with many others) suggest not. Thus, whereas correlation does *not* establish causality, correlational studies can sometimes *disconfirm* the predictions of a causal theory. We see it again: We don't prove theories, we rule out alternatives (Chapter 2)!

A final comment. Looking backward over even just these few examples, I hope the reader is struck (as the writer is) by the sheer number and diversity of questions that can be asked and answered—not with opinions or impressions, but with data!

Do women who were relatively conservative when they graduated from Bennington tend to describe themselves that way 25 years

Table 4.1
Self-Description of Political Attitude in 1960

Final Conservatism Score in College	Conservative	Middle of Road	Liberal
Above median	19	12	30
Below median	4	9	61

Table 4.2
Favor Conservative Political Figures?

Final Conservatism Score in College	Above Median	Below Median
Above median	44 (73%)	16 (27%)
Below median	22 (33%)	44 (67%)

Table 4.3
Candidate Voted for in 1960

Final Conservatism Score in College	Nixon	Kennedy
Above median	40 (61%)	24 (37%)
Below median	13 (18%)	59 (81%)

later, as compared to ones more liberal? Yes, as Table 4.1 shows.* Are they more likely to favor conservative political figures? Yes (Table 4.2). Were they more likely to vote for the more conservative candidate (Nixon) in the 1960 Kennedy/Nixon election? Yes (Table 4.3). And so on—page after page of it.

Again: Schachter tells us how many among his sample of ex-smokers went for professional help, and, among those who did and those who didn't, how much they had smoked. The relation between these variables, in this sample, is not a matter of opinion. There it was in the data: Those who sought help smoked more on average than those who didn't. Will parents spoil a child by responding to her cries? The Bell and Ainsworth data "suggest the contrary—that those infants who . . . fit the stereotype of the 'spoiled child,' are those whose mothers have ignored their cries or have delayed long in responding to them" (1972, p. 1187).

---

*In looking over the tables, do not be confused by the fact that about as many Bennington women were "high" as "low" in conservatism. This doesn't contradict what we've said about the drift toward liberal views. These women scored above or below the median *of graduating Bennington students*. Thus, a person might score "above the median" for students even if she were pretty liberal relative to, say, her parents and home community.

As we continue our journey, notice how often this happens. Questions that could be debated endlessly as matters of opinion can become matters of looking and seeing—if we pose the questions that way, and if we are willing to put our opinions to the test.

SUMMARY

In many research projects, something is manipulated, to see what effect it has. This is an experiment. But much has been learned by observing and describing what happens naturally, without manipulating anything. This chapter focuses on the latter case.

This kind of research can take many forms. These include *case studies*, as in Broca's careful observation of a patient with speech problems. Then there are *surveys*, as in studies of cohabitation; Newcomb's studies of the drift toward liberal attitudes in students at Bennington College; Miller's interviews with people from two different cultures, showing how they tended to explain the actions of others; and Schachter's interviews with people who had smoked or who had had weight problems There is *participant observation*, in which investigators become part of a group in order to study its workings "from the inside," as in the study of the Seekers. Finally, there is the *direct observation of behavior*. Examples of this range from the description of reproductive behavior in sticklebacks, to the details of the "eyebrow flash" and of book-carrying in humans, to the description of mother–infant interactions in Baltimore families.

In each case, the observations bear on much broader issues: for example, the implications of a "speech center" for the unity of mind (Broca); the role of social pressure in attitude formation and the resistance of attitudes to change (the Bennington studies, the Seekers); the differences between cultures in the "preferred" explanations for another person's actions (the comparison of American and Indian respondents); the complexities of instinctive behavior even in simple creatures; and the universality across cultures of certain nonverbal signals and ways of carrying objects such as books.

Observation can be used to test specific hypotheses (predictions), as the Bell and Ainsworth observations supported an "attachment" as opposed to a "reinforcement" theory of mothers' effects on their infants, and as Schachter's interview data on those who had recovered on their own from smoking and weight problems identified a bias in the clinical data for recovery rates.

But even in the absence of specific theories to test, observational data may provide an overview of a problem that tells us what questions need to be asked—we need to know *what* happens before we can reasonably ask *why*. And such studies can lead to further questions that can be answered with further observations. They may even provide jumping-off points for experimental research, as in the experiments that identified "releasing stimuli" for the reactions of stickleback fish. And, again, they can be used to test theories about what causes what. Correlation does not establish causality, but it may provide evidence for or against a causal theory.

Most important, our examples show that questions about behavior need not be argued in a vacuum. Questions that could be debated endlessly as matters of opinion, can become matters of *looking and seeing*.

MAKING FRIENDS WITH STATISTICS: DESCRIPTIVE STATISTICS

In the last chapter, we learned how to simplify and summarize data by turning them into *frequency distributions.* For many purposes, it is helpful to simplify even further. It may be that just a number or two, calculated from our data, can tell us what is most important about them. Such numbers are called *descriptive statistics*.

MEASURES OF CENTRAL TENDENCY

Imagine that you have a bundle of exam scores in your hand, and a friend asks "How did the class do?" You start to read off the exam scores, but your friend says "No, no, don't tell me *all* the scores. I don't have time, and I couldn't keep them all in my head anyway. What was a *typical* score?" He is asking for a measure of *central tendency*—a measure of what score the individual scores *tend* to *center* around.

There are some options here, and it will be important to tell your friend just which of these measures you are giving him as an estimate of the "typical" score. They give different meanings to the word *typical.*

THE MODE

First, you could tell him what score was received by more students than any other. This is the *mode*, the score with the highest frequency of occurrence. In Figure

4.11A, we see that more students received a score of 10 than any other score. Therefore, 10 is the mode of this distribution. The mode is a typical score in this sense: If we were to guess that *every* student in the class received the modal score, we would be exactly right more often than if we guessed any other score.

One disadvantage to the mode is that it doesn't lend itself to further mathematical development, as some other measures do. Another problem is that not all distributions have just one mode. In Figure 4.11B, there are three scores with frequencies of 3, and none with a higher frequency. In such a case, if we want a single "typical" score, the mode would not do.

Yet it does have its uses. In categorical data (Chapter 3), there may be no numbers to calculate with, but only names that describe the categories. Consider that in many elections, the candidate who re-

ceives the greatest number of votes is declared the winner. Why? Because he or she is the choice of the "most typical" voter—the modal one.

THE MEDIAN

The *median* is the score that divides a frequency distribution in half. Half the scores are above it, and half the scores are below it. So the median is a "typical score" in this sense: If we were to guess that *every* student in the class received the median score, we would not be consistently off in either direction. We would guess too high and too low equally often.

As to calculating the median for a frequency distribution, sometimes we can do it by inspection. Thus in Figure 4.12A, knowing that we have 10 cases, we see by simple counting that a score of 7 has three cases above it and three below, so 7

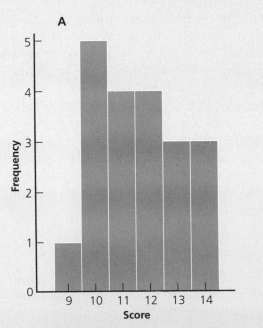
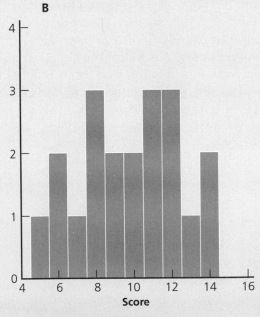

FIGURE 4.11
The mode. In Panel A, 10 is the modal score, but Panel B doesn't have a single mode.

is the median. In Figure 4.12B, half of the 20 scores are at 7 or below, and half are at 8 or above, so we split the difference and call the median 7.5.

Other cases are a bit trickier. In Figure 4.12C, we see that there are again 20 scores, so we would like to find the point such that 10 scores fall above it and 10

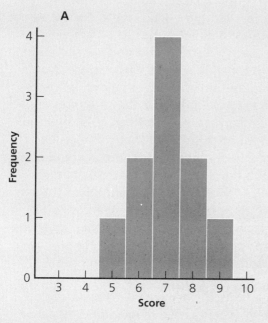

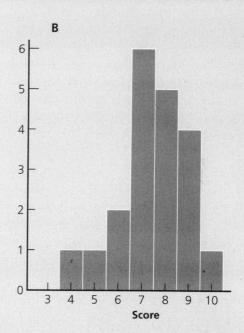

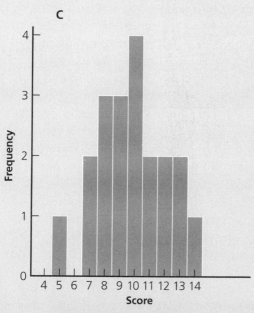

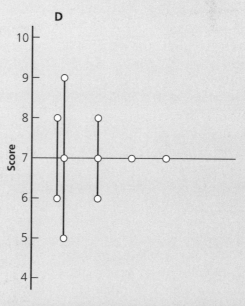

FIGURE 4.12
Medians and means.

below. But there is no such score. If we count scores up through 9, there are 9 scores at or below it—less than half. If we count up through 10, there are 13 scores at or below it—more than half. In such cases, we can get a crude estimate of the median by assuming it to be the score that *includes* the midpoint: here, 10. If we need a more exact measure, there are ways of interpolating within that interval to calculate it. For that, I refer you to books on statistics.

THE MEAN

Finally, there is the familiar *mean* or *average*. We just add up all the scores there are, and then divide the sum by the number of scores. In symbols,

$$M = \Sigma X/N$$

Remember our old friend the summation sign? In words, this just says: The mean (*M*) is the sum of all the scores (ΣX), divided by the number of scores (N).

So for the scores in Figure 4.12A, since there are 10 scores, the mean is simply: $5 + 6 + 6 + 7 + 7 + 7 + 7 + 8 + 8 + 9 = 70$. And 70/10 = 7.0. In this case, the mean happens to equal the median. In other cases, it may not.

Calculate the mean for the scores in Figures 4.12B and 4.12C. You should get 7.45 and 9.80 respectively.

The mean is a "typical" score in this sense: If we take each score and subtract it from the mean, keeping track of minus signs, we will find that these "deviation scores" (i.e., the deviation of a score from the mean) will sum to exactly zero over the class as a whole. In other words, if we were to guess that *every* person in the

class received the mean score, then our *total* error, summed across all scores, would be zero—less than if we guessed any other number.

To get a clear image of what this means, in Figure 4.12D we show the same data as in Panel A, but as a "hanging" frequency distribution, and we represent each individual score with a circle. Now, imagine that the circles below the mean are lead weights, and that the ones above the mean are helium-filled balloons. The length of the thread that connects each circle to the horizontal line, at the mean, is the deviation score for that circle. Finally, if we add up the lengths of thread, treating ones above the mean as "plus" and below the mean as "minus," they will sum to zero. They will do so for *any* frequency distribution—every time.

The mean is a useful statistic, because it permits further mathematical development, whereas the median and mode do not. It does have a potential drawback, however: Its value can be very sensitive to a few extreme scores—maybe only one.

For example, suppose we want to know the "typical" annual income in a community. For simplicity, suppose there are only five families in it—four of modest income, and a fifth family that is very wealthy. We determine that the annual incomes (again keeping it simple) are $20,000, $30,000, $40,000, $50,000—and $1,000,000. If we add these up and divide by 5, we get $228,000 for the mean. Obviously, this gives a misleading idea of the community's affluence. In such a case, the median income—$40,000—would be a better estimate of what is typical for the community as a whole.

The moral of that little story is that, once we have our data in hand, we ought not rush to compute means. We should look at the frequency distribution, to see whether the mean might be misleading because of a few extreme scores. If it is, another measure of central tendency, such as the median, might be a better bet.

A LOOK BACK

We have considered three ways in which we could use a single number to summarize a frequency distribution, by presenting the score that is "most typical" of that distribution. They differ, because they mean different things by "typical."

The mode (if there is one) is most typical in that it is the score that occurs more often than any other.

The median is most typical in that it is at the midpoint of the distribution: as many scores are above it as below it.

The mean is most typical in that it minimizes the sum of the deviation scores. Indeed, it minimizes them all the way to zero. No other number can make that statement.

HOW TYPICAL? MEASURING VARIABILITY

A single "typical" score can tell us the central tendency of a frequency distribution. However, some such scores are more typical than others. It depends on how *variable* the data are within that distribution.

Consider Figure 4.13. Here we see two histograms, both with the same mean: 8. That is the "typical" score, in the sense we

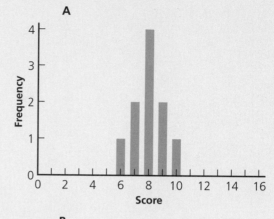

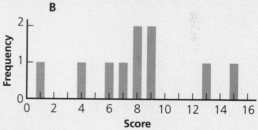

FIGURE 4.13
A histogram with low variability (Panel A) and high variability (Panel B).

noted earlier, for both distributions. Clearly, however, it is *more* typical for the upper than for the lower histogram. In Figure 4.13A, the scores are clustered tightly around the mean; they do not vary much one from another. But in Figure 4.13B, the scores are all over the place; some are much higher, some much lower, than the mean. The scores are *more variable* for B than for A, even though the mean is the same.

Can we develop a numerical measure of the variability of scores within a frequency distribution? Yes, we can. There are several possibilities, but we will focus on only two here—the *variance* and its square root, the *standard deviation*—for

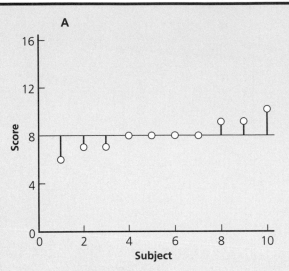

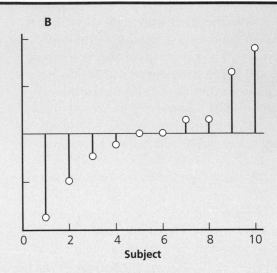

FIGURE 4.14

The data from Fig. 4.13, replotted to show how deviations from the mean (the vertical lines that "tether" the circles to their mean) are shorter when variability is low than when it is high. Each plot was constructed from the histograms in Figure 4.13, plotting scores from lowest to highest. Thus in Panel A we know that one subject received a score of 6, two received scores of 7, four received scores of 8, and so on; and the first seven circles represent those scores in that order.

these are real workhorses. The logic we're about to develop will be useful not just in this context, but in others as well.

In Figure 4.14, we replot Figure 4.13 as a pair of "hanging" histograms, again using circles instead of blocks (so that we can use our image again for clarity). For each case, we represent the mean as a horizontal line running across the histogram from the mean value at the left-hand axis.

Now, look at the "threads" that connect the circles with the line for the mean. Again, imagine that the circles above that line are helium balloons, and that the circles below it are lead weights, all tethered to the mean by the threads. We see that the threads tend to be longer for Figure 4.14B, in which variability is great, than for Figure 4.14A, where it is small. In other words: Greater variability within the distribution implies that the scores, on av-

erage, fall farther away from the mean, above and below it. And the length of each thread tells us *how far from the mean* the corresponding score is. (If a score falls directly on the mean, we still consider it. We treat its "thread" as having zero length.)

Well, the length of the threads could give us our measure of variability right away. We could simply average the lengths of the threads themselves: the higher that average, the greater the variability. In fact, what we are going to do is very much like that. But we cannot do *exactly* that, because if we subtract the mean from each score (thus calculating thread length for each score), some will be positive, and some will be negative, and they will add up to zero as we saw a minute ago. That will be true for both distributions, so the difference between them would be lost.

We could, it is true, just throw out minus signs and deal with the absolute lengths of the various threads. If we averaged those, then the resulting statistic (called the *average deviation*) would be a perfectly good measure of variability. But statisticians prefer another way, more useful for further development. What we do is this: After subtracting the mean from each score, we *square* the resulting deviation scores. The resulting squares are all positive: A positive number, squared, is positive; and a negative number, squared, is positive too. We average these squared deviation scores, obtaining a number called the *variance* (symbolized as SD^2). Then, to reverse the squaring operation, we take the square root of the variance. That gives us the *standard deviation* (SD)—our measure of variability.

In short: The variance is the average of the *squares* of the deviation scores (the thread lengths). The standard deviation, the square root of the variance, is *something like* the average length of the threads themselves.

If we have these ideas in mind, the computation of the variance and standard deviation makes sense. The formula for the variance is:

$$SD = \Sigma(X - M)^2/N$$

In words, this says:

1. From each score X, we subtract the mean: $(X - M)$.

2. We square each of the resulting deviation scores: $(X - M)^2$.

3. We add up all those squared deviation scores: $\Sigma(X - M)^2$.

4. We divide that sum by the number of scores: $\Sigma[(X - M)^2]/N$

And there is our variance. Finally (5), if we take the square root of the whole thing, we have our standard deviation. How simple it is!

In Table 4.4 we present a worksheet for computing the variance and standard deviation for Figure 4.14A. We find that the standard deviation for the "tight" histogram, A, is 1.09. For the all-over-the-

Table 4.4
Worksheet for Computing the Variance and Standard Deviation for Figure 4.14A

Subject No.	Score	Deviation (score − mean)	Deviation Squared
1	6	−2	4
2	7	−1	1
3	7	−1	1
4	8	0	0
5	8	0	0
6	8	0	0
7	8	0	0
8	9	1	1
9	9	1	1
10	10	2	4
	Sum = 80		Sum = 12
	Mean = 8		Variance = 12/10 = 1.20
			SD = 1.09

map one, B, it is 3.82. (I don't show the worksheet for B, because I want you to verify that as an exercise; see the bottom of the page if you need help).*

As estimates of the "typical" lengths of threads in the two cases, these values look reasonable. And the standard deviation is higher for the distribution with the more variable scores, B—just as it ought to be.

STATISTICS AND EVERYDAY LIFE: "PERSONS WHO" AND TESTIMONIALS

Statistical thinking has been described as the Achilles heel of human cognition. We just are not good at thinking statistically, or so it is said. I'm not so sure. My own belief is that we are quite good at statistical thinking, *if we recognize that the problem requires that kind of thinking*. All too often, though, we do not realize that.

THE "PERSON WHO" ARGUMENT

"Men are taller than women, right?" "Right." "So then all men are taller than all women, right?" "No, of course not, and that's not what I said."

What the speaker did say was short-hand for "Men *on average* are taller than women." Or, equivalently: "The frequency distribution for height is farther to the right for men than for women." Now, if we look at a single man and a single woman, we are taking a *sample of one* from each of the two distributions. Since they overlap, sometimes the man we choose will be shorter than the woman we choose—of course! The average difference is still there, and is not challenged by this.

Is this painfully obvious? Perhaps. But surely one of the wonders of the world is how often we overlook it. As Stanovich (1998) noted:

> Consider the testimony of Vincent DeVita, the director of the National Cancer Institute . . . before Congress in 1981. Answering a question about studies of the apricot pit derivative Laetrile, DeVita stated that the most recent NCI research had shown it to be inef-

*Here is what you should have done:

Subject No.	Score	Deviation (score − mean)	Deviation Squared
1	1	−7	49
2	4	−4	16
3	6	−2	4
4	7	−1	1
5	8	0	0
6	8	0	0
7	9	1	1
8	9	1	1
9	13	5	25
10	15	7	49
	Sum = 80		Sum = 146
	Mean = 8		Variance = 14.6
			SD = 3.82

fective. Senator Paula Hawkins of Florida then said, "I know of a person who had skin cancer, who was diagnosed as a terminal case. The person took Laetrile and she's alive 2 years later." Perhaps grinding his teeth at the thought of national policy on multimillion-dollar medical research being determined by another random [person-who], Pitot replied with the polite understatement, "Individual cases don't make a generality." (p. 143)

The senator seemed to regard the matter as a standoff: *one* body of data, involving thousands of cases, against *one* "person who." This happens over and over: A well-established statistical trend is not believed because the listener knows a "person who" is an exception to it: "Whaddya mean, smoking increases the risk of cancer? My Uncle Elbeau smoked heavily for 60 years, and he lived to be 84." But a statistical trend that characterizes a whole sample is not undermined by individual cases.

Nor can it be established by one. Do redheads have hot tempers? It's surprising how often we'll hear an answer of the form, "Well, look at Mary Murgatroyd— she's a redhead, and boy! Does she fly off the handle at every little thing!" So what? That's the "present/present" bias again (Chapter 3)!

Consider the (imaginary) data in Figure 4.15. In these data, we *imagine*—I have no idea what we'd actually find— that redheads are, over a whole sample, actually *less* likely to have hot tempers than nonredheads are. (Notice that we need all four bars to establish this.) Still, if we sample from this whole distribution, with its four bars, we will occasionally

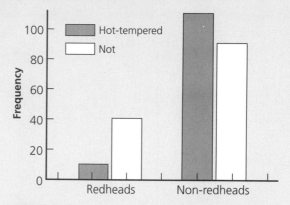

FIGURE 4.15
We could draw a hot-tempered redhead even from this distribution.

sample from the left-most bar. Then we will see a Mary Murgatroyd—a "person who" fits the stereotype—though the data for the whole sample contradict it.

BOUQUETS: TESTIMONIALS

The testimonial is a variant of the "person who" argument. A "person who" was helped, pleased, or gladdened by some product is eager to share his excitement with you. So he tells you how wonderfully the product worked for him. That's a testimonial.

Over and over we hear them. "Here's how I lost 60 pounds while eating anything I like!" Or, "Here's how Elmer Blugg learned French in his sleep!" The idea is, of course, that this or that fad weight-loss program, or this or that subliminal tape, or (who knows) this or that crystal, *really works!*

Well, if it *really works*, this means that two variables are related. People in general should tend to learn more French, or lose more weight, if they use the product advertised than if they do not. If we took the necessary observations, we might

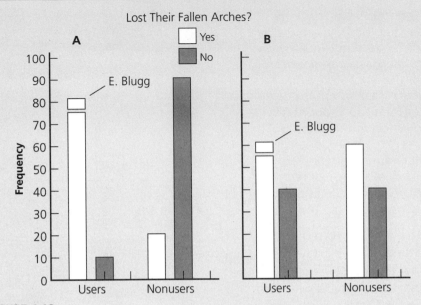

FIGURE 4.16
Mr. Blugg may be very happy with his treatment, whether it really is related to the likelihood of recovery (Panel A) or not (Panel B).

expect to see something like the (imaginary) data in Figure 4.16, which shows that, indeed, a higher proportion of people lost their fallen arches with the product than without it. And we indicate that one of the data "blocks" represents our friend Elmer Blugg, who did indeed do very well, with that product to help him!*

Now, take a look at Panel B. It shows another set of (imaginary) data, carefully constructed so that the proportion improved is exactly and precisely the same in users and nonusers. But lo! Elmer Blugg's data point is in the same column as before: He is a user who improved. Even in

such a case, we will find *some* data points that reflect improvement.

What if Elmer Blugg's data (1) come from a frequency distribution like B, and (2) are the only data we hear about? Mr. Blugg's experience might be very persuasive—but it shouldn't be. His experience could be the same, whether the rest of the plot looks like Panel A or like Panel B!

I'm afraid that Mr. Blugg's personal testimonial—"Boy, Product X really helped me!"—the sort of thing that calls to us from every TV screen and magazine cover—is worth exactly and precisely nothing.

BRICKBATS—THE ANTITESTIMONIAL

The "person who" effect can go the other way as well. Imagine this: We have decided to buy a new car. After careful com-

---

*Remember that histograms are made by stacking up "blocks" at the various scores, where each block represents a single score. In each of the panels, Mr. Blugg's block is added to the same stack of "scores," representing users who were scored as having lost their fallen arches.

parison shopping and consultation of repair records in *Consumer Reports*—statistical data, based on thousands of cases—we decide on Car X.

The trouble is, before we buy the car we have a conversation with a friend. And we learn that this friend has a friend who knows somebody who bought a Brand X car, and found it to be nothing but trouble—breakdown after breakdown and hundreds of dollars for repairs. Question: Would this influence our decision?

It shouldn't. Suppose the *Consumer Reports* frequency-of-repair records are based on the experience of, say, 1,000 owners. Add this poor car owner's data and we have 1001. That miserable experience would lead us to adjust the figures in the third decimal place, but seldom would this change the overall conclusion that Car X has the better repair record. But would we look at it so dispassionately? Could we?

What makes it difficult, I think, is our tendency to think in concrete images. The repair records are numbers; our single case is a drama. It catches our attention and nags at the back of our minds. "First that fancy fuel-injection computer thing went out. 250 bucks. Next there was trouble with the rear end. Had to replace it. Then. . . ." We see and hear the poor person's anguish. We might grit our teeth and buy Brand X anyway, but certainly this *one case* would put a noticeable damper on our enthusiasm for doing so.

This happens even if we *know* that the case is not typical—and we do know it here, for the records tell us that on average the Brand X car is the most reliable one. The records tell us that that lemony car, a sample of one, *cannot* be representative of Brand X's product. But we let it sway our conclusion anyway—knowing that we shouldn't.

The moral of this discussion? There are three. (1) If good data show what value of a variable is most typical, this is not challenged by one or even several "persons who" take on other values. (For further discussion, see Nisbett & Ross, 1980; Stanovich, 1992.) (2) Testimonials from single "persons who" do not establish what is typical. And (3), when you are offered a "person who" argument, form the habit of quietly asking the offerer, "What does the whole frequency distribution look like?" If he doesn't understand your question, explain. He needs you.

CHAPTER 5

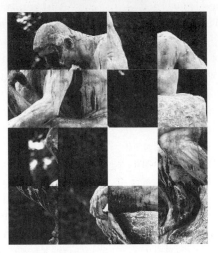

OBSERVATION AND DESCRIPTION II: SOME TECHNICAL PROBLEMS

[A] scientific theory may please you and may seem in accord with your own feelings and beliefs, but your own pleasure is no proof of its possible validity.

—ISAAC ASIMOV

IN THIS CHAPTER, WE'LL DISCUSS:

- Some problems of method that a researcher may face, including:

  Ways of selecting an unbiased sample

  The concept of random sampling

  When, and when not, to be concerned about sampling bias

  Effects of the observer on what the subjects do or say

  Bias in the observations themselves

  Inferential bias, or drawing illogical conclusions from the data

- Some ways of dealing with these problems when they arise

Science bases its conclusions on data (Chapter 3), and we can obtain data by observing nature as we find it, without interfering with it (Chapter 4). But researchers want *good* data—that is, data that really will permit valid conclusions. Data that mislead us are worse than no data at all, for they may make us think we have answered a question when we have not. This chapter is about some ways in which we might gather misleading data, and what we can do to prevent this from happening.

To look ahead: What are some ways we might gather misleading data? First of all, we might observe organisms or events that are different, in some consistent way, from those organisms or events that we want to draw conclusions about. This is the problem of *sampling bias*.

Second, we might distort what we observe by the very act of observing it. If we observe a group of people (or chimpanzees, or whomever), and if they know they are being observed, they may behave differently *because* they are being observed. In such cases, the observer is having an unintended effect on what is going on, so we will call this the problem of *observer effects*.

Third, even if an observer does not distort what happens, she may distort how she *sees* it happening. We can show (with data!) that observers may see what they expect to see, or what they hope to see—as Asimov puts it, what pleases them—rather than what is "out there" to be seen. Such *observer bias* could seriously distort the data we record.

There is a fourth danger. Even if the data themselves are accurate, we may draw conclusions from those data that the data just do not support. Here the problem is with our logic, not our procedures; we *make inferences from our data* in a biased way. So, to have a name for this problem, we will call it *inferential bias*. And we will look later at an instance of it that crops up again and again: the *correlation and causality fallacy*.

Here then are some things we want *not* to happen: sampling bias, observer effects, observer bias, and inferential bias. We want to take steps to ensure that these do not distort our conclusions. Such steps are an integral and important part of the procedures we adopt in gathering our data.

One final comment before we begin: We will discuss these technical problems in the context of observational research; but the problems also arise in experimental research, and there too they can play havoc if they are not dealt with. So many of the ideas that we discuss in this chapter will arise in later ones as well, especially when we talk about experimental control (Chapters 7 and 8).

SAMPLING

In all our examples, we have seen conclusions drawn from observations of what certain people, groups, or animals did or said. A question we have not yet addressed is: Which animals? What people? Whom, or what, are we going to observe? Or, as we say: Which particular people, or groups, or animals, are going to be the *subjects* of our investigation?*

That question is closely related to another one: What people, groups, or animals do we want to draw conclusions about? To what *population* do we want to generalize the results from this *sample* of cases?

As we saw in Chapter 2, science is the search for general principles. We have little interest in just *these particular* monkeys, college students, or stickleback fish that we happened to observe. We want more general conclusions that will tell us about monkeys, sticklebacks, and students (or human beings) in general. So this is our problem: How do we go from particular observations to general conclusions?

This is a topic that many beginning students find confusing. On the one hand, they may have been told that an investigation should *always* begin with a *representative sample* of some *population*. This is especially likely if they have studied such matters as survey methodology, in which representativeness often is a concern.

But when they come to research in psychology, students find that *most* investigations draw their subjects from rather limited populations: Not "people in general" but, for example, college students— and not even college students in general, but students in one college who elect psychology courses and sign up for research participation! Such people are clearly not representative of all the people even in one society, much less of all the human beings there are.

Is something wrong here? Not necessarily, and in the next few pages I will try to clear up the confusion. Briefly, the difference arises

---

*The term *subjects* is a traditional way of referring to the organisms—human or animal—that we observe in a research investigation. Some journals recommend that we refer to them as *participants* instead. That is a useful reminder that if a person comes to our lab, or stops what he is doing to answer our questions, he is doing us a favor by cooperating with us. But the journals are not consistent about this, and it can be misleading. If I collect data on book carrying by watching people from my window, it is not clear that they are "participating" in my project. Still less is it clear that stickleback fish are doing so! Rather than have different words for different cases, I shall use the older term *subjects* throughout this book.

because a survey researcher wishes to draw conclusions about a *specific population*, based on the findings of *just this* survey. Most psychological research is different. Its general conclusions depend on the agreement among *different* investigations. We don't try to let one study do it all.

We'll return to that idea shortly. But first, let's get clear on the ideas of *sample* and *population*.

SAMPLE AND POPULATION

Let us talk about soup for a minute.

Suppose a chef has prepared a large vat of soup. She wonders whether there is enough salt in it, so she tastes a spoonful of the soup. If it tastes salty enough, she will conclude that the whole vat of soup probably is adequately salted.

Some research can be considered directly analogous to this. The big vat of soup is like a *population*. The spoonful that the chef tastes is like the *sample* of subjects that is actually observed. Then, from what is observed in the sample, one draws inferences about the population: If the spoonful tastes all right, chances are the whole vat of soup does.

In other words: There will be some *population* of people (or groups or fish or whatever) about which we wish to draw conclusions. We want to know something, not about the behavior of just the sample (the spoonful), but about the population (the vat).

Now, today's vegetable soup will be different from tomorrow's chicken soup. From this we get to an important idea: We must specify *what* population we are talking about. There is no such thing as "the population" pure and simple. *Our population is whatever we say it is.* I can, if I wish, look over the students in a classroom and say, "You people here in this room are my population." I could then draw a sample from that population.

And I could draw a biased sample or an unbiased one. What do these terms mean?

THE PROBLEM OF SAMPLING BIAS

Returning to the soup analogy, notice that a chef will stir the soup before he tastes it. Why? Because if he didn't, and if (say) the heavier ingredients tended to sink to the bottom of the vat, then his spoonful might not taste at all the way the whole vat tastes. He has, we would say, an *unrepresentative* or *biased* sample of the soup. He would then draw very wrong conclusions if he assumed that all the soup tasted the way his sample did. In short, a sample (like the spoonful) and the population that is of interest (like the vat of soup) may differ in some consistent way (like heavy ingredients in the soup but not in the spoonful). When that happens, we speak of a *biased* sample of that population.*

Some "research" permits sampling biases that are almost laughably obvious. An example is the notorious "Hite report," in which a "researcher" reported a survey of American women's attitudes toward men. The survey distributed some 100,000 questionnaires through various organizations, of which around 4,500 were returned. American males came out looking, shall we say, pretty bad.

A moment's thought tells us that such data are useless if we want to know how American women in general—the intended population—feel about men. This is not because 4,500 is too small a number—it is quite large, as surveys go—but because with a return rate of only 4.5%, the sample we end up with is almost certain to be biased toward people with strong attitudes on the topic. Chances are that it is mostly these people who took the trouble to fill out and return the questionnaires.

Similar limitations attend most of the "survey results" we encounter in magazines and on the Internet, based on readers who bothered to volunteer their responses to published survey questions. Such volunteer or "self-selected" samples are almost certain to be biased toward those who (1) have strong opinions and (2) are eager to express them. Such "findings" are published for entertainment, not for enlightenment.

However, biases can creep in more subtly than that. Consider a political pollster who samples haphazardly, "as he feels like it," within a community—which is *not* what we mean by *random sampling* (see later)! If I were that pollster, I would certainly "feel like" sampling from the lower, rather than the upper, floors of walk-up apartment

---

*The term is unfortunate, perhaps, because the word *bias* may connote prejudice, and perhaps suggest that someone is being malicious. As used here, the term means neither of these. Think of a car, and suppose that the alignment is not quite right, so that the car has a consistent tendency to pull to the right. An engineer or mechanic might speak of a "right-turning bias" in such a case. Of course, the car is neither prejudiced nor malicious. Even so, an engineer will try to design cars so that no such bias occurs!

Now, just as a car can be biased toward a rightward drift, so a sampling procedure can be biased toward certain subgroups within a population. This means that members of that subgroup are likely to be *overrepresented* in the sample—there will be more of them than there should be. When this happens, our inferences about the population can be thrown badly off.

buildings. But what if those who live on lower floors pay higher rent, and so are likely to have higher incomes? A pollster's bias against stair-climbing could become a sampling bias in favor of the higher-income members of a community.

Or consider this: Earlier (p. 118), I mentioned that I had replicated earlier observations about the way men and women carry their books. I did the study at the college where I teach—a "convenience" initial sampling stage (see later). Suppose I had sampled "as I felt like it," tallying the men and the women I happened to notice as I walked around campus. Mightn't I be more likely to *notice* the cases that fit my expectations—men, arms straight; women, arms bent—than those that did not fit them? If so, then the sample I ended up with—those men and women whose book-carrying techniques *were actually recorded*—could have been biased in favor of my expectations.*

Here is another example—a classic cautionary tale, or actually a pair of them. In 1936, when polling was in its infancy, the *Literary Digest* conducted a poll before the presidential election. They confidently predicted victory for the Republican candidate, Alfred Landon, over the Democratic candidate, Franklin D. Roosevelt. Came election day, and there was indeed an overwhelming victory—for Roosevelt!

Why had the *Digest* been so wrong? The story that has been handed down goes like this: They had selected their sample from telephone directories. But in 1936, far fewer voters owned phones than do now. Those who did tended to be more affluent than those who didn't. So low-income voters were underrepresented in the sample, and these voters were overwhelmingly in favor of Roosevelt. The *Digest*'s sample was biased toward high-income voters, and the *Digest* had egg on its face as a result.

But in writing this book I learned, to my surprise, that that story is a myth! What happened was not at all like that (Bryson, 1976; Fowler, 1988). The *Digest* survey was not a phone survey but a mail

---

*I avoided that particular source of bias as follows: I watched the men and the women who passed by my office window (an *accidental sample*) that morning, over a predetermined time period, at a time when classes were in session. That way, there were not too many students to observe, and I was able to tally *every student* who walked past a particular tree I had picked out. Male or female? Books held with arm straight or bent? *All* cases, whether they fit my expectations or not, were included in my sample—that is, were tallied in the appropriate cell of the data sheet. This is a variant of *systematic sampling* (p. 146).

It remains true that students who happened to be in that area at that time may not be representative of all students even at that college. But remember that our sample is to be "like" the population *in ways that matter*. It is unlikely that the book-carrying habits of my sample differ consistently from those of students on other parts of the campus.

survey. Like the Hite report, it had a low rate of return, and those who did return the questionnaire tended to favor Landon, *perhaps* (this is an interpretation) because those who are rooting for the underdog are more likely to take the trouble to express their views.

Thus this little story gives us *two* examples of how a sample can be biased. In the one story, which didn't happen but could have, the sample would have been biased in favor of the *affluent*. In actuality, it was biased in favor of the *vocal*. Either way, we have a sample that differed consistently from the population of interest. It tended to favor Landon, whereas the population as a whole favored Roosevelt—and showed it on election day.

OBTAINING REPRESENTATIVE SAMPLES

To avoid sampling bias, we first define our population, and then seek to obtain a *representative sample* from that population. This is the research parallel to the chef's stirring the soup. We want the sample (the spoonful) to be *like* the population (the vat of soup) in all the ways that matter. How can we encourage that to happen?

RANDOM SAMPLING

The best way of trying for a representative sample from a population is to draw the sample *at random* from that population.* We need to get clear on what that means. It definitely does *not* mean "hit or miss," or "any old way," or "as we feel like it."

No, the phrase *random sample* has a technical meaning. A random sample is one selected in such a way that *every member of the population has an equal chance of being selected*. An easy way to visualize this is to imagine that each member of the population has a name or a number written on a slip of paper, the papers are tossed into a hat and stirred like the soup, and someone reaches in blindly and selects a number of slips equal to the size of the sample we want. The names or numbers on the slips so selected identify the population members who will make up our sample. Or we can replace the hat with a table of random numbers, generated so that at each place in the table all digits (0 through 9) have an equal chance to appear. Appendix A (pp. 504–510) presents a table of random numbers, and shows how to use them for selecting a sample at random from a population.

---

*Pollsters often speak of a "probability sample," which means the same thing.

Alternatively, this manual labor can be replaced by the operation of a computer, which can be instructed to generate a series of numbers that is random or nearly so. Then the numbers so generated will identify subjects for our investigation—provided of course that each population member was assigned a number beforehand.

Such a method assumes a great deal. To use it, we have to (1) list all members of the population, (2) assign each member a number (or name), (3) draw our random sample of numbers, and *then* (4) find the person corresponding to each of the numbers, so as to interview or observe him or her or it. In practice, grave difficulties can arise. Do we want a random sample of all the monkeys in the world, or even in some one country? Just how do we assign a number to every monkey and keep track of who has which number? If our population is a community, we can assign a number to each human being in that community's phone book and select a sample based on those.* But then what about those who have unlisted numbers? Or no phones? If our project involves interviews, what about those who refuse to be interviewed when contacted? In such cases, there may be nothing we can do except to select more subjects (again at random!) to replace the missing ones, and hope that the resulting *bias* in our sample (from the loss of unlisteds, no-phones, and refusers) is not so serious as to affect our results importantly.

Finally, it's important to remember that our population is whatever we say it is; there is no such thing as "*the* population" pure and simple. And so a sample representative of one population may not be representative of another. Thus, I could draw a random sample from the population: *students in this classroom now*. But that same sample would *not* be a random sample of the population *students enrolled in this class*. Why not? Because the students who cut class or slept through it would not have a chance to be selected as subjects, and students who miss class might have different characteristics from those who attend.

VARIANTS OF RANDOM SAMPLING

As we see, strict random sampling from a population can be a real chore, especially if the population to be listed is large. There are shortcut methods to reduce the labor involved.

---

*Today, selecting a random sample from phone owners is less burdensome than it used to be; we can program a computer to dial phone numbers at random. Even so, the unlisteds, the phoneless, and the refusers will not be sampled.

One of these is *multistage* sampling. Suppose we want a random sample of college students in the United States. It would be inhumanly difficult to list all members of that population. Instead we could list all colleges in the United States (a much more manageable task) and take a random sample of the colleges (Stage 1). Then, from every college selected, we could take a random sample of its students (Stage 2). Or, in political polling, rather than list all the *voters* in the country, we might list all the *counties* in (say) the United States (Stage 1); within each county, take a random sample of streets (Stage 2); and, on each street, take a random sample of the voters who live there (Stage 3).

Another variation has been called *systematic sampling*. This method is useful when one cannot keep track of individuals (as in the monkey case), or where the population cannot be listed in advance (e.g., we might want a random sample of transactions in a marketplace). The idea is to observe or interview every mth case, starting with the nth one, where both m and n are randomly chosen.

Thus, suppose I want a random sample from a large classroom. Rather than listing everybody, I might go to my random number table, and point a pencil anywhere on it. Doing that now, I get the number 7. Doing it again, I get 4. So, counting round the room, I would select the fourth student to be in my sample. Then I select every 7th student after that, until I have gone all around the room. In survey research, the parallel case would be to start with the fourth house on a randomly selected street and choose that house, and every seventh house thereafter, as the sample of houses to visit. Or, in the above examples, we could observe every seventh market transaction, or every seventh person (or monkey) that passes some landmark, starting from the fourth one that does so after we begin our observation session.

Random sampling, then, takes many forms. Some variant of the procedure is our best bet if we truly need a representative sample of some population. Random sampling does not *guarantee* a representative sample, but it does make it *unlikely* that the sample will be very different from the population from which it is drawn. And the larger the sample, the more unlikely any large differences become.

Notice something else, too, that is common to all these methods. The researcher sets up a rule, in advance, that dictates whom or what she will observe. After that, she has *no choice at all* in the matter (Fowler, 1988). That way, her own biases—toward lower floors in apartment buildings, or toward more noticeable cases, or toward cases that fit her theory—*cannot* affect the data.

OTHER APPROACHES TO SAMPLING

For certain purposes—like political or opinion polling—representative samples are very important, as we've seen. Yet we noted earlier that much of psychological research pays little attention to representativeness—and here arises the confusion that I promised to address. Not all researchers insist upon a representative sample from a specific population. Nor, for some purposes, would it be sensible to do so.

"PURPOSIVE SAMPLING"

First, we may "purposely" go looking for subjects with certain characteristics—hence the name—where those characteristics make them relevant to the question we are asking. Schachter "purposely" looked for people who had had smoking or weight problems. Such people will not be representative of people in general. Again: To have a strongly held belief sharply and clearly disconfirmed may not be a typical event. But the question was: What happens when such a rare event does occur? Hence the selection of the Seekers for study (Chapter 4). Newcomb chose to study attitude change at Bennington College partly *because* it was not a typical college, but instead had a reputation for unusually liberal views among its students. What happens when students from conservative backgrounds find themselves there? In all these cases, the cases we observe are selected because of the question we ask, not because they are representative of any particular population—though it is true that we can always define a population of "subjects like these" (see below).

"CONVENIENCE SAMPLING"

This kind of sampling is by far the most common in behavioral research. We select our subjects for *accessibility and convenience.* Suppose a researcher teaches at the University of Washington and uses college students as subjects. He will likely use students enrolled at that university. A researcher at the University of Virginia will use students enrolled there. And so on. The initial studies on "bystander intervention," for instance, were conducted with students at just one university. The study of mother–infant interactions was conducted not with college students but with families; these families all lived in Baltimore, where the researchers worked. And even then, they were mothers who were willing to be observed by the researchers—

which probably made them unrepresentative even of Baltimore mothers (or those of any other city)!

Why use such unrepresentative samples? For one thing, research is the art of the possible. A study *could* draw a random sample of, say, college students in the United States, as by multistage sampling. But then what? Do we fly to Seattle to observe one subject, to Baltimore to observe the second, to Iowa City for the third . . . ? Something of the sort could be done for mailed questionnaires or telephone interviews, but for direct observation of behavior, few studies would get off the ground (so to speak) if all good research really required anything of the kind.*

Fortunately, it does not. Let us see why.

The Defined Population: Subjects "Like These." The number-of-bystanders findings would indeed be of little interest if they applied only to students at one particular university. On the other hand, it would also be very surprising if that were so. Even if we use a convenience sample, we can reasonably expect the results to apply to persons who are similar to those subjects in all the ways that matter. We can generalize, in other words, to *"subjects like these."*†

Much of what we do is based on the assumption that people are pretty much alike in the way their minds work, especially in the basic processes like visual perception, or generation of language by the brain. Thus, if we find out something about how vision works in students at one college, it seems safe to assume that it will apply to students at others, and probably to other age and occupational groups as well. (Except perhaps for people with visual defects, and these may be excluded from our study—*purposive sampling* again!)

Now this *is* an assumption, and it will not always apply. Other human beings may be "like" college students in some ways (e.g., how their eyes work), but not in others. Take the study of memory, for instance. College students have had extensive experience at learning things for the purpose of remembering them later. Might they have developed certain strategies for remembering things, strategies

---

*This is all the more apparent if we ask ourselves: Just what population *is* of interest in psychological research? It has been said that we seek the principles of the behavior of *all* species, from humans to flatworms. Yes, but no *individual research project* attempts this level of generality. There are no data on bystander intervention in flatworms, and a random sample of *the Earth's creatures* has never, to my knowledge, been attempted in any investigation.

†Statisticians are familiar with this approach. No less a figure than Sir Ronald Fisher, one of the founders of modern statistics, pointed out that we can always *define our population* in terms of the sample. It can be that population, whatever it is, from which *this* sample can be considered a random one.

that might be quite different from the way an older adult, or an adult from a preliterate society, goes about the matter? Quite possibly; and if so, research on memory that depends heavily on student subjects might turn out to apply less generally than we think.

In short, convenience sampling has its dangers. If we were to restrict our observations to (say) students in college, we would miss the differences there may be—in social relations, use of facial expression, or even strategies for remembering things—in other age or occupation groups, or in other cultures.

Generality from Diversity. In fact, however, our observations are not so restricted as all that. Remember that no general conclusion rests on a single study, and that what one researcher doesn't study, another will. Researchers are in fact studying (for example) memory in children, and in the elderly, and in members of different cultures. These studies will have been conducted in different places and perhaps even with different methods, as well as with subjects drawn from different populations. The generality of the conclusions comes from the consistency among these different findings, not from the "representativeness" of the subjects in any one of them.

So, for example: Does the number-of-bystanders effect occur in other societies? The way to find out is to look and see. If the results can be replicated in other cultures, that supports the original finding and adds generality to them. And if the results do not hold up in other cultures or age groups, we can go on to ask *why* they don't. By checking out possible explanations for this, we may expand our understanding. We'll discuss this further in Chapter 12 (see also Stanovich, 1998).

Now, all this does not mean that we can be complacent. It remains true that a very large proportion of experimental findings comes from a very limited database: college students in the United States. We need to check our conclusions in other age and income groups, and in other cultures, much more carefully than we have done in the past. There are indications that the gap is narrowing (Markus & Kitayama, 1991; Shweder, 1991), but there is much yet to be done.

WHEN DO WE NEED REPRESENTATIVE SAMPLES?

As we've seen, any study has a certain generality built in—we can always generalize to a population of "subjects like these." But then what about the specific *procedures*—like random sampling—by which we try for representative samples of populations? When do we use these methods and when do we not? When do we need them?

I think the answer is: We need them *when there is a real-world population out there*—a specific existing one, not just one that we define—*to which we want to generalize our findings*.

Political polling is an obvious example. We want, let us say, to predict the outcome of an election. It would be foolish to select a sample of very affluent community members, determine whom they will vote for, and say, "Well, *people like these* favor Smith over Jones, so Smith will probably win." Here we are not interested in "people like these" but in what the *whole population of voters* is likely to do. If we don't have a representative sample of *that* population, then we have no business making predictions about it. Or: If we are interested in how *American women in general* (the population of interest) feel about men, we will not find out if our sample is a self-selected one, consisting only of those energetic or angry enough to return questionnaires.

This, clearly, is something we have to decide case by case. Is there a specific population out there to which we want our conclusion to apply? If the answer is yes, we do need a representative sample of that population. But often the answer will be no—we may let our general conclusions rest on the convergence among many findings, not on the representativeness of this one.

OBSERVER EFFECTS

As we observe and describe behavior, we must consider that what our subjects do may be affected by our presence as observers, or by something that we do while observing. Then they may not behave as they normally would. That is the problem of *observer effects*.

EXAMPLES OF OBSERVER EFFECTS

Imagine this: You and I are visiting a first-grade classroom, to observe. We walk quietly to the back of the room and sit down, to see what the kids do. What will we see? Of course—we will see a roomful of little heads swiveled around to observe us! If we concluded that such kids usually spend most of their time staring at the back of the room, we'd be pretty foolish.

"If you're not a good boy, Santa will bring you only educational toys."

FIGURE 5.1
We may be very, very good when we know we're being watched.

Obvious enough. So are some other instances of observer effects. A child may be on her best behavior, rather than her typical behavior, if an adult is watching (Figure 5.1) By the same token, a person may give socially correct rather than accurate answers to an interviewer. Then again, the problem can be much more subtle. The following is a classic cautionary tale.

AN EXAMPLE FROM ANIMAL BEHAVIOR: THE CASE OF CLEVER HANS

This happened in Germany some years ago. A schoolteacher, a certain Mr. Ostler, had discovered a true genius among horses. This horse, whose name was Hans, could do arithmetic! Ask him to add 7 and 4, and he would tap with his hoof 11 times and stop. He was just as gifted at subtraction, and even multiplication and division. He was at least as mathematically skilled as your average fifth- or sixth-grader.

Herr Ostler was not a faker. To his many doubters, he would say in true scientific spirit: See for yourself. Scientists checked out Clever

Hans, and satisfied themselves that Ostler was not feeding him cues on the sly. Ostler didn't even have to be there. He could be far away and out of sight, and still Clever Hans could do his sums, products, and quotients.

But an experimental psychologist, Oskar Pfungst, said in effect: "Let's do one more check." One of the onlookers would whisper into Hans's ear, "Seven." Then another, different observer would whisper into the horse's ear, "Plus four." That way, since neither of the whisperers could hear the other, *none of the observers knew what the correct answer was*. It was up to Hans to tell them.

Well, under these conditions Hans was helpless. He would go on tapping and tapping, indefinitely.

It seems that what had been happening was this: As long as the audience knew the correct answer—7 + 4 = 11—they would wait until Hans had tapped 11 times, and then tense, or lean forward alertly: "That's the right answer. Is he going to stop now?" And Hans would pick up those signals from the onlookers, as his cue to stop tapping.

So Hans was indeed clever. But he was not clever at arithmetic— he was clever at reading humans and their unintended signals. Since his day, the term *Clever Hans effect* has been a standard one, used to remind us of the danger: An observer can give unintended cues that can affect what his or her subjects do.

A CLEVER HANS EFFECT IN HUMANS:
FACILITATED COMMUNICATION

Not all of us have learned the lesson Clever Hans should have taught.

In Chapter 1, we mentioned *autism*, a disorder appearing in early childhood and characterized, among other things, by severe deficiencies in social interaction *and* in language. It was therefore very exciting to hear of a new technique that allowed nonverbal autistic children to communicate. The claim was that such children, even if they did not or could not speak, were able to type coherent messages on a keyboard, if their hands and arms were held over the keyboard by a sympathetic "facilitator."

This "breakthrough" was greeted with a great deal of excitement by educators, and with a great deal of renewed hope by parents. Unfortunately, controlled research showed the "discovery" to be, like the Clever Hans story, a case of unconscious cuing. While supporting the child's hands, the "facilitator" had many opportunities to influence what he or she typed. Certainly some observations—highly literate prose produced by children who did not know the alphabet, for instance—suggested that something of the sort was going on.

Investigators checked that possibility directly, with controls very similar to those that exposed Clever Hans. Perhaps most convincing was a study in which the child and the facilitator were each presented with a drawing and the child was asked to type its name. Neither could see the other's drawing. Sure enough, the child typed out a name that fit the drawing—but it was the drawing the *facilitator* was looking at! Obviously, the response was determined by the facilitator, not the child. The facilitator must have been cuing the child in some way, without being aware of doing so.

This is only one of a large number of controlled studies, and they all conclude the same thing: The child's performance depends on cuing by the facilitator. It is a Clever Hans effect, not a therapeutic breakthrough.

More is involved here than an embarrassed group of would-be helpers. During "facilitated" sessions, some children would type out accusations of abuse or incest by their parents. Sometimes, unfortunately, these were taken seriously. *Newsweek* (September 21, 1992) reported: "Unsubstantiated claims have cast a wide net of damage. Parents have had children taken away. . . . Teachers and aides have had careers ruined simply by the hint of scandal" (Seligmann & Childea, 1992, p. 75).

The possibility of observer effects in facilitated communication would have been obvious to any competent researcher. "Had the professionals involved had minimal training in the principles of . . . control, they should have immediately recognized the parallel to the Clever Hans case" (Stanovich, 1998, p. 91). And there is the flip side of that, too: Many real disasters—children removed from their homes, adults charged with criminal abuse—were averted, or at least corrected, because of researchers who *did* know those principles, and used them to slay a most destructive myth.

AN EXAMPLE FROM MEMORY: LEADING QUESTIONS

Many research situations—and many everyday ones as well—depend on a question-and-answer scenario. A pollster asks a voter whom he will vote for, or how he feels about rent control. A lawyer asks a witness what happened. A clinician asks a client about her relations with her parents. And so on.

Here we face a problem. The answer we get to a question can depend on how the questioner—the "observer"—puts the question.

This has been demonstrated by direct experiment many, many times. Here is just one example of what we see (Loftus & Palmer, 1974). Subjects watched a videotape of an auto collision—the same videotape for all. Later, some of them were asked, "How fast were the cars going when they hit each other?" For others, "hit" was replaced with "smashed into." That's all it took! Subjects who heard the words "smashed into" *now* gave higher estimates of the speeds they had seen earlier. Not only that: Memories for the earlier event could literally be invented, later, in response to questioning. Asked, "Did another car pass the red Datsun while it was stopped at the stop sign?" many subjects "remembered" a stop sign that simply had not been there. Asked, "Was there broken glass?" more subjects in the "smashed" than in the "hit" condition "remembered" seeing broken glass. There hadn't been any.

In this case, the point of the experiment was to demonstrate that such leading questions can and do distort what a subject thinks he remembers. That of course is of interest in its own right. But it also raises the possibility that when we set out to study something else, the same thing may occur: The questions we ask can affect the replies we get, and therefore give us a distorted picture of what is actually going on. Witnesses, clients in therapy, and respondents to a poll might give us misleading answers because of the way we questioned them.

CONTROLLING OBSERVER EFFECTS

What can we do about all this? How can we keep our observations from being distorted by our presence as observers? There is no one neat solution, but here are examples of what we might do in some such cases.

HIDING

Sometimes we can just, well, *hide* from our subjects and so avoid influencing them. If we are observing ducks, we might build a duck blind. If our subjects can be observed in a laboratory, we might hide behind a one-way mirror.

Or sometimes we can hide under a "cloak of legitimacy." Observations have been made of how people eat in restaurants or drink in bars, by scientists who were eating and drinking too, posing as other customers. The scientists might then have scribbled observations as if writing a letter or taking notes on a book. In one case, an

FIGURE 5.2
Jane Goodall and a research assistant who had become accustomed to having her around (courtesy National Geographic Society).

observer in a bar appeared to be muttering into his beer—an action that was not at all unusual in that setting. He was actually dictating his observations into a throat mike concealed under his shirt!

WAITING IT OUT

This is probably what we'd do if we were taking those observations in the classroom that we spoke of earlier. Let the kids get used to our presence, until they lose interest and (we hope) forget about us and go about their business. In her studies of chimpanzees in the wild, Jane Goodall used this tactic. When she began introducing herself to the chimps in the jungle, they fled, or at best dropped whatever else they were doing to focus on her. Eventually, though, the chimps got used to having her around. (See Figure 5.2.) They were no longer frightened, and would go on doing chimp things that she could then record.

DECEPTION

We might decide on out-and-out *deception*. If we wanted to observe the discussions within a secret cult, for example, we might pretend to be converts and actually join the cult. Observers of the Seekers and of the Satanic cult used this tactic.

In less exotic cases, too, it is often thought necessary to mislead the people we are observing. For example, the "cloak of legitimacy" is a form of deception. If we observe people in bars or restaurants, pretending to be patrons ourselves, then we *are* pretending—and are attempting to deceive.

This tactic obviously raises some difficult ethical questions. If our cult is planning some illegal or dangerous activity, what is our ethical position? Do we report it or not? Even short of that, do we have the right to lie to our subjects? We'll alert ourselves to this problem now, and look at it carefully in Chapter 13.

"UNOBTRUSIVE MEASURES"

Still another way around the problem is not to be there at all when the behavior in question occurs. Instead, we can look at *consequences* of the behavior that can be observed later. We will see later, for instance, how police records can be used to test hypotheses about human aggression and its influences.

Such data, made not by observing behavior but by observing its residues and consequences, are referred to as *unobtrusive measures*. The term is unfortunate—hiding makes us unobtrusive too, or is designed to—but the term has stuck.

Much ingenuity has gone into the search for unobtrusive measures. Do we want to estimate how much liquor is consumed in a community? Just asking the residents would, obviously, risk self-presentation effects. Instead we might consider going through a sample of garbage truck hauls and counting the empties (Webb, Campbell, Schwartz, & Sechrest, 1966).

"BLIND" OBSERVERS

Sometimes observer effects occur because the observers know what the results of a study "ought" to be, and communicate their expectations to the subject. The case of Clever Hans is an instance. When Hans's observers were "blind" to the correct answers, Hans's mathematical shortcomings were made plain. Similarly, the "facilitated communication" blunder was revealed when the facilitator was "blind" as to what the child was seeing.

So, in many kinds of research, the experiments will be conducted by students or technicians who are kept "blind" as to who is who, or, perhaps, as to what the researchers are looking for. The point of that is not to add mystery to the proceedings, it is simply to rule out the Clever Hans effect. If observers know how we *expect* the subjects to behave, they may (like Hans's trainer) give the subjects cues that will lead them to behave in the expected way. Solution: Don't tell the observers what the "expected way" is. In the Bell and Ainsworth study of mother–infant interactions (Chapter 4), the students who took the observations did not know what questions the study was asking—not until it was completed.

OBSERVER BIAS

In taking our observations, we don't want to distort what happens; that is the problem of observer effects. But also, we don't want to distort how we *see* it happening. That is the problem of *observer bias* (Figure 5.3).

We saw an example of this earlier (pp. 73–74). Judges who watched a videotape of an interview thought that the interviewee was either a job applicant (for some subjects) or a patient (for others). Their impressions of his attitude and personality were wildly different, depending on who they thought he was—that is, their observations were biased by their preconceptions about what job candidates, or patients, are like.

FIGURE 5.3
Observer bias is a problem in many endeavors, not just science.

"I'm happy to say that my final judgement of a case is almost always consistent with my prejudgement of the case."

Another example: College students from two different universities watched the *same* movie of a football game between the two schools. The students were asked to play official, and to catch the violations on each side. You guessed it: Students at each school spotted more infractions by the opposing team than by their own (Hastorf & Cantril, 1954).

AN EXAMPLE FROM PHYSICS: "N-RAYS"

The classic example of observer bias is that of the scientist who has a pet theory. She may then be more likely to "see" events that confirm her theory than ones that do not. This can and does happen, even in the physical sciences.

In 1903, one of the most distinguished physicists in France, a Professor Blondlot, announced that he had discovered a new form of radiation. He labeled these rays N-rays, in honor of the University of Nancy where he taught. The problem was that other scientists could not verify his findings. Eventually another professor visited Blondlot's lab, where, sure enough, he could see no evidence of N-rays—though Blondlot and his co-workers could! Finally, the visitor craftily removed from the apparatus a prism that was supposed to be important in isolating the N-rays. But his hosts, not knowing this, continued to believe that they were seeing these now-impossible rays. Clearly, what they "saw" was driven by their expectations, rather than by what was (or was not) out there to see.

AN EXAMPLE FROM PSYCHOLOGY: UFOS

Self-delusion—seeing what we expect to see—can lead to distortions that would be funny if they weren't so dangerous. For example: James Randi, "The Amazing Randi," is (like Ray Hyman) a stage magician and, like Hyman again, is concerned about the nonsense that is offered as fact by fakers. He once appeared, in disguise, as a guest on a talk show. There he informed his audience that while driving from New Jersey into New York, he had seen a V-formation of objects flying toward the north overhead. Within seconds, Randi later said, the "station switchboard lit up like an electronic Christmas tree." One "eyewitness" after another called in to confirm Randi's "sighting"—which was purely a product of his own imagination. The observers looked at the skies and saw what they expected to see— the little UFOs that were not there (see Figure 5.4).

"My latest sighting turned out to be just another weather balloon."

FIGURE 5.4
Many dramatic "sightings" turn out to have disappointingly commonplace explanations.

CONTROLLING OBSERVER BIAS

As with observer effects, the danger of observer bias is not an insurmountable barrier to good research, but a technical problem to be solved. Also with observer effects, there is no one solution, but here are some possibilities.

BLIND OBSERVING

This can control for observer effects as we saw earlier, but it can also be a control for observer bias. If we have a theory (or a guess or a preference) about what the outcome on an investigation should be, we may let someone observe who does not know the theory or share the preference. Or that "someone" may not know what observations would, or would not, confirm the theory or support the preference in question.

Consider the cases of bias we surveyed earlier. If clinicians could interview people (or watch tapes of them), *not knowing* whether a given person was a patient or not, their expectations about patients could not have affected their judgments. If Professor Blondlot had checked for his N-rays in his original experiments, *not knowing* whether the prism was in place or not, he would have saved himself embarrassment. The Bell and Ainsworth study of mother–infant interactions used, as their observers, students who *did not know* until the study was over what the research was about; this control was used to minimize both observer effects *and* observer bias. And if people had been asked simply, "What do you see in the sky now" without Randi's prompting about the flying lights, we can doubt that any such lights would have been reported.

OBJECTIVE MEASURES

Whereas you and I may have biases, objective measures do not; that is what *objective* means (Chapter 3). Therefore, if we can bring objective measures to bear, the risk of bias is reduced.

Thus, in Harlow's experiments, a global judgment (How attached to each mother does that baby monkey seem to be?) would have opened the door to biases in judgment. Instead, Harlow's group turned to a physical measure—how much *time* each baby monkey spent with each model mother. Obviously, the risk of observer bias was much reduced. In the Bell and Ainsworth study, when the baby cried audibly, the observer would click a stopwatch, and then click it again when (and if) the mother broke off what she was doing to attend to the baby.

Even where physical measurements are not feasible, one can try to set up definitions of the events in question that are as objective as possible. In the Bennington study, some subjective measures were used: "How liberal would you rate yourself? Your friends?" But these were cross-checked with more objective facts: "Whom have you voted for in the last four presidential elections?"

MULTIPLE OBSERVERS

If different observers agree as to what happened, then it is more likely that that really *is* what happened, and not just something "read in" by any one observer. Therefore, especially if subjective judgments must be made, we often let more than one observer make those judgments and see if the observers agree. Thus, determining *interobserver reliability* (Chapter 3) is in part a check on observer bias.

Notice that this tactic does not get rid of anyone's biases; it simply shows us how serious the problem is. If two observers of the same event agree on what happened, we can be that much more certain that it really *is* what happened. (Unless the two observers have the same biases, and that can happen too!) If they don't agree, then we must approach our problem with more objective methods or, perhaps, better-trained observers.

Bell and Ainsworth used this method as a spot check: For some sessions, more than one observer was present, and their records were compared later. So with the study of the Seekers: For many of the group's meetings, more than one member of the research team was there, and they could compare notes after the session.

OBSERVER BIAS IN EVERYDAY LIFE

Observer bias is not just a problem for scientific observers. It can be a problem for any of us. Let me tell a personal story here, as an example of the kind of "research" that opens the door to it.

An e-mail message alerted me to an amazing discovery. It seems that while a person speaks, he or she is also generating speech *backwards*—without knowing it, for this occurs deep in the unconscious, and, in the mysterious right-brain hemisphere. Nevertheless, the discoverer of "reverse speech" is able to hear these hidden, unconscious, and very revealing messages. He assures us that anyone can learn to hear them with proper training, and offers to teach us how to do it—for a fee, of course. (We can also order his book from his website.)

On the website is a whole series of testimonials from newspaper reporters who had watched his demonstrations. (I was unable to locate these reporters.) They had written that they were, indeed, amazed to hear that there really were messages in the backward-played tapes—just as the researcher had said there were.

Well, I was skeptical and still am. The trouble with all this is: Are the messages really on the tapes, or are they in the listeners' heads? We humans are strongly *biased* toward finding meaningful patterns even in random stimuli; we can, after all, "hear" messages in a seashell that we hold to our ears, or "see" the man in the moon. So, in this case, the first question that would occur to any researcher is: Did two (or more) people ever listen to the *same* backward tape, without communicating with each other, *and* without being told what they ought to hear? ("Blinded" multiple observers, you see, as a check on observer bias!) If they both heard the same message, that would be evidence that the message was in fact on the tape. If they heard different messages, then it would be more likely that each listener was inventing her own.

Strangely, there was no indication that any of the newspersons had asked that elementary question; so I wrote to the gentleman's website and asked it myself. Strangely, he never replied.

CORRELATION AND CAUSALITY

Then there is what we have called *inferential bias*. Even if our data are sound, we (or others) may make unsound inferences from them. And there is a particular instance of this that occurs over and over again: the confusion of *correlation* with *causality*.

The remarkable thing is, everyone knows better! At the age of about Psych 101 or Soc 101, college students are taught to say: *Correlation does not imply causality*. We know this, but one of the wonders of the world is how, when a concrete instance comes along, we forget it. Again and again, a study will claim to demonstrate that some X causes some Y, when all it really shows are that the two are correlated.

Well, what exactly is the difference? *Why* doesn't correlation imply causality? Let me illustrate.

Keith Stanovich (1998), whose "little green men" we've referred to before (Chapter 2), has also revolutionized family-planning research. He discovered the *toaster method of birth control*. In case the reader is not familiar with this scientific breakthrough, it turns out that the more electrical appliances there are in a household, the fewer children there are. So, obviously, if you want to limit the number of children you have, you should have a lot of toasters in your home!

A nonsensical conclusion, you say? Yes—but no more nonsensical than similar conclusions that are drawn from similar data, even by professionals. In the case of the appliance data, the likely reason for the correlation is obvious: Both variables are affected by *income*. Wealthier people tend, on average, to have fewer babies than do poorer people. And since they have more disposable income than the poor, they are also more likely to spend money on luxuries like extra appliances.

In other words, it is most unlikely that a large number of electrical appliances (X) *causes* a small number of babies (Y). It is more likely that a third variable, Z, causes differences in X *and* in Y, without there being any cause-and-effect relation between X and Y at all.

We pointed out this sort of problem earlier, in connection with the Bell and Ainsworth study of maternal responsiveness (Chapter 4). Responsiveness was negatively correlated with fussiness: Responsive mothers tended to have placid babies; unresponsive mothers tended to have fussy ones. Now, those data as they stand *do* make trouble for what we called the "reinforcement" hypothesis, which predicts the opposite relationship. But they *do not* establish that the "attachment" hypothesis is correct.

Maybe it is. Maybe children of responsive mothers form secure attachments, develop basic trust, avoid learned helplessness, and so do not fuss very much. In a word, maybe the mother's behavior (X) affects the baby's behavior (Y).

Then again, it could be the other way around: Maybe Y is affecting X. Perhaps if a baby is placid to begin with (for whatever reason), this leaves the mother time to rest and relax, so that she can be responsive when the baby does cry. Whereas a baby that is fussy and crying, for whatever reason, may exhaust the mother and therefore *make* her unresponsive.

Or, a third possibility: Maybe the two are not affecting each other at all, but perhaps some third variable (Z) is affecting both X and Y. Suppose some homes are noisier than others, or tenser than others because of domestic intranquility between father and mother. High levels of tension or of noise might upset both the mother *and* the baby, leaving the one unresponsive and the other fussy.

Here then are our three possibilities, and *the data do not distinguish among them*. The negative correlation that was found is compatible with all three of them: X might cause Y, or Y might cause X, or Z might cause both.

That is a useful way of thinking through the interpretation of *any* correlational data. Whenever we hear, read, or discover that some X is correlated with some Y, we should think through the *three* possible interpretations. Maybe X causes Y. Or maybe Y causes X. Or maybe neither causes the other, but some third variable, Z, causes both. When we read or hear about correlational data, it is good exercise to think up a way in which *each* of these three possibilities could explain the finding.

Spelled out in this way, the idea may seem painfully obvious, but the mistake is made over and over again. My favorite example is the finding, announced not long ago, that people who drink lots of coffee stay sexually active longer than people who don't! That correlation, you may be sure, was picked up by the nightly news, with jokes about how the prices of coffee and coffee stocks were sure to soar. What a marvelously simple way to prolong one's sex life! Drink lots of coffee. (And this from news commentators who likely had taken Psych 101 or Soc 101, and know about correlation and causality. But, faced with a concrete instance, they forgot.)

It is interesting to apply our X, Y, or Z device to this one. Who knows? Maybe drinking coffee (X) really does cause a prolongation of sexual activity (Y). But not necessarily: Maybe something about some people's body chemistry—the third variable, Z—both prolongs sexual activity *and* leads to a liking for coffee. Or, for all we know, maybe the causal relationship is the other way around. Perhaps sexual activity (Y) induces certain chemical changes that then promote a liking for coffee (X).

Notice that if that last one were so, the practical implications of the discovery would be reversed. The message is not: If you want to stay sexy, drink lots of coffee. Rather, the message would be to the coffee makers: If you want to sell lots of coffee, you should take steps to promote sexual activity. Imagine the TV commercials this could inspire!

Or consider this example: There is a widespread belief that high self-esteem is prerequisite for success at school. Kids with high self-esteem tend to have higher grades, and, for a while there, promoting self-esteem was considered an essential part of a teacher's job description. But in fact, the data are wholly correlational (Dawes, 1994). Self-esteem (X) and academic performance (Y) are positively correlated, yes. And maybe it's because X affects Y. But what if it's the other way around? What if high self-esteem is the result, not the cause, of good performance? Or what about a third variable, Z? For all we know, maybe genetic influences or good nutrition lead to good grades *and* to good feelings about oneself. The data don't tell us which of these is the case (Dawes, 1994).

Yet we see the fallacy again and again. Here are some news stories that have crossed my desk just in the past few days:

> Parents who delay their child's entry into first grade to give the youngster more time to mature may be doing more harm than good, a study suggests. . . . Children who started school when they were a year or more older than their classmates were 70 percent more likely to display extreme behavior problems, said the study, published in . . . [a professional journal]. . . . "We need to concentrate our efforts on getting kids ready to enter school at the age that they're supposed to," [an author] said.

The "more harm than good" remark points us to one possible conclusion: Being held back causes behavior problems (X causes Y). Maybe so; but what if children who already have behavior problems, for whatever reason, are more likely to *be* held back (Y causes X)? Or what if some third variable makes some children likely to be held back *and* to have behavior problems (Z causes X and Y)? What might Z be?

Or:

> "There is a brand new recipe for a healthy life. The basic ingredients are a low-fat diet, regular exercise—and marriage." A re-

searcher found that marriage "lengthens life, substantially boosts physical and emotional health and raises income over that of single or divorced people. . . . In addition, marriage appeared to reduce the degree of depression. Men and especially women whose marriages ended over the five-year period experienced high levels of depression compared with those who stayed married."

A "recipe!" Marriage *reduces* depression, and *lengthens* life—X causes Y. Well, maybe it does. Then again, might happy, healthy people be more likely to marry or stay married than depressed, unhealthy ones (Y causes X)? Or again, think of a third possible interpretation, where Z causes both.

Or:

Here's the lead sentence in a news article: "Musical training may supply a sound method for improving verbal memory." Thirty college students who had had at least six years of musical instruction before age 12 were compared with 30 students who had no such training. The music students were found to be better at recalling lists of words that were read to them. The findings were reported in a prestigious journal, and a psychologist who studies the effects of music was quoted as saying, "[The study] has such huge implications for education."

In fact, the findings are meaningless. We are invited to conclude that musical training (X) caused better memory (Y) in those who received it. This time, I want you to think of *two* equally plausible interpretations: one for which Y caused X, and one for which some Z caused both.

The moral once again: When you come across correlational data, think of *three* possible explanations for them—maybe X causes Y, maybe Y causes X, or maybe Z causes both—and register the fact that the data do *not* tell us which explanation is right. Practice that. You'll find that little device to be one of the best baloney detectors on the market.

SUMMARY

We want conclusions to be based, not just on any old data, but on *good* data. There are many ways in which we could gather data that are not much good. Some of these technical problems are ones that can affect nearly any set of data, unless we take steps to prevent them from doing so.

For some purposes, we need to consider the problem of *sampling bias*. The subjects or events that we observe may differ in some consistent way from those that we are interested in. Often we are interested in a specific *population* of subjects or events, not just the part of the population (the *sample*) that we actually observe. Then we want the sample to be *representative* of that population. This seems an obvious requirement, but it is often ignored, sometimes in ways that should themselves be obvious, as with volunteer or self-selected samples.

The best solution to this problem is to sample *at random* from our population. This does not mean "haphazardly" or "as we feel like it"; it means drawing our sample by a procedure that gives all population members an equal chance to be included in the sample. This may be extremely difficult in practice. Variations on the theme that may reduce the difficulty include *multistage sampling* or *systematic sampling*.

Much of psychological research pays little attention to whether its subjects are representative of any population. One may deliberately seek out subjects with certain characteristics (*purposive sampling*). Or, very often, one chooses subjects that are readily accessible (*convenience sampling*). In such cases, one can *define* a population—"subjects like these"—for which the sample is automatically representative. The question, "What about subjects that are not 'like these?'" will be decided by further research. In such cases, where there is no specific real-world population about which we want to draw conclusions, representative sampling may be of no concern.

The researcher faces other technical problems besides sampling bias. First, we must consider whether we are distorting what goes on by the very act of observing it—the problem of *observer effects*. The case of Clever Hans is a classic cautionary tale: The observers affected Hans's tapping by their unintended movements. Leading questions, which may influence a witness's report, provide another example. In survey research, too, an interviewee may (for instance) give a reply that is socially approved, rather than one that is accurate.

Controls for observer effects will depend on the specifics of the research situation, but some possibilities are: *concealing* the presence of the observers; letting the subjects *get used* to our presence and ignore us (we hope); *deceiving* our subjects; observing the products or effects of our subjects' behavior that are left behind, when the subjects are no longer there (*unobtrusive measures*); or letting the observers be "*blind*" to what the researchers' expectations are.

Then there is the problem of *observer bias*. Even if we do not affect what happens by being there to observe it, our preconceptions or our desires—how we think the data *should* come out—may distort our observations. We may even "observe" things that are simply not there, as in the N-rays story. Or we may "see" very different things in a videotape—the same videotape—depending on whether we think it shows a job applicant or a mental patient. Possible control procedures include *"blind" observing*, by observers unaware of our expectations and preferences; the use of *objective measures*, less susceptible to bias; and cross-checks among *multiple observers*.

In everyday life, as well as in research, we face these traps. Even there, it is sometimes possible to check them, as in the "backward speech" instance. Unfortunately, it may not occur to us to do the checks, and we may be misled by fraudulent or incompetent research as a result.

MAKING FRIENDS WITH STATISTICS: SCATTERPLOTS AND CORRELATIONS

At several points in this chapter and earlier ones, I have sneaked in two concepts: (1) the *scatterplot*, which shows graphically how closely two variables are related to each other; and (2) the notion of *correlation*, which describes that closeness. Let us review these useful ideas and gather them together.

WHAT IS A CORRELATION?

Briefly, a positive correlation says: the more of *this*, the more of *that*. A negative correlation says: the more of *this*, the less of *that*. Now, early in our journey together, we discovered that we already understand a lot about statistics. Correlations are a case in point.

Consider a basketball game again (Chapter 1). If we are two points behind and there is time for one shot at the basket, we want to get the ball to the player with the best shooting record. Why? Because we assume that (other things equal) the player with the best shooting record up to now is most likely to make his shots later on. The higher a player's percentage of hits earlier, the higher his percentage of hits later should be—the more of this, the more of that. So, for example, players' hit rates early in the season should be *positively correlated* with their hit rates later in the season.

SCATTERPLOTS

But is this true? Well, at the end of the season we can check and find out. Suppose we calculate each player's hit rate separately for the first half of the season and for the second half. Then, on a graph, we simply plot one against the other. Figure 5.5 shows (imaginary) data for 10 players who have had a lot of playing time. In 5.5A, the horizontal (X) axis shows each player's percentage of hits for the first half of the season; the vertical (Y) axis, for the second half. If we do that, we get a set of points (one for each player) that are *scattered* over the *plot* we have made—hence, *scatterplot*.

What might the scatterplot look like? First, suppose every player's early percent-

age were identical with his later percentage. Then all the points in Figure 5.5A would lie exactly on the straight sloping line—just as they would be if any other kind of test-retest reliability were perfect. That would be a perfect correlation between X and Y, and the *correlation coefficient* (see later) would be 1.0. That is as high as it can get.

Of course, the data would not actually look like that. There will be some difference between each player's early score and his late score. But, if the relationship is fairly strong, then the points should be fairly close to that straight line, as with

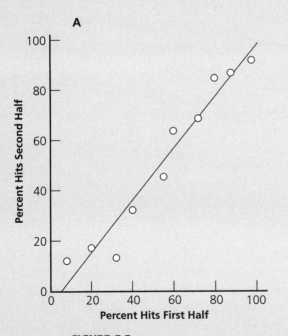 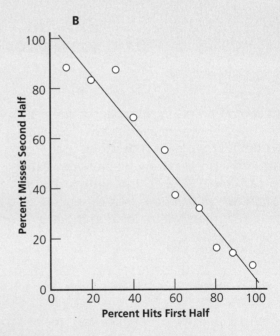

FIGURE 5.5
Correlation between first- and second-half shooting average, shown as a positive correlation (Panel A) and as a negative one (Panel B). Panel A says: The higher a player's hit rate in the first half, the higher it tends to be in the second half (the more of this, the more of that). Panel B says: The higher the hit rate in the first half, the *lower* the miss rate (1 − hit rate) tends to be in the second half (the more of this, the *less* of that). In this case, these are just two ways of showing the same thing.

the data in Figure 5.5A. If it is weaker, they will tend to be farther away. Thus, the closer (on average) those points are to that perfect-agreement line, the stronger the relationship is.

Finally, we could have plotted the same data differently. We could have used hit rate for the first half of the season, and *miss rate*—1 minus hit rate—for the second half. (It is not clear why we would do that—but we could!) That would flip our figure over into Panel B, showing the *same relationship* inverted. Whereas Panel A shows a positive correlation (the more of this, the more of that), Panel B shows a negative correlations (the more of this, the less of that). But they show the same data! So whether a correlation is positive or negative depends on how we label the variables. The strength of the relationship is unaffected by this.

Now in our first case, the X variable (early percentage) and the Y variable (later percentage) were equivalent measures: percentage of hits. But this need not be so—it is the *shape* of the scatterplot that counts. Take the Bell and Ainsworth study, for example. Back in Figure 4.10, we showed the kind of data—the kind of scatterplot—that we would *predict* for each of the theories that were put face to face with each other. In each panel we plotted the responsiveness of each mother (the X variable) against the amount of crying her baby was observed to do (the Y variable). X and Y are different variables now, but still one theory predicts a positive correlation between them, the other a negative one. And a negative one, we recall, was what the data actually showed.

In both cases, we show the relationship as not terribly strong, as in fact it was not. That makes sense; it figures that the baby's behavior will be affected by many things besides what the mother does. But that raises the next question: How can we measure the *strength* of the relationship? There is a way.

THE CORRELATION COEFFICIENT

Just how tightly correlated are two variables, X and Y? We can get an idea of this just by inspecting a scatterplot. But we can also measure it, by calculating what is called a *correlation coefficient*.

VISUALIZING A CORRELATION COEFFICIENT

Look at the scatterplot in Figure 5.6, Panel A. We assume that we have scores on an X and a Y variable for each of our six "subjects"—persons, or chimps, or mother–infant pairs—each corresponding to a dot or, as we say, a *data point* in the plot.

It doesn't matter what the variables are. X could be the score on the first exam, and Y the score on the final exam. X could be hit rate early in the season, and Y could be hit rate late in the season. X could be coffee consumption and Y a measure of sexual activity. What we are going to do is something that we could do with any scatterplot, whatever the variables may be.

In Panel B, we see exactly the same data. But this time, we have drawn a horizontal line at the *mean* of the Y scores. And the vertical lines show how we could

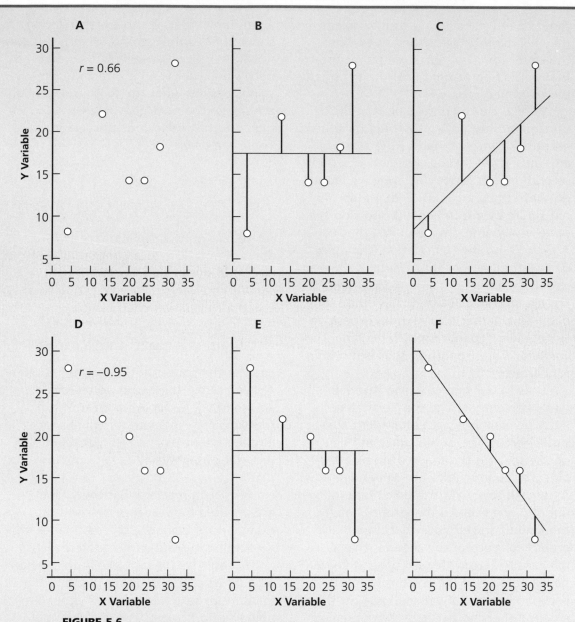

FIGURE 5.6
Where there is a correlation, the variability of scores around the regression line (Panels C and F) becomes less than the variability of scores around the mean (B and E). The greater that shrinkage is, the higher the correlation is.

express each Y score as a *deviation from the mean*. This, you remember, is how we compute a *variance* (Chapter 4). If we square each deviation score and then average the squares, we would have the variance of the Y scores. And taking the square root of the variance would give us the *standard deviation*, SD, which is *something like* the average length of our vertical strings. All this is familiar from the last chapter.

Now comes the new twist, in Panel C. Here we show, not a horizontal line at the mean of the Y scores, but instead the sloping line that *best fits* all the points in the scatterplot. This line is known as the *regression line*.* Again we draw our vertical "strings," but this time we use them to show the deviations of the scores, not from the mean, but instead from the regression line. These deviation scores are called *errors of estimate* (later we'll see why). Now we can go on to compute the equivalent of a variance, but using the errors of estimate. We square them (or they too will sum to zero), average the squares, and take the square root of the result. That gives us a statistic analogous to the standard deviation; it is *something like* the average length of the strings in Panel C. That statistic is called the *standard error of estimate*, abbreviated SE.

How does this help us? It is evident that, on average, the strings are shorter in Panel C than they are in Panel B. That will be true whenever two variables are corre-

lated; and it will be *more* true the stronger the relation is. Look at Panels D, E, and F, in which the X–Y relation is stronger, even though it is negative. Here it is very obvious that the deviations from the regression line (Panel F) are, on average, *much* shorter than the deviations from the mean (Panel D). Some of them are too short to draw at all (although remember that we still consider a string even of zero length). And if there were a perfect, one-to-one relation between Y and X, then all the data points would line up exactly on the regression line. All deviation scores would be zero, and so the standard error of estimate would also be zero.

If we compare the two cases, we soon convince ourselves of this truth: The stronger the relation is (positive or negative), the smaller the standard error of estimate is, relative to the standard deviation. We can use that truth to make a measure of the strength of the relation. This measure—the correlation coefficient, *r*—is defined this way:

$$r^2 = 1 - (SE^2/SD^2)$$

In words, this says: Divide the average of the squared deviation scores (SE^2) by the variance (SD^2). Subtract the result from 1, take the square root of the result, and you have the correlation coefficient *r*.

Then there is just one more step to worry about. Any positive number will have two square roots, one positive, one negative. For 25, $5 \times 5 = 25$, so 5 is the square root of 25; but also $(-5) \times (-5) = 25$, so -5 is also a square root of 25. Do we use the positive or the negative square root for *r*? It depends on whether the re-

---

*More specifically, it is the line that makes the total squared *errors of estimate*—the deviations of the scores from the line, as in Panel C—as small as possible. Statistics texts will show you how to calculate and draw it, should you need to.

lationship itself is positive (as in Panel A) or negative (as in Panel D), and the easiest way to find out is just to look at the scatterplot. The formula for calculating r (see below) gives us the sign directly.

As a measure of relatedness, r has useful properties. If there is a perfect, one-to-one relation between X and Y, then SE^2 will be zero, as we saw earlier. So the ratio will be zero and r will be $1 - 0$, or 1— as high as it can go. If the relation is perfect but inverse (Panel D comes close), again SE^2 will be zero and r will be -1— as low as it can go. If there is no relation at all between X and Y, then SE^2 will be identical to SD^2, the ratio of the two will be 1, and r will be $1 - 1$ or zero—as it ought to be.

Short of these extremes, it is easy to see that as the relationship gets stronger, the errors of estimate get shorter relative to the variance; and, therefore, 1 minus the ratio of the two gets bigger. In other words, a larger value for r means a stronger relationship—again, just as it should.

CALCULATING r

The formula given earlier allows us to *visualize* what r is, but it would be a very awkward and tedious way of actually *calculating* it. A much easier way is given by the following formula:

$$r = \frac{N\Sigma XY - \Sigma X \Sigma Y}{\sqrt{N\Sigma X^2 - (\Sigma X)^2} \sqrt{N\Sigma Y^2 - (\Sigma Y)^2}}$$

In words, this tells us to do the following:

1. $N\Sigma XY$: Multiply each score on one variable (X) by its corresponding score on the other variable (Y). Add the products and multiply their sum by the number of scores.

2. $-\Sigma X \Sigma Y$: Multiply the sum of the X scores by the sum of the Y scores. Subtract the result from the result of Step 1. This gives us the numerator for the above formula.

3. $N\Sigma X^2$: Square each X score, add the squares, and multiply the sum by the number of cases. $N\Sigma Y^2$: Do the same for the Y scores.

4. $-(\Sigma X)^2$: Add up all the X scores (unsquared). Square that sum. Subtract the result from the result of Step 3.

5. Take the square root of the result of Step 4.

6. Repeat Steps 4 and 5 for the Y scores.

7. Multiply the results of Steps 5 and 6.

Then to get r we divide the result of Step 2 by the result of Step 7, and there we are.

The table below is a worksheet, calculating r for the data for six subjects in Figure 5.6A.

Pair number	X Score	Y Score	X^2	Y^2	XY
1	4	8	16	64	32
2	13	22	169	484	286
3	20	14	400	196	280
4	24	14	576	196	336
5	28	18	784	324	504
6	32	28	1,024	784	896
Sums	121	104	2,969	2,048	2,334
Squares of sums	14,641	10,816			

Then, for the numerator of r: $(6 \times 2334) - (121 \times 104) = 14004 - 12584 = 1420$.

For the denominator: $N\Sigma X^2 - (\Sigma X)^2 = (6 \times 2969) - 14641 = 3173$, square root = 56.33;

and $N\Sigma Y^2 - (\Sigma Y)^2 = (6 \times 2048) - 10816 = 1472$, square root = 38.37.

Finally, $r = 1420$ divided by $(56.33 \times 38.37) = 1420/2161.38 = 0.66$, the value shown in Figure 5.6A.

TWO TRAPS

A correlation coefficient can express, in a single number, the direction and strength of a relation between two variables. However, there are some traps that we need to be aware of.

TRAP 1: NONLINEAR RELATIONS

All the above examples have this in common: The relation between X and Y can be summarized reasonably well by a straight sloping line—the regression line. Suppose that is not true? Then this measure of the strength of relation, r, will not be a good one.

Look at Figure 5.7. Here, there is a very strong relation between X and Y, but it is a curved one: As score on X rises, score on Y rises and then falls. We could fit those data quite well with an upside-down U-shaped line.

But r doesn't know anything about U-shaped lines. In the figure, we have drawn the straight line that fits the data *as well as any straight line can*—but, obviously, that is not very well! And if we calculate r

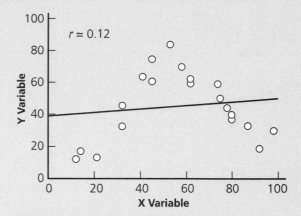

FIGURE 5.7
A curvilinear relation between X and Y. The relation is strong, but r is not a good measure of this.

for these data, we get a measly 0.12—hardly any relation at all. That implies that X and Y are virtually unrelated when clearly, if we look at the data, we see that they are very closely related indeed.

There are ways of measuring the strength of curved relations like that; again, statistics texts discuss them. For us, the moral is: *Look at the data!* When we have our data, we don't, or at least we shouldn't, rush to plug our numbers into a computer that will then calculate r for us. We *plot the data* first; look at the plot; think about what we see; and decide whether the r statistic, which assumes a straight-line relation, is appropriate or misleading.

TRAP 2: THE PROBLEM OF RESTRICTED RANGE

There's another kind of mistake we can make. We could wrongly conclude that two variables are not correlated, when the

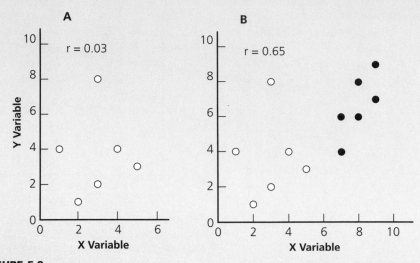

FIGURE 5.8

Attenuation by restricted range. In Panel A, the two variables seem uncorrelated, but that's because we have looked at a restricted range of our X variable. In Panel B, the white circles are the same data as in Panel A, but now we have looked at a wider range of values for the X variable. So in Panel B, we can see the data shown by the filled circles, which we could not see in Panel A. Now we can see that the whole scatterplot shows a quite strong relation.

data would show us that they are—if we had *all* the data we need.

Look at Figure 5.8A. Here we see imaginary data in which the correlation between X and Y is very low—close to zero. Suppose, however, that we had measures only over a limited part of the range of X values. If we had a wider range, the data might look like those in Figure 5.8B. There, the data at the bottom of the X variable (the open circles) are the same as in Panel A, but now the whole scatterplot shows a positive correlation between X and Y. Why don't we see it in Panel A? Because we're looking at only part of the Panel B scatterplot—the open circles—rather than the whole thing.

In constructing Panel B, I assumed that we did have data for the full range of X

values. Otherwise we couldn't have constructed it. But if we collect data so that we have only a restricted range of scores on either variable, we would get *only* the kind of data shown in Panel A. We might conclude that the X–Y correlation was very low or absent, when we really had not given it a fair chance to show itself if it was there.

This problem is often referred to as *attenuation* of a correlation coefficient. Attenuation means something like "shortening" or "cutting off," and that is the problem: Shortening the range of one or both variables "cuts off" part of the scatterplot—and therefore it "cuts off" the possibility of seeing a high correlation even if it is there.

This is a special case of a principle

we've seen earlier (Chapter 3). We cannot expect to see a relation between two variables, X and Y, *unless they both vary*. And now we can add: unless they both vary *enough* to reveal a relation if there is one.

If our data do not show a correlation, or only a weak one, between X and Y, we should ask ourselves whether both X and Y vary over a wide enough range to reveal a correlation even if there is one.

CHAPTER 6

EXPERIMENTS WITH ONE INDEPENDENT VARIABLE

A well-designed experiment is a beautiful thing.

—VINCENT G. DETHIER

IN THIS CHAPTER, WE'LL DISCUSS:

- What an experiment is, and what its advantages are
- What independent, dependent, and control variables are
- Some ways of designing an experiment, and some pros and cons of each:

  The independent-groups design

  Within-subjects designs, with counterbalancing or randomization

  Matched-subjects or randomized-blocks designs
- Some limitations of experiments

As we saw in Chapter 4, not all interesting questions in psychology are concerned with what causes what. However, many are. And if a question does concern what causes what, an experiment is the best way to answer it.

WHAT IS AN EXPERIMENT?

The word *experiment* is likely to bring to mind a laboratory setting, in which white-coated figures preside solemnly over a landscape of high-tech instruments, and little lights blink on and off. The image is misleading. Experiments can be done in any setting. They may be done in schools, in crowded subways, in fields or streams—or they can even be done in a laboratory, and little lights may indeed blink on and off. What defines an experiment is not the setting, but a *manipulation*. An experimenter manipulates something—that is, he *makes something happen*—and observes its effects.

Experiments do specify the direction of causality. In a correlational study, we may find that high scores on some variable A go with high scores on another variable B, and low with low. But what causes what? Does A cause B? Does B cause A? Does some third variable Z cause both? We don't know.

But suppose an experimenter *manipulates* A, causing it to vary. Now we *know* what caused A to vary—the experimenter did! Then if B changes as well, *and* if we can rule out other factors (Zs) that might have made B change (Chapter 9), then the causal picture is clear: A must have caused B.

That's one great advantage of experiments. Another, related one is that they can pull out single threads from a tangled web of possible causal influences. We saw an example early, in Harlow's work (Chapter 2). In nature, monkey mothers offer both food and comfort. But which of all these is relevant to what the baby does? Well, to say that a factor is relevant is to say that it *makes a difference*—that if it were different, what the subject does would be different as a result. Hence, manipulation: We make visible the effect of a factor (if it has one) by *making it different where nothing else is,* and seeing if the difference influences what our subject does.

SOME EXAMPLES

We've seen examples of experiments in previous chapters. Let's see some more, for they will serve to extend our feel for experimentation. They will also serve us later by providing examples of various *experimental designs*.

AN EXAMPLE FROM PSYCHOBIOLOGY: SPEED OF THE NERVE IMPULSE

In discussing *data*, we noted that *time* is often used as a physical measure. We can learn a surprising amount about even very complex events, just by measuring how long they take. Let us see how. And to begin, let me tell you about one of the most famous experiments in the history of psychology—and physiology.

By the nineteenth century, it was clear that the brain and nervous system formed the organ of mind. Mental operations depended on the workings of the physical brain—as in the case of aphasic patients, for instance (Chapter 4). On the other hand, many people then believed (as some still do, though few scientists) that mental events are nonphysical, that they exist in a world separate from the world of physical objects and events. Thus the nervous system, though physical, ought to have special properties.

For example: The movement of a leg is produced by the passage of nerve impulses from the spinal cord to the muscles that move that leg. The sensation of a touch on the foot depends on messages carried by separate nerve cells from the foot up into the brain. So registering a sensation (a mental event), and controlling the movement of our bodies (another), both depend on the integrity of the nerves involved.

But what were the properties of these nervous-system messages? For instance (narrowing down), do they *take time*? At first glance it doesn't seem so. When someone touches our foot, we feel it instantly. When we will our foot to move, it moves—again, instantly. Or so it seems. But it is not so! In 1850, the German scientist Hermann von Helmholz* was able to show that the conduction of nerve impulses

---

*We will call Helmholz simply "a scientist" for short. He was a physicist, nerve physiologist, muscle physiologist, metabolic physiologist, optician, acoustician, mathematician, philosopher, and (for good measure) one of the greatest experimental psychologists of all time. When did he sleep?

from place to place did take time, and a fairly long time at that. To see how he went about it, look at Figure 6.1.

It was also known by then that nerves can be excited by electrical stimulation. So, in an isolated nerve-muscle preparation, Helmholz applied a brief pulse of current to the nerve. That pulse also started a timing device. When the nerve impulse reached the muscle, the muscle contracted, and its movement stopped the timer. Thus Helmholz could measure the time that went by between the stimulation of the nerve and the resulting muscle contraction (Figure 6.1).

Now that does not, by itself, give us the speed of the nerve impulse per se. The total time between timer on and timer off included the mechanical events of the muscle contraction itself. Solution? Move the stimulator! If we stimulate the nerve farther from the muscle, the events at the muscle itself take the same amount of time as before. But now the nerve impulse has farther to travel, so—if it travels at a measurable speed—the total time between stimulus and muscle contraction should be longer.

And it was. Of course the times varied a bit from trial to trial, so Helmholz took many measurements, in many frogs, under both conditions A and B. On average, the total time for conduction-plus-

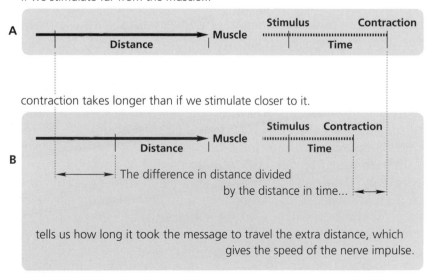

Helmholtz's experiment:

If we stimulate far from the muscle...

A | Distance → Muscle | Stimulus ......|.......... Contraction | Time

contraction takes longer than if we stimulate closer to it.

B | Distance → Muscle | Stimulus ....|.... Contraction | Time

The difference in distance divided by the distance in time...

tells us how long it took the message to travel the extra distance, which gives the speed of the nerve impulse.

FIGURE 6.1
How Helmholtz measured the speed of the nerve impulse. (A) nerve stimulated far from the muscle; (B) nerve stimulated less far from the muscle.

contraction was reliably longer for the more distant stimulus. Then, knowing the distance *d* between points A and B (a physical measure), and the difference in response time *t* (another), Helmholz simply divided distance by time to get *speed*, as in miles/hour (or in this case, meters/second). Helmholz measured this speed at about 30 meters per second—well within the ballpark that more recent methods have established. And it really is not very fast, as fast things go. Far from being instantaneous, the nerve message travels more slowly than sound!

Perhaps this idea is so familiar that it's difficult to get excited about it now. But it would be hard to exaggerate the impact it had when first announced. The nervous system is the "organ of mind," no doubt—but it is a physical system, subject to physical constraints. Its actions take time.

AN EXAMPLE FROM COGNITION: MENTAL ROTATION

The use of physical measures—distance and time—gave rise to a landmark study in physiology. But the underlying logic—we can learn something about an event by observing how long it takes—has much wider applicability. Here's a very different example of the same idea and, in its logic, a similar method.

A number of times in this book, I have asked you to "imagine" this or that. You knew what I meant and were able to do it. And we play with our images. I imagine a conversation with a friend who isn't there, or that I were in Paris or had won the lottery . . . and so on.

We manipulate images, then. What are the properties of these imaginary manipulations? To what extent are they like real manipulations? Well, let's zero in on a more specific question. Manipulation of physical objects takes time. Is this also true of mental "objects"—images in the mind's eye?

Shepard and Metzler (1971) addressed this question in the following way. Look at the two shapes in Figure 6.2A. Are they the same shape, or different? To decide, subjects must rotate one of the figures "in the mind's eye," to see whether they can be rotated into congruence. If they can, they are the same figure; if not, they are not.

Shepard and Metzler presented subjects with slides showing a series of such pairs, some congruent, some not. The subjects made their judgment by pressing a "yes" or a "no" button. What was varied,

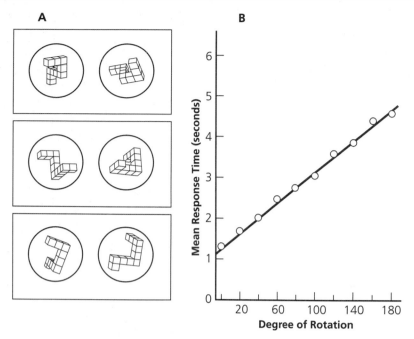

FIGURE 6.2
How Shepard and Metzler measured the speed of mental rotation. (A) sample pairs of shapes; (B) reaction times at varying degrees of rotation (from Shepard & Metzler, 1971).

from one trial to another, was *how much* one figure would have to be rotated, in order to be congruent (if it was) with the other.

Other things equal, physically rotating an object a lot takes more time than rotating it only a little. Is the same true of mentally rotating one? Yes. In Figure 6.2B, we see that the greater the degree of mental rotation, the longer it took subjects to make their judgment. Indeed, the straight-line pattern of the data suggests that such mental rotation occurs at a constant rate.

In these examples, we see a theme that recurs throughout this book: Surface differences can overlie important similarities. One of these experiments dealt with fragments of frogs, the other with intact human beings; the one with simple nerve-impulse conduction, the other with a very complex cognitive process. Nevertheless, in important ways the ideas were the same. At the simplest level, both used *time* as their measure, and both looked at some observable action, leg flexion or button pressing. But the similarities went far beyond that.

Both examples show how a careful experiment isolates one factor in a complex system by *controlling* others. For mental rotation, each subject's task, across trials, was the same; so were the situation and the figures themselves, except for degree of rotation. The use of several different degrees of rotation was also, in part, a control procedure. Some of the time it takes to press a button is, of course, taken up by the mechanics of muscle contraction—just as in Helmholz's case. With only a single degree of rotation (say, 60 degrees), we wouldn't know how much of the reaction time was taken up by mental rotation and how much the time required to perceive the object, make the judgment of congruence or noncongruence, and, of course, by the movement itself. But since these processes are the same for (say) 60 degrees and 120 degrees, any *difference* in reaction time must reflect the difference in how much mental rotation the two conditions required (Figure 6.3). Similarly, it was the *difference*

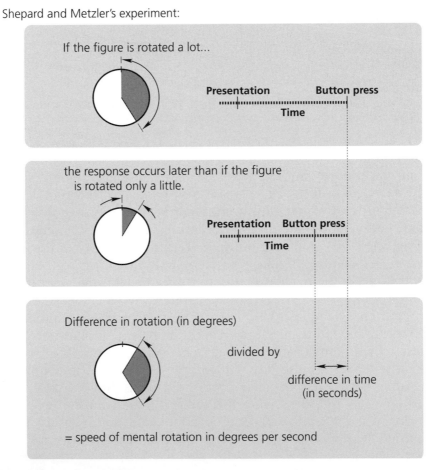

Shepard and Metzler's experiment:

If the figure is rotated a lot...

Presentation   Button press

Time

the response occurs later than if the figure is rotated only a little.

Presentation   Button press

Time

Difference in rotation (in degrees)

divided by

difference in time (in seconds)

= speed of mental rotation in degrees per second

FIGURE 6.3
The subtraction procedure by which the speed of rotation was calculated.

between two placements of the stimulator that allowed Helmholz to calculate conduction velocity. *Comparison*!

Finally, both experiments have ramifications for some very general issues—not only about what the mind or "its" nervous system is like, but also about how it can be studied. At first glance, it's not clear how images can be studied experimentally at all. What can we observe? Images would seem to be locked up inside us. You can "see" your images, I can see mine—but I can't see yours. True, I could ask you to *describe* your images, but attempts to study images that way bogged down in confusion (see Humphrey, 1951).

But Shepard and Metzler's experiment required subjects not to *describe* their images, but to *use* them to perform a task. The task, and the measure (reaction time), are "out there" where you and I can both observe them. Then, by varying the conditions of the task, we learn something about the "hidden" events that allow subjects to perform those tasks. It was recognition of this that made the Shepard and Metzler experiment a landmark in cognitive psychology. And it is a beautiful example of how we can make subjective events into objective ones (Chapter 3)!

Similarly, we can't directly watch a nerve impulse running along a cable of nerve cells. But by arranging things so that the impulse must travel sometimes far and sometimes not so far, we can measure its velocity anyway.

AN EXAMPLE FROM CONDITIONING: TASTE AVERSION IN RATS AND HUMANS

Building on Pavlov's exploratory work, a large literature on classical or Pavlovian conditioning, in animals and humans, developed rapidly. And two principles began to look very well established. First, the development of a conditioned reflex is a gradual process, as we saw earlier (Figure 3.3, p. 70). It requires many pairings of CS (conditioned stimulus) and UCS (unconditioned stimulus). Second, the time between CS and UCS (the "CS–UCS interval") is quite critical. It is best if the onset of the CS (say a tone) precedes the UCS (say a puff of air to the eyeball) by about half a second. If the delay is much more than that, conditioning will be weak or absent.

However, beginning early in the 1960s, some important exceptions to these principles were discovered. Prominent among them is the phenomenon of *taste-aversion learning*, which seems to violate both principles. Conditioning of this sort may take place after only *one* pairing of CS and UCS. And it can occur even if the CS and the

UCS are separated from each other, not by half a second, but by many hours!

In a taste-aversion experiment using rats, the CS is a distinctively flavored food or fluid that the animal eats or drinks; for example, water flavored with saccharin. The UCS is the induction of nausea, by small doses of a toxic drug or by X-irradiation.

THE GARCIA, ERVIN, AND KOELLING EXPERIMENT

In one of the first such experiments (Garcia, Ervin, & Koelling, 1966), rats were exposed to that sequence: saccharin ingestion, followed by illness. Three days later, after the rats had long recovered from their illness, they were offered saccharin water again. The rats showed a clear aversion to saccharin-flavored water—they drank very little of it, whereas most rats will drink it down with enthusiasm. This was so even though the saccharin taste had been paired with illness only once, and even though there had been a delay of a full hour between the initial saccharin exposure and the onset of illness. Later experiments showed that conditioned taste aversion can occur even with a full 24 hours between taste and illness.

But wait a minute! Do we know that the rats' rejection of saccharin was really a *conditioned* reaction? Maybe the experience of being sick (especially in lab-reared rats who had never been sick before) makes rats suspicious of *any* distinctive food—like saccharin in water. In that case, the initial exposure to saccharin, before the illness, might have nothing to do with it.

Garcia and his colleagues anticipated that difficulty. So they added a *control group*: other rats were simply made sick, without prior exposure to saccharin. Then three days later, like the rats in the experimental (conditioning) group, they were offered saccharin water. They accepted it just as untreated rats do.

Figure 6.4 shows the design and procedure of this experiment, and the results. Clearly, the experimental group rejected the sweetened water, not just because they had been made sick (for all the rats had), but because they had been made sick *after* having experienced the saccharin taste.

It's instructive to compare this experiment with the more traditional conditioning experiments—say, Pavlov's. Imagine presenting a dog with the sound of a bell (CS), and then, several hours later, placing food in its mouth! No such dog is going to begin salivating to the sound alone, even after many conditioning trials. But here we see conditioning occurring with just such a long delay, between the saccharin taste (CS) and the onset of nausea (UCS). And we see it

Phase 1

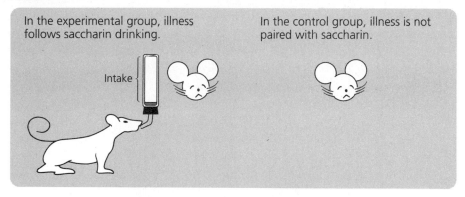

In the experimental group, illness follows saccharin drinking.

In the control group, illness is not paired with saccharin.

Intake

Phase 2

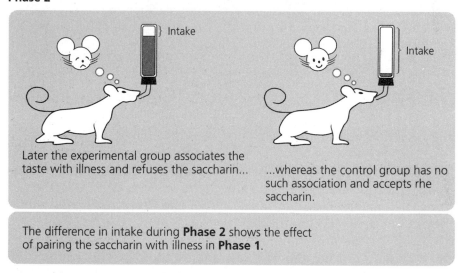

Intake

Intake

Later the experimental group associates the taste with illness and refuses the saccharin...

...whereas the control group has no such association and accepts rhe saccharin.

The difference in intake during **Phase 2** shows the effect of pairing the saccharin with illness in **Phase 1**.

FIGURE 6.4
Garcia and Koelling's conditioned-taste-aversion experiment.

after only one CS–UCS pairing. Clearly, there is something different about this particular CS–UCS combination.

TASTE AVERSION IN HUMANS: BERNSTEIN'S EXPERIMENT

Now let's take another step. Does this kind of conditioning take place in humans as well as rats? A series of experiments by Ilene Bernstein and her colleagues (Bernstein, 1978) showed that it does.

To repeat Garcia's work directly in humans would obviously pose ethical problems. We can't go around making people sick just to answer a scientific question. Instead, Bernstein took advantage of a kind

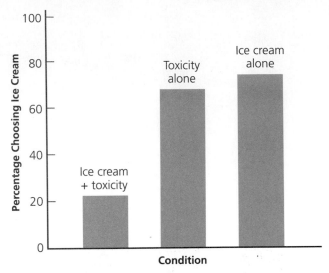

FIGURE 6.5
Results of Bernstein's conditioned-taste-aversion experiment. The group for which the novel ice cream was paired with illness ("toxicity") later ate much less of it than the two control groups did (data from Bernstein, 1978).

of natural experiment, in which people were being made sick anyway, for therapeutic reasons.

Her subjects were a group of adolescents who were being treated for cancer. Their therapy included treatment with drugs that, unfortunately, produce nausea. Question: If the subjects were given something distinctively flavored to eat before the drug treatment, would they come to dislike that flavor?

From the "pool" of hospitalized subjects, the investigators formed three groups. During the first session, children in one group were given a novel, distinctively flavored ice cream (Maple Toff), 15 to 60 minutes before receiving a nausea-inducing drug treatment. Children in a second group (a control group) were not given ice cream prior to drug treatment, but played with a toy instead. And children in the third group (another control group) were given the ice cream but were not made sick with their treatment immediately thereafter.*

Two to four weeks later, in a second session, the acceptance or rejection of the novel ice cream was measured by offering *all* the children a choice between eating that ice cream and playing with a game. The results were quite striking (Figure 6.5): Of the control subjects, 67% chose the ice cream. Of the children who experienced ice cream

---

*For practical reasons, this third group was added later, so we're simplifying the design a bit here.

followed by nausea, only 21% did so. A follow-up measure, offering a choice between Maple Toff and another flavor (Hawaiian Delight), confirmed the effect: Experimental subjects chose the Maple Toff ice cream significantly less often, and ate significantly less of it, than did controls. This was so even though the Maple Toff ice cream had been paired with illness only once, weeks before.

Why was there a third group in this experiment, and not the one by Garcia et al.? It was to check the possibility that that particular flavor of ice cream might just be less attractive the second time it was offered, even without illness. The results from the third group, which was offered the ice cream twice but was not made sick, shows that this was not so. In the rat experiment, no such control was needed, for we already know from an extensive literature that rats, if not made sick, will go on drinking saccharin-sweetened water with gusto, day after day.

COMMENTS

Let us look at some of the ramifications of taste-aversion learning, before we move on.

In the first place, the human experiments in particular bear on a theoretical issue: the question of *awareness* in human conditioning. Does conditioning occur because the subject is consciously *aware* that the tone means the air puff is about to come?

We've seen one experiment suggesting that the answer is no (Chapter 3). Bernstein's experiment supports the same conclusion. In fact, in her experiment, conditioning occurred not because of her subjects' conscious knowledge, but in spite of it! These young people *knew perfectly well* that it was their drug treatment, not the ice cream, that was making them sick. It didn't matter. The people in the experimental group disliked the ice cream anyway, after it had been paired with illness. Apparently there is something about the taste–illness pairing that marches right past our conscious knowledge, and creates an aversion to the taste even if we *know* it has nothing to do with our illness.

A still broader issue is: What is learning like, anyway? Pavlov's experiments suggest that an "association" can be formed between any two inputs we choose—between bell and food, for instance. The mind is like a "blank slate" on which experience writes, and it writes a record of whatever is presented. But the special properties of taste-aversion learning suggest that there is a specialized mechanism or "module" that is designed to associate just *these* inputs—tastes (and smells)—with just *these other* inputs—the sensations of nausea. Other data support this idea (Pelchak & Rozin, 1982), and there is evidence for other specialized "modules" as well (e.g., for language learning in humans; Pinker, 1994). This suggests a different metaphor for the mind: Perhaps it is less like a "blank slate" than like a Swiss army knife, with specialized tools for learning different kinds of things.

Thus again we see how "little" experiments can bear on big issues. No one much cares whether a group of rats does or does not drink saccharin, or whether a group of humans does or does not like Maple Toff ice cream. But such experiments have shed new light on what learning itself—and therefore the mind, which is largely "furnished" by learning—is like.

A LOOK BACK

Finally, let us see what all four of our examples have in common. They all isolated some part of a complex system. And they did it by varying that one part, holding all else constant.

Thus Helmholz on nerve-impulse conduction (Figure 6.1): Under both experimental conditions, the events at the muscle were the same—so the time that those events took could be "subtracted out" of the comparison between them, and only how far the nerve impulse had to travel was different.

In the mental-rotation experiment, not only was the button-pushing response the same under all conditions, but so were all the cognitive operations required: perceiving the geometric shapes, rotating them mentally, and making the judgment of congruence or incongruence. All that varied was how much the figures had to be rotated in the "mind's eye" in order to permit that judgment (Figure 6.3).

Even for the taste-aversion experiments, the logic remains the same (Figures 6.4 and 6.5). The measures were the same across conditions—intake or choice. So was the commodity—saccharin-flavored water for rats, Maple Toff ice cream for humans. In both experiments, all that varied was whether illness had been paired with the fluid—pairing present in one condition, absent in the control condition(s). Thus the influence of the pairing itself—that is, of conditioning—was isolated.

THE ANATOMY OF AN EXPERIMENT

Here and in previous chapters, we have looked over a series of psychological experiments. They are vastly different in the questions they ask, and in the specifics of the situation and procedures, but they also have much in common. There is, so to speak, a skeletal structure that all experiments have; they differ only as to how they put flesh on the skeleton. So let's examine the skeleton itself.

INDEPENDENT AND DEPENDENT VARIABLES

First of all, an experiment is defined by a *manipulation*. The experimenter intervenes in Nature to make something happen; that is, she causes something to *vary*. And she does it by her own action, so that it is *independent* of the natural course of events. Therefore, what she causes to vary is known as the *independent variable*.

Now a *variable* must have at least two *values* (Chapter 3); it isn't a variable if it doesn't. So there will be at least two values of the independent variable. These will often be referred to as different *experimental conditions*, or *experimental treatments* (because they specify how subjects are "treated" under various conditions).

Thus: In the Latané and Darley "bystander" experiments, the independent variable was *number of onlookers*, with its two values a and b: (a) one onlooker, and (b) three onlookers. In the mental-rotation experiments, the independent variable was *degree of rotation*, with its several values—0 to 180 degrees—as shown in Figure 6.2. In the taste-aversion experiments (both of them!) it was *whether or not* the test food—saccharin or ice cream—was paired with illness.

Now we manipulate an independent variable—we make it vary—in order to see its effect. On what? On something about what our subjects say or do. We measure or observe something—in a word, we collect *data*—in order to see how the data are affected by our manipulation. Saying it differently, we want to see how the data *depend on* the value of the independent variable. Does likelihood of taking action in an emergency *depend on* how many onlookers there are? Does a rat's acceptance of a sweet fluid (or a human's acceptance of a distinctive ice cream) *depend on* whether it has been followed by illness? In each case, if we state the question that way, it is easy to see why the measurements or observations we take are referred to as the *dependent variable* or variables.

There is our skeleton. Any experiment will ask: What is the effect *of* an independent variable (what we manipulate) *on* a dependent variable (what the subject says or does).

These are terms we will encounter very often, and we need to be so familiar with them that we dream them. If you have any trouble keeping them straight, here's a handy mnemonic for now, until they become automatic. Just remember that I goes with I and D goes with D. The *Independent variable* is the *Intervention*—what we make happen. The *Dependent variable* is the *Data*—what we observe. That's all.

CONTROL VARIABLES

An experiment, we say, asks how an independent variable affects a dependent variable. Now, if the world were perfectly designed for research purposes, then the independent variable that we manipulate would be the *only* influence on the dependent variable. But it isn't. In practice, our dependent variable will be affected by all sorts of other influences that are irrelevant to our question.

Thus, no matter what we do, some people will be more likely than others to offer help in an emergency. Some, perhaps, will be more altruistic—or less alienated—than others. Some will be very much distracted by their own preoccupations, others less so. One subject will just have had a fight with a significant other and be in a lousy mood; another will not. And so on.

Even if our subjects are laboratory-reared rats, their lives will be filled with uncontrolled influences on what they do. One rat will have eaten more recently than another. One rat will be feeling out of sorts today; another will be feeling just fine. And so on.

So, in real-world research, our subjects' behavior may be affected by our independent variable, but it will be affected by all sorts of other things as well. To best see what effect our independent variable has, we want to get rid of these other influences if we can. If we can't do that, we want at least to equalize them, so that they affect all experimental conditions in the same way and thus drop out of our comparison between them. In a word, we want to *control* them. Hence these nuisance variables are referred to as *control variables*.

Some such extraneous variables can be held constant directly, by the way we set up the situation. Thus in the "bystander" experiment, we make the emergency itself—smoke pouring from a vent—constant from subject to subject.

Other such variables cannot be so directly controlled. We cannot *make* all our subjects equally altruistic, or alienated, or distracted. What we can do is try to make all *groups* of subjects equally altruistic (or alienated or distracted) *on average*. And one way to do that is to assign each subject strictly *at random* to the "alone" or to the "other onlookers" condition. Then, if we have enough subjects, the randomization procedure is likely to assign roughly as many altruistic subjects (or alienated or grumpy ones) to one group as to the other.

The larger the groups, the more unlikely they are to be very different on any variable—those we think of and those we do not.

We will only "look forward" to this topic here, for the following chapters will explore it further. But already we have introduced the fundamental principle of experimental control, which is as follows:

Principle: We control what we can; and what we don't control, we randomize.

Notice that what we control, like what we manipulate and what we measure, depends on the question we are asking. An independent variable in one experiment may be a control variable in another.

Suppose, for instance, that we want to know the effect of food deprivation on food intake. We would then manipulate food deprivation; for example, let different groups of subjects (people or rats or octopi) go without food for different lengths of time. Then we let them eat. In such an experiment, we want to be sure that the attractiveness or *palatability* of the food—how good-tasting it is—is at least approximately equal for all subjects. It would never do to let the severely deprived subjects have good-tasting food and the less-deprived ones have bad-tasting food. If we did that, the effects of deprivation would be thoroughly *confounded* with the effects of palatability, and we wouldn't know which variable was responsible for any difference we might see (Chapter 8). So palatability would be a control variable here.

On the other hand, suppose we want to know the effect of palatability on amount eaten. Now *palatability* is not a control variable; it is the independent variable. We vary it deliberately, perhaps by offering some subjects good-tasting food, others bad-tasting food. And how long the subjects have gone without food, the independent variable in the previous experiment, now becomes a control variable. We want all subjects to be equally hungry, or, if that is impossible, at least we want them to be equally hungry *on average* across experimental conditions.

Speaking of control, there is a popular superstition to the effect that every experiment needs a "control condition" (or, worse, a "control group"). Not so. Harlow's monkey-mother experiment, for example, had neither of these. It is true, however, that *every experiment involves a comparison* between something and something else. What do we compare with what? It depends on the question we are asking. That question specifies our independent and dependent variables.

Thus: If there are others present when an emergency occurs, we ask whether a subject is less likely to offer help, less likely than what? Less likely than when a subject is by himself. So our question defines at least two conditions—other onlooker(s) present, or not—and these are the two values of our independent variable. The likelihood, and/or the promptness, with which a subject offers help should *depend* on which condition is in effect; so these are our two *dependent variables* that we measure.

Or: We ask whether the experience of food paired with illness makes subjects eat less of that food. Less than what? Than they would eat if the food had not been so paired. Our question again defines at least two conditions—presence or absence of such a pairing.

To summarize: Any experiment will incorporate a comparison—that is, there will be an *independent variable* that takes on different values for different *experimental conditions* or *experimental treatments*. And we will see how what our subjects say or do *depends on* the value of the independent variable. So we measure what they say or do as the *dependent variable*.

There will always be other influences on the dependent variable, ones that are irrelevant to the question we are asking. These *control variables* are—well, *controlled*. By careful planning, we can get rid of some of these variables. If we can't do that, perhaps we can hold them constant for all conditions, so that they drop out of the comparisons among conditions. If we can't do *that*, at least we may hold them approximately constant *on average* across conditions, as by randomization.

EXPERIMENTAL DESIGN

Any experiment, we have said, involves a comparison. Or, saying it another way, there will be an independent variable that has at least two values—there will be at least two conditions, or experimental treatments. The question of *experimental design* asks: What subjects receive what treatments, and when? It is concerned with just how the subjects are assigned to different experimental treatments. There are a number of options here.

THE INDEPENDENT-GROUPS DESIGN

In this kind of design, two or more "groups" of subjects will be formed, *at random*, from a pool of available subjects. Each group corresponds to a different experimental condition or experimental treatment—that is, a different value of the independent variable. Except for that, we treat all subjects identically, or as nearly identically as possible—that is, we *control* all other variables as closely as we can.

The Latané and Darley experiments were of this kind. There was a "group" of subjects, each of whom sat by himself in the waiting room when the staged emergency occurred. There was another "group," each of whom waited with other onlookers present.* These were the two values of the independent variable: alone, or with someone else. Each subject was assigned at random to one condition or the other. And the dependent variables—whether the subject took action, and if so, how long it took him to do so—were measured once for each subject.

Similarly for the taste-aversion experiment in rats. The rats were randomly assigned to one or the other condition, resulting in two groups of rats: one that had had saccharin water paired with illness, and one that had not.

This design has the advantage of simplicity, and it avoids some of the control problems that other designs face. It also lacks the advantages of some other designs, as we'll see.

WITHIN-SUBJECTS DESIGNS: CONCURRENT MEASURES

In this design, there are no treatment groups—or, if you like, there is only one. Each subject is confronted with all values of the independent variable and, in the simplest case, is allowed to *choose* among them.

---

*The term "group," used this way, is sometimes confusing to beginners. If we speak of a group of subjects, the term suggests a number of subjects all gathered together in one place, perhaps being introduced to each other. Occasionally an experiment may be conducted that way. Most often, though, it is really the subjects' data that are "grouped," not the subjects themselves—which is why I've put "group" in quotes (though I'll omit the quotes after this section). In the bystander experiment, for instance, the data for all the subjects who waited alone were all put together for statistical analysis after the experiment was done, so they constitute the "group" of observations taken under the "waiting alone" condition. The subjects in that "group" never met each other. Their data were compared with all the data from the subjects receiving the waiting-with-others condition.

Similarly, the rats in the taste-aversion experiments never were introduced to each other. The data from all the rats who tasted saccharin before illness—the "experimental group"— were compared with all the data from the "control group" who experienced illness without saccharin.

So when we use the term "group" this way, we really mean something like "all subjects who are treated *this* way rather than *that*, and whose data are 'grouped' together for statistical purposes." One quickly gets used to this convention.

Harlow's experiment with cloth and wire mothers was of this kind. The independent variable was "kind of mother," and it had two values: Cloth with no milk, and wire with milk. Both these model mothers were made available to each baby monkey, and the experimenters measured how much time the baby spent with each one. That was the dependent variable. Emily Rosa's "therapeutic touch" experiment had the same design: Each subject on each trial reported which hand—left or right—she thought was being almost-touched by the experimenter.

Such a design also has the virtue of simplicity. It has the advantage, too, that we don't have to worry about whether our treatment groups are equivalent, for there is only one group. On the other hand, it is obvious that not all questions can easily be phrased as choice questions; and when they cannot, this design is not an option. Take the number-of-bystanders experiments. Waiting alone must be compared with waiting with others; but, obviously, we can't impose both conditions at once. Separate groups are required.

WITHIN-SUBJECTS DESIGNS: REPEATED MEASURES

Where we cannot present all treatment conditions at one time, we may be able to present them at *different* times to the same subjects. Again we have a within-subjects design: Every subject receives all conditions, all values of the independent variable. But now the different conditions are imposed at different times.

The mental rotation experiments were done this way. The independent variable was degree of mental rotation required. And in each subject, reaction time was measured several times under each degree of rotation. So each of the subjects was *compared with himself* under the various conditions. Again, we don't have to worry about equivalence of groups, for there was only one. That is one bit of good news. The other is that such a design *controls for individual differences*, an important source of variability and inconsistency in experimental data. That too is good news; we'll discuss it later.

THE PROBLEM OF CARRYOVER EFFECTS

Now, the bad news. There can be a problem with this kind of design, and it is simply this: What if being exposed to one condition changes how one will react when, later, one is exposed to another condition? This is the problem of *carryover effects*.

Thus, suppose our subjects all are tested under one condition (A), then later under another condition (B). Suppose they perform better under B. Is this because B really does promote better performance? Or is it because the subjects have had more practice at the task? We don't know.

Or suppose the subjects perform worse under B. Is this because B really leads to lower performance than A? Or are the subjects getting tired? Are they getting bored with the whole business? Maybe it's one or both of these that is making them perform more poorly now. Practice, fatigue, mounting boredom, growing familiarity with the setting—these are examples of carryover effects.

DISTRIBUTING CARRYOVER EFFECTS: COUNTERBALANCING AND RANDOMIZATION

If such things as practice, fatigue, and boredom are going to affect our data, there may be nothing we can do to prevent it. However, it may be possible to *distribute* these effects over all experimental conditions, so that they *affect all conditions equally* when we put all the data together.

One way of doing it is by *counterbalancing*. In the simplest case, let there be two experimental conditions, A and B. All subjects receive both conditions, one at a time. But for half of them (randomly chosen), the A condition comes first, then the B; for the other half, the order is reversed (Figure 6.6). So, if second-time performance benefits from practice or suffers from fatigue, such carryover effects

In a counterbalanced design with two conditions...

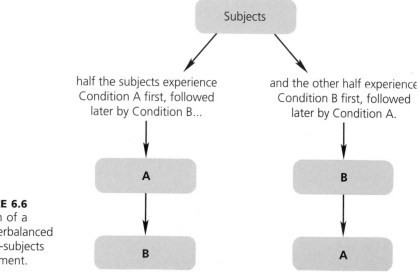

FIGURE 6.6
Design of a counterbalanced within-subjects experiment.

should affect the B condition for half the subjects, and the A condition for the other half. Therefore, they should drop out of the comparison between A and B when all the data are combined.

Here there could easily be confusion, so let's head it off. In setting up this counterbalanced design, we do indeed divide subjects into groups. One group receives the A to B sequence, the other the B to A sequence. But *it is still a within-subjects design*. That's because it still is true that each subject is compared with herself or himself under the two conditions. The counterbalancing is simply an attempt to ensure that both conditions are affected equally by practice, fatigue, boredom, and other effects of repeated trials per se.

An alternative is to present the various conditions in an order that is *randomized* for each subject. This is often done in cases where each observation or "trial" is quickly done, and conditions are easily and quickly changed. Then we can flip back and forth among conditions and, in a short time, we can get for each subject a whole series of trials under each condition. Again, the randomized order means that all the conditions will appear about equally often early in the sequence and late in the sequence, so carryover effects will affect all of them equally.

The mental rotation experiment was done this way. Each subject saw several pairs of shapes, at each degree of rotation; and the various shapes and rotations were presented in random order.

THE PROBLEM OF REVERSIBILITY

Do counterbalanced or randomized sequences then solve our problem of carryover effects? Sometimes. Sometimes not. We just have to think the matter through each time we design an experiment.

To take an obvious case: Suppose we have devised a new way of teaching children how to ride a bicycle. Call it Method A. We want to compare it with the old way (whatever that is); call it Method B. Obviously, we cannot teach a child this skill with Method A, and then return him to baseline and teach him again with Method B. Once taught, he is permanently changed. And that will be true of every child in our sample: Once taught by one method, she or he cannot be taught again, from scratch, by another. In such a case, a within-subjects design—with or without counterbalancing—would make no sense at all.

The same problem can arise in more subtle ways. Take, for example, the bystander experiments. The two conditions are waiting alone, or waiting with others, when smoke begins pouring into the room. In principle, a within-subjects design, with or without counterbalancing, could be used here. But not in practice. Having created an emergency under one condition, it's unlikely that we can plausibly recreate the *same* emergency under another condition, and expect the subject to behave as if the first had never happened.

The moral is: Within-subject designs are a poor choice if any of the experimental conditions produces a *lasting* effect on the subject. Once taught to ride a bike, or once having witnessed the smoke emergency, the subject may be permanently changed in ways that would make later observations misleading.

On the other hand, consider the mental rotation experiments, which are quite different. Making a judgment about one pair of shapes should not warp the subject's judgment about later pairs. True, practice at the button-pressing task may let her respond a bit faster as the session progresses; but again, randomization will equalize that effect across conditions. So in that experiment, a series of trials under different conditions, in randomized order, makes sense. And it is a far more efficient way to proceed than using an independent group of subjects (each of whom has to be instructed, etc.) for each value of the independent variable.

REVERSAL DESIGNS

There is another approach to carryover effects, and that is to "check them out" with a *reversal* design. If we move from Condition A to Condition B and our dependent variable changes, we might *reverse* the manipulation—go back to Condition A—and see if the dependent variable goes back to where it was before.

Figure 6.7 shows an experiment from my own laboratory that illustrates this tactic. Briefly, in rats that were earning all their food

FIGURE 6.7
A within-subjects reversal design. As work requirement (bar presses required per pellet) was raised and then lowered, number of responses went up and then down. The vertical lines show ranges (highest to lowest scores), indicating that the pattern held for all rats without exception (from Mook, Kenney, Roberts, Nussbaum, & Roder, 1972).

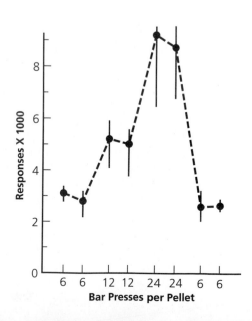

by pressing a lever for small food pellets, we wanted to know how response output varied with the work requirement. So we varied it over successive two-day periods, requiring first 6, then 12, then 24 lever presses per pellet. Sure enough: As the work requirement increased, work output increased too, so that the amount of food earned was nearly constant.

But wait! As we were increasing the work requirement, the rats were getting more and more practice at the task. Could they be responding more for that reason alone, and might that be responsible for their steadily increasing work output? If so, that would be a carryover effect.

To check this possibility, we simply dropped the requirement back to the original 6 responses per pellet (the "reversal"). And response output promptly dropped back to *its* original value. Clearly it was the increased work requirement, not a practice effect, that had caused output to increase before.

This tactic too, however, assumes that a manipulation *can* be reversed effectively. In our earlier example of the two bicycle-training methods, a reversal design would make no more sense than a counterbalanced design would.

To summarize: A within-subjects design has many advantages if it is possible. But in many cases it is not possible, and in many others it would not be wise, especially if one condition has a lasting or irreversible effect that would contaminate performance under other conditions. In such cases we must design the experiment in a different way, perhaps with different treatments for independent groups of subjects—or perhaps with matched groups of subjects, a possibility we turn to now.

MATCHED-SUBJECTS AND RANDOMIZED-BLOCK DESIGNS

There's one other basic design we'll consider. In this one, the various experimental conditions are assigned to different groups of subjects. But rather than assigning subjects at random to groups, we first *match* certain subjects with certain others. Then subjects or blocks of subjects are compared, not with themselves, but with subjects *similar to* themselves with respect to the variable(s) on which the matching or blocking is done. We may think of such designs as an attempt to gain some of the advantages of a within-subjects design, without having to submit to its drawbacks.

For example, suppose we intend an experiment with two conditions, A and B; where A might be waiting alone, and B might be waiting with others. Suppose that, for whatever reason, we feel that *intelligence* might be an important influence on what we plan to measure. We decide to match our two groups for intelligence.

This means that everyone, in our starting "pool" of subjects, will have to be given an intelligence test. Then we might do our matching pair by pair. Take the two people with highest IQs. Assign one *at random* to Condition A, the other to B. Take the next two highest scorers and do the same thing. Do it again for the next two highest . . . and so on down to the two lowest scorers. The result will be two groups of subjects, matched for intelligence (Figure 6.8A). Of course, if we wanted three groups, we would do the same thing with the three highest scorers, the next three highest, and so on.

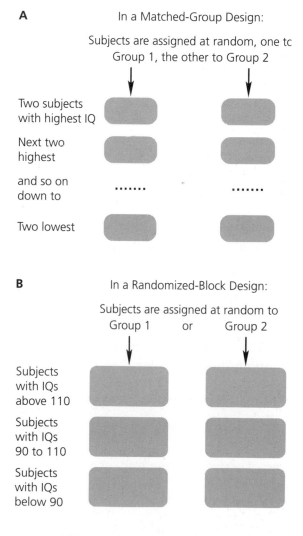

FIGURE 6.8
How matched-groups and randomized-block experiments are designed.

The matching need not be subject by subject. Less precisely (but more efficiently), we could simply divide our subject pool into levels, or "blocks," of IQ scores: say, above 110, 90 to 110, and below 90. Then, within each of the three blocks, we assign each subject *at random* to Condition A or B (or to A, B, or C, etc.). Because we are doing random assignment separately within each block, this kind of setup is called a *randomized-block design* (Figure 6.8B).

Bernstein's experiment with conditioned taste aversion used a randomized-block design. Before forming her groups, she divided her pool of subjects into "blocks" on the basis of age and number of prior drug treatments. Only then, within each block, did she assign subjects at random to one or another group.

This design gives us some control over individual differences, though less than a within-subjects design does. And it provides more assurance than does randomization (the independent-groups design) that our groups are comparable to each other. Finally, since each subject is exposed to only one experimental condition, we avoid the troublesome problem of carryover effects that arises for within-subjects designs.

The chief drawback of such a design is the expense (in money, time, or effort—or all these) of taking the measures with which we will do the matching. If we are going to match our groups for intelligence, for instance, then we need to get a measure of intelligence for all our subjects before we can assign them to groups. This simply makes the matched-groups design more cumbersome than the others. So in deciding whether to match subjects, we do a kind of informal cost/benefit analysis: How much added control would we gain by matching subjects? And is it worth the effort and expense of doing so? Actually, that kind of cost/benefit analysis affects many decisions about control, as we'll see in the next chapter.

These experimental designs—independent-groups, within-subjects, and matched-groups—are the building blocks for more complex designs, for they can be elaborated, combined, and mixed together in various ways. But if we thoroughly understand these, then understanding more complex designs later on will be no trouble at all.

LIMITATIONS OF EXPERIMENTS

The experimental method, as we have seen, has great strengths. But it has limitations too, and three of them are worth noting here.

First, an experiment isn't always possible, for ethical reasons or practical reasons or both. Studies of brain-damaged human beings, for example, have taught us much about the brain; but often they are hard to interpret, because the damage may be extensive, involving many structures within the brain. *Purely from a research point of view,* we could do cleaner research if we could do very selective, controlled damage *just here* in the brain and nowhere else, with subjects randomly assigned to brain-damage and control conditions. But for practical reasons, we can't do such experiments with humans (they would object), and for ethical reasons, we wouldn't do them if we could. Questions about the human brain must be asked in other ways.

Second, the experimental method is sure but slow. In the taste-aversion experiments, we know that the conditioning suppresses later intake of *this* diet under *these* conditions. But what if the diet were more attractive? Less attractive? What if the subjects were hungrier? Less hungry? What if the room had been warmer? And so on for a thousand what-ifs. Each of these questions requires its own experiment to answer. This is one reason why it is very rare that a general conclusion can rest on a single experimental finding.

And third, remember this: If we vary some independent variable that influences behavior, with all else held constant, we will see that influence—but we will see nothing else. The finding may tell us that *this* manipulation makes a difference, but it says nothing about how important other influences are. To know the effect of other influences, we must manipulate *them* in turn.

In other words, an experiment can show that some independent variable, X, is *an* important influence on a dependent variable, Y. But that does not mean that it is the *only* important influence, or even the *most important* one. This may seem an obvious point. But—obviously—it is easy to forget. Indeed, my guess is that many of psychology's sillier arguments arise just because it has been forgotten.

SUMMARY

Any experiment will incorporate a comparison—that is, there will be an *independent variable* that takes on different values for different *experimental conditions* or *experimental treatments.* And we ask what effect it has—how what our subjects say or do is affected by, or *depends on,* the value of the independent variable. So we measure what they say or do as the *dependent variable.*

There will always be other influences on the dependent variable, ones that are irrelevant to the question we are asking. These we want to control, so we call them *control variables*. By careful planning, we can get rid of some of these variables. If we can't do that, perhaps we can hold them constant for all conditions, so that they drop out of the comparisons among conditions. If we can't do *that*, at least we may hold them approximately constant *on average* across conditions, as by randomization.

There are a number of ways to design an experiment. In an *independent-groups* design, two or more groups of subjects are formed at random from our initial pool of available subjects. Then all groups are treated identically, except that they receive different values of the independent variable. Here we depend on the randomization process to make it likely that our groups will be at least roughly equivalent to each other. Such a design has the "pro" of simplicity. Its "con" is that it lacks the control features of the other designs. But then, other designs are not always feasible.

A *within-subjects design with concurrent measures* is again easy to visualize. *Choice experiments*, like Harlow's cloth-versus-wire mothers experiment, are straightforward. Here, we don't have to worry about equivalence of groups, for there are no groups. Each subject is exposed to all values of the independent variable. That is the advantage of such a design. Its drawback is that not all experimental questions can be framed as choices among concurrent options.

When we go to a *within-subjects design with consecutive measures*, everything gets a bit trickier. Again, we don't have to worry about equivalence of groups, for each subject is compared with himself or herself under the different conditions.

The main drawback to this design is the problem of *carryover effects*. These can sometimes be controlled by *counterbalancing* or by a *randomized order* of conditions, or by a *reversal* of the change in conditions. But this is not always possible; and when it is not, a within-subjects design may not be an option.

We may think of the matched-group or randomized-block design as an attempt to gain some of the advantages of a within-subjects design without having to submit to its drawbacks. Subjects or blocks of subjects are compared, not with themselves, but with subjects *similar to* themselves with respect to the variable(s) on which the matching or blocking is done. This design gives us some control over individual differences, and it provides more assurance than does randomization that our groups are comparable to each other; but it adds the cost in time and effort of measuring the matching variable.

These experimental designs can be elaborated, combined, and mixed together in various ways. Those we've considered, however, are the building blocks for more complex designs.

Experiments have limitations. They are not always possible, for practical and/or ethical reasons. And they show the effect only of the independent variable we choose to manipulate, and do not tell us how important it is relative to other possible influences. To see the effect of other variables, we will need other experiments.

MAKING FRIENDS WITH STATISTICS: ANALYSIS OF VARIANCE AND THE *t* STATISTIC

In a previous chapter, we learned one way to test the statistical significance of a finding—the sign test. We now consider another significance test, which can be extended to more conditions than two. This is the *analysis of variance* (ANOVA). It is a real workhorse—an enormously useful technique that we will encounter very often in the published literature.

A THREE-GROUP ANOVA

ANOVA can best be made clear if, first of all, we just do one. In what follows, we'll take an example and work through the arithmetic together. Then, when *what* we do is laid out before us, we can go back to see *why* we do it.

Suppose we do a conditioned taste aversion experiment in humans, guided by Bernstein's work (pp. 185–187). We have a "pool" of (say) 12 subjects who are undergoing radiation therapy, which produces nausea. Now let's divide these subjects randomly into three groups of four subjects each.* (Bernstein did not do her experiment quite this way. But we might.)

A THREE-GROUP EXPERIMENT

There are three experimental conditions. In Condition B, our subjects eat a distinctively flavored ice cream, shortly before they are made nauseous. The other two groups are controls. In Condition A, our subjects eat the novel ice cream, but are not made nauseous. In C, they are made nauseous, but get no ice cream first. This is the training phase.

Then, say a month later, we do the test phase in which we collect our data. We offer all our subjects that same distinctive flavor of ice cream, and we measure how much each subject eats. That is our dependent variable: how much ice cream is eaten in the test phase. Suppose we obtain the data shown in the first column of Table 6.1, and summarized graphically in

---

*We should note that here and elsewhere, our examples may use unreasonably small numbers of subjects. In a real experiment, our groups would be much larger; Bernstein used an average of 23 subjects per group. We use only a few subjects in these examples, just to make the arithmetic go faster. With real data we'd do the same arithmetic, just with longer columns of numbers!

Table 6.1
Worksheet for One-Way ANOVA (Ice Cream Data)

	Intake (gm)	Deviation from Grand Mean	Deviation Squared	Deviation from Group Mean	Deviation Squared
Group A					
Anna	120	45	2,025	25	625
Archie	100	25	625	5	25
Alan	90	15	225	−5	25
Aileen	70	−5	25	−25	625
Mean = 95					
Group B					
Bob	20	−55	3,025	−10	100
Barbara	20	−55	3,025	−10	100
Betty	30	−45	2,025	0	0
Brad	50	−25	625	20	400
Mean = 30					
Group C					
Carol	120	45	2,025	20	400
Carl	110	35	1,225	10	100
Cindy	90	15	225	−10	100
Colin	80	5	25	−20	400
Mean = 100					

Grand mean = 75 $SS_T = 15,100$ $SS_W = 2,900$

Group	Group Mean	Deviation from Grand Mean	Deviation Squared	× Number of Subjects in Group
A	95	20	400	1,600
B	30	−45	2,025	8,100
C	100	25	625	2,500

$SS_B = 12,200$

Figure 6.9. It looks as if the groups differ, with Group B eating much less than the others. But are the differences significant?

ANALYSIS: BREAKING UP THE SUM OF SQUARES

The first step is to ask how much variability there is in the data, from score to score, for *all the scores*, in all conditions. We will therefore compute something like a variance, considering all the scores as comprising a single frequency distribution. To do that, we first need to calculate the *mean of all the scores there are*, in all groups combined. We'll call this the *grand mean*; here it is 75. Then we express each individual score as a *deviation from the*

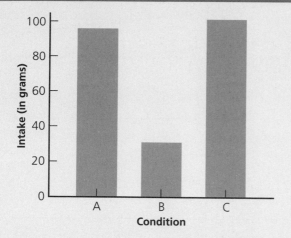

FIGURE 6.9
Mean ice-cream intake under three conditions in an imaginary taste-aversion experiment. Group B, for whom ice cream had been paired with nausea, ate much less later than the two control groups did. But are the differences significant?

grand mean. This gives is the second column of numbers in our worksheet. Figure 6.10A shows graphically what we are doing.

Then, just as if we were going to compute a variance, we square each of these deviation scores (third column) and add those squares together (compare pp. 131–133). The sum of the deviation scores themselves is a check on our arithmetic. If we've done it right, that sum should be zero. And it is.

The sum in the third column is the sum of the *squared* deviation scores from the grand mean, over all our subjects. It is called the *total sum of squares*, or SS_T. Then, to compute a *variance*, we'd divide the sum of squares by the number of subjects (12). Take the square root of the result and we'd have the *standard deviation* of the whole set of scores (compare pp. 131–133). But these steps aren't necessary for ANOVA, so we won't do them here.

Now, the next step is to break up that variability, the total sum of squares, into two components. Each deviation score

consists of two parts: (1) the deviation of each subject's score from his or her own group mean (the "within-groups" component), and (2) the deviation of that group mean from the grand mean (the "between-groups" component). Figures 6.10B and 6.10C show the idea.

And now we begin to see why this technique is called "analysis of variance." *Analysis* means breaking something up into its components. And that's what we do here: We break up the total variance—or more precisely, the total sum of squares—into the two components that it is made of.

Let's look first at the within-groups component—the deviation of each score from *its own group mean* (Figure 6.10B). These deviation scores are the fourth column of our worksheet. We square them (fifth column) and sum those squares to get the *sum of squares within groups* (SS_W). Here it turns out to be 2,900.

Again, to compute a variance we would divide the sum of squares by the number of subjects that went into it. For technical reasons, however, here we divide

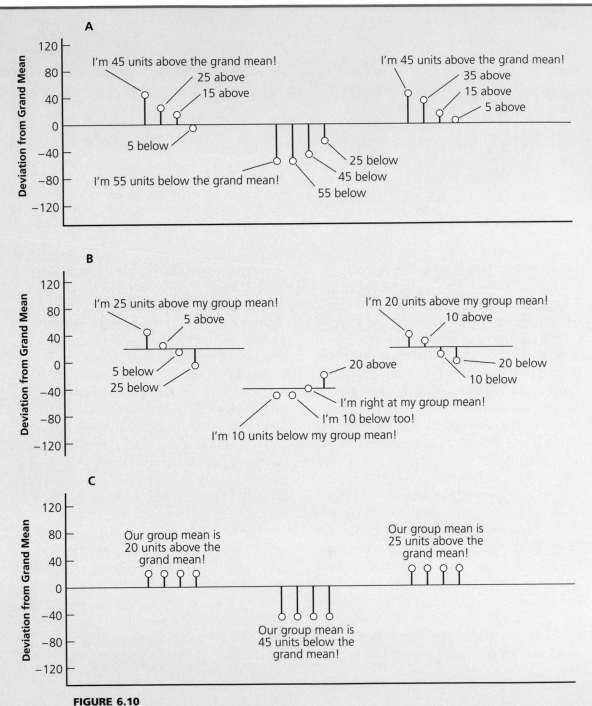

FIGURE 6.10
How the deviations of individual scores from the grand mean (A) can be divided into deviations of scores from the group means (B) and deviations of group means from the grand mean (C).

the sum of squares by the number of *degrees of freedom*. What does that mean?

DIGRESSION: DEGREES OF FREEDOM

The notion is a very simple one. We have a set of scores. Now, how many of these scores are *free to vary*, given what else we know?

Suppose we know that we have three scores, and that their mean is 5. Now, suppose someone tells us a bit more: "Two of the scores are 3 and 10. What's the third score?"

Easy! If the mean is 5, then the three scores must add up to 15, because 15/3 = 5. So if two scores are 3 and 10, the third one must be 2. It can't be anything else, so it is not free to vary. The other two are—we can give them any values we like, and only after that does the third one become fixed.

Thus knowing that there are three scores and the mean is 6, we know the scores must add to 18 (for 18/3 = 6), but we can't specify what any of the scores are. If we know that one of them is 10, we still can't specify either of the other two. But if we know that two of the numbers are 10 and 11, then we know the third one: It *has to be* −3. It can't be anything else.

More generally: If we know the *mean* of a set of N scores, *how many* scores

there are, and *all but one* of the scores themselves, we can calculate what the missing score has to be. So the number of scores that are free to vary is not N, but N − 1.

THE MEAN SQUARES

For the within-groups component, the degrees of freedom turns out to equal the *number of subjects in each group, minus one, summed across groups*. Here we have three groups with four subjects each, so we have $3 \times (4 - 1) = 9$ degrees of freedom. Dividing 2,900 by 9, we get 322.22 as our *mean square* for the within-groups component (MS_w, see Table 6.2).

Then we turn to the *between-groups component*—the deviations of the group means from the grand mean (Figure 6.10C). Here our arithmetic is simpler because we need to consider only the group means and the grand mean. We show that calculation at the bottom of Table 6.1.

Note that we need to multiply each of our squared deviation scores by the *number of subjects* in that group—for that score actually occurs as many times as there are subjects in that group. It is, in other words, a component of *each subject's score*. That is why, in Figure 6.10C, we show four lines, not one, for the deviation of each group mean from the grand mean—there are four subjects in each

Table 6.2
Summary ANOVA Table: Ice Cream Data

Source	SS	df	MS	F
Total	15,100	11		
Between groups	12,200	2	6,100.00	18.93
Within groups	2,900	9	322.22	

group. Adding the results for the three groups, we get 12,200 as the *sum of squares between groups* (SS_B). Then, as before, we divide this sum of squares by the degrees of freedom, to get the *mean square between groups* (MS_B). How many degrees of freedom? It turns out to be the *number of groups, minus one*. So we have two degrees of freedom, and our mean square is 12,200 divided by 2, or 6,100.

PUTTING IT ALL TOGETHER

Now we have everything we need to test the significance of our effect. One way to summarize what we have calculated is to express it as an *ANOVA table* (Table 6.2).

We have another chance to check our arithmetic at this point: The sum of squares between groups, and the sum of squares within groups, should add up to the total sum of squares. And they do. The degrees of freedom within and between groups should also add up to the total degrees of freedom, and they do. Notice, though, that the mean squares are not additive in this way.

What is that last value, F? It is the *ratio of the variability among group means* (mean square between groups) *to the variability within the groups* (mean square within groups). Here, 6,100 divided by 322.22 equals 18.93. It is the statistic that we use to test significance.

As F gets larger, the frequency with which it will occur by chance, if the null hypothesis is true, will get smaller (later we'll see why). Therefore, the probability that that big an F will occur on any given occasion gets smaller, too. Statisticians

know how to calculate these probabilities (compare Chapter 2).

Table B2, pp. 514–516, tells us how big an F we need, in order for it to be significant at various levels of significance. What complicates things just a bit is that we must consider the number of degrees of freedom in both numerator and denominator. Thus here, we have two degrees of freedom (df) in the numerator; so we read across to the column headed "2." We have 9 df in the denominator, so we read down that column to the row for "9." There we find that we need an F greater than 4.26 to be significant at the .05 level.

Ours is larger than that. So, if that is the criterion of significance we have set, then our group means differ significantly from each other. Data such as these, with this number of subjects, would happen by chance less that 5% of the time if the null hypothesis is true. Indeed, these differences would still be significant if we had set our criterion at 0.01, or even at 0.001. These data make the null hypothesis very implausible indeed.

INTERPRETATION

We have shown that the differences among our groups are too large to be plausibly attributed to chance fluctuations. If the null hypothesis were true, we simply would not often see F ratios this large. Where are these differences? Inspecting the original summary figure, we see that Group B subjects on average ate much less than the other two groups, which differed only slightly from each other. It looks as if that low intake for Group B is the source of our significant F. In fact, further statistical analysis will show that this is quite right (see later). Assuming it is true, here is where we are:

We find that if subjects eat an unfamiliar ice cream before they are made nauseous, then they eat relatively little of that ice cream later. This not just because the experience of nausea per se makes children dislike ice cream. Condition C, in which the children were made nauseous without eating the ice cream first, tells us that. And it is not just because children like that flavor less the second time it is offered. Condition A, in which children ate the ice cream but were not made nauseous afterward, tells us that. Rather it is the *pairing* of ice cream with nausea that counts. The children in Condition B have formed a *conditioned aversion* to the taste of that ice cream—after only one conditioning trial! We have successfully replicated Bernstein's original finding.

THE *t* STATISTIC

When there are just *two* treatment groups, there is a closely related statistic known as *t*. For the two-group case, F is simply the square of *t*. So we can calculate F, then take its square root, and we have *t*. But another way of calculating *t*, that may be handier, is to compute MS_w as before, and then enter it into the formula:

$$t = (M_1 - M_2)/\sqrt{MS_w(1/N_1 + 1/N_2)}$$

This is algebraically identical with the other procedure of calculating F first.

As an example, suppose this time we replicate the "bystander intervention" experiment. We have subjects who are witness to a staged "emergency." There are two groups of four subjects each, treated differently. For one of our treatment groups, each subject is alone when the "emergency" occurs; for the other treatment group, each subject has another person with him. We measure the *latency* of each subject's help-giving reaction: How long did it take before he offered help? (We'll assume for simplicity that every subject in both groups did offer help eventually.) We find that for the "alone" subjects the mean latency is 2 minutes, but for the "with another" subjects it is 5 minutes.

We set up our worksheet as before, with the raw data for all subjects in the first column; only this time we need to calculate only SS_w, from the squared deviations of scores from their own group means (third column). SS_w turns out to be 8 , and the within-groups degrees of freedom are $(4 - 1) + (4 - 1) = 6$, so MS_w is 1.33. And the difference between means is 3 minutes. Substituting values in the formula, we get a *t* of 3.659.

Table B3, p. 517, presents critical values of *t*—that is, it tells us the value of *t* that must be exceeded for significance at various levels, for a given number of degrees of freedom. We have (let's assume) set our significance level at 0.05, two-tailed; so under "levels of significance for two-tailed test," we look at the column labeled .05. Following the column down to $df = 6$, we find that *t* must be greater than 2.447 for significance. Our *t* is greater than that, so our results are significant at the .05 level, two-tailed. We have successfully replicated the "multiple bystander" effect.

Table 6.3
Bystander-Intervention Experiment

Condition	Latency (minutes)	Deviation from Group Mean	Deviation Squared
Waiting alone			
Alex	1	−1	1
Arnold	1	−1	1
Andrew	2	0	0
Ali	4	2	4
	Group mean = 2		
Waiting with another			
Brad	4	−1	1
Bart	5	0	0
Bill	5	0	0
Bob	6	1	1
	Group mean = 5		$SS_w = 8$
		$MS_w = 8/6 = 1.33$	

$t = M_1 - M_2/\sqrt{MS_w(1/N_1 + 1/N_2)}$

Since $1/4 + 1/4 = 1/2 = 0.5$,

$t = 3/\sqrt{(1.33 \times 0.5)} = 3/\sqrt{0.67} = 3/0.82 = 3.659 \quad df = 6$

BUT WHAT DOES IT ALL MEAN?

To this point, we have seen what the various sums of squares and mean squares are, and how to combine them to get t or F. But why? What are the numbers telling us?

First, t and F are both *ratios*: One number divided by another. The top term or *numerator* is a measure of *how much the group means vary from one another.* (In the two-group case with direct computation of t, this becomes just the *difference between the two means*.) The bottom term or denominator is, in part, a measure of *how much individual scores vary from each other within groups.*

Now, how much the *group means* vary from one another will depend on how much effect the independent variable has—since the various groups are treated differently, and the difference *is* the independent variable. But *within* each group, all subjects are treated as nearly identi-

cally as possible. Therefore, variability of scores within a group is produced by other, uncontrolled variables: individual differences, measurement error, lapses of attention, and other such things that we'll discuss in the next chapter. So, putting it all together, we have this: *What t or F tells us is how much effect the independent variable had, relative to the effects of other variables.*

Let's look more closely.

THE NUMERATOR:
THE INDEPENDENT VARIABLE

When we test significance, our question is: Can we be confident that our independent variable had an effect? Or is it plausible that it really had no effect, and that the differences we see just "happened to happen" by accident? The latter possibility—that it really had no effect—is our *null hypothesis.*

It is obvious that other things equal, the more the two group means differ from each other, the less plausible it is that the difference "just happened." Suppose the subjects who were waiting alone were, on average, only a *little bit* faster than the subjects who were waiting with others.

Then mere chance is a plausible explanation for that small difference. But if they were *very much* faster on average, then mere chance is a less plausible explanation.

We see this in Figure 6.11. In Panel A, the difference between the two means is quite small, relative to the variability within

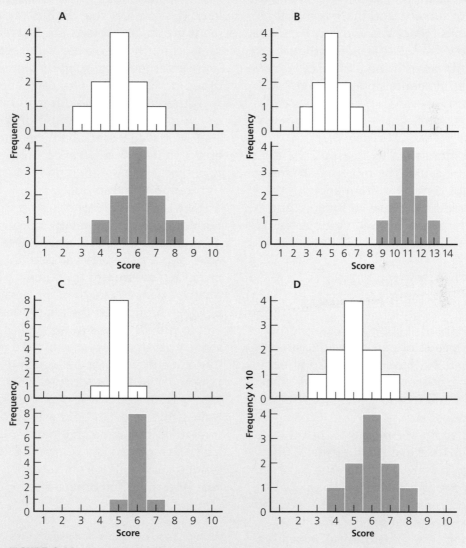

FIGURE 6.11
Some factors that will affect an outcome of a significance test (here, a *t*-test). A non-significant difference between two groups (A) might become significant if the group means were farther apart (B), or if the variability of the data within each group were reduced (C), or if larger groups of subjects were used (D).

the groups. It seems that the difference might easily have happened just by chance. And in fact, if we compute a t on these data, we find that it is only 1.937—not significant with $(10 -) + (10 - 1) = 18$ df (for the distributions show us that there are 10 subjects per group). But in Panel B, the mean difference is much larger, though the number of subjects and the shape of the distributions (hence the within-groups variability) stay the same. Data like that would very seldom occur if the difference was due to chance fluctuations only. And now with the larger numerator ($11 - 5 = 6$ instead of 1), the t is significant: It is 11.628, and we only need a t of 2.01 (Table B.3).

With more than two groups, the argument is the same. The more the means of the groups differ one from another, the greater will be the sum of squares, and the mean square, between groups—and, therefore, the greater F will be.

THE DENOMINATOR:
UNCONTROLLED VARIABLES

So, other things equal, t or F gets larger as the effect of our independent variable gets larger. But other things also affect F or t. One of them is how much the scores vary from one to another *within* the treatment groups.

Look again at Figure 6.11, but this time compare Panel A with Panel C. In these two panels, the difference between the two means is the same. But in Panel C, I have supposed that the variability within groups is very much smaller than in A. That shrinks the value of MS_W, which is a measure of the variability within the groups. And that means in turn that t will

be larger; here it becomes 4.74, which is significant with 18 df. In short, if the scores vary less from one another within treatment groups, MS_W will be smaller, and F or t will be larger and more likely to be significant.

Why? Well, if scores vary one from another, something must be making them vary. But consider that within any treatment group, all subjects are treated the same as much as possible: same setting, same emergency, all subjects alone in one group or all subjects with someone else in the other. If scores still differ from one another, it can only be because of things that we haven't controlled: measurement errors, individual differences from subject to subject, momentary moods, fluctuations of attention, and so on.

Now, if our null hypothesis is true—if our differences in conditions really make no difference—then these uncontrolled variables also are the *only* variables that are producing differences from one mean to another! If that is so, then the mean square between groups and the mean square within groups ought to be about the same. Therefore, F ought to be about 1.* Of course it need not be *exactly* 1—it may be somewhat larger, or somewhat smaller, just by chance. But if it is *very much* larger than 1, then we can be pretty sure that something is making the means different from each other, *over and above* what produces variability from subject to subject. And that "something else" must be

---

*Because of some mathematical complexities, we would expect Fs near 1 and ts near zero when the null hypothesis is true. Advanced statistics texts explain this in more detail.

the differences among conditions—the independent variable.

So we come back to our previous statement: What our *t* or F tells us is how much effect the independent variable had (given by the numerator), *relative to* the effects of other variables (given by the denominator).*

THE ROLE OF SAMPLE SIZE

There's one other consideration. If the null hypothesis is false (there really is an effect), and if all else is equal, we become more likely to detect the effect—that is, get a significant *t* or F—as we increase *the number of subjects per group*.

Look now at the difference between Panels A and D in Figure 6.11. This time, both the mean difference and the shapes of frequency distributions are as they originally were. But in Panel D, I've assumed that we're dealing with groups of 100 rather than groups of 10. Thus the bar that represented one subject before now represents 10 subjects, the bar that represented two now represents 20, and so on. So we just multiply all our frequencies by 10, as shown. And that too changes our original nonsignificant difference into a significant one: now *t* becomes a healthy 6.410, significant at the .05 level with $99 + 99 = 198$ df.[†]

---

*Some find it helpful to think of these statistics as *signal-to-noise ratios*: how much effect our independent variable had (the "signal"), relative to the "background noise" of the effects of other variables. If that way of picturing it helps you, use it; if not, feel free to ignore it.

[†]This table doesn't show 198 df values. But our *t* would be significant even at df = 60, so it must necessarily be significant with df higher than that.

Why? Because a mean is more stable than the individual data points that go into it. Individual subjects' scores will be affected by chance fluctuations that move the scores up or down. But for a mean based on several of those points, the averaging will tend to cancel out those individual fluctuations. The more such data points are averaged together, the more complete the cancellation process will be. So it becomes unlikely that those chance fluctuations will make the means very different from each other. And the more subjects per groups, the more unlikely this is.

Actually, an increase in group size makes a significant outcome more likely in two ways. First, it makes the denominator smaller, and so *t* or F gets bigger. Second, it gives us more degrees of freedom in our denominator, so that our F or *t* does not have to be as large to be significant.

◄ A LOOK BACK

In this discussion, we have found three things that affect the size of our test statistic *t* or F, and so affect whether an effect will be significant. They are:

1. Differences among group means. The greater the differences, the more likely they are to be significant. And we see that how big the differences are depends on the *power of our independent variable*.

2. Variability within groups. The less our scores vary within groups, the smaller MS_W will be and hence the bigger *t* and F will be. What makes this variability large or small? Our *degree of control over other variables*. Tight control means less variability, and a bigger *t* or F. We'll elaborate this in the next chapter.

3. Size of the groups. All else equal, differences among means are more likely to be significant as *sample size* increases.

Be sure you understand these ideas. We will return to them in later chapters.

BETWEEN-GROUPS COMPARISONS AFTER ANOVA

With this background, we can return to the case of more than two groups. Here we would use the F test, as we did in our earlier illness-and-ice-cream example. If we get a significant F (as we did), then what it tells us is: We can be confident that something more than chance is making the group means differ from each other. Our independent variable, therefore, is having an effect. But where is the effect? Are scores under Condition B significantly lower than under A and C? Are the C scores significantly higher than the A scores? Where, among these groups, are the differences we can be confident of?

It might occur to us just to do *t*-tests for all possible two-group comparisons. Using *t*, we could test the difference between Groups A and B, between Groups A and C, and between Groups B and C. Not a good idea, and here's why:

When we do a single *t*-test, we are asking in effect: What is the probability that *this one t*-value will be significant by chance, if the null hypothesis is true? We set that probability at, say 0.05. But what if we do three *t*-tests, and ask: What is the probability that *any of the three* will be significant by chance? Then matters change.

It is easiest to calculate if we turn the problem around. If the null hypothesis is true, then the probability that any particular *t* will *not* be significant is 0.95—that is, $1 - 0.05$. But then the probability that *all* of our *t*s will be nonsignificant—A versus B, and B versus C, and A versus C—is just $.95 \times .95 \times .95$, or 0.857. Therefore, the probability that *at least one t* will be significant, by chance, is 1 minus that, or 0.143—which is much greater than 0.05! If we do it that way, we will run an unacceptably high risk that at least one difference—maybe more!—will be significant just by chance.

There are a number of statistical tests that get around this problem. We will consider only one: the Scheffe test (say Shef-FAY), named after its inventor. It allows us to compare pairs of means with each other, in such a way that the *overall risk* of finding one or more significant *t*, by chance, is no greater than the risk we are willing to accept.

What the Scheffe test does is a bit different from what we are used to. Rather than computing a *t* and looking at a table to see whether it is significant, we compute *how large the difference between two means has to be*, to be significant at the level we have set. We compute it as follows:

$$(M_1 - M_2)_{crit} = \sqrt{[(df_{between})(F_{crit})(MS_W)(1/N_1 + 1/N_2)]}$$

where F_{crit} is the F we need for significance, given the degrees of freedom we have. That, we know (because we have just looked it up), is 4.26. We know that $df_{between}$ is 2; and we calculated MS_W to be 322.22. So, substituting, we get:

$$(M_1 - M_2)_{crit}$$
$$= \sqrt{[2 \times 4.26 \times 322.22 \times (1/4 + 1/4)]}$$
$$= \text{sqr root } (1372.65) = 37.05$$

as the critical value for the *difference between the two means* that we are comparing. In other words, for any two means that are at least 37.05 units apart, the difference between them is significant at the 0.05 level.

Looking back over the group means, we see that the difference between Groups A and B is large enough to be significant. So is the difference between Groups B and C. But the difference between Groups A and C is not. Those two means are not significantly different from each other.

We use the Scheffe test only if—and after—we find that the overall F test gives a significant outcome. That tells us that *some* differences among the group means are significant. Then, using the Scheffe test, we can go on to ask *where* in the data those significant differences are.

ASSUMPTIONS OF THE F AND *t* TESTS

To review, the *t* statistic is used to test the difference between two groups. The F statistic can be used for any number of groups.

There are, as always, some assumptions to be met. First and most important, once again we must be sure that all the observations are independent of each other—that is, no subject's score is affected by anyone else's. In addition, the mathematical derivation of the *p*-values assumes (1) that the different groups have approximately equal variances, and (2) that each group's frequency distribution has the familiar bell shape of the so-called "normal curve." It turns out, though, that F and *t* are not much affected by modest violations of these last two assumptions, *if* the number of subjects is approximately the same in all groups. In setting up an independent-groups experiment, therefore, the careful researcher will ensure that all groups are the same size.

Finally, it should be emphasized that everything we have done in this section, with both *t* and F, is appropriate specifically for *between-groups designs.* We assume, that is, that we have divided subjects *at random* into groups, from an initial "pool" of available subjects. With other designs—for example, matched-pair or within-subjects designs—the calculations of *t* and F must be modified. A full discussion would simply make this book too long. Texts on statistics must be our guides.

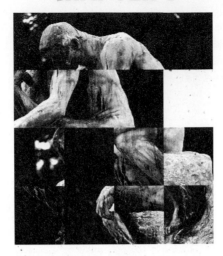

CHAPTER 7

EXPERIMENTAL CONTROL I: OBSCURING FACTORS

I did not imitate the skeptics who doubt only for doubting's sake . . . on the contrary, my whole intention was to arrive at a certainty, and to dig away the drift and the sand until I reached the rock or the clay beneath.

—RENE DESCARTES

IN THIS CHAPTER, WE'LL DISCUSS:

- What experimental control is
- The two kinds of control problem
- Influences that can make an effect difficult to see
  Ineffective manipulation
  Measurement error
  Ceiling/floor effects
  Variability in the data
- Ways of reducing these problems when they arise
- Laboratory and field experiments
- Relation of control procedures to significance tests

Ideally, an experiment would look like this: We cause something to vary (the independent variable), and we can see how this affects our measure (the dependent variable), because *nothing else* affects it (Figure 7.1A).

But of course a real world experiment is not like that. Our measure will be affected by all sorts of other, irrelevant things, as well

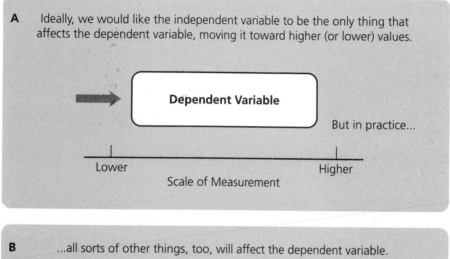

A   Ideally, we would like the independent variable to be the only thing that affects the dependent variable, moving it toward higher (or lower) values.

Dependent Variable

But in practice...

Lower   Higher

Scale of Measurement

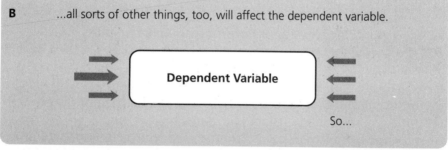

B   ...all sorts of other things, too, will affect the dependent variable.

Dependent Variable

So...

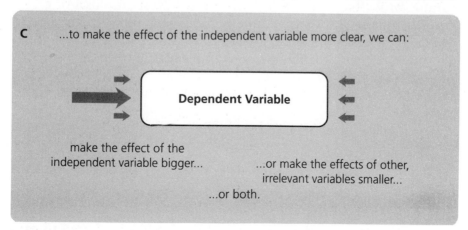

C   ...to make the effect of the independent variable more clear, we can:

Dependent Variable

make the effect of the independent variable bigger...

...or make the effects of other, irrelevant variables smaller...

...or both.

FIGURE 7.1
The problem of obscuring variables, and how we try to solve it.

as by what we vary (Figure 7.1B). All we can do is take steps to minimize the effects of these "other things."

That is what we mean by *experimental control*. It is the attempt to minimize the effects of other influences on our dependent variable, so that we can see most clearly the effect of the variable that is of interest—the independent variable.

TWO KINDS OF CONTROL PROBLEMS

What sorts of "other things" are there? They are of two kinds—which means we face two kinds of control problems in planning an experiment. The two are quite different from each other, and so have separate chapters here.

One kind keeps us from seeing anything at all. They may make the data so unclear that we simply can't draw any conclusions. These are the "drift and the sand" that Descartes wanted to get rid of, so as to see what was going on (the "rock or the clay"). They include ineffective manipulations; ceiling/floor effects; or too much variability in the data, produced by measurement error, individual differences, distractions in the situation, and the like. I call these *"obscuring factors,"* to parallel the standard term *confounding factors*.

That's the other kind of "other thing"—*confounding factors*, or *confounded variables*. We may see an effect, all right, but we may not know what it is an effect *of*. We cannot interpret the effect. This can be true no matter how large, clear, and statistically significant the effect is, if we allow confounded variables to operate.

In other words: When we find, or read, that this or that manipulation *did not* have an effect, then we worry about obscuring factors. The apparent absence of an effect may just reflect poor control over such factors—in a word, a sloppy experiment. In contrast, if we find, or read, that a manipulation *did* have an effect, then we worry about confounding factors. Yes, the effect may be there all right; but can we be sure what produced it? We'll focus on that problem in the next chapter.

HOW TO GET NULL RESULTS: OBSCURING FACTORS

A *nonsignificant*, or inconclusive, set of data is often referred to as a "null finding," or a "null result." "Null" means "nothing" (as in "null hypothesis"), and a null result simply means: We can't be sure that our manipulation did anything. Maybe it did nothing.

There are two possible reasons for a null finding. The first, obviously, is that our independent variable really *does not* affect our dependent variable. We thought it might (or we wouldn't have done the experiment), but it doesn't. The second possibility is that our independent variable really *does* affect our dependent variable, and a more precise experiment would have shown that effect; but the data we obtained did not show it clearly. It is that second state of affairs that we want to avoid if we can.

Now, with that second possibility in mind, let's look at some things that could cause our data to be inconclusive.

INEFFECTIVE MANIPULATIONS

If we vary something, and it has no consistent effect, one possibility is: Maybe we didn't vary it *enough*.

Suppose I want to know whether anxiety affects test performance in a class of students. I divide the class at random into two groups: one to be made anxious, the other not. I stand in front of the experimental group and say to them, "Boo!" Then I give the test. And guess what? The two groups don't differ significantly.

Of course they don't! My feeble manipulation probably hasn't created any anxiety at all. I simply haven't caused anxiety to vary from one group to another, so why should the groups behave differently, even if *real* anxiety would make them do so?

AN EXAMPLE FROM ANIMAL BEHAVIOR

But let us turn to a real example. This one is instructive, because it is a case—and they happen—in which a highly competent experimenter made a mistake.

The experimenter (Adolph, 1947) asked this question: Do rats eat for taste or for calories? More specifically: If we make the food taste especially good, will rats eat more and gain more weight than if we offer them only standard rat food? So one group of rats was offered only the standard food; this was the control group. The other group was offered food sweetened with saccharin. And it made no difference at all. Food intake and weight gain were virtually identical for the two groups.

This flawed study misled research in this area for many years. It gave rise to a myth that still dies hard: that rats regulate their caloric intake, holding it constant in the face of variations in the diet (see Mook, 1990, for discussion).

But subsequent research has made it clear that this is not so. In one experiment (Sclafani & Springer, 1976) rats were offered a "cafeteria" in which a variety of common foods was available: chocolate chip cookies, cheese, bananas, salami, milk chocolate, peanut butter. . . . These rats—perfectly normal rats—gained nearly three times as much weight as their controls over a two-month period! Diets high in fat can produce similar effects (Corbit & Stellar, 1964).

So rats will drastically increase their caloric intake if offered a varied or especially attractive diet. Why did the original investigator not see this effect? Because he didn't vary attractiveness *enough*. Adding saccharin to rat chow increases its attractiveness only very slightly, if at all. It is, in a word, a feeble manipulation. A stronger manipulation shows the effect of diet attractiveness, loud and clear.

MANIPULATION CHECKS

Because a feeble manipulation is so often a danger, many experiments will include what is called a *manipulation check*. This is a separate measure or set of observations designed to tell us whether we have, in fact, manipulated what we intended to manipulate. If an experimental condition is designed to make subjects anxious, one may include some physiological measurements—or, at the very least, some self-report data—to be sure that it really *has* made the subjects anxious (Schachter, 1959).

Or, as a different example: Suppose we have damaged part of the brain in a rat or cat; for example, severed the connections between the two cerebral hemispheres (Chapter 10). After the experiment is over, we will examine stained sections of the brain, under a microscope, to see whether we have severed all and only the connections we intended to sever. That is also a manipulation check.

Now, examining a rat's brain is a far cry, on the surface, from measuring (say) skin conductance in a human subject to check his anxiety level! The underlying logic, however, is the same. We want to be sure that we really have manipulated—and manipulated effectively—what we intended to manipulate.

MEASUREMENT ERROR

Here is another source of inconclusive data: inconsistent measurements.

Suppose we treat some subjects with a drug, one that we think will reduce hunger (or depression, or whatever). A little later, we ask each subject, "How hungry do you feel? Please rate it on a zero-to-twelve scale."

In Figure 7.2A, we suppose that the drug does reduce hunger and has a strong effect. Hunger is consistently lower in the experimental subjects (filled circles) than in the controls (open circles).

But suppose the numbers the subjects give us simply do not reflect how hungry they really are. Thus: John is very hungry and should say "Ten!", but he doesn't like to use extreme numbers, so he gives us a moderate 6. Jean is not very hungry, because of the drug injection, but she knows it's lunchtime and she *should* be hungry, so she calls out a moderately high number. Joan is quite hungry, but in trying to lose weight she consistently denies to herself how hungry she is, and so denies it to us too. Jim is very hungry and should give us a high number, but he doesn't *know* he's very hungry, so again we get a moderate number. (If that sounds strange, consider how we say, "Look how much I ate! I was hungrier than I thought.")

And so on. Let there be much of this sort of thing, and the data will be about as consistent as scrambled eggs (Figure 7.2B). And remember: The numbers the subjects call out or write down are *all the data we are going to have*. In drawing Panel A of Figure 7.2, I pretended to have some sort of crystal ball by which we could know what the data *should* look like. In real life, there will be no such crystal ball. The equivalent of Panel B is all we're going to get.

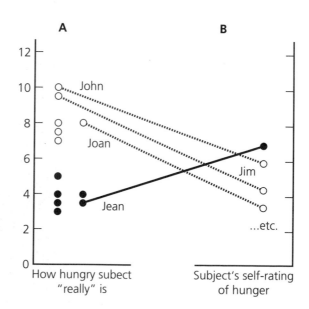

FIGURE 7.2
Measurement errors can make for messy data.

What can we do about this sort of thing? We can try to increase the precision of our measurements.

A lot of time, trouble, and, yes, expense, can go into the search for precise measures. Consider the rat data I collected (shown in Fig. 3.11, p. 93) on the interval between one lick at a drinking spout and the following lick. These intervals are on the order of 150 to 300 milliseconds. Imagine my trying to do that by keeping one eye on the rat and the other on a watch with a sweep second hand, and writing down readings! Out of the question. What I did instead was install a rather expensive gadget that (1) generated an electrical signal when the rat's tongue contacted the fluid, and (2) fed those signals to a quite expensive computer that calculated the intervals I needed.

Or think about the "mental rotation" experiments (Chapter 6). Figure 6.2 showed that the promptness of the subject's response does vary with degree of rotation, but the differences are in fractions of a second. Now, Shepard and Metzler could have set up a human observer and equipped her with a stopwatch: start it when the figures appear on the screen, stop it when the subject *says* "yes" or "no." Almost certainly this would have turned the data into oatmeal. The experimenter's reaction speed would vary from trial to trial, both starting and stopping. Speed of speech itself would vary, perhaps a lot—on some trials the yes/no response may be preceded by "Uh . . . ," on others not. And so on.

Instead, rather expensive apparatus was set up. The same electrical signal that presented the stimulus on the screen also started a timing device. The timer stopped when the subject pressed one or another of two buttons, on which his fingers already rested. Precise measurement allowed precise data, as Figure 6.2 showed.

Where an increase in precision is not possible, one may simply have to live with measurement error. In that case, we must use enough subjects, and try for a powerful enough manipulation, to allow us to see an effect despite it.

CEILING–FLOOR EFFECTS

This problem is a special case of measurement error. But it is a very special case, so we discuss it separately. It is a way of virtually *guaranteeing* null results, if we allow it to happen.

Let's begin with an obvious example. I once collected some in-class data on this question: Do men and women differ in their mathematical skill? I asked the class to write down the answer to this

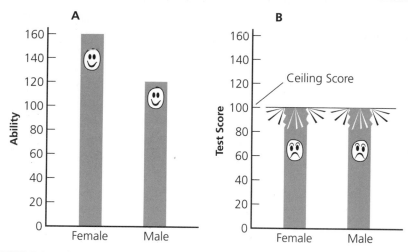

FIGURE 7.3

If scores on a dependent variable are already so high that they can go no higher, differences among subjects or among conditions may be impossible to see.

question: What is 7×5? And guess what? Men and women performed identically!

A silly example? Yes, to make the point. Who knows—perhaps there is a gender difference in mathematical skill, for all I know (Figure 7.3A). But if *all* scores are at 100%, they can go no higher, and we cannot see any difference between groups. The scores are pressed up against a "ceiling" of perfect performance (Figure 7.3B).

In real-life research, we want to be sure that our measurements are not squeezed up against one or the other end of the scale, obscuring possible differences. If a task is so easy that everyone performed perfectly on it (as here), then subjects under one condition *could not* perform any differently from subjects under another. We would speak of a *ceiling effect*. Conversely, if a task were so difficult that no one performed better than chance, then all scores would be at the "floor"—chance level—and again could not differ between one condition and another. We would speak of a "floor effect."

Actually, "ceiling" and "floor" effects are often just different ways of talking about the same thing. If our task is too easy, we might say that performance is so good that it could not be any better—a ceiling effect. Or we could say that number of errors is so low that it could not get any lower—a floor effect.

Anticipating ceiling/floor effects is often in the back of experimenters' minds when they select the conditions of an experiment. Take our hunger experiment, for instance. If the subjects are to be tested for intake of a standard breakfast, we might ask them not to eat for some fixed interval beforehand—say, overnight. This would reduce obscuring variability in how hungry the subjects were when intake was measured (see later discussion). But it also avoids the possibility that all, or many, of the subjects would come to the lab right after eating a big breakfast on their own. If they did that, they might eat very little of the experimental meal, and any differences between conditions could be abolished by a ceiling/floor effect. Again we could express it either way. The subjects might come to the lab so full that they could get no fuller—a ceiling effect. Or, intakes of the test meal might all be so low that they could go no lower—a floor effect.

VARIABILITY I: INDIVIDUAL DIFFERENCES

We turn now to another, major source of null findings: Simple *variability* in the data. This can arise from any or all of several sources.

THE PROBLEM

To get clear on the problem, and on some possible solutions to it, we can get still more mileage out of our hunger experiment. Suppose there are two groups of subjects, one receiving a drug, the other a placebo, before breakfast. And rather than asking the subjects how hungry they are, suppose we measure how much they eat. That's an objective measure, and *measurement error* can be very small: We could weigh each subject's plate to the nearest milligram, if we wished.

Even so, Panel A of the Figure 7.4 shows data that are far from clear. This could happen simply because of *individual differences* in appetite. Thus we suppose that John is a big eater. Maybe the drug has reduced his appetite (we don't know), but it's still big, and so he takes a large lunch. Jo, on the other hand, takes a small meal even under the control condition, because she doesn't eat much for breakfast in any case. And so on. So, looking over the data, we see that on average the experimental subjects did eat less than the controls. But the data are thoroughly mixed and far from consistent; there's a very great deal of overlap. The difference would not reach statistical significance. Individual differences in appetite obscure it.

CONTROL BY EXPERIMENTAL DESIGN

But now, look at Panel B (we'll return to Panel C later). Suppose I tell you that each pair of points, connected by a line, represents a

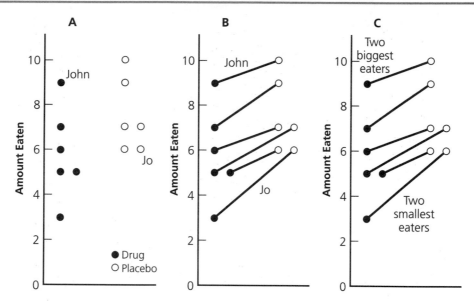

FIGURE 7.4
How a within-subjects or matched design can reduce variability.

single person for whom we took measurements under *both* conditions. Thus the top pair of points represents John's intake under each condition; the bottom pair, Jo's; and so on.

Do you see what has happened here? The individual data points are right where they were in Panel A. But the pairing process has turned a thoroughly scrambled set of data into a clear and very consistent finding: *Every single subject* ate less under the drug condition than under the placebo condition. This includes John, whose appetite was big; Jo, whose appetite was small; and everybody in between. A simple sign test would give us a significant outcome here ($p = 0.031$; why?).

That is how a within-subjects design, which compares each subject with himself or herself, controls for individual differences. Finally, notice that we accomplished all this using only *half as many subjects* as in the original, two-group experiment. Those are the two great strengths of within-subjects designs: They *control individual differences*, and they *require fewer subjects* than between-groups comparisons.

Now, it's true that we buy these advantages at some cost. We must test each subject twice; and since the food we offer should of course be held constant, the subject may just get bored with the food the second time around. If so, this is a "carryover effect" that we can control by *counterbalancing*. If half the subjects get the drug first and the placebo second, and for the other half the order is reversed, then boredom should affect both conditions equally in the data as a whole.

But then again, we recall that counterbalancing is not always possible (pp. 196–197). In some such cases, *matched-group designs* can do a similar job of controlling for individual differences (pp. 198–200). Thus in Figure 7.4C the lines might connect *pairmates*. Thus John and Jan might be the two heaviest eaters, as determined by a previous, "baseline" measure of food intake. So we pair them, and compare them with each other—one receiving placebo, the other drug, before the test meal. Similarly with Jo and Jerry, our two lightest eaters. We would then see the same reduction in variability as before.

Again there are costs. We are back to our original number of subjects, first of all; and, in addition, we have to get the initial "baseline" measurement of meal size that we used to match the subjects. We simply have to decide whether the gain in control is worth the added cost and effort.

Thus, within-subject designs (and matched-group designs) are powerful ways of reducing the variability produced by individual differences. Since individual differences are a major source of variability and inconsistency in the data, this makes them very useful tools indeed.

VARIABILITY II: THE SITUATION

Think again about the mental-rotation experiments. The more rotation required, the longer it took subjects to make their judgments—but the differences were in seconds or fractions of a second.

Now, imagine trying to conduct such experiments on a busy street corner! Out of the question. Apart from the logistical problems—where do we plug in the apparatus?—the sheer amount of distraction in the situation would make a mess of the data. Horns beeping, sirens wailing, people jostling and talking and running to and fro—who could concentrate on judgments of the congruence or incongruence of geometric figures under those conditions? And the amount of distraction would *vary*, from subject to subject and from moment to moment for a given subject. The result? Variability in the data once again.

Thus, *variability in the external situation can create variability in the data*. So can variability in what we might call the "internal situation." Some subjects will be distracted by thoughts of an upcoming exam or a recent fight with a significant other; other subjects will not. Some subjects will have a lot of caffeine in their systems, others little or none. Some will be more tired and/or grouchy than others. And so on. To the extent that these "internal" factors affect the data, they will again tend to make for variability and inconsistency from one subject to another.

For some purposes, adequate control over the external situation requires meticulous attention to detail. For example, here is how Ivan Pavlov described his conditioning laboratory (Figure 7.5):

> It was evident that the experimental conditions had to be simplified . . . eliminating as far as possible any stimuli outside our con-

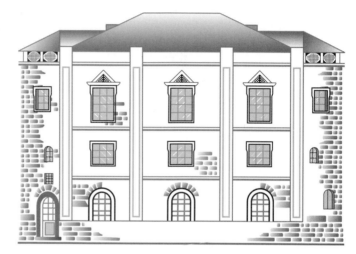

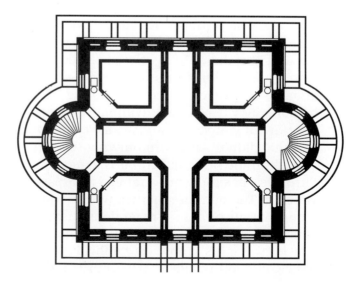

FIGURE 7.5
Pavlov's laboratory.
(Top) The exterior: The beams supporting the entire building are immersed in sand, and a moat filled with straw surrounds it, to deaden vibrations. (Bottom) Floor plan of the first and third floors: The four inner rooms are separated from the outer wall and from each other by corridors, and the first and third floors are separated from each other by the second floor, which houses equipment. Within each room the dog is separated from the experimenter by a partition. The attempt is to ensure that *no* stimuli—no noises, no vibrations, no anything—can affect the dog during an experiment, except those stimuli (CS and UCS) that the experimenter presents (from Kaplan, 1965).

trol which might fall upon the animal, admitting only such stimuli as could be entirely controlled by the experimenter. It was thought at the beginning of our research that it would be sufficient simply to isolate the experimenter in the research chamber with the dog on its stand, and to refuse admission to anyone else during the course of the experiment. But this precaution was found to be wholly inadequate, since the experimenter, however still he might try to be, was himself a constant source of a large number of stimuli. His slightest movements—blinking of the eyelids or movements of the eyes, posture, expiration and so on—all acted as stimuli which, falling on the dog, were sufficient to vitiate the experiments [that is, to make the data muddy by the distractions they produced]. Footfalls of a passerby, chance conversations in neighbouring rooms, slamming of a door, or vibrations from a passing van . . . any of these caused uncontrolled [and distracting] stimuli. . . .

To get over all these disturbing factors a special laboratory was built at the Institute of Experimental Medicine in Petrograd. . . . Inside the building all the research rooms (four to each floor) were isolated from each other by a cross-shaped corridor. . . . Each research room was carefully partitioned by the use of sound-proof materials into two compartments—one for the animal, the other for the experimenter. For stimulating the animal and for registering the corresponding reflex response, electrical methods or pneumatic transmission were used. . . . (Pavlov, 1927/1960, pp. 20–21)

A modern conditioning laboratory could be described in similar terms. For example, in a typical conditioning experiment done with ideal facilities, a rat might be placed in a small box; the box will be placed inside another, soundproofed box; *that* box will be placed on a sheet of foam rubber, to dampen vibrations produced by footsteps and the like; and the whole business will be placed in a small cubicle and the door firmly closed. Electrical devices, with wires fed through a conduit in the wall, will present stimuli and register the animal's responses. Direct monitoring of behavior, if we wish, can be done by videocamera, without telling the rat anything about it.

Now of course not all labs have such facilities. I have taught in labs that didn't. And I can only say this: The farther we depart from that ideal, the more difficult it is to get consistent conditioning data. Sure, we can simply put a rat in a transparent box on a tabletop, and watch it. The odds are that we will be watching it watching *us*—and crouching, in profound rodentious suspicion, at every move, every cough, every approach or departure of a hominid from the group of watchers. . . . It's simply very difficult to demonstrate even the most basic conditioning phenomena in such a situation.

In human research too, *some* research projects demand fanatical attention to detail. Take, for example, research on the sense of smell. To study this sense (a wonderfully sensitive one), we of course want to introduce smells into our subjects' noses. The problem is that we live in a symphony of odors; all sorts of *other* smells, that are not of interest, are already finding their way into our subject's nose. Odorous particles are drifting off the walls and into her nose. Odorous particles are drifting up from her clothing and into her nose. Odorous particles are drifting up from the skin of her face and into her nose, and no amount of scrubbing will remove them.

How to get rid of these extraneous, variable odors? By such means as the following: Place the subject in a steam-cleaned plastic enclosure. Put a steam-cleaned plastic parka around her, snugged tight under the chin, to trap odors from her clothes. Put a layer of Vaseline over her face to trap the odors arising from her skin. *Then* we can let her smell only what we want her to smell, introducing the odors via tubes placed gently in her nostrils. Such experiments have been done—really!

Now for most research, we needn't go to such extremes. The subjects in the mental-rotation experiments, and the bystander-intervention experiments, did not have Vaseline all over their faces; nor, for that matter, did Harlow's baby monkeys or even Pavlov's dogs. For many purposes, it will be sufficient to have a quiet room, free of distractions. Perhaps there will be a sign in the hall: "Experiment in progress. Quiet please," or something of the sort.

All this takes us to the questions: Just how much control over the situation should we try for? How much do we need? Let us discuss these.

HOW MUCH TO CONTROL?

In an ideal world, an independent variable would be varied, with *everything else* held constant. But experiments are conducted in the real world. In that world, it is useless to say: "Control all extraneous variables." We can't.

Consider: When a subject begins his participation, do we control what kind of mood he is in? How? And if we do, do we control his mood on the previous day? Or: Do we control how recently our subject has had a meal? If so, do we control what he ate at that meal? If so, what about the meal before *that*? Clearly, at some point we must stop. To control *everything* is simply not possible.

Here's what we do instead, and it expands on the fundamental principle of experimental control that we saw earlier (p. 191). *We control the extraneous variables that are most important. And what we don't control, we randomize.*

And what do we mean by "most important"? Again, a

Principle: The most important extraneous variables to control are those that have the greatest effect on the dependent variable.

Thus if we are studying the sense of smell, we try to get rid of extraneous odors. Why? Because these will have a big effect on the subjects' responses to the odors *we* present. But if we are studying mental rotation or bystander intervention, we won't worry about extraneous odors (hence, no Vaseline). Why not? Because stray odors will *not* have much if any effect on speed of judgment, or tendency to offer help—our dependent variables.

Again: In our drug-and-hunger experiment, we might control what subjects have eaten recently. Why? Because that could have a big effect on how much they eat now—the dependent variable. Latané and Darley, in their bystander-intervention studies, did *not* control what their subjects had eaten recently. Why not? Because that would have minor effects—some perhaps, but not much—on the dependent variable: willingness to offer help in an emergency.

There are no hard and fast rules here. "How much to control" is a series of decisions and judgment calls.

For example, consider the bystander-intervention studies again. We can imagine that if all subjects had the same amount of caffeine in their systems, the data might be a bit more consistent than if they didn't. Caffeine could affect mood, and mood could affect willingness to help. So, do we control caffeine level? Remember that some people don't drink coffee at all. Others cannot begin a day without two cups at least.

Do we *control* our subjects' coffee intake? Do we force all subjects to drink a fixed amount of coffee (perhaps zero) on the day of the experiment? We could. But it would certainly be an intrusion into our subjects' lives. It might just substitute one source of variability for another: Some subjects would be suffering the discomfort of caffeine withdrawal, others not. All told, we probably would decide that it simply *is not worth it*. It might make the data a bit cleaner, yes; but not *much* cleaner, and not *enough* cleaner to justify the cost—in effort and in discomfort to our subjects.

Instead, we would depend on the *randomization* process to make it likely that, on average, our subject groups are not very different in coffee content. That is what we mean when we say: *What we don't control, we randomize.*

So in deciding whether to control a variable, we do a kind of cost/benefit analysis. We ask: If we control this or that variable, how much would we reduce variability in the data? At what cost—in money, time, effort, and intrusion into our subjects' lives? And finally: Is the benefit worth the cost?

We make these judgments, sometimes guided by the published literature or the advice of older hands; we find out, that is, what has worked for others who have done similar experiments. Or we may make them by intuition, by guess and by golly. And then—why, then we do the experiment and see. The *data can tell us* whether our decisions were good ones.

After all, the whole point of control is to allow our independent variable to have a clear effect. So, if it *does* have a clear effect—if we get a significant effect—then we know that the variables we have left uncontrolled (but randomized) are not important enough to obscure that effect. Hence the rule: If we see a clear effect of our independent variable, then we know that our control *over obscuring factors* is adequate.

Confounded variables are another matter entirely. We will turn to them in the next chapter. First, however, we should look at a different approach to the problem of situational control.

SACRIFICING CONTROL: THE FIELD EXPERIMENT

To this point, we have been focusing on experiments done in laboratories. Now a lab is really just a *simplified situation.* Because it is simplified, we can control what goes on in it. We can eliminate or hold constant many *situational* sources of variability in the data.

It is also possible, however, to do experiments in natural settings. That is what a *field experiment* is: We introduce our manipulation into a natural situation. Rather than controlling situational variables, we let them vary as they normally would, in the hope that our manipulation will have a consistent effect anyway.

AN EXAMPLE FROM SOCIAL PSYCHOLOGY:
THE LIQUOR STORE ROBBERY

As our first example, let's go back to the "bystander" studies. We remember that in response to a staged "emergency," a single onlooker would be likely to take some action and try to help; but if there was more than one onlooker, the chances that any of them would try to help was greatly reduced.

Now these were laboratory experiments. Would the same sort of thing happen in a natural situation? To find out, Latané and Darley (1970) staged an emergency in a natural setting—a liquor store.

The "staging" was of course all worked out in advance with the proprietor of the store. It went like this: Two men (the experimenters) would enter the liquor store. They would send the proprietor to the back of the store to look for some exotic brew or other; then they simply picked up a case of beer near the front, and walked off with it.

The subjects in this experiment were real liquor store customers, who had come into the store to buy liquor and had no idea that they were in an experiment. The "crimes" were staged sometimes when there was only one real customer present, and sometimes when there were two. This was the independent variable: Number of real customers—that is, onlookers to the "emergency" of the apparent theft. Question: Would the customer(s) report the theft to the proprietor when he came back?

Answer: It depended—again—on the number of onlookers. The theft was more likely to be reported if only one customer witnessed it than if two customers did. In other words, the multiple-onlooker effect showed up again.

By the way, here we see another great advantage of experiments: They make things happen at will, as opposed to waiting for relevant events to happen naturally. The liquor store "emergency" was made to happen 96 times in a single week!

In this experiment, some variables were controlled: The liquor store was the same every time, as was the script that the "thieves" followed. But the various customers differed from each other in age, occupation, economic class—all the ways in which customers differ from one another. The environment had all the noise and bustle of a city street and storefront. There was no attempt to control the weather. There was, in short, minimal control over the experimental situation. That is how it is with field experiments.

AN EXAMPLE FROM ANIMAL BEHAVIOR:
AN INJURY-FAKING BIRD

How smart are animals, anyway? The question intrigued many of us when we were little, and it continues to intrigue some of us even now, when we're big.

Recent research on animal behavior, and especially animal communication, has shown us that behavior can display an astounding degree of complexity—and of appropriateness to the situation. Whether it is really "intelligent" or only looks that way is often debatable, but the complexity (and appropriateness) comes as a surprise all by itself, and commands respect. And many of these experiments have been conducted in the animals' natural habitat; that is, as field experiments. Of the many examples we could cite, let us take a study by Ristau and her co-workers on "injury-faking" in the piping plover, *Charadrius melodus* (Ristau, 1991). This field experiment combines experimental manipulation with the careful observation and description of the *ethologist* (Chapter 4).

These shore birds make their nests on beaches or sand dunes; actually, the "nest" is little more than a tiny scrape in the sand. After the eggs are laid, mother and father put in their time sitting on the eggs until they hatch after about four weeks.

Now, before the eggs hatch, suppose an animal comes around who might be a threat to them—a raccoon, for example. If such a creature comes along, we will often see the parent bird (mother or father) make what is called a "broken-wing display," or BWD for short. She* flies a short distance from the nest, and then begins to walk awkwardly, fluttering her wings and dragging them on the ground, as if they were broken (Figure 7.6). Very often, the intruder will turn away from the eggs and follow the parent bird, who seems an easy victim. The parent bird may lead the intruder far away from the nest, 100 meters or more. Then as he closes in—why, then she flies away, that's all. And the raccoon goes hungry.

But now, a question. Does the parent bird know what she's doing? Specifically, is she *trying* to fool the intruder?

Notice what it would imply if she were. It would mean not only that she has mental states herself, but also that these include judg-

---

*For convenience we will call the intruder "he" and the parent bird "she," even though both mother and father bird may do the BWD.

FIGURE 7.6
A piping plover faking an injury (the "broken-wing display"). Notice the awkward position of the left wing, as if it were damaged. It is not.

ments about *another* creature's mental states. If she can say in effect, "I want that intruder to think I'm injured," then her thoughts include thoughts about the intruder's thoughts. Pretty heavy going for a bird of very little brain! (The plover's whole brain is comfortably smaller than the last segment of your little finger.)

But is she really doing that? Can we answer that question definitely? No; we cannot peer into the bird's mind. However, we can entertain the possibility that she *might* be doing that, as a hypothesis that can be tested. We can ask: What should the bird's behavior be like *if* she is trying to fool the intruder? What might she be doing instead, and how would her behavior be different if one of the other possibilities were true?

So Ristau and her colleagues took careful observations of the responses of parent plovers to intruders. Rather than wait for a raccoon to come round, the researchers used "intruders" that could be called on at will: Themselves. One member of the team would approach the nest of an egg-sitting bird, meanwhile dictating observations into a walkie-talkie. Another team member, hiding behind a portable "blind," would make her own observations and also videotape the sequence.

A human "intruder" would indeed evoke broken-wing displays from parent birds. But what exactly do these displays look like? What *should* they look like under various possibilities? These "shoulds" then become hypotheses that can be tested against the data.

Does the bird run or fly away in a random direction, as if disorganized and frenzied, before beginning her display? No. She clearly chooses some directions but not others, in a pattern that is anything but random.* Does she then go straight away from the intruder or from the nest? Again, no. She will fly or run to a position in front of the intruder, quite possibly moving closer to him in doing so, but ending up where he was bound to see her.

Was the display itself fixed and stereotyped, like a chain of reflexes? No. The bird appeared to monitor the intruder's behavior, and she adjusted her actions depending on what the intruder did. If the intruder did *not* follow the parent bird but continued to head for the nest, then the bird would often stop her display, move *toward* the intruder, and display again with greater intensity, flopping and dragging her wings more vigorously than before. It is as if she were saying, "Look, you dummy! Don't you see me, and how helpless I am? Forget the eggs and chase *me*!"

Finally, another testable idea: If the display has the "goal" of fooling the intruder, it should occur only if fooling the intruder is necessary. Making the BWD has costs. The display takes energy; and it presents some risk to the eggs, which may get too warm or too cool without a parent to sit on them. So Ristau and her co-workers asked: Can a bird learn to tell which intruders are a threat to its eggs, and which are not? Can it learn when *not* to make the display, because it isn't necessary?

For this experiment, there were two human intruders, dressed distinctively so that the birds could easily tell them apart. Each of them, at different times, would approach a nest with eggs. But one of them, the "dangerous" one, would always make straight for the nest; pause and hover over it for a few minutes, as if considering eggs for breakfast; and then move on (Panel B in Figure 7.7). The other intruder, the "safe" one, would always walk straight past the nest, not looking at it, and not pausing (Panel A). That was the independent variable: whether an intruder approached the nest in a dangerous way, or safely passed it by. This was the "training" phase of the experiment.

---

*These observations might involve considerable time spent with the videotapes, a protractor, and graph paper, plotting the birds' trajectories. This kind of research is not casual bird watching!

FIGURE 7.7
The conditions of Ristau's field experiment. The independent variable was safe intruder (Panel A) versus dangerous intruder (Panel B).

Then came the test phase. The safe and the dangerous human each approached the nest at different times; but now, *each* of them took the nonthreatening route (Panel A). Which intruder approached first was randomized across birds to control for carryover effects.

Thirteen birds were studied in this way. Of these, 11 were more responsive to the formerly "dangerous" intruder than to the "safe" one; there was one reversal of this, and one tie (the bird was about equally responsive to both). So we have 13 pairs of scores in this within-subjects comparison; 11 of these are in the "predicted" direction, and there are 2 exceptions to the trend. A simple sign test tells us that that trend is significant ($p = 0.022$; why?). It appears that a plover can learn, rather quickly, whether a particular intruder is, or is not, a dangerous one that needs to be led astray, and hence whether or not the BWD is required.

COMMENT

All of this does not *prove* that the parent bird is trying to fool the intruder. We can't look inside the bird's mind and see what her intentions are. We can't even do that for each other, much less for a bird.

So Ristau did not claim proof that the bird is trying to fool the intruder. She did say that some other obvious possibilities can be rejected. (This takes us all the way back to Chapter 2: We don't prove theories; we rule out alternatives!) At the very least, to entertain the possibility that the bird *might* be doing that allows us to make some testable predictions. That in turn suggests experiments that otherwise might never occur to us.

A LOOK BACK

Now let us pause to look over these two examples. Once again, we see two cases that are vastly different on the surface, but have the same underlying logic. We *let the natural situation alone*, except that we introduce a manipulation into it.

In both cases, the weather could be sunny or cloudy, warm or cool. In both cases, no attempt was made to control how recently, or what, the subjects had eaten. No attempt was made to control for distractions produced by street noises in the one case, or by the sounds of insects, birds, and waves in the other.

And yet, in both cases, the manipulation was powerful enough to have a clear effect, despite these sources of variability. We might say that we have all the more confidence in our findings, precisely *because* we see a consistent effect despite all the natural variability that might have obscured it.

FIELD OR LABORATORY? A COMPARISON

The field experiment, we see, takes a different approach to the situation from a tightly controlled laboratory experiment. Actually, field and lab are not fixed categories, but points on a dimension (Figure 7.8). Control is not altogether lacking in a field experiment. If nothing else, the experimenter will take steps to combat our old enemies, unintended *observer effects* and the effects of *observer bias*. Ristau and her co-workers, both for control and for comfort, did not take data in pouring rain—so in that sense there was *some* control over weather. And some labs are more tightly controlled than others. Compare Pavlov's meticulously controlled situation with the relaxed waiting-room setting in which Latané and Darley's "smoke-filled room" bystander experiments were conducted. (Is a waiting room a "natural setting" for college students? Maybe it is!)

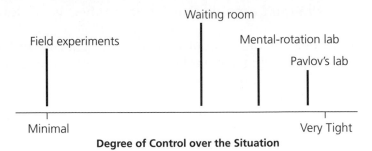

FIGURE 7.8
A situation may be controlled very tightly (toward the right) or very loosely (toward the left).

Clearly, however, in opting for a field experiment we are shifting our emphasis. Rather than *controlling* the situation as much as we can, our attempt is to *let it alone* as much as we can, except for the aspect of it that we manipulate.

How do we choose which approach to take in any given instance? The following are some of the pros and cons we would consider.

FIELD EXPERIMENTS PICK UP POWERFUL EFFECTS

When we do a field experiment, we are betting that our manipulation will be so powerful that the results will be significant, despite the variability of scores that we may expect in our uncontrolled situation. This means that we may not detect small effects this way. We cannot do the mental-rotation experiments, or experiments with weak smells, on a crowded street corner. To detect subtle influences, we must control extraneous ones. Conversely, however, if our manipulation does have an effect in a natural environment, then we know that it is powerful enough to cut through all the "noise" in that environment and have a consistent effect despite it.

In short, we may not see small effects with a field experiment—that's the bad news. The good news is: If we do see an effect, then we know it's a big one.

FIELD DATA MAY BE MORE GENERALIZABLE

Suppose that our dependent variable is sensitive to *temperature*. In a laboratory setting, we may be able to hold temperature constant, and thus get rid of it as a source of variability. But that also means that we cannot see the effect it has, or even that it has an effect. To show that would require a separate experiment, in which temperature is deliberately varied.

In a field experiment, temperature is allowed to vary naturally. If the effect of our manipulation remains the same as it does so, then we know that the effect has *generality* across variations in temperature. Or, if we have had the foresight to keep records of temperature, we can go back through the data to see whether temperature is related to our dependent variable, and whether the effect of our main manipulation *interacts* with temperature (see later). We can get all that information in a single experiment.

This works similarly for all the other variations that will occur naturally in natural environments. If the effect of our manipulation stays the same across these variations, then we know that it *generalizes* across them. If it doesn't, we can discover that too, and it may be important to know.

THE QUESTION OF "REAL LIFE"

A laboratory is a highly unnatural environment. It is supposed to be. It is designed to permit control over extraneous variables, and to permit separations that do not occur in nature—for example, between the food and the comfort that mother monkeys offer their infants. A real mother monkey always offers both. To separate them, we must build our own mother monkeys.

Okay, but we still may wonder: Having stepped out of nature this way, how do we get back in? Will our results, obtained in a simplified laboratory setting, hold up in real-life situations? With a field experiment, we bypass the whole question. We know that our results apply to a natural situation, because we obtained those results *in* a natural situation.

Now, this does not automatically count as a plus for field experiments. It is important to realize that not all laboratory findings are *intended* to be "generalized to real life." Instead, we may be testing a theory or hypothesis (or a hunch) that says, "This is how subjects should behave in *just this* situation." Then the question is: Do they behave that way? And the data are of interest not because they generalize to real-life situations, but because they support or challenge the theory (or hunch). The "naturalness" of the situation (or the lack of it) becomes irrelevant in such cases. We will say much more about this issue later (Chapter 12).

REPRISE: HOW MUCH TO CONTROL?

This chapter has been concerned with some of the decisions one makes in preparing to do an experiment. In addition to selecting and operationalizing our independent and dependent variables, we decide what to control, and how. We make our decisions guided by the published literature, or by more experienced hands, or by careful forethought, or sometimes by careful guesswork, and always weighing gains in precision against their costs.

We might decide to do a small-scale *pilot study*, a preliminary experiment using only a few subjects, just to see how the data might look. Then, for instance, if all subjects under all conditions score very high or very low, we will know that *ceiling/floor* effects are a problem; we had better change our materials or procedures to move the scores away from the ceiling (or the floor). Or, if the data are simply too variable, we might consider changing our experimental design or tightening our control over the situation, before committing ourselves to the full-scale experiment.

And then—why, then we try it and see. We do the experiment. The *data will tell us* whether our decisions were good ones.

If the factor we manipulate has a clearly visible effect, then we know that the factors we left uncontrolled are not important enough to obscure that effect. Or, saying it the other way around: *If we see an effect of our manipulation, we know that our control over obscuring variables is adequate.*

Confounded variables are another matter. They rate a chapter of their own—the next one.

SIGNIFICANCE TESTS AND EXPERIMENTAL CONTROL

Let us look back over what we have learned, and see how the pieces fit together. We will also see how some pieces from previous chapters fit in. Specifically, let us see how the outcome of a significance test—a *statistical tool*—makes contact with the nuts-and-bolts *procedural tools* we employ in conducting the investigation.

Suppose we did an experiment comparing two groups, using a simple between-groups design. We might test the significance of the difference between group means, using a t test (pp. 209–210). Look again at the formula for t:

$$t = (M_1 - M_2)/\sqrt{MS_w(1/N_1 + 1/N_2)}$$

That formula breaks down into the following three quantities: (1) the difference between means; (2) a measure of variability, divided by (3) a quantity that varies with the number of subjects. Summarizing and (over)simplifying:

$$t \text{ equals} = \frac{\text{Difference between means}}{\text{A measure of variability, corrected for number of cases}}$$

We remember that the larger the value of *t* is, the more likely it is to be statistically significant. Well, what makes *t* large or small? The three quantities we identified do.

First, the value of *t* will increase as the *difference between means* increases. And the difference between means will be affected by the *power of the experimental manipulation*. The greater the impact of the independent variable, the more the group means will differ as it varies. Conversely, a feeble manipulation will result in little or no difference between the means. Or, the two means may be *forced* into closeness by a ceiling/floor effect, so that the difference between them is artificially small and, therefore, so is *t*.

Second, we see that the *number of cases* appears in the denominator of *t*. Other things equal, the more subjects there are, the smaller the denominator will be, and therefore the bigger *t* will be.

Third, if we look again at the denominator for *t*, we find that it contains the expression MS_W, which is closely related to the *variance*—a measure of how much the scores vary, one from another, within each of the groups (see pp. 204–207). So, *as the variance within groups gets smaller,* t *gets larger*. What makes the variances small or large? Our *degree of control over extraneous variables*.

Look at it this way. In an experiment, all observations *within a group* are taken under the *same* experimental conditions. So, if those observations differ a lot from each other, it is only uncontrolled factors that can make them differ—individual differences from subject to subject, distractions and internal states (like mood or coffee content) that affect different subjects differently, measurement errors, and so on. The more we control these, the less our scores will vary from one to another within a group; so the smaller the variances will be, and the bigger *t* will be.

To summarize: We are most likely to see a significant difference (1) if our manipulation is powerful, (2) if our control over extraneous variables is tight, and (3) if we have a large number of subjects (see Figure 7.9).

Discovery!

Tight Control   Enough Subjects

Powerful Manipulation

FIGURE 7.9
We become more likely to get significant results, and so make a discovery, as we increase our control over sources of variability,
increase the power of our manipulation, and
increase the number of subjects.

There are trade-offs among these factors. One can compensate
for another. If our manipulation is weak, then we must have more
subjects, or better control over sources of variability, or both, to get
a significant difference. If our manipulation is strong, then we need
less control, fewer subjects, or both. Or, conversely: If our control
over the situation is weak, then we need more subjects, a stronger
manipulation, or both. This is the case, for example, when we opt
for a field experiment.

SUMMARY

Any experiment looks at the effect of one or more independent variables on a dependent variable. Experimental control is the attempt
to minimize the effects of other variables, extraneous to our independent variable, on that dependent variable. Uncontrolled variables
may make an effect difficult to see at all ("obscuring variables," the
focus of this chapter), or difficult to interpret ("confounded variables," the focus of the following chapter).

Among the things that may make an effect difficult to see, and some ways of dealing with them, are:

1. Feeble manipulations of an independent variable; this can be overcome by increasing the range or power of that variable, with perhaps a manipulation check to ensure that it has been varied over a sufficient range.

2. Measurement error, dealt with by increasing precision or, where this is impossible, using enough subjects to make the effect apparent despite it.

3. Ceiling/floor effects, controlled by anticipating them and not letting them happen; a preliminary pilot study may assess their likely impact.

4. Variability in the data, produced by (a) individual differences or (b) variability in the situation. Individual differences can sometimes be controlled by within-subjects or matched-pairs designs.

Variability in the situation can be addressed by holding conditions as constant as possible, especially for variables that have greatest impact on the data. An alternative approach is the *field experiment*, in which an independent variable is introduced into a natural situation that is otherwise allowed to vary naturally. This approach may make the effects of weak variables difficult to see, but it assures us that a variable that does have an influence is a powerful one. Field experiments also assure that findings generalize to the real world, for the research is conducted in that world; but then direct generalization to the real word is not always a researcher's intent.

The outcome of significance tests depends strongly on these control considerations. Other things equal, an effect becomes more likely to be significant (a) as the number of subjects increases; (b) as the power of the manipulation increases, making treatment conditions differ more from each other; and (c) as the variability of the data within conditions decreases, because of better control over the sources of that variability—that is, obscuring variables. These factors trade off, so that weakness in one may be compensated by strengthening another.

In the final analysis, the data tell us whether our control over obscuring factors is adequate. Quite simply: If we see a significant effect of our independent variable, this is evidence that our control *over obscuring factors* is adequate. Confounded variables are a quite different matter, as the next chapter shows.

MAKING FRIENDS WITH STATISTICS: MORE ABOUT SIGNIFICANCE TESTING

In previous chapters, we have discussed some ways of testing the significance of differences or relations: We've made friends with the sign test, F, and t.

Now, there are some decisions we must make about our tests of significance, before we apply them. To this point, we have just assumed that those decisions have been made. Now we will look at them more carefully. But to get clear on them, we must first dip into statistical theory for a few minutes.

FREQUENCY DISTRIBUTIONS REVISITED

Let's look more closely at what we do when we conduct a t-test between two groups. We ask: What is the probability of obtaining a t as high as ours is or higher, if the null hypothesis is true—that is, if there really is no difference?

Suppose we measure the size of a meal in two groups, formed at random from our "pool" of available subjects. Of these, one group is treated with our possible appetite-suppressing drug before the meal. The other group receives a placebo. We measure how much is eaten by each subject; and let's suppose that drug-treated subjects eat less, on average, than placebo-treated ones do. To test the significance of that difference, we compute t.

Statisticians now explore an imaginary scenario. Suppose we were to repeat that experiment an infinite number of times.

(Obviously we're not really going to do that, but statisticians can calculate what would happen if we did.) Suppose we do it the same way every time. In particular, we sample our subjects at random from the same population each time; and we assign them, again at random, to treatment groups. And we do the arithmetic the same way each time. Thus, we might always subtract the drug subjects' mean from the placebo subjects' mean.

Further, we assume that the null hypothesis is true: The drug really has no effect at all. It is important to keep that assumption in mind, and easy to do that if we remember why we make it. We are asking: What is the likelihood—the probability—of our getting a t as large as this one that we have, if the null hypothesis is true? By assuming it to be true, we can calculate that probability.

So, we repeat the whole experiment (in imagination) an infinite number of times. And for each repetition, we compute a value of t. Thus we'll end up with an infinite number of t-values, one for each repetition of the experiment.

Then what we can do—still in our imaginations—is make a frequency distribution of those t-values themselves. Such a theoretical frequency distribution, where what is "distributed" is the value of some statistic (like t), is called a sampling distribution for that statistic: "sampling," because it is based on a (theoretical) infinite number of samples from a (theoretical) population); "distribution," because the exact numerical value of our statistic will *vary* as we take different samples for each (theoretical) repetition of the experiment. So we imagine a frequency *distribution* of the values of that statistic.

Statisticians can calculate what such a sampling distribution would look like. (This may require some high-powered calculus; again, that is the province of statisticians, and we will leave them to it.) In Figure 7.10, we see the sampling distribution for *t*, based on 30 degrees of freedom. (The exact shape of the curve will vary a bit, depending on the number of df; so we do have to specify that.) It is almost (not quite) identical with the familiar bell-shaped "normal curve."

If the null hypothesis is true, the curve will center around zero, as shown. That's because the difference between means, and therefore *t* itself, will average zero. Sometimes, over our (theoretical) infinite number of repetitions, that difference will

be positive (the placebo group on average eats more). Sometimes it will be negative (the drug group on average eats more). Usually it will be small, either way. Then again, sometimes, just by chance, it will be quite large. And *occasionally*, just by chance, we will get a *t*-value as large as 2.042 or larger, or as small as −2.042 or smaller, even if the average *t*-value is zero.

How often will that happen? Just 5% of the time. Why? Because it turns out that just 5% of the area under the curve lies beyond 2.042 in the positive direction and beyond −2.042 in the negative direction—2.5% in each direction (Figure 7.10). And now we're back on familiar ground. As we saw earlier, a *probability* is a *proportion* that can be represented by an *area* in a frequency distribution (pp. 98–99)!

One more step—and here is where all this theory makes contact with our data. We can think of the *t*-value that we actually obtained, in our real-life experiment, as a single case *drawn at random from that distribution of t-values*. So, if the null hypothesis is true, then the probability that *this single* randomly-selected *t* will be greater than 2.042 or less than −2.042 is, again, just 5%.

Finally, notice this. If we know we're going to have 30 degrees of freedom, then we can see what the sampling distribution of *t* will look like, and what the values of *t* are that we would expect to obtain 5% of the time or less. And we can do all this *before we collect any data at all*. We can say in advance: "If we have 30 degrees of freedom, we will need a *t*

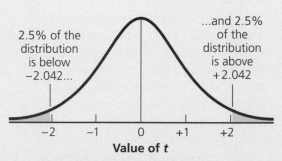

...so 5% of the whole distribution lies outside those values.

FIGURE 7.10
Sampling distribution of *t*, at 30 degrees of freedom. At that many **df** or higher, the *t* distribution is very similar to the bell-shaped "normal curve."

larger than 2.042 or smaller than −2.042, in order for the difference to be significant at the .05 level, two-tailed." We can specify, in advance, what values of *t* will lead us to call the difference significant, and what values will not.

Thus ends our excursion into statistical theory. Now, with these ideas in hand, we can understand some of the real-life, nuts-and-bolts decisions we must make when we plan a study—how it shall be done, and how the data shall be analyzed.

TWO KINDS OF MISTAKE

Some values of *t* will lead us to call our difference significant. Others will not. It follows at once that there are two ways in which we might make a mistake.

First, *we may reject the null hypothesis when we should not*. Suppose the independent variable really has no effect at all (the null hypothesis is true). But by accident we might happen, this time, to get a significant difference between two experimental conditions, even though the "true" difference is zero. This is called a *Type I error*. We could also—less confusingly—call it a *false alarm*. Why "false alarm?" Because we think we've discovered something—"Wow, our independent variable had a significant effect! We've made a discovery!"—when we really haven't. Our significant effect is just an accident that "happened to happen" this time, by chance. So all that fuss is for nothing—it's a false alarm.

Then there is the converse error: We may *fail to find a significant result, even if an effect really is there*. Even if our drug really does have an effect, we might by chance obtain data in which the difference is nonsignificant. In other words, we can "miss" a real effect and, therefore, the opportunity to make a discovery. So I will call this kind of error a *miss*. It is more conventionally called a *Type II error*.

The Type I/Type II terminology is standard; we are going to encounter these terms, and we need to know what they mean. A pity, because it's about the most confusing terminology we can imagine. We simply have to memorize which is which:

A Type I error is a false alarm, and a Type II error is a miss.

Maybe this will help: *f* (for "false-alarm") comes before *m* (for "miss"). And I comes before II. The alphabet and the Roman numerals line up with each other. Okay?

Now in planning our experiment and analyzing our data, we must live with the possibility of one or the other kind of error. If we *do* get a significant result, perhaps we've discovered something, or perhaps we've made a false alarm or Type I error. If we *do not* get a significant result, perhaps it's because there really is nothing there to discover; or perhaps there *is*, but we missed seeing it (a Type II error or miss). There is this much comfort for us: We risk only one or the other kind of error, not both. If the null hypothesis is true, we cannot make a Type II error. If it is false, we cannot make a Type I error. But that is not *much* comfort because, of course, we do not know whether the null hypothesis is really true or not.

The question then becomes: How likely is an error of one or the other kind to occur?

When there really *is* an effect, the risk of a miss, or Type II error, depends on a number of considerations, as we'll see. But when there really is *no* effect, the risk of a false alarm, or Type I error, depends on one thing and one thing only: the *criterion* we set for statistical significance. Let's look first at that.

SETTING THE SIGNIFICANCE LEVEL

In our examples so far, we have adopted the following convention: We call a difference *statistically significant* if such a difference would arise, by chance alone, only 5% of the time or less. Or, we can now say the same thing a different way: We will call a difference statistically significant if the risk that we are making a false alarm in doing so is 5% or less. Or, yet a third way: We consider 5% an acceptably low risk for a false alarm. These are three ways of saying the same thing.

Now, that 5% is quite arbitrary. It has become conventional, but we are free to violate that convention if there is reason to do so.

Imagine this. We are consultants for an industrial firm, and we think we see a better way of training workers than the one currently in use. So we do an experiment, comparing the new way with the old way, to see which way works better. Suppose the new way, on average, does give better results. But before we switch the whole factory to the new method, we want to be confident enough that our re-

sults are not just an accident—a Type I error. Now: How confident is "confident enough"? How confident in our findings do we *have to be* before we base recommendations on them? That is what we are really deciding, when we choose where to set the criterion for significance.

First, suppose that it would be easy and inexpensive to switch to the new method. Then, even if it turns out to be no improvement in the long run, we haven't lost much. In such a case, we might set a less demanding significance level—10% or even 20%, rather than 5%. We can, in other words, accept a greater risk of making a Type I error, or false alarm, if the costs of such an error are small.

But suppose our new method would require retooling the whole plant, retraining the trainers, and generally making a major investment. If our employers do all that, and then it turns out to be no improvement after all, we will be embarrassed (and perhaps jobless). In that case, before recommending a switch, we would want to be *very sure* that our finding is not a false alarm. We might set a *p*-value of .01, or even .001, as our criterion of significance. But if we do set a more stringent criterion, it will be harder for our data to meet it. A glance at Table B.3 shows us that the lower the *p*-value is, the higher is the value of *t* that we will need to reach significance. All told, it is easy to see that the more stringent our criterion is, the more likely a difference is to fall short of significance—even if it reflects an effect that really is there. Thus by making our criterion more demanding, we *decrease* the risk of a Type I error or false alarm, if the effect really isn't there. But we *increase* the likelihood of a Type II error or miss, if the effect really is there.

Thus, in setting our cutoff point, we face a trade-off between our two kinds of error. A more stringent criterion—say, .01 instead of .05—*reduces the risk of false alarm or Type I error if the null hypothesis is true*. That is the good news. The bad news is that it *increases the risk of a miss or Type II error if the null hypothesis is false*.

Where to set it, then? In the case of our factory, it might be possible (with more information) to calculate the optimal setting, balancing, for example, the increase in profits that would result if the new method really is better against the costs of making the change if it is not.

But often this is simply not possible. Especially in basic research, we often cannot assign numerical "costs" to the two kinds of error. If we make a Type I error, announcing a discovery that really isn't there, there are costs. We, and others, may waste a great deal of time following up our false lead. If we make a Type II error, we may fail to pursue a line of research that actually would be informative. But it is hard to translate those costs into dollars and cents. That is why the 5% level has become conventional when there are no other grounds for setting the significance level. It is stringent, but not unreasonably so.

ONE- AND TWO-TAILED TESTS

Here is another decision we must make. Let's begin by showing what the terms

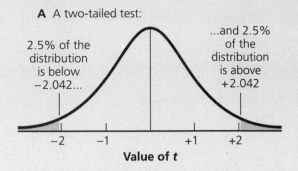

A A two-tailed test:

2.5% of the distribution is below −2.042...

...and 2.5% of the distribution is above +2.042

Value of *t*

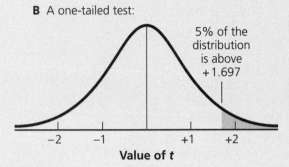

B A one-tailed test:

5% of the distribution is above +1.697

Value of *t*

FIGURE 7.11
(A) A two-tailed test; (B) a one-tailed test.

mean. In Figure 7.11, Panel A shows the setup for our familiar two-tailed test at the .05 level, with $df = 30$. We reject the null hypothesis and conclude that our effect is real, if *t* is greater than 2.042, *or* if it is less than −2.042.

Panel B shows a one-tailed test. We reject the null hypothesis if *t* is greater than 1.697. But if it is less than that, *or if it is negative*, we will consider our difference nonsignificant and draw no conclusion.

Just by looking at the figures, we can see where the names come from. In Panel A, the two critical values of *t*—2.042 or −2.042—each cuts off 2.5% in one "tail" of the sampling distribution. So if there really is nothing going on (if the null hypothesis is true), our total risk of a false alarm or Type I error is 2.5 + 2.5, or 5%

In Panel B our critical value of t, 1.697, puts all 5% in the right-hand "tail" of the sampling distribution. Our risk of a Type I error is still 5%, because now we will not reject the null hypothesis if t is less than 1.69 in the positive direction, or if it is any negative number.

When do we use a one-tailed test, then? Simple. *We use a one-tailed test whenever we are interested only in a difference in one direction, and not in the other.* Let's see how such a case might arise.

When we first introduced significance testing, our scenarios involved two-tailed tests of significance. (You might want to look back over pp. 51–54 at this point.) Say that six out of six baby monkeys preferred cloth mothers to wire mothers. We saw that the probability of getting such consistent data by chance is only .016. But we then doubled that, to get 0.032—still significant at the 5% level. Why did we double? Because we would also have drawn a conclusion if the data had been reversed, six out of six preferring the wire mother. Then we would have said that there was a significant preference for the wire mother. Such data, had they occurred, would not have challenged the "cupboard theory" of attachment but instead would have supported it.

Or: In an upcoming election, 17 out of 20 randomly selected voters prefer Candidate Bit to Candidate Byte. That gives us a p-value of .001, so doubling it gives us .002—a significant preference. We would feel confident in predicting a Bit victory. Again, we double the p-value because, if the data had been equally consistent in the other direction, we would have just as

confidently predicted a victory for Byte. In both cases, we used two-tailed tests because a significant finding *in either direction* would have been of interest.

But now, suppose again that we devise a new method of training employees in a factory. We think it will train them better and faster than the method currently in use, so we design an experiment to test that idea. A pool of new employees is split at random into two groups, one trained with the new method, the other with the old one.

Now, what will we tell the managers of our company? We can (and should) think it through before we collect any data at all. If in this sample the new method works significantly better than the old one, we will advise the managers to switch to the new method. If the new method is *not* significantly better than the old one, we will not recommend a switch. And if the new method comes out *worse* than the old one? Then we *certainly* will not recommend a switch, however loud and clear the difference may be. In other words, *we will make the same decision*—don't switch!—for a difference in the "wrong" direction as for no difference at all.*

In such a case, we can make a costly Type I error only if the new method looks better when it really isn't. So, if we want the risk of such an error to be (say) .05, we would do a one-tailed test such that our critical t value cuts off 5% of the sam-

---

*All this assumes that the research is strictly applied, so that a difference between the two groups in either direction would not have any interesting theoretical implications.

pling distribution, *in the positive direction*: new method better. If scores with the new method are lower than for the old so that *t* is negative, we won't even bother to test the significance of the difference. (We assume in all this that we do the arithmetic so that the difference will be positive if it's in the direction we care about.)

A one-tailed test has this advantage: We need a less extreme *t*-value to be significant. Thus, for a two-tailed test with 30 degrees of freedom, we need a *t* greater than 2.042 or less than −2.042 for significance. But for a one-tailed test, *t*, if it is positive, only has to be 1.697. So it's easier to get significance with a one-tailed test—if the data are in the right direction.

But if we decide in advance to use a one-tailed test, what if the difference turns out to be in the "wrong" direction—and what if that outcome were of interest? Our human drug experiment was done, presumably, because we had some reason to think it would decrease appetite. So, since we predict an outcome in one direction, it seems (and some would argue) that we can justify a one-tailed test of that prediction. But what if the drug enhances intake instead? Wouldn't that be interesting, and important to know if we want to understand what's going on? Yet, if we've committed ourselves to a one-tailed test, strictly speaking we should not even test the significance of that surprising finding.

It might occur to us to use a one-tailed test if the difference is in the predicted direction, and switch to a two-tailed test if it is reversed. Not a good idea. If we follow that strategy, we'll have significance if *t* is in the outer 5% of the distribution, for a difference in the expected direction, *or* if it falls into the outer 2.5% for a difference in the other direction. So we're really doing a two-tailed test with one tail twice as large as the other! And the *total* risk of a Type I error is not 5%, but 7.5%. Too high a risk, if we've set 5% as our significance level.

In short, if we plan to use a one-tailed test, we will be unprepared to deal with surprises. Because of this, my own view is a conservative one: Use a two-tailed test, except in those rare cases where a finding in the unexpected direction really would be of *no* interest—for example, the above comparison of a new training method with an existing one, with an eye to switching methods only if the new one is significantly better. In other cases, I think we should always be prepared to be surprised.

But not everyone agrees. (For further discussion, see Aron & Aron, 1994).

THE CONCEPT OF POWER

The risk of a Type I error or false alarm, we have said, depends on the criterion of significance we have set. The risk of a Type II error, or miss, depends on a number of things. Other things equal, our chances of detecting a real effect—thus avoiding a Type II error—increase as we increase (1) the power of our manipulation, (2) our control over sources of variability, and (3) the number of subjects. And now we've seen that they depend also (4) on whether one uses a one- or a two-tailed test (a two-tailed test makes a miss more likely), and (5) the level of significance we set (a stricter criterion makes a miss more likely).*

We can take these ideas another step. Look at Figure 7.12—and think again about our drug versus placebo experiment testing an appetite suppressant (pp. 244–246). We conduct the experiment, obtain a *t*-value, and test for significance. Let's assume we decide on a one-tailed test, to make the figure simpler.

We've been assuming that the average value of *t*, over our infinite number of (theoretical) replications, is zero (Curve C). That's the null hypothesis. If it is true, then we cannot make a Type II error, but we could make a Type I error or false alarm. Well, we set the critical value of *t* so that that outcome has a probability of 5%. Therefore, with df = 30, Table B.3 tells us that *t* must be at least 1.697 to be significant. All this is familiar.

But suppose the drug really does have an effect. If it does, then the sampling distribution of *t* will not center at zero, but will be shifted to the right. How far it shifts will of course depend on how big the "real" effect is—it might center around a *t*-value of 1, or even 2, as the figure shows (Curves B and A, respectively).

Of course, we don't *know* how big the effect really is. However, we do know this much: (1) If Curve B or A describes the

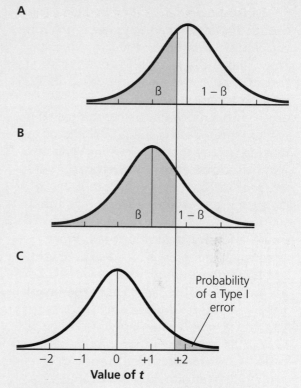

FIGURE 7.12

The concept of power. The shaded area (β) is the probability that we will make a Type II error, for a "real effect" of given size. The unshaded area reflects the probability that we will correctly reject the null hypothesis in each case. The smaller β is, the more powerful the experiment is.

real state of affairs, then we cannot make a Type I error. "There is a difference" would be the correct conclusion to draw. (2) We could "miss" that difference, and make a Type II error. Despite the real effect, and even if the sampling distribution does look like Curve B or even A, still we would get a nonsignificant finding if we happened to draw a *t* lower than 1.697 from the sampling distribution. But also (3) the bigger the real effect is, the less likely that is to happen.

---

*Actually there is yet another factor we may consider here, and that is the power of the statistical test itself. Some tests are more powerful than others, which means just this: For a "real" difference of a given size, one test may be more likely than another to return a finding of significance, and thus avoid a Type II error. Texts on statistics discuss this further.

Okay: How likely *is* it to happen? The probability of such an outcome is given by the *shaded area under the curve* in each case. That is the probability that for an effect of that size, we will *not* get a *t* large enough to be significant. That shaded area has been given a name: it is called β (Greek *beta*). Beta is the probability of our making a Type II error, "missing" the effect, for a true effect of given size. Then the probability that we will get a significant *t*, for a real difference of that size, is simply $1 - \beta$. We refer to $1 - \beta$ as the *power* of our statistical test—or, more broadly, as the power of the experiment itself. It is the probability that we *will* get a significant difference in our experiment, for a real effect of given size.*

As we look at the figures and their shaded areas, we see that the risk of a "miss" can be substantial. Even with a "true" difference of two *t*-units (Curve A), we can expect to get nonsignificant results almost 50% of the time. (And *that* is why we draw no positive conclusions from a nonsignificant finding!)

The three curves show what is intuitively obvious: The bigger the real effect, the more likely we are to get a significant finding (power goes up); conversely, the *less* likely we are to "miss" seeing that effect (β goes down). But now we can say it more precisely: "If the real effect is of a certain size, X, then the probability that our experiment will detect that effect is Y"—where Y is $1 - \beta$. We can specify the *power* of our experiment—the probability that it will detect a real effect of specified size.

APPLICATIONS OF THE POWER CONCEPT

It is possible to do some neat tricks with these ideas. If we know how many subjects we will have and how much variability to expect (previous experiments might tell us that), we can compute the probability that we will find a significant difference—for a "real" effect of such-and-such magnitude. Or, suppose we want to be 95% certain that if the effect is at least as big as so many units, our experiment will be powerful enough to pick it up. (We may decide that if the effect is less than that, we won't care about it anyway.) Then we can calculate how many subjects we would have to have, or how powerful a manipulation, in order to keep the probability of a false alarm at 5%, *and* set the probability of a miss at some low value.

The experiment on "therapeutic touch" did this (Chapter 2). Emily Rosa and her colleagues calculated that β (the probability of a nonsignificant finding) was less than 0.05, if their TT practitioners really could detect the nearness of an "energy field" two times out of three. This is a very generous criterion; actually, if TT theory is correct, practitioners should *always* be able to sense a person's energy field. But the practitioners fell well short of even that undemanding standard.

Not many researchers use this kind of

---

*We are here estimating β simply by inspecting the shaded areas; but by reference to statis-tical tables, we could actually calculate it. Once again, we refer to statistics books for that procedure.

analysis, though it has been argued that more should (e.g., Cohen, 1990). This is partly because it would often mandate an unreasonably large number of subjects, and partly because, especially in basic research, we often have no principled way of deciding how small an effect can be before we cease to care about it. It might be of theoretical interest if a manipulation has *any* effect on a dependent variable, even a small one (see also Mook, 1989; Parker, 1995). But it is worth knowing that such techniques exist; again, statistics texts will take you through them. If we must always live with the risk of one or the other kind of error (Type I or Type II), it is comforting that at least we can know how serious the risk is, either way.

SOME CONFUSIONS ABOUT SIGNIFICANCE TESTS

The relation between statistics and experimental procedures is straightforward. Nevertheless there are some aspects of it that frequently lead to confusion, and it is worth our pausing to get them straight.

p VERSUS N—DON'T CONFUSE THEM!

This one dies hard. It often crops up in reports written by beginning researchers. Very often in the lab reports we see, students will find a significant difference based on (say) 8 or 10 subjects, and then they say, "Of course more cases would have to be studied before we could draw conclusions."

Yes and no.

It is quite possible to get highly significant results with a very small sample—if our manipulation is strong, and/or our control is tight. Suppose we do a two-group experiment with five subjects per group (8 degrees of freedom), and find $t = 2.31$. That is just significant at the .05 level, if we use a two-tailed test of significance.

Now suppose there were 31 subjects per group—60 degrees of freedom—and t turned out to be 2.00. That also is just significant at the .05 level. The results in these two cases are equally unlikely to have come about by chance. Therefore, *our confidence in the results is the same for both cases.* (Or if it isn't, the difference must rest on other, nonstatistical considerations.) A p of .05 is a p of .05—whether based on 6 cases or 6,000.

Now it is true that with larger samples, we can tolerate more variability in the data and still get a significant difference. The high variability inflates the denominator of t (which would make t small), but the larger N deflates it again, so t can still be large. (That is why field experiments often use larger samples than laboratory experiments do.) We saw the same idea earlier with the sign test: With larger samples, we can have more exceptions to the trend and still have a significant trend. And why would there be exceptions to the trend? Because of extraneous, uncontrolled influences that produce exceptions, and a manipulation not powerful enough to overcome these extraneous influences!

Thus we see again there is a trade-off between sample size and our other two influences. The weaker the manipulation and the weaker our control, the larger the sample has to be to produce significant results. But if we *do* get significant results, then our confidence in the finding depends solely on the *p*-value, not on sample size.

This doesn't mean that students are foolish to call for "more cases." First, they may be saying that they would like to see a *replication* of their experiment. If we repeat the experiment and get the same results again, our confidence in those results is very much increased. That is why it has been said that "one replication is worth a hundred *t*-tests." We discuss replication in Chapter 12.

Second, our students may be concerned—rightly—about the *generality* of a finding. Would it hold up under different conditions, or in subjects drawn from a different population? These are good questions. But they are questions for further research. The original experiment is not at fault for not addressing them. Research proceeds in small bites, and we cannot study everything at once.

SIGNIFICANCE VERSUS IMPORTANCE: DON'T CONFUSE THESE EITHER!

We've touched on this before, but it bears repeating. When we say a result is statistically significant, what we are saying is: We can be reasonably confident that the result did not arise just by chance. And that's *all* we are saying. "Significance" in the sense of importance, practical or theoretical, is another matter entirely.

For example, suppose we are dealing with a fatal, and presently incurable, disease. Suppose our demographic data tell us that, once the disease is diagnosed, the victims have an average life expectancy of two years (that figure is made up for purposes of this example).

Now, a drug is developed that we think will extend the lives of those who take it. So we try the drug in a sample of patients. Suppose we find that this drug doubles the average life expectancy of those who take it, from two to four years; but suppose that the finding is significant only at the 10% level (that is, *p* is less than .10 but greater than 0.05). Suppose further that the drug is not expensive and has few side effects.

We would surely recommend that the drug be used for other sufferers. True, there is a risk that we're making a big fuss over nothing—a Type I error. Maybe the drug really has no beneficial effect, and our seemingly positive data are produced only by chance; we would expect that to happen one time in ten, and this could be one of those times. But if we are mistaken, what do we lose? The 10% risk is worth taking.

But now, suppose we're dealing with a truly violent disease. It kills its victims in about two days. We find a drug that, in a clinical trial, doubles the life expectancy of the victim—from two days to four. Suppose further that because of low variability, the effect is highly significant statistically: *p* may be as low as 0.001! But suppose also that the drug is expensive and has painful side effects.

Would we use the drug? Probably not—despite our very high level of confidence that the effect is real. Is the difference between two days and four days worth a painful treatment at high cost to the patients' heirs? We would think not—and my guess is that patients would concur in this.

The point is just this. An effect may be statistically significant: The data cannot be plausibly attributed to chance alone. Whether it is *interesting*, in the practical or theoretical sense, is another matter. It depends, again, on the potential costs and benefits of the decisions we make, if we base decisions on our findings.

CHAPTER 8

EXPERIMENTAL CONTROL II: CONFOUNDED VARIABLES

A lot of people probably think they caused the earthquake, but I'm here to tell you that I'm the one who really did it. At seven forty-two this morning I pressed the button that raises the door of my garage, and all hell broke loose. The first thing I said to myself was "I've got to get this thing fixed."

—*THE NEW YORKER*, OCTOBER 19, 1987

IN THIS CHAPTER, WE'LL DISCUSS:

- What confounded variables are, and why they make data impossible to interpret
- Why significance tests and larger samples are no help against them
- Confounding problems in intervention research, and the "double-blind placebo control"
- How individual differences may be sources of confounded variables, and how random assignment to conditions acts against this problem
- How our procedures may create confounded variables
- How to go about spotting and controlling confounded variables

In the last chapter, we distinguished two ways in which uncontrolled variables can affect data. First, they may make it difficult or impossible to see anything at all. Or, second, they may leave us misled or confused about *what it is* that we are seeing. In the last chapter, we focused on the first kind of problem. Now we turn to the second.

Confounded literally means "confused." In this context, it implies *mistaking one cause for another*—or running the risk of doing so. Our hero confused the real cause of the earthquake (a subterranean happening) with another, irrelevant event—his activating his garage-door opener. Feathers fall more slowly than stones, but Aristotle confused the real cause of this (their susceptibility to air resistance) with another, irrelevant difference between the two (their weight; Chapter 1). Many writers confused the important factor in baby monkeys' preference (contact comfort) with what was really a minor one (food). In the first case, the confusion occurred because the two events happened at the same time. In the second and third it occurred because two variables varied along with each other.

These cases show why confounded variables are so dangerous. Seeing an effect, we may easily conclude that one variable (X) is the cause of it, when really it is the other variable (Z). But we may not realize this—we may overlook the confounded variable(s)—and so we could permit the error to go uncorrected. We may not know when we're wrong.

A confounded variable, then, is some irrelevant variable that *varies along with* the independent variable whose effects we're interested in. Then, if we see a difference between (say) an experimental and a control condition, or between a "before" and "after" set of measurements, we simply will not know what produced that effect. Is it our intended independent variable (X)? Or is it some other variable (Z) that is linked to it? We cannot tell (see Figure 8.1).

A CASE STUDY: INTERVENTION RESEARCH AND ITS PROBLEMS

"Intervention research" means what its name implies: We intervene, in an attempt to make something better. Anxiety attacks, or severe depression, may lead someone to seek professional help; and the professional *intervenes*, perhaps with a drug or with a program of psychotherapy, to improve the situation. *Intervention research* is designed to evaluate interventions. It asks: How much good do they do?

If we allow a situation in which...

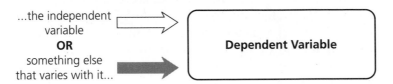

...the independent
variable
OR
something else
that varies with it...

Dependent Variable

...could influence the dependent variable, then which
of them is really producing the effect?

FIGURE 8.1
The problem of the confounded variable: We will not know whether any effect we
see is really the effect of our manipulation, or of something else that varies with it—
if we *allow* "something else" to vary with it. If we do, that "something else" is a
confounded variable.

A FLAWED EXPERIMENT

To begin with, let's look at an intervention project that has, shall we
say, some problems. It will be instructive to see what they were and
how they could have been avoided.

> In 1979, I reviewed the outcome of thirty-seven former patients,
> all of my patients who had had at least a minimum amount of psy-
> choanalytic treatment. Five of these (14 percent) exhibited dramatic
> improvement, that is, improvement so striking that friends or rela-
> tions who hadn't known that the patients were being treated com-
> mented on the distinct change. Nine others (almost 25 percent)
> were considered by themselves and their families to have improved
> impressively, as demonstrated by important changes in their abil-
> ity to function in the several areas of life in which they had previ-
> ously functioned badly. So these two categories together constituted
> about 40 percent of the group. Sixteen patients could be said to
> have achieved limited improvement. They functioned better in one
> or more areas of life but still far from optimally. In general, these
> patients and their families were pleased with the outcome but I was
> less pleased. Seven patients (19 percent) showed no improvement
> at all. . . . Considering the nature of the illness, the duration, and
> in many cases the constitutional basis, these findings are not at all
> discouraging. I should imagine that a more recent cohort would do
> even better (Ostow, 1995, p. 100).

Those data are useless. Why? Because there are too many possible reasons for the patients' improvement (Figure 8.2). Let's look
them over.

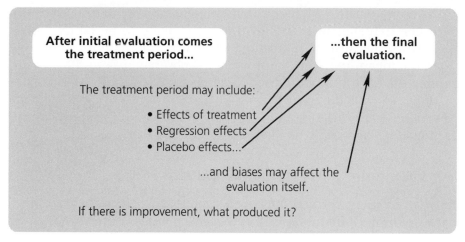

FIGURE 8.2
A poorly designed intervention experiment.

1. SPONTANEOUS REMISSION

We get 40% of the treated group showing considerable improvement. But compared to what? How many of these patients would have shown some, or even marked, improvement without any treatment at all? So-called "spontaneous remission"—a reduction of symptom severity with no known cause—is not at all rare. A percentage-improved figure is meaningless without something to compare it with.

2. REGRESSION

This is a tricky statistical concept, but we can get a feel for it. It says: If a person is feeling particularly bad (or good) now, he is likely to feel better (or worse) later on.

Why? Because feelings of depression or anxiety or, indeed, scores of any kind (happiness, too!) are bound to fluctuate over time, in response to many influences: life circumstances, the season, diet, and much besides. *Right now*, these influences may have happened to combine in such a way as to cause an extreme score; for example, to make a depressed subject very depressed indeed. If he is measured again later, it is unlikely that that especially bad combination will still be there. So the chances are that if his score is very low now, it will not be so low later. At the extreme, subjects who score *very* low now will almost surely score higher later—simply because they have nowhere to go but up!

Now, when does a patient present herself for treatment? When she is doing particularly poorly or feeling especially bad. If we measure her status again at a later time, it is likely to be better rather than worse because of regression, no matter what (if anything) we do in the meantime. The "improvement" observed in our 40% of the sample might, for all we know, have resulted from this alone.

Regression is different from spontaneous recovery because (unfortunately) it works in the other direction as well: A particularly *good* feeling, right now, is likely to be not as good later on.

3. OBSERVER BIAS

Maybe the client seemed improved (to himself and to the therapist) because he, and the therapist, *expected* to see improvement. We know that we can "see" what we expect to see, whether it's there or not; and perhaps this is such a case (Chapter 5).

4. NONSPECIFIC EFFECTS

If patients do improve following psychoanalytic therapy, does this mean that *psychoanalytic treatment* is effective? In a word, no. Maybe patients do better (a) because someone is paying attention to them, or (b) because they are doing something about their problem, or (c) because they *expect* to get better—or all three! All of these are *confounded* with any effect the treatment itself may have. Masses of data are out there, showing the effect that such "nonspecific" factors have—"nonspecific," because they are not "specific to" any particular therapeutic technique. Thus, even if these patients did better than untreated controls, this by itself would be no evidence for the effectiveness of psychoanalytic treatment per se.

5. THE "PLACEBO EFFECT"

This is the name that researchers have given to a well-documented phenomenon. It really is a special case of "nonspecific effects," but it is important enough to warrant separate discussion. In a word: Patients may improve because they *believe* that they are receiving treatment.

This effect is separate from observer bias as we use the term here. The improvement may be real enough, not illusory. The problem is that real improvement may occur even if a patient is given (say) a pill, with nothing active in it—an inert, dummy pill—or even an injection, with nothing active in it. Such a pill or injection is called a *placebo*, and so this effect—improvement that occurs because a patient *believes* he is being treated—is called the *placebo effect*.

Some common misconceptions should be moved out of the way at the outset:

First, a placebo effect is not necessarily imaginary, nor does it affect only imaginary symptoms. In an early and influential review of the literature on this topic, Beecher (1955) cited cases in which placebo treatment abolished the pain of terminal cancer, or even brain-wave abnormalities that are diagnostic of epilepsy!

Second, a placebo is not necessarily harmless. If a "dummy" pill can cure, it can also afflict: "Side effects" such as skin rashes can be produced by placebos. And patients who improve in response to quack treatments, because of the placebo effect, may be led to believe they are suffering from imagined physiological states, or nonexistent allergies, or control by extraterrestrials. Above all, they can be led away from treatments that might do more for them than a placebo does.

Third, the effect is not small; a placebo can be strong medicine. Beecher evaluated over two dozen studies and calculated that about one-third of the subjects in the studies improved because of the placebo effect. Other, more recent studies calculate the placebo effect as even greater than that.

Just how all this works is not clear and is, in fact, a research topic in its own right. (One researcher's confounded variable is another's subject matter!) We can talk about the "power of suggestion," but that tells us little about what actually happens. In some cases, conditioned responses within the nervous system, perhaps affecting hormonal and immune systems, may be part of the story. Also in some cases, the brain's natural painkillers, the *endorphins* (morphine-like compounds produced by the brain) may play a role.

Finally, we should note that the placebo effect is a fertile source of *testimonials* (Chapter 4) for every quack treatment we can imagine. No matter how worthless a "treatment" may be, there will be some who will tell us they are helped by it!

CONTROLS IN INTERVENTION RESEARCH

Now in our case study (the before-and-after comparison), all these things—spontaneous improvement, regression, observer bias, the placebo effect, and the positive effect of the therapy itself, *if* it has one—all act in the same direction. Any or all of them could act to promote the perception, in both client and therapist, that improvement has occurred. If there is that perception, which of these has produced it? We don't know. They are confounded with each other.*

TWO CAUTIONS

All told, this report of therapeutic success is meaningless. We simply don't know how to interpret the findings. And notice two other things as well.

First, the control procedures we looked at in the previous chapter are no help at all here. Shall we add more subjects? We'd just have the same unclear data in a larger sample. Shrink the variability of scores, or increase the size of the effect? These may make it clearer that there *is* an effect, but not what it's an effect *of*.

Second, the data will be uninterpretable no matter how large, clear, consistent, and statistically significant the effect is. We still won't know what produced it. Indeed, this is so important that we should flag it as a

Principle: A significance test is no protection whatever against a confounded variable.

THE "DOUBLE-BLIND" PLACEBO CONTROL

No, we are just going to have to *control* the variables that are confounded with the effect of the treatment. First: What if these patients had not received any therapy? Would they have improved just as much (spontaneous remission)? Since any given patient either receives therapy or does not, individual case studies won't answer that question. We would likely turn to *groups* of subjects, some of whom receive therapy, others not. Then, if subjects who receive therapy improve *more* on average than those who don't, we can say that therapy had an effect *over and above* spontaneous improvement and regression effects, for these should affect both groups about equally.

---

*Perhaps this is the place for a word of warning. It may be tempting to draw a parallel between the two kinds of control problems and the two kinds of statistical errors, thus: Obscuring factors lead to Type II errors, and confounding factors lead to Type I errors. Resist the temptation, for that's not true. In our example, suppose patients improve *significantly*, but because of placebo effects rather than the effects of therapy. That is not a Type I error. The improvement may be real enough, in which case the null hypothesis is indeed false. It's just that we'd be mistaken to think that the *cause* of that improvement is the therapy, if it's really the placebo effect.

That assumes, of course, that the two groups are comparable to begin with. We'll address that matter shortly.

But let's think further. If subjects who receive therapy are compared with a control group who do not, what happens to that control group? Are they just placed on a waiting list? But then the difference between groups—therapy versus no therapy—is still confounded with observer bias and the placebo effect. No one expects a waiting list to make them better!

If we are using drug therapy, with the drug administered as a pill or injection, we have a handy control procedure. Our control subjects may receive a literal placebo—a pill or injection with no drug in it. Then we need to make sure that neither the subject, nor those who will interact with him and evaluate him, knows whether he is in the drug group or the placebo group—not until the experiment is over and all the data are collected. Hence such an experiment is called *double-blind*—both patient and clinicians are "blind" as to whether any given subject is taking drug or placebo. The double-blind precaution, of course, is to control for *observer bias* in clinicians' observations of patients and in patients' observations of themselves, and also for *observer effects*: If the clinicians know who is who, they might treat placebo and drug subjects differently in ways that could affect the subjects' well-being.

This gives us a double-blind, placebo-controlled study. And now if the drug-treated subjects improve more than the ones receiving the placebo do, then we can say that the drug is having a positive effect, *over and above* the effects of regression and spontaneous improvement, *and* that the placebo effect cannot account for this, for it should be affecting both the groups. *Only the drug itself*, as a physiologically active agent, now varies: Present for the one group, absent for the other. So now we can see what the effect is of *just that* variable. The others are controlled (see Figure 8.3).

SOME QUESTIONS

Such a procedure does raise some troublesome issues, and we should pause to consider them. First, if a physician gives a patient a placebo, telling him that it will make him better—is she not lying to the patient? Doesn't this violate the trust that the patient is placing in her? Yes, it does—or would. Today, ethical practice requires that the patient give *informed consent* (see Chapter 13) to the design itself. He should be told, before the experiment begins, that he *might* be assigned to placebo condition. And of course the reasons for this must

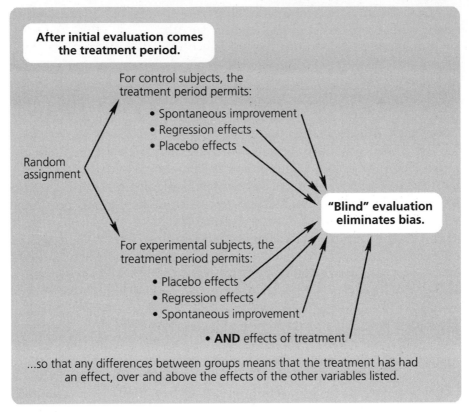

After initial evaluation comes the treatment period.

For control subjects, the treatment period permits:

- Spontaneous improvement
- Regression effects
- Placebo effects

Random assignment

For experimental subjects, the treatment period permits:

- Placebo effects
- Regression effects
- Spontaneous improvement

- **AND** effects of treatment

"Blind" evaluation eliminates bias.

...so that any differences between groups means that the treatment has had an effect, over and above the effects of the other variables listed.

FIGURE 8.3
A better-designed intervention experiment.

be explained. If the patient consents to this, then the experiment can proceed.

The second issue is this: Are we justified in withholding, from the placebo group, a treatment that might benefit them? Well, we must remember that we do not yet know that the treatment will be helpful. We are doing the experiment to find out. In this connection, it is helpful to remember Dr. Benjamin Rush and his bloodletting therapy (see Chapter 1). A patient of his would have been far better off if assigned to the control condition!—if, that is, there had been one.

On the other hand, once it becomes clear that the treatment outperforms the placebo, then it would be appropriate to end the experiment and make the treatment available to both groups. Ideally, patients' progress should be monitored closely enough to permit this.

Third, a question that often arises: *Does it matter?* If a patient is helped by the pill (or whatever) that he receives, do we care whether it is a placebo effect or something more?

I think we do, for two reasons. First, a placebo is likely to be substantially less expensive than a drug. But more important: If we conclude that a treatment is effective, that will also lead us to conclude something about the nature of the disorder we are treating, its causes and its cures. In other words, the research finding will advance our understanding of that disorder, and perhaps lead to treatments that are more effective still. But if we're wrong—if the improvement we see is a placebo effect of the pill, not a physiological effect of the drug itself—then our understanding will be thrown off the track. We could waste much time and resources following up a false lead—at the expense of more informative leads that properly controlled research could provide. And here we find ourselves back home—if we know when we're wrong, we can correct our mistakes. If we don't, we can't.

PSYCHOTHERAPY: WHAT IS THE PLACEBO?

For a drug study, a placebo-controlled, double-blind experiment is reasonably straightforward. These precautions are now routine among competent drug researchers. But similar problems arise with other kinds of interventions, where the cure is not so apparent.

What about psychotherapy, for instance? If we give psychotherapy to one group of subjects but not to another, the control group—what happens to the control group? Do we perhaps put them on a waiting list? That would control for spontaneous recovery and for regression, but not for placebo effects. Instead, we might try for a kind of "dummy" psychotherapy, in which we withhold some presumably critical aspect of a therapeutic "package." We'll see an example of this in the next chapter.

Or we might compare our new treatment (administered to the experimental group) with the best treatment currently available (administered to the controls), and see if the new treatment is better. Notice, though, that this changes our question. We are now asking, "Is this new method more effective than what we already have?" rather than "Is this new method effective at all?" Yet the latter question may be of theoretical, if not practical, importance.

There really is no perfect solution to this problem—no perfect "placebo control" for psychotherapy. The result? After a century of effort, clinicians and theorists—and insurance companies!—are still debating questions like: What sorts of therapy are most effective, and for what problems? Is psychotherapy effective enough to justify its cost? Is it effective at all? If we are still debating these matters, it is because it is extremely difficult to get solid answers—and for exactly the reasons we've discussed.

A FINAL COMMENT

Let us look once again at the flawed study with which we began. These data are offered as evidence for the effectiveness of psychoanalytic therapy. The author is described as a psychiatrist and psychoanalyst practicing in New York City, and as President of the Psychoanalytic Research and Development Fund, among other indicators of prominence. Yet he can write the above-cited passage in 1995, in the face of a massive technical literature—dating back for decades now—*showing* that such data are totally useless, and why.

Now these problems are not buried in obscure statistical journals. They are well known to anyone who does serious research along these lines. By allowing the above passage to be printed, its author shows himself unfamiliar not only with the problems of research, but also with the large literature that *discusses* those problems.

He is not alone. "Research" like that is still done, we may be sure. Indeed, the self-help shelves at the bookstore are filled with books of "case studies" that have all of these problems, undiscussed. Take them with a lot of salt.

INDIVIDUAL DIFFERENCES AS CONFOUNDED VARIABLES

In our double-blind study, as in many experiments, separate groups of subjects are assigned to different experimental conditions. But how do we know that the groups are equivalent in the first place? If they are not, then any difference between them might arise, not because the manipulation made them different, but simply because they were different to begin with. So any "differences" that we "begin with" will be confounded with the independent variable. It's true, we could *match* the groups as to age, education, income level, and so on; but how can we be sure that we have matched on all the important variables? We can't.

THE CONCFPT OF RANDOM ASSIGNMENT

It is good to know that in this case, an apparently impossible problem has a very simple solution: *Randomize*. If we assign subjects strictly *at random* to one condition or another, then in the long run and with enough subjects, our groups will probably not be very different on *any* variables—those we have thought of, and those we haven't. And the larger the groups, if they are randomly formed, the more similar to each other they are likely to be.

As with random sampling (but don't confuse them! see later discussion), random assignment does not mean hit or miss, or any old way, or as we feel like it. It means assignment by a procedure such that *each subject is as likely to be assigned to one group as to another*. If there are two groups, we could flip a coin for each subject. Heads, this subject goes to the experimental group; tails, to the control group. Or, for any number of groups, we could use a random-number table. Appendix A will steer you through the procedure for doing that.

Now, we said that this device will make our groups approximately equivalent "in the long run, and with enough subjects." With fewer subjects (as in most research), the equivalence may be less close. Perhaps (for example) more subjects with less severe symptoms will get assigned to the drug condition than to the placebo condition, just by chance. But two considerations make this less problematic than it looks. First, if the difference between groups is *statistically significant*, then we know that *all* chance factors, taken together, are unlikely to produce such a difference. And that includes the "chance factor" that puts a subject in one condition rather than another, if the assignment is random.

Second, remember that a single experiment does not stand alone. If we have a whole series of experiments supporting the same idea, and if each one used the randomization technique, then *all told* we are looking at a longer run and a larger number of subjects. Thus as *replication* adds to the *weight of evidence* supporting a conclusion, our confidence in that conclusion increases very fast. And rightly so.

RANDOM ASSIGNMENT AND RANDOM SAMPLING—DON'T CONFUSE THEM!

Finally, *do not confuse random assignment to conditions with random sampling from a population*. These two ideas have the notion of randomness in common, but that's all. They are entirely distinct from each other.

Our initial "pool" of subjects, from which we form (say) a drug and a placebo group, might be drawn at random from some population. Or it might not; it might be a "convenience sample" of, say, depressed patients in a clinic near us. *Either way*, we might assign patients strictly at random to one group or another. Or we might not; we might (if we were foolish) let subjects volunteer for one group or the other—a nonrandom procedure.

In short, we could have both random sampling and random assignment. Or we could have either one, without the other. Or we could have neither. The two procedures are independent of each other.

NONRANDOM ASSIGNMENT: SOME CAUTIONARY TALES

Yet another reason for random assignment is just this: If we do not form our groups at random, we will form them in some other way. And "other ways" will almost inevitably open the door to bias in our assignment to groups. Consider some possibilities.

First, suppose we assign to the "therapy group" those who volunteer for therapy, whereas those who don't volunteer are assigned to the control group. If we do that, we can be virtually certain that the two groups will differ as to their expectations of improvement, motivation for treatment, education level, and so on. This is so obvious that it seems inconceivable that such "experiments" should actually be done. But they have been (see Smith, Glass, & Miller, 1980, for discussion).

Second, suppose again that we have a new method for treating depression. And we have a "pool" of available subjects who, we find, are depressed to varying degrees. At first glance, it might seem a good idea to give our new treatment to subjects who are most depressed. They are, after all, the ones who most need help. Then we could use the less depressed subjects as controls.

If we take a second glance, however, we will see that this would be a very bad idea. Remember, we don't yet know whether our "helping" helps. That's why we are doing the experiment—to find out. And if we do it as just described, we will open the door to the dreaded *regression* artifact if nothing else.

The subjects who are most depressed now, are likely to be less depressed later no matter what we do (pp. 259–260). For less depressed subjects, this is less so. Our new treatment could *look* better than control treatment, even if it really isn't, on those grounds alone.

Better to assign subjects strictly *at random* to one condition or the other.

Finally, we could assign hit or miss, or "as we feel like it." As we consider each person in our "pool" of subjects, we could make our decision arbitrarily: Arthur goes to the experimental group, Anna to the control group, and so on. One danger here is that we might, quite unintentionally, "feel like" assigning those with less severe symptoms to the experimental group. Then our groups would not be equivalent, and the effect of therapy would be confounded with that difference. At the end of the experiment, the treated group might look better simply because they were, on average, in better shape to begin with.

It would simply be very dangerous to assume that we, the experimenters, could identify and avoid such biases as these. Far better to adopt a procedure that takes the decisions out of our hands altogether—as a coin toss or a random-number table would do.

THE PROBLEM OF SUBJECT LOSS

This one is an even sneakier trap. Even if our two groups are randomly formed when our experiment begins, they may not stay that way. Suppose that one group receives our new treatment. The other group (the control) is put on a waiting list. But now suppose the treatment itself is stressful and unpleasant. Suppose some subjects decide to drop out of the experiment—something they have an absolute right to do. Then it might be that the subjects who remain in treatment are the ones who are most strongly motivated to do something about their problem. It is these subjects who stay with us despite the stress. With the control group, no such pressure is operating. A waiting list is not very stressful.

If that happened, we could have confounded data at the end of our experiment, even with random formation of groups at its beginning. One group received our new treatment, the other did not. But also, when we collect our final data, the experimental group may now consist mostly of highly motivated subjects—for these are the subjects who stuck with the experimental treatment—whereas the control group does not. Our treatment/no treatment comparison is now confounded with the difference in average level of motivation.

In some cases, it is possible to "control" for such effects statistically (pp. 286–291). In others, there may be little we can do about the problem except be aware of it, and temper our conclusions accordingly. Sometimes the problem is so serious that the whole experiment must be considered a failure—and the worst of it is that we may not know that until we are well into the experiment, and have invested a great deal of time and energy in gathering useless data. It happens!

PROCEDURAL CONFOUNDS: A SUCCESS STORY AND MORE CAUTIONARY TALES

Individual differences, we have just seen, can be confounded variables as well as sources of obscuring variability. Other confounded variables may lurk in the nuts and bolts of our experimental *procedures*—in particular, *the way we make our manipulation*. We may think we are manipulating a variable that is of interest, but we may actually be manipulating something else in addition—or instead.

Let's begin with a success story—one in which a host of confounding problems were thought through in advance, and solved. The example again incorporates a double-blind placebo control, but in a study that was not an intervention one. Let us try to follow the researchers' thinking.

AN EXAMPLE FROM PSYCHOBIOLOGY: HORMONES AND HUNGER

Consider what happens when we eat a meal. We taste the food we are eating. The stomach fills. Digested food is absorbed from the intestine into the bloodstream, which conveys it first to the liver, thence to all the organs of the body, including the brain. And at some point, satiation or *satiety* kicks in. We say, "I've had enough, thank you," and stop eating.

Therefore, some consequence(s) of our eating a meal must act to shut down our hunger. But which consequences? Actually, the answer is probably "All of the above and more besides." The system that governs our food intake is a complex one, with multiple controls (Mook, 1996). For now, let's tease out just one of those controls and take a closer look at it.

When partially digested food is passed from the stomach to the intestine, the intestine senses its presence, and releases into the blood a hormone. The name of that hormone has been mercifully abbreviated to CCK.* And experiments with laboratory rats have found that the injection of CCK, all by itself, is enough to reduce the amount of food that the animals eat (Smith & Gibbs, 1994).

Question: Will CCK also reduce food intake in humans? It will.

CCK EFFECTS ON MEAL SIZE IN HUMANS

The experimenters (Pi-Sunyer, Kissileff, Thornton, & Smith, 1982) invited five adult male subjects to have lunch with them in their laboratory. A standard lunch was presented and the subjects were invited to eat as much as they wished. They also filled out some self-report questionnaires describing their feelings of hunger, fullness, and illness or nausea.

After a few days' adaptation to the situation, the two-day experiment was conducted. On one day, as each subject began eating, an injection of fluid containing CCK was slowly injected into a vein in his arm. (The needle in his arm was connected through flexible plastic tubing to the injection syringe, leaving the arm free to move.) On the other day (the control day), again an injection was given, but the fluid contained no CCK. For half the subjects, the CCK was given the first day, the control injection the second day; for the other half, the order was reversed (*counterbalancing*).

What happened? The subjects did indeed eat smaller lunches on the days when CCK was injected. They began eating at about the same rate on both days, but they stopped eating sooner when the hormone injection was given.

Now let's look at the control procedures here. The setting and the food were constant throughout. The experiment was conducted *double-blind*; that is, neither the subjects nor the experimenters knew, until later, which injection was which. The subject had a needle in his arm, and was given an infusion of fluid, both on test days when the fluid contained CCK and on control days when it did not.

Let us pause and examine that. We might ask: In the control condition, if we're not going to give any CCK anyway, why does the poor subject have to have a needle in his arm? Why not just let him alone and let him eat? Because if we did it that way, the effect of the hormone would be thoroughly *confounded with* the effects of the needle itself—stress of inserting it, stress of having it there, and the like. And any effect of the hormone would also be confounded with

---

*Its full name is *cholecystokinin*, if you really want to know.

A A Poor Experiment:

	Experimental Condition	Control Condition
Effect of hormone	Yes	No
Effect of injection stress	Yes	No
Subject expects effects	Yes	No
Observer expects effects	Yes	No

So which of these is responsible
for any effect we may see?

B A Better Experiment:

	Experimental Condition	Control Condition
Effect of hormone	Yes	No
Effect of injection stress	Yes	Yes
Subject expects effects	?	?
Observer expects effects	?	?

So now the only difference between
the two columns is presence or
absence of the hormone effect.

FIGURE 8.4
Design of a CCK experiment. The first, poor experiment was not the one that was
conducted; the second, better one was.

the effects of the subject's expectations, and of the experimenters'
expectations: Both would expect something to happen if there were
a needle in the arm, but not if there were not. We can lay all this
out in Figure 8.4.

You see the problem. Suppose subjects do eat less with CCK than
with no injection. Is this because the hormone affects feeding? Or
because the stress of the needle does? Or because expectations do?
We simply would not know. All of these are confounded with each
other.

No, here again we are just going to have to control for those confounded variables. We need, in other words, to *separate* the variable
of interest (the CCK effect in this case) from the other variables listed
in the table.

If we look at how the experiment was actually done, we see how
it accomplishes this. The control condition included the famous nee-

dle in the arm. And for any given session, neither the subject nor the experimenters knew whether the injected fluid had any CCK in it or not—the double-blind procedure. Thus we get to Figure 8.4B. (The question marks simply recognize that under these double-blind conditions, neither subjects nor experimenters will be sure just what to expect!)

What a difference! Expectations are constant (if vague). Stress is constant. The *only* difference between the two conditions is the one that is of interest: presence or absence of CCK in the injection fluid. We have separated this difference from all the others. Thus we can see what effect *just that* variable has—which is what we want to know.

Finally, this experiment introduces an idea we've not yet considered. Sometimes we can deal with a suspected confounded variable by "checking it out"—taking another measurement or observation in order to see whether it is a problem or not. If it is, we must find a way to control it. But perhaps we can show that it isn't, and then we need not worry about it.

Thus here: A persisting argument in the rat literature on CCK is whether the compound depresses food intake simply by making the rats feel sick. There is strong evidence against that possibility (e.g., Fedorchak & Bolles, 1988), but some writers still have doubts about it. And we can't ask the rats.

But we *can* ask humans! The investigators did ask their subjects about feelings of illness. Few subjects reported any, and the effect of CCK on intake was the same for those who did not as for those who did. It therefore appears that CCK—or some consequence of its injection—can depress food intake without inducing any unpleasant sensations. Illness, in other words, might have been a confounded variable—but the experimenters checked, and found that it was not.

COMMENTS

Since these experiments were inspired by experiments with animals, perhaps this is a good place to note a misunderstanding about animal research, one that affects many laypersons and, indeed, more than a few professionals. One hears the complaint: "Where do you experimental psychologists get off, generalizing results from rats and pigeons to human beings?"

There are several answers to this. One is that we do far less "generalizing" than is popularly supposed. If we say, "Rats do it; therefore people do it too," that's generalizing. In fact, however, one rarely hears that remark from responsible researchers.

What one does hear is what these researchers did say: "Rats do it. *Let's see* whether people do it." That is not generalizing, for a generalization draws a conclusion, whereas "Let's see" asks a question. And in this case, the final conclusion—generalization, if you like—rests directly on data: "Rats do it, and *we have shown* that people do it too." In such a case, rats guided our question; but human data gave us the answer.*

Another, and separate, general comment: These experiments are an excellent example of the difference between applied and basic research—between research that tells us how to improve or repair a system, and research that tells us how the system works in the first place (Chapter 1).

The experiments with CCK are squarely in the basic-research camp. We should not expect to find CCK placed on the market as an appetite suppressant. First, we cannot swallow a CCK pill; if we do, the digestive tract will break its molecules to pieces and we won't have CCK in the system anymore. We must inject it intravenously. And even if we do that, its duration of action is very short—far too short to do the would-be dieter any good.

No, we study CCK not because it will be useful clinically—it won't—but because, if we understood how it does what it does, we would better understand the workings of the systems that control appetite and food intake. And if we understand *that*, we would be in a better position to manipulate those systems. We might then be able to invent or discover really safe and effective appetite suppressants, though CCK will not be one of them.

AN EXAMPLE FROM PERCEPTION: PERCEPTUAL DEFENSE

When procedural confounds are overlooked, very misleading results may be obtained. This can and does happen in published research, too—as in the following example.

We often hear that human beings "see what they want to see,"

---

*Another answer, less directly pertinent here, is this: Not all animal research is *intended* to apply directly to humans. Animals are interesting in their own right. Moreover, if we know how this or that process works in an animal species, at the very least we have learned *one* way in which it *can* work. That may give us valuable insights about the characteristics that any system must have, if it is to perform the process effectively. In this way, such knowledge can indirectly but importantly affect how we investigate the human case.

with its implied corollary that we resist seeing what we don't want to see. Is this literally truc? Does our perceptual apparatus "defend" against unpleasant or anxiety-arousing inputs, making it more difficult to perceive them?

One experimenter (McGinnies, 1949) asked the question this way. His subjects (college students) were seated in front of a device called a *tachistoscope*, which presents visual stimuli (like words on a screen) for very brief, and controllable, periods of time. In this experiment, a word would be presented very briefly indeed, so briefly that the subject could not tell what the word was. The exposure time would gradually be lengthened, until the subject *could* identify the word. Then the experimenter would go on to the next word on the list and do it again. Thus, for each of a series of words, the subject's *recognition threshold* was measured: How long did the word have to be on the screen, in order for the subject to identify it? The longer the exposure that was needed, presumably, the more reluctant was the subject's perceptual apparatus to accept and recognize the word.

The words were all of equal length (five letters). But of these words, some were nonthreatening and innocuous, like "spoon." Others, however, had sexual overtones that should have made subjects uncomfortable, like "penis" or "whore." Would subjects require longer exposures of these words in order to identify them? They did—very consistently (Figure 8.5). The experimenter concluded that anxiety made the subjects reluctant to *see* the nasty (but not the nice) words on the list. Hence, longer exposures were required

FIGURE 8.5
Results of the perceptual-defense experiment. On average, the threatening words had to be presented about twice as long as the nonthreatening ones before subjects indicated recognition of the words by saying them aloud. But was this reluctance to *see* the words, or reluctance to *say* them? (Data from McGinnies, 1949.)

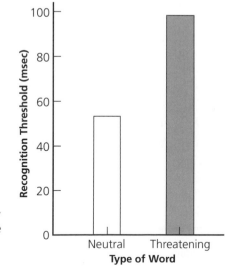

to overcome this *perceptual defense* and permit the word to be recognized.*

But not so fast. There are some difficulties here.

Imagine that you are a subject in this experiment. A string of letters appears on the screen, very briefly; you're not sure what the word is, but it looks as if it might be "spoon." Okay, you go ahead and guess "spoon"—what can you lose? And if you're right, that exposure time is above your recognition threshold for that trial.

But now the next word is flashed. Again you're not sure, but it looks like "whore"! Could it really be *that* word? If you guess it and you're wrong, you'd be pretty embarrassed. (That would have been even more true in the 1940s, when this classic, flawed experiment was done.) Better wait until you're *sure*—which means, wait until the word has been exposed longer—before you call out what you think it is. The subjects in the original experiment might have been showing just that kind of caution.

In short: Were the subjects really reluctant to *see* the nasty words? Or were they just reluctant to *say* them? Reluctance to see, and reluctance to say, are confounded.

As if that problem were not bad enough, there is another. The nasty words used in this experiment simply *appear less often in print* than the nice words do. And, as later research showed, the time it takes to recognize a printed word does depend on how frequently it appears in print. Thus, actual counts of how often words appear in newspapers, magazines, and books show that, for example, the word "smile" is quite frequent, whereas the word "smirk" is infrequent. Sure enough, it takes subjects just a bit longer to recognize "smirk" than to recognize "smile."

That may come as a surprise. "Smirk" is not *that* rare a word; we know what a smirk is, and we can read a sentence about smirks (like this one) without a noticeable pause. But in fact, precise measurement with tachistoscopic presentations show that the relatively rare word does require just a fraction longer to be identified than more commonly used words do. (For review and discussion, see Reisberg, 1997). Perhaps this effect, and not "perceptual defense," was what our original experiment was really showing.

---

*You may be wondering how a subject can "defend" against a threatening word if she doesn't yet know what the word is. The argument was that some unconscious part of the perceptual system does recognize the word, and throws up a barrier that makes its *conscious* recognition more difficult.

	Nice Words	Nasty Words
Reluctant to see?	No	Yes
Reluctant to say?	No	Yes
Infrequent?	No	Yes

FIGURE 8.6
Once again, there are too many differences between the experimental conditions.

Figure 8.6 lays these problems out. And we see that in this new context, we have the same old problem: There are too many differences between columns. We don't know *which* of these differences produced the very clear effect we see. That is how it is with confounded variables.

To solve these problems, we ought first to equate our nice and nasty words for frequency. Then we must do something about "reluctance to say." Some students of mine solved that problem in an imaginative way, in an experiment they did as a class project. In their experiment, there were *two* strings of letters flashed briefly on the screen, side by side. One string formed a word, like "spoon" or "whore"—again, some words were nice, others nasty—and the other string formed a nonword, like "noops" or "rewho." Sometimes the real word (nice for some series of trials, nasty for others) was to the right, sometimes to the left. And the subjects were asked just to say which string, the right- or the left-hand one, formed a word.

Notice that with this procedure, the subjects *never had to say the words*. They had only to call out "left" or "right"—words they should have no reluctance to say, whatever the word on the screen might be. Under these conditions, there was no evidence whatever for "perceptual defense." Recognition thresholds were virtually identical for nice and for nasty words.

AN EXAMPLE FROM MEMORY: HYPNOSIS

Let us look at one more example of confounded variables. There is a very popular myth, which goes as follows: Under hypnosis, one may recall events that one can't remember otherwise. Forgotten memories are retrieved. This includes "repressed" memories—ones that were forgotten on purpose, because they arouse too much discomfort to be held in consciousness. This myth has been the theme of a great many movies and TV shows; and unfortunately some clinicians, unfamiliar with the research on this topic, also take it seriously.

But a myth it almost certainly is.

The problem is: Are these "recovered memories" accurate? Or are they manufactured? A hypnotized subject is going to be very compliant, very eager to please the hypnotist, and very responsive to the hypnotist's suggestions. So, especially if questions are framed as "X happened, didn't it?" or "Don't you remember that X happened?" the hypnotized subject is likely to say, "Yes, yes!" But is this because memory is better, or because the subject is more inclined to say "Yes!" to whatever the hypnotist says? Does hypnosis enhance *memory*, or does it enhance *compliance*? The two are confounded.

What we must do is to separate accuracy from yea-saying. Well, let us ask some questions to which the correct answer is "No!" We might ask, "Do you remember seeing X?" when in fact there was no X. Now, if the hypnotized subject gives more correct "No" responses as well as more correct "Yes" ones, we can say that the accuracy of her memory has increased. But if she says "Yes, yes!" to the false items as well as the true ones, then we know that what has increased is not the accuracy of her memory, but only her readiness to *say* "yes!" when asked.

Simple enough; but notice something more. If we are to do this, then we must know what the answer to each question ought to be. So we must ask about events for which we *know what actually happened*. (The clinician does not know what actually happened between, say, a client and her father when she was 10 years old. All she knows is what the client tells her *now*.)

One way to do this is to bring the subject into a laboratory. Let him witness a staged event, say, or look at a complex picture or film sequence in which a lot is going on. Then, later, we ask him questions about the event, picture, or whatever, either hypnotized or unhypnotized. We include questions to which the correct answer is "yes," and ones to which it is "no." And we know what the correct answers are because we staged the event or made the pictures ourselves.

Much research of this kind has been done, and the answer seems very clear. When we separate effects on memory from effects on compliance, we find that hypnosis does *not* augment memory. It augments yea-saying instead. (For reviews and discussion see Erdelyi, 1985; Reisberg, 1997.)

PSYCHOLOGY AND EVERYDAY LIFE:
THE FALSE-MEMORY SYNDROME

Hypnotized subjects, it seems, are especially likely to say "Yes!" even if the correct answer is "No!" But one doesn't have to be hypnotized to do that. We saw the same sort of thing going on even in non-hypnotized subjects, when we discussed eyewitness testimony and "leading questions" in an earlier chapter (Chapter 5).

Now let us look at an especially important, controversial, and dangerous implication of the yea-saying tendency: the *false-memory syndrome*.

In the fall of 1988, Paul Ingram was accused by his two daughters of having abused them sexually when they were little (they were now young adults). Mr. Ingram first categorically denied the charges; but later he began to "remember" such episodes, and eventually he confessed to the charges and was imprisoned.

Later, the daughters' accusations spread to other members of the family, and friends in the community. These were now "memories" of dreadful Satanic rituals involving torture of animals and sacrifice of babies (in the absence of any babies reported missing). Eventually, the stories became so wild and contradictory that even the prosecution ceased to believe them. In a word, it is likely that none of this had ever happened. These were false memories, "implanted" at the insistence of well-meaning but incompetent therapists who were convinced (1) that a history of abuse underlies many psychological problems, (2) that memories of these episodes are repressed, and (3) that an insistent therapist can break through the repression and "uncover" the memories. So the therapist may say, insistently: "X must have happened. Don't you remember? Try to remember! Allow yourself to remember!" Clinicians unfamiliar with the research literature may use hypnosis to "help" the process along.

The problem is: One can lead a client to *manufacture* memories by just such tactics.

Can memories really be "implanted" in such ways? Yes; it has been shown many times, by direct experiment, that they can (Loftus, 1994). In one case, subjects were led to "remember" an occasion when they hurt their hand in a mousetrap and had to be taken to the hospital. It had never happened (Ceci, Huffman, & Smith, 1994). Other subjects were led to "remember" a birthday party in which a clown entertained everybody. It had never happened (Hyman, Husband, & Billings, 1995). Such an experiment was conducted also with Mr. Ingram as subject, and he too was led to "remember" episodes that were known never to have occurred (Ofshe, 1992). Why then did Mr. Ingram confess? It is likely that he was manufacturing memories, at the insistent probing of police and a "helpful" pastor.

Such findings have sobering implications for law enforcement. They show that *even a confession is not proof positive of guilt*. An accused person may, sincerely, "remember" an event that simply did not happen. We remember, too, that a person's confidence in the accuracy of her memory has little relation to how accurate it really is (Chapter 3).

In recent years, literally thousands of people have come forth with "memories" of sexual or ritual abuse, years earlier, by parents, teachers, or clergy. Now, this might mean that such abuse is in fact widespread, and that because society is aware of the problem, the victims are now bringing their memories out of the closet and confronting their victimizers. That may be true in some instances. But in other cases, the "memories" are so bizarre that they could never have been believed except in an atmosphere of hysteria.

In 1992, a number of accused parents founded the False Memory Foundation, to aid parents who were falsely accused by their children. More than 3,700 people so accused came forward in the first year alone. And in the past few years, therapists have been successfully sued for malpractice as accusers have recanted their accusations, realizing that their "memories" had not been "uncovered," but manufactured at the therapist's insistence.

Do not misunderstand. Child abuse by adults can and does occur. When it does, we should insist that something be done about it. But the false-memory syndrome can and does occur, too. Accusations dredged up from "memory," at someone else's insistence and/or under hypnosis, need to be treated with great caution. At the very least, such "memories" need to be supported with independent evidence. This requirement, where the crime is private almost by definition, will not be easy to fulfill. (For further discussion, see Loftus, 1994; Ofshe & Watters, 1994.)

HOW TO COMBAT CONFOUNDS

We have looked over several examples of the problem of confounded variables, and we have seen examples of how the problem was, or might have been, solved. Now let us generalize what we have learned.

HOW TO THINK THROUGH
CONFOUNDING PROBLEMS

As we have seen, confounding problems come in a variety of sizes and shapes, and there really are no hard and fast rules for spotting them. We simply have to think them through.

Perhaps the best way to do that is as follows. We first "rough out" an experiment in our minds. In light of our question, we decide what we shall manipulate, and how (the independent variable); and we decide what we shall measure, and how (the dependent variable). Then, with this preliminary sketch, we sit down to think—perhaps with more experienced colleagues, over coffee. And our thoughts go like this: "If we do the manipulation as we have planned, are we manipulating *only* what we intend? Is there *anything else* that will vary along with what we intend, if we do it this way? Are we allowing *observer effects* to operate in unintended ways? Might *observer bias* affect the data? And what about the nuts and bolts of our *procedures*? Might these introduce irrelevant differences between conditions—like reluctance to see, along with reluctance to say; or injection stress along with any effects a drug or hormone might have?"

If we get "yes" answers, then our experiment as planned has confounding problems. We must do something about them.

HOW TO CONTROL CONFOUNDED VARIABLES

Do what? If we do spot a confounded variable, how can we control it? As far as I can see, there are three ways (see Figure 8.7).

"TAKE IT OUT"

Ideally, we can set up the experiment so that the confounded variable isn't there at all—we "take it out." An example is the experiment my students did on perceptual defense. Are subjects reluctant to *see* threatening words (the question of interest)? Or are they just reluctant to *say* them (the possible confounding factor)? Well, set up the experiment so that the subjects don't have to *say* the words at all. Then we find no indication that they are reluctant to *see* them.

Often, taking out a possible confound is only common sense. In the hormone experiments, the investigators held the diet constant across conditions (taking out variations in it) so that the hormone/placebo comparison would not be confounded with differences in diet. As experienced researchers, it is likely that they never

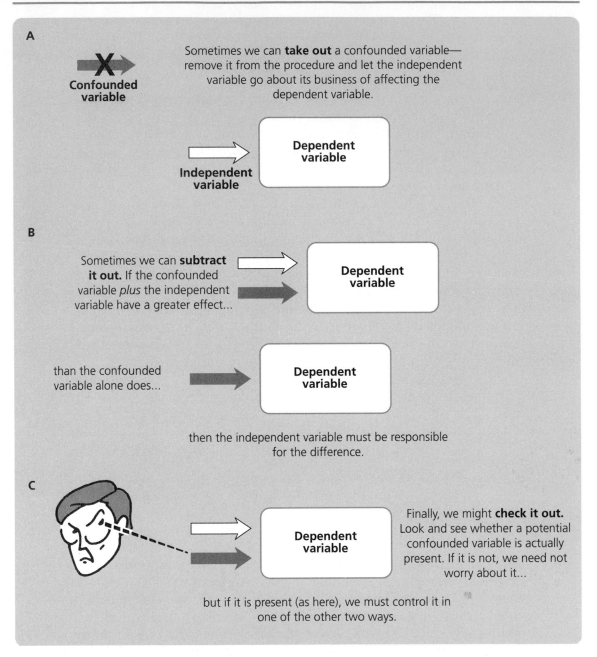

A

Confounded variable

Sometimes we can **take out** a confounded variable—remove it from the procedure and let the independent variable go about its business of affecting the dependent variable.

Independent variable

Dependent variable

B

Sometimes we can **subtract it out.** If the confounded variable *plus* the independent variable have a greater effect...

Dependent variable

than the confounded variable alone does...

Dependent variable

then the independent variable must be responsible for the difference.

C

Dependent variable

Finally, we might **check it out.** Look and see whether a potential confounded variable is actually present. If it is not, we need not worry about it...

but if it is present (as here), we must control it in one of the other two ways.

FIGURE 8.7
How to combat a confounded variable.

even considered doing the study any other way. But this constancy was a control procedure, just the same.

"SUBTRACT IT OUT"

In cases where we cannot take out a confounding factor, we often set up an experiment so that we can "subtract it out." Here is one place where *control groups*, or *control conditions*, come in.

In the CCK experiment, administration of the hormone was accompanied by the stress of injection (among other things). That can't be helped. We can't magically introduce CCK into our subjects' bodies without using a needle ("Beam it in, Scotty!").* But though we cannot take out injection stress, we can set up a control condition in which we have the *same* injection stress, but without the hormone. That isolates the hormone effect by subtraction:

> Effect of CCK plus effect of injection stress (experimental condition)
>
> minus   effect of injection stress (control condition)
> equals   effect of CCK.

This kind of logic underlies the use of placebo controls in a drug experiment. To add a control group—given placebo instead of the active drug—does not get rid of the placebo effect. It just makes it constant across both conditions—if it is present, it affects the drug subjects, but it affects the control subjects too—so that it is subtracted out of the comparison between them:

> Effect of the drug plus placebo effect (experimental group)
>
> minus   placebo effect (control group)
> equals   effect of the drug.

"CHECK IT OUT"

There is a third way of dealing with potential confounded variables. If we are worried about such a variable, we may be able to "check it out" and see whether in fact it is a problem.

Consider two examples of this—again very different in details,

---

*Remember that we cannot have subjects swallow CCK in pill form. If we do, the digestive system will break up the CCK molecule into its amino-acid parts before it is absorbed into the bloodstream, and we won't have CCK anymore.

but the logic is the same. First, look once more at the CCK and hunger experiment. There is a potential problem here: If CCK depresses food intake, is this just because it makes the subjects feel sick? Its effect of producing nausea could be confounded with its effects on hunger per se. Well, the experimenters checked out that possibility simply by asking the subjects, "Do you feel sick?" "No," said the subjects. So illness was probably not a problem. A very simple control. But the experimenters had to be aware of the problem ("think it through!") to include that question in their procedures.

As a second example, consider hypnosis and memory. We plan to ask the subjects a series of questions to which the correct answer is "Yes." Perhaps the subject will say "Yes!" more often when he is hypnotized. But as we think it through, we see a problem: If he does, is this (a) because he remembers better, or (b) because he is more willing to say "Yes!" when asked a question? Here (a) and (b) are confounded. So we check out the (b) possibility by including some questions to which the correct answer is "No." If the subject still says "Yes!" more often when hypnotized (and he does), then we know that the confounded variable *is* a problem. Hypnosis has affected what he *says*, not what he *remembers*.

To anticipate and solve confounding problems, *before* the experiment is done, is the hallmark of a careful experimenter.

SUMMARY

A confounded variable is one that consistently varies along with the independent variable. If this happens, and if we see differences among the experimental conditions, we won't know whether the differences are produced by the intended independent variable or the confounded one—or both.

Confounded variables abound in intervention research, which attempts to evaluate interventions aimed at medical or psychological problems. Patients receiving treatment may show apparent improvement, but we may not know whether it occurs because of the treatment or because of spontaneous remission, regression, observer bias, or nonspecific effects, including the powerful placebo effect.

The control procedures discussed in the last chapter are no help to us here. Nor are significance tests, which may assure us that something more than chance is affecting the data, but won't tell us what that "something more" is.

In such cases, treated persons may be compared with untreated controls. Then spontaneous remission and regression are controlled, for they should affect both groups easily. Observer bias can be controlled by keeping each patient and her evaluator "blind" as to who is in what condition. And the placebo effect can be controlled *with* a placebo, given to the otherwise untreated group. This gives us the *double-blind placebo control.* In research with psychotherapy, this can present real difficulties. What would be the equivalent of placebo psychotherapy? That is one reason intervention research can be so difficult to do.

Differences from one subject to another, in addition to being a source of obscuring variability (discussed in the last chapter), can be confounded variables if, for example, our groups are different from each other at the outset. The best way to avoid this problem is to assign subjects to groups on a strictly random basis. This procedure (1) makes it unlikely that the groups will be very different from each other on *any* variable, those we think of and those we don't; and (2) avoids the biases that attend alternative means of subject assignment. Random assignment can be done whether or not the subjects were selected at random from a population—random sampling and random assignment are two separate concepts. But even if we do everything right, subjects may be more likely to drop out of the experiment in one condition than in another, leaving us with nonequivalent groups at the end.

Confounding problems also lurk in the nuts and bolts of our experimental *procedures*. Three case studies were discussed. In one, double-blind placebo controls were used to avert a number of confounding problems in an experiment on hunger, much as in an intervention experiment. In the second, "unwillingness to see" a threatening word was confounded with "unwillingness to say" such a word, and with differences in word frequency. In the third, it appeared for a while that hypnosis enhanced memory. In fact, memory and compliance were confounded in such studies, and it was actually compliance—"yea-saying"—that was enhanced.

There are no hard and fast rules for spotting confounding problems; we must think the matter through for each investigation. If we do spot a confounding problem, three possible ways of dealing with it are suggested: (1) just take it out of the procedure; (2) set up a comparison (e.g., a control group) that allows us to subtract it out; or (3) check it out by taking a measure or observation that will tell us whether or not it is a problem. Perhaps it isn't, and we needn't worry about it.

MAKING FRIENDS WITH STATISTICS:
STATISTICAL CONTROL

Our discussion has emphasized that a *statistically significant* finding is no protection at all against a confounded variable; we will emphasize this again at the end of this section. If there is such a variable, a difference between conditions may have as low a *p*-value as we please, but still we will not know *what it is* that produced that clear effect.

Other statistical techniques, however, may be helpful in controlling *some* confounded (or obscuring) variables. Using these techniques, we can sometimes control certain variables after the fact, as part of the data analysis, rather than directly when the study is conducted.

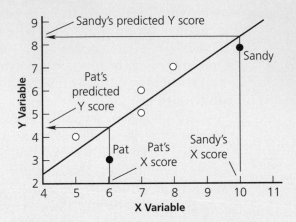

FIGURE 8.8
Predicting scores on the Y-variable from scores on the X-variable, using the regression line.

REGRESSION AND PREDICTION

To see how this can work, we must set the stage a bit. We'll return to statistical control, but we need to have some other ideas in mind first.

Look back for a minute on our discussion of predictive validity (Chapter 3). There we saw that if two variables are correlated, then we can *predict* a subject's score on the Y variable (e.g., sales performance) knowing her score on the X variable (e.g., a test). Now, let's suppose we have a scatterplot in front of us (Figure 8.8), and we know each subject's score on the X variable—but we haven't looked up her score on Y. We can however have a stab at predicting it. What we should predict, for each subject, is the Y score that falls on the regression line for that sub-

ject's X score (look back at pp 167–172).

Thus we know that Pat's score on X is 6. From that point on the X axis, we go up to the sloping line that best fits these data—the *regression line.* From there we go over to the Y axis to find her *predicted* score on Y. It is 4.4, though her actual score is 3. So in predicting or *estimating* Pat's score on Y, we have made an error; our estimate is 1.4 units too high. This we call our *error of estimate* for Pat. (We could just as well call it our *error of prediction.*) Similarly for Sandy: Her score on X is 10, so her predicted score is 8.4, but her actual score is 8.0. So her error of estimate is 0.4 units.*

---

*These things we can see just by inspecting the figure. We could go further and *calculate* where that best-fitting regression line should be, and then calculate the errors of estimate from there. Books on statistics will show us how to do this, if we need to; my intent here is only to show the logic of the procedure.

If we make such predictions for all subjects, we will minimize the total (squared) errors of estimate for the sample as a whole. And the tighter the correlation between X and Y, the smaller this total will be (Chapter 5).

Now, let's see how we can use this idea to *control* a variable statistically.

STATISTICAL CONTROL: ANALYSIS OF COVARIANCE

The logic we have just worked through underlies many methods of statistical control. *Analysis of covariance* is a case in point. The idea is very simple, yet it is a revealing example of what regression methods can do.

Suppose we perform an experiment to test a treatment for depression—a drug, let us say. We divide our subjects at ran-dom into two groups. We administer the new drug to one group; to the other (the control group), we administer a placebo. And—of course!—we do it double-blind. Then after a few weeks, we take a measure of how depressed each subject is.

Suppose that for our "after-treatment" measure, we get the data shown in the "hanging" frequency distribution, in Panel A of Figure 8.9. But also, suppose for now that those are all the data we have; we have no scatterplot, but only that "after" measure in the left panel.

We find that indeed, the drug-treated subjects (solid circles) are less depressed on average than the control (open circles). That is, their depression scores tend to be lower. But obviously the difference is not impressive and would certainly not be significant. The scores for the two groups are thoroughly mixed and the overlap is great.

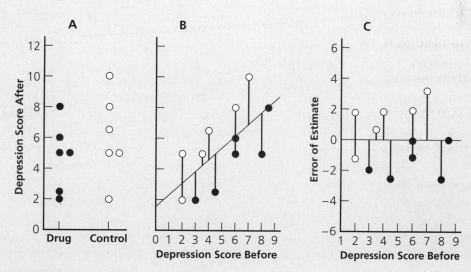

FIGURE 8.9
Analysis of covariance. Treating the scores as deviations from the regression line "controls" the X-variable statistically.

Now, suppose we had the foresight to give a test of depression *before* we began the drug or placebo treatment. And suppose it occurs to us now that we could plot the end scores ("after") against the initial scores ("before").

In Figure 8.9B, we have done that—keeping the "after" scores the same as before, and letting the horizontal axis show what the "before" scenes might be. We see that initial scores are positively correlated with final scores; the scatterplot has a positive slope, as shown by the regression line.

But look again! In these imaginary data, it turns out that every single drug subject scores at or below the regression line. And every control subject but one scores above it. In other words, at the end of the experiment, the people in the drug group are *less depressed than we would have* predicted *them to be, given their scores at the beginning*. For the controls, this is not so.

We can see this even more clearly if we focus on the "strings" that tether the data points to the regression line. Suppose we convert each subject's score to a *deviation score*—that is, express it as so many units above or below the regression line. If we do this, in effect we rotate the regression line to the horizontal and set it at zero (Figure 8.9C). The strings that tether the data (helium balloons or lead weights) to the regression line, keep their lengths as we do this. Then we can treat those string lengths as a new Y-variable. Rather than working with final depression scores as our dependent variable Y, we are now letting our dependent variable be the *deviation of the actual final depression score from the predicted one*—the error of estimate.

Having turned the regression line horizontal, we find that there is now almost no overlap between the two distributions: Drug subjects consistently score below control subjects, on this measure of deviation from expectation. Were we to calculate these deviation measures and compute a t using them, we would find the difference significant. I have done this for us, and I find that $t = 3.510$, higher than the 2.228 we need at df = 10. If we had more than two groups with random assignment, of course, we'd use F instead of t, but the logic would remain the same.

We have turned a very muddy effect into a very clear one, just by statistical analysis—though of course we also needed the forethought that led us to take a "before" as well as an "after" measure in the first place.

STATISTICAL CONTROL II: HOLDING VARIABLES CONSTANT

Let us look again.

In the previous example, we took our final scores, and expressed them as deviations from the regression line. Those deviation scores give us a *measure of final performance that is independent of initial performance.*

Why? Well, looking at the original scatterplot, we see that if we know a person's "before" score, we can do a pretty good job of predicting what her "after" score will be. If her "before" score is high, we know that her "after" score should be high; if low, low. Of course if we calculated the regression equation we could make even more precise predictions.

None of this is possible if we convert our scores to deviation scores. Now, in Figure 8.9C, the predicted deviation score for the "after" score is just zero—for *all* values of the "before" score. Knowing a person's score at the beginning is no help at all in predicting her or his deviation score at the end. So, the deviation score for "after" is independent of the score "before," as we said. By using the deviation scores this way, we have in effect held *initial score constant* (at zero), statistically.

PARTIAL CORRELATION

Suppose some variable, A, is tightly correlated with Variable C. And another variable, B, also is tightly correlated with C. If this is so, then Variables A and B will necessarily be closely correlated with each other.

But is there a relation between A and B, independent of their relation to C? We can ask it this way: If C were held constant, would A and B still be correlated with each other? Or would the A–B correlation weaken or even disappear? In the former case, we say that the *partial correlation* between B and A remains present, with C controlled or "partialled out." In the latter, we would say that the partial correlation between A and B is weak or absent.

It is virtually impossible to answer that question just by staring at the scatterplots. But it becomes very easy if we compute the regression equations for predicting one variable from another. First, we predict the A scores from the C scores, and take the errors of estimate for A; these deviation scores are now independent of C. Then we predict the B scores from the C scores, and take the errors of prediction for B. Now these deviation scores, too, are independent of C. Then we can correlate deviation scores on A with deviation scores on B. Since each of these new scores is independent of C, the effect of that is indeed to hold the C variable constant statistically.

AN EXAMPLE: BENNINGTON REVISITED

An example of the use of partial correlation comes from Newcomb's Bennington studies (Chapter 4). There was, you recall, a drift toward less conservative political and social views as students spent time at Bennington. Despite this, some of the students were more conservative than others, and these differences persisted over time. Thus, scores on a measure of conservatism taken at the beginning of students' college careers, in the 1930s, were correlated with conservatism scores 25 years later, in 1960 ($r = 0.29$). Scores taken at the end of their college careers also were correlated ($r = 0.47$) with the 1960 scores. So, of course, scores early and late in college had to be positively correlated with each other, since both were correlated with the scores in 1960.

Now all this could, it seems, be accounted for very simply. It could be a matter of stable personality or family-background variables. Maybe, because of these, some Bennington students were just more conservative than others to begin with, that's all; and they stayed that way. The difference persisted through the end of college (so early and late scores were correlated); and it persisted further into the 1960s. So early college scores, late college scores, and 1960s scores could all be correlated with each other because a single underlying variable—degree of conservatism—ran through them all.

Very simple. But wrong.

Even if early-college scores are held constant statistically, by partial correlation, late-college scores remain strongly correlated with 1960 scores ($r = .39$). In other words, these sets of scores are related to each other, and not *just* because they are both related to early-college scores.

However, if late-college scores are "held constant" by partial correlation, then the correlation between early-college scores and 1960 scores disappears! The correlation becomes a negligible 0.01.

In other words: Attitudes held at the *end* of college are predictive of conservatism scores 25 years later, even if earlier attitudes are partialed out and so made constant. But attitudes held at the *beginning* of college do *not* by themselves predict conservatism in adulthood. They only seem to do so, because they are correlated in turn with later attitudes, which do predict this. If we take that "bridging" variable out, early scores have no predictive value.

In other words again: Something happened between the beginning and the end of these women's college careers, to change their political attitudes from non-predictive to predictive of their attitudes and actions much later. Something happened to make the later attitudes *more stable* than the earlier ones had been. And though we still cannot establish causality from correlation, we have ruled out an alternative: The "unchanging personality" explanation, as just discussed, will not work. It is therefore that much more likely that, in Newcomb et al.'s (1967) words, "The simple fact of four years in the college had a good deal to do with it" (p. 234).

A LOOK BACK

We have seen some ways in which variables may be controlled statistically rather than procedurally—and, in some cases, after the fact. There are other ways of doing this, too, but most of them are variations on the themes we've explored here. Books on statistics will steer you through them.

I would mislead you, however, if I left you with the idea that we can always use statistics to clean up our messes.

We noted earlier that statistics won't do our thinking for us. That still goes. For instance, suppose we can indeed control some third variable by partial correlation or analysis of covariance. Even so, we must, at minimum, have thought the problem through to the point where (1) we have identified that third variable as one we need to consider, and (2) found a way to measure it. Sometimes, as with variables such as socioeconomic status, we can go back and measure it after the fact. But in the case of our drug-and-depression study, there is no way we can go back and get a pretreatment measure after the experiment is done!

The underlying idea in all this is so important as to be a

Principle: No statistical procedure ever spawned will give us any information about a variable we haven't measured.

So we think it through, carefully. In advance.

CHAPTER 9

EXPERIMENTS WITH MORE THAN ONE INDEPENDENT VARIABLE

IN THIS CHAPTER, WE'LL DISCUSS:

- Experimental designs with two or more independent variables

  Factorial designs

  Mixed between-groups and within-subjects designs

  Mixtures of manipulation and selection

- Main effects of independent variables

- Interactions among independent variables

To this point, we have focused upon experiments in which only one variable—the independent variable—was manipulated directly by the experimenter. Other influences on behavior were removed, or held constant, or at least assessed ("checked out") to the extent possible.

Many experiments are more complex than this. It is quite possible to manipulate more than one independent variable in a single experiment. This can have two advantages. First, there is a gain in efficiency: If the experiment is well designed, we can see the effects of two or more independent variables in a single experiment. In essence, we get two or more experiments for the price of one.

Second, we can see whether the two or more independent variables *interact* with each other. Since the notion of interaction is important, let's talk about it for a minute.

A LOOK AHEAD: THE CONCEPT OF INTERACTION

An interaction is any case in which the effect of one independent variable changes with the value of another one. For example, consider this question: Do you prefer your food hot or cold?

If we think about it for a minute, we see that no simple "yes or no" will do. If the food in question is ice cream, I for one prefer it cold; if a hamburger, then I'd rather have it hot. So we'd have to answer the question with "That depends!" On what? On what the food is.

In this little experiment, preference or liking is the dependent variable. The two independent variables are: kind of food (ice cream vs. hamburger), and temperature (hot vs. cold). The two interact, because the effect of one depends on the value of the other: Cooling the food increases its attraction for us *if* it is ice cream, but has the opposite effect if it is hamburger (Figure 9.1A).

Not all interactions are "crossover" ones of that kind. As a quick example of one that isn't, think again about our lamp in Chapter 2, the one that didn't light. Suppose we replace the bulb, with another one that we know to be good (because we've tested it in another lamp—a manipulation check!). And nothing happens. The light still doesn't work, and we say: "Okay, the problem isn't with the bulb." But at this juncture our roommate chimes in: "Hey, wait a minute! The cord's unplugged! Of course neither bulb will work." So we plug the cord in, and now again test the old bulb. It doesn't work. Re-

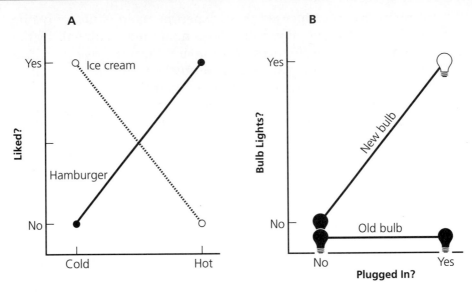

FIGURE 9.1

Two interactions. (A) Do we like food hot or cold? It depends on whether it's hamburger or ice cream. (B) Does the light work if we replace the bulb? It depends. If it's plugged in, yes, but only then.

place it with the new bulb, and that does work. The problem *was* with the bulb after all.

Here again we have two independent variables in this little experiment, and they interact with each other. One is old bulb versus new. Does it have an effect? That depends! On what? On the other independent variable: plugged in versus not plugged in. If the light is plugged in, then the bulb makes a difference; otherwise not (Figure 9.1B). We'll look at more examples as we go, until the notion of an interaction becomes second nature.

But before we go on, a caution. *A dependent variable never interacts with anything.* If we find that, say, the tendency to offer help is affected by the number of bystanders, it is tempting to say that the tendency to offer help "interacts with" the number of bystanders. But such a statement is ungrammatical in the language of research. We just don't use the term that way.

No, an interaction is always between one independent variable and another. We say that the *two or more independent variables interact with each other* in their effect on the dependent variable. Thus temperature of the food and the kind of food it is (the two independent variables) *interact with each other* to affect preference (the dependent variable). And similarly for the other interactions we'll consider.

Please remember that.

FACTORIAL DESIGNS

A *factorial design* is one in which (1) there are two or more independent variables, and (2) a group of subjects is assigned, at random from our initial "pool" of subjects, to *each possible combination* of these independent variables.

Look at Figure 9.2. In the first two boxes, we see a two-group experiment of the kind we're familiar with. There is some independent variable, A, and it has two values, A1 and A2. The subjects are assigned at random to one or another group, one receiving treatment A1, the other A2.

It doesn't matter what A is. It could be number of onlookers, where the A1 subjects witness an emergency alone, and the A2 subjects witness an identical emergency in the presence of others. Or it could be whether a rat has been made sick after eating a particular food, or not. It could be temperature of food—hot or cold. Lamp cord plugged in, or not. It could, in short, be anything an experimenter can manipulate.

In the second two boxes, we assume that in a separate experiment there is another independent variable, B, with its two values B1 and B2. Again subjects are assigned at random to experimental conditions or treatments, B1 and B2. Again, B can be any independent variable—anything we can manipulate.

Now to make a *factorial design*, we just take Panel B, turn it on its side, and superimpose it on Panel A. We now have four groups of subjects, receiving each possible combination of treatments: A1,B1;

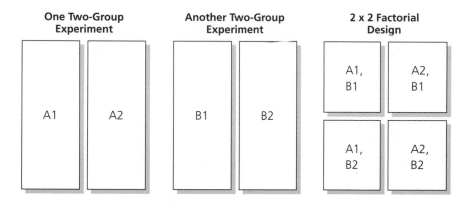

One Two-Group Experiment		Another Two-Group Experiment		2 x 2 Factorial Design	
A1	A2	B1	B2	A1, B1	A2, B1
				A1, B2	A2, B2

FIGURE 9.2

Building a 2 × 2 factorial design out of two independent-groups designs.

A1,B2; A2,B1; and A2,B2. Each subject is assigned at random to one of the four cells. Since both A and B have two values, we call this a *2 × 2 factorial design* (say "two by two").

Again, each of the two independent variables could be anything we can manipulate. But it will be easier to nail the idea down if we see how it works in concrete instances. So let's look at some real examples.

AN EXAMPLE FROM COGNITION: STATE-DEPENDENT MEMORY

Consider what happens when a subject in a memory experiment learns, let us say, a list of familiar words, and is later asked to remember what the words were. To do this, he is not learning the words themselves, for they are familiar. Rather, he is learning that *these* words go with *this* experiment. (We sometimes do the same sort of thing when we study for an exam.)

The subject, we may say, is forming an association between *these* words and the whole experimental situation. But this situation is quite complex. It may include both the external setting, and the subject's internal "situation"—the mood he or she is in, for example. It follows that if the subject is in the *same* mood when he learns the words initially and when he remembers the words later, the mood itself may act as a reminder of the words (because it is associated with them). This may improve his performance. That strange-looking prediction has in fact been confirmed many times.

In a classic demonstration of this effect, Bower (1981) manipulated his subjects' moods by hypnosis. First, the pool of subjects was divided into two groups. One of these memorized some material while they were put in very happy moods. The others memorized the same material while they were put in very sad moods.

Later, retention of the material was tested. And now the groups were split in half: Half the subjects in each original group were made happy, the other half sad. So again we have a 2 × 2 factorial design (Figure 9.3A).

The results are shown in Figure 9.3B. In this case, we see what is called a *"crossover" interaction*. (It is "crossover," of course, because the lines connecting the data points cross.) And it is an "interaction," because the effect of one independent variable (mood when remembering) is different depending on the other independent variable (mood while memorizing). Do subjects remember better when happy or when sad (one independent variable)? That depends! On

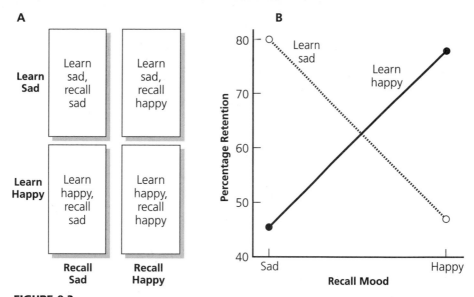

A

	Recall Sad	Recall Happy
Learn Sad	Learn sad, recall sad	Learn sad, recall happy
Learn Happy	Learn happy, recall sad	Learn happy, recall happy

FIGURE 9.3
Another crossover interaction: Subjects who memorized material when happy remembered it better if tested when happy; if sad, sad (from Bower, 1981).

what? On whether they were happy or sad when they first learned the material—the other independent variable.

Any time we have to talk like that—to say that the effect of one independent variable *depends on* the value of another one—we know that we are dealing with an interaction. Here, we say that mood during the memory test *interacts* with mood during memorization, to affect the dependent variable: amount remembered when memory is tested. Not all interactions are crossover, as we'll see; but such cases, where the effect of one manipulation is actually *reversed* when the other changes its value, shows vividly just how important interactions can be.

Many other experiments have shown this state-dependency of memory. Other variations in internal state can produce it: Thus in one experiment, subjects who memorized material when mildly inebriated did better if they were mildly inebriated when tested later; those who learned it when sober remembered it better when sober. External situations, too, can be "states" on which memory depends. In one especially heroic experiment, Godden and Baddeley (1975) used deep-sea divers as subjects. The task for all subjects was to memorize some arbitrary material; but one group of subjects memorized it while sitting on dry land, whereas the other group memorized it while they were 20 feet underwater. That was one independent variable: wet versus dry when memorizing. Then each of the two groups

297

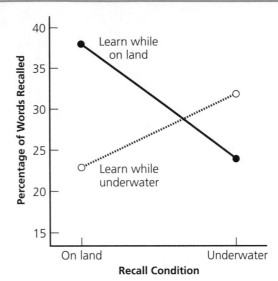

FIGURE 9.4
And another crossover interaction. Subjects again showed better retention if tested under the same conditions (wet or dry) as when they had memorized the material (from Godden & Baddeley, 1975).

was divided in half, with half the subjects tested for memory while on dry land, the other tested underwater. Sure enough: Subjects who learned the material dry remembered it best when dry; and subjects who memorized it wet did better if tested wet (Figure 9.4)—another crossover interaction.

AN EXAMPLE FROM MEMORY OR PARAPSYCHOLOGY OR SOMETHING: SUBLIMINAL TAPES

The idea that material can be recognized unconsciously, and affect our behavior without our awareness, remains a popular one. Certain of us have made quite a good thing of this idea, with the claim that one can boost self-esteem, improve memory, or even master a foreign language, by the use of *subliminal tapes*—ones that have messages embedded in noise or soft music. The messages are so faint that we fail to perceive them consciously; but, the claim is, they bypass our consciousness and speak to the subconscious directly.

Well, what about that claim? A number of research teams (see Pratkanis, 1992) have checked the effectiveness of subliminal tapes, and they have checked something else as well. A typical experiment would go as follows (Pratkanis, 1992).

When subjects appeared at the lab (in response to posters, newspaper ads, or the like), half the subjects were given tapes claimed to enhance self-esteem; the others were given tapes claimed to enhance memory. That is one independent variable: type of tape. The subjects listened to the tapes every day for a few weeks, as instructed by the manufacturer. Then memory and self-esteem were measured.

However, there was a twist to the study. For half the subjects in each group, the tapes were mislabeled. Half the subjects who *thought* they were hearing memory tapes were actually hearing self-esteem tapes; and conversely. This gives us once again a 2 × 2 factorial design, where the two independent variables were type of tape the subjects really were listening to, and the type of tape they thought they were listening to. See if you can diagram the design!

What happened? There was no effect whatever of either tape on either measure—memory or self-esteem—when these were measured.

However, this is not what the subjects thought. They said in effect: "No matter what the objective measures show, I know that these tapes did improve my memory" (for some subjects) "or my self-esteem" (for the others). But there was a problem. The domain in which subjects felt improvement was the domain that they *thought* their tapes were designed to enhance. Subjects who thought they were listening to self-esteem tapes—whether they were or not—reported enhanced self-esteem. Subjects who thought they were listening to memory tapes—whether they were or not—reported better memories. The authors call this an "illusory placebo effect"—placebo effect because it was the result of expectations, and illusory because the improvement that the subjects felt was simply not there, at least as far as objective measures could detect.

To sum up (Figure 9.5), there was no *main effect* of type of tape—memory or self-esteem—on the subject's perception of (say) his or

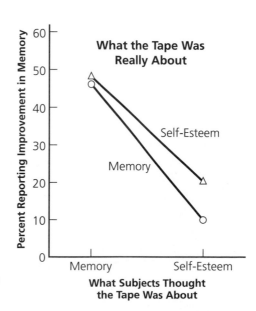

FIGURE 9.5
The effect of subliminal tapes on self-reported memory improvement. Subjects were more likely to report improvement if they *thought* the tapes had to do with memory—whether they did or not (data from Greenwald, Spangenberg, Pratkanis, & Eskenazi, 1991).

[Figure axes: Percent Reporting Improvement in Memory (vertical, 0–60); What Subjects Thought the Tape Was About (horizontal: Memory, Self-Esteem); "What the Tape Was Really About" with Self-Esteem and Memory lines]

her memory. However, there was a significant main effect of what the subject *thought* the tape was for. If she *thought* she had listened to a memory tape (whether she had or not), then she felt that her memory had improved. Finally, there was *no interaction* between type of tape heard and type of tape thought. As the nearly parallel lines in Figure 9.5 show, the effect of type of tape thought was about the same, whether it was a memory tape or a self-esteem tape that was actually heard. It did not all "depend" on the value of the other variable, the real content of the tape.

COMMENTS

Before moving on, let me say three things about this investigation.

First, it does not stand alone. There is now a substantial body of data, and the conclusion it supports is clear: Subliminal tapes are worthless. Indeed, there is no evidence that subliminal stimuli of any kind affect our behavior. They do not, for example, lead us to eat more popcorn at the movies.

The data are out there. No one is hiding them. Yet subliminal tapes continue to be sold—for as much as $400 a set!

What is the appeal of the "subliminal effects" idea? First, I suppose, it promises learning without effort; it may also give us a villain to hate (the "hidden persuader"); and it lends a pleasing aura of mystery to the mind—as if the mind were not mysterious enough without it! But there is this little problem with the idea: It is not true.

Second, the myth of subliminal persuasion can have consequences that would be funny if they were not so serious. Not long ago, charges were brought against the rock group Judas Priest. They were accused of causing the suicides of two teen-age boys, because (it was argued) their music covered the subliminal message, "Do it!"

The charges were rejected by the court, largely on the basis of testimony by research psychologists who pointed out the utter lack of evidence that such subliminal messages have any effect on our actions. But think of the expense of the trial to the defendants! Think of the expense to ourselves, were we ever accused (however witlessly) of subliminal manipulation.

The third comment is a methodological one. The tactic of varying what a subject thinks is happening, independently of what is actually happening, has been used in a number of different contexts, and we'll see further examples. Now, the use of such procedures raises tricky ethical questions, for they necessarily involve deception.

On the one hand, have we the right to lie to our subjects? On the other: It may be important to know whether an effect is produced by (say) what the subject has listened to, or by what he *thinks* he has listened to. The only way to find out is to separate the belief from the reality. And the only way to do that is by deception.

Thus we look forward to a topic we'll consider again later (Chapter 13). To anticipate: We don't (or we shouldn't) ask whether this-or-that experiment is "ethical." Rather, we weigh the ethical costs of doing the experiment against the ethical costs of not doing it. That doesn't make the decision any easier, as we will see.

A LOOK BACK: FACTORIAL DESIGNS AND INTERACTIONS

In all the above examples, we see the great advantages of factorial designs. First, we see the effects of two independent variables in a single experiment. Second, we see how the two interact, if they do. The effect of happiness versus sadness at learning (one independent variable) interacts with the effect of happiness versus sadness at testing (another independent variable) in affecting amount recalled (the dependent variable). The effect of wet or dry during learning (one independent variable) interacts with the effect of wet or dry when tested for memory (another independent variable) in affecting performance on the memory test (the dependent variable). Then again, there may be no interaction. Tape thought heard (one independent variable) did not interact with tape actually heard (the other independent variable) in affecting the dependent variable (self-report of memory enhancement).

MIXED WITHIN- AND BETWEEN-SUBJECTS DESIGNS

In a factorial design, a separate group of subjects receives each possible combination of conditions. Such a design really consists of two or more simple between-groups designs, turned at right angles to each other and superimposed (see Figure 9.2 earlier). But other "simple" experimental designs can also be superimposed on each other. For example, a between-groups design can be turned on its side, as before, and superimposed on a *within-subjects design*. In such a design, all subjects are tested or measured repeatedly; that is the within-subjects component. But throughout these repeated measures,

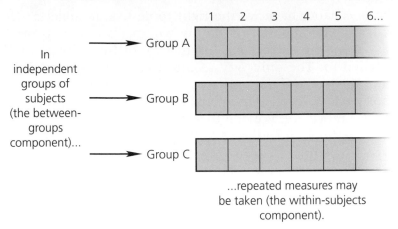

In independent groups of subjects (the between-groups component)...

Group A

Group B

Group C

1 2 3 4 5 6...

...repeated measures may be taken (the within-subjects component).

FIGURE 9.6
Design of a mixed between-groups and within-subjects experiment.

independent groups of subjects (randomly assigned, of course) differ as to something else. That is the between-groups or between-subjects component (Figure 9.6). Let's look at an example.

AN EXAMPLE FROM CLINICAL RESEARCH

Earlier, we saw how within-subjects designs reduce variability in the data by controlling for individual differences. They can still do that when mixed with a between-subjects comparison. And here, as there, they can bring order to what looks at first like chaos.

Let's take an example we have already considered. Suppose we take before and after measures for two groups of subjects, randomly assigned. Between these measures, one group receives therapy of some sort. The other group receives a placebo treatment. Thus one independent variable, treatment versus placebo, is varied between groups; it is the between-groups component of our mixed design. The other independent variable, before versus after, varies within each subject; so it is the within-subjects component.

Look at Figure 9.7, which shows what the data might look like for such a design. Again we find ourselves on familiar ground. Do treated subjects do better than untreated ones? Is there a difference between the scores for treated and untreated subjects? In Panel A, there is certainly not a consistent one; the data are well mixed. And this is true for both the "before" and the "after" scores.

But now look at Panel B. Here, we suppose that each pair of data points, connected by a line, represents the *same* subject, with per-

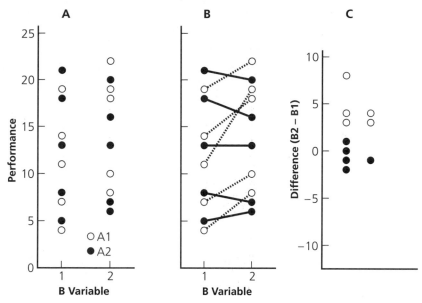

FIGURE 9.7

A mixed within-subjects and between-groups design. A thoroughly mixed-up and in-consistent set of scores (Panel A) becomes much more clear and consistent when the subjects are compared with themselves (Panel B), and even clearer when the raw scores are converted to before-and-after difference scores (Panel C).

formance measured twice. And look at the consistency that emerges! Although the data points themselves are still all scrambled around, we see that *every subject* in the treated group improved more than *any subject* in the placebo group. By *controlling for individual differences* in absolute performance level, we make the data tell a very clear story.

Actually, in this case we could make it even clearer by taking *difference scores*: each subject's "after" score minus her or his "before" score (Panel C), which would give us a measure of *improvement*. Now the two frequency distributions of these difference scores have drawn wide apart, and the movement toward higher scores in the one group, but not the other, is visible at a glance. By shrinking variability *within* each group (by within-subjects comparisons), we make the *differences between groups* consistent and readily visible.

When we take difference scores in this way, in effect we turn the data into a simple between-groups comparison. We can now compare the difference scores between the two groups in Figure 9.7C with a simple *t*-test. In effect, we make the within-subjects variable disappear—from the statistics! But it is still very much present in the experimental *procedure*. And its great advantage is still there: By controlling for individual differences, it reduces variability in the data.

What do we conclude from the data as a whole? If we compare all the "before" scores with all the "after" scores, we see that there is a tendency toward improvement in the sample as a whole. If this tendency is significant, there is a *main effect* of before versus after. But we also see that this effect is more pronounced in the treated patients. We could summarize by saying: All subjects tended to improve, yes (the main effect). But *how much* did they improve? That depends! On what? On whether they received real or placebo treatment—the other independent variable.

And "that depends" tells us that we are seeing an *interaction* between the two independent variables—treatment versus placebo, and after versus before. It is not a crossover interaction this time, but it's still an interaction: The magnitude of the before-versus-after difference *depends on* the other independent variable, placebo versus real.

Now let us look at a real example.

AN EXAMPLE FROM ANIMAL LEARNING—OR IS IT CLINICAL PSYCHOLOGY?

The story of "learned helplessness" begins with an accidental discovery by Maier (1970) in the study of animal learning. In these experiments, the subjects (dogs) were trained in a simple learning task, in an apparatus like the one shown in Figure 9.8. The long enclosure is separated into two compartments by a barrier, adjusted for each dog to shoulder height, over which the dog can jump. The experiment begins when the grid floor of the box is electrified, to provide a mild but unpleasant shock. The dog can turn off the shock by

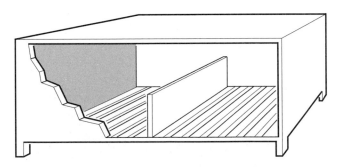

FIGURE 9.8
A shuttlebox. An animal's task is to turn off electric shock by jumping across the barrier from one side of the box to the other.

jumping over the barrier to the other side of the box. That ends the first trial. Then, after a predetermined period of time, shock comes on again and the dog can again escape it by crossing the barrier back to the original side. So, on successive trials, the dog shuttles back and forth between the two sides of the apparatus to turn off the shock each time it comes on. Hence such an apparatus is called a *shuttlebox*.

Dogs usually learn this task very quickly. After a few trials, when the shock comes on, they promptly jump the barrier to turn it off again. But in some dogs, this was not so. Suppose a dog had had experience, prior to this experiment, with shocks that it *could not turn off*. Then, faced with these shocks that it *could* turn off, it might never learn to do it. Instead, such dogs waited passively for the experimenter to turn the shock off for them.

Maier, Seligman, and Solomon (1969) went on to conclude that the dogs had formed a belief in, or expectation of, their own helplessness. It is as if the dogs said: "These experimenters put me in situations where nothing I do does me any good. Well, this must be another such situation. If I have no control over what happens, why try?"*

Let us zero in on one of these experiments.

For this experiment, a pool of dogs was selected. They were assigned, at random, to one of three conditions. In one condition (the control), the dogs were simply given the shuttle-box task and allowed to learn to escape the shocks. They had had no previous experience in an experimental apparatus.

A second group was treated identically, except for this: Before being given the shuttlebox task, they were given a series of shocks, in a different apparatus, that they *could not control*. The experimenter, not the dog, determined how long the shock lasted each time it came on. These dogs, then, should show learned helplessness. Having once discovered that they could not control the shocks in Phase 1, they should make no attempt to control them later, even when they could, in Phase 2—the shuttlebox task.

The third group allowed the researchers to ask another question. The dogs in the second group (but not the first) had experienced shocks, and ones that they could not control. But if they showed poor learning later, would this be because of the shocks themselves, or because of their uncontrollability? The third group, in Phase 1

---

*There were other possible interpretations, but the researchers "checked them out" in separate control experiments and rejected them. We cannot tell the full story here; see Seligman (1990).

Table 9.1

Group	Phase I	Phase II
1	No shock	Shuttlebox task
2	Uncontrollable shock	Shuttlebox task
3	Controllable shock	Shuttlebox task

prior to the shuttlebox learning task, received shocks at the same pattern and intensity as the "helpless" group, but these dogs could turn the shocks off. So the history of shocks per se was the same for the second and third group. Only their controllability varied.*

Thus *prior experience* was one independent variable in this experiment, and it had three values: experience with uncontrollable shock, experience with controllable shock, and no experience with shock, for three independent groups. That was the between-groups component.

The other independent variable was simply *number of trials*. This is a perfectly good independent variable: The experimenters impose a first trial, a second trial, and so on, and we can see how performance changes as the trial number increases. So here: As amount of experience (number of trials) increased, was there a change in promptness of jumping over the barrier—the dependent variable? That was the within-subjects component of the design.

Table 9.1 summarizes this design. In Figure 9.9, we see the results. The vertical axis shows the average *latency* of the barrier-crossing response for each group—that is, from the time each shock came on, how long (on average) did it take the dogs to cross the barrier and turn it off? This was the dependent variable. As we see, the control animals quickly learned to jump the barrier promptly—low latency—and thus turn off the shock almost as soon as it came on. So did the group that had experienced shocks, but controllable ones, before this task.

Not so the previously "helpless" group. The average latency—time from shock onset—was 20 seconds, and it stayed there, trial after trial. Why 20 seconds? Because this was the "ceiling" that the experimenters placed on duration of the shock: On a given trial, if the dog

---

*This was accomplished by what is called a *yoked control* procedure. In Phase 1, each dog in the "helpless" group was assigned, or "yoked to," a pair-mate in the nonhelpless third group. And within each pair, each trial in the apparatus was conducted for the control animal first, then for its "helpless" pair-mate. On each such trial, the experimenters kept track of how long it took the control animal to turn off the shock. Then they left the shock on for just that long, and then turned it off themselves, for the "helpless" pair-mate. Thus the total amount of shock received was held rigidly constant for both groups of dogs. Only its controllability varied: For one group, the animals turned it off themselves; for the other, the experimenters turned it off, irrespective of what the animals did.

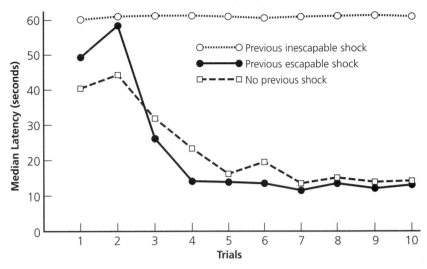

FIGURE 9.9

A conditioned-helplessness experiment. The three groups were treated differently in Phase I (the between-groups component). Then all subjects were given repeated trials at the shuttlebox task (the within-subjects component; from Maier, Seligman, & Solomon, 1969).

had not crossed the barrier by the 20-second mark, the experimenters turned the shock off for that trial. So, since the *average* score for the "helpless" group was right at 20 seconds, this tells us that *every animal in the group* must have waited the full 20 seconds on each trial, never discovering that in fact they could turn the shock off themselves, much sooner. They had acquired learned helplessness.

It is important to realize that the task facing the animals in Phase 2 was identical for all three groups. The apparatus was the same for all, and all groups could have controlled the shock in Phase 2. But only two groups learned to do so. The dogs with a history of helplessness never did.

Finally, Figure 9.9 shows us another example of an *interaction* between two independent variables. Does latency—the dependent variable—change over successive trials—one independent variable? That depends! On what? On the value of the other independent variable—prior history. In dogs with no history of uncontrollable shock, latency goes down—performance improves—over successive trials. In dogs with such a history, it does not.

COMMENTS

From this experiment came many others, and some ideas that have implications far beyond dogs, shocks, and shuttleboxes. First, researchers went on to show that learned helplessness could be produced by similar experiments in monkeys, rats, and even humans.

But there is more. Seligman was struck by certain parallels between the behavior of his "helpless" dogs and the behavior of depressed human patients, whom his colleague, psychiatrist Aaron Beck, was studying intensively. Beck had focused on the disordered and irrational *beliefs* that depressed patients exhibit, focusing on their own unworthiness, incapability, and *helplessness*. Now, "I can't control what these humans do to me" is a belief; and we could say that it is a false one, even an irrational one, if control is in fact available to the animal. And remember that it is the uncontrollability, not the shocks themselves, that made the dogs behave "helplessly" in Phase 2.

Might learned helplessness play a role in human depression? Do depressed patients habitually give helpless, hopeless explanations for the misfortunes that befall them? There is evidence that they do (see Abramson, Seligman, & Teasdale, 1978). Thus the animal-learning lab makes contact with the investigation of habits of thought, and causal attributions, as conducted by cognitive and social psychologists. The whole line of thought is a case study in how different research areas can cross-fertilize each other.

A LOOK BACK

In these examples, once again the specifics are very different, but the underlying ideas are the same. An independent variable is varied, taking different values for different groups, giving us a *between-groups* comparison. But also, a different independent variable—such as successive trials, or before versus after—varies within subjects so that each subject is compared with himself, herself, or itself. This gives us a *within-subjects* comparison.

And once again, the two independent variables may interact with each other. In the learned helplessness experiments, does shuttlebox performance get better over successive trials—the within-groups independent variable? Answer: It *depends*. On what? On whether or not the animal has had a history of helplessness—the between-groups variable. So the effect of number of trials interacts with the effect of history.

Similarly for our hypothetical clinical experiment. Does improvement occur in the sample as a whole? Yes, it does (a main effect); most subjects improved. But how much improvement is there? Why, *that* depends! Improvement is much greater with real than with placebo treatment.

MIXED EXPERIMENTAL AND SUBJECT–VARIABLE DESIGNS

Until now, we have looked at designs in which two independent variables were manipulated experimentally, in a single experiment. However, a manipulated variable may also be combined, in a single design, with another variable that is varied by *selecting* subjects who already differ with respect to it.

An investigation of this type, strictly speaking, is only half an experiment. One independent variable is manipulated experimentally. The other "independent variable" is only measured, not manipulated; and subjects may be selected in accordance with what that measure shows for them. A variable of this sort, on which people already differ, is often called a *subject variable* or, sometimes, an *individual-differences variable*.

AN EXAMPLE FROM COGNITION: RESTRAINED EATING AND "COUNTERREGULATION"

We tend to think of eating behavior as governed by a relatively simple physiological control system. In fact, we find that the amount that is eaten at a meal varies not only with physiological but also with cognitive influences. This is true even in the rat, as the conditioned-taste-aversion phenomenon shows (Chapter 6). And it is true in humans too, as we are about to see.

In our society, many people worry about their weight. Many of us consciously limit our intake of food because of this. An intriguing phenomenon was discovered by C. Peter Herman, Janet Polivy, and their collaborators, in investigating such "restrained eaters" or "dieters."

One study was as follows. Based on questionnaire data, the subjects (female college students, all of normal weight) were divided into "restrained eaters" who deliberately restricted their intake, and "unrestrained eaters" who did not. This was the individual-difference variable. When the subjects came to the lab, they were first asked to drink either zero, one, or two big rich milkshakes. This—number of milkshakes (including zero)—was the other independent variable, and this one was manipulated experimentally. Subjects were randomly *assigned* to one of the three conditions.

Finally, all subjects were offered dishes of ice cream, and were invited to eat as much ice cream as they wanted. How much would they eat? That was the dependent variable.

First, what ought to happen? Having just drunk down a big milk-shake or two, one will be less hungry and so will eat less ice cream, right? Right, for the nondieters in the study. But for the "restrained eaters," quite wrong! These subjects actually ate *more* if they had just had a milkshake or two than if they had not.

Figure 9.10 shows this result, in the form of a beautiful "crossover" interaction. How does drinking lots of milkshake now affect how much ice cream is eaten later? That *really* depends! For nondieters, the more milkshake first, the less ice cream second. But for dieters, the reverse is true: The more milkshake first, the *more* ice cream second.

This effect, which Herman and Polivy (1980) call "counterregulation," makes no physiological sense at all. If we are *regulating* food intake on the basis of internal physiological cues, then the more food there is in the body, the less additional food we should take.

However, it does make cognitive sense, in this way: If a person sticking to a rigid diet drinks down a whole milkshake, then the diet plan has already been violated. The subject may say, "Well, my diet is already ruined for the day. I might as well just go ahead and enjoy myself, and eat." Hence this phenomenon has also been called the "what-the-hell effect."

Now there is an alternative possibility. Maybe the milkshake had internal effects that stimulated hunger or "whetted the appetite."

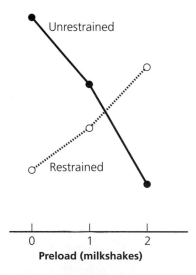

FIGURE 9.10
Amount of ice cream eaten after varying amounts of milkshake (0, 1, or 2 glasses, the manipulated variable), in dieters and nondieters (the subject variable); from Herman & Polivy, 1980).

However, this possibility was checked out, and ruled out, in a separate experiment. Here, counterregulation was shown if the dieters *thought* the milkshake was high in calories. Dieters who drank an identical milkshake, but thought it was low in calories, did not counterregulate. Physiological appetite whetting should have been the same for both, so what matters is what the subject's *beliefs* are. As so often, it's the thought that counts.

COMMENTS

In a provocative paper, Polivy and Herman (1985) relate their extensive research to a problem of human feeding. This is the syndrome known as "binge eating," or *bulimia*. It is characterized by periods of uncontrolled eating, in which a person may wolf down an enormous meal all at once. Typically the bulimic person feels remorseful after the eating binge, and if she is a dieter (as many binge eaters are), she may diet all the more strictly to make up for it.

It seems natural to think of binge eating as a cause of later dieting: One overeats now, so one then diets to make up for it. But Polivy and Herman suggest that we try thinking of it the other way—maybe dieting can cause binge eating!

If a person persistently holds his food intake below where the body "wants" it to be—as determined by internal, physiological signals—then he must suppress or ignore the signals that his body is sending him. He must depend on conscious cognitive controls. But it is just these controls that have that soap-bubble quality: They may collapse after even a minor "violation" of the diet (the "what-the-hell" effect). The resulting bout of eating may escalate into a full-scale binge episode.

Indeed, we can take the argument yet a step further. Suppose one is accustomed to ignoring the body's signals. Then a binge episode could continue even past the point of physiological, as well as cognitive, inhibition. Binge eaters often say things like this: "When I would binge, my stomach would get so full I would feel stuffed. I'd say, 'So what?' and go on eating anyway!" Thus *case study* information can be brought to bear in support of this conclusion.

In short, we see that cognitive factors have powerful effects even on such "basic, biological" behavior as eating. Apparently it is not enough for the body to tell the brain, "Hey, I've had enough!" The brain has to *listen* to those signals. Then it must decide what, if anything, to do about them.

In all of our examples, the underlying logic is the same. In essence, we design the first experiment, with its independent variable; design the second experiment, with *its* independent variable; turn the second experiment on its side, and superimpose it over the first one. If both independent variables are varied using independent groups, we have a factorial design. But a manipulated variable can also be superimposed on a within-subjects variable, like successive trials or a before/after comparison; or with a subject variable, like dieters versus nondieters. In each case, we can see whether each independent variable has an effect across the board—what we call its *main effect*—and also see how the two *interact* (if they do) in affecting the dependent variable. And we get all this information in a single experiment.

HIGHER-ORDER DESIGNS

Our examples thus far have been cases in which *two* independent variables were varied in a single experiment. But no law says there can only be two. In principle, we could vary as many independent variables as we like, all in one experiment.

For example, Figure 9.11 shows what the layout would look like for a *three-way*, $3 \times 2 \times 2$ factorial design. There are three independent variables. The A variable has three values, so there are three groups to begin with. Each of these groups is split in half, to receive

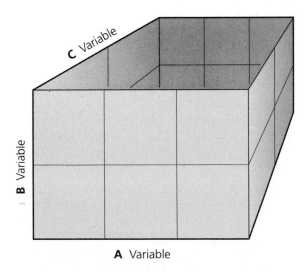

FIGURE 9.11
A three-way design.

different values of the B variable. And each of *those* groups is again split in half, to receive different values of the C variable. The same dependent variable will be measured in all the resulting groups.

Once again, each of the three independent variables can be anything we can vary—by manipulation or by selection. Let's see some examples.

AN EXAMPLE FROM CLINICAL PSYCHOLOGY: DESENSITIZATION THERAPY

Our previous discussions of Pavlovian conditioning have focused on theoretically relevant instances: salivary conditioning in dogs, eyelid conditioning in humans, and taste-aversion learning in rats and humans. However, the principles of conditioning also find direct application to practical human problems. As an example, let's consider an experiment on *desensitization therapy*, in which the principles of conditioning were applied to the treatment of *phobia* (Davison, 1968).

A *phobia* is an intense, irrational fear—of snakes or spiders, of dirt, of enclosed places (claustrophobia), of speaking in public, or of taking tests ("test anxiety"). The person may know perfectly well that the fear is irrational, but it may persist anyway—reason and knowledge, as with taste-aversion learning (Chapter 6), may not be enough. Instead, desensitization therapy attempts to *condition a response* to the feared situation—a response that will reduce the fear. Deep-muscle relaxation is one such response (Figure 9.12).

Here is how it is done. First, the patient practices total, deep-muscle relaxation until he can relax his entire body on command. After that, there follows a series of conditioning trials on which the patient *imagines* the feared situation—an examination perhaps, or a snake, depending on what he is afraid of—and, while doing so, relaxes his body completely at the therapist's command.*

This is done over and over again. Each such pairing—of the image with relaxation—can be considered a conditioning trial. The image is an internal CS (as Pavlov's bell was an external one), and relaxation is the response (like salivation). If one can establish re-

---

*The usual procedure is to take it in stages. The patient first practices the relaxation response while imagining a mild form of the phobia object—for example, a snake 100 yards away, or an exam 24 hours in the future. Once the patient can relax while forming such images, further training will bring the imagined snake (or the imagined exam) closer, little by little.

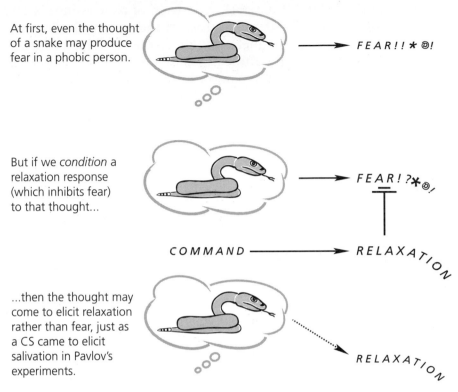

At first, even the thought of a snake may produce fear in a phobic person.

FEAR!! ✳ ☺!

But if we *condition* a relaxation response (which inhibits fear) to that thought...

FEAR!? ✳ ☺!

COMMAND ⟶ *RELAXATION*

...then the thought may come to elicit relaxation rather than fear, just as a CS came to elicit salivation in Pavlov's experiments.

RELAXATION

FIGURE 9.12
The theory of desensitization therapy.

laxation as a conditioned response to the image, then the relaxation will oppose fear and the fear will be reduced.

Then there is the further assumption that the relaxation response will transfer from the image of the feared object to the object itself (e.g., a real snake). One may also try to condition relaxation to actual feared situations rather than imagined ones; but, interestingly enough, it is not clear that this method works any better than the one described here, done with imagery as CS.

Now all this sounds very sensible, if we know about Pavlov's work. Two questions, however: (1) Does it work—is the method really effective in treating phobia? (2) Even if it is, does *conditioning* really have anything to do with it? Not necessarily. There are other possibilities.

First, maybe what matters is just that the subject learn the skill of relaxation—which does take some practice. Once he acquires the skill, he may be able to apply it when snakes (or whatever) are around. The *pairing* of relaxation with snake imagery may not be needed at all.

Second: Maybe just repeatedly imagining snakes permits the fear to die down. This would be an instance of what psychologists call "habituation," not of conditioning. In other words, again the *pairing* of the imagery with relaxation may not be necessary. Maybe the treatment would work just as well with only the imagery. In a word, maybe the subject just gets used to thinking about snakes, and so fears them less.

Davison (1968) asked both these questions at once. His experiment was a 2×2 factorial design (a between-groups component), *and* a before-and-after within-subjects comparison.

Davison was fortunate in that he had access to a reasonably large number of subjects (college students) who reported severe fear of snakes, even nonpoisonous ones. So he compared various ways of treating this "snake phobia." When each subject came to his lab, Davison first took an objective measure of the severity of the phobia. His apparatus consisted of one live snake, with life-support system, and he set up a progression of tasks that brought the subject into closer and closer contact with the snake. These ranged from placing a gloved hand on the glass near the snake, to holding it bare-handed for 30 seconds. Davison's measure was how far along the graded series of tasks the subject could go.

Then, at the end of the experiment, he measured severity of phobia again in the same way. So we have before and after measures for each subject. Comparison of these—the within-subjects component—gives us a measure of before-to-after *improvement*. All these measures were taken by an experimenter who was "blind" as to what group each subject was in (why?).

But before and after what? The second independent variable was the *type of treatment* the subject received between pre- and postmeasures. One group received standard desensitization therapy: repeated pairings of snake imagery with relaxation. A second group repeatedly imagined snakes or snake-related scenes, but without relaxation training and without being asked to relax while imagining. The third group did receive relaxation training, but it was paired with images unrelated to snakes. And the fourth group received no treatment; they were just tested, and tested again, after a period corresponding to the duration of treatment for the other three.

This sequence of events is diagrammed in Figure 9.13A. We could also represent the four groups as a 2×2 factorial design. The two independent variables are: snake imagery, present or absent; and relaxation, present or absent. The combinations of these—the one, the other, neither, or both—give us the four groups shown. We might note too that Groups 2 and 3 give us examples of a possible control

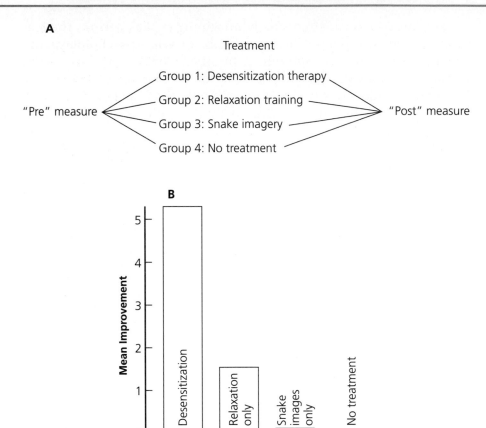

FIGURE 9.13
(A) Design of Davison's experiment; (B) his findings (from Davison, 1968).

condition for therapy: omitting some critical part of a therapeutic "package" (Chapter 8).

But in all groups, severity of phobia was measured before, and then again after, the "treatment" was imposed. This before-and-after comparison was the within-subjects component of the three-way design. So we have a within-subjects comparison superimposed on a factorial design.*

Davison's results are shown in Figure 9.13B. To simplify matters for the reader, Davison opted to collapse his within-subject measures into single *difference scores*, or *improvement scores*. As it turned out, Group 1, for whose subjects the snake images were *paired with* re-

---

*Actually, Davison added yet another complication: His groups were *matched* for initial severity of phobia, based on the pretreatment scores. So this is really a *four-way* design, with pretreatment score (high to low) as the fourth variable. We'll ignore this refinement here.

laxation, improved significantly more than the other three groups. And only in Group 1 was the before/after difference significant in itself.

Notice how comparisons between these scores allow us to answer the questions we began with. Is the method effective? Yes. Group 1 showed significantly more improvement than Group 4, the control. Was this only because subjects were learning to relax? No. If it were, then Group 2 should have improved as much as Group 1; but they didn't. Well, was it because subjects got used to thinking about snakes, and so became less fearful? No. If this were the case, Group 3 should have improved as much as Group 1. They did not.

So Davison concluded that this technique, whose effectiveness is demonstrated by this and many other studies, really does require explicit *pairing* of the snake-imagery CS with the relaxation response. It is not just a case of skill acquisition (learning to relax, Group 2). It is not just a case of habituation (getting used to the thought of snakes, Group 3). It is a case of genuine Pavlovian conditioning. A striking example of how a phenomenon discovered in one context— salivation in dogs—can reveal *principles* that apply in a quite different one—the treatment of phobias in humans.

AN EXAMPLE FROM COGNITION: CONDITIONING AND AWARENESS REVISITED

Actually, we have seen this example before. We need only put it in the present context.

Remember the Clark and Squire (1998) experiment, dealing with the role of awareness in human eyelid conditioning (Chapter 3)? We recall that there were two manipulated variables: (1) successive trials, and (2) whether or not there was a brief delay between the CS (a tone) and the UCS (a puff of air to the eyeball). In addition, the subjects were divided (after the conditioning sessions) into those who were, and those who were not, aware of the relationship between the CS and the UCS—that is, that the tone meant a puff was coming. This "aware/unaware" difference was a subject variable.

In Figure 9.14A, we see the data for the no-delay condition. We see that both groups showed conditioning, and conditioning occurred at about the same rate for the "aware" and the "unaware" subjects. There was no main effect of aware versus unaware (overall frequency of CRs was about the same for both groups). There was a main effect of trials (more conditioned responses occurred as the session went on). And there was no significant interaction between the two

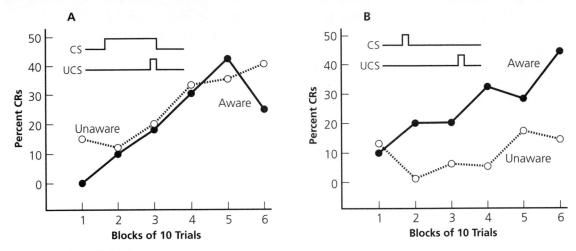

FIGURE 9.14

In the Clark and Squire conditioning experiment there were three independent variables: (1) successive trials (horizontal axis), (2) whether the subjects were or were not aware of the CS-UCS relation (filled versus open circles), and (3) presence versus absence of a silent interval between CS and UCS (Panel A versus Panel B). There was a three-way interaction among these, in their effect on the dependent variable (percent CRs).

(the rate of increase was roughly the same for aware vs. unaware; i.e., the two curves in the figure are roughly parallel).

But now look at Panel B. Here we see the data for the condition in which there was a half-second silent period between offset of the tone, and the puff. Once again, there was an overall trend toward more CRs as trials progressed; there was a main effect of trials. But this time, there was a main effect of condition (overall, more CRs in the "aware" group than in the "unaware" group). And, this time there was an interaction between trials and condition: Frequency of CRs increased much more over trials in the aware than in the unaware group. Indeed, in the unaware group it increased hardly at all.

What do we make of all this? In Panel A, CRs increased in frequency over the session—period. They increased at about the same rate for both—period. Neither of these conclusions "depends." So learning occurred over trials, and at the same rate, whether the subjects were aware or unaware.

But in Panel B, it all does depend! How did the frequency of CRs increase over trials? That depends—on whether the subjects were aware or unaware. If they were aware, it increased raidly; if they were unaware, it didn't. So awareness/nonawareness interacts with trial number in affecting the average score.

Putting these together, we find ourselves with a *three-way interaction*, among trials, awareness/unawareness, and gap versus no-gap

318

condition. Did trials interact with awareness/unawareness? Why, *that* depends! On what? On whether there was a silent period between CS and USC . If there was, the other two variables interacted; if there wasn't, they didn't. That is what a three-way interaction looks like.

A three-way interaction is daunting to look at. It really doesn't have to be, though, if we keep in mind the questions we're asking. If there is no silent period, the subjects learn, and at about the same rate, whether they know what is going on or not (Panel A). So knowledge is not necessary for conditioning. But adding that silent period depresses their learning—it may even abolish it—*if* they do not know what is going on. So that knowledge protects against the disruptive effects of the silent period.

We have worked through an example of a *three-way interaction*. And we've seen that if we stay tuned and keep our eye on the questions we're asking, it breaks down into sensible answers to those questions.

A LOOK BACK

Just as two independent variables can be "crossed" to make a two-way design, so a two-way design can be "crossed" with yet another variable—a within-subjects comparison, a subject variable, or another manipulated variable—to make a three-way design. Indeed, we could add yet more to make a four-way design, a five-way design . . . we could take it to as many independent variables as we like.

The way to avoid confusion in all this is to realize that each of our comparisons *asks a question*: What effect does this variable have across the board (its *main effect*), and how does it *interact* (if it does) with other independent variables in affecting the data we obtain? If we keep that in mind, asking ourselves for each comparison—What question is the investigator asking?—then we will find that even the most complex design breaks down into a set of simple question-and-answer experiments within that design.

SUMMARY

More than one independent variable can be manipulated within a single experiment. This way, we see the effects of each such variable, all in one experiment.

Moreover, we can see if there are *interactions* among our independent variables. An interaction occurs when the effect of one independent variable depends on the value of another. When that happens, if we are asked "What is the effect of this particular independent variable?" we must answer, "That depends!" On what? On the value of the other independent variable.

In a *factorial design*, there are two or more independent variables, and a separate group of subjects is assigned, at random, to *each possible combination* of these independent variables. State-dependent learning, for example, can be shown by an experiment in which there are variations both in conditions at learning and conditions at later test, with a separate group of subjects for each combination.

In other cases, a between-groups comparison can be combined ("crossed") with a within-subjects design. An example is an experiment in which before and after measures (a within-subject comparison) are taken in each of two or more groups which differ along some variable (the between-groups component). Another is an early experiment on "learned helplessness," in which one independent variable (repeated trials, the within-subjects component) was found to interact with another independent variable (prior history, the between-groups component) in affecting the dependent variable, task performance.

Or an experimental manipulation may be combined with "manipulation by selection"—that is, a subject variable. Interactions between these two "kinds" of independent variable may occur. For example, amount of milkshake consumed (manipulated directly) interacts with the subject variable, dieter/nondieter ("manipulated" by selection), in affecting the dependent variable, amount consumed later. The interaction had a surprise to show us: the "counterregulation effect."

Still more complex designs are possible. Thus a within-subjects comparison was superimposed on a factorial design, in the desensitization example. In another case, a variable "manipulated" by selection (aware/unaware) was crossed with a mixed design, in which the independent variables were (1) aware/unaware, (2) presence or absence of a silent period between CS and UCS, and (3) trials. A three-way interaction was found. Did performance improve over time? It depended on whether or not there was a silent period *and* whether or not the subjects were aware of the CS–UCS pairing.

We could extend these complex designs to investigate as many independent variables as we like. If we do, we can avoid being confused by complex designs if we remember that each of our variables *asks a question*: What effect does this variable have across the board (its *main effect*), and how does it *interact* with other independent variables in affecting the data we obtain? Even the most complex design breaks down into simple questions and answers.

MAKING FRIENDS WITH STATISTICS: FACTORIAL ANALYSIS OF VARIANCE AND MORE ABOUT INTERACTIONS

In previous chapters, we have learned how to test the significance of a difference between two or more conditions, in an experiment with one independent variable. But what if there is more than one independent variable, as in a factorial design?

We have already made friends with the *analysis of variance* (Chapter 6) for the case of one independent variable. You might want to review that section before reading further. For now we are going to extend that useful tool to the case of two independent variables in single experiments.

Let us begin by simply doing one. In what follows, we will go through the calculations first. Then, when we have *what* we do laid out before us, we can look at *why* we do it.

EXAMPLE 1

Let us suppose that we have conducted a 2 × 2 factorial experiment. We have two independent variables, A and B; each has two values, 1 and 2; so we have four independent groups who receive, respectively, treatments A1,B1; A1,B2; A2,B1; and A2,B2 (compare Figure 9.2 above).

It doesn't matter what A and B are. They could be any two variables we can manipulate. Variable A might be whether food is hot or cold, and Variable B might be whether it is steak or ice cream; and the dependent variable could be a rating

of liking. Variable A could be whether material is learned on land or underwater; Variable B, whether retention is measured on land or underwater; and the dependent variable could be number of items recalled. The A and B variables might be drug treatment (present or absent) and psychotherapy (present or absent) as treatments for depression; so the 2 × 2 design would have as its four groups drug treatment, psychotherapy, both, and neither. In short, a factorial design using *any* two independent variables would be an example of what we're about to explore.

Figure 9.15 summarizes some imaginary data for our imaginary experiment. (Note that the groups are very small—four subjects each—to save space and make the arithmetic go faster. We'd do all the same things with larger groups, just with longer columns of figures!) The full set of data is

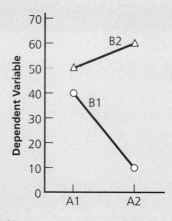

FIGURE 9.15
Imaginary findings from a 2 × 2 factorial experiment.

Table 9.2
Data for Example 1

Group	Score	Deviation from Grand Mean	Dev^2	Deviation from Group Mean	Dev^2
A1,B1	30	−10	100	−10	100
	60	20	400	20	400
	20	−20	400	−20	400
	50	10	100	10	100
Mean =	40				
A1,B2	40	0	0	−10	100
	60	20	400	10	100
	44	4	16	−6	36
	56	16	256	6	36
Mean =	50				
A2,B1	12	−28	784	2	4
	0	−40	1,600	−10	100
	20	−20	400	10	100
	8	−32	1,024	−2	4
Mean =	10				
A2,B2	62	22	484	2	4
	60	20	400	0	0
	60	20	400	0	0
	58	18	324	−2	4
Mean = 60			Sum = 7,088 = SS_T		Sum = 1,488 = SS_W

Grand Mean = 40

shown in Table 9.2 (first column). In the same table we begin our data analysis.

First we compute the *total sum of squares* (SS_T). From each score we subtract the grand mean, 40 (second column). Then we square the resulting deviation scores (third column), and add them. The result is 7,088.

Then we calculate the *sum of squares within groups* (SS_W). Take each score as a deviation from the mean of *its own* group (fourth column), square these (fifth column), and add the results. SS_W turns out to be 1,488.

The table also shows the group means, so we can now compute the *sum of squares between groups* (SS_B) based on them. We list the group means in any order, and do the arithmetic:

Group Mean	Deviation from Grand Mean	Deviation Squared	×4
40	0	0	0
50	10	100	400
60	20	400	1,600
10	−30	900	3,600
			Sum = 5,600

We multiply by four, because the squared deviation score is a component of the score for each of the four subjects in a group. Do the sum of squares between and within groups add up to the total? They do.

All this is familiar. We did all the same things for our earlier one-way ANOVA.

Now comes the new part: We are going to take that between-groups sum of squares and break it down further. How much of the variability from group to group—the between-groups sum of squares—is attributable to (1) the A variable; (2) the B variable; and (3) the interaction between them?

Let's look first at the A variable—that is, the A1 versus A2 comparison (Figure 9.16, left panel). We take *all 8* of the A1 scores—the A1,B1 and A1,B2 scores—and put them all together into an A1 "supergroup." We do the same for all 8 of the A2 scores, combining the A2B1 and the A2B2 scores into a A2 "supergroup." We see that the mean of all the A1 scores is 45, and for all the A2 scores it is 35. These are, respectively, 5 units above and 5 units below the grand mean of 40.

Now those 5-unit deviations from the grand mean are just that—they are perfectly good *deviation scores*! And we can compute a sum of squares based on them, thus:

Super-group	Mean	Deviation from Grand Mean	Deviation Squared	×8
A1	45	5	25	200
A2	35	−5	25	200
				Sum = 400

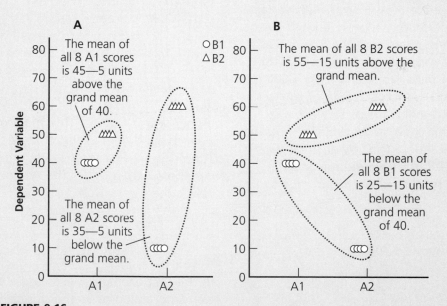

FIGURE 9.16
Analyzing the between-groups variability. Left panel: Dashed ellipses enclose the two "supergroups" for the A variable (A1 and A2). Right panel: Dashed ellipses enclose the two "supergroups" for the B variable (B1 and B2).

Notice that we multiply by 8 here, because there are 8 scores contributing to each supergroup mean. So 400 is the sum of squares for the A variable, SS_A.

We do the same thing for the B variable (Figure 9.16, right panel):

Super-group	Mean	Deviation from Grand Mean	Deviation Squared	×8
B1	25	−15	225	1,800
B2	55	15	225	1,800
				Sum = 3,600

So 3,600 is the sum of squares for the B variable, SS_B.

Now let's look again. Our sums of squares for the A and the B variables add up to 4,000 (3,600 + 400). But we saw that the between-groups sum of squares is more than that; it is 5,600. There are 1,600 units of between-groups variability unaccounted for. Since we've accounted for the effects of the A and the B variables, what's left can only be produced by the *interaction* between A and B. So 1,600 is $SS_{A×B}$, or the interaction sum of squares.

It only remains for us to summarize our results in an ANOVA table, computing each mean square (MS) by dividing each SS by its df, just as we did for one-way ANOVA. Omitting unneeded numbers, we get:

Source	SS	df	MS	F
Between groups	5,600			
A variable	400	1	400	3.22
B variable	3,600	1	3,600	29.03
A × B	1,600	1	1,600	12.90
Within groups	1,488	12	124	

Where did those degrees of freedom come from? The within-groups df, as be-fore, is the number of subjects in each group minus 1, summed across groups; so $(4 − 1) × 4 = 12$. The A variable and the B variable both have two conditions, and the df for each is the number of conditions minus one. As for the A × B interaction, it turns out that its df is the product of the df for the two variables that enter into it; so here it is $1 × 1 = 1$.

Finally, we compute an F for each variable and the interaction by dividing its MS by the MS within groups—once again, exactly as before.

For the A variable, F = 3.22. Table B.2, p. 515, tells us that we need an F of 4.75 for significance at the .05 level, with 1 and 12 df. Our 3.22 is less than that, so the *main effect* of the A variable is not significant. But the B variable does have a significant *main effect*; its F of 29.03 is higher than 4.75. The interaction also is significant: 12.90 is greater than 4.75.

Our conclusion? Across the board, the A variable—the A1 − A2 difference—has no significant effect on the scores. But again across the board, the B variable does: Condition B2 leads to significantly higher scores than B1 (the main effect). How much higher? Why, that depends! The difference is significantly greater under the A2 than under the A1 condition. That's the interaction.

EXAMPLE 2

In the first example, we found a significant interaction as well as a significant main effect of the B variable. If that interaction weren't there, what might the data have looked like?

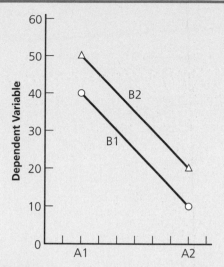

FIGURE 9.17

A 2 × 2 experiment showing no interaction.

In this example, suppose that the A2,B2 mean were not 60, but 20. Then we would get the data summarized in Figure 9.17.

Let us further suppose that although the mean value changes, the distribution of scores within the A2,B2 cell does not change; we still have two scores that are right on the mean, one at two units above, and one at two units below. In effect, we imagine that we slid that cell mean down from 60 to 20, but the "tether" lines that tie each data point (lead weight or helium balloon) to its cell mean have kept their length. So the whole group of data moves together, and the sum of squares within that cell is the same as before. So, since nothing else has changed, the overall SS$_W$ also remains the same.

We're doing it that way for several reasons: to save us some arithmetic, to spare us another big table and so make the book shorter, and because it shows us something worth knowing. *The between-and within-groups sums of squares are independent of each other.* Either can be big and the other small, or both big or both small. The group means are free to vary all over the place; but as long as the distributions of scores retain their shapes *within* each group, the within-group sum of squares will remain the same.

So now, all we need to worry about is the between-groups SS and its components. Let's compute it:

Group Mean	Deviation from Grand Mean	Deviation Squared	×4
40	10	100	400
50	20	400	1,600
20	−10	100	400
10	−20	400	1,600
			Sum = 4,000

Now we break it up into parts (Figure 9.18). For the A variable:

Super-group	Mean	Deviation from Grand Mean	Deviation Squared	×8
A1	45	15	225	1,800
A2	15	−15	225	1,800
				Sum = 3,600

For the B variable:

Super-group	Mean	Deviation from Grand Mean	Deviation Squared	×8
B1	25	−5	25	200
B2	35	5	25	200
				Sum = 400

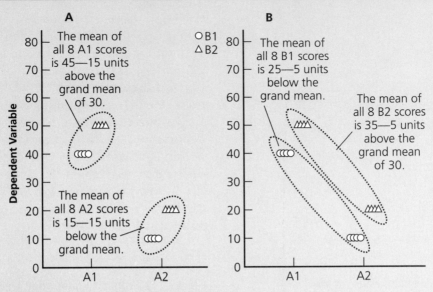

FIGURE 9.18
Again we can analyze the between-groups variability into the variability produced by the A variable (left panel), and the B variable (right panel). Together, these account for all the variability there is among the group means.

And guess what? The SS for A and B sum to 4,000, which is equal to the overall between-groups sum of squares. The interaction SS is flat zero. There is no interaction at all between the A and B variables.

In real research, of course, things would not be so neat. There would almost always be *some* interaction variance. But if the data looked anything like these, the interaction would be very small, and nonsignificant.

But let's see what the data tell us:

Source	SS	df	MS	F
Between groups	4,000			
A variable	3,600	1	3,600	29.03
B variable	400	1	400	3.22
A × B	0	1	0	
Within groups	1,488	12	124	

As before, we need an F of 4.75 for significance at the 0.05 level. Now the *main effect* of the A variable is significant. The *main effect* of the B variable is not. This is what we would expect if we look back at the means (Figure 9.17). We see that as a result of our change, the B1 and B2 means are quite close to each other, so the difference doesn't add much to the variability among means. The A1 and A2 means now differ from each other quite a lot, so that difference influences the between-groups variability, also by quite a lot. Finally, the F for interaction is zero—not about to be significant! The effects of the A and B variables do not "depend" one on the other.

EXAMPLE 3

Finally, let us see how an interaction can be significant in the absence of *any* significant main effects. A *crossover interaction* can swallow up virtually all the between-groups variability there is.

This time let's take a concrete example. Suppose we replicate the Herman and Polivy "counterregulation" experiment (pp. 309–311). On the basis of questionnaire data, we classify our subjects as dieters or as nondieters. Then within each

category, we assign subjects at random to drink down either zero, one, or two milkshakes. So we now have a 3 × 2 mixed design, with six groups of, let's suppose, three subjects each.

After that, we offer all our subjects some ice cream and measure how much of it they eat. Amount eaten is the dependent variable.

Table 9.3, Panel A, lists the cell means; they are also presented graphically in Figure 9.19. This time, we won't do the calculations for SS_W—you know how to do those now. But after making up the data I

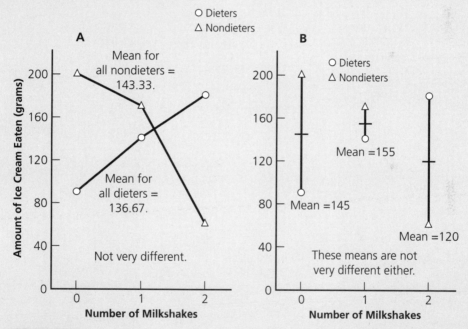

FIGURE 9.19

Between-groups variability in a "counterregulation" experiment. The "supergroups" for dieters and nondieters are shown by the connected points in the left panel (we don't need the dashed ellipses anymore), and the "supergroups" for the three preload conditions by the connected points in the right panel. The overall ("main") effect of the dieters/nondieters variable is negligible (left panel); the means are close to each other. The main effect of number of milkshakes is also negligible (right panel). The interaction accounts for nearly all the between-groups variability there is.

Table 9.3
Data and Analysis for Milkshake Experiment

A. Group means

	No Milkshake	One Milkshake	Two Milkshakes	
Dieters	90	140	180	
Nondieters	200	170	60	Grand mean = 140

B. Calculation of SS_B:

Cell Mean	Deviation from Grand Mean	Deviation^2	×3
90	−50	2,500	7,500
140	0	0	0
180	40	1,600	4,800
200	60	3,600	10,800
170	30	900	2,700
60	−80	6,400	19,200
			Sum = 45,000

C. Breaking up SS_B:

Dieter/nondieter	Mean	Deviation from Grand Mean	Deviation^2	×9
All dieters	136.67	−3.32	11.02	99.18
All nondieters	143.33	3.32	11.02	99.18
				Sum = 198.36

Milkshakes	Mean	Deviation from Grand Mean	Deviation^2	×6
None	145	5	25	150
One	155	15	225	1,350
Two	120	−20	400	2,400
				Sum = 3,900

Interaction   45,000 − 198.36 − 3,900 = 40,901.64

D. ANOVA

Source	SS	df	MS	F
Between groups	45,000.00	5		
Diet/nondiet	198.36	1	198.36	<1
Milkshakes	3,900.00	2	1,950.00	1.42
Interaction	40,901.64	2	20,450.82	14.86
Within groups	16,510.00	12	1,375.83	

calculated it for you. Take my word (you can't verify it from the information given) that SS_W is 16,510.0. (Don't assume you've made a mistake if you get very large numbers like that. In ANOVA, one often does.)

Then, as before, we compute SS_B and then break it up into components. Table 9.3 shows how we compute SS_B for these data (Panel B), and also how we compute the sums of squares for the two independent variables and their interaction (Panel C). Notice that we multiply the squared deviation scores for dieters and nondieters by 9 this time, for there are 9 scores for each of the two supergroups. And we multiply by 6 for each of the preload values—0, 1, and 2 milkshakes—for each of those supergroups contains 6 subjects.

Then we make our summary table (Panel D). Since there are three conditions for the milkshake variable, there are 2 df associated with it—the number of conditions minus 1. And since df for the interaction is the product of the dfs for the two variables that contribute to it, the inter-action now has also $1 \times 2 = 2$ df. The within-groups SS has 12 df, because there are 6 groups of 3 each; and $(3 - 1) \times 6 = 12$.

The dieters/nondieters comparison gives us an F less than 1—of course not significant; we needn't even look it up. For the milkshake variable, F is 1.42, again not significant. But for the interaction, F is a healthy 14.86—higher than the F of 3.89 we need for significance at 0.05, with 2 and 12 df. The interaction is significant, though neither main effect is.

If we go back and look at the picture of the data (Figure 9.19), we see how this happened. If we compare scores of *all dieters combined* with those of *all nondieters combined* (Panel A), we see that the two means are very close to each other and to the grand mean. Similarly, for the "preload" data, if we lump dieters and nondieters together under each of the three conditions, again the means are close to each other (Panel B). *If* the data are lumped together that way, it doesn't seem to matter whether one has had two milkshakes, or one, or none. But that lumping is what we do in computing main effects.

No, the only interesting finding here is the interaction itself. If we go back to the cell means, without lumping *any* cells together, we see that the nondieters ate less

and less as the milkshake "preload" increased in size from zero to two. This is how a physiological regulating system should behave. But the dieters did the opposite, eating more and more. The preloads brought into play a *cognitive* controlling mechanism, one that said, "I've blown my diet today anyway, so I might as well eat and enjoy." So, what effect does a milkshake or two have on intake? That depends! In nondieters, it suppresses it; in dieters, it releases it instead.

A LOOK BACK

In this section, we have learned how to tackle factorial designs with two independent variables. We have done it with pencil and paper and a hand calculator, the better to understand what we are doing.

Actually, most such analyses are done by computer now; various programs exist for this purpose. These are especially helpful with higher-order designs, involving more than two independent variables. To do (say) a three-way ANOVA by hand does require an exhausting amount of penciling, though the logic remains the same. And other kinds of designs, such as repeated-measures and mixed designs, introduce some complications that we cannot get into here.

But these programs give us the *results* of calculations. To actually do the calculations ourselves the first few times, as we have done here, is by far the best way to understand what ANOVA does and how it does it. And we have learned more about how to read an ANOVA table, and how to interpret the F statistic. As we read further in the psychological literature, we find that these are valuable skills to have.

CHAPTER 10

SINGLE-SUBJECT AND "SMALL-N" EXPERIMENTS

I had the clue from Pavlov: Control your conditions and you will see order.

—B. F. SKINNER

IN THIS CHAPTER, WE'LL DISCUSS:

■ How small-N experiments differ from large-N ones

■ Some applications of small-N research in perception, conditioning and animal cognition, neuropsychology (the "split-brain" experiments), memory, and clinical psychology

■ Some experimental designs applicable to small-N research

Stable baselines

Multiple baselines

Reversal designs

■ Some similarities and differences between large- and small-N research

To this point, most of our experiments have been ones in which each subject is treated as part of a *group*. Different groups of subjects have been treated in different ways (between-groups comparisons), or a group has been treated in different ways at different times (within-subjects comparisons). And we have looked at the ideas underlying the statistical analysis of data obtained from such groups.

Research can be done in a quite different way, however: using only a few subjects (sometimes only one), but obtaining a great deal of information from those few cases. Actually, this approach is the older of the two, and many of psychology's classic findings have come from it. It still has its uses today.

CHARACTERISTICS OF SMALL-N EXPERIMENTS

To see what lies ahead, we can look at the characteristics of this kind of research. And we can best do so by contrasting them with the more usual group, or "large-N," research.

Large-N research tends to have these characteristics:

1. The subjects are *grouped*. The data from an individual subject are not of interest in themselves, but are treated as part of a statistical aggregate.

2. The data are typically presented as *group averages*. Variability in the data will be described by a statistical measure of that (e.g., a standard deviation).

3. The *reliability* of differences among conditions is assessed by a test of *statistical significance*.

Now for the typical small-N research project, we can just reverse all of these. Thus:

1. Each subject is treated as a *separate experiment*. Thus, differences among conditions are examined in each subject's data. That means in turn that, with few exceptions, *small-N research uses within-subjects designs*.

2. *Individual subjects' data* are presented. Variability is shown by comparisons between subjects.

3. *Reliability* is assessed by *replication*—that is, repetition—of the experiment, by the original investigator and by others.

We can best make all this clear by turning at once to some examples.

PSYCHOPHYSICS

Among the earliest psychological experiments are those concerned with *psychophysics*. The term means just what it suggests: the relation between mental events (psycho-) and physical events (-physics). In its simplest form, it asks: How does sensory experience depend on physical inputs to the sensing person or animal? Thus it has its roots in the study of sensory processes, though its methods extend far beyond these.

DETERMINING AN ABSOLUTE THRESHOLD

One question we can ask is: How much physics does it take to produce any psychology at all? In other words, what is the least amount of physical energy (physics) that will trigger a sensory experience (psychology)? What is the dimmest light that we can just barely see? The faintest tone that we can just barely hear? The lightest touch that we can just barely feel? And so on.

When we ask such questions, we are asking about what is called the *absolute threshold*. The theory (shown as the solid line in Figure 10.1) is as follows: Below some critical value, an input or *stimulus* is just too faint to be perceived at all. If we gradually increase its intensity, moving from left to right in the figure, at some point it will "cross over" to become perceptible—as if it had walked through a doorway (hence "threshold") separating the unperceived from the perceived.

Now, actual experimental data will not look quite like that. The actual stimulus we use will vary from moment to moment because of "noise" in the apparatus. And the exact location of the threshold will vary too, because of "noise" in the nervous system, momentary lapses in the perceiver's attention, and the like. What we actually see will look more like the open circles in Figure 10.1—an increased *probability* that the stimulus will be perceived, as we make it more and more intense. From the resulting curve, we estimate where the threshold is.

So in practice, we need to present a range of stimulus intensities, bracketing the threshold; and we need to present each intensity a number of times so we can calculate the probability of detection

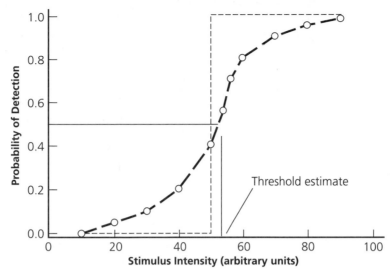

FIGURE 10.1
The theory of threshold measurements. As a very faint stimulus is made more in-tense, it is assumed that there is an abrupt transition point, or "threshold," at which the stimulus becomes perceptible. The actual data will show only a gradual increase in the *probability* that the stimulus will be detected. The point at which detection occurs 50% of the time is taken as the threshold estimate.

for each one.* It is a tedious procedure—which is why such exper-iments typically use the small-N approach!

THRESHOLDS AS DEPENDENT VARIABLES

Even though it takes much effort just to estimate a threshold, in most cases that is only part of an experimental project. We find that the absolute visual threshold is so-and-so many units of light intensity (or that the threshold intensity of a tone is so-and-so many decibels, etc.). So what? We learn about the characteristics of sensory systems by determining how these thresholds vary as other conditions are

---

*There are a number of specific ways of accomplishing this that we cannot explore here; see, for example, Woodworth and Schlosberg (1954). And—to digress for a minute—this is a good place to clear something up that might be misleading. Just because few subjects are used, don't get the idea that small-N research is "research the easy way." Few subjects are used, but one studies each subject in session after session, collecting an enormous amount of information for each. One may end up devoting more time and effort to such an experiment than to the typical "large-N" one.

changed. For if we ask our original questions again—What is the dimmest light we can see, the faintest tone we can hear, the lightest touch we can feel. . .—the answer is in every case the same: That depends on other things!

There is an enormous literature concerned with these matters; and, as so often, we can look at only one example here. So let's zero in on the visual system, and look at some of the variables that affect how sensitive it is.

DARK ADAPTATION IN VISION

Suppose we walk into a dark movie theater from a well-lighted street in the daytime. At first, we see very poorly; we have to grope. After a few minutes, though, our eyes have adjusted to the dim illumination and we can see quite well. Our eyes have grown more sensitive. In other words, our visual threshold is lower now than it was at first. Remember that a *lower threshold* means *greater sensitivity*: The visual system is more sensitive if it takes less light to activate it.

But how does it work, this process of adjustment to the dark or, for short, *dark adaptation*? To begin with, let us try to describe it more precisely.

In Figure 10.2, look first at the open circles. These data are from a single subject (though they were replicated in other subjects). In this experiment, visual threshold was estimated repeatedly as the subject sat in the dark. We notice that there is a distinct "break" in the curve that connects these data points (threshold estimates). Threshold gets lower over the first 4 or 5 minutes, then it levels off. But at about the 7-minute mark, the threshold suddenly begins to drop again, and continues to drop over the next 20 minutes or so. By the 30-minute mark, sensitivity has increased about ten-thousand-fold (four log units) from its original value.

It is as if there were two processes contributing to the complex curve. The first of these is rapid, but relatively small, so that sensitivity increases only moderately before the process is complete and threshold levels off. The second process is slower, but much greater in magnitude. It kicks in only after a delay of about 7 minutes; but then it continues for another 20 minutes or so, making the eye very much more sensitive than it was at the beginning.

Now that idea is suggestive if we look at some facts about the human *retina*—the sensitive surface at the back of the eye. Microscopic inspection of the retina reveals that there are two kinds of cells there, differing from each other anatomically. These are called

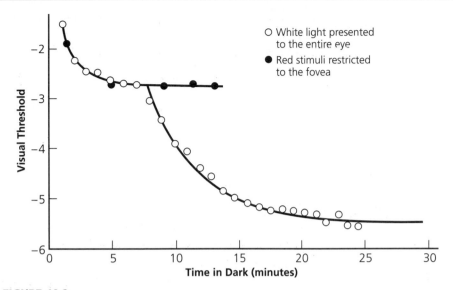

FIGURE 10.2
Visual threshold drops (sensitivity increases) over time in the dark. White light as stimulus gives rise to the two-phase dark-adaptation curve; but red light restricted to the center of the retina, activating core vision selectively, gives only the early shallow component of the curve (from Hecht, 1934).

the *rods* and the *cones*. Many other species also have both these kinds of cells, though some have only one. In species with both (including humans), we find that the cones tend to be clustered at the center of the retina, whereas the rods cluster around the center rather than in it.

Are these cells sensitive to light? They are. If we extract the pigments from rods or cones and put them in test tubes, we find that they undergo chemical changes—literally, they bleach—when exposed to light. Then let them sit in the dark, and the process is reversed; the original pigments are regenerated. We will find that the regeneration process takes longer for rods. We will also see that once regeneration is complete, the rods are much more sensitive than the cones: It takes much less light to set the bleaching reaction going again. Finally, if we vary the wavelength of the light we expose them to, we find that rods' sensitivity is greatest—that is, it takes the least light to get them to bleach—in the blue-green portion of the spectrum. That is also where sensitivity is greatest for the dark-adapted subject, in psychophysical experiments.*

---

*Things are more complicated for the cones, for we now know that there are three cone types in the human retina, having greatest sensitivity at three different bands of wavelength. All three, however, are very much less sensitive than are the rods.

Putting these findings together, we get this suggestion: Maybe the fast, but small, increase in visual sensitivity that we see in Figure 10.2 represents cone function, whereas the slower but bigger increase in sensitivity reflects the contribution of the rods. Well, can we test that idea? Going back to psychophysical experiments in human subjects, Hecht (1934) did test it. He did so by taking advantage of the things we've just learned about rods and cones. He repeated his threshold measurements, but with two changes, both designed to stimulate *just the cones,* and not the rods. First, rather than presenting light to the whole eye, he presented a small dot. That confined the stimulus to the center of the retina (the fovea), where there are many cones but few rods. Second, the dot was red rather than white. Red light is a strong stimulus for the cones (or at least some of them); but it is a relatively weak stimulus for the rods, which are much more sensitive in the blue-green part of the spectrum.

So Hecht was now stimulating the cones selectively. If it is true that the fast-but-small component of the complex curve reflects cone function, then we should see only that component now. And as the dark circles in Figure 10.2 show, that is exactly what happens.

COMMENT

The experiments we've just reviewed are good examples of small-N research. They're good examples of a couple of other things, too.

First, they're good examples of how different findings, from different kinds of experiments, converge to support a conclusion. We have drawn some conclusions about the contributions of rods and cones to vision in the dark. Our conclusion draws on information from psychophysics: This is what humans see, and this is how what they see is affected by illumination level, time, and wavelength of what is shown. But it also draws on information from histology (there are these two kinds of cells, and they look different, and *here* is how they are distributed spatially in the retina). It also draws on comparative anatomy (not all animals have both) and biochemistry (the "bleaching" with exposure to light, and the effects of wavelength on this bleaching). All this and more has contributed to our present understanding of what the eye tells the brain.

Second, they are good examples of how experiments can shed light on occurrences in everyday life, even if the experiments themselves are far removed from everyday settings. In this case, our understanding of vision just might have tipped the balance of a vitally important historical episode. Let us look at something that happened during World War II—a "practical" setting if there ever was one. This story rates a section of its own.

PSYCHOLOGY AND REAL LIFE:
THE BATTLE OF BRITAIN

We pick up the story in 1940, when Western Europe was dominated by Adolf Hitler's armies. In the West, Great Britain stood virtually alone in Hitler's path, for the United States had not yet entered the war. And Hitler's plans for world domination very much included the conquest of Britain.

The German military had plans for an invasion of England; but they hoped, and believed, that such an invasion would not be necessary. Rather, they thought that the German air force could bomb the British into submission from the air. Thus began what historians call the Battle of Britain, which was really a battle for control of the air *over* Britain. At the time we take up the story, German bombers were dropping tons of bombs upon London—at night. The British fighter pilots had to get into the air and intercept these bombers. It was the heroism of these British fighter pilots that prompted Winston Churchill's famous line: "Never in the field of human conflict was so much owed by so many to so few."

But the defending fighter pilots faced a problem. To fly at night, one ought to have one's eyes fully sensitive—that is, to be well dark-adapted. That takes about half an hour (Figure 10.2 above). But when an oncoming air raid was detected by the British, it would be only minutes away from its target. The British pilots didn't *have* half an hour to prepare!

What to do? The pilots who were on call could sit in the dark, *in case* an attack came; but clearly, that would cause morale problems. So the commanders consulted with psychologists and physiologists who knew about the visual system. And they received an ingenious suggestion. Let the pilots wait in the ready room, and let the room be well lit—but let the pilots wear red goggles!

Let's see what should happen. The goggles admit red light into the eye. Some cones respond well to red light, so the pilots had enough cone vision to read, play cards, write letters, and the like. Now, the rods will respond *somewhat* to red light, but they are more sensitive by far in the blue-green part of the spectrum; and it was these frequencies that the red goggles screened out. So while the pilots wore the goggles, their rods were adjusting—adapting!—to what was, for them, relatively dim illumination, just as we adapt to dim illumination in a movie theater. If a raid did come, the pilots could step out into the night, take off their goggles—and there was rod vision, almost fully sensitive, almost at once.

The success of this tactic made everyone happy but the Germans. It made the British pilots and their commanders happy, needless to say; and it made the British and American scientists happy too, (1) because it strengthened the British defense against their would-be conquerors, and (2) because their theoretical understanding of vision gained yet further support from their successful *prediction* that this device would work.

Finally, this story is a good example of yet another important idea. We often ask or are asked, "But do these laboratory results apply to real life?" That may not be quite the question to ask. Consider Hecht's experiments: A subject is staring at a place (perhaps a microscope eyepiece, to control eye position) where a tiny dot of red light will appear, and he tells us when he can see that dot. Do the results apply to real life? Not directly, no; real life never presents us with such a situation!

What applies to real life in such cases is *not the findings*, but the *understanding* of (in this case) the visual system, to which the findings contribute (Mook, 1983). It is that *understanding* that tells us what we know about how to identify and correct visual defects, how best to detect faint objects in darkness (look a bit to one side of them; why?), how to prepare a fighter pilot for night action on short notice—and much besides. In other words, it is understanding that "generalizes to the real world"—not the experimental findings themselves. We will return to this idea in Chapter 12.

CONDITIONING

Another domain in which small-N research has found application is in the study of conditioning. There are two senses in which that term is used in psychology—unfortunately, for the two are quite different as we'll see—and the small-N approach has a place in both.

PAVLOVIAN CONDITIONING

Pavlov's classic experiments were done the small-N way. Back in Figure 3.3 (p. 70), we saw a typical "learning curve" for eyelid conditioning in human subjects, based on group averages. But Pavlov's

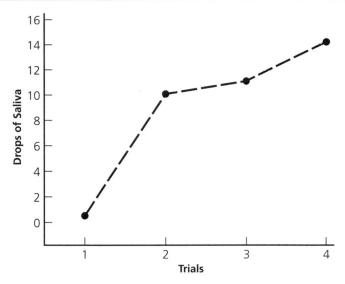

FIGURE 10.3
A learning curve from one of Pavlov's experiments. More salivation occurred in response to the CS as conditioning progressed (from Pavlov, 1927/1960).

own experiments used single animals, with the reliability of the findings shown by their consistency from one dog to another. One of his dogs' "learning curves" is shown in Figure 10.3.

OPERANT CONDITIONING

In Pavlov's experiments, a stimulus is presented that evokes some response—the UCS (thus food in the mouth evokes salivation). It is paired with some other stimulus, the CS, that does not evoke that response initially (e.g., the sound of a bell). After conditioning has occurred, the CS does evoke the response (the bell will trigger conditioned salivation). With this kind of procedure, the focus is on the events that occur *before* the response in question—its antecedents (Figure 10.4A).

Operant conditioning is different. Here, the focus is on the events that *follow* the response in question—its *consequences*. A rat in a Skinner box (or a simple maze) may make all sorts of responses, all on its own—nothing external makes these responses occur. The experimenter arranges matters so that some one of these responses is followed by a *consequence* that affects the animal's later behavior, causing the response in question to become more, or less, likely to occur again (Figure 10.4B). If the consequence makes the response more

A In classical conditioning:

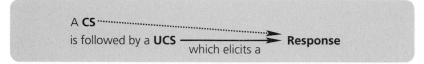

and eventually the CS becomes capable of eliciting the response by itself.

Both the CS and the UCS occur *before* the response in question.

B In operant conditioning, the reinforcing event occurs *after* the response:

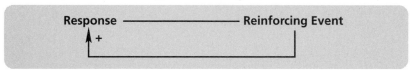

and makes the response more frequent or more probable thereafter.

FIGURE 10.4
Classical and operant conditioning.

likely to occur, then we call that consequence a *positive reinforcer* or, colloquially, a *reward*. Positive reinforcers can include such things as food for a hungry animal, water for a thirsty one, praise or attention from another human being, or even stimulation of certain areas of the brain, within the so-called "reward system."

THE "FREE OPERANT"

The complex mazes we see in cartoons are mythical. No one uses these to study the learning process in animals, nor has anyone tried to do so for half a century. A better prototype is the "free operant" experiment, pioneered by the late B. F. Skinner (1904–1990). A rat may press a lever to earn water, or a pigeon may peck at a disc or "pecking key" (by analogy to a telegraph key) to earn food (Figure 10.5); or a human may press a real telegraph key to earn points. Food, water, points—these are the reinforcers.

Once reinforcement has occurred, the subject need not be caught and put back in a start box (as with a maze); she simply remains where she was, with the lever or key or button still in place. The lever (or whatever) is always available, and the subject is free to press it at any time. Hence the expression *free operant*.

With this method, one can measure the *rate* of response (number of responses per unit time), and watch it change continuously as an experimental session progresses. Reinforce key-pecking with food,

FIGURE 10.5
A pigeon in an operant-conditioning chamber. Pecking at the small illuminated disk is rewarded or "reinforced" with a small amount of food delivered automatically.

and a hungry pigeon shortly comes to peck at a high rate. Stop reinforcing the response and its rate goes down ("extinction"). Reinstate reinforcement, and rate rises once again.* All this we can see without interfering with the animal at all. We just change the settings on the apparatus so that it does, or does not, deliver reinforcement when it detects a response. And we can watch and record these rate changes in individual subjects, establishing their reliability by comparing one subject's results with another's.

AN EXAMPLE: REINFORCEMENT BY BRAIN STIMULATION

One of the most exciting discoveries of modern psychobiology is that the direct activation of certain cell clusters in the brain can act as a positive reinforcer. In a free-operant situation, animals will work away steadily for no other reward than direct stimulation of those parts of the brain that form the "reward system."

What does the experiment look like? First, the rat is "prepared" by having a thin metal wire, or electrode, placed in its brain so that the wire ends within the reward system. Having it there is not painful;

---

*The fact that responding drops out in the nonreward condition provides an answer to the criticism, still made of operant-conditioning experiments by those who know nothing about them: "The animal makes the response because there is nothing else to do." If that were so, response rate would remain high even when reinforcement is not available. It doesn't.

there are no pain-producing cells within the brain, and of course the rat is deeply anesthetized during the placement of the electrode. After the rat wakes up, experimentation can begin.

For the experiment itself, the rat's implanted electrode is connected to a stimulating device, through light flexible wiring that leaves the rat free to move about. Then we can give the rat a lever to press (Figure 10.6). When the lever is pressed, a brief series of pulses of electric current is delivered through the electrode into the brain itself. The effect of this is to activate, artificially, the brain cells that surround the electrode tip.

And if the electrode is within the "reward system," and if the current we apply is within the effective range, we will see a powerful reinforcing effect of this brain stimulation. The rat (or cat or monkey) will press the lever over and over, to deliver these pulses of activation to its own brain again and again.

The effect can be extremely powerful. In one instance, a rat worked away at the lever at a steady rate from 12 noon on one day

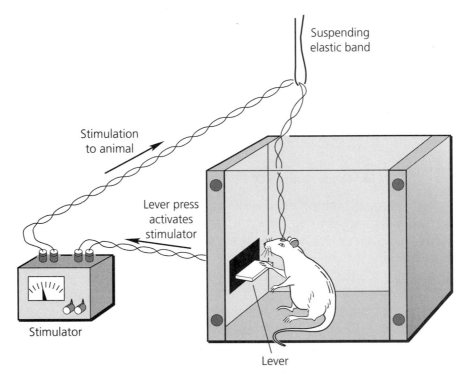

FIGURE 10.6
Setup for an experiment in self-stimulation of the brain. The implanted electrode is attached to flexible wires that allow the rat to move freely. A press on the lever causes the apparatus to deliver a brief series of electrical pulses through the wires to structures deep inside the brain (from Pinel, 1993).

to 2 P.M. the next day—26 hours—pressing the lever more than 50,000 times! Then it rested or slept for about 6 hours and, after that, returned to work at the same high rate as before.

Now, that's one rat; true. But this experiment has been replicated many, many times in laboratories all over the world. It has also been used as a jumping-off point for further investigation; researchers have asked, for instance, whether drugs that produce pleasure (like cocaine) involve the activation of this "reward system" in the brain. (They almost surely do.) Whole new chapters in psychobiology are being written, based on the discovery that direct activation of brain cells can be its own reward.

ANIMAL COGNITION: CONCEPTS IN PIGEONS

The properties of operant conditioning are of interest in their own right. But also, behavior maintained by reinforcement can be used as a tool, to study other things. Operant conditioning can, in effect, give our animal a language with which to tell us something about what it sees or knows.

Suppose the animal is in a box in which a faint light is sometimes on, sometimes off. Suppose too that this rule is in effect: When the light is on, lever-pressing will occasionally be reinforced; but when it is off, the response will never be reinforced. If our animal masters this *discrimination learning*, it will respond only when the light is on, and not when it is off. If so, this tells us (1) that the animal can master the rule, and (2) that it can see the light!

We can go further, using the same logic. We can ask whether our animal subjects are capable of more complex and subtle perceptual and conceptual feats. Here's an example.

For example, and speaking of "how smart are animals?" (Chapter 7): Are pigeons capable of forming and using the concept of *human being*? That is an extraordinarily complex idea, if we think of it. Human beings come in all kinds of sizes, shades, shapes, and so on; a person lacking all four limbs is still a human being. It is an "open-ended" concept, too; we can come across a person who looks quite different from anyone we have seen before, and still recognize him or her as a human being.

How do we do it? We don't know. But if a pigeon can do it, then we can study the process in a simpler system. And we can do experiments—manipulation of the brain, for instance—that would be impossible in human beings. But *can* a pigeon do it? How can we find out? An ingenious series of experiments by Richard Herrnstein and his colleagues (Herrnstein & Loveland, 1964; Herrnstein, Loveland, & Cable, 1976) addressed this question.

Imagine a pigeon in a box, with a pecking key mounted on the wall. But now, there is also a translucent screen mounted on the wall, onto which slides can be projected from outside the box so that the pigeon can see them. In this case, a number of such slides were presented one at a time, each for a few minutes. The slides showed various scenes from natural settings. In some of them, there was a person, or people, in the scene. In others, there was not.

Then the experimenters set this rule: If there was a person or people in the picture, then pecking at the key would occasionally be reinforced with food. If there was no person, then pecking was never reinforced. So—if the pigeon could master the concept of a *person*—then eventually the pigeon ought to stop pecking when pictures with no people were shown, but peck away when the picture did show people.

And that is what the pigeons did—all three of them. Figure 10.7 shows the data, bird by bird in the small-N tradition. The data—which were gathered after extensive training on the problem—show response rates to slides with people in them (open circles), and slides without people (closed circles). We see at a glance that every bird responded at a high rate to people pictures; but that response rate with nonpeople pictures was more variable and, for most slides, lower. The pigeons had grasped the concept of *human being*. They were able to recognize the presence of any instance or instances of human beings, as opposed to the absence of these.

Of course it is possible that the birds had simply memorized which of all the various pictures were worth pecking at, and which were not—still an extraordinary feat of memory, but a different kind of cognitive achievement. But no. This potential *confounding* of conceptualization with memory was "checked out" and ruled out. When the birds were tested with new slides, that they had never seen before, they maintained the discrimination. People, high rate; no people, low rate.

What does it matter that a pigeon can do this? Consider that a pigeon's whole brain is comfortably smaller than your thumb. Yet the cells of the pigeon brain are about the same size as those of a human brain; so it figures that in the pigeon, there must be vastly fewer of them. Thus, this really quite complex cognitive operation can be performed by a system—and studied in a system—that is much simpler than we have supposed. The findings, in other words, give

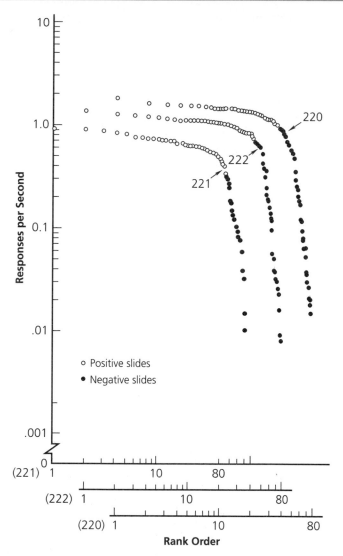

FIGURE 10.7
Response rates when "people" and "no people" pictures were presented. Each set of points represents a single pigeon. Within each, the points are arranged left to right from highest to lowest response rate. Open circles represent pictures showing people, closed circles represent pictures without people. In each bird, people pictures consistently evoked higher rates of response than no-people pictures did (from Herrnstein & Loveland, 1964).

us a whole new way of studying how a brain can form and use complex concepts.

They bear as well on another general issue, concerning the very nature of thought. It has been argued that the use of abstract concepts, like "human being," requires the use of language. One must be able to *label* an object with words, as "human being" or "not human being," in order to have the concept of human being. Well, clearly that's wrong. Pigeons can have a people concept, and pigeons have no language. The point need not be argued anymore.

AN EXAMPLE FROM NEUROPSYCHOLOGY: THE "SPLIT-BRAIN" EXPERIMENTS

To understand the next example, we need to take a look at the layout of the human visual system (Figure 10.8). Light, emitted by or reflected from objects "out there," strikes light-sensitive cells at the back of the eye (the *retina*). This excites nerve cells in the *optic nerve*, which carries messages up into the brain—the two great *cerebral hemispheres*. The hemispheres are joined together by a very large band of nerve fibers, the *corpus callosum*, and it is largely (not exclusively) by

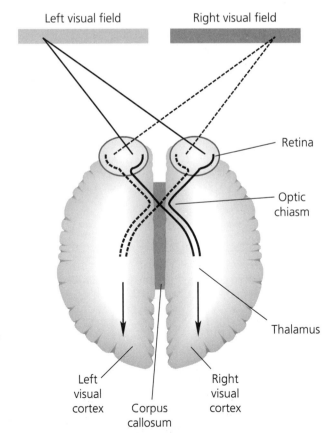

FIGURE 10.8
Layout of the human visual system. The left half of each retina sends information to the left visual hemisphere, the right half to the right hemisphere.

346

way of this band that the two hemispheres communicate with each other.

In the 1940s, neurologists and neurosurgeons discovered that in patients with uncontrollable epileptic seizures, cutting the corpus callosum was often effective as a last-resort procedure. Cutting these communicating fibers could restrict the seizure to one side of the brain, rather than letting it spread to both. But now, if we have cut across a major channel of communication within the brain, what effect is this going to have on the patient's mental functioning?

The answer is: very little, on casual observation. But if we look more closely, we see striking effects. Look again at Figure 10.8. The two cables of nerve fibers, one from each eye, come together at the *optic chiasm*. There a strange thing happens: Half the fibers from each eye stay on the same side as before, and continue up into the brain on the side where they originated. But the other half, those from the nasal or "toward-the-nose" side of each retina, cross over and pass up into the brain on the opposite side. The effect of this is as follows: If a stimulus falls on the left side of the retina, in either eye, its excitation of the retina will affect the left hemisphere of the brain. If it falls on the right side of the retina, it will be relayed to the right hemisphere.

What happens then if we present, to a "split-brain" human patient, a picture of some object, and restrict that picture to the *left* side of the retina? If we ask him, "What do you see?" he can tell us—no problem. But if the picture falls on the *right* side of the retina, such a patient will say, "I don't see anything." Now in some sense he did see it, as we can show in other ways; he may, for example, be able to pick out the object he was shown, by touch, from an array of objects before him. But he cannot *talk* about it. He cannot tell us what he saw.

This finding makes eminent sense if we put it together with the work of Broca and his successors on the localization of *speech* within the brain. We recall (Chapter 4) that the production of speech seems to depend on an area on the *left* side of the brain. So in a split-brain patient, input to the left hemisphere can communicate with the speech-production system that is located there. Input to the right hemisphere cannot. The result is that *speaking about* that input is disrupted.

But speaking of identifying objects by touch, this task also shows how *selectively* impaired the split-brain person is. If we present our picture to the left hemisphere of such a patient, she can identify it by touch using her right hand (which is controlled by the left hemisphere). If we present it to the right hemisphere, she can do so with her left hand (controlled by the right hemisphere). But the left hemisphere cannot tell the left hand, nor can the right hemisphere tell the right hand, where to point; the left brain doesn't know what the left hand should do, or conversely.

We should note that the division of labor is not always so straightforward. For example, it is much too simple to say that speech is localized *in* the left hemisphere. If a split-brain patient is asked to make a fist with his left hand, he can do so. Therefore, understanding of the spoken request does get to the right hemisphere (which controls the left hand) by one route or another. There are other indications too that the right hemisphere does have some linguistic capacity. The attempt to specify just how the two hemispheres divide their tasks is very much in progress (see Gazzaniga, Ivry, & Mangun, 1998).

Now the discovery of these separations took quite some time. When this surgical procedure was first employed with epileptic patients, observers were surprised and puzzled by how perfectly normal the "split-brain" patients appeared to be after the operation. There were no obvious deficiencies in perception, cognition, memory, or language—yet the patients had lost a *major* band of interconnections in the brain. What were the connections *for*, if one could do so well without them?

The symptoms of hemispheric separation were not seen until Roger Sperry, a psychologist, was called in to devise more effective tests of these patients' capabilities.* Among the changes he made was this: We present visual stimuli to the left, or to the right, half of the retina, and we present them *very briefly*. How briefly? So briefly that they appear and disappear *before eye movements can occur*.

Why? Look again at Figure 10.8. We present, let's say, a stimulus (a picture) so that its image falls slightly to the right of the center of the retina. It will then be conveyed to the right (nonspeaking) hemisphere. But only a slight eye movement would be needed to move that image to the left on the retina—and hence to the left, speaking hemisphere! In other words, without the refinement of brief exposure, we have not really manipulated left versus right brain at all. Any input can be relayed to *both* sides of the brain, if the subject can move her eyes before it goes away.

---

*Sperry had already achieved a respected status in the field because of, among other achievements, his studies of learning in split-brain cats. Here is another case in which both questions and methods for research in humans were guided directly by animal research. And to remind ourselves once again: "Generalizing from cats to humans" had nothing to do with it. It is the questions and the methods that were "generalized"—not the answers.

In short, to reveal the deficits that cutting the corpus callosum produces, we have to *really* restrict input to one hemisphere or the other.* If we think we're doing that when we are not, we will have a *feeble manipulation* (Chapter 7)—less kindly, a sloppy experiment. And we will be misled, as early neuropsychologists were.

Now nearly all of these experiments were conducted with a very small number of subjects—of course! Only a relatively small number of people, fortunately, require such surgery. In fact, though the first series of observations were done with a series of 20 cases, the fact is that much of our knowledge about split-brain patients—involving well over a hundred published reports—comes from the intensive study of only five subjects (Gazzaniga, Ivry, & Mangun, 1998). What makes this possible? Two old friends: (a) a high degree of experimental control (e.g., over eye movements), and (b) the power of the manipulation—tasks that are trivially easy for a subject with intact brain may be impossible for a split-brain patient. The result is a level of consistency across individuals that justifies our drawing conclusions even from so few cases.

Two final comments. First, notice that effective manipulation in this case, as in Harlow's (Chapter 2), really requires an artificial situation. In real life, we rarely encounter objects or events that appear on one or the other half-retina, and go away before our eyes can scan them. For just that reason, "real-life" observations could never have shown us this apparent division of labor between the two hemispheres. And, by the same token, the results do not "generalize to real life." The understanding does.

Second: We see again that simple findings can raise some very broad issues. The philosopher Patricia Churchland (1986) has called our attention to a few of them:

> One is accustomed to thinking of oneself as a single, unified, coherent self. . . . [But] hard on the heels of the observations comes the inescapable inclination to infer that [split-brain patients] have two of something where the rest of us have only one. But two of *what*? Two minds perhaps, or two souls, or two selves, or two persons . . . two centers of control, two wills, or what? How do these categories relate to each other? (pp. 178–179)

Churchland points out that the findings even raise problems for the view, still popular among nonscientists, that the mind is a non-

---

*There are other ways of restricting input to one hemisphere; for discussion, see Churchland (1986); Gazzaniga, Ivry, & Mangun (1998).

physical entity separate from the body. If this is so, why should certain *specific* mental operations—as when the brain commands one or the other hand to point to a seen object—depend so much on the integrity of certain connections in the brain?

The split-brain research has already challenged some fundamental assumptions about mind–body relations and indeed about the nature of mind. How many minds *do* we have, anyway?

MEMORY I: EBBINGHAUS'S RESEARCH

Hermann Ebbinghaus (1850–1909) was one of the founding fathers of modern psychology. He was a German philosopher turned scientist, adapting the methods of science to the study of mind. In 1885, he published a book, *On Memory*, that summarized the results of years of experimental investigation of the growth and decline of memories. For this monumental series of experiments, he used a single subject: himself.

He began with some assumptions:

1. Our memories are networks of connections, or *associations*, between one "item" in memory and another.

2. These associations *vary in strength*. If I have met you recently, then when we meet again, I may remember your name (the memory is strong), or I may not; and if I do not, the memory for your name may be lost altogether (very weak), or it may be "on the tip of my tongue" (almost, but not quite, strong enough to be remembered).

3. These connections are *strengthened by repetition*. I am more likely to remember your name later if I repeat it to myself many times just after we've met. We learn that *abogado* is the Spanish word for *lawyer*, by repeating the pair of words together many times.

THE EXPERIMENTAL STUDY OF MEMORY

Guided by these working assumptions, Ebbinghaus began a long and painstaking study of memory in himself. Let us see how he went about it.

First of all, if we want to study the formation and decay of associations, we want to use materials that initially are not associated with anything. That way, we can create a brand-new association from scratch. There are real-life situations that come close to this. If you and I are about to be introduced at a party, I have *almost* no idea what your name will be until I hear it: It could be anything from Abigail to Zelda. But I do have *some* idea of what to expect: Your name will probably not be Aardvark. So even here, *some* prior knowledge is present in me even before I hear your name.

In an attempt to get rid of *all* preexisting associations, Ebbinghaus turned to material that was entirely arbitrary and meaningless. He invented the famous *nonsense syllable*. Choose at random two consonants and a vowel. Put the vowel between the consonants. If the three form a word (like *map*), throw the word out. If not (like *mip*), we have a nonsense syllable. Ebbinghaus made up a large number of such nonsense syllables. Then, for a given experiment, he would make up a list of syllables, memorize the list, and later test his memory for the list he had memorized.

Because the syllables meant nothing whatever, Ebbinghaus assumed that any associations that developed among them were created solely within the experiment itself. We could say that he was doing for himself what Pavlov had done for his dogs (Chapter 3): Start with items that are wholly unassociated with each other at the beginning. Then we can study how associations form, starting at zero and gradually increasing with repetition.

These nonsense syllables, then, were the material Ebbinghaus worked with. Worked how? First of all, how was he to *measure* the strength of the associations he created?

After he had memorized a list of nonsense syllables, he could have come back later and asked how many of those syllables he could remember. In fact, many modern investigators do do that, because it's simple and quick. But Ebbinghaus wanted a more precise measure than this. After all, even "forgotten" associations can vary in strength, as we saw a minute ago. If I can't recall your name, is it "on the tip of my tongue" (strong but not strong enough), or have I lost it completely (weak or nonexistent)? Either way, I can't recall it; so such differences in strength would be obscured by a *floor effect* (Chapter 7) if we used recall as a measure.

To avoid this, Ebbinghaus gave us yet another invention: *savings* as a measure. He would memorize a list of syllables, until he could run through them without making any mistakes. He would note how many trials it took him to do it. Then, after a predetermined interval, he would come back to the list and memorize it again.

Suppose it took him 10 trials to memorize the list initially. Suppose later it took him only 2 trials to memorize it again. Then we can say that the memory of the list gave him 80% "savings"—

because the relearning took only 20% as many trials as the initial learning experience did. The memory traces from the first learning now "saved" him 80% of the effort that had been required to learn the list initially. If it took him 10 trials the first time and 5 trials the second, that would be 50% savings. And of course, if it took him as long to relearn the list as it had taken him to learn it in the first place, then the initial learning might as well not have occurred. That would be zero savings, and would imply that by the time of relearning, the memory had vanished altogether so that he was starting again from scratch.

Finally, we should say something about the nuts and bolts of his experimental *procedures*. The nonsense syllables themselves he had printed on little cards, and he would turn over the cards one by one. For each syllable he saw, he would try to remember what the next syllable would be; then he would expose the next card, to check his memory and provide the cue for the card after that . . . and so on until he had completed the list. Then he'd begin at the beginning and do it again, until the list was memorized. Throughout all this he turned over the cards at a constant rate, governed by the ticking of a metronome.

What about situational control? We know that we will get the most consistent data if irrelevant influences are kept to a minimum, and Ebbinghaus worked hard to minimize all influences on memory except repetition itself. He ran his experiments at about the same time every day, and tried to free his mind of distractions and bring himself into a more or less constant mood each time. The recency of his last meal was held constant.

Ebbinghaus spent years, evening after evening, at this self-investigation. Not only that: He went back later and repeated his earlier experiments, to establish the reliability of his findings. The whole project is a case study in sheer determination, and shows us just how strong scientific curiosity can be.

THE "FORGETTING CURVE"

These are the methods, then, that Ebbinghaus used to study memory in himself. Now let's look at just a sample of the discoveries he made by their use.

Memories, once formed, get weaker over time. But what is the time course of this "weakening"? The way to find out is straightforward: Learn a list of fixed length; later, relearn it and measure "savings"; and, for different lists, vary the time between learning and

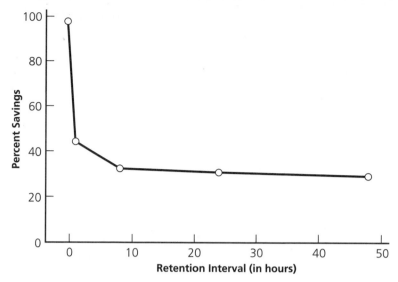

FIGURE 10.9
Ebbinghaus's forgetting curve. Memory for a list (as measured by savings) drops dramatically over the first hour, more slowly thereafter (from Ebbinghaus, 1885/1913).

relearning. The more time we allow to pass, the less savings we should see.

And that is exactly what happens. In Figure 10.9, we see Ebbinghaus's classic "forgetting curve," which is still reprinted in textbooks after more than a century. We see that forgetting is quite rapid; savings drop to less than 50% in the first hour. After that, the decay is slower, so that savings are about 30% after a 48-hour interval.

These findings, by the way, have immediate practical importance. If we are about to take an exam, then there will be some benefit to reviewing the material *immediately* before the exam. A delay of even an hour will reduce the benefit substantially. This is true, that is, (1) *if* the material was well learned to begin with, and (2) *if* the exam tests only for rote memory (a foreign-language vocabulary perhaps, or the valences of elements). If the exam tests for our understanding of concepts, this changes matters, as we shall see.

There was more—a whole bookful more. Ebbinghaus asked such questions as: How does number of repetitions during learning affect the rate of forgetting? If we "overlearn" material, by going over it several times more even after we have learned it, does that aid retention? (Yes.) If the list is long, is it better to learn it all in one session, or in blocks of repetitions spaced apart from each other? (In general, "spaced" learning leads to better retention.) And more. Much more.

This series of experiments is a classic case of small-N research. Ebbinghaus gathered a tremendous amount of information about a single subject—himself. He was able to gather consistent data because he controlled his experimental conditions, used a sensitive measure, and manipulated variables (time since memorization, amount of memorization) whose effects on the data were powerful. Still, some questions arise that we should pause to examine.

Ebbinghaus's book was based on a series of experiments in which he used *one subject*—himself. It is reasonable to ask: How generalizable are his findings? Might not the results apply only to himself? The answer to that question is empirical—that is, we answer it by looking and seeing. The fact is that all of Ebbinghaus's major findings have been *replicated*, countless times, by other researchers—some using groups of subjects, some only one or two. This is how we establish reliability and generality in small-N research.

But there is another issue. Given that Ebbinghaus's findings are reliable (for replication shows that), are they *interesting*? After all, nonsense syllables are highly artificial. Very few of our real-life memory tasks involve associations between one meaningless item and another. What can such limited material tell us about the use of memory in real life? Our memories for persons and events do not seem to fade in a matter of hours. Indeed they may be vivid, and they *may* even be accurate, years later (see for example Linton, 1982).

Moreover, we have already seen that memory is a more complex process than simple "associations" among elements. What about distortions in memory, as in the effect of leading questions (Chapter 5) or false-memory syndrome (Chapter 8)?

Let us admit that these processes are ones that Ebbinghaus could not have discovered with the methods he used. He studied the formation of *just these* item-to-item associations during the initial memorization process. And he assessed the strength of *just these* associations later on, when savings were measured. Is this a criticism of his methods? Yes and no. We can best make the issues clear if we turn to look at another way of studying memory.

MEMORY II: BARTLETT'S INVESTIGATIONS

In 1932, another book on memory was published, by Sir Frederic Bartlett. His book too reported not one but a whole series of experiments on memory. His approach, however, was very different. Rather than "associations" formed from scratch among arbitrary items, he studied memories for organized, structured events—pictures, stories, and the like. The best known of these experiments was his study of memory, among subjects of European ancestry, for a Native American folk legend.

In this experiment, a fairly large number of subjects (20) was used initially, but the logic of the procedure was small-N. Each subject read the story through to himself twice, then tried to reproduce the story 15 minutes later. After that, subjects were asked to reproduce the story again "as opportunity offered"—that is, the number of memory tests, and the intervals between them, varied from subject to subject. Since the "remembered" stories were also idiosyncratic, varying from subject to subject, individual reproductions—individual data!—are presented. (In one case, Bartlett happened to meet one of his subjects six years after the original session—and tested him then.)

These recollections of the story showed consistent changes over time. First, the remembered stories were shorter, so some details had dropped out; but also, they were distorted. Words were replaced by more common words, and often the story line was changed so as to resemble more the format of a European folk tale. Some leaps of logic, or some bits of the story that sounded strange and foreign, were rationalized—either omitted or explained. As well as loss of detail, there were frequent *inventions* of detail that had not been mentioned in the original story. Many subjects reported that, rather than remembering the words of the original story, they remembered the visual images that the story had evoked, and *reconstructed* the story from those.

To Bartlett, this notion of *reconstruction* is the key. When remembering, the subject says in effect, "This and this and this must have occurred, in order that my present set of images should be what it is." It is not a matter of running from one point to another in a network of associations. And it certainly is not "running off" a record of the past with a mental tape recorder. It is more like a process of inference or deduction. Based on bits and pieces remembered now, we *deduce* what the whole experience must have been like back then.

Now that idea, too, fits in with a lot of other data. If we are inferring *now* what must have happened *then*, our inferences should be influenced by what is going on *now*. And they are, as we saw when we discussed leading questions (Chapter 5), state-dependent memory (Chapter 9), and the false memory syndrome (Chapter 7). Our memories may also drift far away from the details of the original events. And they do, as we saw when we discussed "flashbulb memories" (Chapter 3).

So Bartlett's conclusion—memory is not "reading off" a record, nor is it drifting passively through a network of connections, but inferring a whole from remembered parts—is widely accepted now. Yet Ebbinghaus, too, is right. Very often we must "connect" one item with another more or less arbitrarily, as in learning foreign-language vocabulary or, in a roomful of people, learning which name goes with which face.

Maybe we need to consider two "kinds" of memory—one for meaningful episodes or meaningful prose (like this book you are reading), and another for making connections by rote.* And effective use of these systems requires different strategies—so both conceptions of memory have some immediate practical implications. If we're going to be tested on *rote memory*, we should go over and over the material (repetition), and a quick review just before the exam will be helpful, so we can take the exam while memory is strongest. But if we are to be tested on our *understanding* of meaningful, organized material (like this text), then going over it and over it to memorize what it says will be of little help. Rather, we should (1) understand its organization—understand the argument that a text makes, for instance—so that recalling bits here and there, we can *reconstruct* the whole set of ideas. And (2) we should connect the material to other things. We should draw parallels between this text and others we read or lectures we hear. We should look for further examples of an idea, beyond those that a text provides. That way, we will have as many cues as possible (we call them *retrieval cues* nowadays) to jog our memories for parts and fragments. If we have these, and the overall organization of the Big Picture, then we can better reconstruct that Big Picture from those parts and fragments.

In short, Bartlett and Ebbinghaus came to different conclusions

---

*A bewildering variety of divisions among "kinds" of memory has been proposed; see Reisberg (1997) for review and discussion.

about the nature of memory, with different implications. That does not mean that either was wrong. Rather, they were studying different things, different "kinds" of memory. So we have here a good example of how the methods we use determine what we will see. And the disagreement itself has helped us see more clearly the Big Picture of how memory works.

SMALL-N DESIGNS IN CLINICAL RESEARCH

Small-N designs have also found wide application in intervention research. In treating disorders of the nervous system or problems of behavior, some clinicians have found the small-N approach to be of great value.

If a clinician wishes also to be a "research producer," he or she often faces a dilemma. Much research in psychology, as we've seen, is done "large-N," with a group or groups of subjects who are more or less similar to each other—perhaps a "convenience sample" of college students, or a more "purposive sample" of students with snake phobias (Chapter 9). Conditions will be standardized and held constant for all subjects, except of course for the independent variable.

A clinician, treating patients or clients, may not have available a group of patients with similar problems (unless she works in, say, a substance-abuse treatment facility). Moreover, she wants the freedom to adapt her treatment to each individual; what works well for one may not work so well for another. Both these considerations may make statistical treatment of grouped data difficult or meaningless. But consider small-N procedures: each subject a separate experiment, with treatments adapted to individual subjects, and reliability established by replication rather than significance tests. Exactly what a practicing therapist needs (Hayes, 1992; Kazdin, 1992).

In short, one may adapt the small-N approach to the clinical setting. That is also a setting that gives us clear examples of specific *experimental designs* for small-N research.

But before we go further, we need to make one thing very clear. We saw in Chapter 7, and elsewhere, that the usual "clinical case studies" are at best of limited use, even if conducted with a number of subjects. Patients or clients come for help, are treated, and may get better. But even if they do, that doesn't show that the therapy was effective. Why not? Because the effects of treatment are *confounded with* spontaneous recovery, regression, expectations (the "placebo effect"), and often observer bias as well.

That still goes. The problem is to *control for* these sources of confusion. The following experimental designs are attempts to do just that.

STABLE BASELINES

Look first at Figure 10.10 (Moffat, 1989). This experiment was conducted with a patient suffering from Alzheimer's disease, who had particular trouble remembering the names of things ("nominal dysphasia"). Told the name of a familiar object, she could remember it only for a few minutes. The obvious "rehearsal" strategy—going over and over the name of the object while looking at it—produced no improvement.

The experimenters first took a series of "baseline" observations, in which Miss S's memory for the names of 20 familiar objects was tested. Every third session began with a "probe," in which all 20 objects were presented and Miss S was asked to name them all. Performance on these "probes" was the dependent variable, and Figure 10.10 shows these data over successive "probes." It is clear that very few words were remembered during the baseline period, and there was no upward trend. The baseline was "stable," varying only slightly from one day to the next.

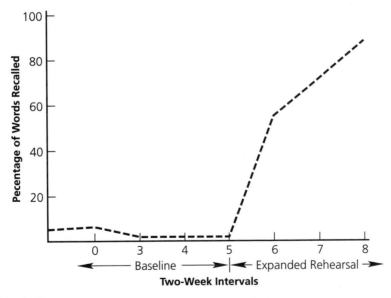

FIGURE 10.10
Memory training in an elderly Alzheimer's patient. A seemingly minor change in procedure produced a dramatic improvement in performance, as compared with low and stable "baseline" performance before the change was introduced (from Moffat, 1989).

Then an experimental program was instituted, in which Miss S memorized words in a different way. Told the name of an object, she was tested for the name after 2 minutes. If successful, she was tested at 4 minutes; and so on. If she correctly named the object after a given interval, then for the next test the interval was doubled; if not, it was halved. This was the independent variable: the new way of memorizing ("expanded rehearsal") versus the old way. As before, each third session began with a "probe" in which Miss S was shown all 20 of the objects and asked to name them.

It doesn't seem as if the new method should have made that much difference, but it did. In the days after the experimental program began, ability to hold onto an item in memory increased dramatically. Whereas before Miss S could hold a name in memory only for a few minutes after being told it, by the third test she was naming most of the objects at the *beginning* of the session, a full day or more after she had last been asked to name them. In addition, her latencies decreased; she named the objects more and more promptly on successive tests (not shown in the figure).

Notice some things. First, the stability of the baseline is important. If the researchers had simply noted that performance was low before the new training and higher afterward (a before-and-after comparison), that would have told us little, for it could happen for any number of reasons; for example, spontaneous recovery or the regression effect. But the initial low performance was *stable over time* until conditions were changed, and it rose soon and sharply thereafter. It is unlikely that sudden spontaneous recovery "just happened" to occur right at the time therapy began. By the same token, we are not looking at a single low point from which improvement was almost bound to occur—the regression effect. Performance began low and *stayed* low until the experimental conditions were changed.

Finally, this of course is only one patient, Miss S. But the experiment was replicated, first by multiple measures for Miss S herself (percentage correct and latency both told the same story), and also in other patients (Moffat, 1989; Wilson, 1989). The replications make it clear that "expanded rehearsal" can be an effective way of retraining patients with nominal dysphasia.

MULTIPLE BASELINES

In Miss S's case, it is unlikely that improvement "just happened" to occur, for some other reason, right at the time that intervention began. Such a coincidence becomes even more unlikely if improvement occurs for the behavior that is the "target" of treatment, but *not* for other behavior. One behavior then serves as a kind of control for another one.

Here again is just one example (from Tawney & Gast, 1994). The subject was a 12-year-old profoundly retarded girl (her measured IQ was 14), and the setting was her classroom. The study focused on certain "inappropriate behaviors" she repeatedly engaged in (among others). These were touching her face, touching her hair, and taking objects. These innocent-sounding labels do not convey the severity of her problems: "[S]he pushed and pulled other children, removed or threw their materials, 'mouthed' her fingers after touching her nasal, genital, and anal areas, and pulled and twisted her hair, resulting in bald spots on her scalp" (Tawney & Gast, 1994, p. 240).

As with Miss S, the therapists first took a series of baseline observations. This time an observer behind a one-way mirror tallied each occurrence of each the three "target behaviors." Spot-checks by a second observer served as control for observer bias. Baselines were obtained in this way for *each* of the three problematic actions (hence "multiple baselines").

Then conditions were changed. Each and every occurrence of a "target" behavior ("touching face") was followed by a 3-minute period of practicing "overcorrection": The child had to sit at a desk in a corner of the room, hands on the desk palms down, with a strip of masking tape across them. At first, this consequence was applied only when "touching face" occurred. A few sessions later, it was extended to include "touching hair"; and later still, it was extended further to include "taking objects."

Figure 10.11 shows what happened. In this case, the baseline data were not very stable, but they were consistently high; so the therapists went ahead anyway. When "touching face" was followed by the "overcorrection" consequence, it was promptly and dramatically reduced, whereas the frequency of "touching hair" and "taking objects" was unaffected. But these actions too were sharply reduced later on, when the consequence was extended to include them.

Here, we see how different actions serve as controls for each other. If it is unlikely that a single action "just happened" to improve right at the time of the new condition, it is all the more unlikely that this would happen for *each of three* actions at different times! This specificity also controls for some other possible confounds. "Touching face" did not improve just because the weather did; and it did not improve just because the added attention of the "overcorrection" procedure put the girl on her best behavior. If it had been either of

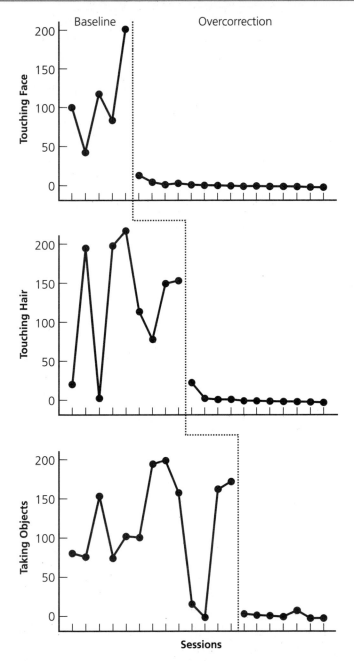

FIGURE 10.11
A multiple-baseline procedure (from Savie & Dickie, 1979, as reproduced in Tawney & Gast, 1994).

these, then *all* of the (mis)behaviors should have decreased in frequency when the first change was made. They did not.

It is true that we don't know just why the procedure worked. Maybe the child's practice at keeping her hands still was an important component of the treatment "package," or maybe it simply acted as a mild punishment. These are questions for further experiments to answer. As they stand, though, the data can be added to many, many other findings showing that behavior can be affected by its consequences even in the severely retarded.

REVERSAL DESIGNS

This design, like the others, depends on repeated measurements of behavior under (at least) two conditions—control and intervention. If there is a measurable change after the intervention begins, and if nothing else in the situation has changed, it is likely that the intervention was responsible for the change. But in some cases we can test that conclusion further by withdrawing or reversing the change in conditions. If then the behavior returns to its former state, we have all the more confidence that it is our independent variable, and *nothing else*, that is controlling that change.

Here's just one example; in this case, a *field experiment* in which a woman who went into severe depression, following the death of her mother, was treated at home by modifying the consequences of her actions. Her actions were typical of depression—lassitude, weakness, and expressions of helplessness. Her husband and children responded with sympathy and consolation to these actions. This is understandable, but possibly short-sighted: What if these attentions were acting to maintain (reinforce?) the unhappy and unproductive expressions? On the advice of therapists, the family members forced themselves to change their reactions, ignoring depressive actions but giving attention and encouragement when positive coping actions occurred.

Figure 10.12 shows the results. Baselines were stable: high for depressive actions, low for coping ones. But when the family's reactions changed, so did the patient's actions; depressive behavior declined, and coping behavior rose. Then (still on advice from the therapists/researchers) the family went back to its original ways of reacting (this is the *reversal*); and sure enough, depressive actions rose again and coping ones declined. Finally, the treatment conditions were reinstated once again. And again, coping behaviors became more frequent, depressive behaviors less so. And they stayed that way. Clearly, it was the family's reactions *and nothing else* that determined whether, in this situation, grieving or coping predominated.

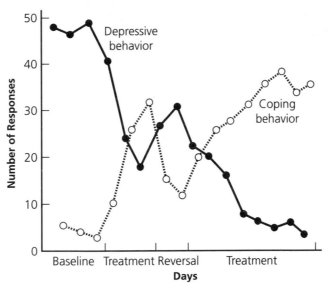

FIGURE 10.12
A reversal design. Changing the consequences of a depressed woman's actions changed the frequency of the actions themselves. Undoing ("reversing") the change in consequences also reversed the change in behavior (from Liberman & Raskin, 1971).

Now, all this is not to discount this unfortunate woman's grief. It was real enough. But the data show that, above and beyond that grief, the family's reactions were of great importance in determining how the patient functioned. We see here yet another example of the powerful role of *situational* factors in determining what we do.

CONTINUITIES WITH LARGE-N RESEARCH

As we saw at the beginning of this chapter, there are ways in which small-N experiments typically differ from large-N ones. But now we see that there are similarities as well. We still have independent and dependent variables. We still take steps to identify and rule out confounded variables, as we have seen at several points.

For instance, in these as in any within-subjects experiments, *order* or *carryover effects* have to be considered as possible confounds. The people-concept pigeons were getting more and more experience with the concept as each session progressed. So, within each session, the various people and nonpeople slides were presented in random order, so that the benefits of practice would be "balanced" between them.

In the clinical experiments, effects of treatment might be confounded with spontaneous recovery or regression effects (compare Chapter 7). This possibility can be checked out, and shown to be unlikely, by (1) stable baselines, (2) multiple baselines, and especially (3) reversal procedures.

What about *observer bias* (compare Chapter 5)? In the experiment with the retarded girl, this was spot-checked by having *multiple observers* record the same actions on occasion. With Miss S, it was dealt with by *objective measures*—either she could name an object or she could not. In the case of the depressed woman, too, there was an attempt to define the relevant behaviors as objectively as possible. Finally, in the pigeon-concept and brain-stimulation experiments, observer bias was again minimized by objective measures: lever presses or key pecks were detected and recorded by automated equipment.

In short, small-N research has characteristics that differ from the (now) more usual grouped-data experiment. But despite these differences, many of the problems and pitfalls—and the solutions to them—remain the same for both.

SUMMARY

Often, experiments in psychology focus on groups of subjects, treated identically except for the independent variable, with data summarized by descriptive statistics and reliability of the finding demonstrated by tests of significance.

Often, but not always. Much has been learned by research in which all of these are reversed: Each subject is treated as an independent experiment, with procedures adapted to the individual; individual data are presented, and reliability is assessed by replication across experiments.

This "small-N" approach has found many applications. Psychophysics, the study of brain function, the study of conditioning and of conceptual learning in animals, rote memory for nonsense syllables and conceptual memory for connected discourse, clinical research—all these have found the small-N strategy useful.

Because they focus on individuals, small-N experiments almost always depend on within-subjects comparisons. As with their large-N counterparts, such experiments must control for carryover effects such as practice and fatigue, or longer-term drifts in a subject's condition. Experimental designs such as stable-baseline, multiple-baseline, and reversal designs can provide such controls.

MAKING FRIENDS WITH STATISTICS: SIGNAL-DETECTION THEORY

Small-N experiments tend to downplay the use of significance testing, preferring to establish the reliability of findings by showing it directly—that is, by *replication*. This does not mean that they don't use statistics! In fact, there is a whole class of situations that (1) are typically studied small-N in the laboratory, but (2) are analyzed in a way that extends ideas we're familiar with into new domains, *and* (3) introduce a new way of looking at many real-life events.

AN EXAMPLE:
A RECOGNITION EXPERIMENT

To start with a specific example, suppose we do an experiment in recognition memory. We make a list of 10 simple words,

and we give the list to a subject, telling her, "Your task is to memorize these." Later, we present her with 20 such words, one at a time. These 20 words include the 10 that were on the list ("signal" or "target" items), and 10 more that were not on the list ("catch" items). Target and catch items appear in random order. For each item, we ask the subject to say either "Yes, that was on the list I saw before," or "No, that's a catch item; it wasn't on the list."

Unless the items are very thoroughly learned, the subject will make mistakes. On some occasions she will say "No" when the correct answer is yes, or "Yes" when she should say no. Specifically, suppose we get the following data (see Figure 10.13) . Of the 10 target items, 8 were recognized: for each of these the subject said, correctly, "Yes, that was on the list." We will

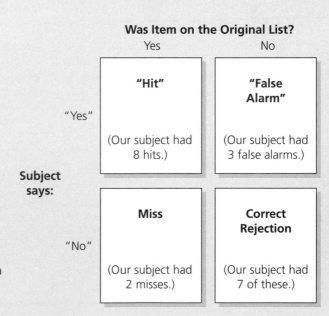

FIGURE 10.13
The four possible outcomes on each trial of a signal-detection experiment, and one subject's data.

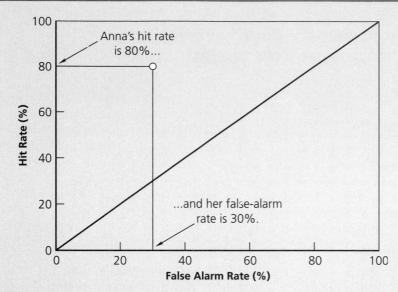

FIGURE 10.14
Anna's hit rate is plotted against her false alarm rate.

call those *hits*. The remaining two items were *misses*: The subject said wrongly, "No, that was not on the list." Of the 10 catch items, 3 were wrongly called target items; these we will call *false alarms*. The remaining 7 were *correct rejections*: The subject said "no," and was right to do so.

Thus, for each word we present in this second, test phase of the experiment, there are four possibilities: The word really was on the original list, or it wasn't; and the subject can say "Yes, it was," or "No, it was not." The resulting four possible outcomes, and our subject's data, are shown in Figure 10.13.*

Another way of plotting the data will make further developments easier to visualize. In Figure 10.14, we present a kind of

scatterplot, in which a point representing a subject's performance is located by two measures: the proportion of *hits*, on the vertical axis, and the proportion of *false alarms*, on the horizontal axis.[†] So our subject's data point falls at hit rate = 0.8 or 80%, false alarm rate = 0.3 or 30%. And now it is time to give our subject a name; let's call her Anna.

---

*We assume in all this that the subject is not allowed to say, "I'm not sure," but is told to guess yes or no if in doubt. We could allow a "not sure" response, but it would greatly complicate the analysis.

If this terminology—especially false alarms and misses—reminds you of our discussion of Type I and Type II errors, respectively (Chapter 7), the resemblance is no

accident. A scientist testing for significance *is* in a kind of signal-detection situation. If she decides that a difference between conditions is "real" when it isn't, she will make a false alarm (a Type I error); and she sets the significance level (the decision criterion) so that the probability of making that mistake is acceptably low. But if her test returns a finding of nonsignificance when the effect is really there, she will have "missed" that real effect (a Type II error). She may be able to calculate the probability of that mistake too (pp. 250–253).

[†]We only need these two, because they provide all the information the whole table contains. If hit rate (saying "Yes" when the answer is yes) is 80%, then the miss rate (saying "No" when the right answer is yes) has to be 20%—since every trial with a target item must be either a hit or a miss. And if false alarm rate is 30%, then the correct-rejection rate must be 70%—since every catch trial must be one or the other.

ANALYSIS OF SIGNAL-DETECTION DATA

And now let us stop and think for a minute.

Anna is making some mistakes, both misses and false alarms. So we can assume that there is some uncertainty in her mind, no doubt greater for some items than for others. If so, then her problem becomes: How sure does she *have to be* that the answer is yes for a given item, before she makes a "Yes" response to that item? She must be setting up in her mind a certain standard, or *decision criterion,* for how sure she has to be that the correct answer is "yes" before she makes that answer.

These assumptions may sound arbitrary but, if we think about it, we see that something like this *has* to be going on.

Otherwise, there would be no misses or false alarms at all. Some items that were, in fact, on the original list, were "missed"—Anna wasn't sure enough to say "yes." Some others were not on the list, but she thought they were; and in three cases she was sure enough of this that she said "yes" mistakenly—hence her three false alarms.

What use can we make of that information? It will allow us to separate a subject's accuracy from her response criterion, or "guessing strategy"—how willing she is to guess "yes" when uncertain. To see how it works, let's say we have four subjects. Anna's data we already have; so let us run Barbara, Carole, and Donna through the same experimental procedure (Figure 10.15).

Barbara correctly identifies 90% of the items on the list, so that is her hit rate. If

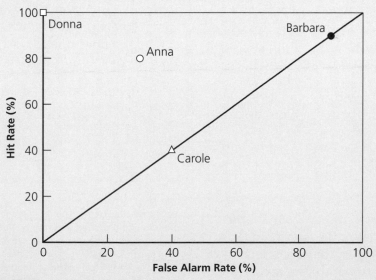

FIGURE 10.15
To the extent that hit rate exceeds false-alarm rate, a subject's accuracy is high. Hit rate and false-alarm rate together permit assessment of accuracy and decision criterion.

we look just at that, it would seem as if she's doing even better than Anna. But wait! Barbara's false-alarm rate is 90%, too. She says "Yes" 90% of the time, *whether she should or not*. Clearly, she is just guessing and her accuracy is zero! She just says "Yes" 90% of the time, on both target and "catch" trials.

What about Carole? She has a hit rate of 40%, but her false alarm rate is also 40%. She also is just guessing—she says "Yes" 40% of the time whether the answer should be "Yes" or "No." Her accuracy, like Barbara's, is zero. More generally, we can say *that any time the hit rate equals the false alarm rate, the subject is guessing and accuracy is zero*. This is shown by the diagonal line in the figure.

Thus accuracy is zero for both Barbara and Carole. The only difference is that Carole is more cautious about saying "Yes" when she guesses, whereas Barbara says "Yes, yes!" nearly all the time. To say the same thing another way: Carole's *criterion* for a "Yes" response is higher than Barbara's. Thus, the false-alarm rate gives us an estimate of how conservative her decision criterion is. (There are more precise ways of locating the criterion [see Green & Swets, 1966], but we don't need to get into them to see the logic of what we're doing.)

What about accuracy, then? Clearly, we *cannot assess accuracy from the hit rate alone*; Barbara's hit rate is higher than Anna's, but her accuracy is lower. Why do we say Anna is more accurate? Because her hit rate is higher than her false alarm rate. She says "yes" more of-ten when she should than when she should not. More generally, we can say that *accuracy is greater, the more the hit rate exceeds the false alarm rate*. (Again there are more precise measures of accuracy, should we require them.) Thus Anna is not performing perfectly—she is making mistakes—but she is still more accurate than either Barbara or Carole.

Finally, look at Donna's data. She has a hit rate of 100%, but that doesn't mean much; she could have been guessing "yes" 100% of the time. But if that were so, her false alarm rate would also be 100%. In fact, it is zero. Her hit rate exceeds her false alarm rate by as much as it possibly could. She turned in a perfect performance.*

Looking backward over this, we find that our data have allowed us to estimate the values of two variables at once. How willing is the subject to guess "Yes" when in doubt? The *false alarm rate* tells us that. How accurate is the subject? The hit rate alone does not tell us that, but the *how much the hit rate exceeds the false-alarm rate* does.

---

*It is true that two people might turn in perfect performances like that, and still one might have learned the list better than the other. If so, we are encountering an old enemy: *ceiling/floor effects* (Chapter 7). If we find many of our subjects turning in perfect performances, we would probably want to revise the task to make it more difficult; otherwise, too many perfect performances might obscure differences among conditions.

EXTENSIONS OF THE METHOD

We have chosen for our example an experiment in rote memory. But the ideas can be extended to other settings and other kinds of experiments. Consider a perceptual experiment—the kind of experiment that gave "signal-detection theory" its name.

Take three subjects, John, Joe, and James. Suppose the experiment is one of auditory signal detection: Each subject is given a series of trials, on each of which a faint auditory signal either is presented (a signal trial) or is not presented (a catch trial). The signal is a very faint one, so that the subject can never be certain whether it was presented or not. The subject must judge on each trial whether the signal was presented or not, saying "Yes" or "No."

Let us think of this situation in the same way as before. The subject will say "Yes, I heard the signal" if what he heard on that trial was "strong enough" to exceed a decision criterion; otherwise he will say "No." Because the signal is faint, it will sometimes be too weak to be heard even when it is present, and we will get misses. Other times, even a no-signal presentation will sound "strong" enough to be a signal (as a result of uncontrolled noise, spontaneous events within the brain, or whatever). Then the subject will say "Yes" when the answer should be "No," and we will have a false alarm. We can then analyze these data in the same way as we did the memory data earlier.

Or consider a real experiment in memory, one we have met before. Remember our discussion of hypnosis and memory? One of the sets of experiments we discussed there was conducted in just this way. Subjects were allowed to inspect complex pictures, and then, after awhile, they were asked a series of questions of the form, "Was there an X in the picture?" "Did the picture show a person doing Y?" and so on. This gives us our familiar four-outcome format: For each such question, we know whether the answer should be yes or no; and we know whether the subject said "Yes" or "No." The memory test was conducted twice: once when the subject was hypnotized, and once when she was not.

When a signal-detection analysis was applied to the data, the results were quite clear. In every case, the measure of accuracy was not affected by hypnosis. What *was* affected was the decision criterion: Under hypnosis, the subjects became more willing to guess "Yes" when in doubt (Erdelyi, 1985).

More generally, the concepts of signal detection can be applied to *any* situation in which we must decide whether some X is the case or not (Was this item on the list, or not? Is he guilty, or not? Did I just hear a signal, or not?) when we cannot be sure. Consider some scenarios:

An accused person is brought to trial, and we as jurors, having heard all the evidence there is, must now vote "guilty" or "not guilty." The evidence, we assume, is strong but not airtight. Now a vote of guilty, if the defendant *is* guilty, is a vote to punish the guilty—a hit (good). But if he is not guilty, then it is a vote to punish the innocent—a false alarm (bad).

Assuming we have all the information we are going to get, our problem comes down to one of *setting our response criterion.* How sure do we *have to be* that the person is guilty, before we vote guilty? And that criterion—how sure is *sure enough?*—will be affected by our beliefs about the likelihoods of various outcomes, and by the costs and values we place on them.

Thus: How likely is it that an innocent person will be brought to trial at all? If we believe that it happens rarely, we will set our criterion lower—we will be more willing to vote guilty—than if we think it happens often. And which is worse, to let the guilty go free or to punish the innocent? Obviously, if we think punishing the innocent is a worse mistake, we will be less likely to vote guilty when in doubt.

One final example—a worrisome one. Recall that in our initial analysis of signal-detection data, our measure of accuracy depended on two things: the hit rate and the false-alarm rate. Looking at hit rates alone does *not* tell us how accurately our subjects were performing.

Barbara had a higher hit rate than Anna. When the correct answer was yes, she answered "Yes" more often than Anna did. If we looked *only at that,* we would conclude that Barbara was performing more accurately than Anna was. She wasn't—she was just guessing "Yes" more often than Anna did. But *we know that only because we can look at the false-alarm rate.* And we can look at that only because we presented some "catch" trials in which the answer should have been no.

In other words, accuracy in any of these yes/no situations depends on how often we say "Yes" correctly, *and* on how often we say it incorrectly. We should think about that when we read of a test, or other diagnostic procedure, that "correctly identified 80%" of the people with such-and-such a condition. That is the hit rate. We should ask ourselves, "What was the false-alarm rate? How many people *without* the condition were wrongly identified as having it? Come to think of it, were people without the condition even included in the study? They are necessary." All this is reminiscent of the "present/present bias" we encountered back in Chapter 3.

We also should think about this when we hear of the extraordinary claims sometimes made by "experts" in psychological assessment. Dawes (1994) quotes the following claim, made by a psychologist on "Good Morning, America!" The "expert" tells us: "I can spot it as a person walks in the door. . . . There's a certain body language . . . [that identifies a person as an incest victim] (Dawes, 1994, p. 8). This psychologist had claimed that "Probably one in four women . . . have been incested [sic]."

It would be very interesting to put that claim to the test. To do it, we would need to let a number of known incest victims "walk in the door," and note the number of "Yes" responses by our expert—the hit rate. She might correctly identify most or all of them—but that high hit rate, by itself, would mean nothing. We would *also* need to let a number of people walk in who are known *not* to be incest victims (how would we know that?) and note the false-alarm rate. To assess accuracy, we need both. (What if the two were equal?)

One wonders whether the expert would submit to such a test! Without it, the claim is no more solid than air. Yet the fact is that accusations of abuse or in-

cest have been made, and enormous damage has been done, on no more grounds than this kind of useless "evidence" (Crews, 1993; Ofshe & Watters, 1994) by counselors who mean well, but who have no way of knowing when they are wrong.

CHAPTER 11

QUASI-EXPERIMENTS

By comparing data patterns under different conditions, scientists rule out certain explanations and confirm others. . . . That is, they try to weed out the maximum number of incorrect explanations. They do this either by directly controlling the experimental situation or by observing the kinds of naturally occurring situations that allow them to test alternative explanations.

—KEITH STANOVICH

IN THIS CHAPTER, WE'LL DISCUSS:

■ What a quasi-experiment is

■ How it resembles, and how it differs from, a real experiment

■ How selection may be used as a substitute for manipulation
   Nonequivalent groups designs
   Time-series designs

■ The danger of confounded variables in quasi-experiments

■ Combinations of methods

Correlation, we all know, does not imply causality. Two variables may be correlated with each other, but from that fact alone we cannot draw conclusions about what causes what. For that, we need experiments. But then we may face a dilemma. The experiments cannot always be performed—either because we can't for practical reasons, or because we won't for ethical reasons, or both.

For example, we might wish to observe how the members of a community react to a natural disaster. But we cannot select some communities to be hit by tornadoes and others not. We cannot produce tornadoes at will (the practical limitation). And we would not do so if we could (the ethical limitation). We must take our tornadoes where we find them.

Or, look again at the study of infant crying and mothers' responsiveness (Chapter 4). We saw that the correlation between the two is negative, and that this raises problems for one theory—the "reinforcement" one. But it does not clearly support any other theory. We don't know that responsive mothers *cause* their babies to be placid whereas unresponsive mothers cause their babies to be fussy. It could be the other way round: Fussy babies might cause mothers to become unresponsive. Or some third variable—noise level in the home?—might affect both the mother and the baby. Such ambiguity always accompanies correlational findings.

Now, we could resolve it all if we could do an experiment. We might take a sample of mother–infant pairs and divide them at random into (say) two groups. In one, the mothers are *told* to be responsive; in the other, unresponsive. Then if babies raised by responsive mothers were less fussy (on average) than those raised by unresponsive mothers, we would know that the difference between "parenting styles" *caused* the difference in babies' behavior. That's because we know what caused different parents to behave differently. We did!

But of course we cannot do that experiment. The parents would object, rightly; and they would not obey our instructions (the practical constraint). And even if we could somehow force them to do so, we wouldn't; we would not make so intolerable an intrusion into their lives (the ethical constraint).

However, we can do this: We can observe young babies in settings where social contact—cuddling and "contact comfort," and responsiveness to social signals like cries—are minimal. Some institutional nurseries, in certain parts of the world, are like that even today. And their babies do tend not to thrive, and are (or become) socially unresponsive and generally unhappy, even if their nutritional needs are met. Here, what we have done is not to *make* some homes unresponsive, as in an experiment; but to *find* some homes that *already are*, and compare these with other, more responsive ones. That is a quasi-experiment. And the findings fit in with the conclusions of Bell and Ainsworth, Harlow, and the many other investigators whose various findings point to the same conclusion: For babies' well-being, nutrition is not enough.

WHAT IS A QUASI-EXPERIMENT?

Quasi- is a prefix meaning "like," or "almost." A quasi-experiment (a term introduced by Campbell & Stanley, 1963) is like an experiment in that it tries to establish a causal relation between one variable and another. But it is not quite an experiment—hence *quasi,*—because it does not directly *manipulate* a variable. It tries to isolate a causal influence by *selection* rather than manipulation. Rather than *causing* some X to vary from one condition to another, we *select* cases in which X *does* vary.

Let us look at some examples of what can be done.

SELECTION OF SUBJECTS: NONEQUIVALENT GROUPS DESIGNS

One kind of experimental design we're familiar with is the *between-groups design*. Such an experiment divides subjects at random into two or more groups, and these groups receive different values of the variable that is of interest. In one group, for example, we might cause each subject to be emotionally aroused in some way, whereas subjects in the other group are not aroused. Then we measure some other variable to see whether the degree of arousal, which we have manipulated, affects it.

That would be an experiment. In a quasi-experiment, we would not *make* some subjects aroused and others not, but rather *select* subjects who are already aroused, and compare them with others who are not. This was done in a famous and ingenious quasi-experiment, in the following way.

AN EXAMPLE FROM EMOTION:
A TALE OF TWO BRIDGES

The question was this: Do we always know what we are feeling? Or can we mistake one emotional state for another?

Do we look inside ourselves and "see," directly, what we are feeling and why we are feeling it? Or, given a feeling, do we make *inferences* about what we are feeling and why? If the latter, then it is not true, as we are so often told, that "our feelings never lie." If we must *infer* what our feelings are, then our inferences could be wrong. A substantial body of literature supports that conclusion. It is clear that—folklore to the contrary—we are capable of being quite mistaken about how we feel, and why we feel that way. We may indeed confuse one emotional state with another.

More specifically, we may experience a state of arousal and excitement—and simply *mistake* it for a more specific emotion—for example, attraction to another person. And here is a study that supports that conclusion.

The researchers (Dutton & Aron, 1974) took advantage of a pair of bridges across a river (Figure 11.1). One of these bridges was made

FIGURE 11.1
The Capilano Suspension Bridge, near Vancouver, British Columbia.

of wooden boards attached to wire cables, with a low wire handrail. Crossing this bridge was a stressful experience, as subjects' self-reports confirmed. The crosser felt that he could be pitched over the side of the bridge at any moment, onto rocks and shallow rapids far below.

The other bridge, upriver, was only 10 feet above the water and was made of solid wood. There was no stress or anxiety attached to crossing it.

The subjects were men who happened to cross one bridge or the other. They were not *assigned* to one or the other—this is important—but *chose* one or the other themselves. They were going about their business, with no idea yet that they were in a quasi-experiment.

Now, as each man finished crossing the bridge he had chosen, he was met by a female experimenter. The men who had just crossed the rickety bridge were in a state of anxious arousal. The question was: Would they *mistake that arousal for attraction to the female*? If so, men coming off the risky bridge should feel more attracted to her than men who had crossed the safe one.

So, it is necessary to find a way of measuring how attracted to the female each subject felt. That is our Y or dependent variable, and we want to see how it is related to the X (independent) variable: whether a subject chose to cross the risky bridge, or the safe one.

How can we measure each subject's feeling of attraction? How do we *operationalize* that variable (Chapter 3)? Let us think about that.

Obviously, it would never do to let the female walk up to the male and ask "Do I attract you?" What could the poor subject say but "Yes, of course"—an unacceptable *observer effect*. We must be less direct than that.

So a little scenario was played out. The female approached each man, and asked if he would help her with a psychology project. At her request, he told a brief impromptu story that later was scored for sexual imagery. (The scoring was done "blind," by scorers who did not know which bridge the subject had crossed. Why?) That was one measure of the subject's sexual arousal. In addition, there was a direct measure of behavior itself. The female explained that she was only beginning the project and didn't yet know how the data were going to come out. So she gave the subject her phone number, saying in effect, "If you'd like to know the results, call me and I'll tell you about them." Then it was a simple matter to count the number of calls she received, from those who had crossed the high bridge and from those who had crossed the low one.

Again, the question was: Would a state of physiological *arousal*, produced by crossing the rickety bridge, enhance the male subject's feeling of *attraction* to a female experimenter? Would he mistake the bridge-induced arousal for a person-induced arousal? If so, then the subjects who crossed the dangerous bridge should perceive themselves as more attracted to the female experimenter. They should (1) show more sexual imagery in their test responses, and (2) be more likely to call the experimenter later.

What happened? Of the men who had crossed the dangerous bridge, fully 50% telephoned the experimenter. Of those who crossed the safe bridge, only 12% did so. The differences in sexual imagery also were as predicted.

Now this finding fits the hypothesis under test. Again, the idea is that (1) after crossing the dangerous bridge (but not the safe one), the men were in a state of physiological arousal produced by anxiety; and (2) that on meeting the woman, they would mistake that arousal for attraction to her (Figure 11.2A).

However, there is another possibility. Remember that the men chose which bridge to cross. Now crossing a risky bridge is, well, risky. But so is calling up a strange woman in an attempt to maintain a relationship with her. One risks rejection. Suppose then that the men who chose the risky bridge were simply *more willing to take risks*—of all kinds—than were the ones who crossed the safe one? That is our old enemy, the "confounded variable" problem (Figure 11.2B).

The researchers spotted that problem. And so they followed up this quasi-experiment with a true experiment, to "check out" the confounded variable. They reasoned as follows. If what produced the difference in the data was the physiological arousal (high in one group, low in the other)—that is a temporary state. It ought to go away fairly quickly once the danger has passed. But "willingness to take risks" is presumably a stable personality trait. It should characterize some men more than others, whatever their momentary state may be.

In the second study, *only* men who had crossed the risky bridge were subjects. But now, they were approached by the female either (1) immediately after crossing the bridge, as before; or (2), some time after they had done so, when anxiety should have gone away. This is a full-blown between-groups experiment (not a quasi-experiment), because men could be *assigned at random* to one or another condition: interview immediate, or interview delayed.

Notice how this change separates the two variables that were confounded before. If the original data only mean that men who

A

Men who crossed the dangerous bridge were more likely to call the experimenter later...

...than were those who crossed the safe bridge.

B

But was this because of the arousal that crossing the dangerous bridge had produced? If it was...

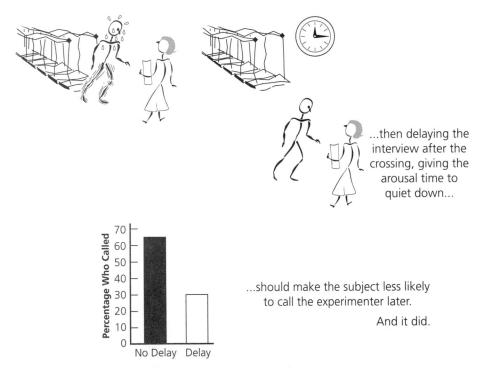

...then delaying the interview after the crossing, giving the arousal time to quiet down...

...should make the subject less likely to call the experimenter later.

And it did.

FIGURE 11.2
Interpretation of the safe-bridge/dangerous-bridge finding, and a follow-up experiment to test that interpretation.

cross risky bridges also make risky phone calls, that presumably is a stable personality trait, and the delay should make no difference. But if momentary state of arousal is the crucial factor, then the delay, which allows time for that arousal to dissipate, should make a difference. And it did. Of the men interviewed at once, when arousal was high, 65% telephoned the female experimenter. Of those interviewed later, when arousal was lower, only 30% did so. And since all these men had risked the dangerous bridge, we cannot attribute the difference to a willingness to take risks, for that was now *controlled*—it was the same for all.

COMMENT

These ideas have a number of immediate practical implications. In light of them, I would suggest that if you're going to have an argument with a Significant Other, don't do it right after a vigorous skating session! Your SO—and you, for that matter—might mistake the increased arousal produced by the exercise for increased anger, making the argument more severe than it has to be.

Or consider a clinical case study. A woman had been feeling so irritable and jumpy that she feared a nervous breakdown. It turned out that she had recently been drinking eight to ten bottles of diet cola a day. Her therapist pointed out to her that the amount of caffeine she was consuming was more than enough to produce jumpiness and jitters. Once she had *reinterpreted* the symptoms, her outlook on life was much improved, even though the jitters remained the same as before.

On the more general, theoretical side, the findings also have a place. They are among the very many studies showing that the old saw, "Trust your feelings. Your feelings are never wrong,"—is simply and demonstrably false. We do not just *experience* our emotions directly. Rather we *interpret* what we feel, and *decide* what emotion it is that we are experiencing. And we can make mistakes, as we have just seen. We *can* be wrong about what it is that we are feeling.

This is not surprising, if we think about it. Think how we say, "I must have been hungrier than I thought. Look how much I ate!" If we can be wrong about so simple a matter as how hungry we are, why should we not sometimes make mistakes in deciding how angry, frightened, or attracted we are?

The question can be raised at a still higher level. We like to think that we can "look inside," or *introspect*, and thus reveal ourselves to ourselves. But can we? Or is there an added step that our cognitive apparatus must supply? Very often it appears that we must *infer* what we must be feeling, rather than just feeling it directly. We often do not really know why we made the decisions we did; and the attempt to list reasons and examine them may lead to worse decisions rather than better ones. A lot of our thinking, many writers point out, is done not to help us make decisions but to justify them, to ourselves and others, after they are made (Zajonc, 1984). Thus they too are inferences we draw, about what our reasons must have been.

In all these domains, we see ourselves making inferences or interpretations about what we experience, just as we do about what we remember (Chapter 10). And the interpretations leave room for error. As one writer put it (Wilson, 1985), we may be "strangers to ourselves" to a much greater extent than we suppose.

AN EXAMPLE FROM CLINICAL PSYCHOLOGY: GENES AND ALCOHOLISM

Now let us compare the tale of two bridges with another instance, in which the same logic is applied in a wholly different domain.

We know—we have known for a long time—that alcohol abuse tends to run in families. Children who come from homes in which one or both parents abused alcohol seem particularly likely to abuse it themselves as adults.

But let us ask two questions here. First, is it true? Or are we giving undue weight to "present-present" cases—parent an alcohol abuser, child becomes one—because these cases are most likely to be noticed and to stick in our minds?

Second: If it is true, why? Two obvious possibilities come to mind. First, there may be some genetically based predisposition to alcohol abuse. Second, the home environment could be the important factor: Children who grow up with alcohol-abusing "role models" may learn habits of thought and action that invite abusive drinking when they are older.

Now, can we separate those two possibilities? Can we find cases in which one of them operates, but not the other? Once we ask the question that way, we see at once what data we need. Look at adoptees! If children get their genes from one set of parents and their home environment from another, we can see which of the two is more closely related to what the children will later do. Notice too that we have an instance of *purposive sampling* here; we will select for our study subjects in which this separation can be made.

So Goodwin and his colleagues (see Goodwin, 1979) undertook studies of the incidence of alcohol abuse among adoptees in Denmark.* They selected a sample of adults who, as small children, had been adopted from one home into another. And they looked for the incidence of alcoholism among those who had an alcoholic parent, and among those who did not.

Notice that by restricting their sample to adoptees, the researchers were attempting to hold constant—that is, to *control for*—the effects of adoption per se, and the stress that may accompany it. Here we see another use of selection: We may use it, not only to vary a variable, but also to keep a variable from varying—to control it. For similar reasons, the researchers restricted themselves to males in this study, thus eliminating gender differences as a possible source of variability in the data.

But now, we face a problem: How do we *operationalize* the important variable here? How, specifically, do we decide who is and is not an alcohol abuser?

We cannot interview everybody; it would be prohibitively expensive and not very informative anyway. Many alcohol abusers vigorously deny that they have a problem with drinking—*self-presentation* perhaps, or maybe simply a *bias in their observations* of themselves. As for friends, relatives, and employers, these too may deny that a problem exists; or, conversely, they may exaggerate it. Thus the problem of *observer bias* is a very serious one here.

Instead, these scientists settled on an *objective* measure. They went through the medical records of adoptees, their biological parents, and their adoptive parents (*unobtrusive measures*, Chapter 5). They asked for each person simply: Does a diagnosis of alcohol abuse appear in the record, or does it not? If it did, the person in question was classified as alcoholic; if not, not.

Aren't mistakes going to be made that way? Of course they are. A drinking problem may be missed by a diagnosing physician. Or a person may have such a diagnosis in his record because of a transient drinking problem from which he recovered on his own, before a child could be affected by it (such "spontaneous" recovery is common). There will be false positives and false negatives. It is a fact of life.

But the researchers opted for this method anyway, for three

---

*Why Denmark? Because there, careful *public* records are kept, showing who has been adopted, from whom, and by whom. Such data can be much more difficult to obtain in the United States.

reasons. First, they decided that they would make even *more* mistakes if they went about it any other way—because of the old problems of observer effects and observer bias. If mistakes cannot be avoided, at least they can be minimized. Second, it would seem that such errors—false positives and false negatives—should be equally likely for both groups. So, on average, they should "subtract out" from a comparison between one group and another.

And third, the readings of the records should have very high *reliability*—someone can check the records a second time (test-retest reliability), or another person can do so (interobserver reliability), or both. To do interviews, instead, might seem on the face of it to be more *valid* as a measure of presence or absence of a drinking problem. But we also remember from Chapter 3 (pp. 90–91) that a measure *cannot be more valid than it is reliable*. And subjective reports by a subject (or ratings by his associates) will not be very reliable. Perceptions of how serious John's drinking problem is will vary from time to time (lowering test-retest reliability), and may well vary with who is asking the questions (lowering interobserver reliability).

On all these grounds, then, the researchers opted in this case for the more remote, but also more objective, way of classifying individuals as having or not having an alcohol problem.

Some typical results are presented in Table 11.1. The table shows what percentage of the children with alcoholic parents, and of those without, later developed alcoholism themselves. Notice that to compute these percentages, we had to have tallies for all four cells—not just the "present/present" one (compare Chapter 3).

Table 11.1
Typical Results

	Father Alcoholic	*Father Not Alcoholic*
Son Alcoholic	20%	5%
Son Not Alcoholic	80%	95%
Total	100%	100%

We see that if a child has an alcoholic *biological* father, the risk of becoming alcoholic himself quadruples. It jumps from about 5% to about 20%. The latter is still a small percentage; the odds are that even the son of an alcoholic will not develop the disorder himself. But the risk, though it remains relatively small, is *not as small* as it is among those with no evidence of alcohol abuse in their fathers' records. Finally, there is little evidence of any such relationship between incidence of abuse in the foster home, and incidence of alcohol problems among the adoptees (the table does not show those data).

These data tell us quite a bit: (1) Along with many other data, they support the idea that alcohol abuse does tend to "run in families." (2) They suggest that the risk of abuse follows biological, not social, parentage; genetic relatedness is of more importance than home environment. But also (3) they remind us that we are speaking of *risk* here, not of inevitability. Even the biological child of an alcoholic is, we might say, relatively safe from developing the disorder. He is just *not as safe* as the child without such parentage. Presumably what is inherited is a *vulnerability* to the disorder. If so, something else must be required to trigger it.

TIME-SERIES DESIGNS

The examples so far are analogues of *between-group designs* in experimentation. One group is compared with another. Now let us turn to the analogues of *within-subjects* designs, where we compare behavior at different times in the *same* subjects.

The study of the Seekers (the group that predicted doomsday and was waiting to be rescued) could be considered a time-series quasi-experiment. It was a before-and-after comparison: Festinger et al. observed the group's behavior before, and after, the times when catastrophe was to strike and rescuers were to arrive. After these things failed to happen, the group's commitment to their ideas changed abruptly—not toward a decrease, but toward an increase!

Let's see another example.

AN EXAMPLE FROM COMMUNITY PSYCHOLOGY: IMPACT OF THE INTERNET

This next example does not grapple with a theoretical issue but with a practical one. It asks: How does usage of the Internet affect our social network, and our psychological well-being?

We could argue it either way. Once logged onto the Internet, we can communicate by e-mail, or even converse by instant messages, with people all over the world. Interest groups have sprung up, as have solid friendships and even romances, some of them lasting. Thus by using this new resource to the full, we might expect to expand our network of friends and interests, and be happier and healthier in consequence.

Or we could reason the opposite way. To the extent that we substitute typing for talking and distant friends for nearby ones, we may be widening our circle of friends at the expense of the quality of friendships. We might end up feeling more alone rather than less, and with a narrower circle of true friends, not a wider one.

Granted that effects of either kind might be seen in individuals, is one more likely than the other? If so, which one? How can we look and see, to find out which impact of the Internet (if either) is the more frequent?

Well, we could simply *correlate* Internet usage with social involvement in a sample of computer owners. But what would that tell us? Some people use the Internet more than others. Okay, but how else do they differ? In many ways—in skills, values, education, and on and on. All these would be confounded with the Internet-usage variable, if we were to just *correlate* Internet usage with—well, with anything!

Specifically, suppose we found that Internet usage was positively correlated with depression. Would it mean that extensive Internet use promotes depression (X causes Y)? Or that depression makes people more likely to turn to the Internet for solace and distraction (Y causes X)? Or is some third variable Z the one that is doing all the work? (Pick your own scenario here.)

So Kraut and his colleagues (Kraut et al., 1998) turned to a *longitudinal study*, in which a group of subjects was followed over time. For all subjects, various measures of social involvement, and of emotional well-being, were taken before, and then again after, a two-year period of Internet access.

Taking a *series* of measures over *time* (hence "time series") permits us to ask questions that would not be possible with a one-shot correlational study. Thus: Suppose depression encourages Internet use. If so, then *how much subjects use the Internet now* should be correlated with *how depressed the subjects were earlier*. The first measure of depression should be correlated with later use of the Internet.

On the other hand, suppose Internet use contributes to depression. Then, *how much the subjects use the Internet now* should be correlated with *how depressed the subjects will be later*. The second measure of depression should be correlated with Internet use. Different ideas make different predictions! So we can test them against each other.

Before we look at the results, we should note some of the control procedures that were used in this study. Some irrelevant variables were *controlled* directly. The subjects were the same throughout—so we needn't worry about whether different groups were comparable, for there were none, just as in a within-subjects experiment. All the subjects were new to the Internet—they were actually given their computers by the investigators! This was a thank-you for participating; it also provided a way that their Internet usage could be tracked automatically—hence objectively. (This tracking was done, of course, with the subjects' knowledge and consent.) As a bonus, it got rid of differences in Internet experience, which might have been a source of obscuring variability. And because of the longitudinal design, initial well-being and social involvement could be held constant statistically (Chapter 8).

The measures themselves were as objective as possible. Not "Did you use the Internet a little, some, or a lot?" but Internet hours per week, number of sites accessed, number of e-mail messages sent and received. Not "How socially involved are you?" but lists of household members and, from each, estimates of minutes per day spent talking with each, number of people socialized with at least once per month . . . and so on. Depression was assessed by responses to standardized questionnaires that, in large populations, are found related to depression; persistent "blues," the effortfulness of everyday tasks, and the like.

What happened? Briefly, depression scores at the beginning of the study did *not* predict Internet use later. But degree of Internet use *did* predict depression scores at the end. Similarly, initial loneliness *was not* correlated with Internet use later. But Internet use *was* correlated with loneliness later. Having a wider circle of social involvement did predict less use of the Internet later; but even holding initial involvement constant statistically, use of the Internet now was correlated with a narrowing of the social circle later. All of these patterns suggest that Internet use was a *cause of* later loneliness and isolation later, and not *caused by* initial loneliness and isolation. These relations were small, but they were there.

Now that conclusion is not airtight—even here, correlation does not really prove causality. As the authors recognize, some unmeasured third factor Z might cause both increased Internet use *and* greater depression and isolation, as time went by. But certainly the picture is clearer than if, say, we had just correlated Internet use with depression at one time.

Of course there are many other variables that could have been measured, such as educational outcome or self-esteem, and families with different characteristics; the results for persons of, for example, limited mobility might be very different. No study can answer all questions at once, and Kraut et al. have no wish to bash the Internet. Their data suggest that it may be a mixed blessing, however, and they encourage the development of ways to use its positives while minimizing its negatives.

MIXED DESIGNS

It is possible to combine our two themes—selection of subjects, and selection of times—in a single investigation. Such a design is like a mixed between-groups and within-subjects experimental design (Chapter 10). Subjects are compared with other subjects, and also with themselves under different conditions.

AN EXAMPLE FROM PSYCHOPATHOLOGY

This example selects time slots before, during, and after a critical episode, and also compares subjects in which such an episode does or does not occur at all.

Lewinsohn and Rosenbaum (1987) studied approximately a thousand people over a 15-month period. Now of these subjects, some were depressed at the beginning of the study, but recovered from it while the study was in progress. Others were not clinically depressed at the beginning, but became so during the course of the research. Still others fell into depression, and also recovered from that state, while the study was in progress.

A dramatic difference was found in comparing interview material for depressed and nondepressed people. If interviewed *while depressed*, subjects reported their parents as much more indifferent and rejecting than did subjects who never became depressed. That in itself would imply an association between parental rejection during childhood, and depression in adulthood. However, it turned out that such rejecting parental care was reported only *while the subjects were in the depressed state*. When interviewed before depression set in *or* after recovery from it, subjects who would be or had been depressed reported, on average, the same kind of parenting as subjects who never became depressed. Thus, before or after depression, the subjects remembered their parents as relating to them in a normal and loving way. Only during depression did they remember their parents as unloving and rejecting.

In other words, how subjects recalled their parents' behavior depended on the state (depressed or nondepressed) that they themselves were in when recall was tested. Now that finding is not an isolated one. Remember the phenomenon of *state-dependent memory* (Chapter 9)? We remember sad things better when we are feeling sad, happy things better when we are feeling happy. If that is so, then the people who were asked about their childhood while depressed might more readily bring to mind more unhappy items, about their childhood or about anything else, because of this state dependency. An unhappy mood hooks onto unhappy thoughts. Perhaps a depressed person's childhood is on average no less happy than anyone else's, but she may remember the unhappy side of it *because* she is depressed. And then these remembered episodes might be used to *reconstruct* memories of indifferent, rejecting parents.

COMMENT

The findings we have just summarized have theoretical implications. Here is yet another case in which memory can be inaccurate, and in this case we can state a reason why this could happen: the "state-dependency" of memory. But their practical implications also are considerable—and worrisome.

When will a person seek treatment for depression? When the depression is severe, of course. Indeed, it figures that some degree of depression might accompany *any* problem severe enough to lead a person to seek help. So, during initial interviews when background information is sought, unhappy memories of childhood may be likely to come to mind and be reported—simply because of the "state dependency" of the memory process.

In a word, clients' memories might be skewed toward remembering early experiences as more unhappy than they were, and/or toward remembering selectively the episodes that were in fact sad or depressing among all those that occurred. Thus a client with a perfectly normal childhood might give, in all honesty, the picture of a joyless and rejected childhood spent with indifferent, critical, or even abusive parents.

I have talked with clinicians about this possibility, and many of them say this to me: "What matters is how the patient/client perceives her early relations with her parents now. It doesn't really matter whether those perceptions are accurate or not. What matters is the perceptions themselves."

With this I have no quarrel. I do say, however: Let's be careful about drawing inferences from what the patient remembers to what actually happened earlier in life. It is one thing to say: Depressed patients *remember* unhappy relations with parents. It is quite another to say: Such patients *had* unhappy relations with parents. And of course it would be yet a third thing to say: These patients are depressed *because* they had unhappy relations with parents (the correlation-and-causality trap). In fact, (3) would not follow from (2) even if (2) followed from (1), which it doesn't. If we think it does, it is because of our tendency to credit memory with more accuracy than it has.

The situation is even more sobering when we recognize that in most instances, the client's recollections now are *all the information a clinician has* about what actually went on in the patient's childhood. Information about what actually happened can obviously be very hard to come by—it all happened long ago, and often there were no witnesses. Yet we have elaborate theories about how early experiences with parents shape the personality problems one confronts later in life. We now see that *all* such theories, if based on the retrospective reports of people now grown, are built on treacherous sand.

LIMITATIONS OF QUASI-EXPERIMENTS: SOME CAUTIONARY TALES

Quasi-experiments, we have said, are like experiments in that they try to isolate a causal variable. They try to isolate it not by *making* it vary, but by *selecting* cases for which it does vary. But in that respect, they are also like correlational studies—they ask how "natural" variation in one variable is related to "natural" variation in another. As a result, they face the same difficulty in determining just what causes what.

EXAMPLE 1: CRIME AND PUNISHMENT

Does the death penalty deter capital crimes? Does having capital punishment on the books cause a reduction in the incidence of capital crimes?

Here is a question that, one would think, could be settled once and for all by data. The comparison we need is obvious enough: between localities that have capital punishment for certain crimes, and ones that don't. We could seek such a comparison in either of two ways.

First, we might compare states (e.g., in the United States) that have capital punishment on the books with those that don't. Such a quasi-experiment is a nonequivalent between-groups design. So we might note that State A, which has the death penalty, has a very high rate of violent crime including capital murders; whereas State B, which doesn't, has a very low incidence of such crimes. So it looks as if the death penalty has no deterrent effect and perhaps even an aggravating one.

But wait! The two states are likely to differ in all sorts of ways: population density, ethnic composition, age composition (it is young males who add most to the capital crime statistics), number of large cities . . . and so on and on. If State A has a higher murder rate than State B, despite its having the death penalty, so what? The rate might be even higher if it didn't.

Or, second, we might compare states before and after a change in the law. That would be a time-series design. There the problem is: Okay, but as the law changes, what else changes with it? If the rate of capital crimes goes down, maybe it's because the possibility of death deters them. Or maybe those localities made the change at a time when the crime rate was high, and therefore more likely to decrease than to increase because of random fluctuations ("regression," Chapter 8). Or, maybe along with the change in penalties, police practices were changed so that crimes were more likely to be prevented. Or, suppose there is no change in the rate of such crimes. Again, if the law was changed at a time of rising crime, and the crime rate levels off, maybe the change in law has prevented a further increase that otherwise would have occurred. We simply don't know.

So neither of these designs gives us a definitive answer to our question.* And the reason is the same: Presence or absence of the death penalty varies over time, or from one community to another, but *something else varies along with it*—or might.

EXAMPLE 2: DISORDER OR DIET?

Here is another classic case of what we worry about. If we want to study the characteristics of, say, schizophrenic patients as compared with "normal people," a quasi-experiment is our only option. We can't *make* some of our subjects schizophrenic, for practical reasons; and we wouldn't if we could, for ethical reasons. The best we can do is *select*

---

*Notice that we have narrowed the question to just this: Does capital punishment deter? There are other arguments. Based on them, some reasonable people argue for abolishing the death penalty even if it does deter; others, for keeping it even if it doesn't. Those issues, though important, are not our concern here.

a group of persons who *already* are schizophrenic, and compare them with a "control" group whose members are not schizophrenic.

In just such a study, it was found that blood drawn from schizophrenic patients had a different chemical composition from blood drawn from nonschizophrenics. The finding was announced with some fanfare, as perhaps showing the way to identifying a toxin in the blood that produced schizophrenic symptoms.

The trouble was: The control, nonschizophrenic blood donors were hospital personnel and medical students. Thus there was indeed a difference in psychiatric status—one group was schizophrenic, the other was not. But there was another difference as well. Back in the 1950s when the study was done, many schizophrenic patients simply received custodial care at hospitals, and stayed there—often for many years—living in the hospital and eating hospital *food*. The controls, of course, had been living normal lives and eating mostly out-of-hospital food.

Question: Was it the disorder, or the diet, that produced the alteration in blood chemistry? As it turned out, it was the diet. The study was repeated, but the control group was changed: It now consisted of a group of patients, hospitalized for as long (on average) as the schizophrenic group, but for nonpsychiatric disorders. When this was done, the unusual chemicals in the blood were the same for both groups. It was the diet, not the disorder, that produced them (Snyder, 1974).

A LOOK BACK

In quasi-experiments, as in experiments, we want to know how some variable, X, affects another variable, Y. Now, if there is some other variable Z that varies along with X, and could cause Y to change, then we do not know whether it is X or Z that causes any change in Y that we might see. We could look at it either way. It's the old "third variable" problem we encountered in Chapter 5. Or it's the "confounded variable" we faced in Chapter 8. Whatever we call it, the problem is the same: too many differences among conditions!

And all of the problems we saw a minute ago were problems of just this kind. Communities differ in that some, but not others, have the death penalty (X); but how else do they differ (Z)? Or the law changes (X), adding or repealing the death penalty; but what else changes along with this (Z)? It is these "else"s, these Z variables, that make the results hard to interpret. And the result of this is that after decades of controversy, the value of the death penalty in deterring crime is still open to debate (Kaminer, 1995).

Our other cautionary tale illustrates the same problem. Some subjects were schizophrenic, others not (X). But also, the former subjects had different diets from the latter (Z). Which of the differences is the important one? We don't know—unless we spot the difficulty and, at the least, "check out" the possibilities.

Even our earlier examples cannot escape this criticism. Suppose two groups of subjects are selected. One group has some feature that was of interest—it consists of aroused men, or children of alcoholics. It is compared with another group, selected as lacking that feature (the "control group")—nonaroused men, children of nonalcoholics. The question, in each case, is whether the control group is equivalent to the experimental group in all the other ways that might matter. In other words: *How else did they differ?*

In the bridge case, subjects differed as to their aroused/nonaroused status (X); but they may also have differed in personality characteristics: risk-takers versus risk-avoiders (Z). (Yes, Dutton and Aron were able to rule out the latter explanation—but that required a true experiment.)

In the alcohol case, we don't know that the children adopted out of one or another kind of home were equivalent. Adoptees were used to form both groups, so that the stress of *having been adopted* was present for all. But maybe alcoholism in the home can increase the stress on a baby even very early in life. So the important variable here might not be presence or absence of alcoholism in the biological parent, but total amount of stress to which the child was exposed when very young.

Stepping back and looking over these examples, we see that in each case we face the same underlying problem. It really is just the correlation-and-causality problem all over again. *If we select subjects or time frames that differ with respect to any variable X, they will also differ with respect to any other variable, Z, that is correlated with X.* If we select subjects that have X and others that don't, they will never be truly equivalent in all other ways. That is because other variables (Z) will inevitably be correlated with presence versus absence of X—and so our groups will differ, on average, on those variables too. That's why we refer to a *nonequivalent control group* in these quasi-experimental designs.

It's true that in some such cases we can rule out a third variable—diet, for example, or being an adoptee—by *selecting* our subjects so as to hold it constant. But of course we can control only for variables we think of. Have we thought of all the important ones? We can't know.

We do know that the danger is real, as our cautionary tales show. What looks like the effect of one variable sometimes does turn out to be the effect of another and quite different one, but one that we have overlooked.

THE USES OF QUASI-EXPERIMENTS

Correlational studies do not permit causal conclusions. Even quasi-experiments leave us in some doubt as to what causes what, as we have just seen. We select subjects, settings, or time slots that differ with respect to some variable, X. But we always need to ask: How else do they differ?

In light of this, one must wonder just what such studies are useful for. In fact, they can be very useful indeed, despite their limitations. They are useful in many of the same ways as the nonexperimental research projects that we looked at earlier, in Chapters 4 and 5.

First, if they cannot establish causality directly, they can *disconfirm* predictions about causality. They can't tell us that a causal theory is right. But they can suggest that a causal theory is wrong.

Second, they may be a *jumping-off point for further research.* Thus, observational (archival) data show that the incidence of violent crimes is higher in some parts of the United States than in others. But why should this be so? As geographic area varies, what else varies with it? And which of these variables is the important one? We can go a long way toward finding out, as we'll see in a moment. We can even bring the phenomenon into the laboratory. But the questions we can ask would not even occur to us without the initial observations that showed the relation in the first place.

COMBINING METHODS: A CASE STUDY

In earlier chapters, we have focused on observational studies (Chapters 4 and 5), experimental ones (Chapters 6–10), and studies that fall somewhere between the two (this chapter). Let's now "look backward" over what these methods can do, by examining a research project that combines a number of them.

This will also give us a feel for what a *research project*, as contrasted with an isolated "research study," looks like—how a team of scientists can come across something interesting, and investigate it in a systematic, stepwise way. We will see how each step is guided by previous ones, how each step can use whatever methods are possible and appropriate—and above all, how guesses may be replaced by data.

GEOGRAPHIC SETTING AND VIOLENT CRIME

The case study we focus on began with a simple set of observations. In the United States, survey evidence suggests that crimes of violence are more prevalent in the Southern part of the country than in the North. And historical evidence suggests that this has been true since well before the Civil War.

Why should that be so? Historians and sociologists have offered various explanations for it, including these:

1. Homicides and other violent acts are more frequent in hot weather than in cooler weather, and the Southern United States is hotter than the North.

2. The South is poorer than the rest of the nation, and crimes of all sorts, including violent ones, are associated with poverty.

3. Historically, the institution of slavery made it both unnecessary and demeaning for white people to work, so at least the landed gentry among them turned to exciting and dangerous pastimes including violent ones.

4. The different ethnic compositions of the North and the South may account for the difference.

Richard Nisbett and his co-workers (Nisbett & Cohen, 1996) saw that these possibilities could be checked out, by appropriate *selection* of data.

The first thing to ask is: Is it really true? So Nisbett and his colleagues first examined homicide rates from Department of Justice data (an *unobtrusive measure*, based on what amount to nationwide *surveys*) for the period 1976 to 1983. Indeed, it was true: Homicide rates were consistently higher in the southern United States than in other parts of the country.

But why? Nisbett and his colleagues pulled out some further comparisons from the records. First, they examined homicide records for small, medium, and large cities in the North and in the South (variation by selection!). Only the data for white, non-Hispanic offenders were used, so that ethnic differences would not be represented in the data (control by selection!). Ethnicity was controlled by selection in another way, too: 100 small- and 60 medium-sized cities, in all of which the population was at least 90% white and non-Hispanic, were examined separately.

Still the difference was there: It was found that even when ethnicity was controlled, the incidence of homicides was correlated with geographical location; such crimes were more frequent in the South by a two- to threefold margin.

Other comparisons yielded further information. It turned out that it is the *smaller* communities that have elevated homicide rates in the South as compared with the North. In the larger cities, the difference is very slight. That suggests that temperature is *not* a critical factor, at least by itself; because of course the North–South temperature difference is as great for large cities as for smaller ones.

What about poverty? Yet another set of data speak to that question. Nisbett and his colleagues compared the data from two kinds of rural communities in the South (where *rural* was operationalized as counties having no town with a population over 2,500). Again they looked at homicide rates by whites, and they classified the counties as predominantly farming, or predominantly herding. In general, farming is encouraged by moist plains areas, herding (as of cattle or sheep) by dry plains. White male homicide rates were substantially higher (over twice as high) in the herding areas (Figure 11.3). These comparisons again argue against temperature as an explanation for the difference; and ethnic composition was in the wrong direction to account for it. Poverty also fails to account for it: Differences in per capita income between moist and dry areas were small, and when income was controlled statistically by *partial correlation* (Chapter 8), still the difference in the crime statistics remained.

THE "CULTURE OF HONOR"

In light of all these findings, Nisbett and his colleagues suggest another way of approaching the North–South difference, one that we have not yet considered.

Historically, herders have faced dangers that farmers do not have to face. Herds can be stolen; crops cannot. A herder may have to

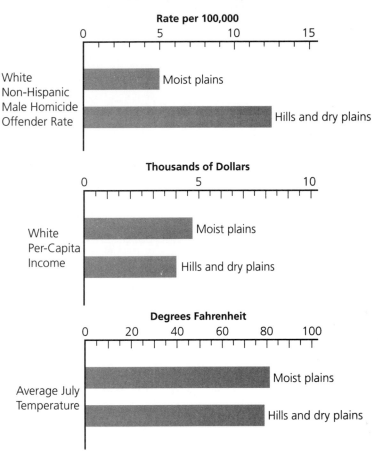

Rate per 100,000

White Non-Hispanic Male Homicide Offender Rate

- Moist plains
- Hills and dry plains

Thousands of Dollars

White Per-Capita Income

- Moist plains
- Hills and dry plains

Degrees Fahrenheit

Average July Temperature

- Moist plains
- Hills and dry plains

FIGURE 11.3
Homicide rates were much higher in the hills and dry plains area of the South than in the moist plains parts. Neither average income nor average summer temperature differed between the two, so neither high temperatures nor poverty can explain this difference (from Nisbett & Cohen, 1996).

protect his very livelihood, and that of his family, against thieves and rustlers. This means not only that he must be prepared to fight for his possessions if necessary. It means also that it is to his advantage to have the *reputation* of a person who is ready to respond violently to threats or insults—to be, as we might put it today, a person "not to mess with."

Thus Nisbett proposed that a "culture of honor" characterizes the communities that grew out of herding economies in certain parts of the South. This culture promotes a readiness for violence, a sense that it is manly, and a willingness to resort to it in the defense of

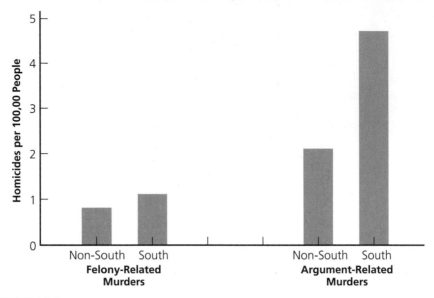

FIGURE 11.4
Murders related to fights or arguments were much more frequent in the South than elsewhere in the country. Murders related to felonies (as during robberies or holdups) were not (from Nisbett & Cohen, 1996).

one's property, one's family, one's self-respect and the respect of the community—one's "honor."*

Well, this idea can be tested! If it is true, homicides committed in the course of a dispute (e.g., a barroom quarrel) ought to be more frequent in the South, whereas homicides not related to personal honor or self-protection (e.g., murders occurring during a robbery or burglary) should not be. Nisbett's group again compared homicides in North and South, but now classified the homicides themselves as "argument-related" or as not. Sure enough, it was only argument-related homicides that were higher in the South—though again, only in the small cities and rural communities (Figure 11.4).

But records of homicide rates can take us just so far. The "culture of honor" idea is a theory about the attitudes and values of people who live in certain communities. If we *measured* those attitudes and values, we could test the theory more directly.

---

*Of course all these differences are less sharp now than they used to be. There are few bands of cattle rustlers today. But the "culture of honor," if there is one, goes back many generations; and the attitudes and values it reflects may be passed on from parent to child, even after the need for them has much diminished. That, Nisbett's group suggests, is what has happened in those parts of the South where the "culture of honor" prevails.

So the researchers turned to a series of *small-scale surveys*, using *interview and questionnaire techniques* and comparing white males in rural areas of the South and the Midwest. Respondents were asked such questions as: Would it be right for a man to respond violently if someone insulted his wife, or called him a liar and a cheat behind his back? Southern men were more likely to reply that it would be right for a person to respond violently, and that he "wouldn't be much of a man" if he didn't. In the South, 47% of respondents thought a man would be justified in shooting someone who had sexually assaulted his daughter, whereas only 27% of the Midwesterners thought so. These differences did not reflect simply a greater tolerance for violence in the South. Some of the scenarios were unrelated to the defense of property, family, or self-esteem (e.g., whether it is permissible for police to use violence on suspects being questioned or attempting to escape custody). For these, Southerners were no more likely to endorse violence than Midwesterners were. There are indications in the same data that these attitudes are indeed transmitted across generations: Southern males were more likely than Midwestern ones to say that a boy should be willing to fight after being hit, or bullied for his lunch money.

TRANSITION TO THE LABORATORY

These survey data tell us what respondents' attitudes *about* violence are. But how do people actually behave when faced with real threats or insults? A series of experiments addressed that question. Here we'll consider just one, conducted in a standardized setting where many variables could be held constant—that is, a laboratory. The "laboratory" in this case was a college library.

The subjects (male, white, non-Hispanic college students) came to a room in the library. They had no idea that they were participating in an experiment dealing with aggression. They were first given a questionnaire to fill out, and were asked to drop it off at a table at the end of a hallway.

To get to that table and back, each subject had to crowd past another "student" who was looking in a file cabinet. This "student" was actually an assistant to the experimenters, and he role-played an insulting scenario: He slammed the file drawer shut to let the subject go past, and he bumped the subject angrily with his shoulder and muttered under his breath, calling the subject, in effect, a lower digestive tract. Two other assistants, sitting where they could watch the subjects' emotional reactions, rated those reactions.

What was varied was where a given subject came from: the northern or the southern part of the United States. Of course a subject could not be *assigned* a northern or a southern upbringing; so the variation, of necessity, was done by selection. Thus, the study thus far was a *nonequivalent control group* quasi-experiment (compare pp. 374–379). The observers, of course, did not know the subjects' regional origins until the study was completed. (Why not?)

Now since the variable of interest—northern versus southern origin—was varied by selection, the two groups of subjects differed (on average) in *all* the ways that Northerners will differ from Southerners. Still, we can test the theoretical prediction that they should differ in *this particular* way: Southerners on average should be more angered by the insult than Northerners.

The prediction was confirmed. Subjects who had grown up in the North were more likely to be amused than angered by the insult. For the Southerners, the difference was sharply reversed (Figure 11.5). Several other such quasi-experiments were conducted as well, using other measures of anger or resentment; and these told the same story.

Here, *comparison by selection* (northern or southern origin) was coupled with *direct observation of behavior*, this time in a standardized situation where an "insult" could be delivered that was the same for all. We might note too that the subjects in this experiment were very likely *not* representative of young white males in the North and the

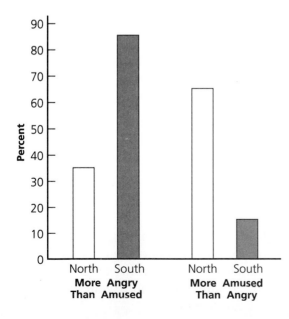

FIGURE 11.5
Reactions of subjects to being insulted, as rated by observers. Most Northerners were rated more amused than angry; for Southerners the opposite was true (from Nisbett & Cohen, 1996).

South of the United States. Their families tended to be affluent, and the Southerners might be unusual too in that they had chosen to come to the North to go to college (the experiment was conducted at the University of Michigan). But as Nisbett and Cohen point out, "We suspect both of these factors worked to mute regional differences [in aggressiveness] and that regional effects would be bigger if more representative samples . . . were drawn" (1996, p. 42). Here, in other words, the biases in the samples worked against the hypothesis. But it was confirmed anyway!

And they comment: "We would never have predicted differences so strong as we found with this college student [sample]. . . . If the reactions of our subjects bear any similarity to the way southerners react to a real insult in their lives, it is easy to understand why violence in response to an insult is more common in the South than in the North" (1996, p. 52).

A LOOK BACK

There is much more—including some ingenious "field experiments" (Chapter 7) and a discussion of women's roles in the "culture of honor"—but we cannot take it further here. The thing to see is how a variety of methods, asking a variety of specific questions, can zero in on an explanation for an otherwise puzzling observation: Why are there regional differences in violence? An impressive number and variety of questions were asked and answered by thoughtful *selection* of observations. Nisbett and Cohen (1996) summarize their work with, I think, a note of justifiable pride:

> With archival methods using census and crime reports, we have collected evidence showing that the homicide rate of the South, especially the rural South, remains high relative to the rest of the country. Using survey techniques, we have collected evidence indicating that the values of southerners favor violence for purposes of protection of property, for retaliation for an insult, and for the socialization of children. Employing [laboratory] methods, we have collected evidence showing that southerners respond to insults in ways . . . quite different from the pattern shown by northerners. And with archival methods, we have collected evidence indicating that many of the social institutions and contemporary public policies of the South have their roots in the culture of honor. . . . The body of evidence . . . presents an overwhelming case for a difference between cultures that one normally thinks of as being essentially similar—the southern and northern United States. (pp. xvii–xviii)

Finally, we may note that even such a far-reaching investigation does not stand alone. The "culture of honor" bears a striking resemblance to the description, arrived at independently by sociologist Elijah Anderson (1994), of the attitudes and values of young inner-city males in the United States. Where other routes to status are limited, a young man's self-esteem may center around (1) possessions, and (2) the esteem of his peers. And, like cattle, these may be stolen away. A man may be robbed of high-status possessions such as a gold chain or leather jacket; and his esteem may be "stolen" if he is treated disrespectfully, or "dissed." Many inner-city young males develop what Anderson calls the "code of the streets," an informal but clearly understood set of rules that virtually *requires* a constant readiness for violent action in response to insult. One retains status by being ready for violence, and by being *perceived* as ready for it—by being, again, someone "not to mess with." The code of the streets and the culture of honor seem virtually identical.

Nisbett and Cohen (1996) close their book with this comment:

> There is great concern with violence in our society today, and much effort is being put into providing young people with "conflict resolution skills." Though such programs may have some value, this book should have made it clear that in some subcultures, conflict is not something to resolve but rather something that one is required to confront or even generate. From that perspective . . . programs that teach ways to get community respect without resort to violence, seem more likely to succeed with some groups. (p. 94)

SUMMARY

An experiment is not always possible, for practical reasons or ethical reasons or both. A quasi-experiment is "like" an experiment in that it seeks to pinpoint causal relations. But it does so, not by *causing* a variable to vary (experiments do that), but by *selecting* cases in which it does vary.

In a *nonequivalent control-group design*, we select groups of subjects such that the groups differ—we hope!—in only one way. And where it is possible that the groups may differ in some other important way as well, sometimes we can make other selections to rule out the importance of that variable. The high- versus low-bridge quasi-experiment is such a case; the genes-and-alcoholism studies are another. Thus selection can be a control procedure as well as a way of varying a variable.

A *time-series design*, rather than comparing different groups, looks at the same subjects at different times; for example, before and after some event, as in the case of the Seekers. Or it may look at two variables over time, to see how closely changes in one are accompanied by changes in the other (as in the study of childhood memories before, during, or after depression), or to track the order in which different variables change (as in the study of Internet use). Since we assume that causes happen first and their effects later, these methods may at least rule out some otherwise possible causal sequences.

In all such cases, the danger remains that we may overlook some important difference, something that varies *along with* the variable(s) in which we are interested. In one classic cautionary case, what looked like a difference between normal subjects and hospitalized schizophrenics (a nonequivalent control-group study) turned out instead to be a difference between people who had, and had not, been eating hospital food for a long time. Thus one variable—clinical status (presence or absence of schizophrenia) was *confounded with* another one—diet.

There is always this problem in nonexperimental research. If two groups differ along Variable X, we must ask: *How else do they differ?* If some event of interest occurs, we must ask: *What else occurred along with it?* We can never be sure that we have even thought of, much less controlled for, all the important variables.

Systematic research projects often use a variety of methods. The study of violent crime and the "culture of honor" is an example of what can be done. Survey and historical data raised the question: Why are there differences between northern and southern parts of the United States, in the frequency of such crime? Appropriate *selections* from these data ruled out some possibilities: ethnic composition of the communities, temperature, and average income level. The suggestion that some cultures within the United States actively promote violent responses to certain kinds of offenses (a "culture of honor") was supported by further comparisons using survey and questionnaire data, and the direct observation of behavior in a controlled setting that permitted variables to be manipulated experimentally.

MAKING FRIENDS WITH STATISTICS:
THE CHI-SQUARE TEST

Back in Chapter 2, we saw a way of testing the *statistical significance* of differences among conditions: the sign test. If monkeys choose a cloth over a wire mother more consistently than random choice between the two could plausibly account for, then we assume that the preference for cloth is real. We've since looked at *t* and F as ways of testing significance. These are more powerful tests. However, and unlike the sign test, *t* and F require that our data be quantitative variables; they can be applied only awkwardly to categorical data.

ONE-WAY χ^2

The χ^2 (say "kai-square") test is another test of significance. Like the sign test, it can handle categorical data, but it is much more versatile than the sign test. For one thing, it can be applied to cases of more than two alternatives.

Suppose there is an election for mayor of the town coming up next month. Suppose that there are three candidates on the ballot: Pat Floppi, Sandy Pixel, and Meredith Rom. We are a team of pollsters, and we ask: Can we predict the results of this election?

We could take a random sample of the population of registered voters in the town; a sample, say, of 1,000 voters. We ask each one whom she or he intends to vote for. Suppose we get the data shown in the first column of the worksheet below: 400 favor Floppi, 350 favor Pixel, and 250 favor Rom. (Assume for simplicity that there are no undecideds.) Notice that Floppi doesn't have a majority, but she does have more votes than anybody else, whereas poor Rom trails badly. Do we predict a Floppi victory? Has the Floppi drive led to success? Or is the race too close to call?

The question is: Do these data mean that the population from which this sample came favors Floppi over the other two? Or are the three candidates equally preferred by the population (the *null hypothesis*)? If the latter, then plurality for Floppi just "happened to happen" in this sample. Could that be so? Yes, of course. But how often would that happen?

Well, if the null hypothesis were true (no preference in the population), and if the sample matched the population *exactly*, we would expect the sample to be evenly divided: $1/3 \times 1,000$ or 333.33 preferring each candidate. A quick word of explanation! To be sure, we are not going

Candidate	Obtained (O)	Expected (E)	O − E	$(O − E)^2$	$(O − E)^2/E$
Floppi	400	333.33	66.67	4,444.89	13.33
Pixel	350	333.33	16.67	277.89	0.83
Rom	250	333.33	−83.33	6,943.89	20.83
					$\chi^2 = 34.99$

to see 1/3 (0.33) of any voter preferring any candidate. It is a mathematical "expectation," and it means this: If we were to take repeated samples of 1,000 from the population, and do this many times, the tallies for each candidate would *average* 333.33 if the null hypothesis were true. So an "expected" tally refers to a (theoretical) average, not to data from any one possible sample. We put those expected tallies as the second column in our table.

But of course the sample will not exactly match the population, and different samples would give us different results. Most samples would give us something close to 1/3 for each candidate, but some would be more lopsided than that; and occasionally we would get a sample that gave us such data as the ones we obtained. The question is: How often would that happen? Obviously, if the population is split 1/3 each, then the more the sample differs from that, the less often will such a difference happen. So let us see how different the obtained data are from the expected data. We simply subtract the expected scores from the obtained one, $O - E$ (third column).

If we added those third-column difference scores, we would have the *total amount of discrepancy* between the numbers we obtained, and the numbers the null hypothesis would lead us to expect. We cannot do that, and for the familiar reason: They will sum to zero every time. So, as we do when we compute a variance, we avoid that problem by squaring the deviation scores, to get $(O - E)^2$ (fourth column).

One final step. Suppose that our sample size were only 9 cases, and our data were 7 for Floppi, 1 for Pixel, 1 for Rom. That looks like a big lead for Floppi; she leads each of the others by over four to one. The expected tally is 3 for each, so deviations from expected values are $7 - 3 = 4$ for Floppi, $1 - 3 = -2$ for Pixel, and $1 - 3 = -2$ for Rom. But suppose we had a sample of 900, with the same deviations: $300 + 4 = 304$ for Floppi; $300 - 2 = 298$ for Pixel, and $300 - 2 = 298$ for Rom. These deviations would obviously be trivial.

So we must correct for sample size. It turns out that we can best do this by dividing each squared deviation score by the expected score: $(O - E)^2/E$. This gives us the fifth and last column in our worksheet. Sum these *corrected squared deviation scores*, and we have χ^2. A few strokes of a calculator does it all: χ^2 is 34.99.

In short: χ^2 is an *adjusted measure of the discrepancy between the tallies we see and the tallies that the null hypothesis would lead us to expect*. Therefore, very large values of χ^2 would seldom occur if the null hypothesis is true. In the appendix, Table B.4, pp. 519, there are *p*-values associated with various values of χ^2. We go to the table taking into account the number of *degrees of freedom* in the data.

Here the number of degrees of freedom is 2. Why? Well, we know that we have a thousand cases, and that there are three candidates; this we know before we even look at the data. But now suppose that in addition, we know *any two* of the actual tallies. If we do, then we know the third one as well. If 600 favor Floppi, and 300 favor Pixel, then the number who favor Rom has to be 100—it can't be anything else. Only two of the tallies are free to vary—hence, we have only two degrees of freedom. Once we know two of the tallies (any two), the other one is fixed. We can calculate what it has to be. More generally: In any one-way χ^2 table like this, the number of degrees of freedom is the *number of rows, minus one*.

What then of the upcoming election? If we look at Table B.4 with two degrees of freedom, we find that we need a χ^2 of 5.99 for significance at our conventional $p = 0.05$. Our χ^2 is larger than that—it is 34.99—so we have a statistically significant finding.

And now we have to be careful. What we know is that the total corrected squared discrepancy between expected and observed tallies is too big to be plausibly attributed to chance. But we don't yet know *which* discrepancies are doing the work. Maybe Floppi is driving significantly ahead of the others; maybe Rom is lagging significantly behind. Or maybe both. We don't yet know.

But we can find out; for a nice thing about χ^2 is that we can look separately at parts of it. We can ask: Given that there is a significant discrepancy somewhere, is the difference between Floppi (the leader) and Pixel (the next highest) significant? It is. If we consider just those two rows and add their corrected squared deviations, we have

$$\chi^2 = 13.33 + 0.83 = 14.16.$$

We have only one degree of freedom now (the two rows minus one), but we only need a χ^2 of 3.84 for significance at the .05 level. Our χ^2 exceeds that. So, the difference between Floppi and Pixel, the closest competitor, is significant. Floppi, we'd predict, should win.

ASSUMPTIONS OF THE χ^2 TEST

One advantage of the χ^2 test is that it requires few assumptions. There is, however, one that remains with us: our old friend the *independence* assumption. Once again, this assumption comes to this: Which cell a given score falls in must be unaffected by where any of the other scores fall.

Now this might not be true. Take our preelection poll, for instance. Suppose we were so foolish as to conduct our poll at a party, in which the people we interviewed could hear each other. Suppose further (1) that the null hypothesis is true—the population is equally divided—but also (2) that just by chance, the first three people we interviewed happened to be pro-Rom. (That could easily happen.) Then the fourth person, hearing this, might also tell us she favors Rom—so as not to look weird perhaps, or because she fears starting an argument—even if she really favors Floppi. And then the social pressure would be even greater on our fifth interviewee . . . and so on. We could get a very misleading set of results, and all because we've allowed some sample members to affect what other members said.

ALTERNATIVE FORMS OF THE NULL HYPOTHESIS

With that caution in mind, let's look at some further uses of the χ^2 test. In the survey example, our null hypothesis was that the population was equally divided among Floppi, Pixel, and Rom. But what we see is that 40% favor Floppi, 35% Pixel, and 25% Rom. And we found that distribution to be significantly different from the "expected" 33.33% for each.

Now we could do the same study in a different community (assume the same candidates there), and again ask if the data differ significantly from an even division. But we might also be interested in this question: Does the second community *differ significantly from the original one*? Does it show (within chance fluctuations) the same distribution of voter preference?

Suppose our new survey gives us these data: 450 for Floppi, 300 for Pixel, and 250 for Rom. These are our "obtained" tallies. In this case, our null hypothesis is that there is no difference between this new community and the original one. So now our expected values are just our original data: 400, 350, and 250 for Floppi, Pixel, and Rom, respectively.

Does the new community differ significantly from the old one? Take a minute to calculate χ^2 for these data. How many degrees of freedom, and is the χ^2 significant? See if you can do it before looking at the bottom of the page.*

THE χ^2 TEST FOR CONTINGENCIES

The χ^2 test can be extended. We can use it to ask, not only whether the tallies in different rows are significantly different from each other, but also whether there is a significant relationship between two variables.

Here, as an example to work with, are some data I collected not long ago (as this is written). Remember about how men and women carry books differently (Chapter 4)? I spent a few minutes tallying the men and the women who passed by my office window (a "convenience sample") during a 10-minute period. For each person, I noted whether he or she carried books with arm straight or bent. (People bearing backpacks were excluded from the sample.) And the data were as follows:

Gender	Arm Straight	Arm Bent	Total
Female	1	16	17
Male	11	0	11
Total	12	16	28

Question: Does this 2 × 2 table show a significant relation, or *contingency*, between gender and arm position? We speak of a "contingency" here because we are asking: Is arm position dependent on, or *contingent on*, gender? Therefore, this kind of layout of the data is referred to as a *contingency table*.

The first thing we do is ask: If there really is *no* relation between these two variables (the null hypothesis), what should the data look like? We see that of all the 28 people I observed, 12, or 42.8%, carried their books with arms straight. Now if males and females were equally likely to carry their books this way, then about 42.8% of the males, and about 42.8% of the females, should have done

*We get 13.393, with 2 df. The new sample differs significantly from the original one.

so. (Again these are mathematical "expectations"; see p. 402.)

So we can begin filling in a table of *expected* tallies. We say that 42.8% of the 11 males should carry "straight." Well, 42.8% *of* 11 is the same as 0.428 *times* 11, so we get 11 × .428, or 4.71, as our expected tally in the "male/arm straight" cell. And 42.8% of the 17 females gives us 17 × .428, or 7.28, as our expected tally for "female/arm straight." Similarly, since 57.2% of the sample carried with arms bent, we would have 11 × .572 = 6.29 as our expected tally in the "male/arm bent" cell, and 17 × .572 = 9.72 as our expected tally in the "female/arm bent" cell.*

The degrees of freedom in a contingency table is given by the *number of rows minus one,* times the *number of columns* minus one. Here we have (2 − 1) × (2 − 1), or just 1.

With our observed and expected values in hand, we line up the cells in our worksheet (the order doesn't matter), and compute χ^2 exactly as before. We get a χ^2

---

*Actually we're doing much more button pushing here than we need to do. We know the column and the row totals; we have to know those to compute any expected values at all. So if we know that we have 11 males, and we calculate that 4.71 males would be expected to carry with arms straight, then the expected tally for males with arms bent would *have to be* 11 − 4.71, or 6.29. Then, since a total of 12 people walked with arms straight, the number of females expected to do so must be 12 − 4.71, or 7.29. And the number of females walking with arms bent must be 17 − 7.29, or 9.71. These numbers agree with the previous ones within rounding error. Knowing any *one* of the cells, we can calculate all the others by simple subtraction. That's why we have only one degree of freedom in our 2 × 2 table.

of 24.16 (verify that). Table B.4 tells us that with df = 1, we need a χ^2 of 3.841 or higher for significance at the .05 level. My finding is significant; I can confidently conclude that, in these real data, book-carrying position is *contingent* on gender. So I have successfully replicated the earlier findings by other researchers. That's exciting!

χ^2 AND DEGREE OF RELATEDNESS: CRAMER'S PHI

There is yet another use for this very useful tool.

In a previous chapter, we talked about the correlation coefficient *r* as a measure of the strength of a relation between two *quantitative* variables—variables for which there is a numerical measure on each of two variables, X and Y. With *categorical* data, like political preference, geographic origin, or book-carrying style, it is awkward to use *r* as a measure. But it turns out that a χ^2, computed on a contingency table, can be transformed into a measure of the degree of relatedness between the row variable and the column variable.

This measure, Cramer's φ, is defined this way:

$$\Phi = \sqrt{\frac{\chi^2}{(N)(df_S)}}$$

That is, we divide χ^2 by the total number of cases in the sample, times the number of degrees of freedom for the row variable (number of rows minus one), *or* for the column variable (number of columns minus one), whichever is *smaller*—hence, df_s. We then take the square root of the whole thing. Thus for the book-carrying data, where $\chi^2 = 24.16$, I get a respectable 0.93 as the strength of the relation.

Phi has a minimum of zero and a maximum of 1. We interpret it just as we would a correlation coefficient.

CHAPTER 12

THE RELIABILITY AND GENERALITY OF FINDINGS

When evidence from a wide range of experiments, each flawed in a somewhat different way . . . points in a similar direction, then . . . a reasonably strong conclusion is justified even though no one experiment was perfectly designed.

—KEITH STANOVICH

The most exciting phrase to hear in science, the one that heralds new discoveries, is not "Eureka!" (I've found it!), but "That's funny. . . . "

—ISAAC ASIMOV

IN THIS CHAPTER, WE'LL DISCUSS:

- The concepts of reliability and generality
- Statistical significance and reliability
- Replication

  Direct

408

Systematic

Conceptual

- What external validity is
- The "generalization" and "theoretical" conceptions of research
- What research is "about"

When we encounter any research finding, there are two questions we might reasonably ask about it. First, is it *reliable*? Would we see it consistently if we repeated the experiment, or did it just "happen to happen" this time?

Second, how *general* is it? Does it hold only in a specific, restricted set of conditions? Or does it hold up under a wide variety of conditions? It would seem at first glance that a finding with high generality, telling us something about a wide rather than a limited set of conditions, would necessarily be a much more interesting finding. (Later on, however, we'll take a second glance at that idea. It may not always be true—or so, at least, I intend to argue.)

But let's see some examples.

STATISTICAL SIGNIFICANCE AND RELIABILITY

If a result is *statistically significant*, then we have some confidence in its reliability on those grounds alone. We can be confident that our results are not just a matter of chance. Rather, there really *is* a relationship between two variables: between two measures, in a correlational study; or between an independent and a dependent variable, in an experiment. (Of course, we hold in the backs of our minds that chance alone *could* produce even a significant finding [a Type I error or "false alarm", Chapter 7]. We can never rule out that possibility absolutely.)

That conclusion in turn implies another: If the effect is real, then, if we were to repeat the study exactly, we should get the same results. (Except of course that chance fluctuations *could* give us a nonsignificant outcome even if the relationship is real [a Type II error or "miss"]. Again we cannot rule out that possibility; we must simply learn to live with it.)

A significant finding, then, gives us reasonable confidence that *if* we were to repeat the study exactly, then we *would* see the effect again. Well, suppose we do in fact perform the study again (or one like it), and see if the results do hold up. That would be *replication*. Let us turn to that topic.

EXPERIMENTAL RELIABILITY: REPLICATION

Whereas statistical significance rests on treatment of the original data, *replication* of a study means gathering more data. To *replicate* a study means to *repeat* it—do it again, and see if the results hold up. (If they do, we sometimes speak of "replicating the findings," as shorthand for "replicating the study and confirming the findings.") We can do this in several ways.

DIRECT REPLICATION

In *direct replication*, we repeat the original study as closely as we can, to see if the original effect shows up in the newly collected data. The original investigator may do a direct replication. Dr. Modem performs an experiment, obtains a finding, says, "Very interesting! Does it hold up? Can I get the same effect again?"—and does a direct replication to find out.

Or a different investigator may do it. Dr. Hardrive reads about Dr. Modem's finding in a journal, or is told about it in conversation or by e-mail, says, "Very interesting! Can I get the same effect in my laboratory?"—and repeats Dr. Modem's experiment as exactly as possible. In either case, if replication is successful—if the original findings hold up—then our confidence that the effect is real, so that we can *rely* on it, increases very rapidly.

We might sum it up by saying that direct replication, if successful, gives us somewhat the same information as does the statistical significance of the original findings. If the findings are significant, this means that *if* we were to repeat the experiment exactly, we are pretty sure we would get the same results. In direct replication, we *do* repeat the experiment exactly and see if we *do* get the same results.

But notice that in both cases we specify: *Repeat the experiment exactly*. Same manipulation, same measurements, same experimental conditions, subjects drawn from the same population. Same everything. And so we have not yet addressed at all the question of *generality*. The finding holds under *these* conditions, but what is the range of conditions over which it holds? The subjects in this experiment, let us say, were females; but then what about males? The CS was a bell; what about visual or tactile or other kinds of stimuli? The room was painted blue; what about red rooms? And so on for zillions of what-abouts. These questions of generality are not addressed by either significance tests or direct replication.

Of course, it is true that the original experiment will never be repeated *exactly*. If Dr. Hardrive in Argentina repeats the experiment of Dr. Modem in New England, obviously there will be differences. The climate will be different; the student populations will be different, if students are used as subjects; the rat supplier will be different, if rats are. . . . The list is long. Even if Dr. Modem herself repeats her original experiment, her lab assistants may have changed, and she herself will be a little older and more experienced if nothing else. The idea is to come *as close as possible* to exact repetition of the original experiment. But because these differences will necessarily be there, direct replication shades into the topic of *systematic replication*, to which we now turn.

ADDING GENERALITY: SYSTEMATIC REPLICATION

Whereas direct replication means that we repeat the original experiment as closely as possible, *systematic replication* means that we repeat it with variations. We change something, or a few things, and see if the results hold up when those changes are made. If they do, then (1) our confidence in the original finding is increased, and (2) we have established something about the *generality* of that finding.

Thus suppose Dr. Modem's original finding was obtained in female rats. She says: "Very interesting! Can I get the effect again, if I repeat the experiment? And what if I used male rats this time? Will the effect hold for males as well as females?" So she repeats the experiment, using males.

Suppose the results are the same. Then Dr. Modem will say, "Now I can be all the more confident of the original finding, for I have just seen it again (reliability). And I have learned something more: It holds for male rats as well as for females (generality)." And if the results are *not* the same, Dr. Modem may say, "That's funny . . . why should females be different?" and go on to explore that question.

Real examples of this process abound, and since the logic is straightforward, we will run through a few of them quickly.

AN EXAMPLE FROM LEARNING: PAVLOV'S EXPLORATIONS

Pavlov's original experiments with conditioning used the ticking of a metronome as CS, or conditioned stimulus. But having shown that conditioned salivation occurs, one of the first things Pavlov did was to ask: What if some of the conditions were varied? For instance, does the CS have to be a metronome? He checked this with experiments, and the answer was no. It could be a tone, or a light going on, or a light going off, or the sound of bubbling water, or even a mild pinprick. The conditioning phenomenon was seen time and again (reliability), and it held up across variations in the signal that was used (generality).

And did the UCS have to be food? Again, no. If a dilute acid is placed in a dog's mouth, one sees "defensive" salivation: a flow of saliva that dilutes the sour-tasting fluid. Here too the conditioning phenomenon can be obtained (reliability), and such conditioning has the same characteristics with acids as with food (generality).

Now, we also recall that some of Pavlov's *principles* of conditioning, though they hold over a wide range of CSs and UCSs, do not hold for all. Experiments with conditioned taste aversion show that at least some of these principles—conditioning occurs gradually, and it requires that the CS and the UCS be close together in time—do not always hold. But it can be instructive and important to know the limits of the original findings, so that we know when they do not hold as well as when they do (see "When Replication Fails," later).

AN EXAMPLE FROM SOCIAL PSYCHOLOGY: BYSTANDERS REVISITED

Think again about the "bystander intervention" effect—the finding that if there are many onlookers to an emergency, it is less likely that anyone will offer help than if there is only one. Latané and Darley first showed this by staging one kind of "emergency"—smoke pouring out of a vent in the room where the subject or subjects were sitting. But then they repeated the experiment, using different kinds of "emergency" (e.g., the sounds of someone falling off a stool and hurting herself in an adjacent room). The results were the same: A subject waiting by himself would usually offer help. If subjects were waiting in groups, it was less likely that anyone would help. Therefore, we can be that much more confident of the original findings (reliability); and we know that they hold up despite differences in the precise nature of the emergency (generality).

In all these examples, we see that if a result holds up under variations in conditions—the nature of the CS and UCS, the nature of a staged emergency—then our confidence in a finding is increased, just as it is increased by direct replication and by the statistical significance of the original findings. However, successful systematic replication adds information that neither significance tests nor direct replication can give us. It tells us that the finding has *generality* across whatever changes in conditions we have introduced.

Now we noted earlier that even with direct replication, there are bound to be *some* differences between the replication and the original study. In that sense, direct and systematic replication shade into each other, and you may wonder: Why distinguish them at all?

It's a matter of the researcher's intentions. In direct replication, one comes as close as possible to an exact repetition of the earlier study. Differences will remain, unfortunately; but one gets rid of as many as possible. In systematic replication, the differences are not unfortunate; they are introduced deliberately, to see whether or not the original finding holds despite them. If it does, that again speaks to the generality, as well as the reliability, of the original finding.

GENERALITY OF IDEAS: CONCEPTUAL REPLICATION

In systematic replication, one repeats the original study, but with variations. Conceptual replication is still more abstract. The idea is: *Ask the same question, but with different procedures.* Again we can best make this clear with examples.

AN EXAMPLE FROM SOCIAL PSYCHOLOGY: MORE ABOUT HELPING

Let's return to the topic of bystander intervention. Both the smoke-from-a-vent study and the falling-off-a-stool study were conducted in a laboratory setting. But when we discussed *field experiments* (Chapter 7), we saw that the question could also be asked in a natural setting, as in the liquor store robbery experiment.

Now the robbery experiment differed in every way imaginable from the smoke experiment. In the smoke experiment, the emergency was, well, smoke; in the liquor store experiment, it was a theft. In the one case, subjects were college students; in the other, liquor store customers. In the one case, the setting was controlled, in the other it was not. And so on. The only thing the two studies had in common was the *conceptual* question: Do multiple onlookers inhibit helping? Since the answer remained yes, we have more confidence in the original findings (reliability), and we also know that the answer remains the same, even if the question is asked with wholly different methods (generality). So what is generalized is the conceptual, or theoretical, conclusion.

We can push it further—for, as we saw in Chapter 2, there is a ladder or hierarchy of theoretical principles. Thus here. The conclusion—multiple onlookers inhibit helping—is a low-level generalization that summarizes many specific findings (not all, as we will see). But it is also a special case of a still more general principle: *Situational factors can be of overwhelming importance in determining what people do.*

At this more abstract level, even experiments that have nothing to do with number of onlookers could be considered conceptual replications of ones that do. Consider the following experiment (Darley & Batson, 1973).

The subjects were students at the Princeton Theological Seminary. They were told that they were to prepare themselves for a brief extemporaneous talk on the parable of the Good Samaritan (a neat touch, for reasons that will soon be clear), in a nearby building. Then subjects in one condition were told, "It will be a few minutes before they're ready for you, but you might as well head on over." In the other condition they were told: "You're late; they were expecting you a few minutes ago, so you'd better hurry." Subjects of course were randomly assigned to one condition or the other.

On the way to the talk, each subject was faced with a staged "emergency": a man lying slumped in a doorway, coughing and groaning. Would the theology student stop to help the person in distress? It depended on the situational manipulation. Of subjects who thought they had plenty of time, 63% stopped to help. Of those who were in a rush, only 10% did (Figure 12.1).

Now, number of bystanders was not manipulated in this experiment, and so we cannot think of it as a replication of the bystander effect except at a very abstract, conceptual level. But at that level, it does fit in. Both sets of experiments say: Situational factors—number of bystanders in one case, time pressure in the other—have a very great impact on what people do (Figure 12.2).

And this general conclusion is important, and often comes as a surprise. If we describe a situation and ask a person to predict whether John will offer help to someone in trouble, most people—in this so-

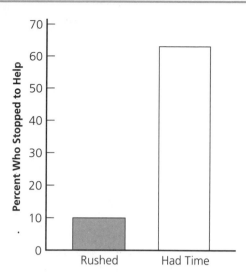

FIGURE 12.1
Time pressure greatly reduced the likelihood that a passerby, even one who had devoted his or her life to helping others, would stop to do so now (from Darley & Batson, 1973).

ciety at least (Chapter 4)—will want to know more about John. Nice guy or nasty guy? Self-centered or sensitive to others? Altruistic or callous? And so on. So common is this outlook, and so often mistaken, that it has been called the *fundamental attribution error* (Ross, 1977). It is fundamental because we do it so often. And it is an error, because it overlooks the overwhelming importance of the *situation*. Time after time, situational factors have been found to swamp such "inner" factors as personality differences as determinants of the

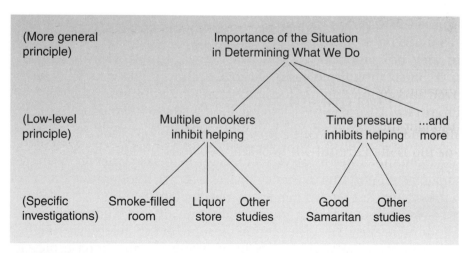

FIGURE 12.2
The Good Samaritan findings fall into place with many others, including the multiple-onlookers ones, in supporting a very general conclusion: Situational factors are powerful influences on what we do.

"I've heard that outside of working hours he's really a rather decent sort."

FIGURE 12.3
The situation plays an important role in what we do, whatever our personal characteristics may be.

actions people take (see Figure 12.3; for further discussion see Ross & Nisbett, 1991).

AN EXAMPLE FROM COGNITION AND EMOTION:
MISATTRIBUTION

As another example, let's go back to the high bridge/low bridge quasi-experiment (Chapter 11). We remember that male subjects were much more likely to call up a female experimenter if, when they met her, they were aroused by the stress of having crossed a high, dangerous-looking bridge. And a follow-up *systematic replication* of this study by the same researchers, varying the delay variable, suggested that the important influence here was the momentary state of arousal, not lasting differences like personality.

Now consider a conceptual replication of this study, conducted in the laboratory. In this experiment, some male subjects spent a few minutes arousing their bodies by working on an exercise bicycle. Others did not. Sure enough: The aroused subjects showed a greater sexual response to erotic films, when tested a few minutes later! Same question, drastically different procedures—but the conceptual finding holds. An emotional reaction, like attraction or sexual arousal, can be enhanced (or appear to be) by physiological arousal. This is true even if the arousal comes from a source that has nothing to do with the emotion in question—a dangerous bridge in one case, an exercise bicycle in the other.

CONCEPTUAL REPLICATION AND "NEXT STEP" RESEARCH

Conceptual replication, we say, is asking the same question with a different method. But another kind of conceptual replication changes the question as well! Given the original findings, it may ask: Why do they happen? What is going on, and how does it work? If one can answer such a "next step" question, that will (1) tell us more about the original findings, and in doing so (2) increase our confidence that the original findings were reliable.

Look again at the findings just summarized. Their conclusion, shown in many ways, is that physiological arousal can be interpreted as an emotional state, even if the arousal has nothing to do with that emotion.

There are two ways of interpreting these findings. One is called "misattribution": We *mistake* our inner arousal for some other, more specific emotional state, so that a subject *thinks* he is more attracted to a woman than he really is. The other we might call "spillover." Maybe the arousal "spills over" so that other emotional states are enhanced. The difference is that in the "spillover" case the subject is not making a mistake; he really *is* more attracted to the female.

An ingenious experiment by Valins (1966) showed that a pure "misattribution" effect can occur. Each subject, a male college student, looked at a series of pictures of women, while listening to what he *thought* was the sound of his own heartbeat, fed back through earphones. With some slides, but not others, the subject was made to hear an increase in what he thought was his heart rate. It was these slides that the subjects rated most attractive. And when they were invited to take some of the pictures home as a reward for participation, it was the pictures they *thought* had made their hearts go pitty-pat that they were likely to choose.

Here, there is no question of spillover from general arousal. There was no general arousal! It was a purely cognitive phenomenon: The subjects received (false) signals that suggested that they were aroused, and they misinterpreted the *perceived* arousal as increased attractiveness of the picture they were viewing.

This study, then, supports the earlier ones in their conclusion: We can mistake one source of arousal for another. But it also adds something new: The "arousal" need not even be there. If we *think* it is there, that is enough! We go on to make inferences about that.

COMMENT

Let me point out several things about this series of studies. First, notice how, taken together, these studies fill up each other's gaps and cross-check each other. In the high bridge/low bridge study, the results could have been confounded by personality differences. In the laboratory bicycle experiment, we can eliminate this worry by assigning subjects at random to the various conditions; and the heart-rate study was a within-subjects design, so individual differences (as in personality) were not a factor at all. But then we may wonder whether the effect is important enough to affect behavior in the real world. Well, the bridge study, which was conducted *in* the real world, strongly suggests that it does. And the effect—mistaking one source of arousal for another—holds up across a number of studies (reliability), even though they differed as to the setting, as to how the emotional response was measured, and as to how arousal, or the perception of arousal, was manipulated—and even whether or not there was really any arousal at all (generality).

Second, the theoretical conclusion has both practical and theoretical implications. On the practical side, it tells us things like this: As pointed out earlier, if we are about to have an argument with our Significant Other (SO), and expect such SO to be angry—then right after a vigorous game of tennis might not be the best time to raise the issue!

On the theoretical side, if we think about it we realize that these findings are quite surprising, and go against much common sense. It seems as if we ought to be able just to look inside ourselves, and *see* how angry we are, or how fearful, or how attracted. Again as noted earlier: We are often told something like "Trust your feelings. Your feelings are never wrong." Not true. We can be quite wrong about what we are feeling and why we are feeling it. We don't just feel, we *interpret* our feelings—and the interpretation can be way off base.

One other point before we move on. Think for a minute about how ridiculous these studies could be made to sound, if taken out of their theoretical context. Bicycles and sexual arousability! Think what a journalist or a politician could do with that: "Researchers are spending taxpayers' money, by way of grant support, to find out whether riding an exercise bike is a sexual turn-on! Who cares? Why waste time and money on such foolishness?"

But if we remember the theoretical issue these studies address, they look much less ridiculous. The authors of the bicycle study really had no interest in bicycles, or even in sex. They were interested in the theoretical issue: How well do we identify our feelings? Can we just look within ourselves and know for certain what we are feeling? Conversely, to what extent are we "strangers to ourselves"? That doesn't sound like so trivial an issue, does it?

In the same way, the Dutton and Aron study was not about bridges, or even about sex; it was about the same theoretical issue. We'll talk some more about this at the end of the chapter, when we ask: What is research really about? But for now, we might do well to remember this the next time we read in the paper about some seemingly "ridiculous" study. There are indeed ridiculous studies out there. But we cannot judge the worth of a study just by looking at what the specific measures and manipulations are. The study may not be "about" these at all.

A LOOK BACK

We have now considered four ways of establishing reliability, and sometimes generality, of research findings. Two of these ways address the question of reliability only. Statistical significance tests ask: Can we be confident that these results, obtained under *just these* conditions, were not a fluke? And direct replication asks: If we do it again, under *just these* same conditions, do we get the same results? To the extent that the answer to either or both questions is yes, our confidence in the reliability of the findings increases. Neither, however, addresses the question of generality: Over what range of conditions do the findings hold?

The remaining two approaches do address that question as well as the reliability one. In systematic replication, we ask: Do the results remain the same if we change something, or a few things? If so, that increases our confidence that the original findings are reliable, and it also tells us that they hold up across whatever changes we have made—they have generality.

In conceptual replication, we ask: Does the answer to a question remain the same, even if we ask it with a different method? Here we may change virtually everything from an original experiment: How the independent variable was manipulated, how the dependent variable was measured, the setting, the subject population. Only the question itself remains the same. And if the answer to that question also remains the same, then, as before, our confidence in the original answer increases (reliability); and we know that the answer holds up across *all* the changes we have made (generality). This process can occur at any level of theoretical abstraction, from relatively low-level and specific questions (Does the presence of bystanders inhibit helping behavior?) to much more abstract and general ones (Are situational factors important influences on altruistic behavior?).

WHEN REPLICATION FAILS

Thus far, we've been talking about success stories. We have looked at examples in which systematic or conceptual replication has succeeded, thus bolstering our confidence in the original findings *and* saying something about how general they are. But what if the new findings do *not* support the original ones?

That too can be instructive. It tells us that the changes we made, from the original experiment to its replication, make a difference. Suppose we do an experiment in male rats, and get such-and-such a result. So we do a systematic replication: We repeat the experiment using female rats. And the original finding does not emerge. What then?

Well, assuming that both findings hold up under direct replication, this tells us that the effect of our manipulation depends upon—*interacts with!*—something about the gender of the subject. And we check out the possibilities one by one in further experiments. If successful, we can pinpoint the important source of the difference, thus teaching us still more about the original finding.

But let us turn to some real examples of this process in action.

AN EXAMPLE FROM CONDITIONING

Our first example we can run through quickly, for we have discussed it earlier. Early investigators quickly showed (by conceptual replication) that Pavlov's conditioned-reflex findings held in a variety of species, humans included. Now, certain principles also seemed to apply across the board: for example, that conditioned reflexes formed slowly, with many pairings of CS and UCS; and that they would not form at all unless the CS and UCS were close together in time. But, we recall, the *conditioned taste aversion* experiments showed that these principles do not always hold (Chapter 6). There are limits on their generality. If we think of these studies as further conceptual replications of Pavlov's work, we would have to say that in these cases, replication fails.

But this "failure" was itself instructive. Certainly it did not lead us to scrap all the work on conditioning where the principles do apply—they are much too well established for that! Rather, it suggested that there are limits on their generality. Certain particular CS-USC combinations seem to have special status. And that has led us to rethink a great deal of what we thought we knew about how learning works.

AN EXAMPLE FROM SOCIAL PSYCHOLOGY

In several places, we have looked at a series of studies showing that the presence of more than one onlooker to an emergency actually makes helping less likely, not more, than the presence of only one. But this is not always true. There was another experiment (Piliavin, Rodin, & Piliavin, 1969) in which an experimenter faked a collapse in a subway car. In this case, the likelihood that someone would offer help was quite unaffected by the number of onlookers there were. There was no "danger in numbers." This experiment failed to replicate the earlier findings.

Let us assume that neither of these sets of findings was a fluke. Then the very inconsistency of the data has taught us something. We know that the presence or absence of the "danger in numbers effect" depends on something else. Like what? Darley, Teger, and Lewis (1973) suggested one possibility: It may depend on the signals the onlookers give each other.

Suppose we witness an emergency. We ask ourselves, "Is something really bad happening? Should someone do something? Should *I* do something?" While asking ourselves that, we may be standing there giving the appearance of calmness, even if our minds are racing; and others, whose minds may also be racing, can be looking quite calm to *us*. In light of all this apparent tranquillity, we may decide, "Well, no one else seems much worried. It can't be all that bad"—and take no action.

Suppose, on the other hand, we are face to face with another onlooker when a sudden emergency happens. We see him jump; he sees us jump. We see his startled face; he sees ours. It will be less easy to discount the seriousness of the emergency in that case.

Well, this idea can be tested. Darley et al. did an experiment in which, again, an accident was staged: A loud crash and the sounds of an injured person came from a room adjacent to the one in which the subjects (male college students) were sitting. How likely was it that someone would come through the door into that adjacent room to offer help? This was tallied by an experimenter who could see that adjacent room, but not the waiting room, so that he could be "blind" as to the experimental conditions (why?). The likelihood of offering help was the dependent variable.

There were three experimental conditions, and the differences among them constituted the independent variable. Some of the subjects were waiting alone, others in pairs. Of the pairs, half were seated facing each other. The remaining pairs were seated back to back. They could not see each other's startled reactions when the emergency occurred—not, at least, until they had time to turn around, and the initial startles might have faded by then.

Face to face, or back to back? It seems unreasonable to expect such a subtle situational factor to affect a complex decision such as "Should I help?" But in fact, it made a very great difference (Figure 12.4). Of the pairs of subjects who were back to back, and could not see each others' immediate reactions, in only 20% of the pairs did either member go to offer help. Among those seated face to face, at least one member took action in a full 80% of the pairs. This was only slightly lower than the tally for subjects waiting alone, of whom 90% offered help.

Thus we see one way in which two sets of contradictory findings can be reconciled with each other. It is a sort of double conceptual replication, two findings for the price of one experiment. Comparing the back-to-back pairs with the subjects who were alone, we replicate the "danger in numbers" finding. Comparing the face-to-face subjects with the alone ones, we replicate the "no-danger-in-numbers" finding. And comparing the face-to-face and back-to-back conditions with each other, we isolate *one* set of factors (for there surely are others too) on which the difference depends: It depends in part on the cues that onlookers give each other when there is more than one.

FINDINGS VERSUS THEORY: THE EXTERNAL-VALIDITY CONTROVERSY

In 1963, Campbell and Stanley coined a couple of terms—*internal validity* and *external validity*—that have been with us ever since, and that we should be familiar with. The latter idea (not the former) has been the subject of some controversy.

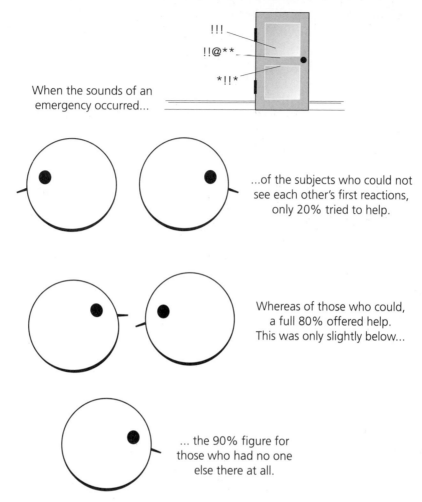

FIGURE 12.4
The back-to-back or face-to-face experiment. A seemingly minor situational variable had a very great effect.

The term *validity* here is not quite the same as when we speak of the validity of a test or a measurement procedure (Chapter 3). Rather, we will speak of a study as *valid* if it teaches us something that is reliable and worth knowing.

When we ask if a study has *internal validity*, we are asking: Is the study a good study on its own terms? Does it really justify the conclusion it draws? Is it adequately controlled? Is it free of confounded variables? If not—if a study lacks internal validity—then we say that it cannot teach us something interesting, because it really hasn't taught us anything at all. We cannot safely draw a conclusion from it.

External validity, on the other hand, means what we have been calling *generality*. "To what populations, settings, treatment variables, and measurement variables can this effect be generalized?" (Campbell & Stanley, 1963, p. 5). The idea is that if we have a finding that applies only in a very limited set of subjects and procedures, then, even if it is an internally valid finding, it simply isn't very interesting. It lacks external validity.

Thus Pavlov discovered a new way to make dogs salivate. But if his discovery had been *only* that, then it would have interested only those very few researchers who are really interested in why dogs drool! In fact, of course, his discovery had much more generality (external validity) than that. As he saw it, it was a discovery not about salivation, but about how the brain forms connections. The process of *systematic and conceptual replication* showed that the principles held up in a variety of species including humans. And the principles have found direct application of a variety of kinds, from treatment of phobia (Chapter 9) to the loss of appetite (anorexia) that cancer patients so often display (Bernstein, 1978).

But in thinking about that, we realize something: The generality of Pavlov's findings had to be *demonstrated* by systematic and conceptual replication. The question of generality, in other words, was what we call an empirical question—we answer it by gathering more data. It *could not be determined by examining Pavlov's original experiment, taken by itself.* Maybe the idea of "external validity" should be applied, not to individual experiments, but to whole bodies of data!

Thus we see that the notion of external validity is more complicated than it looks. And it has been the topic of some controversy. The controversy is important, for it leads to some very general questions about just what psychologists are trying to do. So let us look more closely.

TWO MODELS FOR RESEARCH

There are two ways of looking at the problem of external validity. The first sees the problem as arising for any investigation, and best solved by the notion of *representative sampling*: One can generalize to populations from which the sample is representative (Chapter 5). The second sees the problem as arising only for certain kinds of research. For other research—indeed, most research—the problem does not arise at all for individual studies and experiments. It is settled by the convergence of many diverse findings on a general conclusion.

THE GENERALIZATION MODEL

The first model for research treats external validity as arising for individual studies. Within this framework, the more *generalizable* the study's findings are, the greater is its external validity and the more important are the findings.

In research of this kind, one wants to generalize findings directly, from a small sample to a larger population, and from a setting (perhaps an artificial one) to natural ones. Of course, survey research fits this model nicely. From what the sample wants, believes, prefers, or is concerned about, one wants to infer what is wanted, believed, preferred, or of concern to the population from which the sample was drawn.

But not only survey research fits in here. Marketing research does, too. Or consider clinical research. Often one tries out (say) a new therapeutic technique on a limited number of patients or clients. If it is effective in this sample, one wants to be able to predict that it will also be effective in the more general case of people with that disorder (the population). If we are to do that, then the sample must be representative of that population.

In such cases, the logic of the research is as shown in Figure 12.5A. From the sample, we generalize to a population. In such cases, the issue of representativeness is squarely before us. Suppose our sample is special in some way that makes them different from the rest of the population of interest. Then we don't, or at least we shouldn't, generalize to that population. And we have to ask whether

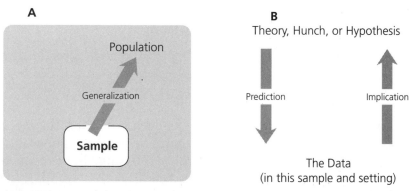

FIGURE 12.5
Two models of the research process. In (A), we think of the subjects, setting, and procedures as samples from populations of these; so we are concerned with their representativeness. In (B), we are exploring or testing a theory (or hunch or hypothesis) that predicts what *these* subjects, in *this* setting, will do. In the latter case, the notion of "generalizing to a population" may not even arise.

our setting is so different from natural ones that what we find in that setting simply has no relevance to the real-world events we want to know about. Similarly for our experimental manipulation: If nothing like it ever occurs in the real world, what can we predict about the real world by knowing its effects? In a word, for research of this kind, the *external validity* of the study is a perfectly valid concern.

Let me make clear that my intent is not to criticize that kind of research. There is absolutely nothing wrong with it; it is necessary and valuable. But I think it is a mistake to treat *all* research as fitting that mold. There is another model, which we'll look at in a minute.

From this perspective, a frequent criticism of most psychological research is that it deals with small and biased samples, not just of subjects (though probably those too), but also of settings and experimental manipulations. Suppose we do an experiment on helping behavior. The subjects we use can be a sample from some population. But the setting in which we do the research can also be considered a sample (of one) from a population of possible settings. And whatever manipulation we make—the independent variable—can be considered a sample (of one) from the population of things that could happen to the subject, or from the population of ways in which one setting might differ from another. We should, it is often argued, pay more attention to the representativeness of our setting and manipulation, as well as of our subjects.

However, there is a different way of looking at the research process—another model for research. Let us look at it.

THE THEORETICAL MODEL

A great deal of research does not, in fact, generalize directly to the real world, and *is not intended to*. What "generalizes" is not the results themselves, but the understanding of general principles to which the results—usually many results, taken all together—give rise. We may test theories, for example. And when we do, our interest may not be in generalizing the findings to natural settings or populations. Rather, we ask: Do *these* subjects, in *this* setting, behave as our theory—or hunch, or hypothesis—predicts that they should? And from the answer we draw conclusions, not about populations, but about the theory, hunch, or hypothesis.

The logic of this kind of research is shown in Figure 12.5B. We see at once that it is quite different from that shown in Panel A. There is no "population," so there is no step called "generalization."* Rather, we ask a question with our experiment. And based on what we observe in *these* subjects under *these* conditions, we answer our question. In answering it, we may find the data supporting or disconfirming a hypothesis. Or we may not be testing a fully developed theory, but checking out a hunch, or just exploring: "I wonder what would happen if we did thus and so—with *these* subjects in *this* setting . . . ?" In either case, we have here an instance of the old "theory-data cycle" that we explored way back in Chapter 2.

In this kind of research, the issue of external validity, or "generalizability," does not arise. But again, let us turn to examples.

The Sample: Baltimore Revisited Way earlier in the book, we looked at the study by Bell and Ainsworth (1972) on mother–infant interactions. Recall that a popular theory said: Promptness in responding to a baby's cries will reward crying, or spoil the child, causing increased fussiness in either case. Bell and Ainsworth tested a prediction based on that idea, and failed to confirm it (Chapter 4)—at least *in the families that were observed.*

Consider how wildly unrepresentative these families were—of families in general, or American families, or even families in Baltimore where the study was done. At minimum, the families had to be well-enough educated, and sympathetic enough to the notion of research, to allow a gaggle of psychologists armed with stopwatches and tally sheets to eavesdrop on their interactions with their children! Surely, the only population we could generalize to is the after-the-fact population: Sympathetic Baltimore families *like these* (see Chapter 5).

That would place serious limitations on the study's generality, but Bell and Ainsworth were little concerned about this. Rather, their logic went like this: "One theory tells us that responsive parents should tend to have fussy babies. Do they—in *these* families?" The answer was no. The prediction was disconfirmed.

And *that* conclusion does not depend on generalizing the find-

---

*It is true that many statistical procedures make implicit references to populations. Often we have come across the notion of taking repeated samples from the same population, an infinite number of times, and working out what the sampling distribution of a statistic would look like were we to do this. These, however, are "thought experiments" that aid statisticians in their calculations. Obviously, we aren't really going to repeat a study an infinite number of times. Likewise, the population we have in mind may not correspond to anything real. It might be "the population of all white rats of the Sprague-Dawley strain, living, dead, and yet to be born"—not a population we will find walking around the real world!

ings to any population whatever. It is based on what happened *in the sample itself*, and on the failure of that sample to support the theory's predictions.

It is at this point that students, when I talk with them about this matter, get uncomfortable. "But," they say, "don't we want to know whether the results hold for other cities and other cultures? What if they hold true *only* for sympathetic Baltimorians?" Yes, we do want to know that. Two points, however:

First, these are questions for further research to answer. We may do some of this research ourselves, but if we don't, someone else will. And the research may consist of conceptual, rather than direct, replication.* As we develop better theories of social development, sooner or later we will discover whether the *principles* hold up in different cities or cultures. And the original findings will have played a part in the development of those new and better theories.

Second, suppose the findings did hold up only in sympathetic parents—perhaps only ones who live in Baltimore! Then, rather than dismissing the findings as ungeneralizable, it would be instructive to ask why *that* is so. What is going on among these families that so affects parents' reactions to what their children do? A failure of replication, as we've seen, is an invitation to the success of further discovery.

The Setting: Harlow Revisited Let's think once more about Harlow's cloth mother/wire mother monkey experiments. Harlow found, we recall, that baby monkeys attach themselves to the mother that offers "contact comfort," and not to the one that offers food.

Do his results apply to real life? Well, first of all, *whose* real life? The real lives of monkeys in the wild? Just when are they going to encounter either a wire mother *or* a cloth one? What a silly question!

The real lives of lab-reared monkeys? But even *they* will not encounter a mother of either kind, unless a Harlow builds the contraptions and wheels them in. Moreover, they're a highly restricted and unrepresentative sample of the monkeys in the world. So who cares what their behavior is like?

In short, we have artificial mothers, in an artificial setting, with, in a sense, artificial baby monkeys—lab-reared ones—as subjects. Surely all this would be a terrible way to learn anything about real monkeys in natural environments.

---

*In fact, Ainsworth did take some observations on mother–infant interactions in a very different culture—Uganda (Ainsworth, 1967). Here the specifics had to be very different from the original study in Baltimore, but the conceptual conclusions held.

Yes, but—and this is the point—Harlow was not *trying* to learn about real-life monkeys. That was not the point of his study at all. He was testing a theory, and his logic went like this: If the cupboard theory of infant–mother attachment is correct, then *these* infant monkeys, in *this* situation, should go where the gravy lies. They should attach themselves to the mother that offers food. "Well, do they?" asked Harlow. "No, we don't," the monkeys told him. And the cupboard theory, and the drive-reduction theory that subsumed it (Chapter 2), received a stiff challenge—one among many!—from these disconfirming data.

The Manipulation: Split Brains Revisited In Chapter 10, we looked at some characteristics of patients who had undergone section of the corpus callosum—the great band of nerve fibers that connects the two hemispheres. We recall that if they were shown objects or pictures of objects, and the visual input was confined to the left hemisphere, subjects could describe what was shown, in words. If the input was restricted to the right hemisphere, subjects could not talk about it—though they could identify the object by touch, for example, and thus show us that they had seen it and knew what it was.

Remember about that? Okay, now: Do these findings apply to real life?

No. They do not. Not even to the "real lives" of the split-brain patients who were in the study.

Why not? Because in real life, a split-brain patient can move her eyes! Suppose some object of interest does fall on the right side of the retina. A quick movement of the eye can shift the input from the right to the left side of the retina; and from there it can access the speaking half of the brain, even in a split-brain patient. The difference between left and right can be erased in, literally, the flick of an eye.

That is why, when the experiments were done well, the inputs to one or another hemisphere were extremely brief—so brief that they were gone before an eye movement could occur. All told, about as unnatural a set of inputs as we are likely to find. Yet they have taught us much about how the parts of the brain divide their duties.

Another way of saying it is this: If natural stimuli were presented in a natural way, eye movements would wipe out any effect of left versus right—thereby making it a feeble manipulation (Chapter 7)! And, for a long time, poorly controlled experiments allowed just that. The fact is, we *have* to make the conditions unnatural if we are to see any difference at all. Do the findings then apply to real life? No, and it doesn't matter.

THE MODELS AND THE REAL WORLD

The difference between these two models—the generalization model and the theoretical model—is not the same as the difference between lab studies and field studies done in the real world. Rather it cuts across that distinction, producing the fourfold division shown in Table 12.1.

Table 12.1
Comparison of Research in Two Settings

Laboratory Research	*Research in Natural Settings*
Generalization Model	
A. Laboratory research intended to generalize to the natural world.	B. Research in natural settings intended to generalize to the natural world.
Theoretical Model	
C. Laboratory research designed to test a hunch or hypothesis.	D. Research in natural settings designed to test a hunch or hypothesis.

In Cell A, we have laboratory research in the "generalization" mode. The studies are done in a laboratory under controlled conditions, but one intends the results to apply to the natural world. Much medical research is of this kind: One does laboratory tests for the effectiveness or toxicity of a drug, for instance, in order to know what to expect if we administer it to populations of patients living their real-world lives. In psychology, any case in which laboratory research is designed to model and predict real-world phenomena falls here.

In Cell B, we have research done in natural settings, and again designed to model and predict what will happen in the general case (the population) and in the natural world. Survey or marketing research obviously fits nicely here. So does some clinical research, where the treatment and the follow-up evaluation occur in natural settings. So too, incidentally, does the field from which many of our statistical techniques are borrowed—agricultural research!

In Cell C, we find laboratory research in theoretical mode. Here, the results may not apply directly to real life. What does is the understanding we gain from such research. The examples we ran through earlier—monkey mothers, split-brain patients, Pavlov's work—fit nicely here, as do many of the studies we've used as examples throughout this book.

Finally in Cell D, we have theoretical research conducted in a natural environment. Here we place any experiment or correlational study that is conducted in a natural setting, but is concerned not with generalizing the findings, but with whether *these* subjects in *these* settings behave as a theory predicts. Examples would include the study of infant crying and maternal responsiveness, the liquor store robbery, and the high bridge/low bridge quasi-experiment.

MIXING THE MODELS

To this point, we have presented the two models—generalization and theoretical—as if they were either-or. Actually, it is quite possible for an investigation to fit both models at once. It depends on how we think about the findings, how we talk about them, and how we use them.

Suppose a theoretical advance suggests to us that a new way of treating, say, depression ought to be effective. So we try out the new treatment in a sample of depressed persons. Suppose we find it effective (as compared to placebo treatment). What can we say? Ideally, two things.

First, we can say: "Since the treatment had a significant beneficial effect in this sample, it ought to benefit depressed persons generally" (the population). Here we are in *generalization* mode. And before we draw our conclusion about a population, we do want to be sure our sample does not differ in important ways from depressed persons in general; if it does, that obviously limits the generalizability of our findings. Similarly, we want to be sure that our treated subjects are actually leading less depressed *lives*, and not just (say) scoring lower on a paper-and-pencil test of depression in a therapist's office! The generalizability of our setting and measurement procedure must be considered. In a word: If we think and speak about the findings this way, then the external validity of the experiment is an important concern.

But we could also say this: "Our theory predicts that the new treatment we've developed should be effective—in *these* people, in *this* situation, as measured *this* way. It is. So we have supporting evidence for the theory that gave rise to it." Now we're in theoretical mode. The issue of representativeness does not arise. And the generalizability of the findings is an empirical question, to be decided by replication. Of course, if systematic and conceptual replication show that the findings hold up under a variety of conditions, this strengthens our confidence in the underlying theory as well as in the practical usefulness of the findings.

GENERALIZATION OF WHAT?

Now, does all this mean that studies in the theoretical mode have no relevance to the real world? No, it does not mean that at all. What we've said is that the *findings* may not generalize directly to the real world. What does generalize, and in spades, is the *understanding* that the findings give us.

Thus Pavlov found something that affects salivation in dogs. Who cares? Well, very few care about that specifically. But very many care about the *principles* of conditioning that Pavlov pioneered. These principles make the world more understandable—besides having some direct practical applications, as noted earlier.

This generality had to be *shown*. We could not have established it just by inspecting Pavlov's original experiments. It might, indeed, have turned out that his principles applied only to salivation, and only to salivation in dogs—in which case his work would have been much less interesting to most of us. But, of course, it didn't turn out that way at all.

WHAT THEN OF GENERALITY?

Okay, but the reader (like the author's students) may still feel a twinge of discomfort. If we study (say) salivary conditioning and nothing else, we may be able to test a variety of theories, hunches, and hypotheses in that context. That still won't tell us whether the principles we develop have application beyond the salivation laboratory. Or suppose that people doing memory research had depended exclusively on work with nonsense syllables. Then we might have developed what we thought were theories of memory in general, when in fact the theories might only apply to disconnected, arbitrary material. We would have missed the many influences that require organized, meaningful material for their expression—the drifts in memory for events, for example.*

---

*There is real risk of this sort of provincialism, and I don't mean to dismiss the danger. In the 1930s and 1940s, three immensely influential books were written. One was titled *Purposive Behavior in Animals and Men*—presumably all animals and humans besides. The second was titled *The Behavior of Organisms*—presumably all behavior in any organism. The third was titled *Principles of Behavior*—any behavior, one presumes, by anybody. Yet all three books dealt *exclusively* with the behavior of white rats in experimental apparatuses!

This is a perfectly valid concern. But I think there are ways of addressing it that do not revert to the "generalization model" of research.

THE "WEIGHT OF THE EVIDENCE" REVISITED

Back in Chapter 2, we noted that very rarely does a single experiment either establish, or overthrow, a theory. Rather it adds its "weight" to one or another pan of a balance, which weighs "evidence for" against "evidence against." When a balance tips strongly one way or the other, a theory may come to be thought of as "well established" in one case (like the theory of evolution), or as "no longer a serious contender" (like drive-reduction theory). General principles rest, not on single studies, but on whole bodies of findings.

Again, let's take Harlow's work as an example. His experiment alone was a sharp challenge to the "cupboard theory," yes. But there was already some contrary evidence, and much more has been gathered since—in monkeys and in humans, and in a number of countries and cultures. For example, the Bell and Ainsworth findings on infant crying and mothers' responsiveness fit in. All mothers in this study met their babies' physical needs, but it was the mothers who also responded to their *social signals* who tended to have contented, noncrying babies. Nutrition is not enough.

GENERALITY AS DIVERSITY

As another case in point, think back over some of our examples from memory research. And think about the *principle* implicated by many of them: Memory is not just "reading off" a record of what happened, but involves reconstruction. That conclusion is supported by a large *and diverse* body of findings. Subjects of European ancestry reconstructed a Native American folk tale so that it resembled more closely a Western folk story (Chapter 10). Other subjects "remembered" things about the *Challenger* explosion that were simply wrong (Chapter 3). Others, asked about a stop sign that hadn't been there, "remembered" seeing one (Chapter 5). And so on.

Now, not one of these studies tried for a representative sample of any known population of subjects, much less of settings and manipulations. Rather, what impresses us is the wide variations—the diversity—of subjects, settings, and manipulations under which the principle—memory is reconstructive—is seen to hold. All these differences, and still the same underlying principle holds up! It must indeed be a generalizable principle.

But that still means that what is generalizable—what has "external validity"—is not a single investigation or its findings, but the general principles that are supported by a solid body of evidence. And the generalizability depends on the diversity—the range of conditions—under which the principle holds. This cannot be established by any single finding.

A LOOK BACK

We have presented two "models" of the research process—two sets of ideas as to just what the researcher is trying to do. They have quite different implications as to how research psychologists should go about their task.

The first, the "generalization model," says: What we are after is *generalizable findings*. To obtain these, we ought to try for representative samples—certainly of subjects, but perhaps also of settings and manipulations. Maybe we pay too much attention to subject representativeness, and not enough to the representativeness of our settings and experimental manipulations.

The second, the "theoretical model," does not deny that there is research—market research, survey research, and some clinical, educational, and industrial research—that fits that mold. What it denies is that all research does. It says: Very often, what we are after is not generalizable findings, but *generalizable principles*. These principles will not be established by any single study, but by a whole body of studies. And the generality of a principle (and its limits) will be established by systematic and conceptual replication. The representativeness (or lack thereof) of any particular study has little to do with the case, and the "problem" of external validity simply does not arise.

Actually, this is not (I think) a revolutionary view at all. It is just a description of what we actually do. In practice, most researchers usually do not worry very much about the representativeness even of our sample of subjects—unless we are doing, say, survey or market research or other research that fits the "generalization" model. For most research, we take our subjects where we can find them: student volunteers at the college where we teach, or those parents in our town who are willing to be observed. And we select or construct a setting, and an experimental manipulation, not to mimic the real world but (as in Harlow's case) to permit our theory to be tested, or our hunch to be checked out.

As for generality, this we determine by the processes of systematic and conceptual replication. The more findings there are that support a general conclusion, the more confidence we have in that conclusion. And the more *diverse* those findings are, the more confidence we have that the conclusion is a general one.

WHAT IS RESEARCH "ABOUT"?

Is it worth damning your own soul and risking everybody else's in order to learn something about a dog's spittle?

—GEORGE BERNARD SHAW

The controversy about external validity makes contact with a broader issue. One thing that impresses a beginning student is that some psychological research looks pretty weird! It just is not clear how the questions it asks can tell us anything interesting about ourselves and others.

Now, as we near the end of our journey, we have the background we need to give that impression another look. We just might want to reconsider it.

CONCEPTS VERSUS SPECIFICS

Back in Chapter 3, we saw that research usually begins with a rather broad question—too broad to be investigable. "How does the brain work?" or "How do we learn?"—we don't know how to design experiments that would answer such questions as these. So we narrow our question, zeroing in on some small part of the complex system, until we find ourselves asking how one variable is related to another. *Then* we have a researchable question. But now, as a further step, we must "operationalize" our variables. (Recall that that expression can be roughly translated into English as "Look, we have to do something specific. What shall it be?")

And because the operationalized variables, our manipulations and measures, are so specific, they may easily look trivial. In themselves, they may *be* trivial! And if we focus on them, a whole research project can be made to look trivial even when it is not.

As an example, let's take Pavlov's work (since Shaw raises the issue). On the surface, what did Pavlov discover? Why, something about "a dog's spittle." He found a new way to make a dog drool! All the expense that went into building his lab, and the endless hours that went into the experiments themselves—and *that* is the outcome?

Well, you surely know by now what my answer will be. The specific materials used in these experiments were incidental. The research was not "about" drooling. It was "about" how learning takes place. Not a small question!

We have emphasized this source of confusion many times in this book. To emphasize it once more in this context: The bridges study was not about bridges. The bicycle study was not about bicycles. The false heart-rate study was not about hearts. All these studies were about a theoretical issue: Can we look inside and see directly what we feel? Or must we *interpret* what we see, and can we be mistaken? (Yes.) And the findings invite further discoveries: When, and under what conditions, are we such "strangers to ourselves"? And why?

This, then, is the danger in focusing on the specifics of a study (Figure 12.6). It can lead us—and journalists, and government agencies, and even our colleagues on occasion—to dismiss informative research that bears on important problems, because the specifics look trivial—as in fact they often are.

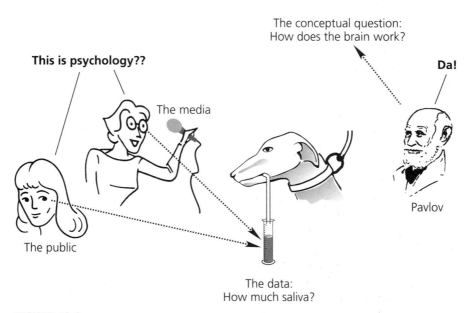

FIGURE 12.6
Focusing on the specifics of an experimental procedure can cause us to miss the real point of research.

But I think it worth our while to remember this: We can't determine how general a conclusion is by examining a single set of findings. Similarly, we can't determine the importance of a study just by examining its *procedures*! We must work back to the questions the study is asking—the general ones, not the specific operational ones—and weigh the importance of those.

Pavlov's experiments were not "about" a dog's spittle. George Bernard Shaw missed that point; but Pavlov knew it well.

SUMMARY

Two questions arise about any research finding. First: Should we believe it? That is the question of *reliability*. Second: How generally does it hold—over what range of subjects, settings, and procedures? That is the question of *generality*.

One way of establishing the reliability of findings is by demonstrating their *statistical significance*. A significant finding means that we can be reasonably confident that the finding we saw, under the conditions in which we saw it, is not just an accident. But that confidence applies only to the investigation as we conducted it. It says nothing about the generality of the finding.

The process of replication also addresses reliability, and sometimes generality as well. In *direct replication*, an investigator repeats the original study as exactly as possible. Here again, therefore, the emphasis is on reliability, not on generality.

Systematic replication repeats the original study but with variations. If the results hold, then our confidence in the original finding is increased, and also we have established something about the generality of that finding. If the findings don't hold up—if replication fails—we may wonder why that is so, and explore the matter further to try to find out.

These ideas apply to *conceptual replication*, too, but here we go further. We ask the original question, but with an altogether different method. Or it may take the original finding a "next step," asking why it came about. That can tell us more about the original findings, and in doing so increase our confidence that the original findings were reliable. Either way, different studies using different methods can cross-check each other and fill in each other's gaps.

This also means that the importance of a set of findings depends on their context—the other findings, and theories, that gave rise to them. A study that looks trivial or even silly when considered in isolation can look much more interesting when that context is taken into account. Who cares whether a bicycle is a sexual turn-on? No one, not even the experimenters. Who cares whether we know our own feelings accurately? Many!

The concept of *external validity* is closely related to the notion of generality. To the extent that a finding applies across a wide range of settings and subjects (especially in the natural world), it has external validity. Such validity, it is argued here, really applies to theoretical conclusions, or to whole bodies of data, rather than individual experiments. Few real-world dogs get attached to apparatus for measuring salivary flow. This does not diminish the importance of Pavlov's experiments.

Considering all this, we see two ways of conceptualizing research. One, the "generalization model," sees research as an attempt to *draw conclusions about populations*—populations of subjects, but also of settings and procedures. Much research—survey research, for instance—fits that model well. It raises the quite legitimate concern that our sample—of subjects, but of procedures too—be representative of the populations of interest.

But another way of thinking about research is the "theoretical model," which sees research as an attempt to *draw conclusions about theories*. Results may not even be intended to apply to the "real world." In such cases, there may be no definable "population" to generalize to. We ask whether the results, in *these* subjects and in *this* setting, confirm or disconfirm the predictions made by the theory in question. It may even be that the setting and procedures have no real-life counterpart, as when we restrict visual input to one cerebral hemisphere or the other.

Such studies' findings may not "generalize to the real world" at all—but the understanding to which they give rise may do so. Again, though, that understanding comes from the convergence of many diverse studies, not from any single specific one. Much misunderstanding comes from confusing the specific details of a research project (which can often look trivial) with the broader theoretical issues it addresses.

MAKING FRIENDS WITH STATISTICS: META-ANALYSIS

In this chapter and elsewhere, we have emphasized that theories or general conclusions are rarely overthrown, or accepted, on the basis of single findings. Well-supported conclusions rest on whole literatures—whole collections of findings that are placed in the balance pan, and together contribute to the "weight of the evidence" pro and con (Chapter 2).

In recent years, methods have been developed that bring the "balance pan" metaphor closer to reality. It is possible to measure—not in single studies, but across whole bodies of research—just how strong the overall evidence for a conclusion is. One such method is known as *meta-analysis*. It is a way of statistically combining the results of different experiments, so that we see what conclusion the whole body of evidence supports, and how strongly.

A CASE STUDY: THE EFFECTIVENESS OF PSYCHOTHERAPY

To have a specific example to work on, let us ask this question: Is psychotherapy effective?

The question has been bitterly debated. In the 1950s, the prominent psychologist H. J. Eysenck reviewed six controlled experiments on the efficacy of psychotherapy. His conclusion: About 75% of troubled clients will get better no matter what we do. About three-quarters will improve who receive psychotherapy; about three-quarters will improve who do not. On the strength of these and other discouraging findings, one psychologist proposed that clinicians should hand a card to prospective clients, explaining that the therapy being offered them had never been proven superior to a placebo (Smith, Glass, & Miller, 1980).

Should they? It is *not* an adequate answer to say: "Surely all these people would not be spending all this time and money on something that doesn't help!" Remember that not many years ago, we could have said the same thing about blood-letting (Chapter 1). In the treatment of disorders, we have chased wild geese many times before. Is psychotherapy another wild goose? We need to show *with data* that it is effective—if it is.

But how to do that? The literature on psychotherapeutic effectiveness includes studies of clients with radically different kinds of problems, treated with different forms of psychotherapy, and with very different measures of therapeutic outcome—clients' own subjective reports of their well-being, ratings of their well-being by therapists or families or friends, frequency of problematic behavior, or scores on paper-and-pencil tests of depression or self-esteem or mood. . . . Surely comparing one study with another is meaningless. Apples and oranges!

Then again, combining apples and oranges is not always a mistake. If we want to talk about *fruit*, it would be a sensible thing to do. But just what do we combine with what? In one outcome study, a sample of depressed clients is assigned at random to a psychotherapy group or a control group. We compare their scores on, say, a paper-and-pencil test of depression. In another study, a sample of alcohol abusers is divided at random into a psychotherapy group and a control group, and we measure, say, number of days abstinent from alcohol over a year.

Within each study, we can compare the experimental (psychotherapy) group with its untreated control group. But how can we compare these studies with each other? How many days of abstinence are equivalent to how much reduction in depression score? It looks much worse than the apples-and-oranges problem!

But there is a way. We can compare apples and oranges or, indeed, apples and orangutans, by moving from the data to the statistics that summarize them.

THE *z*-SCORE

To explain it, we must back off for a minute. Suppose we have a frequency distribution of scores—on any measure. Suppose we know its mean and its standard deviation. Now, we can take any score, X, in that distribution and express it as a *deviation from the mean, in units of the standard deviation.* Arithmetically, this becomes

$$z = (X - M)/SD.$$

That *z-score* tells us this: *How many standard deviations*, above or below the mean, is this score X? A score that has a *z*-value of 1 is one standard deviation above the mean of its distribution. A score that has a *z*-value of −0.5 is half a standard deviation below the mean of its distribution. A score with a *z*-value of 2 is two standard deviations above the mean of its distribution. And so on.

EFFECT SIZE

Now let's take another step. Let us look at our experiment dealing with psychotherapy and depression. At the end, we have test scores for all our control and experimental subjects. (And to simplify, assume that our test is scored so that a higher score means less depression.) We compute the mean and the standard deviation for the control group. Then we compute the mean for the experimental group, and *convert it to a z-score on the distribution of control-group scores*. We are asking, in other words: How many standard deviations above the control group mean is the mean for the experimental group? Suppose we find that the mean score for the treated group falls one standard deviation above the mean for the controls. It then has a *z*-score of 1.

This kind of *z*-score is referred to as the *effect size* for the psychotherapy treatment in this experiment. How big an effect did psychotherapy have? Big enough (we have supposed) to make the average score for treated clients one standard deviation above the average score for the controls.

Now look at the scores for the clients with alcohol problems. We determine, over a year, how many days each subject abstained from alcohol. Suppose the average score for our untreated control subjects was 190 days, with a standard deviation of 40 (these again are made-up numbers). For subjects given therapy, the mean number of days abstinent might be 250 days. Then, since

$$(250 - 190)/40 = 60/40 = 1.5,$$

we have an effect size of 1.5. How big an effect did treatment have? Big enough to make the average score for treated patients one-and-a-half standard deviations higher than the average score for controls.

And now we see the point of all this. By converting our data to effect sizes, we can take data of vastly different kinds and convert them to a scale that is common to all. That scale is *effect size*. We can compare the weights of apples and oranges, in grams (a common scale). We can compare their caloric values in kilocalories (a common scale). And—we can compare the effects of psychotherapy on a depression scale, with its effects on abstinence from alcohol, by converting *these* to a common scale: effect size, in units of z.

THE SMITH AND GLASS META-ANALYSIS

Let us turn to an actual example of meta-analysis. Smith and Glass (1977) searched the literature for studies of the effectiveness of psychotherapy, selecting 375 of these that met the criteria for meta-analysis: There had to be a group of subjects who received psychotherapy, and a control group either untreated or receiving a different kind of therapy. The studies were very diverse as to the measure that was used: measures of self-esteem or of anxiety, physiological stress, achievement at work or in school, and many others. But these measures could all be converted to effect sizes, and thus compared with each other.

First, then, the overall question: Is psychotherapy effective? Averaging effect size across *all* of these studies, Smith, Glass, and Miller found a mean effect size of 0.68 standard deviation units. That is, the mean of *all* the treated groups combined was .68 standard deviations above their control-group means. That may not sound like much, but by reference to statistical tables we find that it means this: The *average* treated patient or client was better off at the end of treatment than 75% of the untreated controls (Figure 12.7).

Smith and Glass went further. Using effect size as a measure of effectiveness, one can correlate this with other variables across the entire sample—of experiments, not of subjects! Effect size was not correlated with how experienced the therapists were—a disturbing finding (see Chapter 14)—nor with the duration of therapy. Interestingly, it *was* correlated with the average IQ of the clients, and with "similarity" of client and therapist: Therapists who resemble their clients in ethnic-

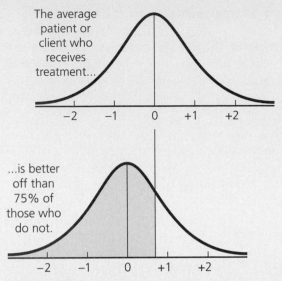

The average patient or client who receives treatment...

...is better off than 75% of those who do not.

FIGURE 12.7
Meta-analysis applied to clinical evaluations of psychotherapy. The mean of the treated group falls at a z-score that exceeds 75% of the untreated group.

ity, age, and social class tend to get better results.

Again: Using the effect-size measure, it is possible to compare the impact of psychotherapy on different kinds of problems. Some of the studies surveyed were concerned with anxiety problems, others with self-esteem, yet others with performance on the job or in school. We can compare *all* the studies that dealt with one of these problems with *all* the studies that dealt with another, by comparing their average effect sizes.

The data show that psychotherapy has greatest impact on fear or anxiety reduction, and on improvement in self-esteem; the average effect sizes here were 0.97 and 0.90, which means that the average treated client was better off than 83% and 82%, respectively, of the controls. Psychotherapy had least effect on school or work achievement; here the average effect size was 0.31, which still places the average treated client as better off than 60% of the untreated ones.

What about type of therapy? We can compare the effect sizes for all studies using one approach to therapy (e.g., psychoanalytic) with all studies using another (e.g., behavioral therapy). (Selection again!) Briefly, the overall differences were quite small, a finding that fits most reviews of the literature on therapy: The personal characteristics of the therapist (and of the client) are probably more important than the "school" of therapy in which the therapist was trained. And, of course, one approach to therapy may be better for one kind of disorder, another for another.

Well, meta-analysis can combine and compare whole literatures to check that possibility too.

There is still more—but that is enough! The point is that by use of this technique, which allows us to combine different studies even if they use different methods, we can look at whole literatures and, considering all available studies, measure the "weight of the evidence" (Chapter 2) on this or any other research question.

CHAPTER 13

ETHICAL CONSIDERATIONS
IN RESEARCH

First, do no harm.

—FROM THE HIPPOCRATIC OATH

IN THIS CHAPTER, WE'LL DISCUSS:

- The ethical issues that arise in research
- The guidelines of the American Psychological Association
- The subject's right to safety and to respectful treatment, and some dilemmas that arise from these, especially the problem of deception
- The role of "debriefing"
- Weighing the ethical costs or risks of doing an investigation against the costs of not doing it
- Consultation, oversight, and the role of review boards
- Ethical issues in animal research
- Oversight and the role of institutional committees
- The debate over animal rights

The research setting is a minimal social situation: One organism observes what another one is doing. Especially in research with human subjects, however, we have seen one organism (an investigator) relate to another one (the subject or participant) in ways that would not be tolerated in normal social intercourse. Subjects have been observed without their knowledge or consent. They have sometimes been told outright lies.

The investigator's purpose, of course, is not "normal social intercourse"—it is to learn something about human behavior. Therein is the difficulty. To what extent may one violate social rules in the search for knowledge? What, in other words, is one's ethical position as a researcher, when the research requires breaking the rules of normal social interaction (Figure 13.1)?

Serious attention to ethical considerations has greatly increased in recent decades. Take, for instance, the study of the Seekers, the "doomsday group" that was awaiting the end of the world (Chapter 4). We saw that a team of researchers infiltrated the group, posing

FIGURE 13.1
What would be an experimenter's ethical position here?

as believers, in order to study that group. Now, nowhere in the book that resulted (unless I have missed it on several readings) is there any mention of the ethical issues that are raised by this. Do researchers have the right to lie to their subjects? Do researchers have the right to observe them secretly at all, knowing that the subjects would almost certainly not consent to being observed if they were asked?

Let me say at once that I raise these questions not to criticize the authors. It is rather to show how times have changed. Ethical issues that simply did not occur to investigators 40 years ago would certainly be debated now. Indeed, if scientists had to obtain permission from one of today's review boards (see later discussion) in order to conduct such a study, I am not at all sure that permission would be granted.

In any case, the ethical position of an investigator nowadays is carefully assessed *before* research begins. And this is not done by the researcher alone, who may be too close to his research plans to be the best judge of their acceptability. Oversight committees review the research plans, must approve a research project before it begins, and have the power to prevent an unacceptable project from being conducted.

THE APA GUIDELINES

The American Psychological Association (APA) published a series of guidelines for the ethical treatment of human research subjects or "participants." The following discussion is based on the 1992 version of these guidelines, the most relevant parts of which are reproduced (in abridged form) below.

Ethical Principles of Psychologists and Code of Conduct
(APA, 1992, abridged)

6.06 Planning Research.
(a) Psychologists design, conduct, and report research in accordance with recognized standards of scientific competence and ethical research. . . .
(c) In planning research, psychologists consider its ethical acceptability under the Ethics Code. If an ethical issue is unclear, psychologists seek to resolve the issue through consultation with institutional review boards, animal care and use committees, peer consultations, or other proper mechanisms.

(d) Psychologists take reasonable steps to implement appropriate protections for the rights and welfare of human participants, other persons affected by the research, and the welfare of animal subjects.

6.07 Responsibility.

(a) Psychologists conduct research competently and with due concern for the dignity and welfare of the participants.

(b) Psychologists are responsible for the ethical conduct of research conducted by them or by others under their supervision or control.

(c) Researchers and assistants are permitted to perform only those tasks for which they are appropriately trained and prepared.

(d) As part of the process of development and implementation of research projects, psychologists consult those with expertise concerning any special population under investigation or most likely to be affected.

6.08 Compliance With Law and Standards.

Psychologists plan and conduct research in a manner consistent with federal and state law and regulations, as well as professional standards governing the conduct of research, and particularly those standards governing research with human participants and animal subjects.

6.09 Institutional Approval.

Psychologists obtain from host institutions or organizations appropriate approval prior to conducting research, and they provide accurate information about their research proposals. They conduct the research in accordance with the approved research protocol.

6.10 Research Responsibilities.

Prior to conducting research (except research involving only anonymous surveys, naturalistic observations, or similar research), psychologists enter into an agreement with participants that clarifies the nature of the research and the responsibilities of each party.

6.11 Informed Consent to Research.

(a) Psychologists use language that is reasonably understandable to research participants in obtaining their appropriate informed consent (except as provided in Standard 6.12, Dispensing With Informed Consent). Such informed consent is appropriately documented.

(b) Using language that is reasonably understandable to participants, psychologists inform participants of the nature of the research; they inform participants that they are free to participate or to decline to participate or to withdraw from the research; they explain the foreseeable consequences of declining or withdrawing; they inform participants of significant factors that may be expected to influence their willingness to participate (such as risks, discomfort, adverse effects, or limitations on confidentiality, except as provided in Standard 6.15, Deception in Research); and they explain other aspects about which the prospective participants inquire.

(c) When psychologists conduct research with individuals such as students or subordinates, psychologists take special care to protect the prospective participants from adverse consequences of declining or withdrawing from participation.

(d) When research participation is a course requirement or opportunity for extra credit, the prospective participant is given the choice of equitable alternative activities. . . .

6.12 Dispensing With Informed Consent.
Before determining that planned research (such as research involving only anonymous questionnaires, naturalistic observations, or certain kinds of archival research) does not require the informed consent of research participants, psychologists consider applicable regulations and institutional review board requirements, and they consult with colleagues as appropriate.

6.13 Informed Consent in Research Filming or Recording.
Psychologists obtain informed consent from research participants prior to filming or recording them in any form, unless the research involves simply naturalistic observations in public places and it is not anticipated that the recording will be used in a manner that could cause personal identification or harm.

6.14 Offering Inducements for Research Participants.
(a) In offering professional services as an inducement to obtain research participants, psychologists make clear the nature of the services, as well as the risks, obligations, and limitations. . . .

(b) Psychologists do not offer excessive or inappropriate financial or other inducements to obtain research participants, particularly when it might tend to coerce participation.

6.15 Deception in Research.
(a) Psychologists do not conduct a study involving deception unless they have determined that the use of deceptive techniques is justified by the study's prospective scientific, educational, or applied value and that equally effective alternative procedures that do not use deception are not feasible.

(b) Psychologists never deceive research participants about significant aspects that would affect their willingness to participate, such as physical risks, discomfort, or unpleasant emotional experiences.

(c) Any other deception that is an integral feature of the design and conduct of an experiment must be explained to participants as

early as is feasible, preferably at the conclusion of their participation, but no later than at the conclusion of the research.

6.16 Sharing and Utilizing Data.
Psychologists inform research participants of their anticipated sharing or further use of personally identifiable research data and of the
possibility of unanticipated future uses.

6.17 Minimizing Invasiveness.
In conducting research, psychologists interfere with the participants
or milieu from which data are collected only in a manner that is
warranted by an appropriate research design and that is consistent
with psychologists' roles as scientific investigators.

6.18 Providing Participants With Information About the Study.
(a) Psychologists provide a prompt opportunity for participants to
obtain appropriate information about the nature, results, and
conclusions of the research, and psychologists attempt to correct any misconceptions that participants may have.
(b) If scientific or humane values justify delaying or withholding
this information, psychologists take reasonable measures to reduce the risk of harm.

6.19 Honoring Commitments.
Psychologists take reasonable measures to honor all commitments
they have made to research participants.

I shall not, in this space, attempt a point-by-point discussion of
these guidelines (though the APA monograph, which does that,
should be read carefully by every research producer). Instead, I shall
focus on just a few of the issues that seem (1) most instructive and
(2) most likely to be encountered by the beginning investigator.

The guidelines seem to me to break down into two more general
principles of ethical treatment. First, the subject has a *right to safety*.
He or she is not to be exposed, without volunteering, to physical or
mental danger or discomfort, either during the investigation (6.11b,
6.15b) or afterward as a result of participation (6.13, 6.16).

Second, the subject has a *right to respectful treatment*. The subject
in our investigation is not "our" subject; she is her own person. She
has the right to know exactly what she is doing as a research participant (6.10, 6.11a, b) and to decide whether or not to do it or to
continue doing it (6.11b); and her participation or continued participation may not be coerced (6.11c, d). At minimum, she can expect
information about the study after its completion (6.18). She is entitled to assume that her privacy will be protected (6.16). Thus her
participation is the result of a clear agreement with the investigator,

whose commitments she can rely on (6.19). In short, the subject should be a willing collaborator in the search for knowledge.

But these guidelines, apparently straightforward, can in practice be enormously difficult to implement. And in some cases they can collide head on with the scientific requirements of the investigation, giving rise to conflicts that no simple formula can resolve. Let us see some examples of the dilemmas that arise.

THE RIGHT TO SAFETY

Perhaps it should go without saying that an investigator may not risk physical harm to his subjects, unless they know and accept the risk. What may need to be stated, however, is the implication of this rule. The investigator must know, and consider, *all* the possible consequences of what she intends to do.

An obvious example: Do not build your own apparatus for delivering shocks to human beings. Not unless you could qualify as an electrical engineer. A little knowledge is a most dangerous thing, especially about electricity.

THE PROBLEM OF PSYCHOLOGICAL HARM

Considerations of safety become even more difficult when we consider the possibility of mental harm or discomfort. We need to give some thought to this matter in virtually every laboratory investigation.

Consider an experiment in memory, for example. We tell the subject that he will be asked to memorize a list of words, and to recall them later on. If the subject consents, it would seem that we could proceed under this "clear and fair agreement." But suppose the subject finds the task difficult, and leaves thinking, "I'm stupid!" Have we harmed him?

We cannot dismiss such feelings as an overreaction. If our procedures gave rise to the feelings, we are responsible for them, and must take steps to deal with them. Therefore, the postexperimental interview or *debriefing* cannot be a casual affair—even in a memory experiment. The subject must understand that experimental tasks usually are difficult—they are made so, to avoid ceiling effects—and that performance in such a task has little to do with the subject's abilities, personality, or worth.

More difficult is the case in which "uncomfortable" mental states are specifically under study. Suppose that the effects of self-esteem are of interest, and some subjects are made to fail at a task or are made to overhear other people downgrading them, in an attempt to produce a state of low self-esteem.

It seems inconceivable that such an experiment would be conducted without some attempt to remove any depression of self-esteem that may have been induced. Yet it has happened. If we agree that it is mandatory to undo any damage we may have done, how shall we undo it? A careful debriefing, explaining the deception and the reason for it and assuring the subject that the demeaning information was faked, might seem to be enough, but there is evidence that feelings of low self-esteem can persist even after such explanation (e.g., Wegner, Coulton, & Wenzlaff, 1985). The search for more effective means of debriefing, therefore, may itself become a focus of research activity.

A CASE STUDY:
THE OBEDIENCE EXPERIMENTS

Most difficult of all is the possible damage to self-esteem produced, not by an experimental treatment, but by the findings themselves. Let us look at a case where the problem is squarely before us.

Imagine yourself as a subject in one of these experiments (Milgram, 1974). There are two subjects (or so you are told). One is a "learner," and the other—you—is a "teacher." As teacher, your job is to punish the subject when he makes mistakes in a learning task. The "learner" slips into a cubicle where you cannot see him, and the "learning session" begins (Figure 13.2).

As the task goes on, you are told to deliver electric shocks at greater and greater intensity, as indicated on the shock generator. Actually, the "learner" is an assistant to the experimenter; he is playing a role, and in fact is receiving no shocks at all. But *you do not know that.*

You (the reader) are probably familiar with these experiments, but I'm going to describe in detail how the scenario played itself out. Familiarity should not be allowed to blunt the horror of what took place, with perfectly normal people like you and me as subjects ("teachers"). Here is a typical scenario.

At first, with low-voltage shocks, the "learner" does not complain. But as voltage was increased, he begins to grunt with pain. At about 120 volts (the voltage supplied by wall sockets in the United States), the learner shouts that the shocks are very painful and he

A

B

C

D

FIGURE 13.2
The Milgram situation. (A) The shock apparatus. (B) The "learner," who was really an actor and never received any shocks. (C) The "learner" cries out in pain, but the white-jacketed experimenter insisted that the subject continue to deliver more and more intense shock. (D) This subject did quit the experiment and leave, but he was in the minority.

wants to quit the experiment. At 300 volts, he screams that he will no longer make the responses his learning task requires. And he stops responding. But the experimenter tells you to treat nonresponding as an error and continue delivering shocks, increasing the intensity still further, even though you cannot even tell whether the learner is conscious. And—chances are—you do so.

Not that you obey mindlessly. You protest, but the experimenter says, "Continue." You say, "We ought to see if he's okay," but the reply is, "The experiment requires that you continue." If you press the matter, you are told, "You have no choice; you must go on."

You may feel very strongly that you would refuse to obey such inhuman orders. Most people do say that, if asked. And maybe you would refuse. But the *fact* is that in the original study, with ordinary people like you and me as subjects, *a full 68%* followed orders to the very end—delivering, as they thought, the highest possible voltage to the now-silent learner.

Milgram went on to vary the conditions of this experiment, and to learn more about what he had discovered (*systematic replication*, Chapter 12). For instance, he showed that what he saw was a matter of *obedience to authority*, not of *conformity to a group* (though his work is often erroneously discussed under the latter heading). If the person who demanded that the "shocks" continue was not a "scientist," but a group of peers (who actually were playing the role of co-experimenters), then the subject was much more likely to refuse to continue. If the effect were a matter of "conformity to a group," the group of peers should also have led the subjects to comply. It didn't. From these explorations, Milgram learned much about obedience in this society (not, by the way, an authoritarian one as societies go), including some of the factors that acted to oppose it.

Now what is Milgram's ethical position here? The question arises on two levels. First, the experiment itself was—we may be glad to note—extremely stressful for the subject "teachers." Milgram says:

> I observed a mature and initially poised businessman enter the laboratory smiling and confident. Within 20 minutes he was reduced to a twitching, stuttering wreck, who was rapidly approaching a point of nervous collapse. He constantly pulled on his earlobe, and twisted his hands. At one point he pushed his fist into his forehead and muttered "Oh God, let's stop it." And yet he continued to respond to every word of the experimenter, and obeyed to the very end (Milgram, 1963, p. 377).

Did Milgram—does anyone—have the right to put unsuspecting volunteers through such an experience?

And yet that is not the only issue. Bad as the experience was, the subjects could be—and were—assured later, at a postexperimental interview or "debrief," that it had all been staged. No one had actually received any shocks at all. No doubt they were much relieved to hear this. But then what? Milgram's subjects walked away from the experiment knowing this: "I was willing to risk harm to another human being, just because someone in authority told me to do so." No "debriefing" could mitigate that knowledge (except to make it clear that most subjects do the same). It was the simple truth.

Might not that knowledge do irreparable damage to the subjects' images of themselves? Actually, most of Milgram's subjects thought not. Most of them felt that they had learned something important and valuable about themselves. But Milgram had no way of knowing in advance that this would be so, and we cannot be certain that it will always be so.*

On the other hand, if we refuse to learn unpleasant truths about ourselves, what hope is there for us? We could well argue that what Milgram found is something we had *better* know and understand about ourselves. But on the other hand again: Is this for us scientists to say?

As I read the situation now, it is the opinion of most psychologists that these experiments would be considered unethical if they were conducted today. The result is an extraordinary situation. The findings and their implications are discussed in every introductory textbook as important information. It is as if we were saying, "The work should not have been done—but it's a good thing that it was. We have learned from it something about ourselves that is of potentially vital importance."

The tension between these considerations—the value of the information on the one hand, and the danger of psychological harm to the subjects on the other—cannot be resolved by a neat formula. What this case study makes clear is that questions of ethics are double-edged ones. What we must do is weigh the ethical costs and risks of doing an experiment against the costs and risks of not doing it. That theme will recur in what follows.

THE RIGHT TO RESPECTFUL TREATMENT

I do not consider myself a lab animal to be experimented upon.

—A STUDENT

This comment was made by a student in a lab course taught by the author some years ago. Students in this class ran some reaction-time, concept-learning, and motor-skills experiments, using each other as subjects. At the end of the semester, that student expressed his outrage in the words quoted above.

Was he overreacting? That is not for me to say. If the student held that view, he had a right to it. I now believe that some alternative to participation in experiments, even in-class ones, should

---

*In fairness, we should note that Milgram was as surprised as anyone else at his initial data. He did not anticipate that normal, decent subjects in the United States would behave as his did. After his first experiment, however, this could no longer be said.

have been made available to that student and others who might feel the same way. Even in a class on research methods, that should have been done.

What of students in introductory classes, many of which require participation in research for course credit? In this case, it is mandatory today that there be an alternative way of fulfilling that requirement; for example, writing a short paper based on library research.

Finally, when a human subject does become a participant in our experiments, she does not surrender any of her rights just because she walks into a laboratory. Full respect for her autonomy requires that if she does us the *favor* of participating—for that is what it is— then she must consent to do so, knowing what she will be doing. Even if she is paid for participating, she should have the job description before her before she signs on. And she may be paid, but not coerced (Principles 6.11c, d; 6.14).

THE PROBLEM OF INFORMED CONSENT

One of the issues that arises here is: When is consent really voluntary? Suppose a student is taking an introductory psychology course—as many do—that requires participation in an experiment as a course requirement. A student will lose credit and grade points if he does not do so. Is his participation truly voluntary, then? And what about the student who, quite simply, does not want to be experimented with? If that is her wish, shouldn't she be allowed to follow it, without having to justify it to the course instructor or anybody else?

The answer is yes. Today, if departments set up a research-participation requirement, they will also set up alternative ways of fulfilling it: a paper, for example, that may describe a series of journal articles that the student will have read.

That solution provides for students who do not want to be in experiments at all. But what about informed consent for a *particular* experiment? This right is compromised whenever the subject is deceived, or is less than fully informed, about the research.

This problem becomes especially acute if the subject has not consented to be a subject in the first place. This happens, as we've seen, when experiments are conducted in a natural setting—for example, the liquid-store robbery experiments (Chapter 7). The subjects may not even know that they are under observation—and it may be important that they not know, since they might behave differently if they do know (observer effects).

In some such cases one can compromise by approaching the subjects after the observations are taken, and asking permission to use their data. (Of course, this *is* a compromise. Even if the subject consents, it still means that he has already revealed something about himself at least to one person—the observer—without having consented to do so.) But this compromise can present difficulties in practice. Suppose we note whether or not at least one member of a crowd offers aid to someone in distress. Do we then approach the members of the crowd to explain the study? *All* of them?

We could argue that the actual data collection is the kind of "naturalistic observation" that does not require informed consent, even if we have manipulated something. For such cases, the informed consent requirement is relaxed (see 6.10). But consider this example (Campbell, 1969). An investigator entered a shoe store. She rejected all the shoes shown her by the beleaguered salesman, whose behavior was observed by another experimenter posing as another shopper. The two experimenters then left the store.

Now it could be argued that in this case nothing happened to the salesman that would not happen anyway in the course of the day. Should the salesman be debriefed? On the one hand, if he is not, then his informed consent has not been obtained even after the fact. Indeed, technically speaking, the investigators may have violated the law against trespass, by which they have permission to enter the store only for the purpose of buying shoes, and such was not their purpose (cf. Silverman, 1975, for a discussion of such legal issues in research). And if the salesman had to neglect actual customers, one could argue that he ought to be reimbursed for loss of potential sales.

On the other hand, as Campbell (1969) points out, "Debriefing would probably not reduce the salesman's frustration, but merely change its target . . . it would be painful to learn he'd been had. Some damage to the future utility of natural settings would result . . . and the possibility of journalistic publicity would be greatly enhanced" (p. 377). In other words, debriefing in such cases could upset the subject and give the profession a black eye, while benefiting no one.

These are the costs of seeking informed consent. They must be weighed against the costs of not doing so: the compromise of the investigator's integrity and the insult to the principle of honesty in human relations.

THE PROBLEM OF PRIVACY

The problem of privacy is closely related to the informed-consent issue. Ideally, the subject should have the right not to reveal anything about himself or herself to an investigator, without having agreed to do so. Thus, we must wonder whether observation of a shoe salesman's behavior, by observers who were interested in behavior rather than shoes, is a violation of the salesman's privacy.

The problem may not be acute if what is observed is in the "public domain," so to speak; that is, if the scientists are observing only what might be observed by any random people-watcher. But what if the observers took movies of the salesman? What if they then showed those movies around the country in discussing their work, or published frames from the movies in journal articles? The APA guidelines are clear in such cases: No such films should be used without the participant's consent, if he or she can be identified. If permission is refused, the films should be destroyed.

Then again, what observations can be considered in the "public domain"? The facial expressions of couples in restaurants may be, but their conversations are certainly intended to be private. Placing hidden microphones to record these conversations would be considered unethical by virtually all investigators. But if we agree about that, then what of the one-way mirrors, often used in conjunction with microphones, through which subjects are observed without their knowledge in some experiments?

The fact is that the line between observing and snooping is a thin one. There are no fixed rules for drawing it. Again, we must weigh the very real ethical costs of such a study against the value of the information it may provide.

THE RIGHT TO CONFIDENTIALITY

"An ethical researcher does not run around saying things like 'Bobby Freshman is stupid; he did more poorly than anyone else in my experiment" (Kantowitz, Roediger, & Elmes, 1994, pp. 89–90). Actually, an ethical researcher would not say anything, good or bad, about any subject's performance. It is simply no one's business. For this reason, a subject's data will typically be kept in some coded form, so that the individual subject cannot be identified.

Even here, though, dilemmas can arise. Take this case, for example: Suppose we plan to compare depressed and nondepressed students on some measure. So a sample of students, who are willing to participate in our experiment, take a paper-and-pencil test of depression.

Now one student, let us say, scores as very severely depressed. Do we inform anyone of this—the student's dean or a counseling service? It is a violation of confidentiality to do so. On the other hand, we may feel that it would be dangerous not to.

In the event, when this happened, in at least one case the investigator did decide that a student's counselor should be informed. Then, under the guise of a routine interview, the counselor did see the student and refer him for help.

THE PROBLEM OF DECEPTION

Here we come to the most difficult issue of a difficult lot, and the one that has given rise to the most heated debate. We dislike liars and lying. Yet there are cases in which research simply would not be meaningful if the subjects knew what it was about. What sort of data would we get if we said to subjects: "We want to know how far you will go in obeying repugnant orders. I am going to tell you to do some lousy things and see whether you do them. . . ." Obviously the data would be useless.

Then there are the cases in which deception is built into the very question one is asking. Consider the experiments on subliminal tapes (Chapter 9). The subjects were very sure that the tapes had helped them—but in the domain they *thought* the tapes were about, not the domain the tapes really were about. Now, the only way we can make that separation—the real content of the tape, and what the subject thinks its content is—is to let the subject think she is listening to one kind of tape, when she is actually listening to another kind. And that's deception!

A similar separation has been made in the study of alcohol's effects on a variety of social behaviors, like aggressiveness or sexual arousal. Many such studies have employed a 2×2 factorial design of the kind shown in Figure 13.3.

This design allows us to see the effect of alcohol itself (comparing rows), and also of the subject's expectations (comparing columns)—that is, what the subject thinks alcohol ought to do. And in a surprising number of such studies, what the subjects think they have drunk has a much greater effect than what they have actually drunk. Again, the only way we can vary these two things indepen-

**What Subjects Thought
They Were Drinking**

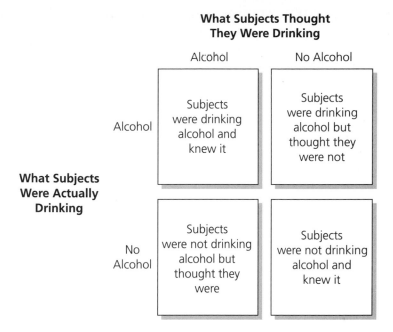

FIGURE 13.3
A placebo-controlled factorial design separates the physiological effects of alcohol from the effects of expectancies. It necessarily involves deception.

dently is (in two of the cells) by leading the subject to think he is drink-ing one thing when he is actually drinking another. Again, that's deception.

Having said that, however, we should introduce a qualification: The doses of alcohol used in these studies were quite low. Why? For ethical reasons! To turn a subject loose from a laboratory session with a high alcohol level would simply be too dangerous. She might have an accident, or hurt herself or others in some way. In this case, clearly, the physical safety of the subject and other people takes precedence over the scientific merits of studying alcohol's effects in large doses. In a hospital setting, where safety can be more closely monitored and assured, such studies can be done.

Thus we see again that the ethical decisions we make are not black-or-white judgments. They are more like cost/benefit analyses. We don't, or at least we shouldn't, ask: Is such-and-such a study ethical? Rather we ask: What are the ethical risks and costs of doing the study, compared with the risks and costs of not doing it? It is important to know whether subliminal tapes are an educational revolution or a fraud. It is important to know to what extent the effect of alcohol on behavior is cognitive, based on expectations, rather than physiological. And in such cases the deception was harmless, and was the sort of deception subjects readily understand when it is explained to them at debriefing. On balance, the gain in knowledge seems worth the cost of lying (temporarily!) to the subjects.

Sending a subject out into the world drunk is quite another matter. Yes, the information gained might be valuable. But that simply does not justify our making a subject drunk and then turning him loose, a danger to himself and others. The balance tips hard the other way in this case.

Is deception then justified when the research question requires it and it presents no danger? Reasonable people have disagreed as to the answer. For some, the maintenance of honest relationships with other human beings and the avoidance of deceptive, manipulative ones is an ethical absolute. Others, recognizing the importance of these values, insist that they must be weighed against "the moral value of producing a nontrivial . . . science" (Campbell, 1969, p. 370). All agree that the use of deception is, or ought to be, a last resort, to be applied only after an investigator has honestly convinced herself that the information to be obtained is important *and* that it is obtainable in no other way. The most recent APA guidelines reflect this consensus (6.15).*

When deception has been used, a debriefing is considered mandatory as an attempt to restore the honesty of the relationship between investigator and subject. Aronson and Carlsmith (1968) comment: "Perhaps the one essential aspect . . . is that the experimenter communicate his own sincerity as a scientist seeking the truth and his own discomfort about the fact that he found it necessary to resort to deception in order to uncover the truth" (p. 31). When taken into the experimenter's confidence in such a way, most subjects understand the necessity of deception and "seem to accept this as part of an implicit bargain" (p. 35).

But the guidelines also say: Deception is admissible only when it is clear that "equally effective alternative procedures that do not use deception are not feasible" (6.15a). Investigators have looked hard for an alternative to deception, in situations where it might appear necessary. Suggestions include such procedures as asking the subject what he *would do* in a situation, rather than imposing the actual situation on him (a curious solution, since the Milgram obedience experiments

---

*But notice clause 6.15b: "Psychologists never deceive research participants about significant aspects that would affect their willingness to participate, such as . . . unpleasant emotional experiences." That would seem to rule out the Milgram obedience experiments today.

that gave rise to much of the controversy in the first place showed how useless the answers would be). A problem with all of them is that we would never know whether they were effective—not until we had done the full-blown experiment, with deception.

Thus, whereas most psychologists would welcome a truly viable alternative to deception, most feel that for certain purposes none is yet in sight. Where there is no alternative, then, is the use of deception justified under any conditions?

I think it unrealistic to expect a simple answer to this question. It confronts us with a conflict between irreconcilable values—just as the public's right to a free press and a defendant's right to a fair trial sometimes collide. Which brings us to the familiar bottom line of this discussion, as of so many others: We must weigh costs against benefits. And we should not do so ourselves, but with advice and guidance from others who are less caught up in the research question than we are. Let us turn to that topic.

OVERSIGHT COMMITTEES—THE IRB

As we'll see in both human and animal research, some razor-edged questions can arise when we weigh the ethical costs against the potential benefits of research. The scientist, involved in her subject matter and eager to gain new knowledge, should not make these judgments alone. Getting a second opinion would be a wise step in any case. And in many countries, including the United States, such a second opinion is mandatory.

In the United States, any institution that receives money from the federal government—which means virtually every research institution—must have an Institutional Review Board, or IRB, that oversees the protection of human subjects (there will be a separate board for animal research, as discussed later). Federal regulations require that any experiment performed be approved, in advance, by the IRB. In practice, this means that an experimenter must submit what is called a "protocol"—a full and detailed statement of what all procedures will be. Then, if a member of the IRB sees problems with subjects' rights or safety, a discussion with the investigator will be in order. In any case, the research cannot proceed without approval by the IRB.

Federal regulations require that each such board have at least five members qualified to review research. There must be at least one member whose area of expertise is in a scientific area, at least one whose area is outside of the sciences, and at least one who has no other

461

FIGURE 13.4
If experimenters cannot give a clear reason for doing the experiment, it will not be permitted. This one would be unlikely to pass an oversight committee.

affiliation with the institution (i.e., a representative of the community at large).

Anyone who has worked with such oversight panels can tell you that they are anything but rubber stamps. They take their responsibilities seriously as protectors of the institution, the subjects, and the scientists themselves. A researcher must be able to defend his procedures, demonstrating to the committee that adequate safeguards are in place for the safety, privacy, and dignity of the participants in his research.

On balance, most researchers agree that such oversight committees serve a valuable function in checking scientists' judgments with their own. Research that seriously violates human subjects' rights or animals' welfare will not be permitted. And research that asks no intelligible question or has no sound rationale simply will not be allowed to pass Go (Figure 13.4). And that is as it should be.

ETHICS IN ANIMAL RESEARCH

It's very easy for agitators to create the impression that mad scientists are doing horrendous stuff to helpless pet kitties when it isn't true at all. They never mention the anesthetics we use or the benefits we obtain.

—VISION RESEARCHER COLIN BLAKEMORE

Our comments to this point have focused on human research. But psychologists use animals in research too, as we have seen. And ethical practice requires that these subjects be treated humanely and, yes, respectfully.

Consider one scientist's comment:

> I remember once seeing the inside of a space rocket and being told by my engineer guide how every inch of space had been utilized and how beautifully minute all the working parts were. The thought that crossed my mind was that there was still space for a goodly number of cockroaches to stow away and that each cockroach has more working parts and was more versatile than the whole rocket (Dethier, 1962, pp. 44–45).

Once we get to know an animal personally—a rat, or even a cockroach—we develop a profound respect for its complexity. We do not like to see such a fine "machine" mistreated.

In the United States, surveys find that a great majority understand the need for animal research, but also feel strongly that animal distress should be minimized and mistreatment abolished. On the other hand, relatively few understand the circle of safeguards that exists to serve just these goals—to protect animals from needless suffering. So let's begin with those.

OVERSIGHT AGENCIES AND THE IACUC

In the United States, the two major government bodies that regulate animal research are the Public Health Service and the Department of Agriculture, the latter operating under the authority of the Laboratory Animal Welfare Act, passed by the U.S. Congress in 1966 and revised several times since. In addition to these, many of the individual states have their own standards and enforcement agencies. And many professional societies publish their own sets of guidelines for proper animal care and use, the APA among them.

The liaison between these oversight agencies and the individual researchers is the Institutional Animal Care and Use Committee, or IACUC (say "EYE-a-kuk"), which every institution (such as a college or university) is required to have if it maintains an animal laboratory. The IACUC must have at least three members: a veterinarian; a practicing scientist familiar with animal research; and a member of the community at large, unconnected with the institution.

Like an IRB, the IACUC must approve any research project before it can begin. Also like an IRB, it is no rubber stamp. It requires—it is required to require—an extensive protocol that specifies exactly how many animals will be used, what will happen to each one, what precautions will be taken to minimize distress (e.g., what anesthetics or analgesics [pain-killers] will be used during and after surgery), and how the animals will be disposed of at the end. It may require the report of a literature search—complete with the keywords used in the search!—to be sure that the proposed research does not needlessly duplicate what has been done. Finally, it requires a clear rationale for the research. "Curiosity" is not enough.

Once the research is approved, it is monitored by frequent IACUC inspections and periodic inspections by the government regulatory agencies. These oversight groups have teeth. Violations of proper procedures can be grounds for stopping an experiment or closing a laboratory. Severe and persisting violations can result in the withdrawal of all federal research support from the *institution*—not merely the individual investigator—so that all researchers at that institution are affected. This step is, of course, last-ditch and extremely rare, but it has happened.

THE THREE Rs

Finally, the IACUCs work with investigators toward the long-term reduction of distress in animal research, guided by what are called the Three Rs: *reduction, refinement,* and *replacement. Reduction* means using fewer animals. This may be achieved by avoiding wasteful duplication of existing research (though the need for *replication* is recognized [Chapter 12]). It also means more efficient experimental designs and analyses. *Refinement* means improved care for those animals that are used, including improved procedures and training of animal personnel and, where possible, concern for animals' psychological as well as physical well-being. *Replacement* means the search for alternatives to research in living animals, and includes such techniques as computer modeling and use of tissue cultures or isolated organs instead of whole animals.

"The three Rs of reduction alternatives, refinement alternatives, and replacement alternatives are considered by many to be the middle ground where scientists and animal welfare advocates can meet to reconcile the interests of human health and animal well-being" (Zurlo & Goldberg, 1998, p. 7).

COSTS AND BENEFITS REVISITED

In many experiments described in this book, animals have been subjected to discomfort for research purposes. They have been made hungry, or have been given electric shock, or have been subjected to surgical operations. Indeed, one of the reasons (but only one) for the use of animals in research is that procedures can be applied to them that cannot be applied to human beings.

Should such procedures be applied even to animals? To most of us, the question again is whether the gain in knowledge outweighs the suffering imposed. That question must be considered separately for each investigation. Once it is decided that the answer is yes, the scientist and her co-workers may develop a self-protective callousness about it, and speak of food deprivation or electric shock with the appearance of casualness. Do not be misled. Few people enjoy making animals suffer, and the laboratory is no place for anyone who does.

The direct human benefits of animal research should not need elaboration (Figure 13.5). Most Nobel prizes in physiology and medicine have been awarded for research with animal subjects. Animal research has led to methods for prevention or treatment of polio, diabetes, strokes . . . the list is long. And today, animal research holds the promise of treating Alzheimer's disease, Parkinson's disease, and many other disorders of the nervous system.

And those are only the *direct*, obvious benefits. It is important to remember that the benefits of animal (or human) research may be very indirect. And as we saw in the last chapter, looking only at the

FIGURE 13.5
This ad was placed by advocates of animal research. Most people in the United States support the view it expresses. The text at the bottom reads: "Without animal research, we couldn't have put an end to smallpox, rubella, and diphtheria. Now some would like to put an end to animal research. Obviously, they don't have cancer, heart disease, or AIDS."

surface of an investigation can make it look trivial even if it isn't, and give a very wrong view of what the research is "about."

Thus many critics of animal research argue that animal experiments are of limited use, because results cannot be generalized across species. Animal findings, in other words, cannot be "generalized to human beings." We have touched on this matter before: The argument rests on a misunderstanding of what it is that is "generalized"—it is not findings, but principles.

Miller (1985) has summarized just a few of the ways in which human beings—and animals as well!—have benefited from application of the *principles* discovered through research using animals. One example: "Experiments on the chemical signals (pheromones) that insects use to attract mates have greatly increased the ability to trap them and to discover the first signs of infestation of a new area by an insect, such as the medfly or gypsy moth, that can devastate orchards or other trees" (p. 424).

Now that's true enough—but there is even more to it than that. Let's take the pheromone example, and back up a few steps.

Before such work could be done, it had to be known that some animals *do* attract mates using chemical signals. That had to be discovered by research. And—working back from there—it had to be discovered that there are such things as *mates*—that is, that some animals, us included, reproduce sexually. That was a major discovery, if we stop to think about it. How did our ancestors ever discover that what two adults do now has any bearing on the appearance of a new neighbor nine months later? Not all adult humans have made the connection even today. It must have taken careful observations and tallying of data to make that momentous discovery. And my guess is that observations in animals with shorter gestation periods may well have played a role.

Let's take one more example, to dramatize the point. Surely one of the most important ideas in the history of medicine is the *germ theory of disease*—that is, that disease may be caused by microscopic organisms. And the research that led most directly to the germ theory was the experimental work of Louis Pasteur in the nineteenth century, using an animal model: the silkworm. The applications have been immense, of course—not because any experimental findings "generalize from silkworms to humans," but because the germ theory does.

Thus the point of animal research is not always to "model" the human case directly. It is to discover principles. It is the principles, not the findings, that "generalize," and open up whole new horizons to explore.

THE ANIMAL RIGHTS MOVEMENT

[Even if animal experimentation would find a cure for AIDS], we'd be against it.

—INGRID NEWKIRK, NATIONAL DIRECTOR AND CO-FOUNDER OF PEOPLE FOR THE ETHICAL TREATMENT OF ANIMALS (PETA)

We have been discussing what we might call the *animal welfare* point of view. It recognizes the importance of animal research (the benefits), but insists that it be done humanely, responsibly, and so as to cause as little distress as possible (the costs). It sees that animal experimentation weighs its costs against its benefits, and it welcomes the Three Rs as guidelines. Most scientists would fit into this camp.

The "animal rights" movement takes a different view. We'll use this term to refer to those who oppose the experimental use of animals at all—as well as other exploitation of animals for human purposes, as when we eat them or steal their furs. To animal-rights advocates, we are not speaking of cost-to-benefit ratios, but of actions that are morally wrong, whatever their benefits may be. Thus: "The animal rights view holds that human utilization of nonhuman animals . . . is wrong in principle and should be abolished in practice. . . . Whatever humans might gain from such utilization (in the form of money or convenience, gustatory delights, or the advancement of knowledge, for example), are and must be ill-gotten" (Regan, 1998, p. 42).

"SPECIESISM"

The principle advocated here is that we should not subordinate the rights of other animals to human desires. Even if the experiments are painless, the argument goes, we have no business intruding into other creatures' lives just to advance our own understanding. We are one species among many. The idea that humans are *automatically* more important than other animals has been called *speciesism,* by analogy to *sexism* or *racism.*

The full implications of these arguments are seldom explored. Do they extend to mosquitoes? Including the mosquitoes that are vectors for deadly yellow fever? And what about bacteria? Shall we stop sterilizing baby bottles and surgical equipment, on the grounds that bacteria have as much right to life as the baby or the patient?

I'm not being facetious here. I am pointing out that we do draw a line somewhere, beyond which we do put human benefit above the rights of other creatures. The debate is about where and, above all, *how* to draw that line.*

MISINFORMATION ABOUT ANIMAL RESEARCH

Many advocates of the animal-rights position argue and demonstrate in responsible ways for their point of view, something they have a perfect right to do. However, in their zeal to discourage animal research, some animal-rights groups have disseminated "information" about research that is so misleading as to constitute outright lies.[†] Much of this reflects the confusion about "generalizing findings" that we have already discussed, but some of it is harder to excuse.

One such group, calling itself Mobilization for Animals (MFA), staged a protest at a meeting of the American Psychological Association in Toronto in 1984. To rally support, they published a statement accusing experimental psychologists of a variety of inhumane practices. So serious were their accusations, and so blatant their falsifications, that a team of psychologists surveyed the literature to reply to them.

Specifically, Coile and Miller (1984) combed through all the articles over the previous five years, in journals published by the American Psychological Association, that dealt with animal research. There were a total of 608 such articles. To put it briefly, *not one* of the abuses listed by MFA appeared *even once* in the published literature over the time in question.

As Coile and Miller note, "It might be argued that the accusations were true but were not reported. But, if the purposes and results were as alleged, there would have been no point in not reporting

---

*On such grounds, many animal-rights advocates restrict their concerns to animals that can think and feel, have beliefs and desires—ones that are, as we say, sentient. But this criterion seems arbitrary—as any criterion will—and it presents obvious difficulties in application. Can a mosquito learn? (I don't know, but it wouldn't surprise me.) If it can, is it sentient? And if it is, what then of the next one that lights on our arm? The philosophical issues that arise here are intriguing and difficult, and I pass them by not because they are unimportant but simply for lack of space. For a very readable introduction to them, see Russow (1999).

†I omit from this discussion the criminal fringe that any reform group is likely to attract. In attempts to prevent the use of animals in research, some animal activists have vandalized laboratories and threatened animal researchers physically. As this is written, a prominent vision researcher in England is literally in hiding after receiving death threats from a group calling itself the Animal Liberation Front. His mail is examined closely, because the police intercepted a wrapped "Christmas gift" for his teenage daughter that turned out to be a cardboard tube filled with high explosives and needles (Hoge, 1999).

them" (p. 700). I would add that there would be no point in doing the experiments at all unless they were intended to be reported. Animal research is expensive and requires grant support, and continued grant support depends in large part on productivity in the form of published research reports. No investigator is going to perform elaborate experiments that are not intended to be made public by reporting them. Nor will he or she perform experiments out of idle curiosity—granting agencies demand a clear and sound rationale for the research they support. The "mad scientist" who torments his subjects out of "idle curiosity" is a mythical beast.

Yet the distortions continue. Medical research is repeatedly hit by them. As just one example, consider the drug Thalidomide, which produced severe birth defects in pregnant women. We are told by animal-rights groups that this effect was missed by the preliminary tests in animals, because animals respond differently from people. But the fact is that Thalidomide was not tested in pregnant animals. Here is a clear case in which more animal research—not less—would have saved real tragedy to thousands of people.

Coile and Miller conclude: "By misleading humane people, the radical animal activists are in fact diverting the energy and funds of humane groups away from areas where animal abuse is common (such as the abandonment of 10 million pet dogs and cats each year to die of starvation, disease, and road accidents) in order to focus upon an area in which it is rare" (p. 701).

Something to think about.

SUMMARY

The scientist, observing the behavior of humans or animals, has ethical obligations to them. Today, this issue is carefully addressed before research begins, by the investigator but also by advisory and oversight groups.

The American Psychological Association (APA) publishes a set of guidelines, updated periodically, for the ethical treatment of human (and animal) research subjects or participants. These seem to me to be based on two ideas. First, the participant has a *right to safety*. He or she may not be subjected to the danger of physical or mental harm, without prior informed consent—that is, he must know the danger(s) and consent to be subjected to them.

Second, the participant has a *right to respectful treatment*. She is entitled to know what she is doing, and has a right not to do it or to stop doing it; the right to quit an experiment is absolute. And she is entitled to protection of her privacy.

In practice, it is not always easy to judge what would violate these rights. Even a harmless experiment in memory or reaction time could do psychological harm if the person leaves the experiment feeling inept or stupid. Still more do we risk harm if the subject is led to believe that he has performed poorly, or that he has committed acts of cruelty (as in the obedience experiments).

What of the cases in which people do not know they are being observed? The line between observing and snooping is a thin one, and no fixed rules for drawing it apply. We must weigh the ethical costs of such a study against the value of the information it provides.

Even more difficult is the problem of deception. Its use may be essential (1) to head off observer effects, as in the case of the Seekers; or (2) to separate actual effects of some manipulations from the effects of expectations, as in exploring the effects of alcohol or of subliminal tapes. The fact remains that it violates the principles of trust that we feel ought to apply to any relationship, including the scientist/participant one.

There is no formula for resolving this tension. We simply have to weigh the ethical costs of doing the proposed investigation against the ethical costs of not doing it—that is, the costs of not obtaining the knowledge the investigation could provide. At minimum, ethical practice requires a postobservation interview or "debrief" when it is possible to conduct one. The researcher takes the participant into her confidence, explaining the reasons for the procedures used, including the need for deception if there was any. Most subjects understand this when it is explained.

Animal research also raises ethical questions. If painful procedures are required, pain must be minimal—and we must first make sure there is truly no alternative way to ask the research question, and that the question is worth asking. In other words, we once again must weigh the costs of doing the research against the benefits the knowledge may provide. For both animal and human research, the investigator does not make these determination by himself. In the United States, virtually every research institution is required to have an Institutional Review Board overseeing human research, and a similar body, the IACUC, for animal research. Research cannot proceed until the oversight board is satisfied that the health and comfort of animals, and the safety, dignity, and privacy of human participants, are protected—or, if they are compromised, that the compromise is minimal, and required by the research. Research that seriously violates human subjects' rights or animals' welfare will not be permitted. And research that asks no intelligible question or has no sound rationale will not be allowed; the stereotype of the scientist who torments her subjects out of "idle curiosity" is a very false one. Finally, IACUCs and investigators seek improvements in animal care and usage, guided by the Three Rs: reduction, refinement, and replacement.

In recent decades, animal-rights groups have objected to the use of animals in research. Some do so on the grounds that animal results cannot be generalized to humans (overlooking the fact that it is principles that "generalize," not findings). Others take the view that other species have as much right as our own to live their lives without interference, and that to think otherwise is "speciesism."

Most scientists have disagreed with these positions, but they also have recognized the right to voice them in public debate. Sometimes, though, this advocacy has taken the form of gross distortions, ones that scientists should be prepared to rebut. And the efforts of animal activists may be drawing attention away from problems of animal suffering that are much more frequent and severe, and very much less necessary.

CHAPTER 14

RESEARCH PSYCHOLOGY, POP PSYCHOLOGY, AND INTUITIVE PSYCHOLOGY

Not everyone is bold enough to make judgments about questions of physics; but everyone—the philosopher and the man in the street—has his opinion on psychological questions and behaves as if he were at least an amateur psychologist.

—SIGMUND FREUD

IN THIS CHAPTER, WE'LL DISCUSS:

■ The ambivalent "image" of psychology in the public mind

■ The myth of "special insight" into others' minds

■ The image of research as trivial, and of psychology as "all a matter of opinion"

■ Distortions of the research process in the media

■ The idea that we are all pretty good "intuitive psychologists" who do not need research findings

- Some limitations of everyday experience as a source of understanding
- Overconfidence in our conclusions
- The advantages of systematically collected data
- Peer review and replication as ways of correcting our mistakes

Psychology has been described as the Rodney Dangerfield of the sciences: It "don't get no respect" (Stanovich, 1998). As I see it, that is not quite right. Often indeed, psychology gets no respect; but sometimes, too, it is respected more than is warranted and for the wrong reasons.

PSYCHOLOGY'S IMAGE PROBLEM

In Figure 14.1, we again present the two popular images of what the psychologist does: therapy or research.

The rat-runner and his little lab partners figure in quite a few cartoons. None of these make clear just *why* he might be running rats. What question is he asking? Where that question is raised about research, often it will focus on the specifics rather than the underlying theoretical issue; and this, as we've seen, can make research look trivial even if it is not. We have not done a good job of explaining what research is "about."

"Are you there now, Linda? Are you in that happy, safe place that brings you peace and assurance, and deep contentment?"

"Oh, not bad. The light comes on, I press the bar, they write me a check. How about you?"

FIGURE 14.1
Again, the two popular stereotypes of psychological research.

As to psychology as a "helping" profession, many people think of psychology as a bunch of theories spun from the armchair, where one person's opinion is as good as another's. And it doesn't help that much of what passes for psychology is, in fact, just like that. Sometimes it is simply unsupported opinion, based on oodles of intuition and no research. If we ask the author "How do you know?" we usually are invited to "see if your experience doesn't confirm this."* That's exactly the kind of "evidence" by which Ray Hyman's subjects "confirmed" the accuracy of palm-reading (Chapter 1)! Or we get "research" that looks very much like what we examined at the beginning of Chapter 8: a nestful of uncontrolled confounded variables.

We can visit any bookstore and learn that *Men Are from Mars, Women Are from Venus* (no wonder there are so many *Women Who Love Too Much*), but that a book can give them the *Courage to Heal*, especially if they *Feel the Fear and Do It Anyway*; and that it will all work out because *I'm OK/You're OK*. And we do not get much guidance in how to distinguish psychology from pseudopsychology from pure baloney.

Mind you, I'm not saying that all such books are worthless. (Though some are, and some do enormous damage; see Ofshe & Watters, 1994.) As with works of fiction, the good ones can put a different perspective on our experience; they can say in effect, "Try looking at it *this* way." We just shouldn't confuse their imagery and intuitions with well-supported data about human behavior.

At the same time, and inconsistently, we credit mental-health professionals (MHPs) with almost magical powers. And certainly some practitioners (not all!) have claimed powers for themselves that would indeed be magical—if the claims were justified. All too often they are not. At times, they cross the border into sheer absurdity. Thus:

> In my mind, I know what she was thinking and feeling at the time of her death.

This from a Harvard professor of psychiatry, testifying at a trial for child abuse following the child's suicide. (We need go no further than Chapter 2 here. Just how does the practitioner know that? If he was wrong, how would he discover *that*?)

---

*One author (Gray, 1992) safeguards himself against even this feeble test: If you don't find that your experience confirms his ideas, he says, you must not have examined your experience closely enough. So the theory wins, either way.

Or the therapist on "Good Morning, America":

I can spot it as a person walks in the door. . . . There's a certain body language . . . [that identifies a person as an incest victim].

We've been through that one (Chapter 10) as a signal-detection problem. Has the therapist checked her false-alarm rate?*

Another recovered-memory team gives us a list of "warning signs," typical of patients whom they diagnosed as abused. Checks for these "signs" include questions like: "Do you feel different from other people? Are you afraid to succeed? Do you have trouble feeling motivated?" (quoted by Ofshe & Watters, 1994, p. 31). (Do the answers to such questions really differ as between abused persons and nonabused persons? Or might they apply to just about everybody? No such comparison was made; see Chapter 3).

How can professionals make such claims? One reason—and it is worth remembering—is that many highly trained, fully credentialed MHPs have had *no training at all in research methods*. They may simply not understand what it takes to support a claim. You yourself, Reader, now that you've worked through this book, are already better equipped than many professionals to evaluate the claims that some (not all!) professionals make—as we saw in the above examples.

Then too, all too many professionals simply aren't familiar with what research has taught us. Thus: "The subconscious mind has a memory bank of everything we ever experienced, exactly as we perceived it. Every thought, emotion, word, taste, and sight. Everything is faithfully recorded somehow in your mind. Your subconscious mind's memory is perfect, infallible"—a remark (by a licensed psychologist) that simply ignores all we have learned about memory in the past century.

Or, from a psychiatrist: "Events thus relegated to the unconscious remain unaltered unless they are hypnotically recovered and reinserted into the stream of consciousness." The effects of hypnosis on *suggestibility* were already well known to the research community when this was written.

Professionals competent in research would have known about the Clever Hans effect, and the "facilitated communication" embarrassment would have been averted (Chapter 5). They would have known about implanted memories, and false imprisonments and

---

*Both these remarks are quoted by Dawes (1994, p. 8).

shattered lives would have been avoided (Chapter 8). Real tragedies can occur if we don't know when we're wrong.

MHPs who make such claims will often justify them with the further claim that their years of experience give them a special "clinical insight" into people's minds, making it unnecessary to test their conclusions. Now, this is itself a testable assertion. If it were true, then effectiveness as a therapist should increase with experience; that is, effectiveness and years of experience should be positively correlated. There is now a very large research literature that shows that they are not. Experience does *not* make one a better therapist— surprising as that may be. This is not my opinion, or anyone else's; it is a consistent empirical finding, supported by a mass of data.

This doesn't mean that therapists are inept. On average, they do help people, as we saw earlier (Chapter 12). It just means that (1) they are not magicians, and (2) the claim to special "clinical insight" based on experience, made by some (not all!) practitioners, is largely myth. The danger is that many MHPs *believe* the myth—as do many of the rest of us. (For further discussion see Dawes, 1994; Stanovich, 1998.)

THE INTUITIVE PSYCHOLOGIST

There's yet another reason for the dismissal of psychology by intelligent people. We may simply feel that it is not needed. We understand ourselves and others quite well enough now, thank you kindly.

We are all "intuitive psychologists," in this sense: We have been dealing with other people all our lives; we have had extensive experience with them; and we are able to say, within limits but with reasonable confidence, what sorts of things to expect from them. In that sense, we have (or think we have) intuitive understanding of what makes people tick.

Nonetheless, I am going to suggest that, in fact, personal experience is *not* a very reliable guide to a real understanding of ourselves and others; and that there are good reasons why this should be so. It is a very good source of the *illusion* of understanding—that comforting feeling that we understand, when we do not.

This may sound arrogant. That's ironic, because later I will suggest that it is quite the opposite—it counsels modesty in the conclusions we draw from our daily lives and the confidence we place in them. The fact is that our daily lives offer many ways in which we can draw wrong conclusions—"things we know that aren't so." There are whole books about this alone (e.g., Gilovich, 1991; Nisbett & Ross, 1980; Stanovich, 1998), and much of it we have spoken of before in this book. Looking again in this context will serve as a "look backward" over where you and I have been.

PERSONAL EXPERIENCE AND ITS PITFALLS

Why is personal experience suspect? Because of confounded variables (Chapter 8) and uncontrolled observer effects and observer bias (Chapter 5); because it focuses on positive instances rather than comparisons (Chapter 3); and perhaps above all, because it does not test its conclusions in a way that would show them to be false if in fact they are (Chapter 2). And so we are much too confident of our conclusions. We resist changing our minds; and so our ideas resist change, even for the better (Chapter 1).

Why do we fall into these traps? For one thing, we are busy. We have only so much time and energy to expend in checking our conclusions and gathering data. Basing our beliefs and judgments on a thorough gathering and weighing of evidence could take too long, and often would not be worth it, for ordinary living. This is one reason why the scientist, who does have time and whose "ordinary living" is devoted to the task, will in the long run be a more reliable guide. We will circle back to that idea too at the end of this chapter.

CORRELATION, CAUSALITY, AND CONFOUNDING

If we see that some Y varies with some X, and we want to say that X causes Y, we must be sure that nothing else (Z) varies along with X that could cause Y instead. If some Z does vary with X, then the effects of X and Z are *confounded*.

SOME CASE STUDIES

Return to the example we began this book with: The notion, which once was just "common sense," that women are intellectually unsuited for higher education. Now, there were data from everyday experience that could support that idea—women once were, on average, less interested in, and less accomplished at, intellectual pursuits. But how to interpret that? Is it a male–female difference (the "common sense" of not long ago)? Or is it an effect of differences of encouragement and opportunity? When we unconfound these, by moving toward equality of encouragement and opportunity, we find that women can in fact handle a college curriculum just fine. Common sense was dead wrong.

Similar controversy has swirled around the issue of race and IQ. There is about a 15-point average difference between IQ scores for African Americans and for Caucasian Americans. That difference is *there*; no one can seriously dispute it. The problem is: What does it mean? Does it reflect a genetic difference, or is it the result of systematic exclusion and deprivation? The two are confounded. And it is extremely difficult to unconfound them—to *control for* one or the other. But it is true (and the statistics tell us this, too) that as we come closer to providing equality of opportunity and encouragement, that 15-point difference has a way of shrinking (e.g., Scarr & Weinberg, 1976).

CAUSAL EXPLANATION AND THE THE GOOD STORY HEURISTIC

Why do we so often overlook the problem of confounded variables, even obvious ones? I have a modest suggestion to make.

We want to be able to explain things to ourselves. We like the feeling of understanding. But also, we're busy, and we can only afford so much time and effort in seeking explanations. As a compromise, we may adopt what I call the *Good Story heuristic* (a *heuristic* is a rule of thumb). This rule of thumb says: Find a plausible explanation for the event in question—one that makes a Good Story. Then stop thinking. Rest content with that explanation and go on about your business.

What happens then when we confront a set of correlational data? There are two stages. First, we look for a causal theory, a Good Story that helps us feel, rightly or wrongly, that we understand the correlation. Very often someone will offer us a plausible theory to account for it. (She might say: Why do the races differ in IQ? Because some races are smarter than others, that's why.) But if not, we will invent our own (see for example Taylor, 1989). Then we *believe the theory*—we feel that the task of explanation is done, and no further thought is required—so we do not think the matter through any further, to see that other explanations are just as possible.

A study the author conducted with Timothy Wilson lends some support to this idea. College students, all of whom had heard the correlation-and-causality problem discussed in class, were asked to explain a correlation between two variables, X and Y. Almost without exception, these students gave the three possibilities; maybe X causes Y, maybe Y causes X, or maybe they do not affect each other at all but some third variable, Z, causes both. So far so good.

For other students the problem was logically the same: Two variables were correlated with each other. But this time the variables had *names*. The amount that art history majors drank per week, for example, was described as positively correlated with the amount of studying they did per week. What explanations could our (real) students give for that?*

The difference was dramatic. Where subjects in the "X-Y" group gave all three likely interpretations, most subjects in the "named variables" group offered only one explanation *and then stopped*. It is as if, having constructed a plausible scenario—a Good Story—by which one named variable could cause another, they felt that the job of explanation was done. No further thought was required. The X-Y group, on the other hand, had no concrete material from which to spin a causal story, and had to think the problem through logically. Then, all three possibilities were easy to see.

Clearly, such students were perfectly capable of seeing the ambiguities of correlational data. They understood, in the abstract, that correlation does not imply causality, and why. But in concrete instances, a Good Story—a specific scenario by which something could plausibly cause something else—preempted this knowledge. The invented scenario took over.

In short, while we can *say* "Correlation does not imply causality" as often as we like, we may simply *not bring that caution to mind* when faced with a real-world instance of correlation. (See the "pop-up principle" later.) Rather, we invent a causal theory (because we like to have explanations) and then rest content with it (because we're busy). And so we omit the crucial step for the scientist: *checking our conclusions* (Chapter 2).

"NATURAL CONFOUNDS"

In the everyday world, some variables will inevitably be confounded with others. We really cannot see which of them is actually doing

---

*Many of the examples we gave were bizarre ones like that, in hope that our students, having trouble finding a causal explanation, would be more likely to consider all three possible interpretations. We underestimated our students' ingenuity at inventing causal connections. In this case, one student suggested the following: Maybe hard-drinking students want to do well at art history so they'll have something to talk about at cocktail parties!

the work, unless we *create* a situation that separates them. No amount of "experience" in natural settings will do the job.

The "subliminal tapes" story is an example (Chapter 9). A person feels that his French has improved after a subliminal course of instruction. Does he feel that way because of the tapes, or because of his expectations? We have no way of knowing, as long as what he thinks is on the tape really *is* on the tape. We must create mislabeled tapes to separate the two possibilities.

Similarly for the Therapeutic Touch practitioner (Chapter 2). In any natural situation, where a practitioner is "looking" for an energy field emanating from another person, she will *know where that field ought to be.* To decide whether she really detects an energy field, or only thinks she does, we must create an artificial situation in which that knowledge is taken away. Emily Rosa's experiment did just that. The "facilitated communication" idea was exposed by similar artificial separations (Chapter 5).

SAMPLING BIAS

An important source of our personal experience is the people whom we observe and talk to. If we draw conclusions about human nature based on these, we are in effect generalizing from a sample (the people we encounter) to a population (people in general). But there is every reason to suppose that the people we encounter will make up a sharply biased sample. It is likely, for instance, that the people who are our neighbors and co-workers and friends will be roughly similar to ourselves in socioeconomic status. A homeless person meets more homeless people, and fewer suburbanites, than the suburbanite does. This may be one reason why we consistently overestimate the extent to which other people believe as we do or would act as we do (see Gilovich, 1991).

Thus our sample of *persons* is biased. So are our samples of *behavior*. We see "samples" of a person's behavior, and from these we draw conclusions about the kind of person he is (the "population" of his actions). From this we predict how he would likely react in other situations as well.

But what if the sample of behavior is biased? For a concrete example, consider the interview situation. A candidate (for a job or college or whatever) is very much on the spot. She is likely to be tense and nervous. She is engaged in a task ("impress the interviewer"), and the skills required for that task may be very different from those required for successful performance on the job or in school. Her behavior during the interview may not be at all "representative" of what it is like in other settings. And *we know this*. But we insist on interviewing anyway. The fact is that interviews have very low predictive validity—and no wonder! The only thing surprising is that we continue to depend so heavily on them in making decisions on such matters as hiring or admission to college.

Now sometimes we do correct for this sampling bias. We would not marry someone after a single date, if only because we know that a "first date" evening (1) gives us too small and limited a sample of the other person's actions, attitudes, and values; and (2) gives us too biased a sample, because the other person is likely to be putting his or her best foot forward for us to admire.

But do we apply that kind of good sense consistently? We do not. Indeed, the conclusions we draw can be influenced by data even if we *know* them to be biased. Later, we'll see an experimental demonstration of this (pp. 499–500).

In short, our personal experience gives us biased samples both of persons and of their actions. We should temper our generalizations accordingly. Sometimes we do. Often we do not.

OBSERVER EFFECTS

Back when we first discussed control procedures, we discussed two ways in which a researcher might get misleading data. First, he could affect what happens in an unintended way—*observer effects*. Second, he could distort how he sees it happening—*observer bias*. But these are problems not only for the researcher. They can lead all of us to draw wrong conclusions from our everyday observations. Let's consider observer effects first.

One way to make sure that our theories will be supported by life's events is to *make* life's events support them. Here we meet the famous *self-fulfilling prophesy*.

Suppose a person believes that she is no good at math and will do poorly in a math class. She may fail to study—and thus do poorly, so her low opinion of herself (right or wrong) is supported.

Suppose her math professor also believes that she is—or that women in general are—poor at math. He may be reluctant to help the student, or he may make his encounters with her unpleasant. She may not receive the help she needs and, again, do poorly—so *his* low opinion of her (right or wrong) is supported (Figure 14.2).

"I see by your résumé that you're a woman."

FIGURE 14.2
Stereotypes can easily create self-fulfilling prophesies.

Another real-life example, and a grimmer one, is the false memory syndrome (Chapter 8). A well-meaning but incompetent therapist may "uncover memories" of childhood abuse that, *in some cases*, turn out to be demonstrably false. The therapist may never consider that he might not have "uncovered" these memories, but *implanted* them himself. And he may be unaware of the data which *show* that this can happen.

OBSERVER BIAS I:
PRECONCEPTIONS AND SELF-DELUSION

Where observer effects are distortions in what actually happens, observer biases are distortions in how we see it happening. And a theme that has occurred over and over in this book is just this: How often and how easily we can delude ourselves, seeing what we expect to see—whether it's there or not.

Therapeutic Touch practitioners were convinced that they could detect a human being's "energy field." But they couldn't (Chapter 2). Subjects were convinced that subliminal tapes had raised their self-esteem. They hadn't (Chapter 9). James Randi's listeners "confirmed" his imaginary flying lights (Chapter 5).

And so on.

OBSERVER BIAS II:
AVAILABILITY AND THE POP-UP PRINCIPLE

Besides tending to see what we expect to see, we tend to see what is most obvious and to remember what is most memorable. Thus the obvious and the memorable are most *available* to us as things to think about, when we think about our everyday experience. This is technically known as the *availability heuristic*, but I call it the *"pop-up principle"*: What is most vivid or memorable, or most closely associated with the situation, is most likely to "pop up" into mind when we try to think about something.

THE POP-UP PRINCIPLE

The trouble is that the information most available may not be the most accurate. An example? Give a quick, intuitive answer to this one, before reading on: Which is more frequent, death by drowning or death by fire?

If you answered "death by fire," you are as wrong as most people who are asked that question. Death by drowning is far more frequent. But drownings seldom get much press, unless of course the victim is a celebrity. Fires do. So deaths by fire are more available—they *pop up* more readily into our minds—and we inflate the risk we associate with them.

The effect of this is that we may worry about, or draw conclusions from, very rare events if they are events that come quickly to mind. One survey (MacDonald, 1990) of what parents worried about most where their children were concerned, found them to be more worried about kidnapping than about death in a car crash, though the latter was over 100 times more likely to occur.

THE POP-UP THEORY

There is another way the pop-up principle can throw us off the track. That is by reminding us of a theory or a preconception, when (and only when) it is confirmed. It works like this:

Suppose we have read or been told that redheads have hot tempers. Will our experience confirm this? We see a redhead responding violently to some emergency, and the theory pops up into mind: "Yes. This is a redhead and she does have a hot temper." But suppose we see a redhead enduring the slings and arrows with calm efficiency. Do we tally that in our mental notebook on the negative side? Quite possibly not, simply because *the theory may not come to mind at all*. We are busy, remember. We can't be thinking about the feisty-redhead theory all the time. And so whereas we may notice positive instances *as* positive, we may fail to relate negative ones to the theory at all, because it does not pop up into mind when they occur.*

THE POP-UP CONFIRMATION

A theory can look well supported, when it isn't, in another way. Rather than having a theory pop into mind when a confirming instance occurs, we may begin with the theory and search our memories for confirming instances. And *they* will pop into mind.

Hyman's palmistry experiment, that we met early on, is an example (Chapter 1). Suppose we are told, "Your palm says you're an introvert; are you?" We search our memories looking for evidence of introversion, and find it. "Your palm says you're an extrovert; are you?" We search our memories looking for evidence of extroversion, and find that. Thus we go about our business with the comforting feeling that our ideas are supported by experience, even if they are not—because the supporting data, but not the contradictory ones, pop readily into mind.

THE POP-UP GALLERY: FOLK WISDOM

Now let's consider a phenomenon that illustrates the point especially well. This is the collection of "principles" variously known as Folk Wisdom, or What They Say, or Things Grandmother Could Have Told Us. Together, they offer us a comforting "explanation" for any event whatever. Like Stanovich's little-green-men theory (Chapter 2), folk wisdom can never, ever be shown to be wrong.

Suppose two lovers are separated for a long time. Do they break up? Well, that's just common sense: "Out of sight, out of mind" pops up. Does the relationship endure instead? Just common sense: "Absence makes the heart grow fonder" pops up.

A person grabs impulsively at a business venture without checking it out thoroughly first. Does he thrive and prosper? Common

---

*All this is aside from the fact that we also need a tally of *placid nonredheads* to complete our fourfold table, and thus know whether redheads are more feisty *per capita* than anyone else (Chapter 3). *That* fact—that we need these seemingly irrelevant data—will almost certainly not pop into mind, unless we have formed the habit of looking at such questions in such a way.

sense: "He who hesitates is lost," or "Strike while the iron is hot." Does it turn out disastrously? Common sense: "Look before you leap."

Birds of a feather flock together, but opposites attract. A stitch in time saves nine, but let's cross that bridge when we come to it. And so on . . . and on.

See how it works? We have a collection of folk sayings, organized neatly into pairs like that (but no fair comparing the members of a pair with each other). No matter what happens, a saying that covers it will pop up into mind. And so the episode will be seen as nicely confirming folk wisdom. We can easily forget that the opposite outcome would have popped the opposite Wise Old Saying into mind, and confirmed folk wisdom just as nicely. Thus we have a body of "knowledge" that could survive *any* test, and therefore cannot be tested at all. It is good only for the illusion of understanding.

OBSERVER BIAS III:
THE RESEMBLANCE PRINCIPLE

In searching our memories or thinking about a problem, we assume implicitly (without thinking about it) that the most available memories are the most important—the pop-up principle. There's another implicit assumption we often make, and that is that certain things naturally "go with" certain others. It's often called the *representativeness heuristic*, but we will call it the *resemblance principle*. We are likely to assume that actors resemble their actions, that causes resemble their effects, that things that are similar in one way are similar in others. The part is *representative* of the whole—hence the term.

One example of this is the *halo effect*. This the tendency for persons high in one "good" attribute to be judged high in others too. Good qualities "should" go with good people; bad qualities, with bad people. In one experimental demonstration of this (Dion, 1972), a child's misbehavior was judged as a worse offense if an ugly child committed it than if an attractive child did, though the offense was the same. And the ugly child was judged more likely to misbehave again.

Another example of this kind of thinking is the "just world hypothesis." If actions "should" resemble actors, consequences "should" resemble the actions. Good things should follow good actions, and we implicitly assume that they usually do; that people tend to get what they deserve (Lerner & Miller, 1978). This assumption reached absurd heights in a public statement by an official of the U.S. Department of Education in the 1980s. Handicapped individuals, he told us, "falsely assume that the lottery of life has penalized them at random. This is not so. Nothing comes to an individual that he has not, at some point in his development, summoned. . . . [A] person's external circumstances do fit his level of inner spiritual development" (quoted by Gilovich, 1991, pp. 143–144).

As Gilovich wryly notes, "This is not exactly the philosophy that one would want in the upper reaches of the . . . department that is responsible for overseeing educational opportunities for the handicapped." We also wonder how that official would have responded to our questions: How do you know? Why do you think so? Are your reasons good ones?

DEFENDING OUR BELIEFS: COGNITIVE CONSERVATISM

Earlier, we suggested that a natural tendency when looking at data is to spin an explanatory theory (because we like explanations), and then to stop thinking about the matter (because we're busy). Thus we miss confounded variables and alternative explanations. But there is an important exception to this. It shows just how good we can be at spotting confounded variables or alternative explanations. This happens when the data *challenge* our preconceptions. Thus:

> One of the authors, in his first years of teaching, was amazed and disturbed by the tendency of many of his female undergraduate students to maintain negative stereotypes of their mathematical abilities even though their successes belied such stereotypes. Often, a student would succeed admirably in a statistics course that, on the first day of class, she had tearfully predicted she would fail. Such a student usually proved capable of readily assimilating her unanticipated success to her previous view of herself, assigning credit to the lucidity and patience of the instructor, to her strenuous efforts, or to the "easiness" of the course. It was quite difficult to get such a student to entertain the possibility that her previous theory about herself was simply wrong (Nisbett & Ross, 1980, pp. 143–144).

We like to understand things (or to feel as if we do), but we do not like to spend a lot of time and energy thinking through alternatives or testing the "Good Stories" for truth. Still less do we like to go back and *rethink* a conclusion we've already reached. So we resist changing our minds, a tendency that has been called *cognitive conservatism* (Greenwald, 1980).

Take a student whose self-concept contains the belief "I can't do math." If she must drop that belief, she will have to modify her self-concept appropriately. It may be easier to hold onto the belief and dismiss the contrary evidence. So in the example, rather than dismantle and rebuild her beliefs about herself, the woman inferred that her success was due to luck and effort, not to ability. Thus the belief could stay as it was.

Explaining away contrary data, then, is one way to keep from having to change our beliefs. Another is to let our beliefs color the information we take in. We saw an example earlier: Subjects who watched a videotape, thinking they were seeing a job candidate, saw the person as poised and thoughtful. Those who watched the same videotape but thought they were watching a patient, saw him as hostile and denying. Of course, these interpretations supported the watchers' existing beliefs about what patients, or job candidates, are like.

Once information is taken in, we can work on our memories to make *them* fit our beliefs. In a word, we can and do rewrite our memories. We saw some instances of this earlier too, in connection with eyewitness testimony and the false memory syndrome. We need to be aware that such distortions of memory are very real, and, as in the false memory syndrome, are capable of doing enormous damage.

Finally, there is what historian Barbara Tuchman (1984) has called *wooden-headedness*. This is a simple failure (or refusal) to consider what the data imply for our theories. It says: "My mind is made up. Don't confuse me with facts." We saw an example earlier in the case of the Seekers, a group of rational, intelligent people—like you and me—who nonetheless persisted in their belief, despite the clearest possible evidence that it was false.

OVERCONFIDENCE

We have noted before that in the busy world in which we live, we don't have time for careful and thorough investigation prior to forming beliefs and opinions. We compromise by accepting biased samples and observations that may be contaminated by our own actions (observer effects). We base our opinions partly on quick-and-dirty rules of thumb (availability and resemblance) that may bias our observations. Having drawn a conclusion, we find that supporting evidence pops readily into mind, whereas disconfirming evidence may be overlooked. So may alternative explanations of the data, if the first explanation tells a Good Story and lets us rest content.

It all makes it look so *easy* to draw conclusions from our experiences! Perhaps it is this, plus the fact that we can defend our conclusions against challenge, that leads to a pervasive *overconfidence* in the things we think we know (Figure 14.3). Perhaps it is this more than anything else that stands in the way of our knowing when we're wrong, and so correcting our errors.

There is plenty of evidence for overconfidence in daily life. Think about the college students who were certain, three years later, that they remembered how and where they had heard about the *Challenger* explosion—their memories were clear and vivid, as if the scene were lit up by a flashbulb. They were overconfident: Their clear and vivid memories were as likely as not to be flat wrong. Or think about the Therapeutic Touch practitioners, who were *certain* they could detect human energy fields—but could not.

How about you and me? We are routinely overconfident about how quickly we can finish a task, like writing a book or a term paper. That remains true after years of experience, during which time you'd think we'd learn! But it seems we don't.

"What do you mean 'Your guess is as good as mine'? My guess is a hell of a lot __better__ than your guess!"

FIGURE 14.3
Overconfidence in our abilities, judgments, and memories can make us feel that we don't need to check our conclusions. But then we don't know when we're wrong.

We are overconfident in our predictions—even about ourselves. In one study, Vallone, Griffin, Lin, and Ross (1990) asked students to predict, at the beginning of the school year, whether or how often they would do various things: call home, drop a course, vote in the November election, and the like. The subjects also rated how *confident* they were in their predictions. Those ratings averaged about 84%. But accuracy, checked at the end of the year, was only about 71%. Even the predictions that were rated 100% sure things were correct only 85% of the time.

Finally, we are overconfident of the accuracy of our explanations. Let's look more closely at one experiment (among many) that show this very clearly (see Nisbett & Ross, 1980).

In this experiment, subjects (college students) were divided into two groups. Subjects in one group were told about some (fictitious) data, showing that success as a firefighter was *negatively* correlated with risk-taking tendencies, as measured by a paper-and-pencil test. The *best* firefighters were the ones who scored *most cautious*. The subjects were asked to write down an explanation for those findings. They had no trouble doing so, of course: a burning building is a dangerous, unpredictable place where it is important to proceed with caution.

The other subjects were told that the data had shown the opposite. Success as a firefighter was *positively* correlated with risk-taking. The *best* firefighters were the *least cautious*. These subjects had no trouble explaining *that*. Firefighters have to take risks to save lives and property; that is what they are paid for. A timid firefighter who will not face danger is not doing his job.

Then came the crucial step: The subjects all were told that the information given them was bogus. There had been no such study, and it is not known whether the correlation would be positive or negative if it were determined. Then the subjects were asked: What do you think the correlation *would be*, *if* it were to be determined in an actual study? Would it be positive or negative?

Overwhelmingly, the subjects argued that the relationship they had been told about was the one that would actually be found. Thus the subjects who had been told the correlation was negative now said, in effect: Of course the relationship would be negative! Who could possibly think otherwise? Well, the subjects in the other condition could, that's who. They said just as firmly: Of course the relationship would be positive! Who could be silly enough to doubt it?

The important point is not that the subjects could spin a Good Story to account for either a positive or a negative relationship. (Though this should give us pause when we dismiss a research finding as "obvious common sense." Would we have said the same thing if the data had shown the opposite?) Rather it is the confident adoption of one conception of the relationship, together with a *confident discounting of the other possibility that was, in fact, just as plausible.* And we know that because the subjects who were given that "other possibility" held to it with just as much vigor.

← A LOOK BACK

I beseech you . . . consider that ye may be mistaken.

—OLIVER CROMWELL

In skimming over the problems of "personal experience" as a source of belief or knowledge, we have met a number of old enemies—confounded variables, sampling bias, observer bias, and more. And we see that they can lead not only the research scientist, but also the intuitive psychologist, to conclusions that are simply wrong.

We are forced to the conclusion that "personal experience" or "intuition based on experience" simply *is not a very reliable guide to an understanding of each other or of ourselves.*

Now, just what am I saying? That we should draw no conclusions about anything until we have gathered systematic data—with unbiased samples of humankind, all needed comparisons incorporated, and controls for observer bias in place? Of course not. If nothing else, who would have time? Nor am I suggesting that we approach new experiences with no preconceptions. Even if we could do that, think what it would mean. We would have to approach each new restaurant, meet each new professor, as if we knew nothing about how to behave in the one or toward the other. We could not bring our general knowledge—knowledge about this or that kind of thing—to bear on new instances. Surely that would be a recipe for paralysis, and it's not what I am suggesting.

Rather I am suggesting two things. One is that we use our understanding of these pitfalls to combat *overconfidence*. Perhaps we can form the habit of alerting ourselves to these sources of mistakes, and hold our conclusions, not as the Last Word to be defended, but tentatively and subject to correction—as a scientist does. That is what I meant in remarking earlier that I counsel not arrogance but humility—that we consider that, indeed, we may be mistaken.

Second, I am suggesting that "personal experience" just doesn't stand up against systematically collected data, controlling for biases, based on many cases, and incorporating the needed comparisons.

Where such data exist, we should not automatically swallow them whole, but we should take them seriously—especially if they challenge our beliefs.

Let's see why.

THE SCIENTIST'S ADVANTAGES

It is not what the scientist believes that distinguishes him, but how and why he believes it.

—BERTRAND RUSSELL

We have seen that personal experience or everyday observation has limitations: biases, confounded variables, and missing comparisons can lead us astray. Am I suggesting then that the research scientist is somehow immune to these errors? That would be arrogant indeed!

But no. I am suggesting quite the opposite—the scientist is fully as subject to these errors as anyone else. The difference is (1) that the *scientist knows it* and tries to remember it, and (2) that she often knows how to *do something about* these ways of being misled.

Training in research, in other words, makes available a set of cognitive skills or mental habits. These amount to being *alert to* the ways in which we can draw wrong conclusions, and to some of the ways of avoiding these traps. (Whether at a given time a person uses his available skills—well, that is another matter. We all fail to use our heads at times—scientists along with the rest of us.)

HABITS OF THE HEAD

Because of his training and experience, a scientist has developed certain *ways of thinking* that have become habitual. Certain ideas are readily *available* to him, as habits of thought. It is because of this availability—not because he is smarter than anyone else—that certain ideas, problems, and perhaps solutions will "pop up" into his mind when he thinks about data or theories or their interplay. Let's see some examples.

"IT'S AN EMPIRICAL QUESTION."

I am often struck by how often, in conversation, a point will be argued on which there is, or ought to be, an empirical answer—that is, for which there ought to be data available so that we can *look and see*. Very often the argument will proceed in a vacuum. That we could go to the data, and find out, seems to come as a whole new idea.

As one example, we are often told that one needs religious beliefs as a basis for standards of ethics and morality. This is argued pro and con (e.g., Kaminer, 1995), and it does not seem to occur to either side that this is a researchable question: Do people who identify themselves as religious *in fact* profess higher moral standards, or behave in more ethical ways, than people who don't? In fact, there are quite a few studies out there, and they suggest that the answer is no.

The point is that the mindset—the habit of asking, What are the facts? Can we look and see?—*is* a habit. It is not automatically *available* for use where it could be of help. Training in this habit of the head can make it more so.

SYSTEMATIC DATA COLLECTION

When we draw a conclusion based on our experience, our tendency is to notice, and then remember, events that confirm it. We're not in the habit of actively looking for cases that might prove us wrong. The practicing scientist does just that.

Back in Chapter 2, we looked at an idea that is fundamental to the enterprise: the notion of *falsifiability* (pp. 32–35), or knowing when we're wrong. Even if we pile up oodles of confirming instances, still we do not know that the theory is correct. But even *one* disconfirming finding—if it is reliable (Chapter 11)—tells us that something is wrong. The theory thus challenged may need to be modified, or qualified (it may hold under certain conditions but not others), or perhaps discarded—but we know that we cannot rest content with it. In short, a search for disconfirming evidence is simply *more efficient* than totting up tallies of confirming instances.

Of course, if we are to see these important disconfirming findings, they must be tallied when they happen. We cannot allow a theory to "pop up" into mind when a confirming instance happens, and remain asleep when a disconfirming instance does. Yet exactly this is what we tend to do in our busy everyday lives.

The trained scientist also will have in mind the importance of *comparison* (Chapter 3). If we ask, "Do redheads have hot tempers?" the scientist will realize that the question, despite its form, is *not a question about redheads*. It is really asking: "Do redheads tend to have hotter tempers *than the rest of us*?" Tallying instances of feisty redheads will not tell us this. We need observations on "the rest of us"—

including a tally of those placid brunettes we have met before (pp. 60–62).

Finally, the scientist knows that she is not immune to biases and may, as observer, have unintended effects on what she observes. She will adopt specific procedural safeguards, to keep *observer effects* and *observer bias* from distorting her observations. *Sampling bias* too is a problem for some investigations; and where it is, the scientist has ready to mind some methods for dealing with it.

"IT'S OUR BEST CONCLUSION—FOR NOW"

The theory of the Big Bang, like the theory of evolution, is so well supported that we can consider it a fact in science, if we define fact as something so well supported that it would be perverse to withhold our provisional assent.

—MICHAEL SHERMER

Our tendency is to lock on to a Good Story and, having done so, place too much confidence in it and resist changing our minds. Here, perhaps, is the greatest difference between scientists' and nonscientists' habits of the head. The scientist holds his conclusions tentatively, as ones that are consistent with the data *thus far*, but are subject to correction as further data come in (Figure 14.4). He gives them what Shermer calls "provisional assent."

Not that this is always a calm, dispassionate process. A scientist— of course!—may fall in love with a pet theory as easily as anyone else. When contrary data come in, he may challenge them or try to explain them away. Even so, what he will *not* do is ignore them. If the contrary data continue to pile up and cannot be explained away, then sooner or later even the most cherished theory must respect them—and give way. The *self-corrective* nature of science will correct even the stubbornness of individual scientists, in the long run.

FIGURE 14.4
A lesson in modesty, perhaps?

THE BACKSTOPS: PEER REVIEW
AND REPLICATION

Any individual investigation can reach a wrong conclusion. A scientist can make a mistake, like anyone else. Or simple chance fluctuations may produce an error of Type I, a false alarm, or Type II, a miss (Chapter 7). However, even then there are "backstops" in the scientific community that provide some further safeguards.

PEER REVIEW

When a scientist completes a study, she will write a full report of it, with detailed descriptions of what was done, what was found, and how she interprets her results. That report will go to a scientific journal, and the editor will send it off to one or more practicing scientists in that research area. These are known as "reviewers," and they are the author's scientific "peers." Hence this practice is known as *peer review*.

The reviewers will read the report carefully. If there are mistakes in the method, or if the results don't really support the conclusions, there is a very good chance that the reviewers will spot these flaws. They will write back to the editor and the author, recommending either that the research be improved and a new report submitted; or, if the research is really bad, that it be flatly rejected. A research study will be published in a peer-reviewed journal only if the reviewers and the editor are satisfied that its methods are adequate and its conclusions sound.

This can be of help to the research consumer, too. One question we can ask when offered a conclusion is this: Has the research been published in a peer-reviewed scientific journal? If it has, we know that it has survived at least *some* inspection by people who are trained at separating good from bad research. Indeed, one commentator (Stanovich, 1998) states it as a rule: If the "latest scientific breakthrough" has not passed the test of peer review, it's a good sign that the breakthrough is bogus.

REPLICATION AND VERIFICATION

The report of a research study will include a full description of the methods that were used and the results that were obtained. That means that *everything a scientist says is subject to verification by others*.

This is a tremendously important safeguard. It means that in the long run, frauds or honest mistakes will be detected. Other scientists will repeat, or *replicate*, the experiments to see if they can obtain the same results. If they cannot—then we know that something is wrong.

In the physical sciences, this happened not long ago with the notorious "cold fusion" experiments. A team of researchers reported a tremendously exciting discovery (the details don't matter). But the first thing that happened was that other teams of scientists, all over the world, repeated the experiments and tried to verify the results. They couldn't verify them. The results simply didn't hold up. And so it became apparent, very quickly, that the original claims had been mistaken.

In psychology, the subliminal tapes story is an example. Given the claim that one could learn (say) French while snoring away, many teams of scientists tried to verify the claim. They could not. These repeated failures make it pretty clear that something was wrong with the original claims, for they simply do not hold up. The replication process has shown us that.

This sort of thing has happened repeatedly in, for example, the literature on parapsychology. Time and again, this scenario has been played out: Researchers have claimed to demonstrate some paranormal phenomenon. Other scientists, inspecting their methods, have realized that those methods do not rule out other, perfectly normal explanations of the findings. So they have repeated the experiments, *adding the necessary controls*—which simply means changing the experiment so that normal explanations *would* be ruled out if the findings held up. But they have not held up. And so we strongly suspect that the original findings did have perfectly normal explanations.

Despite more than a century of effort, researchers have not given us a single solid, *replicable* demonstration of a paranormal phenomenon. Not one. Claims have been made over and over, but if they cannot hold up under replication, then the chances are that they are—well, simply wrong. And thus far they have not yet held up. Not once.

Therefore, here is a second question we can ask when we are offered "information." We can ask: Has the research been independently replicated by other scientists? If it has, then it is likely—not guaranteed, but likely—that it is sound.

However, all this does not mean that we don't need to develop our own critical habits of the head. We do. That's because we are offered a great deal of "information" in ways that bypass the inspection process. A bogus researcher may, rather than submit to peer review, go directly to the local newspapers or television with his "breakthrough." He may write for general circulation magazines. He may write a book, and the book may be reviewed, but not by scientists. In all such cases—and they abound—it is up to the reader to ask: What evidence is offered to back up this "advice" or "information"? And is it *good* evidence? To think about these matters intelligently, we need well-developed "baloney detectors" (Sagan, 1995) of our very own.

← A LOOK BACK

In this section, we have seen how the scientist can avoid some of the errors of the "intuitive psychologist." This is not because he is smarter, but simply because he is aware of the sources of error and of what sorts of things can be done about them. If he makes a mistake anyway—and he may—further quality control is offered by the whole scientific community, in the form of peer review and replication.

The result is just this: Well-done systematic research is simply *more reliable*, as a guide to knowledge, than the "experience" of everyday life. Not that even good researchers do not make mistakes. They do. But they will make fewer, in the long run. And when they do, others may catch those mistakes either before they are announced (peer review), or after (replication). Further research will correct these; so, knowing when we are wrong, we will correct our mistakes, again in the long run.

If we are willing to do so.

And that, Gentle Reader, brings us full circle. Our ideas change—and they improve, if we check our ideas, know when we're wrong, and allow our errors to be corrected. That's what science is.

I have enjoyed writing this book—truly! If you have comments, by all means pass them on to me. And good luck to you.

SUMMARY

The public image of psychology is ambivalent and contradictory. On the one hand, it is widely believed that psychologists and others in the mental health professions have a special insight, honed by clinical experience, into the causes of our actions. Many mental health professionals believe this too, but the evidence does not support it.

On the other hand, in the public view, psychologists run rats through mazes or do other "trivial" research. Few are aware of the solid body of knowledge that research offers us, and too few know how to distinguish good research from bad. It doesn't help that many "experts" offer unsupported opinions that are well publicized, lending credibility to the notion that psychology is "just a bunch of opinions." In part, this is because too many credentialed professionals know little about research and its pitfalls—that is, about what it takes to support a conclusion.

Most of us think of ourselves as pretty good "intuitive psychologists" who do not need research findings in order to understand ourselves or others; personal experience is enough. But much of this "understanding" is illusory, for personal experience has limitations. Many of these we have met before: sampling bias, observer effects (as in "self-fulfilling prophesies"), or observer bias that can easily lead to self-delusion. Then there are confounded variables, as in the correlation-and-causality fallacy. In some cases, two or more variables will necessarily vary with each other in the real world ("natural confounds"), so that we really need an artificial situation to separate their effects.

There are also our tendencies to notice, remember, and call to mind the evidence that supports our preconceptions, and to save ourselves time and trouble by jumping to a single explanation of what we observe (a Good Story), rather than exploring alternatives. Or, among our various preconceptions there may be one or more that would fit any possible event, so that our storehouse of preconceptions will be "verified" and "validated" no matter what happens. "Folk wisdom" provides many examples. And we seem to operate with the unexamined assumption that like goes with like: Effects resemble causes, actions resemble the actor (the "similarity principle").

The result of all this is a tendency to be overconfident about our preconceptions. They can look much better supported than they are. In fact, though, all the sources of distortion we've considered should make us much more willing to "consider that [we] may be mistaken," and be willing to change our minds if well-conducted research tells us we should.

For another consequence of all these pitfalls is that our everyday observations cannot stand up against systematic scientific data. This is not because scientists are smarter than anyone else, but because they are trained to be aware of the traps and of what can be done about them. Conclusions are held tentatively, subject to further observations, rather than dogmatically. Finally, the scientist's conclusions are checked by others, through peer review before they are made public, and through replication afterward.

The result is that science is simply a more reliable guide to knowledge than everyday experience is. It makes mistakes—of course! But the mistakes are likely to be detected in the long run, so, knowing when we are wrong, we will correct our mistakes. That is the great strength of the scientific method.

MAKING FRIENDS WITH STATISTICS:
WHEN IS A PROBLEM A STATISTICAL PROBLEM?

The race is not always to the swift nor the battle to the strong—but that's the way to bet.

—DAMON RUNYON

Like psychology itself, statistics has a double image in the popular mind. On the one hand, statistics are "cold, hard, unfeeling, and inhuman." But statistical *statements* are "soft and squishy." We want to know: Does smoking cause cancer? If we get an answer like, "Well, it's more likely if you smoke than if you don't," we get hungry less than two hours later. We want a straight answer, not an evasion like that! (We *might* even say, "Whaddya mean? I know a Person Who . . ."!)

But we can't always have what we want. And if a problem is in fact a statistical problem, then we need to think of it as one as we work it out. It is soft and squishy thinking not to.

FREQUENCIES VERSUS STEREOTYPES

Here's a little demonstration you can try on your friends.

The author has a friend. This friend is short and balding, and writes poetry in his spare time. Question: Which is he more likely to be: a teacher of psychology, or of Chinese?

The phrase "more likely," of course,

makes this a problem in judging *probability*. Yet you'll find that many of your friends reply either "A teacher of Chinese" or else "There's no way to judge."

But there is. He is much more likely to be a teacher of psychology than a teacher of Chinese. Why? (1) Because there *are* more teachers of psychology than of Chinese, and (2) because the author meets more teachers of psychology than of Chinese, and so is more likely to make friends with them.

We tend to overlook these quite obvious facts, and give a wrong answer. Why? Because we *do not treat the problem as a question of probability*. We turn it into a question of *resemblance*: "Which does that description resemble more—my stereotype of a psychologist, or my stereotype of a Chinese scholar?" If we do that, we will neglect what statisticians call the "base rates" and what we've called the *frequency distribution*—that is, how many people or events there *are* in each of the relevant categories. But "base rate" information is what one needs to use, in order to make sensible probability estimates.

Look at it this way. The frequency distribution of the author's friends will include many more tallies for psychologist than for Chinese scholar. If we sample one case at random, we are necessarily more likely to sample a psychologist. Simple. But we miss it.

We've seen a number of instances of this sort of thing. The dreaded "person-who" argument, and its relatives the brickbat and the testimonial, depend on a similar mechanism: Rather than the base rates, we tend to focus on the vivid, dramatic, person-who (smoked and lived a long healthy life, or bought a Brand-X car that gave nothing but trouble, or was cured by a crystal, and so on—and on).

These are imaginary examples, but a large number of real ones also show the lure of the single case. A classic experimental demonstration was as follows (Hamill, Wilson, & Nisbett, 1980). In one condition, subjects were given a vivid description of a single case of a woman on welfare, a Ms. Santana:

> [The description] painted a vivid picture of social pathology. The central figure was an obese . . . and irresponsible Puerto Rican woman who had been on welfare for many years. Middle-aged now, she had lived with a succession of "husbands," typically also unemployed, and had bore children by each of them. . . . Her children showed little promise of rising above their origins. They attended school off and on and had begun to run afoul of the law in their early teens, with the older children now thoroughly enmeshed in a life of heroin, numbers-running and welfare.

In a second condition, the article was omitted. Instead, the subjects were given accurate statistical summaries, showing for example that the average stay on welfare for the middle aged was only about two years (subjects originally had thought it was about ten years).

Now, the statistical information was clearly more informative than any single case could possibly be. What can you tell from one case? Not much, of course—but it had an impact anyway! The experimenters measured the subjects' attitudes toward welfare recipients in general, before and after exposure to the information. It was found that exposure to the vivid story moved subjects' attitudes toward welfare recipients downward. In contrast, the abstract statistical information had little effect on attitude. This was so even though it was shown, by questionnaires after the experiment, that the subjects did remember the statistical data (a manipulation check! p. 220). So it was not that they were bored by the statistical information and tuned it out. They were just not much affected by it. But similar subjects were very much moved by the close to useless, but concrete and vivid, single instance.

That's scary enough, but there is worse. The subjects who were given the horror story about Ms. Santana were in turn divided into two groups. One group was told, specifically, that the case was typical of welfare recipients. The other group was told, specifically (and truthfully), that it was *not* typical (and they registered and remembered that information too). It didn't matter (Figure 14.5). Subjects who knew the case was atypical were as much affected by the concrete, vivid description as were those who thought it was the norm.

It seems that the subjects were thrown off the track by a variation of the "person who" argument. If we're not used to visualizing statistical trends (see later discussion), we visualize instead a "person

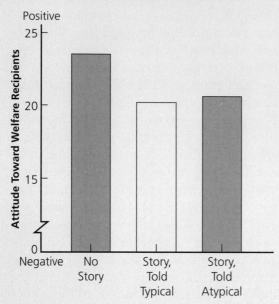

FIGURE 14.5
Mean attitudes toward welfare recipients in general, in the Hamill, Wilson, and Nisbett experiment. A vivid story led to less favorable attitudes, even in subjects who were told specifically that the story described an atypical case (data from Hamill, Wilson, & Nisbett, 1980).

who," and think in terms of that image thereafter—just as your friends do if they visualize the author's friend, and judge whom the image most resembles, psychologist or Chinese scholar. It is harder (without practice) to generate an image of abstract statistical data, even if those data are much more informative.

IN DEFENSE OF STATISTICS: THREE BUM RAPS

If we're going to think straight about statistics, we ought to be prepared to meet certain objections to statistical thinking. Here we'll consider three of them. I think

all three are mistaken, and I'll tell you why.

STATISTICS AND INDIVIDUALS

What we are discussing is the difference between two sources of information: (1) base rates, correlations, and other statistical summaries, and (2) "persons who." At this point we may hear, "Well, statistical trends don't apply to individuals."

Tell insurance companies that. True, they make no attempt to predict whether a given *individual* will or will not have (say) an accident. But probabilities—statistical trends—are precisely what *do* apply to individuals. If you and I are statistically at "high risk" for accident, then you and I, as individuals, will be charged higher premiums. And rightly so, because we are *more likely* to have accidents—a statement about probabilities, based on statistical trends, that *is* applied to individuals right in their pocketbooks.

Actually, what the remark probably means is that for any statistical prediction, there will be "persons who" exceptions, for whom the prediction is way off. That's true. But "person who" arguments will lead to mistakes too, and they will be bigger and more frequent mistakes—on average! And if errors are costly, in money or in human unhappiness, that means a lot.

THE "DEHUMANIZATION" OBJECTION

In comparing statistical trends with living individuals, there is another objection one meets very frequently. That is ". . . that making predictions about people using statistical formulas is 'dehumanizing,' that

"Ah, Mr. Bromley. Nice to put a face on a disease."

FIGURE 14.6
A doctor can use the most objective methods available and still be humane and caring.

it treats people as 'mere numbers.' There is nothing in the approach that implies a judgment about what people *are;* the point is to make the best possible predictions, which can then be used to everyone's benefit" (Dawes, 1994, p. 103).

Statistical summaries can sound like something cold and inhumane. But this reaction confuses the method with its user. A cold and inhuman computer is doing the number crunching, perhaps. But no one says that statistical judgment must be *used* in a cold and inhumane way.

Suppose a doctor is afraid that you might have cancer. So he runs some tests to find out. Now, let's assume that the doctor is a humane and caring one, who treats you as the individual you are (Figure 14.6). Indeed, suppose further that he,

like you, desperately hopes that you do *not* have cancer.

But would you want that hope to influence his diagnosis? Wouldn't you want that diagnosis to be based on the most accurate, *objective* information we can get? I certainly would. If the diagnosis is positive, both we and any humane doctor will be upset by this—of course! But if we are armed with the most accurate information we can get, then we'll be in the best position to decide what to do about it. Isn't that what we want?

"YOU CAN USE STATISTICS TO PROVE ANYTHING!"

This is quite false if taken literally (there are no statistics to prove that light can't travel in a vacuum). But it is a reaction to the *misuse* of statistics that unfortunately is common.

To overlook confounded variables, or (a special case of this) to jump from correlational data to causal conclusions, is a mistake we see over and over again. Perhaps it is this that leads many of us to throw up our hands and say, "You can use statistics to prove anything!"

But the problem is not with the statistics. It is with the conclusions we draw from them. Perhaps we could think more clearly if a different aphorism gained currency instead: "Statistics don't lie, but they don't interpret either." *We* must do the interpreting, and we may do it very badly.

We might also do well to keep in mind yet another popular one-liner, which is sadly true: "Figures don't lie, but liars figure."

CODA

Roommate: So what are you saying, Doug? That statistics are infallible?
Author: Why, no. Neither is a hammer.

—OVERHEARD IN A CHAT ROOM

VISUALIZING STATISTICS

Suppose it's true, as I have suggested, that a major source of mistakes is our tendency to think in concrete images rather than statistical trends. One wonders, then: What if we were in the habit of *visualizing statistical information concretely*?

Your author has formed that habit. If I'm told, for example, that the *average* stay on welfare is about two years, I visualize a frequency distribution—a bar graph—centered at two years, but with bars to the left and to the right of that, their heights trailing off as we move from the center. Then it's easy to see that if we take a sample of one case from the whole distribution—why, sometimes we'll sample from the tail of that distribution and come up with a Ms. Santana! The whole bar graph is unaffected by this, and any one case does not show us what the whole thing is like.

Or: If told that poor Elmer Blugg suffered from some difficulty, and a crystal cured him, I again visualize a frequency distribution, comparing (say) crystal users and nonusers in the proportion of cases improved or not improved. Mr. Blugg could be one of the users who improved, even if only a few did. Or we might visualize a scatterplot, with dosage of preparation J on the horizontal X axis and therapeutic outcome on the vertical Y axis. Then if Mr. Blugg takes a lot of preparation J and has a good outcome, we're invited to think of the two variables as correlated (Figure 14.7A). But if we visualize the whole scatterplot, we see at once that Mr. Blugg's data point could be the same even if the X–Y correlation were precisely zero (Figure 14.7B). And if all we know about is Mr.Blugg's data, we don't know which is the case. Another testimonial bites the dust.

That idea underlies the visual, geometric approach to statistics that I have used throughout this book. I want the reader

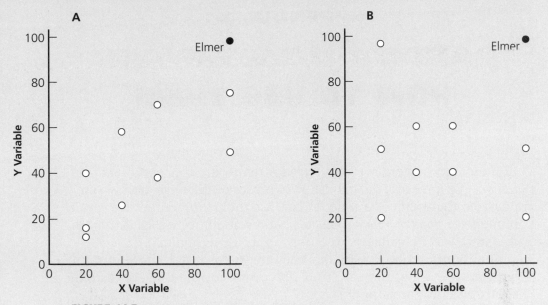

FIGURE 14.7
Elmer Blugg may be a "person who" scores high on both X and Y; but that doesn't show that X and Y are correlated.

to *see* the way we summarize data statistically, and how we can read information from those visual images—information about the general case, and about how individual data points are related to it. I hope it has been helpful here and will continue to be, in the many, many cases the reader will encounter.

APPENDIX A

RANDOM NUMBERS AND HOW TO USE THEM

In previous chapters, we've referred often to the concept of *randomization*. We have also distinguished two uses of the term, and we emphasized that is important not to confuse them. Sometimes we speak of *random sampling from a population*, and sometimes we speak of *random assignment* of subjects to groups in an experiment.

Random number tables, like the one in Table A.1, are useful for both purposes, but they are used differently for the two. Let us talk about random sampling first.

RANDOM SAMPLING

Suppose we wish to select a sample at random from some specified population. Table A.1 is a random series of two-digit numbers, from 00 through 99.

Let's assume for now that we have a *population* (not a sample) of no more than 100 cases. (If we do have a larger population than that, we can just take the numbers in pairs; thus the first entry in the table will become 7917. Then we can handle populations of up to 10,000 members [0000 through 9999]).

Specifically, suppose we have a classroom with no more than 100 people in it; that is our population. Suppose we want to draw a sample of 20 cases at random. The first step would be to let everyone in the classroom be assigned a number, 0 through 99; we might let the members of the class just "count off" around the room. Then, we look at the random number table and enter it anyplace. We might close our eyes and point with a pen. I have done that, and my pen came down on the third entry in the first row: 78. So Person Number 78 will be included in my sample. Then I could just continue around the table from there: Persons 71, 21, 28 . . . and so on until there were 20 numbers selected. (If a number were repeated, of course, I'd ignore the duplicate.) Then, if we go back and select the real people who correspond to the numbers 78, 71, and so on, we know we will have selected an *unbiased* sample of the population in question: the people in this room.

It doesn't matter where we enter the table, or, having entered it, whether we move to the right or down or diagonally. However we do it, a random number table is one in which the probability that *any* given number will appear at *any* position is the same for all numbers.

If the sample is very large, there are shortcuts. Suppose, for example, we define our population as *all students enrolled in our college,* and that there are much more than a hundred of these. Rather than assigning a number to each one, which would be tedious, we might go to *multistage random sampling* (see Chapter 5). We might get out the student directory. Suppose, for simplicity, that it turns out to have exactly 90 pages. Then we can take a random sample of those pages. The procedure would be the same as before: We would go to the random number table, enter it anywhere, and read off the next 20 digits from that point of entry, ignoring any entries greater than 90. That gives us a sample of *page numbers,* and that is the first stage of our multistage sampling procedure. The second stage would be to select one individual at random within each selected page.

What if the individuals to be sampled cannot be identified in advance? In the previous examples, we had a list of students in the class, or we had the student directory. But what if there is no such list? What if, for example, we wish to sample from the population "students emerging from our college's library between noon and 1 P.M. today," to note whether male and female students carry their books differently? (Remember that our population is whatever we say it is. In this case, we're choosing a population for convenience—library users at our college at the noon hour—but we still want a random sample of cases within that population we have defined. Why? Because a random sample is unbiased! See Chapter 5).

In such a case, *systematic random sampling* can be helpful. Let's go back to our random number table, and as before, enter it anywhere. Suppose my pencil points to the 7th entry in the first row—49. I will consider that as two digits, 4 and 9 (we'll see why in a minute). So, starting the following day at noon, we would tally the fourth person we saw leave the library, and every ninth person after that, until the hour is up. (And now you see why we consider the table entry as two digits for this purpose! If we had had to wait until the 49th person emerged from the library to begin our observations, we might not have had much observation time left.) This procedure, of course, can be repeated any number of times, until we have the total number of observations we require.

RANDOM ASSIGNMENT

Now let's talk about *random assignment* to experimental conditions. Remember that this is a different problem. We assume that we have already selected the people who are going to be subjects in our experiment, and now the only question is: Who is going to be assigned to what experimental condition? For simplicity, we'll assume that we're doing a between-groups design throughout this discussion.

Here again there are two possibilities: We know in advance who our subjects are going to be, or we do not. If we do, we can make the assignments in advance.

Let's suppose that we have three experimental conditions, and we have before us a list of 30 subjects who agreed to participate. Suppose we want to have 10 subjects in each of our three groups. The simplest way to make the assignment is as follows.

We first number our groups arbitrarily, as Group 1, Group 2, and Group 3. Then we consider our list of subjects three at a time. We start anywhere in the random number table and read along, considering only the numbers 1, 2, and 3. Other numbers are ignored.

Suppose the first of these numbers we come to is a 3. That tells us to assign the first subject on our list to Group 3. Then we continue to read along in the table, looking for 2 or 1. If the next number we come to is 1, then our second subject goes to Group 1. And then, of course, our third subject has to go to Group 2, so we are finished with our first block of 3 subjects. We do the same thing with the next three subjects, and continue until all blocks of three have received their random assignments, one to each of the three groups.

Of course, if we had four groups, we'd consider the numbers 1, 2, 3, and 4. If we had only two groups, then we might only consider numbers 1 and 2 in the table. Or, alternatively, we could consider any odd number as telling us to assign the first subject to Group 1 and the second subject to Group 2; whereas an even number would tell us to do the reverse. We proceed similarly through all pairs of subjects, until all of them have been assigned.

In the two-group case, flipping a coin for each pair of subjects would do just as well. Heads, the first subject goes to Group 1 and her pairmate goes to group 2; tails she goes to Group 2 and her pairmate goes to Group 1; and similarly for all remaining pairs of subjects.

Then there are the cases in which we do not know in advance who our subjects are to be. Then, of course, we can't assign treatment conditions to our subjects until they actually appear. What we can do, however, is make up in advance a schedule, or "protocol," that tells us what treatment each subject should receive, whoever he or she may be. The procedure would be just as before: If we have two conditions, we consider our subjects in groups of two (first and second, third and fourth, etc.). If our first random number is even, then the first subject who comes along will be assigned to Condition 1, and the second subject who comes along will go to Condition 2. If the first number is odd, we reverse these assignments. Similarly for the second number and the second two subjects; and so on for all subjects.

Thus our experiment might be concerned with men who have chosen to cross a swaying, dangerous bridge (Chapter 11). One member of our experimental team is going to interview each subject. But for each one, shall the interview be conducted right away, or after a delay (the independent variable)? We won't know who a given subject is until he comes along. But we do know, if we've set up our protocol in advance, which of the first two subjects who shows up is going to be interviewed at once, and which will be interviewed later. Similarly for the next two (the third and fourth subjects who come along); and so on for as many subjects as we've decided we need.

TABLE A.1
Random Numbers

79	17	78	71	21	28	49	08	47	79
17	33	72	97	86	45	44	65	97	29
27	65	06	82	98	28	36	03	72	93
33	57	70	34	39	91	78	99	64	53
76	81	31	42	31	04	00	10	82	13
27	72	54	77	94	97	92	56	20	98
97	95	39	36	02	43	10	08	19	00
87	84	51	57	65	03	46	70	94	69
40	80	05	81	12	90	02	90	44	38
21	90	78	37	47	61	92	69	35	30
40	61	04	23	42	76	72	13	08	83
59	02	28	10	82	77	75	89	13	34
91	37	80	64	61	39	19	38	91	28
24	42	44	77	45	44	03	46	25	94
66	49	81	89	88	40	81	60	25	26
57	55	52	54	53	31	49	38	14	72
83	26	59	05	42	05	89	74	68	10
16	97	26	84	41	14	94	94	94	03
53	16	08	29	29	28	19	28	01	83
87	73	84	55	94	57	52	68	56	90
56	55	60	96	53	21	18	59	55	86
83	59	56	38	86	84	07	40	77	20
37	39	88	49	43	00	49	13	02	51
14	20	68	04	90	94	70	05	83	10
11	16	82	54	39	36	56	00	52	07
46	97	32	82	63	13	42	30	20	64
25	04	76	44	88	19	61	20	56	97
05	54	35	78	93	94	17	15	28	07
16	87	66	77	22	06	50	76	95	09
67	78	65	43	99	96	82	04	48	30
50	70	46	81	33	52	89	59	09	49
57	90	31	77	96	04	97	17	87	54
51	85	26	99	70	46	88	58	00	99
45	07	47	13	64	79	44	06	15	07
46	72	46	81	14	12	17	48	07	33
04	62	90	98	01	48	00	54	91	65
75	83	67	58	01	28	14	42	41	00
84	72	63	83	39	67	62	67	28	05
61	91	27	17	24	76	64	22	20	75
01	05	20	78	51	19	23	31	44	61
71	71	55	10	29	62	30	90	52	04
08	98	57	51	73	55	96	67	02	36
57	83	20	73	45	93	21	48	23	95

TABLE A.1 Random Numbers (*continued*)

33	51	57	26	11	16	82	56	63	55
10	35	48	50	12	09	09	83	81	46
26	07	34	35	97	89	11	71	88	75
94	08	05	65	43	55	83	00	20	64
03	80	52	12	55	86	62	79	39	72
50	86	61	36	18	43	48	01	71	04
24	58	31	51	91	55	43	43	17	27
76	96	32	12	33	99	74	96	26	65
41	63	83	68	38	74	97	45	30	82
22	25	34	52	80	38	18	62	53	15
79	88	43	73	32	02	38	51	22	47
28	37	38	51	44	13	10	03	18	97
95	09	89	59	94	87	96	44	55	82
53	37	57	01	72	33	79	00	85	10
84	83	02	29	98	81	77	79	49	28
86	67	93	57	32	17	50	69	42	12
18	61	05	12	59	12	71	25	42	60
26	09	16	23	90	39	33	49	11	64
48	83	61	38	67	06	46	03	18	83
88	46	69	96	53	83	10	91	06	15
89	34	46	69	45	65	42	29	04	04
58	06	18	26	65	07	55	36	54	05
85	87	13	15	14	37	25	31	61	36
01	81	81	80	61	99	67	81	14	25
14	46	11	80	94	45	75	84	92	28
17	04	08	18	02	51	04	84	31	76
79	72	38	16	74	54	22	00	51	22
71	17	12	26	47	03	30	51	27	95
08	64	24	69	14	90	49	53	37	89
65	79	53	49	56	27	20	15	10	59
33	13	86	60	94	48	27	27	98	84
14	78	26	31	01	57	02	92	55	81
56	57	03	39	92	45	53	36	69	25
42	54	21	57	40	71	99	66	91	48
93	10	88	86	67	14	03	16	38	89
32	61	47	42	04	94	25	65	84	76
60	44	66	51	94	34	21	32	12	86
06	70	13	90	90	05	68	01	98	87
76	38	70	73	55	62	94	24	47	06
66	22	83	26	59	77	97	79	04	97
80	38	89	80	14	96	13	64	16	12
51	16	75	12	20	77	85	30	59	76
87	74	55	86	74	38	76	81	30	94

TABLE A.1 Random Numbers (*continued*)

00	16	08	49	50	55	59	33	65	93
75	61	81	62	03	92	94	27	41	67
23	87	37	06	08	56	34	86	06	86
41	48	68	45	23	89	04	83	37	38
84	34	63	36	22	31	02	53	42	53
35	20	23	20	76	56	73	88	60	17
80	49	38	13	41	00	93	37	62	53
70	35	78	06	05	91	52	81	98	14
33	14	40	54	94	39	20	69	69	15
54	42	74	80	12	98	76	28	42	91
30	55	14	38	26	06	33	44	94	24
96	28	58	93	82	45	63	13	15	79
85	46	30	34	09	39	37	55	46	01
53	57	10	83	57	51	79	05	90	76
17	19	89	90	27	01	50	84	55	09
40	09	81	67	07	32	52	40	68	71
49	17	66	61	97	30	20	66	54	53
22	32	35	81	47	32	70	73	87	77
89	97	08	70	87	39	11	40	15	46
46	74	00	02	80	39	85	92	57	65
42	75	86	23	09	75	28	28	40	73
94	43	80	48	64	63	01	02	80	22
54	72	93	31	34	07	50	42	60	66
55	16	04	74	47	21	43	16	70	89
07	92	33	15	38	36	86	79	95	71
54	11	73	86	13	49	10	10	89	36
05	52	32	81	69	27	76	65	87	73
93	65	64	46	20	42	68	34	85	95
09	38	86	01	19	06	94	71	04	16
71	01	97	48	42	07	38	90	53	56
37	65	03	46	22	79	31	84	70	20
04	81	54	72	34	51	85	03	07	83
13	57	23	30	11	58	68	32	83	96
67	61	33	63	86	59	14	58	99	17
60	35	99	45	88	44	76	17	69	96
22	03	82	01	22	27	58	50	89	24
87	30	73	72	02	93	22	09	27	89
99	94	97	86	75	02	95	33	44	88
45	52	41	35	79	56	51	82	60	26
41	94	12	01	61	24	15	62	89	77
52	14	05	73	11	94	46	70	97	64
60	00	84	59	49	21	31	13	02	92
39	68	23	26	03	47	31	65	19	44

TABLE A.1 Random Numbers (*continued*)

75	13	26	61	84	80	01	03	68	47
27	97	18	67	27	04	78	25	08	44
91	57	66	46	33	86	53	92	06	18
01	27	28	26	57	42	54	96	59	57
27	20	92	69	21	66	61	26	42	49
02	50	90	88	07	29	00	31	28	37
18	65	98	52	80	62	69	95	93	15
78	03	44	65	65	95	79	40	18	16
38	35	22	57	31	12	26	91	84	06
64	57	05	57	88	08	43	09	09	86
36	45	40	89	71	45	92	65	10	93
76	15	46	64	02	20	02	70	80	04
80	46	64	08	14	05	97	40	14	91
44	06	76	09	27	64	96	16	88	45
40	96	57	18	29	57	93	17	51	16
22	44	15	74	06	20	01	87	96	41
73	74	62	72	62	44	14	80	35	21
40	80	02	83	30	70	32	71	67	55
80	18	00	89	50	03	36	98	28	43
00	58	81	60	69	31	04	00	72	88
42	90	04	88	39	50	08	68	83	05
17	67	53	59	58	16	77	35	69	27
65	79	70	89	83	92	93	52	67	42
67	44	99	46	06	68	99	61	51	59
95	97	55	13	90	37	34	05	22	59
92	66	90	62	13	82	06	53	82	34
75	48	61	03	24	99	44	91	39	42
61	44	61	22	16	78	68	61	63	39
43	55	63	52	90	27	81	38	62	62
05	01	10	11	11	23	68	48	83	09
25	81	88	75	58	95	52	75	23	56

APPENDIX B.1

BINOMIAL PROBABILITIES

This table shows the probability that, for a given number of "cases" (e.g., tosses of an honest coin), a given number of "exceptional cases" *or fewer* will occur. Thus if five out of six coins landed heads, the remaining "tails" coin would be one "exception." The table tells us that the probability of obtaining *five or more* heads—that is, either *one or zero* tails—is 0.109. (Decimal points are omitted from the table.)

We can use this table for any situation that is analogous to a coin-tossing one: There are two possibilities for each "case," and the null hypothesis is that the two are equally likely (Chapter 2). Thus:

1. A coin may land heads *or* tails, and each is equally likely for an honest coin.

2. A baby monkey may choose a cloth *or* a wire mother, and each is equally likely.

3. A person may judge that another person's hand is close to her own left *or* right hand, and she is as likely to judge one as the other.

And so on.

NUMBER OF CASES	NUMBER OF EXCEPTIONS								
	0	1	2	3	4	5	6	7	8
5	031	188							
6	016	109	344						
7	008	062	227						
8	004	035	145	363					
9	002	020	090	254					
10	001	011	055	172	377				
11		006	033	113	274				
12		003	019	073	194				
13		002	011	046	133	291			
14		001	006	029	090	212			
15			004	018	059	151			
16			002	011	038	105	227		
17			001	006	025	072	166		
18			001	004	015	048	119	240	
19				002	010	032	084	180	
20				001	006	021	058	132	252

APPENDIX B.2

CRITICAL VALUE OF F

This table can handle up to 7 independent treatment groups. To use it, decide your level of significance (.01, .05, or .10). Determine degrees of freedom for the numerator (number of groups minus 1), and degrees of freedom for the denominator (sum of the number of subjects, minus one, in each group). The table then gives the value of F that must be *exceeded* to be significant at the specified level.

Thus if we have three treatment groups with 10 subjects each, we have 2 df for the numerator and $9 + 9 + 9 = 27$ df for the denominator. If we set our significance criterion at .05, we need an F larger than 3.36.

DENOM-INATOR df	SIGNIF-ICANCE LEVEL	NUMERATOR DEGREES OF FREEDOM					
		1	2	3	4	5	6
1	.01	4,052	5,000	5,404	5,625	5,764	5,859
	.05	162	200	216	225	230	234
	.10	39.9	49.5	53.6	55.8	57.2	58.2
2	.01	98.50	99.00	99.17	99.25	99.30	99.33
	.05	18.51	19.00	19.17	19.25	19.30	19.33
	.10	8.53	9.00	9.16	9.24	9.29	9.33
3	.01	34.12	30.82	29.46	28.71	28.24	27.91
	.05	10.13	9.55	9.28	9.12	9.01	8.94
	.10	5.54	5.46	5.39	5.34	5.31	5.28
4	.01	21.20	18.00	16.70	15.98	15.52	15.21
	.05	7.71	6.95	6.59	6.39	6.26	6.16
	.10	4.55	4.33	4.19	4.11	4.05	4.01
5	.01	16.26	13.27	12.06	11.39	10.97	10.67
	.05	6.61	5.79	5.41	5.19	5.05	4.95
	.10	4.06	3.78	3.62	3.52	3.45	3.41
6	.01	13.75	10.93	9.78	9.15	8.75	8.47
	.05	5.99	5.14	4.76	4.53	4.39	4.28
	.10	3.78	3.46	3.29	3.18	3.11	3.06
7	.01	12.25	9.55	8.45	7.85	7.46	7.19
	.05	5.59	4.74	4.35	4.12	3.97	3.87
	.10	3.59	3.26	3.08	2.96	2.88	2.83
8	.01	11.26	8.65	7.59	7.01	6.63	6.37
	.05	5.32	4.46	4.07	3.84	3.69	3.58
	.10	3.46	3.11	2.92	2.81	2.73	2.67
9	.01	10.56	8.02	6.99	6.42	6.06	5.80
	.05	5.12	4.26	3.86	3.63	3.48	3.37
	.10	3.36	3.01	2.81	2.69	2.61	2.55

DENOM-INATOR df	SIGNIF-ICANCE LEVEL	NUMERATOR DEGREES OF FREEDOM					
		1	2	3	4	5	6
10	.01	10.05	7.56	6.55	6.00	5.64	5.39
	.05	4.97	4.10	3.71	3.48	3.33	3.22
	.10	3.29	2.93	2.73	2.61	2.52	2.46
11	.01	9.65	7.21	6.22	5.67	5.32	5.07
	.05	4.85	3.98	3.59	3.36	3.20	3.10
	.10	3.23	2.86	2.66	2.55	2.45	2.39
12	.01	9.33	6.93	5.95	5.41	5.07	4.82
	.05	4.75	3.89	3.49	3.26	3.11	3.00
	.10	3.18	2.81	2.61	2.48	2.40	2.33
13	.01	9.07	6.70	5.74	5.21	4.86	4.62
	.05	4.67	3.81	3.41	3.18	3.03	2.92
	.10	3.14	2.76	2.56	2.43	2.35	2.28
14	.01	8.86	6.52	5.56	5.04	4.70	4.46
	.05	4.60	3.74	3.34	3.11	2.96	2.85
	.10	3.10	2.73	2.52	2.40	2.31	2.24
15	.01	8.68	6.36	5.42	4.89	4.56	4.32
	.05	4.54	3.68	3.29	3.06	2.90	2.79
	.10	3.07	2.70	2.49	2.36	2.27	2.21
16	.01	8.53	6.23	5.29	4.77	4.44	4.30
	.05	4.49	3.63	3.24	3.01	2.85	2.74
	.10	3.05	2.67	2.46	2.33	2.24	2.18
17	.01	8.40	6.11	5.19	4.67	4.34	4.10
	.05	4.45	3.59	3.20	2.97	2.81	2.70
	.10	3.03	2.65	2.44	2.31	2.22	2.15
18	.01	8.29	6.01	5.09	4.58	4.25	4.02
	.05	4.41	3.56	3.16	2.93	2.77	2.66
	.10	3.01	2.62	2.42	2.29	2.20	2.13
19	.01	8.19	5.93	5.01	4.50	4.17	3.94
	.05	4.38	3.52	3.13	2.90	2.74	2.63
	.10	2.99	2.61	2.40	2.27	2.18	2.11
20	.01	8.10	5.85	4.94	4.43	4.10	3.87
	.05	4.35	3.49	3.10	2.87	2.71	2.60
	.10	2.98	2.59	2.38	2.25	2.16	2.09
21	.01	8.02	5.78	4.88	4.37	4.04	3.81
	.05	4.33	3.47	3.07	2.84	2.69	2.57
	.10	2.96	2.58	2.37	2.23	2.14	2.08
22	.01	7.95	5.72	4.82	4.31	3.99	3.76
	.05	4.30	3.44	3.05	2.82	2.66	2.55
	.10	2.95	2.56	2.35	2.22	2.13	2.06
23	.01	7.88	5.66	4.77	4.26	3.94	3.71
	.05	4.28	3.42	3.03	2.80	2.64	2.53
	.10	2.94	2.55	2.34	2.21	2.12	2.05
24	.01	7.82	5.61	4.72	4.22	3.90	3.67
	.05	4.26	3.40	3.01	2.78	2.62	2.51
	.10	2.93	2.54	2.33	2.20	2.10	2.04
25	.01	7.77	5.57	4.68	4.18	3.86	3.63
	.05	4.24	3.39	2.99	2.76	2.60	2.49
	.10	2.92	2.53	2.32	2.19	2.09	2.03
26	.01	7.72	5.53	4.64	4.14	3.82	3.59
	.05	4.23	3.37	2.98	2.74	2.59	2.48
	.10	2.91	2.52	2.31	2.18	2.08	2.01

DENOM-INATOR df	SIGNIF-ICANCE LEVEL	NUMERATOR DEGREES OF FREEDOM					
		1	2	3	4	5	6
27	.01	7.68	5.49	4.60	4.11	3.79	3.56
	.05	4.21	3.36	2.96	2.73	2.57	2.46
	.10	2.90	2.51	2.30	2.17	2.07	2.01
28	.01	7.64	5.45	4.57	4.08	3.75	3.53
	.05	4.20	3.34	2.95	2.72	2.56	2.45
	.10	2.89	2.50	2.29	2.16	2.07	2.00
29	.01	7.60	5.42	4.54	4.05	3.73	3.50
	.05	4.18	3.33	2.94	2.70	2.55	2.43
	.10	2.89	2.50	2.28	2.15	2.06	1.99
30	.01	7.56	5.39	4.51	4.02	3.70	3.47
	.05	4.17	3.32	2.92	2.69	2.53	2.42
	.10	2.88	2.49	2.28	2.14	2.05	1.98
35	.01	7.42	5.27	4.40	3.91	3.59	3.37
	.05	4.12	3.27	2.88	2.64	2.49	2.37
	.10	2.86	2.46	2.25	2.11	2.02	1.95
40	.01	7.32	5.18	4.31	3.83	3.51	3.29
	.05	4.09	3.23	2.84	2.61	2.45	2.34
	.10	2.84	2.44	2.23	2.09	2.00	1.93
45	.01	7.23	5.11	4.25	3.77	3.46	3.23
	.05	4.06	3.21	2.81	2.58	2.42	2.31
	.10	2.82	2.43	2.21	2.08	1.98	1.91
50	.01	7.17	5.06	4.20	3.72	3.41	3.19
	.05	4.04	3.18	2.79	2.56	2.40	2.29
	.10	2.81	2.41	2.20	2.06	1.97	1.90
55	.01	7.12	5.01	4.16	3.68	3.37	3.15
	.05	4.02	3.17	2.77	2.54	2.38	2.27
	.10	2.80	2.40	2.19	2.05	1.96	1.89
60	.01	7.08	4.98	4.13	3.65	3.34	3.12
	.05	4.00	3.15	2.76	2.53	2.37	2.26
	.10	2.79	2.39	2.18	2.04	1.95	1.88
65	.01	7.04	4.95	4.10	3.62	3.31	3.09
	.05	3.99	3.14	2.75	2.51	2.36	2.24
	.10	2.79	2.39	2.17	2.03	1.94	1.87
70	.01	7.01	4.92	4.08	3.60	3.29	3.07
	.05	3.98	3.13	2.74	2.50	2.35	2.23
	.10	2.78	2.38	2.16	2.03	1.93	1.86
75	.01	6.99	4.90	4.06	3.58	3.27	3.05
	.05	3.97	3.12	2.73	2.49	2.34	2.22
	.10	2.77	2.38	2.16	2.02	1.93	1.86
80	.01	6.96	4.88	4.04	3.56	3.26	3.04
	.05	3.96	3.11	2.72	2.49	2.33	2.22
	.10	2.77	2.37	2.15	2.02	1.92	1.85
85	.01	6.94	4.86	4.02	3.55	3.24	3.02
	.05	3.95	3.10	2.71	2.48	2.32	2.21
	.10	2.77	2.37	2.15	2.01	1.92	1.85
90	.01	6.93	4.85	4.01	3.54	3.23	3.01
	.05	3.95	3.10	2.71	2.47	2.32	2.20
	.10	2.76	2.36	2.15	2.01	1.91	1.84

APPENDIX B.3

CRITICAL VALUES OF *t*

To use this table, first decide whether a one- or a two-tailed test is appropriate. Decide the level of significance. Then read down the corresponding column to the number of degrees of freedom. The tabled entry gives the value of *t* that must be *exceeded* in order to be significant. For example, if we do a two-tailed test with 20 degrees of freedom, our *t* must be greater than 2.086 to be significant at the 0.05 level.

	ONE-TAILED TESTS			TWO-TAILED TESTS		
df	.10	.05	.01	.10	.05	.01
1	3.078	6.314	31.821	6.314	12.706	63.657
2	1.886	2.920	6.965	2.920	4.303	9.925
3	1.638	2.353	4.541	2.353	3.182	5.841
4	1.533	2.132	3.747	2.132	2.776	4.604
5	1.476	2.015	3.365	2.015	2.571	4.032
6	1.440	1.943	3.143	1.943	2.447	3.708
7	1.415	1.895	2.998	1.895	2.365	3.500
8	1.397	1.860	2.897	1.860	2.306	3.356
9	1.383	1.833	2.822	1.833	2.262	3.250
10	1.372	1.813	2.764	1.813	2.228	3.170
11	1.364	1.796	2.718	1.796	2.201	3.106
12	1.356	1.783	2.681	1.783	2.179	3.055
13	1.350	1.771	2.651	1.771	2.161	3.013
14	1.345	1.762	2.625	1.762	2.145	2.977
15	1.341	1.753	2.603	1.753	2.132	2.947
16	1.337	1.746	2.584	1.746	2.120	2.921
17	1.334	1.740	2.567	1.740	2.110	2.898
18	1.331	1.734	2.553	1.734	2.101	2.897
19	1.328	1.729	2.540	1.729	2.093	2.861
20	1.326	1.725	2.528	1.725	2.086	2.846
21	1.323	1.721	2.518	1.721	2.080	2.832
22	1.321	1.717	2.509	1.717	2.074	2.819
23	1.320	1.714	2.500	1.714	2.069	2.808
24	1.318	1.711	2.492	1.711	2.064	2.797
25	1.317	1.708	2.485	1.708	2.060	2.788
26	1.315	1.706	2.479	1.706	2.056	2.779

df	ONE-TAILED TESTS			TWO-TAILED TESTS		
	.10	.05	.01	.10	.05	.01
27	1.314	1.704	2.473	1.704	2.052	2.771
28	1.313	1.701	2.467	1.701	2.049	2.764
29	1.312	1.699	2.462	1.699	2.045	2.757
30	1.311	1.697	2.458	1.698	2.042	2.750
35	1.306	1.690	2.438	1.690	2.030	2.724
40	1.303	1.684	2.424	1.684	2.021	2.705
45	1.301	1.680	2.412	1.680	2.014	2.690
50	1.299	1.676	2.404	1.676	2.009	2.678
55	1.297	1.673	2.396	1.673	2.004	2.668
60	1.296	1.671	2.390	1.671	2.001	2.661
65	1.295	1.669	2.385	1.669	1.997	2.654
70	1.294	1.667	2.381	1.667	1.995	2.648
75	1.293	1.666	2.377	1.666	1.992	2.643
80	1.292	1.664	2.374	1.664	1.990	2.639
85	1.292	1.663	2.371	1.663	1.989	2.635
90	1.291	1.662	2.369	1.662	1.987	2.632
95	1.291	1.661	2.366	1.661	1.986	2.629
100	1.290	1.660	2.364	1.660	1.984	2.626
∞	1.282	1.645	2.327	1.645	1.960	2.576

APPENDIX B.4

CRITICAL VALUE OF χ^2

Using this table is straightforward. We decide the level of significance; that determines which column we consult. Then, knowing how many degrees of freedom we have, we read down the appropriate column to that many df. The tabled value is the value our χ^2 must exceed, to be significant at that level.

	LEVEL OF SIGNIFICANCE		
DEGREES OF FREEDOM	**0.10**	**0.05**	**0.01**
1	2.71	3.84	6.64
2	4.60	5.99	9.21
3	6.25	7.82	11.34
4	7.78	9.49	13.28
5	9.24	11.07	15.09
6	10.65	12.59	16.81
7	12.02	14.07	18.48
8	13.36	15.51	20.09
9	14.68	16.92	21.67
10	15.99	18.31	23.21
11	17.28	19.68	24.73
12	18.55	21.03	26.22
13	19.81	22.36	27.69
14	21.06	23.69	29.14
15	22.31	25.00	30.58
16	23.54	26.30	32.00
17	24.77	27.59	33.41
18	25.99	28.87	34.81
19	27.20	30.14	36.19
20	28.41	31.41	37.57

APPENDIX C

HOW TO REPORT RESEARCH

A scientist is usually judged by his published works. In them he is exposing his very soul. In the long run, incompetence and fraud will out, because every statement is open to verification.

—VINCENT G. DETHIER

This process of verification is one great strength of the scientific method. It is one of the most important ways in which we discover when we are wrong.

But findings are of no use unless they are reported. Locked up in the investigator's skull (or in her filing cabinets), knowledge is withheld from the rest of us. By reporting, the scientist gives away to all humankind what he or she has discovered.

Many who read this book will be doing so in connection with a course in research methods. The chances are that such a course will include practice in research-report writing. If you're a potential "research producer," you'll see that scientific writing is a necessary professional skill. But practice in scientific writing has benefits for the research consumer as well. You will—if you take the exercise seriously—develop skill at a style of writing in which your words say exactly what you want to say, say it with crystal clarity—and then stop.

Different scientific journals specify different formats for reports that are submitted to them for publication. Here, we will follow the format and style set by the American Psychological Association (APA). This is a way of organizing and writing research reports that you will find in journals published by the APA, and by many other (not all) psychological journals as well. We cannot consider all facets of APA style, but your library will have available the APA *Publication Manual*, which will guide you through any problems that we don't cover here.

THE ANATOMY OF A JOURNAL ARTICLE

We assume that we are writing for professional readers. That means that our readers will be (a) professionals in the field, familiar with its terminology; (b) interested in the topic of our investigation; and (c) busy. We want them to be able to read our paper *once*, and, from that single reading, understand clearly what problem we were addressing (introduction), what we did (method), what we found (results), and how we interpret it (discussion).

As to how to go about doing that, there is some very old and very wise advice to writers and speakers, and it goes like this: Tell 'em what you're going to tell 'em; then tell 'em; and then tell 'em what you told 'em. That's what a research report does.

And how do we organize a report so that it will do that? Why, that's what I'm going to tell you!

THE TITLE

In the *title* of the paper, we tell 'em what we're going to tell 'em *about*.

The title is the first thing readers will see. On the basis of it, they will decide whether to read further or to pass us by. Since we want readers who are interested in our topic to read further, we must show them that the paper would in fact be of interest.

So we want the title to be brief, but not mysterious. It should tell the reader what the general topic of the paper is, and proceed perhaps one level down from there: What, within that general topic, is our specific one?

It might do this by specifying directly what variables we are relating to each other. For one example, Bell and Ainsworth (1972) titled their paper "Infant Crying and Maternal Responsiveness." For another, Jenni and Jenni (1976) titled theirs "Carrying Behavior of Humans: Analysis of Sex Differences."

Perhaps our paper tests a specific hypothesis—for example, that subliminal tapes can enhance memory or self-esteem. This is implied in the title of the report by Greenwald et al. (1991): "Double-Blind Tests of Subliminal Self-Help Audiotapes."*

---

*Specifying "double-blind" was a nice touch. This gives the reader some assurance that the study was well done, in a research area where very many studies are not.

We might be reporting an extension of previous findings. Bernstein (1978) extended the work on conditioned taste aversions, previously done with animals, to humans. Her title said so: "Learned Taste Aversions in Children Receiving Chemotherapy."

Or our paper might describe a wholly new finding. When Olds and Milner (1954) discovered that electrical stimulation of the brain could act as a reward or reinforcer, their title said so: "Positive Reinforcement Produced by Electrical Stimulation of Septal Area and Other Regions of Rat Brain."

There are other ways of doing it. An investigation asks a question. Our title might indicate what the question was. Thus Darley, Teger, and Lewis (1973) asked: "Do Groups Always Inhibit Individuals' Responses to Potential Emergencies?" as their title shows.

As we see, the title can tell the reader in very few words what the study was about. If it can also pique the reader's curiosity, so much the better. If you came across a paper titled "From Jerusalem to Jericho: A Study of Situational and Dispositional Variables in Helping Behavior" (Darley & Batson, 1973), wouldn't you be curious as to what the paper was all about? Yet even here we're not left wholly in the dark: We know that it was about helping behavior. This is the paper in which the "good Samaritan" study was reported.

THE ABSTRACT

The abstract tells the readers all you're going to tell 'em, in one terse paragraph. This, after the title, is the first thing the reader of your paper will see if she is reading through a journal. Or, if she has found your article by way of a computer search, it's likely that the title and abstract are all she will see. Either way, on the basis of the abstract, a professional reader would decide whether to read any further or whether to seek out our entire article, or not. The abstract should provide enough information so that she or he can make that decision.

Although the abstract comes first, it's easiest to write it last. That way, we can go back over our paper and, in three sentences or less per topic, give the bare essentials of each topic in order: what problem we addressed (introduction), what we did (method), what we found (results), and what it means (discussion). That last sentence you just read is an abstract of the whole discussion that follows, about what the parts of a report are and what goes where.

THE BODY OF THE PAPER

The *body* of the report comes next, and this is where we tell 'em. For most research reports, the body is divided into the following sections: *introduction, method, results,* and *discussion.* After that come the *references*, the *figures and/or tables*, the *figure captions* on a separate page, and an *appendix* (if there is one). Each of these is indicated with a topic heading, except for the introduction; it is assumed that an introduction begins the body of the report. But we'll title it here, for clarity, thus:

INTRODUCTION

The introduction is the section that motivates the reader's reading: Why should he be interested in what we found? The best way to get that across in a few words is to explain why *we* were interested in it. Why did we do the investigation in the first place? Try organizing the section under the following topics, in order:

1. What is the problem we are addressing? The first sentence identifies the topic area; for example, "This investigation is concerned with human memory." Then we narrow it down: What about human memory are we going to focus on? We zero in on the point of the paper, as quickly as we can.

2. What is known about the specific problem? Here we cite the work of previous investigators that has led directly to our own work. If we discuss someone else's investigation, we cite it, and describe in a sentence or two what it showed and why it is relevant to our work. If we are manipulating some variable, it's usually because existing data suggest that its effect should be of interest. Okay, what existing data (with references), and how did those data affect our thinking? Are we testing a theory? Whose theory (with references)? Briefly, what does it say? If it makes predictions that are important to us, what are they?

3. Now we want to know *this* about the problem: why? Specifically, what light will be shed on the problem by the data we're going to report?

In all this, the progression of ideas is very much like the one we discussed back in Chapter 3. We begin by identifying the general topic of the investigation. Then we narrow it down to a statement of the specific variables with which our work is concerned. In doing so, we explain to the reader what we were investigating, and why we chose to investigate it in the way we did.

We do this briefly. If we are reporting an experiment on memory, for example, we say so; but we avoid the temptation to begin with a discussion of why memory is such an important thing to have. We can safely assume that the reader knows that. Go quickly to the point: What specific question about memory are we asking in the investigation we report here?

METHOD

In the Method section, we continue to follow Chapter 3's progression. We've identified the variables that we're going to relate to each other. Now, how did we *operationalize* those variables (pp. 65–66)? What did we actually *do*? How did we manipulate the independent variable (if there was one)? How did we measure the dependent variable? The rule for this section is: *Give enough information so that any reader could repeat our study exactly, having only our report to go on.*

The method section will often break down in turn into the following topics:

SUBJECTS

Did we observe college students? Other adults? Members of another species? If the last, it is customary to give the taxonomic name as well as the common name. For example, Ristau, in describing her studies of the piping plover, gave the scientific name of the species: *Charadrius melodus*. If we used laboratory rats, we give the strain and the supplier.

What gender were the subjects—or, if mixed, how many males and how many females? Give the approximate age range. Were there any special criteria on the basis of which subjects were selected or ruled out? For example, in an experiment on vision, subjects with visual defects might have been deliberately excluded from the study. This should be stated.

If we used college students as subjects, it's a good idea to tell the reader which college they came from. People say that students from different colleges do have different characteristics, and they just might be right. For the same reason, indicate why the subjects were there. Were they volunteer subjects, paid subjects, or subjects fulfilling a course requirement? Again, all these might have different characteristics, so a reader who wished to repeat our study would want subjects with the same characteristics as ours, as far as possible.

APPARATUS

What instruments did we use for manipulation and measurement? They should be described unless they were obvious, or unless it doesn't matter. For instance, if we were conducting a survey, we need not specify the paper on which the survey questions were written (unless there was something special about it), nor whether the responses were recorded with a pen or pencil. Since these will not affect the data, the reader would not need to know them in order to repeat what we did. But if, for example, we were presenting material on a computer screen, and measuring reaction time (as in the mental-rotation study discussed in Chapter 6), we should specify the size of the screen, how far the subject was placed from it, and how the subjects made the responses that we measured. If we used a commercially available program to do this, specify the program; if we wrote it ourselves, indicate that.

Or if our study dealt with rats in a Skinner box, specify its dimensions, and what the reinforcement was (food, fluid, or whatever). If the apparatus was bought, specify the manufacturer and model number. The reader, if she wishes to repeat our experiment, can then be sure that she's using a Skinner box with the same properties as ours. Through all this, remember the rule: The information we give must allow a reader to repeat our study exactly.

DESIGN

This should be specified if there is anything unusual about it, or if the necessary design is not obvious. Otherwise, this section can be omitted. For example, if all subjects received a series of learning trials at some task, it is obvious that the design is within-subjects, and this need not be specified as a separate section. But if some subjects received those learning trials under one set of conditions, and another group received them under a different set of conditions, it may help the reader to see at a glance what we did if we note that the design was a mixed between- and within-subjects design.

If it was a factorial design, again it will help the reader if we say so, and if we identify each independent variable and how many values it had. It'll save space and the reader's time if we identify the experiment as an $n \times m$ factorial design and then specify the number of values for m and for n, thus: "The actual content of the tapes (memory or self-esteem), and what subjects were led to believe was the content (memory or self-esteem), were varied in a 2×2 factorial design." As we see, this can be done very briefly if we assume (as we should) that the reader is familiar with standard design terminology.

PROCEDURE

What, specifically, did we do? If a series of trials was given, what happened on each trial? And how were the trials sequenced? Was the order of conditions random for each subject, or counterbalanced, or the same for all subjects, or what? If the procedure involved a large number of steps, it may help the reader if we present a table or flowchart to give an at-a-glance summary of what was done.

RESULTS

Okay, the reader now knows precisely how we did the investigation. What did we find? We told the reader what question we are asking (introduction), and how (method). Now that we have the data in hand, we are in a position to answer our question or announce our discovery, and to back up what we say with data and analysis.

We do it in that order. The rule is: *First present the results in plain English* (or whatever is the language in which the report is written). If it will help the reader (and it usually will), we present whatever graphs and/or tables will most clearly show the important aspects of our results (see below).

Then, and only then, we back up those results with statistical analysis. But first, how do we present the data?

GRAPHS AND TABLES

Readers like to *see* the data—literally. If we say only something like "Scores under condition A were greater than those under condition B," the reader doesn't know whether the difference is negligible or substantial. Graphic or tabular presentation of summary values (such as mean scores) lets the reader take in our message at a glance.

Shall we show the reader a graph or a table? We make that decision from the reader's perspective. How can the reader most easily see what we want to show? Other things equal, a graph is usually easier to absorb at a glance. But there are exceptions. For example, if an investigation took a very large number of measures, a graph for each measure might simply make the paper too long. Here, a table would be better. Then the text should guide the reader through the table, noting, one by one, each important comparison and what it shows (see below).

If we opt for graphs, the figures we have seen in this book should make clear the conventions of graphic presentation. By convention, the independent variable in an experimental investigation is plotted on the horizontal axis. Corresponding values of the dependent variables are represented by the height of the bars or position of the data points, and numerical values can be read off the vertical axis. Where there is more than one dependent variable, different ones can be distinguished by such devices as shaded bars or different symbols for the data points, or by labels close to each.

Line graph or bar graph? Often the choice is arbitrary, and we simply decide which method is clearer and most pleasing to the eye. For example, Figure C.1 shows two ways of presenting our hypothetical data on milkshake preloads and subsequent ice cream intake in dieters and nondieters (Chapter 9). One panel shows a line graph,

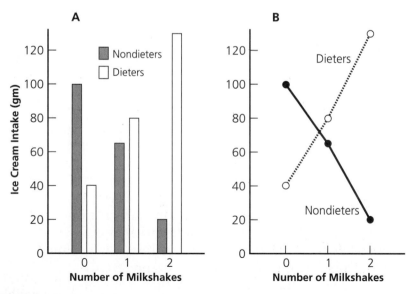

Figure C.1
Data from our hypothetical replication of the "counterregulation" experiment. (A), a bar graph; (B), a line graph. Either one would do.

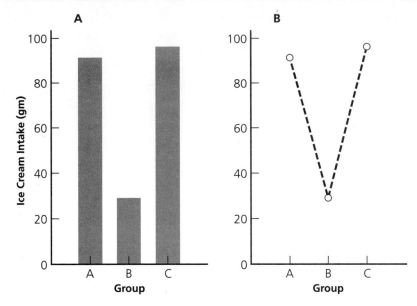

Figure C.2
Data from our hypothetical replication of the conditioned-taste-aversion experiment.
(A), a bar graph; (B), a line graph. In this case, the line graph suggests a progression
that is not there. A bar graph is preferable.

the other a bar graph. But each one shows clearly that as the number of milkshakes increases, the amount of ice cream eaten afterward goes down in nondieters, but rises in dieters. My own judgment is that the line graph makes these progressions a little bit more clear, but it really is a judgment call. Either way would do.

There are cases, however, in which one way of doing it is clearly better than the other. Take a look at Figure C.2, from our hypothetical replication of Bernstein's conditioned-taste-aversion experiment (Chapter 6). The bar graph shows us that of the three conditions, condition B led to substantially lower intake than the other two conditions did. If we look at the line graph, our impression is of something that falls and then rises again as the X-variable increases—but wait! There is no *increase* of anything on the horizontal axis as we go from left to right. They are just different conditions, not a progression. It is even an arbitrary matter how we arrange the groups left to right. In such cases as this, a bar graph prevents the reader from being misled and is to be preferred.

Such guidelines, however, are only that. Very often it will be an arbitrary matter whether to use table, line graph, or bar graph. The only rule is: *Remember the readers*. Choose a means of presentation that will make it easy for them to absorb the important information.

One final, important note: The results section is a section of the *text* of the report. The graphic and/or tabular presentations of the data are a *supplement* to the description—in the text—of our findings. They are not a *substitute* for it. A reader looking at a graph or table still needs to be told what to look for in that graph or table. To simply label a section "Results," throw some graphs or tables at the reader, and then walk away does not make an acceptable results section. We never take the view that "the data speak for themselves." That's *our* job.

STATISTICAL ANALYSIS

In writing the results section, we assume the reader knows at least as much about statistics as we do, so we can be very brief. We can say something like, "The two variables (specified) were positively correlated ($r = 0.64$)." The professional reader will know what we mean.

Or, if we're comparing two groups, we might simply point out that group 1 scored higher on average than group 2, and add something like: "$t(18) = 4.36$, $p < 0.01$)." That's enough! The reader knows that the difference is significant, that we tested significance by t-test, that the value of t was 4.36, that there were 18 degrees of freedom (the number in parentheses), and what the p value was. (Actually, if a reader knows the value of t, he could look up the p-value in a table, and by referring to our method section he could see how many degrees of freedom there had to be. But, as we see, we can save him all that trouble in very little space by specifying those numbers ourselves; so we do so.)

DISCUSSION

The previous section has presented our findings. Now we present our *interpretation* of the findings. The discussion is separated from the results section, for the same reason that editorials are presented separately from news articles in a newspaper. We want the readers to be in no doubt as to whether they are reading "just the facts" (results), or our interpretation of them (discussion).

To organize this section, try taking up the following topics in order: Where are we now? Where do we go from here? What have we learned on the way?

WHERE ARE WE NOW?

In the introduction we set up the context for our findings, telling the reader what the problem was and why we decided that our results would advance the problem. Well, now that we have that information (the results), how *have* we advanced the problem? We can treat this topic as a direct extension of the introduction, in light of the data. If we were testing an hypothesis, do the data support it? If we set out to repeat someone else's investigation, do these results agree with the earlier ones? In short: Our introduction asked a question. Our discussion answers it.

WHERE DO WE GO FROM HERE?

Having shown how our findings advance the problem, we might suggest some further steps. What do we need to do next? What new hypotheses are implied by our findings? If our findings and those of others don't agree, what factors might account for the disagreement? How might we design a new investigation to test our suggestions about that?

In the introduction, we cited the work of earlier investigators whose results bear directly to the question we asked. But now, with our data in hand, we might see relations between our work and some other data, in other contexts not directly related. Or maybe our findings have practical implications. Note them. It is in seeing such relationships that your creativity and insight can have their greatest impact.

But keep it brief and keep it sensible. The reader doesn't need a long list of strained implications or sci-fi applications. Stay close to what the data actually show.

WHAT HAVE WE LEARNED ON THE WAY?

We learn about research by doing research; we learn what to do and what not to do. Perhaps in doing our research we neglected to control some factor that turned out to be important. Perhaps we now see a better way of measuring the dependent variable than the one we used. In general, if we now see how the investigation could have been improved, we can share it with the reader. In lab-report writing, this section lets an instructor see how our skills develop. It has a place in professional writing too, in that it is a way of saving the reader from repeating our mistakes.

But if we do criticize our own work, we should keep it brief and keep it well thought out. Brief means: Avoid piling up a list of trivial criticisms. Well thought out means: Show *how* the criticism applies, and be sure it really *is* a criticism. When, for instance, a student writes, "The fact that the subjects were all males may have affected the results," a reader isn't sure what she means. Affected the results how? Does this really *affect* these results, or does it only raise the question of their *generality*—a question that arises for any findings whatever? If the latter, there's no need to raise it at all. Similarly, there is no need to say that "more subjects would have to be studied." If that's true, the reader knows it, and it may not even be quite true (see Chapter 12)!

At the end of the discussion section, it never hurts to tell 'em what we told 'em. We can end the text with something like, "In summary, the data show that baboons under X condition behave in Y manner. That finding implies. . . ." Such a wrapup helps fix your message in the reader's mind, and gives a satisfying conclusion to the text.

One final plea. If we do not want the reader to grind his or her teeth with vigor and curse us under her or his breath, let's not end our discussion with the ringing sentence: "More research is needed."

Please. The reader knows that.

After the discussion section comes a list of the *references* that we've cited in our paper. But before we discuss that, we should say some more about how the body of the paper should be written.

STYLE

Your reader is busy. He wants to absorb your news as quickly as possible. If we help him do it, he will both appreciate your courtesy and admire your writing skills. Hence, all the suggestions that follow reduce to one:

Principle: Do not slow the reader down.

How might we slow the reader down? There are several ways, and these are the don'ts of writing style. We slow the reader down if we waste words; our writing must be *compact*. We slow the reader down if she has to stop to wonder what we mean; our writing must be *clear*. Finally, we slow the reader down if we give her a headache. And she can get a headache from snarling at bad grammar, from re-arranging long twisted sentences, or from bumping over awkward prose. Our writing must be *literate and easy to read*. Yes, even in a lab report.

Is this difficult? Yes, it is. It's a skill, and as with other skills, if you practice it, you'll find it gets easier and easier with time.

COMPACT WRITING

Do not [use so many verbal units that they form themselves into winding twisted compound complex sentences like this one, studded with sesquipedalian words like *sesquipedalian,* or that are redundant in that they say the same thing twice or more, or that in other ways] waste words.

We can cross out everything between the brackets. And we should.

CLARITY

But don't withhold important words, either. We are holding a conversation with the reader; we are explaining something to him. After all, we know what we did and what we found and what we make of it; the reader does not. We can't afford to omit important steps in our procedure (for example) because we take them for granted. A reader cannot take them for granted, for he doesn't know them until we tell him.

This is why, after we have drafted a paper, it's very good idea to get a second opinion. Let someone read our draft who has no idea what we did or why. If that reader, with only our paper to go on, can understand what we did and why, what we found, and what we make of it, the professional writer for whom we are writing can probably do so as well. A second reader can also catch unclear phrases, sentences, or whole passages, and, after we've explained more clearly, can do us the great favor of asking us: Why not say it that way?

EASY READING

Students often imagine that in order to sound scientific, text must be written in a dull, stodgy way, filled with big words in long sentences. Not so.

Remember that we are explaining something to the reader. So our text should read like an explanation, saying things in the simplest way. In fact, if we're not sure how to say something, often the best thing to do is to ask ourselves: How would we explain this to someone who was sitting across the table from us? And then: Why not say it that way?

There will be times when we are told that this or that passage in our draft isn't clear, and we'll feel the urge to snarl just a bit. We ask ourselves, "How could he or she *not* understand that passage?" Resist the temptation. *If this reader misunderstands, so will others*. It's our job to go back and reword it until it *is* clear to our readers, and not just to ourselves.

By the way, your present author, who has been writing since the late Middle Ages, still gets another opinion—sometimes several—on everything he writes for publication. He did so for this book you are reading, you may be sure.

USAGE AND MECHANICS

Professional writers and professional readers (college teachers are both) develop a certain respect for language, and they don't like to see it abused. Bad spelling and bad grammar, like it or not, turn them off as with a switch. I can't write a style menu in this limited space, but many good ones are available in bookstores—for example, *Elements of Style*, by Strunk and White. Invest in one, and consult it when uncertain as to punctuation, grammar, or usage. Mistakes do show, and they do turn readers off. Get used to it.

PERSON, VOICE, AND TENSE

"I" (or "we") is first person; "you" is second person; "he, she, or it" is third person. Thus, when we write "I (or "we") did thus and so," we're writing in first person.

In active voice, the actor is the subject of the sentence. In passive voice, the object of the action is. Thus, "We injected the rats with ethanol" is active voice. "The rats were injected with ethanol" is passive voice.

There is a tradition that scientific writing should use third-person, passive voice, where the choice exists. Thus, "The rats were injected with ethanol" is by tradition preferred to "I injected the rats with ethanol." This can sound stilted and it often wastes words. But it does get the emphasis where we want it; what matters is what was done with the rats, not who did it.

Different journal editors and lab instructors differ in their preferences on such matters as these. Find out your lab instructor's preference; or, if you write for a professional journal, flip through recent issues of it to see which style is preferred by its editor.

Which tense to use seems to be a frequent source of confusion. Actually, it's strictly logical except for one arbitrary convention: In stating something that is generally true—hence true today, but also in the past and the future—we use present tense.

Thus, the subjects in your experiment (now completed) *performed* in such and such a way (past tense, for here we are describing what happened *then*, when we conducted the investigation). But such a finding may suggest the general conclusion: "Such subjects under such conditions *perform* in such and such a way" (so we expect that they would do so next month as well). This goes beyond the data to a statement about the general case, so present tense is used.

Finally, in reporting a finished investigation, we don't end the introduction with "Subjects *will be* treated in such and such a way." That's all right in a proposal, for the events in question haven't happened yet. But if we are reporting an investigation that is now complete, then it has already happened when we write the paper, even if we haven't described it yet. Use past tense here.

REFERENCES

Throughout the paper, we'll be referring to the published work of other investigators. The body of the paper will contain these citations; and at the end of the paper, for the reader's convenience, we list all citations and indicate where they came from. The purpose of this is to allow the interested reader to find any of the reports, books, or chapters we cite, so that she can read the original reports or discussions we refer to.

That gives us two sets of conventions to guide us. One tells us how to refer to other publications *within the body* of the paper. The other tells us how to organize the list of references *at the end* of the paper. Since they are so closely related, we'll consider them together here.

REFERENCE TO A BOOK

Early on in this book, we encountered the following citation:

> The effect of all this was to place a decades-long guilt trip on already stressed and desperate real-life parents (Dolnick, 1998).

This tells you right away that what I say is supported by something that a person named Dolnick has written. If you want to follow this up, either to check me or to explore the matter further, this citation tells you to go to the list of references in the back of the book, where all such citations are listed in alphabetical order by author.

The citation turns out to be a reference to a *book,* as we see when we look it up. In the reference list we find:

> Dolnick, E. (1998). *Madness on the couch.* New York: Simon & Schuster.

Author's name; date in parentheses; title of the book (in italics); city of publication; publisher.

The text might have said it this way instead:

> As Dolnick (1998) points out, the effect of all this was to place a decades-long guilt trip on already stressed and desperate real-life parents.

Notice that if the author's name is not part of the text, as in the first version, we enclose the author's name and the date in the parentheses. If it is part of the text, as in the second version, we enclose the date only.

Another example brings up some further points. On p. 41 of the book we find a direct quote:

> No one even so much as calls the police. She dies (Latané & Darley, 1970, p. 1).

(The block indentation on p. 41 shows that this is a direct quote.)

This is another book reference. In the list of references at the end, we see:

Latané, B., & Darley, J. (1970). *The unresponsive bystander: Why doesn't he help?* New York: Appleton-Century-Crofts.

Here there are two authors, so we list them in the order in which they appear (not alphabetically). They are separated by an ampersand (&) in the paper and also in the bibliography. And now, since this is a direct quote, our citation also gives the page on which the quote occurs.

Again we might have said it differently:

Latane and Darley (1970) tell us that no one even called the police.

Here, we use *and* instead of the ampersand, for the *and* occurs as part of the text, not part of the citation. And since this is not a direct quote, we omit the page number if we do it this way.

REFERENCE TO A BOOK CHAPTER

In the sciences, many books are actually collections of independent chapters, each with its own author or authors. These will be put together and published as a book, perhaps with commentary, by an editor or a team of editors. An example from this book (p. 49) is:

In our own time, for example, we find that social isolation in monkeys—even if they are not hungry, thirsty, or in pain—can actually affect the chemistry of the body (Suomi, 1991).

In the reference list we find that this is a chapter:

Suomi, S. J. (1991). Primate separation models of affective disorder. In J. Madden IV (Ed.), *Neurobiology of learning, emotion, and affect* (pp. 768–777). New York: Raven Press.

Chapter author's name; date; chapter title; name(s) of the editor(s); book title (in italics); city of publication; publisher; inclusive page numbers. Here the word *In* is the tipoff that we're dealing with a chapter in an edited book.

And once again our text might have said it differently:

Suomi (1991) reports that social isolation . . . (etc.).

But either way, the entry in the reference list at the end would stay the same.

REFERENCE TO A JOURNAL ARTICLE

We read (p. 35):

> As a result, we cannot speak of psychoanalysis as a well-established theory that has survived repeated tests. It hasn't survived *any* tests, because no tests are possible (Crews, 1996).

Or we might have said:

> Crews (1996) points out that. . . .

But either way, the reference at the end is the same:

> Crews, F. (1996). The verdict on Freud. *Psychological Science, 7,* 63–68.

Author's name; date; title of article; title of journal, in italics; journal volume number; pages.

Articles with multiple authors are handled in the same way. On pp. 71–72 we read:

> In one experiment, Clark and Squire (1998) paired a tone with a puff of air in human subjects, with a seemingly minor difference between two conditions. . . .

Or we might have said something like:

> In one experiment (Clark & Squire, 1998), a tone was paired. . . .

Again, if the citation is all within parentheses, we use & to separate the authors. Either way, the reference list gives us:

> Clark, R. E., & Squire, L. R. (1998). Classical conditioning and brain systems: The role of awareness. *Science, 280,* 77–81.

Authors in the order in which they appear, separated by &; date; title of the article; title of the journal, underlined; volume number; page numbers.

What if there is a large number of authors? Here, the rule is: If there are more than two but fewer than six, we cite them all the first time we refer to the paper, thus:

> We find that if the subject reports a visual dream, parts of the brain involved in processing visual information become active (Hong, Gillin, Dow, Wu, & Buchsbaum, 1995).

But after that, we refer to the first author only and add *et al.* (which means "and others"). Thus, later in our report we might say:

> Recall that Hong et al. (1995) found. . . .

Finally, if there are six or more authors we use the *et al.* format throughout.

But here again the citation in the final reference list is always the same, whatever format we use in the text:

> Hong, C. C., Gillin, J. C., Dow, B. M., Wu, J., & Buchsbaum, M. S. (1995). Localized and lateralized cerebral glucose metabolism associated with eye movements during REM sleep and wakefulness: A positron emission tomography (PET) study. *Sleep, 18,* 570–580.

THE FINAL REFERENCE LIST

This, the last part of the text of a report, lists all the references we've referred to in the report itself, alphabetically by first author's last name. The bibliography at the end of this book follows APA format, so you can use it as a model for your own.

What to include? The rule is: We list *all and only* the items we've referred to in the body of the text. If you're not going to list it in the reference list, don't cite it in the text. If you haven't cited it in the text, don't list it in the reference list. If you *have* cited it, *do* list it. Nothing annoys a reader more than this: He reads a paper and finds something interesting, and he says, "Gee, I'd like to read more about this myself." A source is cited, so he goes to your reference list at the end to see where to find it—and the reference is not there. He will scowl—as well he should.

* * *

This brief guide covers the kinds of referencing we are most likely to be confronted with in writing a lab report. There are (I assure you) many more rules to follow in special cases. The APA *Publication Manual*, which your library will have available for use when questions of format arise, discusses these.

Remember that all these rules are never (well, hardly ever) laid down without reason. As the authors of the manual say early on, "These rules . . . spare readers from a distracting variety of forms throughout a work and permit readers to give full attention to content" (APA, 1984, p. 11). In other words, these rules follow our own rule: Remember the reader!

WRITING THE REPORT

Stephen King was once asked how he managed to write so much. He replied: "One word at a time." When all is said and done, to get the final copy out, you have to apply seat of pants to seat of chair and write one word after another.

The process can be made a great deal less painful, however, if we are guided by Mook's Three Laws of Report Writing. These simple laws will save you much perspiration in the long run. Here they are.

1. *You will write a better paper—much better—if you organize it in advance.* On paper. Swallow your pride and begin writing by making a detailed topic outline. Jot down, within each section, the order in which ideas can most logically be presented. Do that for all sections, and once the actual writing begins you'll find that the work is virtually done. The primary headings are sections of the report (e.g., Method); secondary headings are subsections or major topics (e.g., Subjects); tertiary headings are paragraphs; quaternary headings are sentences. Add the inevitable drudgery of drawing figures and writing references, and you are finished.

2. *Let it cool.* Make your first draft far enough in advance that you can put it aside for a few days before you write the final version. While you are doing something else, something within you will go on working on the paper. Better organizations will to come to mind and, very often, difficult passages that you're not sure how to write will write themselves. Jot down the results in your outline. We don't know how this works, but it does.

3. *It takes less total time—much less—to organize a paper and then write it than to write it without organizing first.* If you doubt it, time yourself and try it. Do the experiment! You'll find that if you proceed that way, you will have more time for yourself than you expected to have. Enjoy.

THE FINISHED PRODUCT:
THE PROFESSIONAL-LOOKING MANUSCRIPT

It should go without saying that your report should be typed, on $8^1/_2 \times 11$-inch paper, double-spaced. This gives a professional look to the manuscript, and makes a good initial impression on an editor or an instructor.

The manuscript begins with a *title page*, which gives the title of your paper, the authors' name or names, the institutional affiliation (Dearold University), and the addresses (mail and e-mail, if any) for the authors. If you're writing the paper in connection with a course, the course number and section also go here.

Next, on a separate page, comes the *abstract*. Then, again beginning on a new page, the body of the paper begins.

The sections themselves are laid out in the typescript as they were above. The order of sections, and the section headings, are again designed to help the reader know exactly where he is in your presentation.

Primary headings are centered, thus:

Method

Major subheadings are to the left and underlined, as in

Apparatus*

And the topic of Apparatus can be further broken down into subtopics with subheadings if necessary:

Stimulus presentation
And text follows. . . .
Response measures
Text follows. . . . And so on.

The sample lab report that follows this section shows the layout again.

Finally, after the discussion, comes your list of references, the figures and/or tables you wish to include in the paper (each on a sep-

---

*We indicate italics by underlining. Text that is underlined in the typescript will be set in *italics* in the final, printed version.

arate page), and (again on a separate page) the captions for these. Your instructor may also ask for an appendix in which your raw data are presented. Journal submissions do not include this.

A SAMPLE REPORT

If a picture is worth—well, many words—so is an example. In what follows, I have supposed that you and I, reader, working with a group of classmates, have conducted the *wholly imaginary* experiment I'm about to describe, and analyzed our *wholly imaginary* data. Now we're ready to write a final report—the three of us: One Good Student, Another Good Student, and This Very Author. Like as not, we'd sit around a desk or table with a lot of coffee available, deciding how to tell the story of our investigation. The result might look like the following sample, except that all parts of the typescript would be double-spaced.

My comments on our paper are in boldface.

The Bystander Effect: A Field Replication
O. G. Student, A. G. Student, and T. V. Author
Dearold College
[address]

[new page]

Abstract

In the natural setting of a college campus, a field experiment was conducted. As each male subject approached, a minor "emergency" was staged: A female experimenter stumbled and dropped an armful of books and papers. This was done under either of two conditions, to which subjects were randomly assigned. In the "with others" condition, two male experimenters were standing near the female, but made no offer of assistance. In the "alone" condition, the two males were a short distance away, so that in effect the subject was alone with the person needing assistance. Subjects who were "with others" were less likely to offer assistance and, if they did offer it, were slower to do so, than those who were "alone." These findings extend the familiar "bystander effect" to a new setting and subject population.

[new page]

This experiment is concerned with helping behavior. If a person sees that someone else needs help, what factors affect the likelihood that the person will offer help? There are a number of such factors (see Sabini, 1992, for review). We focus on one of these: the number of persons who are present when the opportunity to help, or the need for help, arises.

The introduction begins without a heading, and it wastes no time. In this paragraph, we identified the general context in which our research takes place, referred the reader to a source that gives more background, and then zeroed in on the specific variables that we intend to investigate.

Folklore tells us that there is "safety in numbers." Intuitively, it seems obvious that if there are many onlookers to an emergency, the odds that at least one of them will take action will be increased. However, a number of studies have shown quite the opposite: Multiple onlookers may actually reduce the likelihood that helping will occur. This has been shown in both laboratory and field situations (Latané & Darley, 1970, 1976). It has even been found in on-line chat rooms: A person requesting help is likely to receive it more slowly, the more group members are present (Markey, 2000).

The present study is a conceptual replication of these studies, in a new situation and with a different population of subjects. Our question is: What is the effect of number of onlookers on the likelihood that a subject will offer assistance to someone who is in trouble? More specifically: Is a person more likely to offer help in an emergency if he or she is alone, or if other people are present?

Having identified the general question, we zoomed in on the specific one that this study is asking, and we have identified our independent variable (number of onlookers), and our dependent variable (offering or not offering help).

Method

This was a field experiment, conducted on the campus of Dearold College. As in the original experiments, subjects were made witness to a staged "emergency." Some subjects saw the "emergency" in the presence of other onlookers, whereas other subjects saw it when they were alone.

This last sentence is not strictly necessary, for it anticipates the later description of the procedure. But it gives the reader an overview at the outset; this makes the following more detailed description easier to follow.

Observations were made on a lawn in front of the library, on which there were several trees. One of these trees was used as a landmark as described below. Observations were made at times during which classes were in session, so that relatively few people would be passing by the tree at any time.

Subjects

The subjects were undergraduate male students. Each subject was "selected" as he walked past the tree that had been designated as landmark. Persons who were walking with others were not considered, nor were those who were able to see the "emergency" that was staged for another person.

Random assignment to conditions was accomplished as follows. A coin was tossed 20 times, and each result was applied to a set of two subjects. For example, if the coin was heads, the first subject to appear would be assigned to the "alone" condition and the second to the "with others" condition; if tails, the reverse. Similarly for the third and fourth subjects, and so on, until we had specified the conditions for 40 subjects (20 per group). The resulting sequence was written on a sheet of paper that served as a protocol for the experimenters in assigning conditions during the conduct of the experiment.

Notice that there was no attempt here to make a random selection of subjects from the population of students at Dearold College. It was an accidental sample—and appropriately so, for our concern was not with making inferences about that population, but with testing a theory. Nevertheless, the assignment of subjects to experiment conditions was done by a bias-free random procedure.

Procedure

Two conditions were compared. In one, an emergency took place when a subject was by himself. In the other, it occurred when two other onlookers were present.

The emergency was as follows. An undergraduate woman, carrying a large armload of books and papers, passed by the subject as he walked. She was an assistant to the experimenter, and she created a standardized "emergency" as each male subject approached: She stumbled and dropped the books and papers she was carrying. She did this at a distance of about 6 feet from the subject. She then began to gather together the material she had dropped. The question was whether the male subject would stop to help her and, if so, how long it would take him to do this.

Two experimental conditions were imposed on independent groups. In the "other bystanders" condition, two other men were standing close to the woman (about 6 feet away) when the accident took place. These two men were also assistants to the experimenter, and, in this condition, they made no move to assist the woman after the accident had taken place. They simply stood where they were and watched.

In the "alone" condition, the two men were also present, but they were at some remove from the accident (at least 20 feet away), and they were not looking at the woman but conversing with each other when it occurred. In effect, they were removed from the situation, and the subject was alone with the woman in her distress.

Notice that this gives us a direct experimental manipulation. Under the experimenter's control, either there were onlookers immediately present or there were not. Instead, we might have selected cases in which one student, or a group of students, were present when the emergency occurred. This, however, would have been a very much weaker procedure. Why?

The dependent variables were, first, whether the subject would offer assistance to the woman during the 1-minute interval following her dropping her books. This was approximately how long it took her to collect her possessions in the absence of any help. Thus, it provided a kind of natural "ceiling" for helping behavior on the subject's part. Second, latency of helping was recorded in the following way. When the woman dropped her books, one of the onlookers clicked a stopwatch that was hidden in his pocket. If the experimental subject turned from his path to offer assistance, then the watch was stopped, so that latency of helping behavior could be read off the stopwatch and recorded after the subject had gone away.

Again a very brief section, but it gives the procedure in complete detail. Do you think that you, having read that section, would be able to repeat the experiment and do what these imaginary investigators did?

Results

In Table 1, we see the number of subjects who came to the woman's assistance under each of the two conditions. In the "alone" condition, 14 of the 20 subjects offered help before 1 minute had elapsed. In the "other bystanders" condition, only 4 of the 20 subjects offered help. The resulting 2 × 2 contingency is significant: x^2 (1) = 10.10, $p < 0.05$.

[Insert Table 1 about here]

Our figures and tables are not inserted into the text, but instead are assembled at the end of the manuscript, as described later.

The latency data permit a similar conclusion (Figure 1). To examine these data, we consider the time between the occurrence of the emergency and the time at which help was offered, for each subject. If the subject did not offer help at all, he was assigned a "ceiling" score of 60 seconds.

[Insert Figure 1 about here]

The mean latency to offer assistance was 36.150 seconds for the "alone" condition, as compared with 57.650 seconds for the "bystanders" condition. The difference is significant, $t(38) = 4.826$, $p < 0.05$. That finding should be interpreted with caution, however. Since most of the scores in the bystander condition were at the "ceiling" of 60 seconds and therefore identical, the distribution of the data in that group is very far from normal. Since the t-test assumes distributions that are at least approximately normal, the results may be misleading. In addition, this 60-second ceiling might have made the variability within that group artificially low, which would make the t-value artificially high.

So, in a separate analysis, we compared only those subjects who did offer help, four in the "with others" condition and 14 in the "alone" condition. Still the difference was significant: Mean latencies were 48.252 and 25.928 respectively, $t(16) = 3.338$, $p < 0.05$. Therefore, even those subjects who did offer help were slower to do so if other onlookers were there.

Actually, the chances are we would not use the t-test for such data if this were "for real." Instead, we would use one of the "nonparametric" tests of significance, which make fewer assumptions. However, we have not discussed those, so for present purposes we will stick with the t-test, and add appropriate notes of caution.

And that is all we need for a results section! We summarized the data with a figure and a table, told the reader what to look for in the figure and the table, and presented our significance tests. Notice further that we don't take the reader through the logic of significance testing, or explain what a t-test is. We assume the professional reader will know these things.

The present $t =$ values are for imaginary data.

Discussion

Our results confirm and extend the major findings of a number of previous investigations. Witnesses to an "emergency" are much more likely to offer assistance if they are alone than if other onlookers are present (Latané & Darley, 1970, 1976).

Here, in this paragraph, we briefly relate our findings to those of others. We show, in other words, how our findings fit into the literature on this topic that already exists.

It is worth noting that the latency measure we chose to use might have introduced an artifact. Since the maximum score each subject could obtain was capped at 60 seconds, there was the danger that all scores might have been close to or at that maximal possible value, producing a "ceiling effect." However, the data show that this problem was not serious, for it would make a significant difference more difficult to obtain. In fact, despite it, we did obtain a significant difference between the two groups.

This is frequently done. The authors will anticipate a criticism that might be made, and meet that criticism in the text of the report—heading it off in advance, as it were.

It is also possible that our results might have been different if the behavior of the "onlookers," when they were present, had been different. Our two onlookers deliberately made no gesture toward helping the person in distress. Had they done so, or even shown some indication of concern, then subjects in the "bystander" condition might have been more likely to offer assistance themselves. In a sense, however, this is our point. The subjects were taking their cues not from the emergency itself but from the behavior of the bystanders. One might have supposed that the indifference of the bystanders might itself have encouraged helping behavior on the part of the real subject. He might have said in effect, "Why aren't these guys offering any help? I guess I'd better do it myself." Clearly, however, this did not occur.

Again the authors are anticipating a possible misunderstanding and are heading it off by discussing it in advance.

Quite possibly, what was occurring was the kind of "diffusion of responsibility" that Latané and Darley (1970, 1976) discuss. If multiple onlookers are present, whose job is it to offer assistance? If that is ambiguous, then the chances that any onlookers will offer assistance are correspondingly reduced. Direct evidence for this was found in Markey's chat-room experiment (2000), which showed that if an individual were asked directly for help, he or she was likely to give it.

In summary, we have found in a new setting, and with a different subject population, the same phenomenon that has been reported many times before, in many different contexts. Far from there being "safety in numbers," it appears that "numbers" actually reduce one's safety, if "safety" means the likelihood of getting help if one needs it.

[new page]

References

Latané, B., & Darley, J. (1970). The unresponsive bystander: Why doesn't he help? New York: Appleton-Century-Crofts.

Latané, B., & Darley, J. (1976). Help in a crisis: Bystander response in an emergency. In J. Thibaut, J. Spence, & R. Carlson (Eds.), Contemporary topics in social psychology (pp. 822–832). Morristown, NJ: General Learning Press.

Markey, P. M. (2000). Bystander intervention in computer-mediated communication. Computers in human behavior, 16, 183–188.

Sabini, J. (1992). Social psychology. New York: W. W. Norton.

After the reference section we start a new page and present the tables if there are any, each on its own page (here there is only one). Then, again on a separate page, we list the figure captions (here there is only one caption). Then come the figures themselves, each again on a separate page if there is more than one. Therefore, if we were submitting this report to a journal, our table and figure would not be inserted into the text; that would be done at a later stage as the journal issue is prepared for printing. So we have:

[new page]

Table 1
Number and Percentage of Subjects Offering Help

Condition	Number	Percent
Alone	14	0.70
With Others	4	0.20

[new page]

Figure Caption
Figure 1. Mean latency of helping response. Failures to help were assigned a "ceiling" score of 60 sec.

All the figure captions, if there were more than one, would be listed in order on this page. Finally would come the figures themselves, each on a separate page, as glossy prints or other "camera-ready" graphics. Our

one figure, therefore, would be the last item in the assembled stack of pages that would be mailed off to the journal's editor:

[new page]

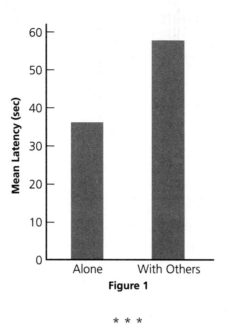

Figure 1

* * *

There we have our research report! Notice two more things about it before we leave the topic. First, it is very brief—but not so brief as to be unclear or incomplete. It does give the reader all the information that would be required if he or she should wish to repeat the experiment.

Second, a report should allow the busy reader to absorb all essential information in a single reading. To that end, it is written very simply. The style is formal, yes, but it is not stuffy and pedantic—at least I hope it isn't—and it is not filled with jargon. It states, as simply and clearly as possible, what the question was, what was done, what was found, and what the authors think it means—as a lab report should do.

And that's what I told you.

REFERENCES

Abramson, L. Y., Seligman, M. E. P., & Teasdale, J. (1978). Learned helplessness in humans: Critique and reformulation. *Journal of Abnormal Psychology, 87,* 49–74.

Adolph, E. F. (1947). Urges to eat and drink in rats. *American Journal of Physiology, 151,* 110–125.

Ainsworth, M. D. S. (1967). *Infancy in Uganda: Infant care and the growth of love.* Baltimore: Johns Hopkins University Press.

Ainsworth, M. D. S., & Bell, S. M. (1977). Infant crying and maternal responsiveness: A rejoinder to Gerwitz and Boyd. *Child Development, 48,* 1208–1216.

Anderson, E. (1994, May). The code of the streets. *Atlantic Monthly,* pp. 80–94.

Aron, A., & Aron, E. N. (1994). *Statistics for psychology.* Englewood Cliffs, NJ: Prentice-Hall.

Aronson, E., & Carlsmith, J. M. (1968). Experimentation in social psychology. In G. Lindsey & E. Aronson (Eds.), *Handbook of social psychology* (p. 179). Reading, MA: Addison-Wesley.

Astin, A., Korn, W. S., & Riggs, E. R. (1989). *The American freshman: National norms for Fall 1993.* Los Angeles: Higher Education Research Institute, Graduate School of Education, UCLA.

Babbie, E. (1989). *The practice of social research* (5th ed.). Belmont, CA: Wadsworth.

Balakrishan, T. R., Rao, K. V., Lapierre-Adamcyk, E., & Krotki, K. J. (1987). A hazard model analysis of the covariates of marriage dissolution in Canada. *Demography, 24,* 395–406.

Bartlett, F. C. (1932). *Remembering: A study in experimental and social psychology.* Cambridge, UK: Cambridge University Press.

Beecher, H. K. (1955). The powerful placebo. *Journal of the American Medical Association, 159,* 1602–1606.

Bell, S. M., & Ainsworth, M. D. S. (1972). Infant crying and maternal responsiveness. *Child Development, 43,* 1171–1190.

Bennett, N. G., Blanc, A. K., & Bloom, D. E. (1988). Commitment and the modern union: Assessing the link between premarital cohabitation and subsequent marital stability. *American Sociological Review, 53,* 127–138.

Bernstein, I. L. (1978). Learned taste aversions in children receiving chemotherapy. *Science, 200,* 1302–1303.

Bower, G. H. (1981). Mood and memory. *American Psychologist, 36,* 129–148.

Bryson, M. C. (1976, November). The literary digest poll: Making of a statistical myth. *American Statistician,* pp. 184–185.

Bumpass, L. L., & Sweet, J. A. (1989). National estimates of cohabitation. *Demography, 26,* 615–625.

Campbell, D. T. (1969). Prospective: Artifact and control. In R. Rosenthal & R. L. Rosnow (Eds.), *Artifact in behavioral research* (pp. 351–385). New York: Academic Press.

Campbell, D. T., & Stanley, J. C. (1963). *Experimental and quasi-experimental designs for research*. Chicago: Rand McNally.

Ceci, S., Huffman, M., & Smith, E. (1994). Repeatedly thinking about a non-event: Source misattributions among preschoolers. *Consciousness and Cognition, 3*, 388–407.

Churchland, P. S. (1986). *Neurophilosophy*. Cambridge, MA: MIT Press.

Clark, R. E., & Squire, L. R. (1998). Classical conditioning and brain systems: The role of awareness. *Science, 280*, 77–81.

Cohen, J. (1990). Things I have learned (so far). *American Psychologist, 45*, 1304–1312.

Coile, D. C., & Miller, N. E. (1984). How radical animal activists try to mislead humane people. *American Psychologist, 39*, 700–701.

Corbit, J. D., & Stellar, E. (1964). Palatability, food intake, and obesity in normal and hyperphagic rats. *Journal of Comparative and Physiological Psychology, 58*, 63–67.

Crews, F. (1993, November 18). The unknown Freud. *The New York Review of Books*, pp. 55–66.

Crews, F. (1996). The verdict on Freud. *Psychological Science 7*, 63–68.

Darley, J. M., & Batson, C. D. (1973). From Jerusalem to Jericho: A study of situational and dispositional variables in helping behavior. *Journal of Personality and Social Psychology, 27*, 100–108.

Darley, J. M., Teger, A. I., & Lewis, D. L. (1973). Do groups always inhibit individuals' responses to potential emergencies? *Journal of Personality and Social Psychology, 26*, 395–399.

Davison, G. C. (1968). Systematic desensitization as a counterconditioning process. *Journal of Abnormal Psychology, 73*, 91–99.

Dawes, R. M. (1994). *House of cards: Psychology and psychotherapy built on myth*. New York: Free Press.

Dement, W. C. (1990). A personal history of sleep disorders medicine. *Journal of Clinical Neurophysiology, 7*, 17–47.

DeMyer, M. (1979). *Parents and children in autism*. Washington, DC: V. H. Winston.

Dethier, V. G. (1962). *To know a fly*. San Francisco: Holden-Day.

Dion, K. K. (1972). Physical attractiveness and evaluations of children's transgressions. *Journal of Personality and Social Psychology, 24*, 207–213.

Dolnick, E. (1998). *Madness on the couch: Blaming the victim in the heyday of psychoanalysis*. New York: Simon & Schuster.

Dutton, D. G., & Aron, A. P. (1974). Some evidence for heightened sexual attraction under conditions of high anxiety. *Journal of Personality and Social Psychology, 30*, 510–517.

Ebbinghaus, H. (1913). *Memory: A contribution to experimental psychology*. New York: Columbia University Press. (Orginal work published 1885).

Eibl-Eibesfeldt, I. (1970). *Ethology: The biology of behavior*. New York: Holt, Rinehart, & Winston.

Eibl-Eibesfeldt, I. (1972). The expressive behavior of the deaf and blind born. In M. von Cranach and I. Vine (Eds.), *Non-verbal behaviour and expressive movements* (pp. 510–527). London: Academic Press.

Ekman, P. (1973). Cross-cultural studies of facial expression. In P. Ekman (Ed.), *Darwin and facial expression* (pp. 390–442). New York: Academic Press.

Ekman P., & Friesen, W. V. (1975). Unmasking the face: A guide to recognizing emotions from facial clues. Englewood Cliffs, New Jersey: Prentice-Hall.

Erdelyi, M. (1985). *Psychoanalysis: Freud's cognitive psychology*. New York: W. H. Freeman.

Fedorchak, P. M., & Bolles, R. C. (1988). Nutritive expectancies mediate cholecystokinin's suppression-of-intake effect. *Behavioral Neuroscience, 102,* 451–455.

Festinger, L., Riecken, H. W., & Schachter, S. (1956). *When prophecy fails.* Minneapolis: University of Minnesota Press.

Fowler, F. J., Jr. (1988). *Survey research methods.* Newbury Park, CA: Sage Publications.

Garcia, J., Ervin, F. R., & Koelling, R. A. (1966). Learning with prolonged delay of reinforcement. *Psychonomic Science, 5,* 121–122.

Gazzaniga, M. S., Ivry, R. B., & Mangun, G. R. (1998). *Cognitive Neuroscience.* New York, NY: W. W. Norton.

Gewirtz, J. L., & Boyd, E. (1977). Does maternal responding imply reduced infant crying? A critique of the 1972 Bell and Ainsworth report. *Child Development, 48,* 1200–1207.

Gilovich, T. (1991). *How we know what isn't so.* New York: Free Press.

Godden, D. R., & Baddeley, A. D. (1975). Context-dependent memory in two natural environments: On land and under water. *British Journal of Psychology, 66,* 325–332.

Goodwin, D. (1979). Alcoholism and heredity. *Archives of General Psychiatry, 36,* 57–61.

Gray, J. (1992). *Men are from Mars, women are from Venus.* New York: HarperCollins.

Greeley, A. M. (1991). *Faithful attraction.* New York: Tor Books.

Green, D. M., & Swets, J. A. (1966). *Signal detection theory and psychophysics.* New York: Wiley.

Greenwald, A. G. (1980). The totalitarian ego: Fabrication and revision of personal history. *American Psychologist, 35,* 603–618.

Greenwald, A. G., Spangenberg, E., Pratkanis, A., & Eskenazi, J. (1991). Double-blind tests of subliminal self-help audiotapes. *Psychological Science, 2,* 119–122.

Grice, G. R., & Hunter, J. J. (1964). Stimulus intensity effects depend upon the type of experimental design. *Psychological Review, 71,* 247–256.

Hamill, R., Wilson, T. D., & Nisbett, R. E. (1980). Insensitivity to sample bias: Generalizing from atypical cases. *Journal of Personality and Social Psychology, 39,* 578–589.

Harlow, H. F. (1958). The nature of love. *American Psychologist, 13,* 673–685.

Harrington, A. (1987). *Medicine, mind, and the double brain: A study in nineteenth-century thought.* Princeton, NJ: Princeton University Press.

Hastorf, A., & Cantril, H. (1954). They saw a game: A case study. *Journal of Abnormal and Social Psychology, 49,* 129–134.

Hayes, S. C. (1992). Single-case experimental design and empirical clinical practice. In A. E. Kazdin (Ed.), *Methodological issues and strategies in clinical research* (pp. 491–522). Washington, DC: American Psychological Association.

Hecht, S. (1934). Vision II. The nature of the photoreceptive process. In C. Murchison (Ed.), *Handbook of general experimental psychology* (pp. 704–828). Worcester, MA: Clark University Press.

Herman, C. P., & Polivy, J. (1980). Restrained eating. In A. J. Stunkard (Ed.), *Obesity* (pp. 208–225). Philadelphia: Saunders.

Herrnstein, R. J., & Loveland, D. H. (1964). Complex visual concept in the pigeon. *Science, 146,* 549–551.

Herrnstein, R. J., Loveland, D. H., & Cable, C. (1976). Natural concepts in pigeons. *Journal of Experimental Psychology: Animal Behavior Processes, 2,* 285–301.

Hoge, W. (1999, January 10). British researchers on animal-rights movement's death list. *The New York Times,* pp. 61–62.

Hong, C. C., Gillin, J. C., Dow, B. M., Wu, J., & Buchsbaum, M. S. (1995). Localized and lateralized cerebral glucose metabolism associated with eye movements during REM sleep and wakefulness: A positron emission tomography (PET) study. *Sleep, 18,* 570–580.

Hong, C. C., Jin, Y., Potkin, S. G., Buchsbaum, M. S., Wu, J., Callaghan, G. M., Nudleman, K. L., & Gillin, J. C. (1996). Language in dreaming and regional EEG alpha power. *Sleep, 19,* 232–235.

Humphrey, G. (1951). *Thinking.* New York: Wiley.

Hyman, I., Husband, T., & Billings, F. (1995). False memories of childhood experience. *Applied Cognitive Psychology, 9,* 181–198.

Jenni, D. A., & Jenni, M. A. (1976). Carrying behavior of humans: Analysis of sex differences. *Science, 194,* 859–860.

Kaminer, W. (1995). *It's all the rage: Crime and culture.* Reading, MA: Addison-Wesley.

Kantowitz, B. H., Roediger, H. L., & Elmes, D. G. (1994). *Experimental psychology: Understanding psychological research.* St. Paul, MN: West Publishing Company.

Kaplan, M. (Ed.) (1965). *Essential works of Pavlov.* New York: Bantam.

Kazdin, A. E. (1992). Drawing valid inferences from case studies. In A. E. Kazdin (Ed.), *Methodological issues and strategies in clinical research* (pp. 475–490). Washington, DC: American Psychological Association.

Kolata, G. (1998, April 1). A child's paper poses a medical challenge. *The New York Times,* pp. 46–47.

Kraut, R., Patterson, M., Lundmark, V., Kiesler, S., Mukophadhyay, T., & Scherlis, W. (1998). Internet paradox: A social technology that reduces social involvement and psychological well-being? *American Psychologist, 53,* 1017–1031.

Langer, E. J., & Abelson, R. P. (1974). A patient by any other name . . . clinician group differences in labeling bias. *Journal of Consulting and Clinical Psychology, 42,* 4–9.

Latane, B., & Darley, J. (1970). *The unresponsive bystander: Why doesn't he help?* New York: Appleton-Century-Crofts.

Lawick-Goddall, J. van. (1971). *In the shadow of man.* Boston: Houghton Mifflin.

Lerner, M. J., & Miller, D. T. (1978). Just world research and the attribution process: Looking back and ahead. *Psychological Bulletin, 85,* 1030–1051.

Lewinsohn, P. M., & Rosenbaum, M. (1987). Recall of parental behavior by acute depressives, remitted depressives, and nondepressives. *Journal of Personality and Social Psychology, 52,* 611–619.

Liberman, R. P., & Raskin, D. E. (1971). Depression: A behavioral formulation. *Archives of General Psychiatry, 24,* 515–523.

Linton, M. (1982). Transformations of memory in everyday life. In U. Neisser (Ed.), *Memory observed: Remembering in natural contexts* (pp. 72–92). San Francisco: Freeman.

Loftus, E. F. (1979). *Eyewitness testimony.* Cambridge, MA: Harvard University Press.

Loftus, E. F. (1994). The repressed memory controversy. *American Psychologist, 49,* 443–445.

Loftus, E., & Palmer, J. C. (1974). Reconstruction of automobile destruction: An example of the interaction between language and memory. *Journal of Verbal Learning and Verbal Behavior, 13,* 585–589.

Lundberg, G. D. (1998). Editor's note. *Journal of the American Medical Association, 279,* 1004.

Maier, S. F. (1970). Failure to escape traumatic shock: Incompatible skeletal motor responses or learned helplessness? *Learning and Motivation, 1,* 157–170.

Maier, S. F., Seligman, M. E. P., & Solomon, R. L. (1969). Pavlovian fear conditioning and learned helplessness: Effects on escape and avoidance behavior of (a) the CS–US contingency and (b) the independence of the US and voluntary responding. In B. A. Campbell & R. M. Church (Eds.), *Punishment and aversive behavior* (pp. 299–342). New York: Appleton-Century-Crofts.

Markus, H. R., & Kitayama, S. (1991). Culture and the self: Implications for cognition, emotion, and motivation. *Psychological Review, 98,* 224–253.

McGinnies, E. (1949). Emotionality and perceptual defense. *Psychological Review, 56,* 244–251.

Milgram, S. (1963). Behavioral study of obedience. *Journal of Abnormal and Social Psychology, 67,* 371–378.

Milgram, S. (1974). *Obedience to authority.* New York: Harper & Row (Colophon Books).

Miller, J. G. (1984). Culture and the development of everyday social explanation. *Journal of Personality and Social Psychology, 46,* 961–978.

Miller, N. E. (1985). The value of behavioral research on animals. *American Psychologist, 40,* 423–440.

Moffat, N. J. (1989). Home-based cognitive rehabilitation with the elderly. In L. W. Poon, D. C. Rubin, & B. A. Wilson (Eds.), *Everyday cognition in adulthood and late life* (pp. 659–680). Cambridge, UK: Cambridge University Press.

Mook, D. G. (1983). In defense of external invalidity. *American Psychologist, 38,* 379–387.

Mook, D. G. (1989). The myth of external validity. In L. W. Poon, D. C. Rubin, & B. A. Wilson (Eds.), *Everyday cognition in adulthood and late life* (pp. 659–680). Cambridge, UK: Cambridge University Press.

Mook, D. G. (1990). Satiety, specifications, and stop rules: Feeding as voluntary action. In A. N. Epstein & A. R. Morrison (Eds.), *Progress in psychobiology and physiological psychology* (Vol. 14, pp. 1–65). New York: Academic Press.

Mook, D. G. (1996). *Motivation: The organization of action.* New York: W. W. Norton.

Mook, D. G., Kenney, N. J., Roberts, S., Nussbaum, A. I., & Rodier, W. I. III. (1972). Ovarian-adrenal interactions in regulation of body weight by female rats. *Journal of Comparative and Physiological Psychology, 81,* 198–211.

Neisser, U., & Harsch, N. (1992). Phantom flashbulbs: False recollections of hearing the news about Challenger. In E. Winograd & U. Neisser (Eds.), *Affect and accuracy in recall: Studies of "flashbulb" memories* (pp. 9–31). Cambridge, UK: Cambridge University Press.

Newcomb, T. M. (1943). *Personality and social change.* New York: Dryden.

Newcomb, T. M., Koenig, K. E., Flacks, R., & Warwick, D. P. (1967). *Persistence and change: Bennington College and its students after twenty-five years.* New York: Wiley.

Nisbett, R. E., & Cohen, D. (1996). *Culture of honor: The psychology of violence in the south.* Boulder, CO: Westview Press.

Nisbett, R. E., & Ross, L. (1980). *Human inference: Strategies and shortcomings of social judgment.* Englewood Cliffs, NJ: Prentice-Hall.

Ofshe, R. (1992). Inadvertent hypnosis during interrogation. *International Journal of Clinical and Experimental Hypnosis, 11,* 125–155.

Ofshe, R., & Watters, E. (1994). *Making monsters.* New York: Scribner.

Olds, J., & Milner, P. (1954). Positive reinforcement produced by electrical stimulation of septal area and other regions of rat brain. *Journal of Comparative and Physiological Psychology, 47,* 419–427.

Ostow, M. (1995). Exchange. In F. Crews (Ed.), *The memory wars: Freud's legacy in dispute* (pp. 97–102). New York: The New York Review of Books.

Parker, S. (1995). The "difference of means" may not be the "effect size." *American Psychologist, 50,* 1101–1102.

Paul, G. L. (1966). *Effects of insight, desensitization, and attention placebo treatment of anxiety.* Stanford, CA: Stanford University Press.

Pavlov, I. P. (1960). *Conditioned reflexes* (G. V. Anrep, Trans.). New York: Dover. (Original work published 1927)

Pelchak, M. L., & Rozin, P. (1982). The special role of nausea in the acquisition of food dislikes by humans. *Appetite, 3,* 341–351.

Pelkwijk, J. J. ter, & Tinbergen, N. (1937). Eine reizbiologische analyse einiger verhaltensweisen von gasterosteus aculeatus. *Zeitschrift für Tierpsychologie, 1,* 193–200.

Pi-Sunyer, X., Kissileff, H. R., Thornton, J., & Smith, G. P. (1982). C-terminal octapeptide of cholecystokinin decreases food intake in obese men. *Physiology and Behavior, 29,* 627–630.

Piliavin, I., Rodin, J., & Piliavin, J. (1969). Good samaritanism: An underground phenomenon? *Journal of Personality and Social Psychology, 13,* 298–299.

Pinel, J. P. J. (1993). *Biopsychology* (2nd ed.). Boston: Allyn & Bacon.

Pinker, S. (1994). *The language instinct.* New York: HarperCollins.

Polivy, J., & Herman, C. P. (1985). Dieting and binging: A causal analysis. *American Psychologist, 40,* 193–201.

Pratkanis, A. R. (1992). The cargo-cult science of subliminal persuasion. *Skeptical Inquirer, 16,* 260–272.

Pugh, E. N., Jr. (1988). Vision: physics and retinal physiology. In R. C. Atkinson, R. J. Herrnstein, G. Lindzey, & R. D. Luce (Eds.), *Stevens' Handbook of Experimental Psychology* (Vol. 1, pp. 75–164). New York: Wiley.

Regan, T. (1998). Animal rights. In M. Bekoff with C. A. Meany (Eds.), *Encyclopedia of animal rights and animal welfare* (pp. 42–43). Westport, CT: Greenwood.

Reisberg, D. (1997). *Cognition: Exploring the science of the mind.* New York: W. W. Norton.

Ristau, C. A. (1991). Aspects of the cognitive ethology of an injury-feigning bird, the piping plover. In C. A. Ristau (Ed.), *Cognitive ethology: The minds of other animals* (pp. 91–126). Hillsdale, NJ: Lawrence Erlbaum Associates.

Rosa, L., Rosa, E., Sarner, L., & Barrett, S. (1998). A close look at Therapeutic Touch. *Journal of the American Medical Association, 279,* 1005–1010.

Ross, L. (1977). The intuitive psychologist and his shortcomings: Distortions in the attribution process. In L. Berkowitz (Ed.), *Advances in experimental social psychology* (Vol. 10, pp. 173–220). Orlando, FL: Academic Press.

Ross, L., & Nisbett, R. E. (1991). *The person and the situation: Perspectives of social psychology.* Philadelphia: Temple University Press.

Rozin, P., & Zellner, D. A. (1987). The role of Pavlovian conditioning in the acquisition of food likes and dislikes. In N. S. Braveman & P. Bronstein (Eds.), Experimental assessments and clinical applications of conditioned food aversions. *Annals of the New York Academy of Sciences* (Vol. 443, pp.189–202). New York: New York Academy of Sciences.

Russow, L.-M. (1999). Bioethics, animal research, and ethical theory. *ILAR Journal, 40,* 15–21.

Sagan, C. (1995). *The demon-haunted world.* New York: Random House.

Sarner, L. (1998). The "Emily event": Emily Rosa and the Therapeutic Touch wars. *Skeptic, 6,* 32–37.

Savie, P., & Dickie, R. F. (1979). Overcorrection of topographically dissimilar autistic behaviors. *Education and treatment of children, 2,* 177–184.

Scarr, S., & Weinberg, R. A. (1976). IQ test performances of black children adopted by white families. *American Psychologist, 31,* 726–739.

Schachter, S. (1951). Deviation, rejection and communication. *Journal of Abnormal and Social Psychology, 46,* 190–207.

Schachter, S. (1959). *The psychology of affiliation.* Stanford, CA: Stanford University Press.

Schachter, S. (1982). Recidivism and self-cure of smoking and obesity. *American Psychologist, 37,* 436–444.

Schick, T., Jr., & Vaughn, L. (1995). *How to think about weird things: Critical thinking for a new age.* Mountain View, CA: Mayfield.

Sclafani, A., & Springer, D. (1976). Dietary obesity in adult rats: Similarity to hypothalamic and human obesity syndromes. *Physiology and Behavior, 17,* 461–471.

Seligman, M. E. P. (1990). *Learned optimism: How to change your mind and your life.* New York: Simon & Schuster.

Seligmann, J., & Childea, F. (1992, September 21). Horror story or big hoax? *Newsweek,* p. 75.

Shepard, R. N., & Metzler, J. (1971). Mental rotation of three-dimensional objects. *Science, 171,* 701–703.

Shweder, R. A. (1991). *Thinking through cultures.* Cambridge, MA: Harvard University Press.

Silverman, I. (1975). Nonreactive methods and the law. *American Psychologist, 30,* 764–769.

Smith, G. P., & Gibbs, J. (1994). Satiating effect of cholecystokinin. *Annals of the New York Academy of Sciences, 713,* 236–241.

Smith, M. L., Glass, G. V., & Miller, T. I. (1980). *The benefits of psychotherapy.* Baltimore: Johns Hopkins University Press.

Snyder, S. H. (1974). *Madness and the brain.* New York: McGraw-Hill.

Stanovich, K. E. (1998). *How to think straight about psychology.* New York: Longmans.

Stevens, S. S. (1951). Mathematics, measurements, and psychophysics. In S. S. Stevens (Ed.), *Handbook of experimental psychology* (pp. 1–49). New York: Wiley.

Suomi, S. J. (1991). Primate separation models of affective disorder. In J. Madden IV (Ed.), *Neurobiology of learning, emotion, and affect* (pp. 195–214). New York: Raven Press.

Tawney, J. W., & Gast, D. L. (1994). *Single subject research in special education.* Columbus, OH: Merrill.

Taylor, S. E. (1989). *Positive illusions.* New York: Basic Books.

Thompson, R. F. (1986). The neurobiology of learning and memory. *Science, 233,* 941–947.

Tinbergen, N. (1951). *The study of instinct.* London: Oxford University Press.

Tuchman, B. W. (1984). *The march of folly.* New York: Knopf.

Tversky, A., & Kahneman, D. (1973). Availability: A heuristic for judging frequency and probability. *Cognitive Psychology, 5,* 207–232.

Valins, S. (1966). Cognitive effects of false heart-rate feedback. *Journal of Personality and Social Psychology, 4,* 400–408.

Vallone, R. P., Griffin, D. W., Lin, S., & Ross, L. (1990). Overconfident prediction of future actions and outcomes by self and others. *Journal of Personality and Social Psychology, 58,* 582–592.

Webb, E., Campbell, D., Schwartz, R., & Sechrest, L. (1966). *Unobtrusive measures: Nonreactive research in the social sciences.* Chicago: Rand McNally.

Wegner, D., Coulton, G. F., & Wenzlaff, R. (1985). The transparency of denial: Briefing in the debriefing paradigm. *Journal of Personality and Social Psychology, 49,* 338–346.

Wilson, B. A. (1989). Designing memory-therapy programs. In L. W. Poon, D. C. Rubin, & B. A. Wilson (Eds.), *Everyday cognition in adulthood and late life* (pp. 659–680). Cambridge, UK: Cambridge University Press.

Wilson, T. D. (1985). Strangers to ourselves: The origins and accuracy of beliefs about one's own mental states. In J. H. Harvey & G. Weary (Eds.), *Attribution: Basic issues and applications* (pp. 9–36). Orlando, FL: Academic Press.

Woodworth, R. S., & Schlosberg, H. (1954). *Experimental psychology.* New York: Holt, Rinehart, and Winston.

Zajonc, R. B. (1984). On the primacy of affect. *American Psychologist, 35,* 151–175.

Zurlo, J., & Goldberg, A. M. (1998). Alternatives to animal experimentation. In M. Bekoff with C. A. Meany (Eds.), *Encyclopedia of animal rights and animal welfare* (pp. 4–8). Westport, CT: Greenwood.

CREDITS

Figures

Figure 1.1: © by Sidney Harris.

Figure 2.3: Peanuts © UFS. Reprinted by permission.

Figure 2.5: Harlow Primate Laboratory, University of Wisconsin.

Figure 3.1 (left): © The New Yorker Collection 1998 Leo Cullum from cartoonbank.com. All Rights Reserved.

Figure 3.1 (right): © The New Yorker Collection 2000 Pat Byrnes from cartoonbank.com. All Rights Reserved.

Figure 3.4: Peanuts © UFS. Reprinted by permission.

Figure 3.7: © Hank Morgan.

Figure 4.2: © The New Yorker Collection 1989 George Price from cartoonbank.com. All Rights Reserved.

Figure 4.3: Photo courtesy of Crossett Library, Bennington College.

Figure 4.4: © The New Yorker Collection 2000 Mick Stevens from cartoonbank.com. All Rights Reserved.

Figure 4.5: From N. Tinbergen, *The Study of Instinct*. Copyright © 1951. Reprinted by permission of Oxford University Press.

Figure 4.6: Photos by Dr. Irenäus Eibl-Eibesfeldt.

Figure 4.7 (left): Ekman, 1972.

Figure 4.7 (right): Ekman & Friesen, 1975.

Figure 4.8: Photo by Dr. Irenäus Eibl-Eibesfeldt.

Figure 4.9: Photo courtesy of Bea Mook.

Figure 5.1: © The New Yorker Collection 1997 Barbara Smaller from cartoonbank.com. All Rights Reserved.

Figure 5.2: Hugo Van Lawick/NGS Image Collection.

Figure 5.3: © The New Yorker Collection 1973 Dana Fradon from cartoonbank.com. All Rights Reserved.

Figure 5.4: © The New Yorker Collection 1996 William Hamilton from cartoonbank.com. All Rights Reserved.

Figure 6.2: Reprinted with permission from R. N. Shepard & J. Metzlar, "Mental rotation of three dimensional objects," in *Science, 171*, pp. 701–703. Copyright © 1971 American Association for the Advancement of Science.

Figure 6.7: From "Ovarian-adrenal interactions in regulation of body weight by female rats," by D. G. Mook, N. J. Kenney, S. Roberts, A. I. Nussbaum, & W. I. Rodier III. In *Journal of Comparative and Physiological Psychology, 81*, p. 206. Copyright © 1972 by the American Psychological Association. Reprinted by permission.

Figure 7.5: Copyright © 1928 International Publishers Co., Inc. Adapted with permission.

Figure 7.6: Illustration by Julie Zickefoose.

Figure 9.3 (right): From "Mood and memory," by G. H. Bower. In *American Psychologist, 36*, p. 132. Copyright © 1981 by the American Psychological Association. Reprinted by permission.

Figure 10.2: Figure by S. Hecht. From *A Handbook of General Experimental Psychology*, by C. H. Murchison (ed.). Copyright © 1934 by Clark University Press. Reprinted by permission.

Figure 10.5: Photo by W. Rapport.

Figure 10.6: From J. Pinel, *Biopsychology* (second edition). Copyright © 1993 by Allyn & Bacon. Adapted with permission.

Figure 10.7: Reprinted with permission from R. J. Herrnstein & D. H. Loveland, "Complex visual concept in the pigeon," in *Science, 146*, pp. 549–551. Copyright © 1964 American Association for the Advancement of Science.

Figure 10.11: From P. Savie & R. F. Dickie, "Overcorrection of topographically dissimilar autistic behaviors," in *Education and Treatment of Children, 2*, pp. 177–184. Reprinted by permission.

Figure 11.1: Courtesy of Capilano Suspension Bridge and Park.

Figure 11.3: From *Culture of Honor*, by R. Nisbett and D. Cohen. Copyright © 1996 by Westview Press, Inc. Reprinted by permission of Westview Press, a member of Perseus Books, LLC.

Figure 12.3: © 2000 Charles Addams from cartoonbank.com. All Rights Reserved.

Figure 13.1: © by Sidney Harris.

Figure 13.2: From the film *Obedience* © 1965 by Stanley Milgram and distributed by Penn State Media Sales. Permission is granted by Alexandra Milgram.

Figure 13.4: The Far Side © 1993 Farworks, Inc. All rights reserved.

Figure 13.5: By permission of Foundation for Biomedical Research, Washington, DC. Copyright © 2000 by Foundation for Biomedical Research.

Figure 14.1 (left): © The New Yorker Collection 2000 Gahan Wilson from cartoonbank.com. All Rights Reserved.

Figure 14.1 (right): © The New Yorker Collection 1993 Tom Cheney from cartoonbank.com. All Rights Reserved.

Figure 14.2: © The New Yorker Collection 1996 Danny Shanahan from cartoonbank.com. All Rights Reserved.

Figure 14.3: © The New Yorker Collection 1983 Al Ross from cartoonbank.com. All Rights Reserved.

Figure 14.4: Peanuts © UFS. Reprinted by permission.

Figure 14.6: © The New Yorker Collection 1998 Mike Twohy from cartoonbank.com. All Rights Reserved.

Text excerpts

Excerpt page 164: From "Debunking the marriage myth," by H. E. Marano. Copyright © 1998 by the New York Times Co. Reprinted by permission.

Excerpt pages 164–165: Reprinted with the permission of the Associated Press.

Excerpt pages 446–449: From *Ethical Principles of Psychologists and Code of Conduct*. Copyright © 1992 by the American Psychological Association. Reprinted by permission.

Name Index

Subject Index